THIRD WORLD 91/92

Third Edition

A Library of Information from the Public Press

Editor

Jeffrey M. Elliot
North Carolina Central University

Jeffrey M. Elliot is professor of political science at North Carolina Central University. He received his Doctor of Arts from the Claremont Graduate School in 1978. In 1985 he was awarded an honorary Doctor of Humane Letters degree from Shaw University, and in 1986 California State University, San Bernardino, established The Jeffrey M. Elliot Collection, a permanent archive of his published works. He is the author of 62 books and over 500 articles, reviews, and interviews. His work has appeared in more than 250 publications, both in the United States and abroad, and has been nominated for numerous literary awards. Recent book titles include: *Voices of Zaire: Rhetoric of Reality?* (The Washington Institute, 1990); *The Arms Control, Disarmament, and Military Security Dictionary* (ABC-Clio, 1989); *The State and Local Government Political Dictionary* (ABC-Clio, 1987); and *The Trilemma of World Oil Politics* (The Borgo Press, 1987). A free-lance journalist, he has conducted over 350 interviews, among them: President Jimmy Carter, Nobel Prize-winner Bishop Desmond Tutu, Cuban President Fidel Castro, Zairian President Mobutu Sese Seko, UNITA President Jonas Savimbi, PLO Chairman Yasir Arafat, Contra leader Adolfo Calero, and Jamaican Prime Minister Michael Manley. In addition to his academic duties, he serves as Distinguished Advisor on Foreign Affairs to Congressman Mervyn M. Dymally (D-Calif.) and as editor of the *Journal of Caribbean-American Studies* and *Journal of Black Political Studies*.

Cover illustration by Mike Eagle

The Dushkin Publishing Group, Inc.
Sluice Dock, Guilford, Connecticut 06437

The Annual Editions Series

Annual Editions is a series of over fifty volumes designed to provide the reader with convenient, low-cost access to a wide range of current, carefully selected articles from some of the most important magazines, newspapers, and journals published today. Annual Editions are updated on an annual basis through a continuous monitoring of over 200 periodical sources. All Annual Editions have a number of features designed to make them particularly useful, including topic guides, annotated tables of contents, unit overviews, and indexes. For the teacher using Annual Editions in the classroom, an Instructor's Resource Guide with test questions is available for each volume.

VOLUMES AVAILABLE

Africa
Aging
American Government
American History, Pre-Civil War
American History, Post-Civil War
Anthropology
Biology
Business and Management
Business Ethics
Canadian Politics
China
Comparative Politics
Computers in Education
Computers in Business
Computers in Society
Criminal Justice
Drugs, Society, and Behavior
Early Childhood Education
Economics
Educating Exceptional Children
Education
Educational Psychology
Environment
Geography
Global Issues
Health
Human Development
Human Resources
Human Sexuality

Latin America
Macroeconomics
Management
Marketing
Marriage and Family
Microeconomics
Middle East and the Islamic World
Money and Banking
Nutrition
Personal Growth and Behavior
Psychology
Public Administration
Race and Ethnic Relations
Social Problems
Sociology
Soviet Union and Eastern Europe
State and Local Government
Third World
Urban Society
Violence and Terrorism
Western Civilization, Pre-Reformation
Western Civilization, Post-Reformation
Western Europe
World History, Pre-Modern
World History, Modern
World Politics

Library of Congress Cataloging in Publication Data
Main entry under title: Annual editions: Third World. 1991/92.
1. Underdeveloped areas—Periodicals. I. Elliot, Jeffrey M., *comp.* II. Title: The Third World.
ISBN 0–87967–942–5   303.4′4

Third Edition

Manufactured by The Banta Company, Harrisonburg, Virginia 22801

Editors/ Advisory Board

EDITOR

Jeffrey M. Elliot
North Carolina Central University

ADVISORY BOARD

STAFF

To the Reader

In publishing ANNUAL EDITIONS we recognize the enormous role played by the magazines, newspapers, and journals of the *public press* in providing current, first-rate educational information in a broad spectrum of interest areas. Within the articles, the best scientists, practitioners, researchers, and commentators draw issues into new perspective as accepted theories and viewpoints are called into account by new events, recent discoveries change old facts, and fresh debate breaks out over important controversies.

Many of the articles resulting from this enormous editorial effort are appropriate for students, researchers, and professionals seeking accurate, current material to help bridge the gap between principles and theories and the real world. These articles, however, become more useful for study when those of lasting value are carefully *collected, organized, indexed,* and *reproduced* in a *low-cost format,* which provides easy and permanent access when the material is needed. That is the role played by *Annual Editions.* Under the direction of each volume's *Editor,* who is an expert in the subject area, and with the guidance of an *Advisory Board,* we seek each year to provide in each *ANNUAL EDITION* a current, well-balanced, carefully selected collection of the best of the public press for your study and enjoyment. We think you'll find this volume useful, and we hope you'll take a moment to let us know what you think.

Traditionally, the study of international relations has focused primarily on East-West relations—that is, the post–World War II struggle between the Soviet bloc countries and the West. This collection of readings examines the social, political, and economic status of the recently emancipated Third World nations of Africa, Asia, the Middle East, South and Central America, the Caribbean, and the South Pacific.

Annual Editions: Third World seeks to define, explain, and analyze the myriad issues and problems facing the developing world—a widely divergent group of states that defy sweeping generalization. An intelligent examination of the Third World demands an interdisciplinary approach, one that welds the analytical tools of the political scientist, historian, economist, and sociologist. Such issues as institutional stability, economic development, human rights, environmental protection, ethnic strife, regional cooperation, and national security require this interdisciplinary perspective.

The readings explore sundry topics of current interest and controversy. The selections are written by knowledgeable and recognized scholars, journalists, and practitioners. In selecting the articles, I have placed special emphasis on accuracy, readability, objectivity, and currentness. In addition, I have eschewed readings that are overly abstract or empirical, lack focus or definition, fail to ask basic questions or raise critical issues, or ignore or misinterpret the conventional literature on the developing world.

The third edition of *Annual Editions: Third World,* like the previous two, seeks to provide a selection of the most useful and interesting articles on the developing world. My aim is to give students a general sense of the complexities and dynamics of the Third World while providing background information on specific issues. Since books on the developing world become dated very quickly, this new issue of *Annual Editions: Third World* has retained fewer than one-third of the readings from the previous edition. The new articles presented here have been chosen from more than 500 pieces examined in an extensive investigation of the major journals and periodicals which cover the developing world.

Obviously, the Third World is a complex topic, one that cannot be adequately covered in any one book. Most of the selections presented here are fresh, current analyses. I do not agree, nor will you, with all the views expressed in this collection—but no one will read this volume without acquiring new insights and valuable perspectives that can enrich his or her understanding and appreciation of the challenges and opportunities of this vital part of the world.

While this anthology treats much of the information traditionally covered in introductory courses in international relations, comparative government, foreign policy, and area studies, my primary goal has been to draw the reader into the great controversies and debates surrounding the future of the Third World. To this end, I hope that this collection will stimulate rather than inhibit creative thinking, and that it will spark further study and discussion. I owe a special thanks to Ian Nielsen, publisher of the *Annual Editions* series, who played an important part in the creation of this volume and provided many perceptive comments and suggestions.

Readers may have input into the next edition by completing and returning the article rating form in the back of the book.

Jeffrey M. Elliot
Editor

Contents

Unit 1

Understanding the Third World

Five selections examine what is meant by the term "Third World." The topics covered include political development in the Third World, the conditions of structural dependency, and Soviet policy in the Third World.

Unit 2

People, Power, and Leadership

Six articles examine some of the leaders who are important in the Third World. Included are the dynamics of leadership change in, and assessments of, selected Third World leaders.

The concepts in bold italics are developed in the article. For further expansion please refer to the Topic Guide and the Index.

Unit 3

Stability, Crisis, and Revolution

Ten selections discuss the current state of crisis in the Third World. The areas considered include the Middle East, Latin America, Africa, and the Far East.

The concepts in bold italics are developed in the article. For further expansion please refer to the Topic Guide and the Index.

The concepts in bold italics are developed in the article. For further expansion please refer to the Topic Guide and the Index.

Unit 4

The Limits of American Power

Seven selections examine the limits of American power. Considered are American policies toward the Third World, with specific attention to U.S. policy toward Third World dictatorships, U.S.-Asian relations, and the current U.S. relationship with the Middle East.

Unit 5

Human Rights and Democratic Rule

Seven articles discuss the current state of human rights policy in the world. Considered are the use of torture, Pol Pot, and the struggle for human rights in South Africa.

The concepts in bold italics are developed in the article. For further expansion please refer to the Topic Guide and the Index.

Unit 6

Easing the Debt Crisis

Six articles examine the impact of the debt crisis on the Third World. The selections consider the ethics of international debt, the consequences of defaulting on debt, and the positive effects of available funds on Third World nations.

The concepts in bold italics are developed in the article. For further expansion please refer to the Topic Guide and the Index.

Unit 7

A World in Change

Ten selections consider how our world is changing. Topics include the drug war, world terrorism, the Third World arms race, Third World urban growth, and world hunger.

The concepts in bold italics are developed in the article. For further expansion please refer to the Topic Guide and the Index.

The concepts in bold italics are developed in the article. For further expansion please refer to the Topic Guide and the Index.

Topic Guide

This topic guide suggests how the selections in this book relate to topics of traditional concern to students and professionals involved with the study of the Third World. It is useful for locating articles which relate to each other for reading and research. The guide is arranged alphabetically according to topic. Articles may, of course, treat topics that do not appear in the topic guide. In turn, entries in the topic guide do not necessarily constitute a comprehensive listing of all the contents of each selection.

TOPIC AREA	TREATED IN:	TOPIC AREA	TREATED IN:
Agricultural Development	21. Passage to Power 48. World Hunger Amidst Plenty 49. Concern Rising Over Harm From Pesticides in Third World 50. The Kerala Experiment	**Environment (cont'd)**	46. Third World Metropolises Are Becoming Monsters 47. Weeding Out Waste 49. Concern Rising Over Harm From Pesticides in Third World 51. Grass-Roots Groups Are Our Best Hope
Apartheid	29. The Human Rights Imperative 34. Normalizing the Political Process in South Africa 35. Apartheid Has No Future	**Food Programs**	48. World Hunger Amidst Plenty 50. The Kerala Experiment
Civil War	11. Mending Broken Burma 15. Nicaragua's Election 19. The Apocalypse in Ethiopia	**Foreign Aid**	3. What the Third World Really Needs 8. Semper Fidel 22. Policies Toward the Third World 23. The U.S. and Third-World Dictatorships 24. The Third World Is Not a Hopeless Place 25. Refugee Concerns and U.S. Interests 48. World Hunger Amidst Plenty
Debt Crisis	16. Panama: Whose Agenda? 22. Policies Toward the Third World 36. Mortgaging a House of Cards 37. Will the Planet Pay the Price for Third World Debt? 38. It Won't Go Away Alone 39. A Way Out for the Debtors 40. Risking the Lifeboat 41. Going It Alone	**Health Care**	3. What the Third World Really Needs 50. The Kerala Experiment
Democratic Reform	2. Ethnocentrism and Third World Development 15. Nicaragua's Election 16. Panama: Whose Agenda? 17. The People's War 18. South Africa on the Move 29. The Human Rights Imperative 34. Normalizing the Political Process in South Africa 35. Apartheid Has No Future	**Human Rights**	6. When Leaders Fall 12. The Struggle to Build a Nation 15. Nicaragua's Election 23. The U.S. and Third-World Dictatorships 29. The Human Rights Imperative 30. The Fight to Stop Torture 31. The Scandal of the Boat People 32. The Second Coming of Pol Pot 33. Iraq's Fleeing Kurds 34. Normalizing the Political Process in South Africa 35. Apartheid Has No Future
Drug Trafficking	17. The People's War 42. The Drug War	**Insurgents**	5. Gorbachev's Global Doughnut 11. Mending Broken Burma 15. Nicaragua's Election 16. Panama: Whose Agenda? 19. The Apocalypse in Ethiopia 34. Normalizing the Political Process in South Africa 35. Apartheid Has No Future
Economic Development	2. Ethnocentrism and Third World Development 4. The North-South Affluence Gap 8. Semper Fidel 9. Chadli's Perestroika 10. After the Fall of a Dictator 16. Panama: Whose Agenda? 21. Passage to Power 22. Policies Toward the Third World 23. The Third World Is Not a Hopeless Place 26. United States Security Policy and ASEAN 28. Saving Central America 48. World Hunger Amidst Plenty 50. The Kerala Experiment 51. Grass-Roots Groups Are Best Hope	**Intifada**	12. The Struggle to Build a Nation 13. Gunless in Gaza
		Khmer Rouge	20. Cambodia and the International Community 25. Refugee Concerns and U.S. Interests 26. United States Security Policy and ASEAN 32. The Second Coming of Pol Pot
Environment	23. The Third World Is Not a Hopeless Place 45. The North's Garbage Goes South	**Malnutrition**	19. The Apocalypse in Ethiopia 48. World Hunger Amidst Plenty

TOPIC AREA	TREATED IN:	TOPIC AREA	TREATED IN:
Nationalism	1. The Third World 2. Ethnocentrism and Third World Development 5. Gorbachev's Global Doughnut 12. The Struggle to Build a Nation 16. Panama: Whose Agenda?	**Religious Fanaticism**	12. The Struggle to Build a Nation 27. The United States Role in the Middle East
Overpopulation	2. Ethnocentrism and Third World Development 19. The Apocalypse in Ethiopia 21. Passage to Power 24. The Third World Is Not a Hopeless Place 46. Third World Metropolises Are Becoming Monsters	**Soviet Foreign Policy**	5. Gorbachev's Global Doughnut 8. Semper Fidel 19. The Apocalypse in Ethiopia 22. Policies Toward the Third World 27. The United States Role in the Middle East 44. Missile Mania
Palestinians	12. The Struggle to Build A Nation 13. Gunless in Gaza 27. The United States Role in the Middle East	**Technological Revolution**	2. Ethnocentrism and Third World Development 3. What the Third World Really Needs 4. The North-South Affluence Gap
Poverty	4. The North-South Affluence Gap 19. The Apocalypse in Ethiopia 21. Passage to Power 24. The Thrid World Is Not a Hopeless Place 46. The World Metropolises Are Becoming Monsters 50. The Kerala Experiment	**Terrorism**	12. The Struggle to Build a Nation 13. Gunless in Gaza 43. State-Sponsored Terrorism
Refugees	25. Refugee Concerns and U.S. Interests 31. The Scandal of the Boat People 33. Iraq's Fleeing Kurds	**United States Foreign Policy**	15. Nicaragua's Election 20. Cambodia and the International Community 22. Policies Toward the Third World 23. The U.S. and Third-World Dictatorships 24. The Third World Is Not a Hopeless Place 25. Refugee Concerns and U.S. Interests 26. United States Security Policy and ASEAN 27. The United States Role in the Middle East 25. Saving Central America 29. The Human Rights Imperative
Regional Security	26. United States Security Policy and ASEAN 44. Missle Mania		

Understanding the Third World

The term "Third World" is typically used to describe the over 100 economically underdeveloped and developing nations in Asia, Africa, and South America. It can be distinguished from the First World (the United States and its industrialized allies) and the Second World (the Soviet Union and its East European partners). In recent years, the United Nations has employed the term "Fourth World" to identify those countries with an extremely low annual per capita income. Unfortunately, nomenclature in this area is quite imprecise; the Third World is also referred to as the South, the poor countries, the underdeveloped nations, and the less developed, or developing, nations.

Most Third World nations (which now include over one half of the world's population) have achieved independence since World War II. Generally, these countries are poor, weak, and unstable; they produce primary and semi-finished products; and their population growth precludes sustained economic progress (as measured by living standards in the industrialized world). The developing nations represent a majority in the General Assembly of the United Nations. To maximize their influence in this body, they have formed a caucusing bloc, called the Group of Seventy-Seven (G77), in order to shape the agenda and call attention to their special concerns. Although many Third World nations meet regularly to discuss common problems, unified action is difficult to achieve because of the diversity and complexity of these problems. Most developing countries participate in the Nonaligned Movement.

Over the last several decades, these newly independent nations have struggled to improve their standards of living and eliminate the debilitating poverty and misery of past centuries. Since achieving independence, the nations of the Third World have made enormous strides in achieving self-determination, equality, and dignity. However, economic progress has proven more elusive. Many Third World peoples continue to practice subsistence agriculture, deprived of the modern tools they need to increase productivity. In addition, many of these countries lack the political machinery, social structures, and cultural traditions required of industrialized nations. Despite countless initiatives, a majority of these nations have failed to realize sustained economic growth.

Unfortunately, the economic challenge is not the only obstacle facing the developing world. Many Third World countries are still wrestling with the problem of nation-building—that is, attempting to build viable political institutions that meld the various tribal, religious, racial, and linguistic interests of the nation. This is no mean feat. In many cases, public attitudes are parochial and particularistic; formidable barriers prevent integration and assimilation. Many Third World nations are plagued by deep disunity, engendered by a host of competing values, beliefs, and traditions.

The developing world also must wage a concerted campaign to stem the population explosion. Although this problem is not universal in the Third World, it does affect many nations. For those countries, it has prevented significant economic growth. Obviously, a nation cannot spend huge sums on industrial development if it is unable to feed, clothe, and shelter its people. Many of these countries have attempted to reduce their fast-rising populations by initiating birth control campaigns, often with minimal success. The problem has reached epidemic proportions in some Third World countries, where the population has continued to double every 20 years.

Clearly, economic growth is not solely dependent on the development of industry. It is not enough simply to build new factories or dams or steel mills. The developing world must redefine many of its social, political, and economic beliefs. Indeed, modernization requires the complete transformation of the entire society. To achieve this objective, nations must rethink their beliefs on such matters as economic competition, savings, investments, profits, and economic growth.

Unless the Third World solves these and other problems, it is likely to face unprecedented chaos, disorder, and violence, not to mention instability, insecurity, and dependence. As these nations wrestle with the problem of nation-building, they must develop the conditions necessary for economic growth. In many ways, the battle for independence pales by comparison. To survive, Third World nations must promote both agrarian and industrial development. They must not only be able to feed their burgeoning populations, but must devise new ways to produce the goods and services necessary to achieve modernization. The clock is ticking away. The future demands bold action; anything else will invite catastrophe.

Looking Ahead: Challenge Questions

Has independence significantly improved the quality of life in the developing world?

What are the most common sources of conflict in the Third World?

Why is sovereignty a major obstacle to peace in the developing world?

Is underdevelopment a problem indigenous to the Third World?

What explains the North-South affluence gap?

Why is the Third World so susceptible to fluctuations in the international economy?

Is economic progress incompatible with the value systems of the developing world?

Does the West suffer from intellectual imperialism in its dealings with the Third World?

Do shifts in Soviet pronouncements about the developing world signal a retreat from established policy?

How has Soviet strategy changed in the Third World?

How will improved U.S.–Soviet relations affect the plight of the developing world?

The Third World

David W. Ziegler

David W. Ziegler, Professor of Political Science at Western Washington University, received his M.A. and his Ph.D. degrees from Harvard University. He also has received Fulbright, Danforth, and Woodrow Wilson Fellowships.

The concept of sovereignty, as developed in Europe in the seventeenth and eighteenth centuries, was until recently applied only to the most powerful states, most of which were located in Europe. The rest of the world, lacking sovereignty, could therefore legitimately be "discovered" and then "claimed" by these powerful states and added to their own territory. It was only with the League of Nations in the 1920's and 1930's that some inroads were made on the traditional view that the non-Western world was territory in which the inhabitants had no legitimate claims of their own. The League provided for what it called "mandates" in some areas of the world. Although the effect on the inhabitants of mandated territories was not very different from colonial rule, the presumption was that the major power in charge of the mandate would not rule indefinitely but only as long as it took to prepare the people for self-government. This system provided some hope for the future, but it did little to change the day-to-day realities. In 1935, 70 percent of the world's population was still under the control of Western governments.[1]

RISE TO PROMINENCE

It was only with the foundation and growth of the United Nations that a significant number of non-Western states began to play an important role in world politics. The UN Charter mentions as a basic principle the self-determination of peoples. Although in its first years the membership of the UN was confined to just about the same countries that had composed the League of Nations, this balance began to change as former colonies acquired their independence. The year 1960 marks an important turning point. In that year sixteen newly independent African states were admited as members of the UN. The number of such states has continued to grow, and at present they make up more than half of the states of the world.

The term often used to describe these new states is remnant of Cold War thinking. In the bipolar conception developed in the 1950's, states belonged to the world of the United States and its allies or to the world of the Soviet Union and its allies. The remaining countries were said to make up the *Third World*.

DEFINITION OF "THIRD WORLD"

People use the name "Third World" as though it referred to a coherent group of states—much in the way "the Soviet bloc" refers to centrally planned economies ruled by Marxist-Leninist parties with close ties to the Soviet Union. But Third World is a label lacking precision. Both Sweden and Switzerland were neutral states, yet they were not considered Third World countries. The Third World countries were said to be located in Asia, Africa, and Latin America, but that area includes Taiwan, Israel, and South Africa, which were not considered part of the Third World. Most Third World states were poor and struggling with problems of economic development, yet so were Greece and Turkey, both members of NATO. In short, Third World is a residual category, where we put what is left over.

Efforts to define Third World positively—as the membership of some group—are more useful. In political terms, the most significant such group is the Non-Aligned Nations. President Sukarno of Indonesia called the first conference of states wishing to avoid involvement with the major powers at Bandung in 1955. Six years later, Sukarno, along with Nehru of India, Nasser of Egypt, and Tito of Yugoslavia, turned it into a permanent organization, with twenty-five members. The movement grew to almost one-hundred members, with yearly meetings of foreign ministers and summit conferences of heads of state every three years.

Yet divisions within the movement began to appear in 1975, when it added to its membership North Korea and North Vietnam, states that were by any reasonable definition not non-aligned but members of the Soviet bloc. Internal divisions appeared in 1978 as some of the original members tried to resist attempts by Cuba, Angola, and Vietnam—all of whom had pacts with the Soviet Union—to take consistently pro-Soviet positions on foreign policy issues. A summit conference in Havana in 1979 was dominated by Castro, with only minor concessions to the more traditional aims represented by Tito, the last of the original founders to attend. The final declaration of the Havana Conference included numerous attacks on the United States—for example, for its colonialism of Puerto Rico—but none on the Soviet Union. The unity of the movement and the influence of Castro as its chairperson received a sharp setback, however, in early 1980, when half of the membership in a United Nations vote condemned the Soviet Union for its invasion of Afghanistan.

The disunity of the Non-Aligned Nations illustrated a basic

feature of the concept of the Third World. Despite the desire by many members of these states to think of themselves as a unified group, they are beset by serious differences. Even if alliances with major powers are discounted, the political differences among these states are very great. Saudi Arabia, which has a conservative monarchy, is a member; so is its radical neighbor South Yemen. In fact the only ideology they share is that of nationalism, but because nationalism stresses the particular state, it tends to divide and not to unite.

The emphasis in the 1950's and 1960's was on defining the Third World politically. Recent years have seen more emphasis on economic condition as a defining characteristic. Thus, the twenty-four wealthy states known as "industrially developed market economies" are members of the Organization for Economic Cooperation and Development (OECD). States modeled on the Marxist-Leninist ideal of a "centrally planned economy" are members of the Council for Mutual Economic Assistance (CMEA). The remaining states are members of the Group of 77, a somewhat misleading name that was taken from the actual number at the time of its formation in 1964 but which today comprises well over one-hundred states. Because the most prominent OECD countries are in the northern hemisphere—United States, Japan, Western Europe—and many of the Group of 77 are in the southern, they are sometimes referred to as the North and the South. (The CMEA has tried to attract little attention, claiming that whatever poverty exists in the poor countries is the result of imperialism and so they share no responsibility.)

An economic definition of the Third World is not particularly helpful. At the one extreme are countries with suddenly very high incomes per capita because of oil wealth—Saudi Arabia, Kuwait, United Arab Emirates. At the other extreme are countries so poor they are often put in a separate category of "Fourth World." Over 1 billion people live in countries where the per capita income is under $220 a year. These are countries with no natural resources and a growth rate of under 1 per cent a year—enough to add only two dollars to each person's yearly income.

In between the oil-rich and the low-income are the "newly industrialized" countries—South Korea, Brazil, India, Mexico. In some ways these countries are much closer to the OECD countries than they are to other members of the Group of 77. They have no interest in the cancellation of debts, for example, because much of the high growth rate they have achieved (an average in 1979 and 1980 of 5.5 per cent) results from international loans. Defaulting on loans or having them cancelled would deprive them of loans in the future to sustain their growth rate.

The differences among countries generally considered Third World—whether defined politically or economically—are so great that we cannot reasonably speak of the Third World as a unified actor in international politics.

THIRD WORLD INFLUENCE ON WAR AND PEACE

The participation in international politics by over one-hundred new states in Asia, Africa, and Latin America poses two obstacles to peace. On the one hand, it has vitiated some of the traditional approaches to peace. On the other, it has been the source of many new conflicts.

. . . The extent and force of international law have been seriously restricted by the anti-colonial revolution promoted by and working to the benefit of these states. Legal principles of long standing, such as freedom of the high seas or immunity for diplomats, are disregarded in the name of anti-imperialism. Likewise the focus of international organizations such as the United Nations has been shifted away from issues of war and peace toward support first of liberation from colonial rule and then economic development.

The gap between the Third World's new aspirations and traditional ways of conducting international relations is a source of conflict. It widened particularly in the 1960's and 1970's, as people's attitudes in one group of states—above all our own, but also many of the states of Western Europe—were moving in one direction while the people's attitudes in the Third World were moving in another. Many of the states in the Third World had been part of larger, multinational political units, usually colonial empires. As these empires ended they were replaced by more numerous, smaller states.

At the same time, many people in long-established states were calling for a broadening of horizons beyond the nation, for seeing problems in global terms, for viewing ourselves as travelers on "Spaceship Earth." Among many young people patriotism came to be seen as old-fashioned. Proposals to reinstitute the draft were greeted by students holding signs proclaiming, "Nothing is worth dying for." National barriers seemed less important to Europeans, as more states joined the European Community.

These trends were not mirrored in the Third World. The opposite was more likely to be the case. States jealously defended their sovereignty. Young people seemed to find many issues worth dying for, as they joined armies to liberate unredeemed territory (Somalis in the 1970's), to aid other members of their national group (Turks in 1974), or expel foreigners from their land (Iranians in the 1980's). While the United States worried about the proper way to deal with an increase in illegal aliens, the government of Nigeria one day simply announced the forcible expulsion of all foreigners without work permits. According to the Nigerian government's own estimate, 2 million aliens were deported.

Many states have tried to remove foreign influences in a process called *indigenization*. Joseph Mobutu changed the name of his country from the "Congo" to what he saw as the more native name "Zaire," then changed his own name to Mobutu Sesu Seko. In Libya and Iran street signs in English or even ones using the Latin alphabet have been removed, leaving only signs in Arabic script.

Sometimes attempts by international organizations to implement policies were vigorously resisted in the name of sovereignty. Out of sensitivity to the charge that they were not managing their affairs as well as they had been under colonial rule, states tried to cover up health problems, even if the latter were not the result of government policy. Most African states denied for a long time that they had any cases of acquired immune deficiency syndrome (AIDS), despite an international obligation to report all cases to the World Health Organization; exercising their sovereignty they routinely denied visas to reporters investigating AIDS. Ethiopia expelled foreign doctors who reported cases of cholera after the government had denied that such cases existed.[2] Many other states objected to the austerity measures demanded by the International Monetary Fund (IMF) as a condition for loans to support collapsing economies; blame for the resulting rise in cost of living was placed on the IMF, not their own countries' mistaken policies, and governments were tempted to repudiate the IMF rather than face down rioters.[3]

We have seen repeatedly how sovereignty is a major obstacle to peace. The increase in the number of states enamored of it and glorifying it multiplies the obstacles to international agreement and cooperation.

SOURCES OF CONFLICT WITHIN THE THIRD WORLD

The Third World is an important source of conflict quite apart from great power interests. One study has put the total deaths from 1945 to 1967 resulting from violence within and among these countries at 7,480,000.[4] If we add to that the deaths from only two of the conflicts that have occurred since 1967 the Nigerian civil war (2 million deaths) and the Pakistan civil war (500,000 deaths)—we already exceed the number of battle deaths of World War I. With violence of such magnitude, the disputes are worth looking at for their own sake, but in addition they frequently have repercussions in international politics. After looking at the origin of many of these disputes, we shall see why their effects spread so far.

Conflict in the Third World has been attributed to a number of factors—the desire to acquire modern industrial technology, resentment at higher standards of living in economically developed countries, colonial exploitation in the past, and racial discrimination in the present. Important as these may be, they are overshadowed by another source of conflict: national sentiment.

The word "nation" is often inappropriately used (as in the name the United Nations), and so it is necessary to first define carefully what we mean. By *nation* we mean a distinct ethnic group that is clearly set off from its neighbors by such features as a separate language, separate customs, and separate traditions. One important feature of a nation is that you have no control over which one you belong to—you are born into it. Nationality is sometimes called a "primordial tie," a primary bond as opposed to second-order ties or associations. You can choose to join the Audobon Society or the Democratic Party or the Free Will Baptist Church; you can also choose to quit these associations if you desire. The element of choice is absent from a primordial tie.[5]

Conflict resulting from nationalist and other primordial ties is not limited to the Third World. Canada's problems with Quebec and Britain's problems with Northern Ireland are conflicts that have their origin in primordial ties. But it is in the Third World that the problems are most severe. For in the Third World the conditions that facilitated secondary or associational ties are becoming weaker and the conditions that activate primordial ties are becoming stronger. The British Empire, like other colonial empires, was an association. Although membership in it was not always strictly voluntary, no group was excluded because of a primordial trait. Nigerians and Indians alike were free to embrace Anglican or Catholic Christianity, learn English, study at Oxford, and participate in whatever other privileges were extended to British subjects. But Nigeria and India were themselves composed of many ethnic groups. These groups united to free themselves of British rule, but once the British left, the primordial ties reasserted themselves. In Nigeria 250 different languages are spoken; in India the number is 1,652. With

the British imposing English on the entire country, it was possible to have a uniform school system and a common government language. With the departure of the British, the question of what language would be used for instruction and government business became a hotly contested political issue.

It is precisely those developments to which we refer as modernizing and progressive—such things as increased industrialization, improved means of communication, and higher standards of education—that increase the importance of primordial ties. This is so because all these developments mix together people from different groups who previously had no contact with each other. By increasing contact you increase the possibilities for conflict. We might take the case of Nigeria. Suppose several Ibo-speakers from the east take advantage of a new highway to travel north to the part of Nigeria inhabited by Hausa-speakers. Perhaps they open a shop there to sell products newly imported from Europe or Japan, such as sewing machines. The Ibos are likely to be Christians and offend the Muslim Hausas by raising and eating pigs (which are forbidden to Muslims). The language of trade between Ibos and Hausas may be English but among themselves the Ibos use their own language, which arouses suspicions among the Hausas that the Ibos are saying things about them, making fun of them, plotting to cheat them. This example is not a hypothetical one. It was precisely such movement by the Ibos and such hostility that it aroused that it led to a massacre of 50,000 Ibos in northern Nigeria in 1966. Another 1 million Ibos were driven out. They fled back to the east and demanded their own state as the only sure source of protection, an event that led to a bloody and ultimately unsuccessful civil war.

It was precisely the modern developments such as better roads and imported sewing machines that generated this conflict. In the past diverse ethnic groups had little contact with each other. Colonial rule by the British set in motion the process by which the groups came in contact, although the British also were able to prevent tensions from erupting into violence. When the British departed, the process continued, now without any effective central control.

PRIMORDIAL TIES AS A SOURCE OF CONFLICT

The experience of the Ibos in Nigeria illustrates what many people have come to believe, that security for an ethnic group can be found only when that group controls its own state. With thousands of ethnic groups in the world and only about 150 states, it is clear that not all groups control their own states. The most obvious problem is that one state may include many ethnic groups.

But this is not the only problem. In some places states' borders cut right through the territory inhabited by an ethnic group. Sometimes the group so divided is only one of many; this is the case in many African countries where the boundaries were drawn by European colonial powers with no concern for local inhabitants. In other cases the group divided by a state boundary makes up the entire population of each political unit—in other words, a single nation is divided into several states. It was this condition that led to the German wars of unification in the nineteenth century. A century later the division of Vietnam and Korea caused wars for the same reason.

Even though these few cases have been the source of international conflict, they are far outnumbered by the cases in which one state embraces many nations. Only fourteen states (or fewer, if you treat Germany, Vietnam, and Korea each as one), about 10 per cent of the world's states, are homogeneous in ethnic makeup. In another 40 per cent, one ethnic group is dominant, making up 75 per cent or more of the population. But, as Cyprus showed, this is no guarantee of peace; although the Greeks made up more than 80 per cent of the population, the Turks were not willing to submit to rule by them. The problems are even more acute in those states in which no one group makes up even as much as half the population. Almost 30 per cent of the states of the world fall into this category. Nigeria is one example; India and Pakistan are others.

The conflicts generated by ethnic questions within such states are a threat to international peace because they frequently spread beyond the borders of a single country. There are a number of reasons why this happens. When one nation is divided among several states, the issue is by definition international. When one ethnic group finds itself divided between two states, efforts by the group to ignore the border may provoke international disputes. This has been the case when Somali nomads ignored the borders between Somalia and the neighboring countries of Ethiopia and Kenya that cut across their traditional grazing land.

Another reason why conflict spreads is that ethnic ties are valued so highly in the world today that actions taken to support members of one's own ethnic group are considered justification for violating the basic principle of noninterference in the internal affairs of a sovereign state. India felt justified in entering Pakistan's civil war in 1971 because the massacre of Bengalis in Pakistan could not be tolerated by the Bengalis in India. The internal governance of Rhodesia and South Africa is a major concern to black African states; support for guerrillas seeking to overthrow regimes in these countries is not seen as illegitimate. The conflict over Israel has been escalated into a world conflict by primordial ties. Countries as distant as Morocco send troops to fight because of solidarity with other Arabs. American Jews translate their solidarity with Israel into active pressure on the United States government for greater commitment to Israel.

NATIONALISM AND WAR

In states that have been established for a long time, primordial ties are often weaker. Many Latin American states have been independent for over a century and in their populations nationalism is the primary emotion. (In states only recently independent, however, ethnic ties are still major factors. Guyana, a British colony until 1966, is split between groups originating in Africa and ones from the East Indies.) Conflicts between states in Latin America have been made more difficult to solve by intense nationalist feelings and in some cases have led to war. In 1969 El Salvador and Honduras fought over a disputed border. Argentina and Chile have gone as far as mobilizing troops over disputed islands in the sea south of Argentina. Argentina, to most people's surprise, landed troops on islands claimed by them in 1982. The British, who ruled the islands under the name of the Falklands, underestimated the intensity of nationalist feeling that led the Argentines to challenge a superior military power.

The war in the Falklands illustrates how conflicts in the Third World draw in other powers. The British felt directly challenged because of political claims for British protection by the people living on the Falklands, most of whom were of British origin. (Had the islands been uninhabited, the British would have turned them over to the Argentines years ago.) Sometimes outside powers are drawn in in less direct ways. Third World states may actively seek the support of major powers in their quarrels. India actively solicited the support of the Soviet Union in its quarrel with Pakistan. Pakistan in turn sought support from both China and the United States. Thus the war between India and Pakistan in 1971 over an essentially ethnic issue became a potential confrontation between the major powers.

The conflict between India and Pakistan also appears to have been the major motivation for first India and then Pakistan to try to acquire nuclear weapons. In 1974 India exploded a nuclear device that it termed "peaceful." In the absence of any clear-cut need for such a device or any subsequent use of nuclear technology for peaceful purposes, the impression remains strong that India was interested mainly in demonstrating its potential to acquire nuclear weapons. Pakistan's prime minister certainly perceived such an intent, because he declared, "We will eat leaves and grass, even go hungry, but we will have to get one."[6] By April 1979 Pakistan's program was so advanced that the United States government cut off all aid to Pakistan under the provisions of a law requiring such termination to countries acquiring nuclear weapons.[7]

NUCLEAR PROLIFERATION

The Indian explosion of a nuclear device in 1974 was important for three reasons. It was the first acquisition of nuclear capability by a country in over a decade (China's had been the most recent, in 1964). It was the first by a country not generally considered a great power (all other acknowledged nuclear states were permanent members of the Security Council). And it was the first nuclear device built with fuel diverted from power reactors. This last feature was the most alarming. A standard 1,000-megawatt thermal power reactor of current design produces over 200 kilograms of spent fuel a year, enough to make forty small nuclear explosives. With over 200 such reactors operating in more than forty-two countries, the potential for the spread of nuclear weapons to more countries is very great.[8]

Reaction to the Indian explosion illustrates again the essential lack of cohesion in the Third World. Although most of the Third World states adhered to the Non-Proliferation Treaty of 1968 (and thereby made it possible in the first place), when India exploded its nuclear device in 1974, Pakistan was the only member of the Third World to criticize India in the subsequent United Nations General Assembly. Some of these states may have been contemplating nuclear programs of their own; there is evidence that Iraq and Argentina were. Others may have been reluctant to criticize so prominent a member of the Non-Aligned Movement; they may even have enjoyed the technological triumph of what was once called a "backward nation."

But these feelings of solidarity among members of the Non-Aligned Movement have generated anxieties in states not accepted by the Non-Aligned Movement and not fitting comfortably into any grouping. Such states are sometimes called ''pariah'' or outcast states and many of them are considered the most likely to acquire nuclear weapons of their own—for example Israel, South Africa, Taiwan, South Korea. Although not normally considered Third World states, these states are geographically in the middle of the Third World and have Third World states for neighbors.

The proliferation of nuclear weapons to Third World states makes the Third World an even more serious source of international conflict. The use of such weapons in local or regional quarrels would quickly turn such quarrels into world crises. In another round of war between India and Pakistan or between Israel and its Arab neighbors, one can imagine the losing side resorting to nuclear weapons in desperation. Had Argentina possessed nuclear weapons when it was fighting Britain for the Falkland Islands, it might have been tempted to use them to save its position or even as an emotional reaction to the British sinking of one of their ships.

In response to evidence that Pakistan was building nuclear weapons, the United States suspended military aid; India, feeling more directly threatened, considered stronger measures. In 1982 United States intelligence officials suspected that India was developing a plan for a preemptive air strike to destroy the Pakistani facilities.[9] Israel carried out such a strike against Iraq in 1981, and although that strike did not escalate into war, an Indian strike against Pakistan could have. The Israelis struck against a small program, still far from completion, and evidently were completely successful. An only partially successful strike against an extensive program might provoke the target state to retaliate with whatever nuclear weapons remained.

Some analysts have speculated that some of Pakistan's weapons could find their way into the hands of Libya's President Muammar Qaddafi, perhaps in return for his financial support. Some of Qaddafi's public statements suggest he would be more willing to use such weapons against his avowed enemies, particularly Israel, than many other leaders would be. Or Qaddafi might transfer such weapons to a terrorist group, putting that group beyond the control of any state.[10]

We might recall the arguments of those who advocate a balance of terror. According to this line of thought, the possession of nuclear weapons by Third World states might make war less likely just as nuclear weapons have restrained the United States-Soviet rivalry. The argument has some merit but is not completely comforting. The United States and the Soviet Union have ample arsenals, not just a few weapons they would be tempted to use or lose. They have had years to consider carefully the implications of such weapons and to devise doctrines that try to deal with the complexities. They have invested in control devices to prevent unauthorized use. Neither the United States nor the Soviet Union is plagued by the problem common to most Third World states—military coups or takeovers by rival factions within the military.

The internal problems of Third World states are the most common cause of conflict in the world today. Tension between the superpowers occupies the attention of many people, but the actual fighting and dying occurs in countries such as Cambodia, Iraq, and Chad. In the older states, the conflicts generated by primordial ties have been largely settled. This has been the result not of superior wisdom or inherent virtue but simply of the relatively long time these countries have had to work on the problem. In some cases the problem was solved by the creation of separate states. Norway and Sweden became separate countries in 1905, for example. In other cases ethnic minorities were subdued by military conquest, as happened in the English wars against the Welsh and the Scots. In 1945 the Poles adopted an equally drastic measure against the Germans, expelling 10 million Germans from the territory they claimed as the Polish state. But even in the older states, not all conflicts over ethnic issues have been settled. The British have been struggling with the Irish for hundreds of years, and it appears that they will continue to do so for many more. With such struggles just beginning in many parts of the Third World, we can expect conflict there to continue for a long time to come.

NOTES

1. Grover Clark, *A Place in the Sun* (1936), cited by Harold Isaacs, *Idols of the Tribe* (New York: Harper & Row, 1975), p. 6.

2. Lawrence K. Altman, ''In Africa, Problems Change But the Frustrations Go On,'' *The New York Times*, December 10, 1985, p. Y18.

3. It is generally accepted that the government of Sudan was overthrown in 1985 because it tried to implement austerity measures demanded by the IMF.

4. Robert D. Crane, ''Postwar Ethnic Cultural Conflicts'' (1968), cited by Isaacs, p. 7.

5. There is some disagreement about terms. ''Primordial'' is used in approximately this way by Clifford Geertz, ''The Integrative Revolution: Primordial Sentiments and Civil Politics in the New States,'' in *Old Societies and New States*, ed. Clifford Geertz (New York: Free Press, 1963), especially pp. 109-119. See also the definition by Walker Connor, ''The Politics of Ethnonationalism,'' *Journal of International Affairs*, Vol. 27, No. 1 (1973), p. 2n.

6. Donna S. Kramer (Congressional Research Service), *Nuclear Energy: The Threat of Pakistan Going Nuclear*, Issue Brief No. IB 79093, October 23, 1979.

7. U.S. Senate, Committee on Governmental Affairs, Subcommittee on Energy, Nuclear Proliferation, and Federal Services, *Nuclear Proliferation: The Situation in Pakistan and India: Hearings*, 96th Congress, 1st sess., May 1, 1979.

8. Walter Marshall, ''On Plutonium Fears,'' *The New York Times*, April 18, 1978, p. 33.

9. Leonard S. Spector, *Nuclear Proliferation Today* (New York: Vintage, 1985), p. 48.

10. Steve Weissman and Herbert Krosney, *The Islamic Bomb* (New York: Times Books, 1981).

Ethnocentrism and Third World Development

Howard J. Wiarda

Howard J. Wiarda is professor of political science at the University of Massachusetts at Amherst; a research scholar at the American Enterprise Institute for Public Policy Research in Washington, D.C.; and a fellow of the Foreign Policy Research Institute. Among many books, he has written Ethnocentrism in American Foreign Policy: Can We Understand the Third World?

That body of literature focusing on political development has come under severe attack. Once the dominant paradigm within the discipline, the political development approach has been strongly criticized in various ways. Among these is the charge that political development heretofore has been conceived in almost exclusively Western (Northwest European and North American) terms. That is, that the categories and understandings of extant political development are derived ethnocentrically from the EuroAmerican experience and have little or no relevance to the non-Western world.

This charge is serious from several vantage points. First, it has major implications for the Third World: whether the development process is universal, whether Third World nations are but pale and retarded versions of the Western model, whether they will repeat the experience of the early developers, or whether they will fashion an indigenous model of development—or some blend of the Western and the indigenous. Second, it has important ramifications for the social sciences, with most of their concepts based on the Western developmental experience which may or may not be relevant to the Third World. Third, it has important implications for the foreign assistance donor nations—chiefly the United States but increasingly those of Western Europe—concerning the relevance of the developmental models and programs they seek to export to the Third World.

This article explores the problem of ethnocentrism in the study of political development. It is part of a larger project examining both Western and non-Western theories of development. This work suggests that the models of development most familiar in the literature are all derived from the Western experience, of a particular time and place, and therefore have but limited relevance to today's Third World nations. The study emphasizes the efforts of various Third World areas to devise indigenous models of development or to blend these with the Western and presumably more universal models. It suggests that Western foreign assistance programs, largely based on the older ethnocentric understandings, have seldom been successful; yet it concludes pessimistically that because Western policymakers, regardless of party, generally lack the comprehension and knowledge base to understand the Third World on its own terms, in its own language, and in its own cultural and institutional terms, the mistakes of the past are likely to be repeated.

In other papers and publications I have dealt with the ethnocentric assumptions of the social sciences, as well as the effort by Third World leaders to articulate and fashion an indigenous developmental model. In one paper I considered this issue as it affects human rights and United States human rights policy; in another, the revived effort to export democracy abroad; in still another, the ethnocentrism of United States economic assistance programs, expectations regarding the political role of the middle class, the armed forces and "professionalization," and the model of trade unionism the United States has tried to implant abroad.

I concentrate here on a series of other, but closely related, development assistance efforts: agrarian reform, community development, the United States-sponsored law and development program, and family planning. All of these programs derive from the same ethnocentric assumptions; together they form a social and political history (a pathology?) of developmentalism. I touch briefly on the common intellectual and programmatic assumptions of all these efforts, as well as Third World attempts to devise their own developmental paradigms. The theme and cry of "let us do it our way" is now becoming a global chorus. I also deal with the politics of the developmentalist approach and why it will be such a difficult paradigm to change or supersede.

I conclude that the often misguided and misdirected developmentalist programs analyzed here grow chiefly out of naiveté and wrong assumptions, not from venality, malevolence, or even "imperialism." American development assistance programs are generally based not on evil scheming but on good intentions gone awry for various reasons. I question as to where, other than their own experiences, Americans could conceivably have derived their developmentalist models. I fault them here for their biases and ethnocentrism, but realistically it seems unlikely that any model other than their own could have been used. Additionally, the Third World lack of under-

---

Misguided development programs grow chiefly out of naiveté and wrong assumptions.

---

standing of the United States is often at least as great as our malcomprehension of them. Here I concentrate on the latter theme, but the former also requires attention.

Development and Developmentalism

The literature of development and the practice of developmentalism, as an approach to alleviate underdevelopment, were uniquely American phenomena—although scholars and political leaders from other areas also accepted and participated in the formulation of this paradigm. It was uniquely American in that it was extremely, perhaps excessively, optimistic; it derived from the American experience of development (including Lockean liberalism and pluralism); it was largely written by Americans; it reflected a long American "missionary" tradition to bring the benefits of our civilization to other lands; and it became an integral part of American foreign policy toward the Third World, particularly Latin America.

The development literature and developmentalism were not just some abstract intellectual formulations confined to the academy. Rather these ideas had both direct and indirect impacts on policy. Through the incorporation into the Kennedy administration of intellectuals associated with developmentalist themes—such as Walt W. Rostow, McGeorge Bundy, John Kenneth Galbraith, Adolph Berle, Arthur Schlesinger, Jr., and Lincoln Gordon—the ideas of developmentalism were often translated directly into policy. Indirectly this body of literature also had a major impact: as developmentalism became something of the leitmotiv of the 1960s, the thing to do,

and the basis for United States policy toward the Third World, the ideas of the leading theorists of development were gradually infused into the bureaucracy. This came about by the developmentalist intellectuals attending the almost endless conferences that agencies such as the U.S. Agency for International Development (AID) and the Department of State organize, and by the widespread dissemination of the intellectuals' ideas through the universities and among university-trained technocrats of development. Just because a government bureaucrat did not know specifically that it was Walt Rostow's or Seymour Martin Lipset's ideas that he was implementing is hardly sufficient reason to deny the immense impact on United States foreign assistance programs that these ideas had for a long time, and that they continue to have in many government circles today.

Two themes particularly command our attention here. The first is the need for a social and political history of the idea of development itself, tracing its rise in the 1950s and 1960s, its gradual decline in the 1970s and 1980s, and the reasons for this decline. The second involves a history of the rise and fall of various developmental panaceas—agrarian reform, community development, infrastructure development, family planning, basic human needs, the democracy agenda, and private sector initiatives—that have been proffered by the developmentalist school over the years. Such a history would examine the often fickle elevation and then abandonment of these ideas, their intellectual and political origins, and their fate when tested against the hard realities of Third World and non-Western areas.

Agrarian reform in the Third World is part of a larger scheme to promote economic development, build a stronger middle class, and, from the point of view of its United States sponsors, reduce or eliminate the appeal of radical groups. Agrarian reform must thus be looked at in the broader context of the United States effort to fashion a Marshall Plan-like assistance program for the Third World, one component of which was designed for the rural sector. Walt W. Rostow's significantly titled *The Stages of Economic Growth: A Non-Communist Manifesto* served as a key volume in providing the intellectual rationalizations for such an effort. Rostow argued that the stages of economic growth (such as "preconditions for take-off" and "take off") outlined in his book were universal, that all societies (including those of the Third World) went through the same processes, that the United States was the most advanced nation and therefore provided the model for others, that the United States should assist the Third World in its growth, that the funds thus generated would trickle down, that by our assistance a middle-class society would be created that looked just like our own—stable, moderate politically, socially just, and so on. I have dealt critically with the Rostow arguments in other writings. Here, I hope to show that agrarian reform was simply one aspect of a much larger assistance program which had at its base a definite political agenda.

I favor agrarian reform under the proper circumstances and am supportive of the other social assistance programs discussed here: community development, law and development, and family planning. My purpose is not to attack these programs as such but only to discuss the context out of which they emerged and the particular biases of United States official efforts in these areas. I seek not to tear these programs down but to provide a basis to refashion and foment them in ways that make them culturally and socially relevant to the societies in which they are applied and that enable them to take hold and have more lasting effects than they have in the past.

Agrarian reform, as part of a broader United States assistance program, was viewed as an extension of the Rostow analysis to the Third World countryside. It was aimed, especially in Latin America, at creating a rural middle class where none had existed before. According to much lore and popular literature, the Latin American countryside was characterized by immensely large landholdings, latifundia, and dominated by a rapacious oligarchy more interested in exploiting the peasants and using land as a symbol of social status than for greater production. By dividing up this land, the argument maintained, the back of this quasifeudal system could be broken, the oligarchy destroyed, and a new class of medium-sized rural landholders created. Because they would own their land and thus have a stronger stake in their own futures, these new middle-class family farmers would be loyal to the system and would no longer be prey to the appeal of either fascism or communism. Agrarian reform was seen as the rural counterpart to what overall United States economic assistance a la Rostow was designed to create in urban areas: a prosperous middle class that could serve as a bastion of democracy, stability, and anticommunism.

Agrarian Reform

As a form of social engineering, agrarian reform originated in the postwar United States occupation of Japan and in the nationalist occupation of Taiwan. Initially, virtually everyone involved in the agrarian reform programs promoted by the United States in Latin America had first learned their lessons through experience in Japan and Taiwan. Indeed, Japan and Taiwan served as the models for the programs in Latin America. Scholars are still discussing whether and to what degree the programs in Japan or Taiwan may be termed "successes." I concede that the successes in these two countries outweigh the failures, but, aside from that, we must have doubts about the applicability of the Japanese or Taiwanese "models" to Latin America, where conditions are entirely different. Far more open space exists which gives agrarian reform less immediacy; there is no occupation army to enforce the program as there had been in Japan and Taiwan, and (although I hesitate to use the term) the Latin American ethos, behavior patterns, social structure, and attitudes toward land are different than those of the two Asian nations. The contrast is so great that we can doubt the feasibility and appropriateness of transferring a Japanese or Taiwanese model to a set of societies in Latin America.

While the "model" and experience of those active in the agrarian reform movement came from Japan and Taiwan, the real example, as might be expected from Rostow's analysis, was the United States. Agrarian reform in Latin America and other Third World areas derived from an idealized version of the American family farm. That farm was medium-sized—neither too big (latifundia) nor too small (minifundia); it was managed by self-sufficient yeoman farmers who were educated and used the most modern techniques. These farmers were civically conscious, active participants in local government and town meetings; they were politically moderate, not subject to the appeal of radical ideologies of Left or Right. Although the foreign experience of the early agrarian reform practitioners was in Asia, the real model was in the United States: the American midwest or the New England family farm.

Whether or not the American farm and farmer was portrayed accurately, whether the family farm was really the rock of stability it was imagined to be, or even whether the family farm has any future in America—all serious concerns—we must question the applicability of this model to Latin America and other Third World areas. Upon close examination, the differences between the United States and these other areas are more significant than the similarities. The social structure is entirely different (there is no rural middle class in most of Latin America), class and ethnic differences are large, economies are different (capitalist versus neomercantilist), and political structures are different. These differences are so pronounced that it is far-fetched and beyond the realm of possibility to expect a North American rural structure to ever be transplanted into Latin America.

The United States' effort to bring agrarian reform to Latin America and the rest of the Third World was born of the cold war and launched in the wake of the great fear following the Cuban Revolution that all of Latin America was about "to go communist." Agrarian reform was in part a cold war strategy initiated in some desperation and without its prospects and possibilities having been thoroughly thought through. The arguments seemed so plausible: American technology and funds would help the Latin American nations to achieve democracy, development, and stability through the reform of the rural sector. At the time, no one paid much attention to the impossibility of the United States transferring its institutions to societies where they did not fit, or could fit only imperfectly. John F. Kennedy was in office, the United States was at the height of its power and influence, optimism and hope ran high, Vietnam and Watergate had not yet occurred, and the United States still seemed to be both policeman and inspiration to the world. Only later would we come to see why the program not only did not work but could not work.

1. UNDERSTANDING THE THIRD WORLD

Agrarian reform was not just a program the Latin Americans could take or leave; rather, the adoption of an agrarian reform law was the condition by which a country qualified for Alliance for Progress assistance. Hence **most** of the Latin American countries dutifully enacted an agrarian reform law. Since their hearts were not really in it, or not fully committed, or because they soon developed other priorities, relatively little agrarian reform was ever implemented. Some peasants received titles to land under the program; this was usually accompanied by presidential helicopters, expansive media coverage, and great celebratory outpourings. But in no country was the structure of rural life fundamentally affected by the United States-inspired agrarian reform efforts.

There are various forms of agrarian reform. The one at which the United States is most successful involves technical assistance, farm credits, agricultural extension, and the like. None of these involve changing the pattern of ownership; instead they provide aid to those who already own land. We must also distinguish between an agrarian reform carried out for economic purposes versus one carried out with social or political goals in mind. The conclusion of the experts is that in general agrarian reform does not make sense economically because production falls, at least initially, as a result; whether agrarian reform makes much sense sociologically or politically is more difficult to decide. It could be argued that agrarian reform has helped buy the United States some time and perhaps some limited stability in Latin America, but the revolutions in Nicaragua and El Salvador as well as ferment in a number of other countries seem to indicate that it may not have been enough.

Eventually the United States itself lost interest in agrarian reform—except in emergency cases such as El Salvador. The results were generally disappointing; the Latin American governments were not cooperative; and other agendas came to the fore. Agrarian reform was the great developmentalist panacea of the 1960s; by the 1970s there were other concerns.

Overall, pervasive ethnocentrism characterized many aspects of the United States' efforts to export agrarian reform. This is evident by: (1) the political agenda and cold war considerations that undergirded the United States agrarian reform efforts; (2) the strong influence on these programs of the Japanese and Taiwanese experiences which had little relevance for Latin America; (3) the implicit reliance on the United States family farm model, as if that could be transferred to Latin America; (4) the heavy grounding of these programs on United States political assumptions; and (5) the naiveté and lack of knowledge or sophistication about Latin America of so many of the United States officials and technicians involved in the program. It is small wonder that the program produced only limited results.

Community Development

The social and political history of community develop-ment is remarkably parallel to that of agrarian reform. Both programs flourished with considerable romance and pizzazz in the early 1960s. Both emerged as major public policy agenda items during the era of Camelot, the presidency of John F. Kennedy. Both were products of what has been called the "Peace Corps mood" of those times—that is, the urge not just to study development but to bring its agreed-upon benefits to less-favored lands. By the end of that decade both programs had faded. They did not entirely disappear. There are still some true believers, although they are a dwindling number and without the levels of enthusiasm and support that characterized the earlier halcyon and optimistic years.

The community development programs of the 1960s grew directly out of the United States programs of the same name and era. In Latin America and elsewhere in the Third World a large share of the program was carried out by American Peace Corps volunteers. In addition, there was a cottage industry of community development experts—all trained in the United States, deriving their models from the United States, and often closely connected with the United States civil rights movement and other forms of political activism. In those Latin American countries where there was little or no community development, the United States proceeded, as it did with agrarian reform, to create a special agency to administer the program within the host country government structure.

Again, I add a cautionary note: I have nothing against community development; indeed I tend to favor such programs. The problem is not community development but rather the models used and the appropriateness of these in a non-Western, partially Western, or Third World context.

Community development was the special preserve of the Peace Corps, and considerable literature developed out of that experience. Some of this literature even had more ambitious general and theoretical pretensions. In their training programs, Peace Corps volunteers "majored" in community development. Most of the volunteers, in those early days, had been liberal arts students as undergraduates; they often lacked necessary technical expertise or experience. What they meant by "community development" was often rudimentary: building latrines, digging ditches, aiding various self-help projects and what was called "organizational literacy." The latter referred to the basic organizational principles of running a meeting; talking in order; contacting a local official or congressman; forming a cooperative; or lobbying local authorities for housing materials, well-drilling equipment, sewers, roads, and electricity.

These Peace Corps activities were generally harmless enough and sometimes something positive was accomplished. In the long run, the advantages of Peace Corps service were probably greater for the volunteers themselves (in learning a new language and culture) than for the host community. The model with which the volunteers had to work was a major problem.

That model was derived almost entirely from the United States experience. The kind of community-based, grass-roots, self-help programs the Peace Corps sought to initiate came from the North American experience; they were grounded in the tradition of the New England town meeting and local self-governance. They were based upon a liberal, Lockean, Jeffersonian notion of direct and participatory democracy that had almost no basis in Latin America. The historical base of the Latin American systems is not Lockean; it is derived from the organic monism and unity of Saint Thomas and Francisco Suárez. Lockean liberalism is a relatively recent implant in Latin America, and in most countries it remains a minority strain.

The other major problem pertained to the structure of Latin American local government. Local government in Latin America is patterned after the French system. Almost all power is concentrated in the central state and its agencies. Local governments have almost no independent authority. They have almost no power to tax, to set policy, or to initiate new programs. Activities which in the United States are administered at the local level—con

---

Agrarian reform was in part a cold war strategy initiated in some desperation.

---

cerning schools, utilities, health care, police, water supplies, sewers, and so on, the activities with which Peace Corps volunteers were trained to assist—are in Latin America handled not at the local but at the national level. The national government and its ministries determine educational policy, health policy, and so forth. Even if the Peace Corps volunteers could convince local authorities that they needed roads or well-drilling equipment or virtually anything else, the local government had no funds, no authority, no requisitioning power to get any of those things done. The result was a great deal of unhappiness and disillusionment on all sides.

The response took various forms. To overcome these bottlenecks, the United States helped create in several Latin American countries a national Office of Community Development that would help organize and facilitate development activities. These agencies were almost 100 percent United States agencies: staffed, funded, and largely run by the United States or by nationals trained in the United States—so much for self-help. To compound the problem, these offices tended to serve as agencies for even further centralization in countries already highly, some would say overly, centralized. In many instances they took away the already slight residual power that had been located at the local level.

The Peace Corps volunteers were also frustrated. In some notorious early cases they all but completely took over the local communities to which they had been as-

signed. At least one was elected mayor of his town—a perfectly rational step from the point of view of local townspeople who felt they would get more for their community that way, but unacceptable to Peace Corps officials who rightly pointed out to this particular volunteer that he was there to help at the local level, not to take over the place. Many volunteers put to work the lobbying and political organizational skills they had learned in the United States by leading demonstrations, marching on town hall, or leading delegations to the capital city to push for their particular projects. Again, Peace Corps officials had to suggest that such activities, heretofore largely unheard of in Latin America, were not what they had in mind by "community development." After considerable comings and goings, many volunteers ended up teaching English at the local level—a useful contribution, but one far removed from the more grandiose designs of community development theory.

I do not mean to imply that either the Peace Corps or community development are bad ideas. Their accomplishments have been many and significant. I do maintain that the model was flawed, perhaps mortally so, from its inception. It was: (1) based upon a set of liberal-Lockean United States political perceptions and understandings about participatory government that had little basis in Latin America; (2) grounded on the model of a decentralized political system that was different from that of Latin America's centralist tradition, and (3) responsible for producing the opposite effect from that intended—greater centralization, often at the expense of local units. By the end of the 1960s, the community development panacea had also run its course.

Law and Development

Compared with the others, the American-sponsored program on law and development in Latin America was modest. Nevertheless, it was cut from the same cloth as the ones I have discussed, and it exhibited all the familiar biases. For this program, we already have James A. Gardner's thorough, well-researched, scholarly study, *Legal Imperialism*, that recounts its social and political history.

In a manner remarkably parallel to that of a myriad of other United States-conceived programs fashioned in the early to mid-1960s, the law and development program was an effort to bring to bear American legal expertise and ways of doing things for the benefit of Third World development. In part it reflected the aspiration of American lawyers to get in on the same travel and consulting opportunities as economists, sociologists, and political scientists; more fundamentally it reflected the belief among lawyers that they too had major contributions to make to Third World development.

Unfortunately, American concepts and models underpinned and defined the program. The model used was an idealized vision of law and the lawyer—pragmatic, omnicompetent, problem-solving—in United States society. No attention was paid to Latin American law or legal precepts. These were swept aside as "traditional" in favor of the new American conception. The program was also strongly conditioned by cold war considerations and a strident anticommunism. It was bolstered, as were the other programs I have discussed, by a Marshall Plan-like vision, as well as the confidence that we could do it. As Gardner, the foremost student of this program, has written, it was inept and fatally flawed from the beginning.

The program relied exclusively on an American conception of legal culture: It was based on and tried to implant an American system of legal education; it used the case method; it was grounded in American legal thought; it employed the Socratic dialogue of United States law schools; it taught the adversarial approach of American law; it was pragmatic, issues-oriented, and problem-solving. The United States model that these legal advisers sought to export contained a benign view of the state—that it was or would be liberal, pluralist, developmental, impartial, and progressive—which soon ran head-on into the authoritarian statism of Latin America.

The program was initiated on the basis of American

Community development was the special preserve of the Peace Corps.

---

notions of political democracy, liberal capitalism, and non- or anticommunism. There is nothing wrong with these values; the question is one of their relevance to Latin America. United States lawyers would presumably help engineer freer and more democratic societies in Latin America, as—in their own eyes, at least—they had done in the United States. They viewed Latin America as not having viable institutions of its own and hence as a social laboratory for a United States-based program of law-and-development assistance. As in other programs, it was a missionary call that went out, a particularly American one. The program, having as its goal the advancement and implanting of a particularly American legal model, was, as Gardner put it, a "tropical New Deal."

According to Gardner, the American lawyers and law schools who were part of the law and development program in Latin America were poorly equipped by training or background for their assignments. Typically they had no understanding of the local language, customs, or law. They were culturally unaware, sociologically uninformed, and ethnocentric—consistently viewing Latin America in the self-image of the United States. They found, apparently to their surprise, that the goals and methods they brought with them from the United States, and which they assumed to be universal, were not necessarily shared in the Third World. They found the local legal cultures to be resilient and resistant to change. Many apparently lacked the tact to deal with their local counterparts. Rely-

ing on an American legal system and methods which they carried abroad with almost crusading zeal, and often inept and insensitive in dealing with local practices they—or at least the program's administrators—soon discovered that the model used was wrong and inappropriate. The overall result, by common consensus of both the host countries and the program's United States administrators, was failure.

The Latin American legal tradition was entirely different from that of the United States, being based on a code or civil law tradition, not on a common law tradition as in the United States. Most of the United States lawyers involved in the program knew that, but they were not aware of the full implications, of the wide-ranging ramifications of this distinct jurisprudential tradition. At a most basic level, it is doubtful whether this tradition in Latin America is even compatible with a law-and-development orientation. The Socratic method is of doubtful utility in a system based on rote memorization. The use of cases is not appropriate in a context in which the role of the judge is to find the applicable provision of the code, not to induce a general principle from a series of cases. The system of law school training in Latin America and even the role of the law school teacher is entirely different than in the United States. In Latin America there is little judicial review. Rather, as in the French system, these are administrative states, bureaucratic states that are grounded on a system of state positivism, not American-style separation of powers and interest-group pluralism. Prior to plunging headlong into the field, there were almost no preparations, no grounding in Latin American law, no studies of the implications of bringing an American legal system in contact with an undeveloped Roman-Iberian one. As a result, the program had what one author calls "unexpected vulnerabilities" even in those countries of Latin America (for example, Colombia) that were most democratic and therefore closer to the American system.

Three aspects of the law and development program especially command our attention. First, although neither the Latin American governments nor their lawyers or law schools especially wanted the program, the American government brought it anyway. Law and development was like many United States programs then and now: it was grounded on the notion that "we [North Americans] know best," not "they [Latin Americans] know best." Latin Americans not only had different expectations of the program, but they knew from the beginning that it would not work in their context. Bringing in a program anyway that was considered folly, and was known in advance not to work—by the locals if not by the Americans—seems the height of insensitivity.

Second, this program closely complemented and reinforced other United States ideas about foreign aid. It was entirely grounded in the American experience, with little reference to Latin American realities. It viewed Latin American realities with considerable disdain, its legal institutions as a "problem to be overcome." Since Latin America's history had been, by common consent, a "failure" and its institutions unresponsive and "dysfunctional," these could be cavalierly and precipitously discarded in favor of a presumably better model. Attempting naively and ethnocentrically to recast Latin America in the United States mold, and without any consideration for the possible viability of indigenous institutions, the program was bound to be a failure, as proved to be the case. The strong criticisms, even the language, leveled by critics seems equally applicable to the other programs I am describing.

Third, the program had a not very thinly disguised political agenda. Although small in comparison with other programs, it was neither harmless nor "benignly neutral." The program was to be, along with a number of others promulgated in this period, an agency of advanced, even radical change. It was designed to break down the existing legal system of Latin America and to substitute another, more "progressive" one for it. The notion that we and our assistance programs, however well-intentioned, should sweep away another country's (actually a whole set of countries') legal system and replace it with our own presumably better one would seem to be arrogant, misguided, and shortsighted.

Family Planning

Family planning was to the late 1960s and early 1970s what agrarian reform and community development had been in the earlier 1960s; the great panacea that would solve all of Latin America's problems. Impressionistically, I believe there were, and are, more true believers in family planning than in agrarian reform. Among certain cadres, family planning and population control are believed in with fervor and quasi-religiosity. Such attitudes may be useful when recruiting new supporters for the programs envisioned, but in foreign policy that can easily become a formula for disaster.

The language I use here in describing family planning and population control activities is sometimes biting and caustic, but I am sympathetic to family planning. To the extent that these are effective and well run programs reflecting the desires of the local population, I am supportive of them. The problem here as elsewhere is not family planning or the activity per se but the particular model used by the United States to export it.

We do not as yet have a social and political history of family planning programs comparable to the one available on law and development. We need an insider account by someone in the Ford Foundation, the Population Council, the Population Crisis Committee, or the U.S. Agency for International Development, by one of those dozen or so key persons who has been influential in designing and implementing population policy over the last quarter-century.

The most successful early family planning programs in which the social engineering of the population control experts was put to work may have been those in Taiwan. A

significant decline in birth rates began there in 1951 and, after a brief interruption, continued from 1955. Many of the giants in the family planning/population control community first earned their spurs by studying the Taiwanese model. Other places where efforts to reduce fertility have attained at least the appearance of success include Puerto Rico, Jamaica, Singapore, South Korea, and Thailand. The model of these programs has been carried over to the rest of Latin America.

I say the "appearance of success" because it is not clear whether the decline in the birth rate in these societies was due to the actual program to induce smaller families or to broad, "natural" changes in the society itself. It is clear that the societies from which the "population model" (like the agrarian reform and other "models") derives may not be representative of the Third World. Taiwan, Puerto Rico, Jamaica, Singapore, South Korea, and Thailand have a number of characteristics in common that may make them atypical of much of the developing world. All are relatively small, homogeneous, stable, and generally

---

Family planning was seen as the great panacea that would solve all of Latin America's problems.

---

well administered, so that the substantial financial assistance from the United States government and the population agencies could be put to good use. These countries are also among the most advanced of the developing nations, typically already transitional to a developed economy rather than truly underdeveloped. Nor could it be said that Jamaica with its high literacy rate and Westminister political institutions, or Puerto Rico with its special relationship (and outlet for surplus population) to the United States, are at all typical of Latin America. As demographer and population expert William Peterson has written in *Population*, Taiwan is not India and Puerto Rico is not Mexico or Brazil. Nevertheless, despite its ill fit, this is the model that served as the basis for the family planning programs in Latin America.

These programs have been designed, launched, inspired, funded, and in large part administered from the United States; but considerable pains have been taken to disguise that fact. Much of the funding has been channeled through third-party agencies to disguise the extent of United States involvement. Various fronts have been set up to make it appear, particularly in the early stages, as though it is a private association that is supporting the program, not the United States government. But when an agency receives, directly or indirectly, 90 percent to 95 percent of its funds from AID, we are probably safe in considering it a front agency. Care has also been taken to find local doctors and concerned citizens in the countries

17

affected so as to provide the appearance of local control, even though the funding and much of the direction may come from outside.

An elaborate scenario has been worked out to bring family planning and population control to the Third World through a somewhat secretive, furtive, and back-door route. First, a group of doctors are found, usually gynecologists and health care specialists, who receive specialized training in the United States and begin to talk about and publicize population-related topics: abandoned children, illegal and dangerous abortions, crowding, population growth rates that exceed economic growth, and so on. They provide a climate conducive to family planning activities. Then, typically, a private family planning association is formed consisting of these same doctors, demographers, and interested persons. United States aid is provided, usually funneled initially through private agencies. A pilot program of family planning clinics is begun; more publicity is generated; and a lobbying effort is begun with the government. In the third stage, the government, through its health or social assistance ministry, is persuaded to take over a program of family planning that is already in existence and to incorporate it into its nationwide system of maternity and child health care. This third and final step makes the program also eligible for large-scale foreign assistance, from AID, the United Nations, the Pan American Health Organization (PAHO), and other donors. At that stage the program is, presumably, well established, on its way, and on its own. These furtive and often secretive strategies have often generated resentments in the Third World and made the population programs objects of suspicion or hostility.

While these maneuverings were under way to establish a population program, in accord with a model imported from the outside, no one had bothered to check with Latin American countries to see if they wanted family planning, or wanted it all that much. My argument is complicated by the fact that survey data indicate Latin Americans do, overwhelmingly, want to limit family size, to have fewer children. Moreover, most influential groups in society—the army, the elites, even the church or some sectors of it—now see the need for some form of family planning. The problem is that they often see the issue in different terms than the population control donor agencies. The "population problem" in Latin America is variously defined from country to country, but it is usually put in terms of dealing with the problem of abandoned children, of illegal and often dangerous abortions, of resettlement of population and colonization, of squaring population growth with social and economic growth and ensuring that the former does not outstrip the latter. These Latin American concerns most often are barely given lip service by the donor agencies, whose overriding concern has been to limit population growth. It is not family planning per se that is at issue; rather, it is the particular model used and the insensitivity of the major population agencies to the wishes of Latin Americans.

Unless population programs are carried out in accord with the wishes of the host countries, they are unlikely to produce successful results.

At this stage there are so many problems with the population programs that I can only list some of them here. First, the model may not be appropriate: what worked in Taiwan or even Puerto Rico is unlikely to work in Peru or Colombia. Second, the three-stage plan for population policy development can be and has been, in various countries, short-circuited and stalled at any one of several points; there is nothing inevitable or unilinear about the model. Third, while population growth rates are falling in Latin America, we are still not sure—as we are still not sure for Taiwan itself—whether this is due to natural causes (rising literacy, better education, urbanization, greater numbers of women in the work force) or to the efforts of the family planning agencies. Resolving that issue before plunging further ahead would seem to be an important task.

Fourth, there are major problems with the population agencies responsible for carrying out these programs. Their accounting method often leaves much to be desired; some have been guilty of doctoring population statistics to suit their own purposes; they have sometimes presented misleading information to the United States Congress and to AID; and some have been guilty of violating if not the letter then probably the spirit of United States law. Whatever one thinks of the legislation, there are now clear legal guidelines prohibiting the use of United States government funds in support of abortion services; yet some of the population agencies have continued to provide abortion information and equipment—although under pressure from Washington they have been discouraged from direct involvement in actual abortion services. In addition, a key problem has been that the population agencies are full of globalists and generalists, and their knowledge of particular regions such as Latin America has often been minuscule. Indeed, since the population problem is global and the solutions universally applicable, in their view, they see no need to acquire specialists or expertise in specific cultural or geographic areas.

Fifth, and most importantly, there is the true believer syndrome. The population issue is defined differently in Latin America, but it is difficult to convince the population control advocates that such differences are important and should be given serious consideration. They see the population problem as a world problem demanding immediate and emergency measures, and they see it as unidimensional: too many people. Since it is an emergency problem, they feel that time and energy should not be wasted paying serious attention to cultural differences across continents or to the nuances of individual nationalistic preferences. It is hard for these population true believers to comprehend that once the demographic facts are presented all right-thinking people would not see the solution in the same terms. They, in short, already know all the answers. They may give some limited attention to the broader and more intricate Latin American views of the problem, but first and foremost their conception is with global population control. They may even be right, but it is unlikely that they will ultimately win the war in Latin America without seriously taking into account Latin Americans' own perceptions and definitions of the problem. These are increasingly nationalistic, assertive, and resentful of outsiders who tell them what to do.

In the case of population policy it is not so much an American model that is being exported, although Americans have been the chief agents involved. Ironically, although Americans have served as the architects of the program, the United States itself has no national population policy—and could not conceivably pass such a program through Congress—yet we insist that Latin American countries adopt one as a condition of foreign aid largess or, it is strongly suspected, World Bank subsidies. Inspired by the United States, it is nevertheless a global model that is being exported, a perception of spiraling population growth that must be checked at all costs worldwide through the use of a plan of action universally

---

Population control has been brought to the Third World through a secretive, furtive, and back-door route.

---

applicable and emanating from the United States. It cannot possibly work. As sociologist William Peterson concludes in *Population*:

> Those [population] analysts in each social discipline who have attempted to transcend the bounds of a single case have very often erred on the side of too facile generalization, and repeatedly we have been put to the task of freeing our thoughts from one or another monistic bond—in earlier generations racial or geographic determinism and, more recently, their economic or demographic analogues. How much of a guide is the past development of advanced countries for mapping the future modernization of presently backward areas? In some overall sense, obviously; the world is becoming more homogenous, and it is just this metamorphosis that we mean by modernization. But to assume the details of the process must follow a known course, or that the homogenization must eventually eliminate all fundamental differences, is to commit the most egregious error of comparative analysis.

In general, ethnocentrism is strong in virtually all aspects of United States foreign policy toward the Third World. All these programs are based on and derive from the peculiarly Western experience with development and are of limited relevance to the Third World. They are based on particular and special experience with develop-

ment, of a particular time and period, whose economic, sociological, and political laws may not apply to the Third World—or may apply only partially and incompletely.

Whether we are discussing agrarian reform, community development, law and development, or family planning/population control, or referring to other contexts of economic development strategy, military modernization, the democracy agenda, human rights concerns, trade unionism, or any one of countless other programs, the problems have been remarkably parallel. They were all born of a particularly Western experience with development, were based on Western assumptions about the modernization process which were then overgeneralized to the rest of the world, and have not adequately taken into account local and indigenous institutions and ways of doing things.

We may understand why this is so, why we use our own models to understand other areas of the world, why our ethnocentrism is so pronounced; but we must also be aware of the consequences of such ethnocentrism. By this time the policy failures have been so numerous and the Third World resentments engendered so strong that the notion of "let us do it our way" is becoming widespread. The Third World is increasingly inclined to reject the models and recommendations imposed as suggested by the West and is more and more searching for and asserting indigenous models and institutional arrangements more attuned to their own preferences, histories, and ways of doing things.

A long time must pass before policies based on the developmental assumptions of the past will change. These assumptions are strongly entrenched in the foreign assistance bureaucracies; and we know that a policy consensus on these or any other issues once arrived at is difficult to alter. Change will be difficult because these assumptions about agrarian reform, community development, the role of the middle class, and so on are closely associated with the history, culture, and ethos of the Western countries. They are embedded deeply in our educational system, our values, and our civic consciousness and ideology; and these will not be changed quickly or easily. They are part of a powerful social science tradition which sees the Western nations as most "developed" and leading the way and providing the example for the "less developed countries" to follow.

Change will be difficult to achieve because the more nuanced and less ethnocentric ideas I have suggested may be too complex for nonspecialist policymakers and the general public to grasp. I do not say this in a condescending or patronizing fashion but with the frank realization that in political Washington it is the image, the brief phrase, the lowest common denominator that usually counts in policymaking; the substance of the whole argument is often too complicated to get across. It is hard enough to get a consensus in Washington on such programs as agrarian reform and family planning; to say now that these programs will require far greater refinement and diverse adaptations to distinct local conditions is too difficult to convey to lawmakers or the public—and it may have the political side effect of scuttling the whole program or making it impossible to pass through Congress. For these and other reasons, it will likely take considerable time, perhaps a generation, for the changes I have suggested to reach fruition, for us to become less convinced that our own particular model is universal, and for us to take seriously the efforts of various Third World peoples to chart and institutionalize their own developmental routes.

The implications of the trends I have discussed are that the already developed donor nations will have to considerably reorient their assistance programs if they are to succeed in the Third World of the future. They will have to genuinely, not just with lip service, pay attention to local wants and aspirations. They will have to come to grips with models of development different from their own Western one. Far better and more thoroughly than in the past, they will have to learn the language, culture, and institutional procedures of various Third World areas.

The Third World is searching for and asserting indigenous models of development.

They will have to accept the notion now widespread in the Third World that "they know best" instead of the older one that "we know best for them." They will have to empathize and listen seriously for the first time and be prepared to support some of the Third World notions of development as distinct from the Western one. In the Islamic world, in Africa, Asia, and Latin America the sense is now well-nigh universal that the Western models, in their several varieties, have not worked very well, and therefore a social science model of development more attuned to local ways will have to be created. Strenuous efforts are now under way in various areas of the Third World to fashion such indigenous models or to achieve a better blend and fusion between imported and indigenous ones.

It is likely that this will be the next great innovative frontier in the social sciences and in development and foreign assistance research and theory. The foundations, various think tanks, and some within the academy—to say nothing of the Third World itself—are all moving in this direction. It is time for political development theory also to rethink its earlier premises and assumptions, all based strongly on the Western experience, and to move toward greater cultural relativism and an understanding of the Third World and the various parts thereof, on its own terms rather than through the prism of the earlier Western experience which fits the Third World only partially and incompletely. Once this new revolution in the social sciences and in development theory has taken place, it may be that the foreign assistance programs emanating from the Western nations can also be reoriented.

Four major questions come immediately to mind: (1) Are there still universals in the development process and, if so, what are they and how do we go about implementing and bringing about their more positive ends and features? (2) How do we make wise decisions in our foreign policy if not from the matrix of our own being and experience of what we understand to have been good in that experience? (3) Where do we draw lines in terms of the limits of the cultural relativism implied here—that is, once we are agreed that Hitler and Bokassa are unacceptable, what do we do about the tougher cases: Pinochet, South Africa, Zia, the Ayatollah, and Central America? (4) Suppose we heed the admonitions I offer, and then find that there are no Third World models of development worth hanging our hats on; what then do we do—not just intellectually but also from the point of view of policymakers who must make the decisions and carry our policies for these countries?

If past experience is any guide, it will likely take at least ten years (we are already half way through the generation change I referred to, marking a move away from the earlier development literature) before these newer models of development are reflected in more realistic assistance programs, reflecting a more accurate portrayal (as distinct from a wishful one, which far too often constituted the older approach) of Third World realities and institutions. It is, nevertheless, important to begin making the case now, both for educational purposes and because we may still hope to convince policymakers—hard though that is—that the success of their development programs must finally depend on their being adapted to the realities of distinct Third World areas. Success, after all, ultimately reflects the bottom line of American commitment to such programs.

READINGS SUGGESTED BY THE AUTHOR:

Bendix, Reinhard. "Tradition and Modernity Reconsidered." *Studies in Society and History* IX (April 1967).

Gardner, James A. *Legal Imperialism: American Lawyers and Foreign Aid in Latin America.* Madison: University of Wisconsin Press, 1980.

Inter-American Foundation. *They Know How . . . : An Experiment in Development Assistance.* Washington, D.C.: Government Printing Office, 1977.

Nisbet, Robert A. *Social Change and History: Aspects of the Western Theory of Development.* London: Oxford University Press, 1969.

Packenham, Robert. *Liberal America and the Third World: Political Development Ideas in Foreign Aid and Social Science.* Princeton: Princeton University Press, 1973.

Veliz, Claudio. *The Centralist Tradition in Latin America.* Princeton: Princeton University Press, 1980.

Wiarda, Howard J. *Ethnocentrism in Foreign Policy: Can We Understand the Third World?* Washington, D.C.: American Enterprise Institute for Public Policy Research, 1985.

What the Third World really needs

Abdus Salam

Abdus Salam is director of the International Center for Theoretical Physics in Trieste, Italy, and president of the Third World Academy of Sciences.

NINE HUNDRED YEARS AGO, a great physician of Islam living in Bokhara in central Asia, Al Asuli, wrote a medical pharmacopeia which he divided into two parts, "Diseases of the Rich" and "Diseases of the Poor." If Al Asuli were alive and writing today, I am sure he would divide his pharmacopeia into the same two parts. One part of his book would speak of the threat of nuclear annihilation inflicted on humanity by the rich. The second part of his book would speak of the great affliction that the poor half of humanity suffers: underdevelopment, attended by undernourishment and famine.

He would add that both these diseases spring from a common cause: excess of science and technology in the case of the rich, and the lack of science and technology in the case of the poor. He might also add that the persistence of the second affliction, underdevelopment, is the harder to understand, considering that scientific and material resources are available to eradicate poverty, disease, and early death for the whole of humankind in this age of scientific miracles.

What do I mean by scientific miracles? Take the miracle of abundant food in the United States and Europe, leading to the scandal of food mountains. This cornucopia may be due to temperate weather, to good husbandry, and to wise investment policies. But let us not forget the scientific basis of modern agriculture. Similar methods could make the whole world into a granary rather than one marked by deficits.

Another example "potentially even more important than the Green Revolution" has been emphasized by the director general of the United Nations Children's Fund (UNICEF). It concerns the recent decline in child mortality in the Third World due to simple advances in the treatment of diarrhea, the immunization of children, and the quick publicizing of these practices through satellite television.

The director general of UNICEF, in recounting the South's dramatic health developments, concluded that those countries need more help of a similar nature from the North. My own conclusion is just the opposite. In order to achieve long-term health progress, I would like to see the South acquire the ability to conduct its own research on its diseases such as diarrhea. It should also develop immunization vaccines, and it should eventually create its own satellite networks for the dissemination of information.

Similarly, the economists of the world have never appreciated the poor countries' need for scientific prowess; they have concentrated instead on the need for capital investment. But poverty in the developing world can be ameliorated, in the long run, only through a massive implanting of modern scientific technology.

Science and technology are so much a part of European culture today that it is hard to appreciate that European ascendancy in these areas is a relatively recent phenomenon. Science is the shared heritage of all humanity; some of the present developing countries were ahead of Europe in science and technology until the fifteenth century. But now the South looks longingly and hungrily toward Japan, the Soviet Union, Brazil, and South Korea, all of which have improved over the last 100 years. These countries have had the foresight or the good fortune to harness scientists and technologists as well as economists and entrepreneurs in their development.

There are four areas that constitute science and technology:

- *basic sciences:* physics, chemistry, mathematics, and biology;
- *applied sciences:* agriculture, energy, environmental and earth sciences;
- *classical technology:* bulk chemicals, iron and steel, metals, and power generation; and
- *science-based high technology:* new materials, microelectronics, microprocessors, computer-aided design, superconductors, lasers, fiber optics and photonics, space science, fine pharmaceutical chemicals, and biotechnology.

IN ORDER TO DEPLOY science and technology to help the poor, I propose, first, a means-related international levy on all humanity in order to pay for research on global scientific problems. This was one of the suggestions made at the United Nations Conference on Science and Technology held in Vienna in 1979. The global problems which most deserve international research are problems of applied science, such as universal disease (AIDS is a good example), global ecology, weather modification, alternative energy, earthquake prediction, the greening of deserts, and the productivity of marginal soils.

While research on global problems could start today both in the well-equipped laboratories of the North and in the sparsely equipped South, scientific research and education should be enhanced in poor countries in order that they learn to solve their own peculiar problems. For instance, it is incredible but true that in all the studies that have been done on the Sahel in Africa, no scientific study has yet been made of the hydrology of the region. Locally based research would remedy this puzzling gap in practical knowledge.

Thus I propose, second, that a strategy of specialization be implemented, to go into effect in the year 2000. For example, a consortium of universities in the United States, Britain, and France could be encouraged, with their governments' aid, to enhance university science in all developing countries that desire it. The Netherlands and Belgium could look after the building up of libraries and laboratories worldwide. Germany and Japan could sponsor technical education at all levels. Scandinavia could take responsibility for the scientific aspects of ecology. Switzerland and Austria, with their well-known pharmaceutical expertise, could look after medical education. Italy, drawing on its experience of setting up international centers in physics and biotechnology, could attend to the creation of similar institutions in all disciplines of science, in concert with developing countries. Canada, Australia, New Zealand, and Spain could initiate education for agriculture and for prospecting. The Soviet Union could take care of primary, secondary, and vocational education, in order to eradicate illiteracy by the year 2000 — the same way it did in 15 years in Soviet Central Asia. The above merely illustrates what a possible division of the relevant tasks might be.

I have in mind something patterned along the lines of the four Indian institutes of technology built in the 1960s. The one in Kanpur was created by a U.S. consortium of universities which helped to construct and furnish it, besides supplying the higher cadres of teaching staff for a number of years. The founding of the one in Delhi was assisted by a consortium of British universities; the one in Bombay, by the Soviet Union; and the one in Madras, by West Germany. Each nation helped to build the institute under Indian auspices, contributed staff, and left behind a tradition of teaching and research which has persisted after the original contracts have expired. Competition among the donor nations guaranteed excellent standards in the Indian institutes. At present, each of these institutes is producing 1,000 first-rate engineers and scientists yearly.

I envisage similar cooperation in the worldwide development project I have outlined. If the plans are drawn up now, many of the objectives will have been achieved by 2000. The twenty-first century will then dawn with a higher level of scientific and technological expertise in the developing countries themselves, which will make monetary investment in science-based projects there worthwhile.

Specialization would increase efficiency. Take science education as an example: A delegated-nation building plan would reduce costs in the standardized building of schools, in equipping them, in teacher training, and in providing textbooks for schools. Carrying out projects for the entire developing world would enable donors to do the work less expensively than tailoring a system to a single nation. Of course, contributing countries would have to guarantee that they would not interfere ideologically with the receiving countries, under the guise of technical help.

Money is generated chiefly through high technology today, as demonstrated by the experience of Japan, South Korea, Taiwan, Singapore, and others. For example, bio-technology — one of the newer science-based technologies — is likely to revolutionize agriculture, energy, and medicine in the next century. The higher echelons of the Third World educational system will need to create a network of basic sciences and high technology institutions.

In 1975, at the height of the OPEC (Organization of Petroleum Exporting Countries) price war, U.S. Secretary of State Henry Kissinger promised that the U.S. government would found several institutions in poor countries to meet the needs of cooperative world development. Two of these entities were to be "a development security facility to stabilize prices of commodities against crude cycles of export earnings" (although "indexing" was decisively ruled out) and "measures to improve access to capital technology and managerial skills — in particular, an international energy institute, an international center for exchange of technological information, and an international industrialization institute." The Third World still awaits the creation of these institutions.

The Third World Academy of Sciences has recommended that the equivalent of 4 percent of developing countries' education budgets should be spent on research in basic sciences, 4 percent on research on applied sciences, and 8 percent on the development of science-based high technology. This would constitute around 0.6 percent of these countries' GNP and would supply resources for science from the Third World itself of $14 billion — $7 billion for basic and applied sciences and $7 billion for science-based high technology.

The science community in the poor countries has received scant help from its peers in the richer countries.

To put this recommendation in perspective, during the 1979 U.N. Conference on Science and Technology in Vienna, the poor countries presented a case for $2 billion in aid for science and technology, particularly for applied sciences. They were promised assistance of no more than $70 million, which dwindled to $40 million in 1981. The main provider of the funds was the government of Italy. This amount had shrunk to zero by 1987, less than a decade later. Unfortunately, the science community in the poor countries has received scant help from its peers in the richer countries in keeping such aid alive.

LET US RETURN FROM THE SUBJECT of self-help efforts to the discussion of international aid. Donating agencies should have qualified natural scientists and educators on their staffs and governing boards. In addition to funds made available through the official aid agencies, the educational and scientific institutions in developed countries may consider contributing in kind in their own ways, according to the well-known United Nations formula whereby most developed countries have pledged to donate 0.7–1 percent of their GNP for world development.

The Pearson Commission set up by the United Nations in 1969 recommended that aid should be fixed at 0.7 percent of the GNP of donor countries—a recommendation later endorsed by the Brandt Commission. These figures, then accepted, have never been met except by a very few donors, such as Scandinavia and the Netherlands. The U.S. share has fallen to less than 0.2 percent; the contributions of Britain, France, West Germany, Japan, and others have also dropped. The Eastern bloc has never joined the aid consortium; its portion is much smaller, 0.14 percent of each country's gross domestic product (GDP). The OPEC countries started aid in the early 1970s with 1.18 percent of their GDP, went up to nearly 3 percent in 1975, and then declined to 1.4 percent of their GDP in 1981.

In the end, it is a moral issue whether the better-off segments of the educational and scientific communities are willing to look after their own deserving but deprived colleagues, helping them, if necessary, from their own resources. This is a question not only of materials but also of joining these colleagues in their battle to secure recognition within their own countries as valid professionals who are crucial to development.

What funds will be needed? I would estimate that around $100 billion will be used by this development project by the year 2000. This may sound excessive, but such sums can be found. Some part of the deep reductions that President Reagan and General Secretary Gorbachev are considering in the strategic arsenals as well as in the conventional armaments of the two superpowers could be converted to the development of science in the Third World.

It has been estimated that at least $60 billion—some 7 percent of the $900 billion the world now spends on the military, according to Ruth Leger Sivard's estimates for 1987—would be saved *every year* through the projected military reductions. I suggest that of this $60 billion savings, one-sixth—at least $10 billion—should be spent yearly on the development projects I have outlined, rather than on reducing taxes for the rich. Over a period of 10 years, this sixth would add up to $100 billion. Proposals for using money that would become available as a result of disarmament for the creation of a development fund have been advocated in the past at the United Nations by French President Valery Giscard d'Estaing, by the Soviet Union and other nations, and, more recently, by Mikhail Gorbachev in an eloquent plea in his book *Perestroika*. A variant approach has been discussed by former West German Chancellor Willy Brandt, in the famous report in which he advocated a developmental levy—a form of automatic world taxation—on seabed exploitation or armament sales.

The important thing, to my mind, is that we should not wait for a general agreement on these ideas. Rather, every rich country should make a start on Third World technological development by allocating funds from its own resources.

G LOBAL economic development simply isn't working. That's a stark assessment. But that's where Rodrigo Botero begins his analysis of the yawning gulf that separates the wealthy, consumer-oriented industrial nations from the impoverished, developing nations.

"If I were to make one recommendation for the the year 2000," says Mr. Botero, a journalist, author, and former finance minister of Colombia, "it would be simply to drop the goal of closing the gap – understood as it has been understood in the past 30 years."

That last phrase is crucial. Botero wants the gap closed. He's not arguing for the status quo. Nor is he calling for "zero growth" economies. Instead, he's seeking a new method of measurement.

Traditionally, the gap between North and South, the developed and the developing world, has been measured in a number of ways. The commonest is by charting gross national product (GNP) per capita. This measure shows the breadth of the gap in no uncertain terms: According to World Bank figures for 1985, the United States has a GNP per capita of $16,690, while Ethiopia (for example) has $110.

But there are other ways to assess the differences in well-being among the world's nations:

• Population. In 1950, one-third of the world's people lived in industrialized nations. By the early decades of the 21st century, that number will be less than one-sixth, as population pressures intensify in the developing world.

• Age. In the large group of developing nations that lie within the tropics, says Peter Raven of the Missouri Botanical Garden, an average of 40 percent of the population is under 15. The corresponding figure for industrial nations: 22 percent. Result: a built-in certainty of much more rapid growth rates in the tropics, as this young population reaches child-bearing age.

• Poverty. The World Bank estimates that about 40 percent of the 2.7 billion people in tropical and subtropical regions outside China

THE NORTH-SOUTH AFFLUENCE GAP

CONFERENCE STATEMENT:

THE PROBLEM: Per capita gross national product (GNP) has been the traditional means of measuring national progress. The goal of raising per capita GNP has guided international development programs. Such programs have failed. The gap between rich and poor countries has grown, and within many countries the gap between rich and poor groups has widened. Absolute poverty has increased.

Development efforts can be refocused to address human well-being more directly. Data increasingly available can be used to provide more useful measuring criteria. These must include clear, easily understood descriptions of the human condition so that programs can be designed and improvement in the human condition can be easily assessed and compared from nation to nation.

live in absolute poverty – unable to count on adequate food, clothing, and shelter from day to day. In those regions, according to UNICEF, more than 14 million children under age 5 starve to death or die of disease each year.

● Delivery of services. Despite some cases of positive rates of growth in per capita income, many countries are falling behind in meeting the demand for clean water, adequate nutrition, education, medical services, and transportation and communication. Fewer and fewer children are going to school in Nigeria, reports Gen. Olusegun Obasanjo, that country's former head of state. "More people are not able to go to hospital because there are no facilities, no drugs, in the hospital," he says. "All these things are going down, and then we are told that GNP is going up."

That point is an example of what Botero calls "an idea that led us in the wrong direction" – the idea that the growth of per capita GNP measures real development.

For the last four decades, he says, the industrial world's answer to the challenges of global development has been the same: money. "Well-intentioned, intelligent people looked at the [developing] world and said, 'If the conditions are set whereby they're supplied with the necessary capital, then the rest will follow.'" As a result, he notes, a developing nation's progress was usually measured by charting per capita GNP.

The result has been bitter disappointment on the part of many developing nations – not simply because their lot has not improved, but because the promised goal of narrowing the differences in income among the world's people appears unreachable.

If GNP is the only measure of progress, says former World Bank president Robert McNamara, "it's absolutely impossible – mathematically and economically – to significantly close the gap [for most nations] within the next 50 years. There's no way."

Estimates based on World Bank figures confirm his point: If current rates of growth continue, the closing of the income gap with the industrial nations would take Thailand 365 years, China 2,900 years, and Mauritania 3,224 years.

Yet there are bright spots in the picture. In China, Sri Lanka, and the Indian state of Kerala, for example, per capita GNP is still low by Western standards. But other indicators – infant mortality, life expectancy, literacy, nutrition, employment, numbers living in poverty – show real progress.

Such indicators, in fact, may provide sounder measures of a developing nation's progress than per capita GNP. They chart what Botero calls "levels of human welfare, levels of well-being, that are relatively simple [and] not necessarily ethnocentric – [in that] they don't necessarily imply the values of one society."

For many developing nations, that centuries-old question of values remains a crucial one. The very kind of development that could lift them out of poverty might also destroy their cultures

RODRIGO BOTERO
Colombia

'Lowering the
infant mortality rate
means much more to the
ordinary man and woman of
a developing country
than obtaining an
X percentage of growth
in the GNP per capita.'

and traditions. Nazir Ahmad, a graduate student from Bangladesh, warns against "an element of interventionism" that comes when development projects bring Western values with them. "Maybe we need to create a little bit more isolationism in the West – to give us breathing room," he says.

Filmmaker Vineet Narain agrees. "The focus of our attention should be human," he says. It should center on the people themselves – "their welfare, their pleasure, their joy, and their spiritual and mental development. So far, it seems that most of the attention

within the West has been on improving the material lot," under the mistaken assumption that "this increases human welfare and joy." What is needed, he says, is "to restore people's faith in things which are traditional."

Kenyan Patrick Mungai notes

**KATHARINE
WHITEHORN**
Britain

'We are trying to look for
something which you can
measure – and most of the
things that matter cannot be
measured. The reason we've
grasped GNP is because it's so
easy to measure.'

the bad impression left by cash-heavy development projects that failed. "We have in the third-world countries what are now popularly called 'white elephant projects' – projects that have been financed by Western donors, where a lot of money has been poured in, but that can't function."

All of which supports the case for measuring progress by something more meaningful than income. "Lowering the infant mortality rate," says Botero, "means much more to the ordinary man and woman of a developing country than obtaining an X percentage of growth in the GNP per capita, which to the majority of [those] people is an absolutely abstract and mysterious concept."

But there is another important reason for changing the way the gap is measured: Income figures can distort the overall condition of a nation. A small country where the majority lives in poverty, but where a thin layer at the top possesses extravagant wealth, may show a high per-capita income. But that, says Botero, "does not necessarily mean development."

"The $12,000 of income per capita of Saudi Arabia does not

mean that Saudi Arabia's a developed country," he adds by way of example, noting that Saudi levels of literacy, infant mortality, and life expectancy are still well below the Western standards.

The issue, then, is not one of *total* benefit as much as *distribution* of that benefit across the entire society. When a country's progress is measured by something other than wealth, the results cannot mask a lack of distribution.

"You cannot lower the infant mortality rate," says Botero, "unless you offer to *all* of the population a minimum of medical service – instead of offering it to the 10 percent wealthy urban elite. You cannot achieve 70 years of life expectancy at birth unless you extend to *all* of your population, to all social classes, minimum conditions of hygiene, nutrition, education, and literacy."

Zhang Yi, from the Institute of American Studies in Beijing, agrees – although he notes that the issue of distribution applies differently to different nations. "For some countries," he says, "where there is a high degree of wealth polarization, there should be an effort to redistribute the wealth. But in countries where there is too much equality – which I think there is in China – there should be more stratification, there should be people who should be richer."

He also raises an issue of high concern to those seeing new measurements: whether the developing nations will embrace a different set of goals. "You can't *make* the developing countries accept the goals," he says. Acceptance, he says, "really depends on the internal, political interaction inside the particular country itself."

British columnist Katharine Whitehorn agrees. "None of [these goals] will really work unless you consider their relation to the social structure in which they are working," she says. The problem, she suggests, is that "we are trying to look for something which you can measure – and most of the things that matter *cannot* be measured. The reason we've grasped GNP is because it's so easy to measure."

Shifting goals, however, will take time. "Very few developing countries are deliberately seeking these goals," says Botero, "and in fact, very many of them don't even track those indicators."

Yet for General Obasanjo, the very fact that such goals are being considered is encouraging. By searching for something other than GNP per capita as the measure, he says, "we are admitting that we have failed in the past. I think that is significant. Up until now we were not even admitting that we had failed. I think maybe that is a beginning of success for us. Indicators [such as] wholesome drinking water, nutrition, education, health – we just cannot run

away from them, because if those things are there then the absoluteness of poverty will be removed." Countries that do well on such indicators "may not be wealthy, but they will not be poor."

But is absolute wealth a necessity if these other indicators are to improve? No, says Botero, who points to countries as different as Barbados, Chile, Costa Rica, and Cuba. None has a high level of per capita GNP. They have different political systems. Yet each has reached high levels of well being as measured by literacy, infant mortality, and life expectancy.

On one point, however, there is widespread agreement: That while money is not the only answer, it's a necessary part of the solution. On that point, says Mr. McNamara, "I think we in the developed world have failed miserably" by not finding ways to contribute more to the progress of the developing world.

With a different set of goals, however – and the political leadership in developing countries to support them – the problem of so-called "aid fatigue" could be eliminated. If and when it is, however, the goal should be something other than raw wealth.

"Let us try to center them on things that are fundamental for having a decent society," concludes Botero, "even if it's not rich."

Gorbachev's Global Doughnut
The Empire with a Hole in the Middle

Charles H. Fairbanks, Jr.

Charles H. Fairbanks, Jr. is a research professor at the Paul H. Nitze School of Advanced International Studies. In the Reagan administration he served on the State Department's Policy Planning Staff and as a deputy assistant secretary.

T HE ABANDONMENT of the Eastern European communist regimes by the USSR has astonished everyone. Less spectacular, but equally unexpected, has been the substantial continuity of the Soviet commitment to its many Third World communist clients: Afghanistan, Cambodia, Ethiopia, Angola, Cuba, Nicaragua, the Salvadoran guerrillas.

With the striking exception of the Salvadoran guerrillas, it is true that Soviet policy has changed in each of the conflicts in which these clients are engaged, and in a direction more acceptable to the West. In Afghanistan, Cambodia, and Angola, as earlier in Ethiopia, the foreign troops that supported weak communist regimes have been or are being withdrawn. In Angola, Ethiopia, and Nicaragua, regional or internal negotiations have taken place that may hold out the promise of ending civil wars. While internal and U.S. domestic factors have played a role in some of these developments, their appearance in sequence is clearly linked to a shift of Soviet policy.

But the overall picture of Soviet policy in these "regional conflicts" shows a continuing commitment to shoring up the threatened communist regimes. According to U.S. government officials, Soviet security assistance to the Third World in general has been going down—but apparently not to Afghanistan, Cuba, Angola, Cambodia, Vietnam, and the FMLN in El Salvador. Soviet military assistance to the communist government in Afghanistan was increased to $200-$400 million a month, after U.S. aid to the *mujaheddin* was drastically cut. In Cambodia, the first nine months of 1989 saw an approximate doubling of Soviet arms deliveries over 1988 levels—an all-time record. Soviet assistance to Vietnam itself has remained the same or even increased. In Central America, Soviet-bloc military assistance to Nicaragua decreased only about 20 percent from the 1988 level, despite the fact that U.S. military support for the *contras* went down to nothing. A larger share of these munitions was evidently passed through to the FMLN in El Salvador—including the previously withheld SA-7 surface-to-air missiles—enabling them to mount a Tet-style offensive against the capital in late 1989.

The willingness to increase support for some Third World clients raises important questions in its own right. But the combination of this willingness and the withdrawal of support from the Eastern European communists presents an intriguing paradox. Gorbachev has abandoned his country's old servitors, the Honeckers and Husaks, at the same time that he continues to nurture communist client states in the Third World. This has overthrown all our expectations. Ever since the consolidation of the Soviet Empire in Eastern Europe after World War II, the predominant American view has been that Eastern Europe, and above all East Germany and Poland, constitutes a "vital interest" of the Soviet Union that could never be relinquished and, therefore, should never be

From *The National Interest*, No. 19 (Spring 1990), pp. 21–33. Copyright © 1990 by The National Interest. Used with permission.

threatened by the United States. This feeling underlay the inaction of the United States during the various crises in Eastern Europe. But at the same time we generally assumed that Soviet gains in the Third World could be reversed by some combination of American policy and local nationalism, and that the Soviet side would accept setbacks, including expulsion.

The opposite has turned out to be the case. Gorbachev has hastened the loss of his "vital" interests in Eastern Europe while clinging tenaciously to his vexing burdens in the Third World. Of course, this contradiction may turn out to be temporary. In a period when every week brings something that we never expected to see in our lifetimes, we could see Gorbachev renouncing his Third World outposts as well. But, as of now, the divergence in stance toward the two groups of clients represents a clear paradox, one worth thinking through.

The Logic of Ideological Empires

THIS PARADOX is not unprecedented in history. It has been the pattern of many ideological empires to rot at the core but remain vital at the periphery.

To give one example: During the long "ideological" struggle between the Fatimid (Shi'ite) Caliphate of Cairo and the Abbasid (Sunni) Caliphate of Baghdad from the tenth to the twelfth century, the Fatimid Caliphate collapsed at the center from the dead weight of arbitrary rule, but the Fatimids continued to make gains beyond the caliphate's frontiers, in what are now Iraq, Iran, Yemen, India, and Afghanistan. When, in 1059, Baghdad and the rest of Iraq was finally seized by local Shi'ites, the Fatimid Caliphate had lost all authority in its own capital, Cairo, disordered by famine, cannibalism, and civil war between rival army groups. The path of the Isma'ili Shi'i revolutionary movement through the Islamic world was thus from the west, from its original hearth in Algeria, toward the east, with its old centers abandoned or demoralized as new areas were converted or conquered. That is, its movement was like a fire, which burns outward leaving ashes in the center. If not for the existence of the Mediterranean and the Sahara, which channeled the shift of Fatimid zeal in a west-east direction, it would have assumed the shape of a ring or, better still, a doughnut. The doughnut shape is the one now being assumed by the Soviet bloc: it is falling in at the center, still fairly vigorous at the periphery in the Third World.

This shape is not altogether surprising. Revolutionary movements are given their early impetus by hatred of the existing reality, by the hope for an improvement that is rapid and decisive, by the desire to implement abstract formulae never tested against reality, and by personal desires to transform the world and one's position in it. All of these motives are most vivid at the beginning and in the presence of the enemy; but they are attenuated by having to run an established political order and by the passage of time. In addition, where they were victorious, both the Fatimid Caliphate and the Bolsheviks established repressive regimes, ones in which most of the people, while nominally co-participants in the loftiest of human undertakings, were actually excluded from any responsibility for governing themselves. As Tacitus was the first to argue, despotic power kills energy and ambition in the citizens; it nourishes apathy. Meanwhile the shining dreams that had originally motivated attachment to the new political order are stifled by the contrast with the prosaic reality, and by the artificiality with which they are propagandized.

The human costs of centralized power also affected Soviet foreign policy. Because all human activity in the USSR and in Eastern Europe was so tightly controlled, the Soviet Union was deprived of the influence exerted abroad on behalf of the West by independent business and journalism, and by the independent foreign policy activity of America's allies. (The activities of France in Africa and the Middle East and of Britain in the Persian Gulf are cases in point.)

The tendency of ideological empires to gradually assume a ring-like form has, in the postwar era, been increased by certain characteristics of the international system. In any period of history, conflicts that are likely to be very costly or risky for the participants are less likely simply to disappear than to be "displaced" to other areas where the stakes are not as high. In the nineteenth century, for example, the conflict between Britain and France that began in 1882 over Egypt was "fought out" not in Egypt but in confrontations in West Africa (Borgu, 1895–98), in the Southern Sudan (Fashoda, 1898), and even in

Thailand (1893). The incentives for such "displacement" have been vastly increased by the arrival of nuclear weapons. Because nuclear war cannot be regarded as a way of resolving contested issues, and the specter of nuclear war discourages recourse to force in Europe, conflicts have been pushed into the Third World, where the risk of escalation is lower. This accounts in large part for the fact that, despite the acute tensions that have characterized the era of the Cold War, it has been simultaneously a time of almost unprecedented peace between the major powers, and one of continual terrorism, guerrilla struggles, proxy war, and superpower confrontations over Third World issues.

The Importance of Eastern Europe

IN THE postwar era, the Soviet client states in Eastern Europe and in the Third World were useful to the USSR in very different ways. The acquisition of Eastern Europe after World War II powerfully reinforced the central myth of communism, that it represented the future. Our failure to anticipate that communism could be displaced in Eastern Europe shows how successfully this myth was propagated even among noncommunists and anticommunists. Keeping the myth alive was the first useful function Eastern Europe served for the USSR.

The second was the military advantage conferred by geography. Eastern Europe, by providing strategic depth, assured that another war, to the extent it was a conventional one, would not be fought on Soviet soil. But Eastern Europe also created offensive superiority that had immense political weight. Stalin created the greatest concentration of military power in Europe since the time of Charlemagne. But the Soviet Union of the 1930s, which already had more soldiers, tanks, and aircraft than any nation in the world, was not a superpower; it was the location of vast military power in the very heart of Europe, in Germany, after 1945 that first made it one. Militarily, the blitzkrieg strategy taken over from the Nazis depended on a short war, on the ability to reach the English Channel quickly—that is, on a combination of military power and geography. Politically, it was the presence of military power (and of client states) in the center of Europe that settled the recurring issue of whether Russia is a European power (as under Alexander I and Nicholas II) or an Asiatic power essentially outside Europe (as under Nicholas I and between the world wars). By being a preponderant factor *in Europe* the USSR became a superpower.

The occupation of part of Germany and Austria was particularly crucial to the Soviet Union's security and political status. By splitting Germany, the USSR prevented a revival of the dangers it faced in 1917–18 and again in 1941–42. Because the German Question was left undecided, and could not be decided without the USSR, the USSR became not only a military but a diplomatic factor in Europe.

But these advantages of holding Eastern Europe did not come without major liabilities. To hold Eastern Europe against the will of the inhabitants required erecting an Iron Curtain. This prevented Eastern European governments and people from being active on behalf of the Soviet Union on a wider scale. The Iron Curtain was ambiguous: it was simultaneously the wall of a fortress and the wall of a prison. While Western culture and business freely ranged the globe, the Iron Curtain tended to keep its own architects cooped up in the center of Eurasia.

A second liability was that Eastern Europe was hard to hold. Yugoslavia and Albania broke away completely, Romania broke away diplomatically events almost entirely overlooked by Western opinion in judging that Eastern Europe was a vital Soviet interest which could and would be held in spite of everything. As terror lifted and civil society revived in Eastern Europe, it became a more and more open fact that communism was unpopular there: part of the center of the Soviet empire had begun to weaken, and a more ring-like physiognomy was emerging in the empire. When rebellions were suppressed, it was at the cost of weakening communism's legitimacy both within Eastern Europe and internationally.

As time went on Eastern Europe became a small but persistent drain on Soviet resources, a drain that became more nagging as the Soviet economy began failing in the 1970s. The military and political advantages of holding a political base in the center of Europe were slowly depreciated by the emergence of strategic nuclear forces, which reduced the significance of geography. Detente made the Soviet empire in Eastern Europe less threatened politically, but more exposed to different threats, arising out of increased economic, cultural, and political contact with the West. As it became clearer that there was to be no revival of the German military threat, the value of a geographical position to cope with it diminished. Finally, the passage of time and the blurring of human memory worked their inevitable decay. Only new acquisitions, not old ones, could continue feeding the myth of communist momentum. The advantages conferred by the Eastern European client states were obvious to Stalin because they had been missing earlier. As time went on, the advantages of Eastern Europe began to be taken for granted by Soviet leaders, while it was the disadvantages that had novelty.

The Discovery of the Third World

AS THE Soviet Union became increasingly aware of Eastern Europe's limited usefulness for an activist foreign policy, the dismantling of Western empires offered growing temptations to increase Soviet global influence by an "indirect approach" through the Third World. The Soviet Union began to acquire non-Western clients, both states and insurgent movements. As instruments of Soviet foreign policy, these had uses and liabilities very different from those of the Eastern European clients.

One important difference was that the policies of the new Third World clients were usually less fully controlled by the USSR. We have tended to assume that Soviet clients are useful to the USSR to the extent that their activity is controlled or coordinated by Moscow, with the Eastern European satellites being the model. This assumption is plausible but wrong.

The policies pursued by the Soviet Union and its clients have frequently not coincided. To take only a few examples, the Soviet Union has guided Ethiopian efforts to crush the Eritrean insurgency, but Cuba, conscious of its old links to the Eritreans, has abstained even while it has protected the Ethiopian regime. In Grenada, there is evidence that the Soviet Union supported the conspiracy against Maurice Bishop, while Castro wrote to the New Jewel Movement that "Everything which happened was for us a surprise, and disagreeable." In North Yemen, the Soviet Union has armed the government generously, while the People's Democratic Republic of Yemen (PDRY) has conducted the insurgency against the government. In the Iran-Iraq War the Soviet Union armed mainly Iraq, while North Korea gave huge quantities of military aid to Iran.

The partial independence of Soviet clients' activity enhances rather than diminishes their usefulness to the USSR, in several ways. When the Soviet Union and one or more of its clients are active in a country, it creates multiple channels of influence. It is also an insurance policy, a safeguard against the sudden expulsion of the Soviet presence, as happened earlier in Egypt and Ghana. In the Iran-Iraq War the Soviet Union would be connected with whichever side won, or with both if the war ended in a stalemate. In Yemen, whoever wins the internal struggle, the outcome will probably not be the ouster of Soviet bloc influence. This would not be the case if the client had been rigidly guided by the Soviet Union in its policy. Ethiopia—where the channels of Soviet-bloc influence included Cuban troops, Soviet arms (and arms debt), and the Communist party organization formed at Soviet insistence—provides another example. Independent but parallel activities by different pro-Soviet actors reinforce and support one another.

In addition to this, many clients have channels the Soviet Union and its Eastern European clients would never have. Libya and Syria have access to the Arab world because they are Arab and Moslem states, Cuba has access to Latin America because it is Spanish-speaking. Thus the existence of client states widely distributed around the globe and with varying cultural and religious backgrounds, increases the political resources available to the Soviets.

A third crucial fact which makes Soviet Third World clients more effective is that they are not understood to be Soviet clients by a large part of international opinion. Even Cuba has been able to head the Non-Aligned Movement, and a number of clients are seen as less implicated than Cuba in Soviet designs. Grenada provides a striking case. The cooperation of the New Jewel Movement with Cuba and the Soviet Union was extremely close across a great range of foreign policy issues, yet most interested international observers labeled Grenada as a Third World socialist country rather than communist. The somewhat disguised character that many Third World clients of the USSR have springs partly from the absence of tight control already mentioned, but also from the international climate of opinion about the Third World.

Because many client states are not understood to be acting on behalf of the Soviet Union, they can carry out actions against the United States and its friends that the Soviet Union itself could never attempt. It is difficult to imagine that there could be tens of thousands of Soviet troops in Angola and Ethiopia without provoking a strong reaction in the West and among other African countries. Yet the presence of such a number of Cuban troops in these countries did not have that impact. Again, Libya was able to bomb the capital of the Sudan during the decline of Nimeiri's authority without provoking any retaliation. The event would have been far more dramatic, and would have drawn a much more hostile reaction, if a Soviet airplane had bombed Khartoum.

We can draw the following general conclusion: *Third World clients have increased the reach of Soviet world power and reduced the risks of Soviet action.* They have enabled the Soviet Union to damage or threaten Western interests in ways that would not otherwise have been possible. This was not true of the clients in Eastern Europe. Indeed, at the very time that the uses of Third World clients were becoming clearer, the usefulness of the Eastern European clients was being diminished by time and changing circumstances.

One important consequence of the political independence of Third World clients is that they may engage in local initiatives drawing the USSR into attacks on Western interests which it would not otherwise undertake. As with other countries, the relationship between Soviet goals and Soviet instruments is a dynamic one: What the Soviet Union cannot find a way of doing, it ultimately gives up; what it finds itself able to do, it is tempted to undertake. If client initiatives develop in a successful way, opportunities may impel the Soviet Union to follow. Thus the existence of Third World clients with special interests, superior access, and greater immunity from international criticism tends to make the Soviet Union more activist, more adventurous.

This is not a merely theoretical conclu-

sion. In Central America, the support of the Sandinistas was originally a Cuban initiative, which accorded with the historic Cuban preference for armed struggle in Latin America. Not until the Sandinistas overthrew Somoza in 1979 was the Soviet Union converted to a strategy of armed struggle. Those concerned about Soviet power have been accustomed to speak of "Soviet subversion" in places such as Nicaragua, Angola, Ethiopia, and Grenada. This is misleading in that it assumes one-way traffic. Perhaps we need also to speak, coining a deliberate paradox, of Cuban and Nicaraguan subversion in Moscow. Because of its greater vitality and zeal, the periphery of the Soviet empire has sometimes led the flagging center: again, a growing emergence of the ring-like structure latent in ideological empires.

Global Clients

THE EASTERN European clients of the Soviet Union were among the countries most shut off from the rest of the world. But two of the new Third World clients—Cuba and Libya—were (together with the superpowers, China, and France) among the six countries most active in the widest range of places around the globe.

Cuba was regarded by most Americans in 1959 as an obscure "banana republic," unimportant in the Latin America context and negligible in the world balance. Since then, Cuba has become a major problem for the United States; not merely a local problem, but a worldwide one. Cuba is playing a larger role in world politics than any Latin American country has played since 1492. To appreciate the magnitude of this transformation, consider the reception that would be given today to a prediction that, over the next two decades, Ecuador (a country with a population and GNP roughly similar to Cuba) is destined to become a significant global actor—that it will have stronger armed forces than any Latin American country other than Brazil; that it will be coordinating and supplying guerrilla movements throughout Latin America; that it will have over 60,000 troops on another continent as well as a significant presence in half a dozen other parts of the world. Such a prediction would simply be dismissed as mad. Yet this is precisely what has occurred in the case of Cuba over the last quarter century.

1. UNDERSTANDING THE THIRD WORLD

A similar transformation has occurred in the case of Libya, which (to give only a partial list) has been active against American interests in Tunisia, Egypt, Sudan, Somalia, Lebanon, Iran, the Philippines, Western Sahara, Upper Volta, Mali, Chad, Central African Republic, Burundi, Uganda, Grenada, Nicaragua, St. Lucia, and Antigua.

The *global* roles of Cuba and Libya have made them quite different international actors from equally powerful countries that pursue merely regional roles. This global reach presents Soviet foreign policy with special opportunities and risks, and makes the problem they set for American foreign policy quite different. Some other Soviet clients show a tendency to emulate Cuba or Libya by becoming active on a global scale. Vietnam and Ethiopia still pursue predominantly local interests, but the Vietnamese have sent arms to the Salvadoran guerrillas and Ethiopia has been active in destabilizing the southern Sudan, an area traditionally outside Ethiopian imperial ambitions.

We have usually been more worried by the kind of local activity characteristic of Nicaragua and the PDRY in North Yemen than by the Cuban and Libyan type, fearing subversion in our "backyard" and a "domino effect" on nearby countries. This is probably an error, for there is a reason why the "domino effect" usually does not go very far. Local activity by Soviet clients tends to be self-limiting in that it creates and stiffens local opposition and causes the threatened states to seek stronger ties with the U.S. or some other protector. The Sandinista threat caused the United States to establish a quasi-institutionalized military presence in Central America. PDRY subversion deepened the intervention of Saudi Arabia in Yemeni affairs, and brought Iran into Oman. To avoid such developments, Soviet clients have an interest in showing restraint and not using all the power available to them. Nicaragua has reasons not to antagonize Costa Rica, Honduras, and El Salvador. Ethiopia, thanks to massive Soviet military aid, has unquestioned military dominance in the Horn of Africa, but the knowledge that a more aggressive use of that power against Somalia would antagonize and activate other neighboring countries, such as Kenya and Saudi Arabia, has caused it to be utilized moderately. Thus the domino effect is countered by an intrinsic tendency back toward equilibrium in local conflicts. Brushfires have a tendency to put themselves out.

This local tendency toward equilibrium, however, does not operate against *global* client activity. Honduras can act effectively against Nicaragua, but not in the same way against Cuba. Somalia and the Sudan have cards to play against Ethiopia—weak ones, to be sure—but none against Cuba. The global activity of Cuba and Libya is a very powerful weapon in the hands of a revisionist power. By the time that Gorbachev was named general secretary in 1985, Cuba had shown itself to be an instrument many times more powerful on the Soviet side than any Eastern European country.

The Arrival of Gorbachev

THESE WERE the ways in which the two groups of Soviet clients had evolved when Mikhail Gorbachev became leader of the Politburo. As a member of the Communist party apparatus, Gorbachev was a member of a very specialized subculture, like the old Jesuit order or the clergy in Iran. Unlike Western politicians, the members of the nomenklatura spent their entire lives in this career, lived in different apartment buildings from other people, went to different stores and resorts. They were unusually *isolated* from the people they ruled. This group possessed a distinctive world view, comprising a distinctive idea of leadership and distinctive political tactics. The concept of leadership in the CPSU has not been one of managing problems but transforming society, as Lenin and Stalin did. The view of tactics, or "operational code," comprises a complex and sophisticated doctrine that can be summarized only briefly here.[1]

Politics, both domestic and foreign, is, in the traditional communist view, *always* a struggle. The outcome of this struggle depends on the correlation of forces, and success depends on the realistic estimation of that correlation. Because that correlation varies, success ebbs and flows. Consequently, as Lenin said in 1921, "Our strength will always be a capacity to take account of the real relationships and not to fear them, however disagreeable they may be."[2] Sometimes it is necessary to retreat even when pride rebels against it. Stalin elaborated: ". . . there are moments when one must. . . begin a planned retreat and give up, without fighting, whole cities and areas for the sake of winning time and collecting forces for new decisive battles in the future."³ The classic example, taught to every Soviet schoolchild, is the 1918 Brest-Litovsk Treaty with Germany in which the Bolsheviks surrendered vast tracts of territory to survive. Lenin sometimes spoke of the possibility of retreating to the Urals, or even to Vladivostok.

In the traditional communist operational code, skill in attacking and skill in retreating are regarded as equally important. To determine the appropriate moment for maneuvering and for giving in is a key part of the Bolshevik's political training. In phases of retreat it is necessary to be flexible and to accept noncommunist allies such as the Left Social Revolutionaries, the NEP traders, and the Social Democrats in the Popular Fronts of the 1930s. Leninist tactics include a complex array of means by which temporary allies can be manipulated, as some peace movements, front organizations, and the Eastern European Popular Fronts of 1945–48 were manipulated. But retreat does not mean giving up. An important part of Gorbachev's training included mastering tactics for turning a forced retreat into an advance by different means.

Gorbachev, as I have argued elsewhere,⁴ was given his political direction by the crisis of the communist system, by his own ambition which was stimulated by the magnitude of the challenge, and by the ingrained habits of the Bolshevik operational code. He felt increasingly pressed by a need to make drastic changes in the society, changes blocked by a divided Politburo and a bureaucracy that resisted change and eluded control. Thus consolidating his personal power was essential, even disregarding his own ambition. Gorbachev sought to do this by discrediting earlier rulers and institutions (through glasnost); by forcing structural changes in governing institutions in order to give himself a power base independent of the party apparatus; and above all by mobilizing forces outside normal politics (as Mao Zedong did in his Cultural Revolution).

One might consider this strategy cynical if it did not dovetail so neatly with the transformation of society Gorbachev wanted. Gorbachev felt that the Soviet public had become apolitical, bored with communism, apathetic, and lazy. By mobilizing the public,

he hoped both to involve them in a new revolutionary struggle under the banner of communism and to reinvigorate the party by forcing it once again to compete for the people's allegiance. This was a project of noble daring, but not of prudence: it rested on large and untested assumptions about the motives of the Russians and their subject peoples. Gorbachev proclaimed that "perestroika is a revolution": he wanted to re-live the revolution within a civil order settled and petrified for seventy years. Such a possibility was inherent in the communist project, but by its very nature it threatened to shatter the existing order, the communist regime. During 1989, Gorbachev's cultural revolution went out of control. The popular forces mobilized by Gorbachev turned against the regime with demands for national self-determination and political freedom. Eastern Europe was the first part of the Soviet Empire to be shattered by the explosion Gorbachev had ignited.

The Loss of Eastern Europe

IN THE FIRST years of Gorbachev's reign, the news from Eastern Europe was such as to allow a certain overconfidence. Nowhere were there moves away from old political patterns that were not sponsored or regulated by the ruling Communist parties. The Eastern European countries remained isolated from each other and from the USSR. Their limited international usefulness made it easier to neglect them.

In Poland and in Hungary the ruling parties felt the need, in the tradition of Brest-Litovsk, to retreat in the face of looming economic disaster. In Hungary, Imre Poszgay tried, like Gorbachev, to bring noncommunist forces into politics and manipulate them. In Poland, such a strategy had been explicitly sketched by Jerzy Urban as early as 1981⁵ and it guided the roundtable negotiations with Solidarity and the June elections. The Polish Communists, with Soviet assent, bungled the elections and the negotiations before and after, so that these two events led to the wholly unexpected result of a Solidarity-led government.

During these early Gorbachev years Soviet officials wrestled with the issue of redefining their attitudes toward the Brezhnev Doctrine for a largely different audience. Gorbachev finally unambiguously disavowed the doctrine in a July 6, 1989 speech at Strasbourg to the parliamentary assembly of the Council of Europe. The communique of the Warsaw Pact immediately afterward was much vaguer, showing a continued nervousness about pulling out the ultimate prop of the Eastern European regimes. But of course, Gorbachev's words, uttered before there was an acute general crisis in Eastern Europe, could not easily be recalled. They conditioned everything that happened shortly afterwards.

The conflagration was triggered by the concatenation of events as small as the removal of the border wire between Hungary and Austria (May 2) and the Hungarian willingness to allow East Germans to leave through that border (August 22). From this point a chain reaction started, spread to enough countries to create a "critical mass," and then rapidly consumed the entire Warsaw Pact. The unpredictable nature of the process and Gorbachev's shocked reaction to the likelihood of German reunification after early November strongly suggest that he intended none of this. The military and psychological keystone of the Warsaw Pact was the German Democratic Republic. Once it had fallen, the other Eastern European peoples knew that the Soviets would not avert the fall of their own masters. The decisive event occurred at the beginning of October. In the conditions created by Gorbachev's July 6 repudiation of Soviet intervention, Honecker suddenly halted emigration again, goading the public to fury. At this perfect moment Gorbachev arrived on his scheduled visit, repeating the slogans about the need for change designed to achieve a different result in different circumstances. It was Gorbachev who precipitated the avalanche.

From the communist point of view, Gorbachev is a jinx, a hoodoo, a Jonah. His arrival anywhere presages disaster. Like Jaruzelski and Poszgay, he did not understand the people's deep weariness of communism, nor could he sense the people's mood at a particular crux. Perhaps Gorbachev's soaring ambition, his splendid vision of the future, and his courage are spoiled by his lifetime as a member of an isolated priestly caste, whose pride was its ability to manipulate people.

Gorbachev sensed, with Bolshevik lack of sentimentality, that the decomposition of the East German regime signalled the end. In this crisis he seems to have reverted to the ingrained example of Brest-Litovsk. He retreated to the next defensible position: the boundary of the USSR. The communists of Eastern Europe were simply abandoned, an act made easier by their diminished usefulness. The new strategy combined an attempt to contain by diplomacy the movement toward German reunification and an attempt to put himself at the head of the process, urging the Czech party not to use the iron fist and arranging a coup in Bulgaria (November 6–10). These efforts did not change the reality of a forced retreat. What Stalin and his successors had built up over decades with unceasing effort and the expenditure of vast resources, Gorbachev had lost in three months.

The Fate of the Periphery

AFTER GIVING up Eastern Europe, the Communist party of the Soviet Union is faced with the possibility of annihilation as a political entity. Most of the factors that produced the collapse in Eastern Europe are present, to a lesser degree, in the Soviet Union itself: the combination of rage against the rulers; new expectations; a demoralized and divided party apparatus; and Gorbachev's overconfidence in his ability to persuade people to do what he wants rather than what they want. As it is subsiding and partly falling in, the Soviet empire is more and more assuming the doughnut form latent in ideological empires. As Radio Free Europe's Vladimir Kusin has argued, exaggerating only somewhat, "the geographical focus of communist rule thus shifted from Europe to the Third World."[6]

The seeming paradox of abandoning the Eastern European communists while continuing to shore up the Third World regimes emerged from the interaction between specific policy choices and the divergent paths of development experienced by the two groups of clients. The winter of 1989–90 displayed a vivid contrast in morale: in El Salvador, guerrillas spent their lives for communism in suicidal attacks; in Berlin and Prague, the leaders would not defend communism even to save themselves. The historical development had both sapped the vitality and reduced the usefulness of Eastern Europe in an active foreign policy strategy, while making the Third World the arena of active international conflict and the point of the West's greatest vulnerability.

The very different practical benefits offered by the two sets of clients may very well have been decisive in Gorbachev's mind when he made the specific policy choices to retreat in one place and not in the other. Certainly, as some Soviet clients in the Third World—Afghanistan, Ethiopia in 1989—have been under pressure as acute as the Eastern European clients were under in the fall of 1989, it is impossible to explain the different Soviet policies as a mere adaptation to circumstances.

The tactics suggested by the communist operational code may also have affected the different outcomes. In the Eastern European case the code held out the hope that communist leaders could manipulate public opinion during a retreat so as to avoid giving up the position altogether. This hope was a fatal delusion. Gorbachev is not tempted in the same way in the Third World: he will not go to the Panjsher Valley, as he did to East Berlin and to Lithuania, to try to persuade people to like what they don't like. The methods by which the Third World outposts

---

Faith at the Rim

Early in January the liberal Institute for a Democratic Alternative in South Africa (IDASA) played host to the first two Russian academics to visit South Africa in nearly 40 years. Professors Irena Filatova and Apollon Davidson of Moscow State University toured the country giving talks about Soviet foreign policy in Southern Africa and about the collapse of communism in Eastern Europe and the U.S.S.R. To their surprise, their account met with indignant resistance. At one gathering in a Transvaal township more than 100 local leaders and citizens sharply questioned the Russians about this rejection of socialism, and criticized IDASA for bringing them to South Africa.

Robert K. Massie, Jr.,
The New Republic
February 26, 1990

---

are held are simpler—fighting, security assistance, diplomacy—and at this point the Soviet Union probably knows how to employ them more successfully.

We cannot predict Soviet conduct toward the periphery of its empire; we do not even know whether, in five years, the government framing policy will be communist, democratic, or fascist. We can only specify the conditions that will shape Soviet conduct. At the center of the empire, these will be a declining interest in foreign policy, and, to some extent, a concern to save money. Subsidies to Third World clients may be reduced, but these clients are not particularly expensive. They are in fact so cheap compared to the staggering outlay on Soviet military forces that they are not the first place from which funds are likely to be taken to shore up the economy, if a communist oligarchy survives in Russia. On the other hand, a system in which public opinion and elected deputies shaped policy more significantly would be much less attracted to the defense of Third World clients; they are unpopular with the Soviet public.

On the outer periphery of the ring, in the Third World, communism will have continued vitality and appeal, as Peru and the Philippines currently demonstrate. It was an important insight of the Western Left that people in the Third World are not attracted to communism and to the Soviet Union for Soviet reasons, but for their own, local reasons. The crisis of faith in the center is therefore likely to affect the periphery only slowly.

Third World clients will hold a continuing interest as long as the USSR wants to show the continuing vitality of its foreign policy. Beyond the usefulness they displayed in earlier years, they hold out some opportunities specific to the present moment. Because many Soviet clients are clients in disguise, they are compatible with the "New Thinking" in foreign policy. At the Malta summit, Gorbachev could deny Nicaraguan arms were his arms. The New Thinking, while fundamentally of Western origin, is close to the Third World's conceptual framework, as displayed in the international organizations in recent decades. If it fails to satisfy expectations as a general basis for Soviet foreign policy—as is very likely—Soviet clients will provide a bridge to the Third World as an arena of future Soviet leadership. The Soviet clients can, for example, help the USSR to refocus American foreign policy. As the Cold War appears to many to be over, the tendency is already evident to push the United States out of Europe. This has been a long-standing objective of Soviet policy and, after an interval during which the USSR may need the United States to create an appearance of stability, will probably be so again. To the extent that the United States faces concrete, difficult, and divisive problems in the Third World—like El Salvador—a pull is added to this push out of Europe.

Another motive for supporting Third World clients stems from the loss of Eastern Europe itself. The sense of the Soviet Union as a superpower rested heavily on the presence of vast armies on the Elbe, in the heart of Europe, with a firm base behind them. If the Soviet Union wants to retain the sense of being a powerful player in world politics in the absence of such a presence, its Third World outposts will be increasingly important as its image suffers and its status-anxieties increase.

Soviet commitment to Third World clients is likely to continue above all because, as argued above, the Soviet-client relationship is not one-way: the Soviet Union becomes active in response to invitations from friendly states and forces, as well as in pursuit of its own agenda. Once an opportunity is offered to the Soviet Union, the inherent advantages of working through clients make it difficult to refuse. This may become even more true when the Soviets want to stop their global retreat without endangering detente, for Third World clients provide them with an opportunity to stay in the game of world politics without having to take full responsibility for conflict, and thus without attracting too much hostility.

Directions for Western Policy

TODAY THE periphery of the Soviet empire is more of a problem for us than the center. But the damage done by the periphery is now limited by the quiet emanating from the center. Will this situation continue? It is probably best to think of the future in terms of two very different periods. In the present one we have a breathing space (perhaps a year, perhaps several years). In this phase there are enormous opportuni-

ties—if we have the imagination to seize them—to strengthen the Western position in both Eastern Europe and the Third World.

In the second phase we will be hit by the consequences of the instabilities now being created every day. The terminal crises of empires are *dangerous*. The collapse of the Old Regime in France led quickly to the conquest of Europe by revolutionary armies. The long decline of Austria-Hungary was marked by civil war, regional wars, the emergence of new ideological solutions (Hitler was a product of Linz and Vienna), and finally by the abrupt decision to attempt to check the growing threats to the system's existence through the ultimatum to Serbia in July 1914.

Various factions and ideologies will struggle to inherit the former Soviet empire, and the host of historic problems artificially "frozen" by communist order will come alive: Moldavia, Transylvania, the Dobruja, Macedonia, Turks in Bulgaria, Russian settlers and Muslim natives in Kirgizia and Kazakhstan, the relationship between Soviet and Iranian Azerbaijan—this list is long. In this very complex, rapidly changing, and charged atmosphere, saturated with newly-awakened fears and hopes, the vast military power accumulated by Soviet rulers during the rigid and unchanging era of bipolarity will be available—to someone. It is unlikely that it will go unused.

In making this point one frequently encounters the cynical admission that there will, of course, be massacres right and left, but how will they affect us? This is a valid question, but one should not assume an answer that justifies complacency. A situation in which 25,000 nuclear warheads are up for grabs and a secular faith faces annihilation is intrinsically a dangerous one, even if we cannot foresee (as we could not in the 1920s) in what exact form the dangers may arrive.

Of course, these dangers will not simply be a continuation of those we face today. The Soviet capability to wage a general war without long mobilization is ebbing; financial stringencies and the withdrawal of Soviet forces from Eastern Europe will accelerate this process. Any projection of the dangers we are likely to face in the second phase is hazardous; nevertheless, we need to begin thinking about them now. Low-intensity conflict (e.g., terrorism) is likely to become more important; it requires few resources, is deniable, and can be used to shape Western public attitudes on political issues. The Third World, of course, has been the basic arena of low-intensity conflict.

A second source of danger will be civil wars and other domestic conflicts that, together with irredentist ambitions, lead to military clashes. The likely source of many of these problems will be the periphery of the Soviet empire, but some of them will be "displaced" to the Third World, where the stakes are lower.

Iranian militants have already crossed into Azerbaijan, and Turkish public opinion is increasingly called to take sides in the bloody struggles unfolding across the border. The last struggles, in 1918, were decided when the Turkish army marched to Baku. The most readily available and the least risky way for the Soviet Union to prevent Turkish and Iranian involvement is through terrorism and the use of its client states—Syria, Afghanistan, to some extent Iraq—to make it clear to the Turks and Iranians that intervention would involve serious costs. More generally, we should anticipate that during the time of troubles in which it has now entered, the Soviet Union will attempt to use its Third World clients to create diversionary measures intended to keep the West preoccupied.

While the exact nature of these diversions is beyond our vision, we need to get ready for them. We need to do two things above all. The first is to maintain our military forces (although we can and should restructure them). The second is to change the nonmilitary correlation of forces in the world, to take advantage of the benign first phase of the current evolution, the breathing space, in order to strengthen the West's position in the coming era of instability.

If the reasoning above about the potential of Third World clients as instruments of Soviet strategy is even approximately correct, forcing Soviet client regimes from power—the objective of the Reagan doctrine—must be an important element in the needed shift in the nonmilitary correlation of forces. To displace Soviet clients is easier because they are not acknowledged to be such, and because of Gorbachev's peace offensive; such actions need not rupture our better relations with the USSR itself. They serve the purpose of denying the bridge to the Third World provided by Soviet clients; of depriving the

Soviet Union of positions that may be used to put pressure on us in the next phase; and of controlling beforehand the tendency of radical Third World regimes to lead the Soviet Union into adventures it would not otherwise undertake.

While accumulated American blunders have made the Sandinistas largely immune for the time being, the repressive regimes in Afghanistan, Ethiopia, and Angola are as vulnerable as those in East Germany and Czechoslovakia. The fall of communism in Eastern Europe has suggested that regimes such as Cuba's may already be more fragile than we had thought. It would be hard for anyone to deny that a world without communist rule in Afghanistan, in the Horn of Africa, in Southern Africa, and, if possible, in Central America and the Caribbean would be a better world for the people who live in those parts. It would also be a safer world for us.

Because of the breathing space we have in this phase, it is now easier and less risky for us to take the necessary measures; and because we are moving almost inexorably toward a more dangerous second phase, it is more urgent that we take them. Recent events in Eastern Europe have shown that communism will retreat under pressure, but only under pressure, as the communist operational code has always recommended. If that is true at the core, why don't we find out whether it also applies at the rim?

---

[1]The description of the "operational code" that follows is drawn particularly from the work of the late Nathan Leites, beginning with *The Operational Code of the Politburo* (New York: McGraw-Hill, 1951) and *A Study of Bolshevism* (Glencoe, IL: Free Press, 1953).

[2]*Sochineniya*, 3d edition (Moscow: Gospolitizdat', 1928–1937), vol. 27, p. 126.

[3]*Sochineniya* (Moscow: Gospolitizdat', 1948), vol. 5, pp. 167–8.

[4]See "La revolution culturelle de Gorbatchev," Part I, *Commentaire* (Paris), no. 48 (Winter 1989–90); Part II forthcoming in no. 49. Originally published (in shorter form) as "Gorbachev's Cultural Revolution," *Commentary*, August 1989.

[5]Jerzy Urban, letter to the Polish first secretary, translated in the journal *Uncaptive Minds*, November-December 1988, pp. 2–7.

[6]Summarized in RFE/RL *Soviet/East European Report*, VII, no. 13, p. 1.

People, Power, and Leadership

Third World leaders have much in common with the leaders of the industrialized world, yet some facets of their jobs are unique. Unlike most Western heads of state, many leaders of developing nations face persistent attacks on their legitimacy—that is, they lack a popular mandate or broad-based support. Some leaders seized power, others manipulated the election process, others intimidated the electorate, and still others prohibited, harassed, or imprisoned rival candidates. In many cases, this was accomplished through force or threat of force, thereby denying the voters a meaningful say in the selection of their leaders.

Additionally, most Third World leaders face severe social, political, and economic problems, and are forced to manage with extremely limited resources. Indeed, widespread poverty and illiteracy, coupled with the lack of a viable industrial base and few economic alternatives, compound their problems and make it difficult, if not impossible, to solve them.

Furthermore, leaders in the developing world confront myriad cultural, religious, and ethnic problems that undermine national unity and jeopardize the success of official policy. In these countries, the leaders are forced to walk a delicate line between opposing groups, wary of initiating any action that could trigger a major social explosion. Many of these leaders are compelled to share power—both formal and informal—with sundry other figures, many of whom have vastly different perspectives.

Moreover, many Third World leaders face numerous institutional problems, such as the lack of a clearly defined political infrastructure and an unresponsive bureaucracy, plagued by divisive partisan wrangling, pervasive corruption, undefined rules and procedures, and contempt for democratic rights. As a result, these heads of state, however well-meaning, lack the ability to implement their agendas.

Frequently, Third World leaders are also prisoners of the policies and practices of the superpowers and are helpless to steer an independent course. Indeed, in some instances, they function as satellites; their rhetoric and actions must reflect the goals and objectives of those nations upon which they depend for political, economic, and military support. Clearly, these leaders are prevented from formulating policy, expressing dissent, or establishing alliances that may be in the best interests of their peoples.

Obviously, heads of state in the developing world are extremely limited in their ability to solve such pressing problems as hunger, poverty, illiteracy, disease, pollution, and war. They know that they will inevitably arouse both internal and external opposition if they adopt a policy that threatens the ruling elite or a major ally, whose support they need to maintain their position. Thus, many Third World leaders are forced to operate in an untenable situation, one that precludes autonomy and independence.

Somewhat paradoxically, many Third World peoples expect more from their leaders, while denying them the authority and flexibility they require to perform their duties. In many developing nations, the people expect their leaders to produce instant results, even when objective reality would appear to make such changes impossible. When the new leader fails to produce the desired "miracles," he or she quickly becomes the object of derision and scorn—the target of a potential purge, coup, or revolution. Clearly, winning office is only part of the problem, perhaps the easiest part. Far more difficult is the challenge of governing a Third World nation.

Looking Ahead: Challenge Questions

What are the main problems of leadership succession in the Third World?

What conditions are most likely to lead to the demise of authoritarian regimes?

Does the election of Prime Minister Benazir Bhutto signal a new era in Pakistan's political history?

In what ways, if any, does Benazir Bhutto differ from here famous father, the late Zulfikar Ali Bhutto, who served as president and prime minister of Pakistan in the 1970s?

In what ways, if any, have recent developments in Eastern Europe affected Cuban leader Fidel Castro's revolutionary consciousness?

Is Fidel Castro's socialist revolution doomed to collapse?

Why is Algerian President Chadli Benjedid unwilling to

abandon authoritarianism in favor of a democratic political system?

What can or should President Andrés Rodríguez do to establish political legitimacy in Paraguay?

Does Andrés Rodríguez's election promise an end to anarchy and tyranny in Paraguay?

How does the stereotypical image of the Latin *caudillo* fit the newly elected Paraguayan president?

Why does the existence of a new underground organization of young monks frighten the Burmese army?

Is it likely that Aung San Suu Kyi will be able to rescue Burma from the civil war that grips that war-weary nation?

When Leaders Fall: Succession Systems in the Non-Industrialized World

Michael Nacht

Michael Nacht is the Dean of the School of Public Affairs at the University of Maryland. Author of The Age of Vulnerability: Threats to the Nuclear Stalemate *(Brookings, 1985), he is currently editing a volume on forceful regime change in developing countries.*

The problem of leadership succession in the non-industrialized world is among the most vexing issues facing both students of political development and the policy-making community. Despite the considerable efforts of many leading scholars over a sustained period of several decades, there is no single coherent theory that provides a persuasive explanation for the dominant causes of leadership change in developing countries. In the absence of a theoretical or conceptual framework, much policy-making in the United States and elsewhere concerning the nature of regime change and regime stability is understandably guided more by *ad hoc* predilections than by evidence and analysis.

Consider first the nature of the overall problem. According to reasonably reliable statistics (see for example the annual *World Development Report* published by the World Bank), there are 128 nation-states with populations in excess of one million (this includes all UN and World Bank members; additionally, there are thirty-four nations with populations of less than one million that are UN and World Bank members). Of these 128 states, the Soviet Union and seven others are classified as "East European non-market economies;" each is ruled by its respective communist party whose leaders have, without exception, selected the general secretary of the party who is the *de facto* head of state and head of government. Nineteen states are classified as "industrial market economies," ranging in gross national product (GNP) per capita from Spain and Ireland (less than $5,000) to the United States and Switzerland (greater than $15,000). Each of these states has a democratic political system with regularized and legitimized forms of political succession that are determined at the ballot box. This leaves 101 countries, almost all of which are located in Asia, Africa, and Latin America. Thirty-six are classified as "low-income economies" (GNP per capita less than $400); forty are "middle-income economies" (between $450 and $1700); and five are "high-income oil exporters," all located in the Middle East/Persian Gulf region.

The low-income group includes a few communist or "totalitarian" regimes (e.g., Vietnam, Kampuchea, China) and one democracy (India); all others are "authoritarian" regimes led by civilian or military leaders who remain in power until they are forced out by others, unguided by any form of legitimized political succession process. The middle-income group includes communist regimes in the Democratic Republic of Yemen, Nicaragua, Angola, Cuba, North Korea, and Mongolia; and democratic governments in the Philippines, El Salvador (arguably), Jamaica, Colombia, and Costa Rica. Virtually all the others are ruled by an authoritarian form of government. Among the upper-middle-income countries there is one communist regime (Yugoslavia), and democracies of various forms in Brazil, Portugal, Uruguay, Mexico, Venezuela, Argentina, Greece, and Israel. Finally, all five of the high-income oil exporters are authoritarian.

Although there are many cross-currents running through these data, there is one central tendency: the richer the group of nations, the greater the percentage of democratic regimes (with the exception of the five high-income oil exporters). The vast majority of the states in Asia and Africa as well as many in Latin America are ruled by authoritarian regimes.

In overall perspective, there is a second general pattern: regimes of particular types are succeeded most often by regimes of the same type. This pattern is most pronounced among totalitarian regimes: no communist government, once having seized power, has ever relinquished authority to a non-communist regime. With only slightly less consistency (the Turkish *coup d'etat* in 1980, for example),

From *Harvard International Review*, February/March 1988, pp. 6-7, 31. Reprinted by permission.

Democracies and totalitarian regimes tend to be more stable than authoritarian ones.

democracies also tend to perpetuate themselves. Authoritarian regimes exhibit the least consistency in terms of political succession. Some, such as Bolivia, have experienced a consistent pattern over many decades of one authoritarian regime replaced by another. What is striking since 1970, however, is the number of authoritarian regimes that have either been replaced by communist systems (e.g. Vietnam, Cambodia, Nicaragua, Angola) or have shifted to democratic systems (Philippines, Greece, Spain, Portugal, Brazil, Argentina, and several other South American states). South Korea now appears to be ready to join the group of states to make the transition from authoritarianism to democracy.

What leads to the demise of authoritarian regimes? There appear to be several indicators of difficulty. These include:

A protracted economic downturn after extensive economic improvement: If a nation has only known deep poverty, then poverty *per se* may not be a grievance against the regime. Extensive economic improvement, however, generates significant changes in expectations among the populace. A protracted economic downturn then stimulates intense disillusionment that is often channelled into a commitment to forceful regime change.

Ideology of opposition: Different societies have different expectations as to what is acceptable in terms of regime behavior. In the case of the Shah of Iran, for example, he was hounded because of his blatant irreligiosity and the fact that he was thought to have been installed by the Central Intelligence Agency. The central grievances against

Marcos of the Phillippines were, first, the belief that a return to democracy in a country that had previously experienced it was not feasible under his rule, and, second, that the levels of corruption had exceeded the accepted norms of Philippine society.

The state of civil-military relations: In most cases a regime change cannot be effected in an authoritarian system without the support of the uniformed military who have the weapons to determine the success or failure of the change. Senior military officials less often promote change because they are usually part of the ruling elite and enjoy the benefits of their position. What is crucial, therefore, are the political allegiances of the second- and third-echelon military who do not share in the material rewards offered by the regime. In the Philippines, for example, the opposition of recent military academy graduates to the Marcos regime and to the "overstaying generals" was a key ingredient in the regime's demise.

Relative attitudes toward corruption and repression: In the vast majority of non-industrialized countries there is extensive corruption (perversion of behavior for private gain) and repression (removal of political opponents). Their presence thus tells us little about regime stability. What is more significant is the rate of change of these characteristics and whether they reach levels that are unacceptable based upon the norms of the society.

The role of external actors as agents of change: In the modern world virtually no nation lives in isolation from the world community. Great powers such as the United States and the Soviet Union as well as regional powers such as

2. PEOPLE, POWER, AND LEADERSHIP

France and China sometimes adopt explicit policies of military and economic aid to foster regime change or to forestall it. Sometimes the suspension of economic assistance by the World Bank or the International Monetary Fund can have profoundly destabilizing effects on a politically fragile regime in the non-industrialized world. This, for example, was the case in Cuba in 1958.

The issue of corruption is especially relevant both to regime change and to the stability of the successor regime. Recent research has revealed that several common assertions concerning corruption are false: that corruption always tends to destabilize regimes; that corruption alone can induce a forceful regime change; and that there is no corruption in socialist countries. What has been found is that corruption needs to be disaggregated into a number of discrete aspects to assess its effect on political stability. These include answers to the following questions:

- Has the scale of corruption deviated significantly from accepted norms?

- Are powerful rivals to the regime excluded from the rewards of corruption?

- Are military officers other than the top leadership excluded from the rewards of corruption?

- Do groups excluded from the rewards of corruption reflect deep social, ethnic, or geographic cleavages in the society?

- Is the overall economic condition perceived as being severely damaged because of corrupt practices?

- Have the rewards of corruption been reduced in the face of a major economic downturn?

- Has corruption undermined the ability of the armed forces to protect the nation from threats to its security?

- Has corruption undermined external support for the regime?

- Has criticism of corruption stimulated increased repression by the regime against these critics and other groups?

- Is corruption a rallying cry for opposition groups?

- Is the leadership vulnerable to the criticism that its corrupt practices are antithetical to the moral basis of its authority?

- Has a catalytic event (e.g., a political assassination, a major natural disaster) exacerbated corruption or its effects?

- Does the pervasiveness of corruption increase at higher levels of the power structure?

- Are the demands of pressure groups for material rewards not being satisfied by corrupt practices?

- Is the elite too large to be fully rewarded through corrupt practices?

By systematically addressing these questions, one can assess the extent to which corruption would tend to stabilize or destabilize a regime. In the case where corruption is a major grievance against the regime, the successor regime would be expected to remedy these conditions. If the new leadership in turn is found to adopt similar practices, it would also be vulnerable to the same criticism. The Aquino regime, for example, swept into power on the promise of restoring democracy, improving the economy, dealing with the insurgency, and reducing corruption. Subsequent difficulties experienced by the regime have related to the inability to address the second and third conditions effectively. If, in addition, it is found that extensive corruption is practised at the highest levels, then this regime could meet the fate of its predecessor. In South Korea, on the other hand, corruption has not been a central grievance. The absence of democratic reform has been the principal rallying cry. Corruption is only likely to surface as a major issue if the successor to President Chun suspends democratic practices or deals ineffectively with economic or national security issues.

These considerations lead to the following overall conclusions:

- A system of leadership succession is greatly influenced by the political history of the society. A nation with a totalitarian or democratic system is likely to have established institutional, legal, and coercive safeguards to ensure that successor regimes maintain the same type of political system. Authoritarian regimes are more vulnerable to systemic change because of the lack of institutionalization and political legitimacy of the current system.

- A particular system of leadership succession is likely to be sustained if the successor regime redresses the central grievances that brought about the original regime change.

- Ideology and the national experience are pivotal factors in establishing the process of political succession. Societies that have experienced democratic procedures, that practise economic pluralism, or that have well-developed economies, are more likely to turn toward democratic modes of political succession.

Pakistan under Benazir Bhutto

"Unlike her father, Benazir Bhutto has had to be sensitive to the concerns of a constitutionally strong President and a respected military leadership. . . . Even if she wanted to become an autocrat, the current configuration of power in Pakistan would probably thwart her ambitions."

WILLIAM L. RICHTER

William L. Richter is head of the department of political science at Kansas State University and has written widely on Pakistan and South Asia.

DURING the last half of 1988, Pakistan experienced the dramatic end of one era in its turbulent political history and the cautious beginning of another. The death of President Mohammad Zia ul-Haq in a mysterious air crash on August 17, 1988, abruptly terminated his domination of Pakistan's political life and made possible much freer elections than anyone had anticipated. Those elections, held in mid November, and the resultant appointment in December of Benazir Bhutto as Prime Minister ended a decade of struggle and political change. At age 35, Benazir Bhutto became Pakistan's youngest Prime Minister and the first woman to hold that position. Indeed, she is the first woman Prime Minister of any modern Muslim nation.

One day after her appointment, Bhutto addressed the people of Pakistan via nationwide television. Prominently displayed on the wall behind her was a photograph of her father, the late Zulfikar Ali Bhutto, who had served as President (1971–1973) and Prime Minister (1973–1977) of Pakistan. The picture of the elder Bhutto was obviously intended as a symbolic link with that earlier era and with the leader whom Zia had overthrown and executed.[1]

The new Bhutto era, however, is not simply a restoration of the earlier one. Benazir Bhutto is by no means a carbon copy of her father, and the circumstances she faces are different in significant respects from those that prevailed in the early 1970's. She has inherited a large array of political, economic and foreign policy changes, including a continuing civil war in neighboring Afghanistan and a formidable domestic opposition. Nonetheless, she appears to be providing Pakistan with the leadership it needs; she is avoiding the most obvious pitfalls and is now building the foundation for a more enduring democratic political system.

Benazir Bhutto's path to power has not been easy. She returned to Pakistan from overseas study in June, 1977, two weeks before her father's downfall. She had spent four years at Harvard University (Radcliffe College), graduating cum laude in government in 1973, and then had taken a degree in politics, philosophy and economics at Oxford University. While there, she pursued a foreign service training program and served as president of the Oxford Union debating society, the first Asian woman to do so.

Her plans to enter Pakistan's foreign service were radically changed with her father's overthrow. During her father's imprisonment and after his execution, Benazir and her mother, Begum Nusrat Bhutto, assumed the leadership of the Pakistan People's party (PPP). Throughout the period of Zia's rule, the PPP pressed for the restoration of the 1973 constitution and the reestablishment of democratic political parties and representative institutions. Many PPP workers suffered imprisonment, flogging and death at the hands of the military rulers. During much of this period, Bhutto herself was imprisoned or held under house arrest. In 1984, she was released and allowed to go into exile, in part for medical reasons.

General Zia's more than 11 years of rule in Pakistan—the longest of any individual—may be regarded as comprising three broad phases. During the first phase, from the 1977 coup until November, 1979, Zia attempted twice to hold elections that would produce an "acceptable" government, that is, one that would be adequately pro-Islam and pro-military. In both instances (October, 1977, and November, 1979), Zia canceled the elections when it became obvious that the Bhuttos and the PPP still retained popular support. During the second phase, Zia imposed harsh military rule, radically altered the constitution, introduced Islamic reforms and experimented with a variety of alternative political options, including the creation of a 300-member appointed *Majlis-i-Shura* (consultative assembly) The third phase of Zia's rule featured processes of

During the first week of August 1990, the ouster of Prime Minister Benazir Bhutto became a widely circulated rumor. The following week President Ghulam Ishaq Khan confirmed the rumor and announced her dismissal on national television charging that "corruption and nepotism in the federal government" had undermined Bhutto's ability to rule. Free elections were promised in October 1990, with Bhutto's rival Ghulam Mastafa Jatoi appointed interim prime minister.   —Editors note.

Reprinted with permission from *Current History* magazine, December 1989, pp. 433–436, 449–451. Copyright © 1989, Current History Inc.

civilianization and democratization. In August, 1983, Zia announced a program of gradual restoration of representative democratic institutions, with provincial, parliamentary and presidential elections to be held before March, 1985. He failed to hold the presidential elections, substituting instead a misleading plebiscite on his Islamization policies, which he then interpreted as a mandate to stay in power until 1990.

The national and provincial elections were held in February, 1985. Since political parties were still prohibited, the PPP and other anti-Zia groups chose to boycott both the 1984 plebiscite and the 1985 elections. Despite this boycott, the elections served as an effective basis on which to establish a civilian government, with veteran Sindhi Muslim League politician Mohammad Khan Junejo as Prime Minister.

Junejo was not regarded as a forceful leader, but in the months that followed he managed to make several advances in the direction of a more democratic political system. Most notably, martial law was formally lifted on December 30, 1985, and shortly thereafter political parties were again allowed to operate legally and openly.

Three months later, in April, 1986, Benazir Bhutto returned from exile. She toured Pakistan and was greeted by tumultuous crowds. She led the PPP in a series of protest movements calling for new elections. Ultimately, Prime Minister Junejo and President Zia withstood her demands. Bhutto was jailed again for a few weeks in August, after which she shifted to a less agitational strategy of rebuilding support. She was also married, in December, 1987, to Sindhi businessman Asif Zardari. The arranged marriage and the subsequent birth of a son proved to be politically astute.

THE 1988 ELECTIONS

On May 29, 1988, just as Prime Minister Junejo returned from a tour of several East Asian countries, President Zia summarily announced that he was dismissing the Junejo government, dissolving Parliament and the provincial assemblies, and calling for new elections. The ostensible reasons for these abrupt actions included Junejo's alleged failure to check corruption or to enact new Islamic reform legislation; but other reasons appeared more plausible, including the Prime Minister's increasing assertion of his authority over military matters and foreign policy.

General Zia waited for several weeks to set the date for the elections. He was widely regarded as having chosen November 16 on the mistaken calculation that the date would roughly coincide with the birth of Bhutto's child. In any case, the

child was born in September and Bhutto was back on the campaign trail by early October.

Zia's abrupt removal from the scene brought brief uncertainty as to whether elections would be held. Senate President Ghulam Ishaq Khan became Acting President of Pakistan, in accordance with existing constitutional provisions, and reaffirmed the fact that elections would take place as scheduled. His decision was given strong public support by the new Army chief, General Mirza Aslam Beg.[2]

Zia had indicated earlier that the November elections would be held on a nonpartisan basis, like those of 1985. On August 17, just hours before the fatal air crash that killed Zia, Benazir Bhutto filed a court petition to allow political parties to participate. Acting President Ishaq agreed to abide by the court's decision, which ultimately came down in favor of partisan elections.

Throughout the last half of the martial law period, the PPP had functioned as a major component of the Movement for the Restoration of Democracy (MRD). Formed in 1981, the MRD had fought for an end to martial law and the restoration of the 1973 constitution. After Bhutto's return to Pakistan in 1986, the PPP increasingly went its own way and the MRD disintegrated. In anticipation of the elections, new political alliances were made and unmade. The PPP fought the elections alone, but agreed not to field candidates against the leaders of its former MRD allies. Recognizing the PPP as the strongest single contender, another nine-party alliance was created, the Islami Jamhoori Ittehad (IJI, the Islamic Democratic Alliance).[3] Within the IJI, however, there was considerable factionalism. Its largest component, the Pakistan Muslim League (PML), split temporarily between a group led by former Prime Minister Junejo and another led by the chief ministers of Punjab and the North-West Frontier Province (NWFP).

Although there were charges of malpractice, the elections were regarded as among the fairest in Pakistan's history. The major complaint, raised by the PPP, was the requirement of voter identity cards, an eleventh-hour requirement that was seen as disfranchising the PPP's poor, rural and female supporters.

Despite this impediment, the PPP emerged as the largest party nationally, with 93 of the 205 contested Muslim seats in the National Assembly to the IJI's 55. The third largest national winner, with 13 seats, was the Muhajir Qaumi Movement (MQM), a regional-ethnic party representing the Urdu-speaking people of urban Sind (i.e., Karachi and Hyderabad), most of whose families had immigrated from India at partition in 1947. The remaining seats were divided among smaller parties and independents.[4]

In order to establish a majority, the PPP forged a coalition with the MQM, based on a 55-point agreement formulated after the elections. Despite her success in the elections and in the post-election maneuvering for allies, Benazir Bhutto was forced to wait two weeks before being named Prime Minister on December 1. Meanwhile, Acting President Ishaq conducted extensive discussions with political leaders to consider alternative government combinations.

The provincial elections, held on November 19, yielded more mixed results. The PPP won in Sind, but ran second to the IJI in Punjab and the NWFP and secured only 3 seats out of 40 in the Baluchistan Assembly. The PPP suffered the most serious losses in Punjab, Pakistan's largest province. There, the PPP's 94 seats were surpassed by the IJI's 108, out of a total of 240. Both parties attempted to form coalitions, but the IJI was more successful, and Mian Nawaz Sharif was named chief minister. He thereby became Benazir Bhutto's most formidable political opponent; subsequent months brought several instances of confrontation between the two. For the first time in its history, Pakistan has different parties ruling in Islamabad and in Lahore, Punjab's provincial capital. In the NWFP, the PPP was more successful, forming a coalition government with Khan Abdul Wali Khan's Awami National party (ANP) to place PPP leader Aftab Sherpao in the chief ministership.

BHUTTO IN OFFICE

During her first year in office, Benazir Bhutto cautiously attempted to parlay her somewhat precarious position into a position of greater power and authority, and to address the political, social and economic problems she inherited after 11 years of Zia's domination. In her inaugural address to the nation, delivered in Urdu over nationwide television on December 2, she announced the release of political prisoners and the abolition of the National Press Trust, the government agency that had been regarded as a tool of authoritarian control over the media. Among her political appointments were, surprisingly, some holdovers from the Zia period, most notably Foreign Minister Sahabzada Yaqub Khan. Ghulam Ishaq Khan, who had served as Zia's economic adviser and finance minister, was elected to a full term as President with Benazir Bhutto's endorsement. Despite criticism from leftist members of her own party, Bhutto's actions provided a modus vivendi with the bureaucracy and the military; therefore there was a degree of continuity and stability as the new government addressed its challenges.

Benazir Bhutto's first year as Prime Minister has not been easy. She has had to fend off well-entrenched political antagonists led by Punjab Chief Minister Mian Nawaz Sharif, while at the same time attempting to manage precarious national and provincial coalitions. All the while, Bhutto's powers have been circumscribed by a President wary of her intentions and by recalcitrant bureaucrats resentful of the PPP politicians who have become their new bosses.

Bhutto's relationship with Sharif has been especially volatile. After some initial threats and skirmishes, the two arrived at a temporary truce in late December, 1988. Later, however, the Prime Minister attempted to transfer the chief secretary of Punjab, the top bureaucratic official in the province; Sharif and the IJI kept political pressure on central interference in provincial affairs. Meanwhile, Sharif and the IJI kept political pressure on Bhutto in Islamabad and in the other provinces. In mid-1989, the IJI-led Combined Opposition party (COP) was created in the National Assembly, with Ghulam Mustafa Jatoi as its leader. Though comprising seemingly incompatible components like the rightist Jamaat-i-Islami and the leftist Awami National party, the COP shared an interest in keeping the Prime Minister in check.

In the NWFP, the Awami National party, led by Wali Khan and Begum Naseem Wali Khan, split with the PPP-led provincial government, but Chief Minister Aftab Sherpao maintained enough support among provincial assembly members to stay in power. Nawaz Sharif wooed the MQM in Sind and the ruling Baluchistan National Alliance (BNA) in Baluchistan. BNA Chief Minister Nawab Akbar Bugti, however, refused to support the IJI against the PPP. As the government of Benazir Bhutto neared the end of its first year, many opposition groups, with the obvious exception of the IJI, were apparently content to weaken the PPP government, not necessarily to replace it.

Bhutto's relations with President Ishaq have apparently been conditioned by a tacit understanding between the two at the time of her appointment as Prime Minister. That understanding is generally perceived to have included a promise by the Prime Minister not to interfere with Pakistan's military interests or with the broad thrust of Pakistani foreign policy. Whatever the nature and extent of such agreements, Bhutto has made several attempts to increase the power of her office, the most direct of which was an unsuccessful movement to repeal the controversial Eighth Amendment to the constitution, introduced under Zia to give greater powers to the President. Later, she removed General Hamid Gul from the highly sensitive post of chief of the Inter-Services Intelligence directorate (ISI), a position he had held under Zia. Although the move was criticized by people in both the military and the opposition, it did not lead to any major reaction.

When the Prime Minister announced in early August, however, that Admiral Iftikhar Ahmed Sirohey, chairman of the joint chiefs of staff committee, would be retired August 14 at the end of his term as admiral, President Ishaq responded with a public announcement that only the President had the authority to appoint the service chiefs. Ultimately, the President, the Prime Minister and Army Chief Aslam Beg arrived at a compromise; Admiral Sirohey would be retired (as Bhutto had announced), but his successor would be appointed by Ishaq.[5] Although the issue blew over fairly quickly, at least temporarily it created the appearance of a constitutional crisis, with rumors of a possible military coup, Bhutto's resignation or some other dramatic action.

Many of the disputes that have arisen during the first year of Benazir Bhutto's government may be seen as a legacy of General Zia's decade of domination. It was Zia who pressed for the enactment of the Eighth Amendment to the constitution, strengthening the position of the President vis-à-vis the Prime Minister. It was during the Zia decade that Nawaz Sharif gained experience, prominence and power, and his PML built its political base. In other respects, however, Bhutto's political troubles have deeper historical roots. Her father's own record of authoritarianism and his penchant for abusing his political enemies left many opposition politicians wary of giving his daughter too much power.

From a still longer perspective, however, Pakistan under Benazir Bhutto is only undergoing a political transformation that many other countries have encountered earlier in their period of independence. In Pakistan, power has seldom been shared among top leaders; rather, it has been concentrated in the hands of the Governor General, the President or the Prime Minister. Similarly, whoever held power in Pakistan's central government also controlled the provinces, particularly Punjab. Thus, disputes in the past year over the Eighth Amendment, military and provincial appointments, and the relative authority of the Prime Minister, the President and the Chief Ministers represent a working out of power-sharing arrangements for which the country has virtually no precedent. Given this circumstance, it is remarkable that such disputes have not been more disruptive and that workable solutions have been found for each crisis as it has arisen. Nonetheless, the situation continues to remain unpredictable.

THE ECONOMIC AND SOCIAL AGENDA

Benazir Bhutto and her government inherited a mixed economic legacy from President Zia. On the one hand, Pakistan has enjoyed remarkable economic growth since 1977, averaging an annual growth rate of six percent per capita in real income. On the other hand, important economic disparities and a heavy burden of foreign debt remain.

Pakistan's impressive growth is attributable to a variety of factors, most notably the professional management of the economy by experienced civil servants during the martial law period, and sizable foreign inputs in the form of remittances from overseas workers and from foreign assistance.[6]

To varying degrees, each of these factors has become somewhat more tenuous just as the new democratic order has begun. In some respects, the timing is coincidental. Throughout most of the past decade, worker remittances from the Middle East have constituted the largest single component of Pakistan's foreign exchange earnings, but the end of the oil boom in the Persian Gulf has led to a leveling-off, and then a drop, in remittances to Pakistan.

The threat to future foreign assistance has thus far proved to be more imagined that real. Much of Pakistan's foreign aid over the past decade has been related to the war in Afghanistan. Assistance from the United States alone has been around US$5 billion since 1982, making Pakistan the third largest recipient of United States aid in the 1980's. Many Pakistanis feared that the end of the Afghan war might lead to a rapid decline in American interest in Pakistan, given the traditional fickleness of American policy. Although the continuation of the war makes it too early to tell whether these fears are valid, the administration of President George Bush has certainly given no indication that such changes are in the offing. In fact, following Benazir Bhutto's visit to Washington, D.C., in June, 1989, the United States agreed to sell an additional 60 F-16 aircraft to Pakistan, bringing the authorized total to 100.

Perhaps the greatest uncertainty is the future management of the economy, although here again it is too early to make a detailed assessment. In some respects, the bureaucracy has maintained continuity in its management of economic affairs, regardless of frequent changes in the political regime. However, the first Bhutto government (1971–1977) undermined that continuity in several ways. Z.A. Bhutto expanded the public payroll to reward party workers and supporters, weakened the bureaucracy by introducing a system of lateral entry and frightened away capital by nationalizing several industries.[7] Finally, the period of turmoil that followed the disputed March, 1977, elections had further harmful effects on the economy.

Benazir Bhutto appears determined not to repeat her father's economic mistakes, but she is frequently criticized for failure to move quickly enough on economic and social legislation:

> Given that the budget in Pakistan is also a statement of the government's official economic policy, some of the more pertinent issues missing from the 1989–1990 budget include plans to curtail the debt-servicing burden in the future, effective strategies to foster industrial growth, reduction of unemployment and underemployment, and the absence of a long-term vision to mobilize revenues in a democratic and just manner.[8]

Repayment of interest and principal on foreign debts is likely to be on the Bhutto agenda for some time. Pakistan has one of the highest debt-service ratios in the world, and the 1989–1990 budgeted allocation for debt servicing is larger than either the Annual Development Plan or the defense budget.[9]

One controversial component of Pakistan's total foreign debt is a US$833-million package from the International Monetary Fund (IMF). The IMF deal was negotiated before Zia's death, and Bhutto reluctantly agreed to abide by its terms, which will include pressure to restructure Pakistan's economy in accordance with IMF guidelines.

World Bank economist Shahid Javed Burki has argued that Pakistan's future growth is likely to encounter difficulties unless adequate attention is paid to the distribution of economic benefits in Pakistani society. In many respects, he argues, Pakistan is a middle-income country, potentially comparable to the newly industrialized countries (NIC's) of East Asia and Southeast Asia. By certain social indices, however, it remains underdeveloped, particularly in terms of female literacy, infant mortality, infant health care and related areas.[10] The Bhutto government has included sizable increases in the allocations for health and education in the 1989–1990 budget.

FOREIGN AFFAIRS

Just as Prime Minister Bhutto's domestic actions have been sharply circumscribed by opposing political forces, she has not had a free hand in shaping Pakistan's foreign relations. She has tried to take new initiatives with regard to India and Afghanistan, but for the most part she has continued the policies she inherited from the previous regime.

Benazir Bhutto's victory in the November elections was greeted with great enthusiasm in neighboring India. After she became Prime Minister, she capitalized on that goodwill by meeting with Indian Prime Minister Rajiv Gandhi. The two leaders jointly expressed their confidence

that, as "new generation" leaders, they would find ways to reduce the long-standing enmities between their two countries. They also reached some substantive agreements, including a formal agreement not to attack one another's nuclear facilities.

In subsequent meetings, the same cordial spirit has prevailed, although symbolic gestures have largely outweighed substantive change. During a summit meeting of the South Asian Association for Regional Cooperation (SAARC) in Islamabad, Bhutto paid "tribute to the memory of Mrs. Indira Gandhi," Rajiv's mother and predecessor. She abandoned the "No-War Pact" proposal that General Zia had raised in 1981, indicating instead that Pakistan would revert to the 1972 Simla Agreement as the basis for Indo-Pakistani relations. She and Foreign Minister Sahabzada Yaqub Khan offered to initiate mutually agreed-on reductions in conventional arms.[11]

India and Pakistan had haggled over the no-war pact notion, along with an Indian counterproposal for a mutual friendship treaty, for seven years without reaching agreement; therefore, abandoning the idea was understandable, particularly given its identification with Zia. The Simla Agreement, negotiated between Indira Gandhi and Zulfikar Ali Bhutto, also had obvious personal symbolism for the two Prime Ministers.[12] However, many Pakistanis see the agreement, which requires that neither country seek outside support on bilateral issues, as appeasement of India's "hegemony" in the region.

Clearly, Bhutto has made the improvement of relations with India a foreign policy priority, but any Pakistani leader is limited in the pursuit of this goal. A variety of issues between the two countries have remained intractable for several years, with no clear solution in sight. Kashmir has remained disputed territory for four decades. During the 1980's, Indian and Pakistani troops have clashed several times over the undemarcated Siachen Glacier in northern Kashmir.

A second issue that is likely to remain troublesome is nuclear weapons capability. India exploded a nuclear device in 1974, and demonstrated its delivery capabilities in 1989 by successfully testing its Agni long-range ballistic missile. Although Pakistan has not exploded a nuclear device, such an event has been rumored for nearly a decade.[13] India's policy of not producing nuclear weapons, despite a vocal lobby in favor of such a strategy, is coupled with active Indian attempts to deny Pakistan the nuclear option.

American foreign assistance legislation, based on long-standing nuclear nonproliferation policies, provides for the immediate cancellation of assistance to Pakistan if the latter should explode a nuclear device, or even if Pakistan can be shown to be developing nuclear capabilities. Such a cancellation took place in 1979, but during the 1980's security interests related to the Afghan war tended to overlook Pakistan's apparent development of nuclear weapons technology. India and several members of the United States Congress have continued to call for stricter American control over Pakistan's nuclear options, but an assurance from the American President each year has been sufficient to keep the aid flowing.

For several years Pakistan's stance has been that its nuclear technology is directed primarily toward the production of electrical power; that it does not intend to develop nuclear weapons; and that it is prepared to enter into regional agreements with India, including the mutual inspection of nuclear facilities, but not to concede unilaterally an option that India will not even discuss. Benazir Bhutto has reiterated this "regional solution" to the nuclear proliferation problem, which the United States now largely endorses but India rejects out of hand, citing the threat of China on its northern borders. Neither India nor Pakistan sees possession of nuclear weapons as beneficial to its national interest, but neither is prepared to abandon the nuclear option.

India's relations with its other neighbors, particularly Sri Lanka, Nepal and Bangladesh, also limit any possible improvement in Indo-Pakistani relations. India's involvement in Sri Lanka's civil war, its deployment of troops to put down a 1988 coup in the Maldives and its crippling trade pressures on Nepal in 1989 have all served to reinforce Pakistani concerns about Indian "hegemony" in the subcontinent.[14] If Benazir Bhutto ignores these concerns in her attempt to build Indo-Pakistani friendship, she may risk both the goodwill of other South Asian countries and strong criticism at home.

Although India remains Pakistan's top foreign policy concern, the war in neighboring Afghanistan has occupied much of its attention for the past decade. On February 15, 1989, ten weeks after Bhutto became Prime Minister, the Soviet Union completed its withdrawal from Afghanistan, in accordance with the Geneva Accords signed in April, 1988. Despite expectations that the Marxist regime in Kabul might easily fall after the Soviet withdrawal, it has remained remarkably strong, reinforced by massive Soviet arms assistance and aided by growing factional divisions among the anti-Marxist mujahideen.

Under Benazir Bhutto, Pakistan has largely continued the policies it inherited, supporting the mujahideen and maintaining close cooperation with the United States. Continuity of its policy toward Afghanistan was one of the concessions Bhutto apparently made to ensure a peaceful political transition in late 1988.

The failure of the mujahideen forces to capture the city of Jalalabad, despite months of siege after the Soviet departure, has led to reconsideration of Pakistan's Afghan policy. The interim Afghan government in Peshawar and the United States maintain the hard-line expectation of ultimate military victory over Afghan President Najibullah's government. Benazir Bhutto has increasingly urged a more flexible response to the possibility of a negotiated settlement. She raised this issue with United States President George Bush during her visit to the United States in June, 1989; more recently she asked her country's intelligence services to carry out an extensive review of Pakistan's Afghan policy.[15]

CONCLUSION

The second Bhutto era in Pakistan's political history differs in many respects from the first. Although Benazir Bhutto's PPP was unable to secure a majority of seats in the November, 1988, elections, she has been able to maintain PPP governments at the national level and in two of the four provinces. She has had to deal with formidable challenges, however, including the unprecedented situation of having the largest province in the hands of the political opposition.

Unlike her father, Benazir Bhutto has had to be sensitive to the concerns of a constitutionally strong President and a respected military leadership. Whereas Zulfikar Ali Bhutto was able to act virtually as a dictator, silencing any domestic opposition he could not control, his daughter must operate with powers more circumscribed than those of almost any other Prime Minister. Even if she wanted to become an autocrat, the current configuration of power in Pakistan would probably thwart her ambitions.

The key question is whether she has enough power to lead the country, to address its many economic, social and foreign policy issues, and to continue to build its democratic system.

---

[1]Zia, then serving as Army Chief of Staff, led the military coup that deposed Zulfikar Ali Bhutto on July 5, 1977. He promised to hold new elections and restore democracy "within 90 days," but subsequently canceled the elections and had Bhutto brought to trial for complicity in a murder. Following Bhutto's conviction, upheld by a split decision of the Supreme Court, Zia refused widespread appeals for clemency; Bhutto was executed on April 4, 1979.

[2]The air crash that took Zia's life also killed United States Ambassador Arnold Raphel and United States Military Attaché Herbert Wassom, as well as top-ranking Pakistani military officers. Investigation of the crash by Pakistani and American experts was not conclusive. There appears to have been sabotage, using an explosive canister of gas smuggled aboard

the flight, but by whom and at whose orders remain highly speculative questions.

[3]The IJI is sometimes designated IDA in the English-language press. See Rasual B. Rais, "Pakistan in 1988: From Command to Conciliation Politics," *Asian Survey,* vol. 29, no. 2 (February, 1989), p. 202.

[4]For a brief report on the national and provincial elections, including discussion of the fairness issue, see *Pakistan Elections: Foundation for Democracy* (Washington, D.C.: National Democratic Institute for International Affairs, 1989).

[5]These developments are covered in Zaffar Abbas, "Who's in Charge?" and Makhdoom Ali Khan, "Constitutionally Speaking . . . ," both in *The Herald* (Karachi), vol. 20, no. 9 (September, 1989), pp. 53–61 and 64–70, respectively.

[6]President Ghulam Ishaq Khan and former World Bank official Mahbubul Haq were two of the key economic bureaucrats during this period.

[7]W. Eric Gustafson, "A Review of the Pakistan Economy under Bhutto," in Manzooruddin Ahmed, ed., *Contemporary Pakistan: Politics, Economy and Society* (Durham, N.C.: Carolina Academic Press, 1980), pp. 146–162.

[8]Ihteshamul Haque, "Balancing Act," *The Herald,* vol. 20, no. 1 (July, 1989), p. 91.

[9]Ibid.

[10]Shahid Javed Burki, presentation at annual meeting of the Association for Asian Studies, Washington, D.C., March, 1989. Cf. Nasra M. Shah, *Pakistani Women: A Socioeconomic and Demographic Profile* (Honolulu: East-West Population Institute, East-West Center, 1986).

[11]Mushahid Hussain, "The Birth of a Superpower?" *The Herald,* vol. 20, no. 9 (September, 1989), p. 14.

[12]Benazir Bhutto, then barely 19 years old, accompanied her father to the conference at Simla, the Indian hill station that served during British times as the viceregal summer capital.

[13]Cf. Gerard C. Smith and Helena Cobban, "A Blind Eye to Nuclear Proliferation," *Foreign Affairs,* vol. 68, no. 3 (Summer, 1989), pp. 57–59; and Thomas P. Thornton, "The New Phase in U.S.-Pakistani Relations," *Foreign Affairs,* vol. 68, no. 3 (Summer, 1989), pp. 153–155.

[14]For a more general discussion of these issues, see William L. Richter, "Indira Gandhi's Neighborhood: Indian Foreign Policy Toward Neighboring Countries," in Yogendra K. Malik and Dhirendra K. Vajpeyi, eds., *Indira: The Years of Indira Gandhi* (Leiden: E.J. Brill, 1988), pp. 118–131.

[15]Ahmed Rashid, "Give Peace a Chance," *Far Eastern Economic Review,* August 31, 1989, p. 24.

Semper Fidel

'Forward to Socialism!
He Who Doesn't Like It Can Take a Laxative!'

Marc Cooper

HAVANA – Sitting on the meeting room floor of the Fifth Congress of the Cuban Women's Federation were thousands of overdressed, mostly plump, mostly middle-aged, matronly delegates and bureaucrats who—after three long days of approving preordained, undebated, verbose resolutions by unanimous vote and having suffered through scores of sisterly speeches from invited party hacks world round—were now, frankly, beginning to wilt, if not just plain cave in. That is, until the main attraction got underway—that is, the main event of *every* significant meeting in Cuba. The one rock-solid, you-can-count-on-it invariable in a society where hard facts tend to be scarce. The *Comandante-en-Jefe* would, of course, personally wrap up the congress.

At 7 p.m. on that last night of the women's meeting, Fidel mounted the podium. And the near narcoleptic crowd was suddenly electrified, clapping and shouting on its feet. Fidel hitched his military belt over his thickening middle, stroked his longish, now all-gray beard, and futzed with the bank of microphones—giving Rebel Television enough time to adjust their nationwide feed. It was a speech that was vintage Fidel, a two-and-a-half-hour pleading, punching, soothing, seductive, threatening, altogether

---

Some of the names in this article have been changed.

awesome exhibition of world-class oratory.

And though the topics Fidel touched on ranged, superficially, from women's rights to watermelons to washing machine production, the speech was really about that one Big Question that is today on every Cuban's mind: what in the hell is the future of Cuba in a world where its allies have crumbled like stale bread?

In case you didn't want to sit through the whole speech to get Fidel's answer, it was spelled out on the 30-foot-long red-and-white banner over his head: "Socialism, No Matter What!" But if you did bob and weave through the entire speech, as I did, you could see that Fidel, after 31 years in power, was still lightning-quick on his intellectual feet, dangerously unpredictable in his political moves, and that his full answer to the Big Question is much more nuanced than any American newspaper characterization (or, better, caricature-ization) of him as the "Last Stalinist."

Fidel used as his foil an incident 24 hours earlier in Geneva, where Poland, Hungary, Bulgaria, and Czechoslovakia voted for the first time *with* the United States to open a UN investigation of human rights in Cuba.

"Things are taking place that a few years ago would have been difficult to imagine. Indeed, the socialist camp has collapsed," Fidel told his audience, his palms up and his eyes wide. And then, switching to a mocking tone, he continued: "Thank you,

leaders of Poland, Czechoslovakia. Thank you Hungary and Bulgaria! Thanks for the lesson you have taught us! For your contribution to our revolutionary consciousness, for making us feel ever more proud and dignified, for making us feel, as if it were possible, even *more* revolutionary! More socialist! . . . Thank you for deepening our convictions! For making us harder, for making us firmer!"

After detailing the aid that will now *not* be forthcoming from Eastern Europe, Fidel poured on the sarcasm—sarcasm that tickled his audience and that would probably delight Lee Iacocca.

"Let's speak clearly once and for all . . . We Cubans don't export garbage. But often what we get back in trade [from the East] is junk!"

"No one else in the world buys Bulgarian forklifts. They are such garbage, only we bought them! How many hundreds, thousands of them stand idle today in our warehouses? The Hungarian buses we have get four miles to the gallon! They pollute the city with fumes and poison everyone around. Who knows how many people have died from the fumes of those buses just because they put in a defective fuel pump! On top of it all, those buses have a two-speed Czech transmission that alone wastes 30 per cent of the fuel! Oh, how happy I am to speak with such openness! It's been difficult to talk about these things in the past,

 From *The Village Voice*, May 1, 1990, pp. 21–26. Copyright © 1990 by Marc Cooper. Reprinted by permission.

but thanks to these new circumstances, we have been relieved of our previous compromises!"

After the laughs came the really bad news. The Soviet Union was still, more or less, standing by its $5 billion-a-year commitment (including supply of 100 per cent of all petroleum), but no one could guarantee for how much longer. Cuba was being squeezed, Fidel said. And now, he warned, if the Soviets should cut Cuba off, the island should be prepared for an economic Götterdämmerung, something Fidel called a Special Period. "In this Special Period . . . that could last one, two, three, maybe five years . . . we would have to totally halt development of all social programs, schools, day-care centers, clinics." Electrical consumption would be cut in half and strictly rationed, thousands would be laid off their jobs (but not off the state payroll), and Cubans would have to learn to wear the same clothes for months at a time.

But would this mean an end to Cuban Socialism? "We don't care who or what falls from power elsewhere, but here nothing is going to fall!" Fidel vowed, rabbit-punching the air. "The Yankees can dream on, but we tell them straight out, just forget about it! Is there really anybody in this country, anyone with honor, with dignity, who is willing to surrender if we have to stand alone? And when we stand alone how can we really be alone when we defend the most beautiful ideals in the world!"

The women roar to their feet and shout in unison: "Socialism! Forward to Socialism! He who doesn't like it can take a laxative!"

Fidel wasn't quite finished. "There used to be those who berated us because they said we were a Soviet satellite. And now they insult us because we don't follow the Soviets. When are they going to just let us do what we want to do? When will they allow us to declare our own independence? What country can be more independent than ours, a country willing to confront an empire on its own doorstep, and the rest of the world if necessary!"

To watch Fidel deliver that speech to that convention was to look at the best and the worst of Cuba all in one room. The dreary, party-orchestrated Women's Congress smelled of braindeath, of the mind-numbing ossification that drove Romanians to revel in the Christmastime execution of the Ceauşescus. But to reduce Fidel Castro to a tropical version of the Romanian dictator is to not understand either the Cuban leader himself, or his revolution. Partially, because Fidel *is* the Cuban revolution. And to the degree that he is, he is both its saving grace and its potential ruination. Castro is the maverick who made his revolution in spite of the pro-Moscow Cuban Communists' opposition. He is the man who later

absorbed the Communists into his own party.

And while Castro molded the party in the *image* of its Soviet counterpart, he guaranteed that it would, in reality, respond only to his personal political agenda. Hence, the anomaly of an apparently orthodox Cuban Communist Party spending most of the 1960s shitting all over the hemisphere's other Communist parties for too closely mirroring Moscow's revolutionary timidity. When Fidel muted his criticism of Moscow in the 1970s, it was on the heels of domestic economic failure and subsequent further dependence on the Soviets.

Now Fidel has recovered some of that distance he put between himself and Moscow 25 years ago. Those who would have expected Castro to do otherwise are either ignorant of Cuban history or downright disingenuous. Cuba's de facto break with a disappeared "socialist camp" allows it the possibility of recouping its own independent course . . . albeit at enormous, potentially fatal, economic cost. The Cuban leadership is rejecting the sort of transformations taking place in the East, transformations they see as "surrender."

But at the same time, even party bureaucrats now openly criticize, by name, the "Stalinism" they correctly blame for the East's downfall.

Some Cubans, probably many, are dissatisfied enough with their lives to want to chuck the whole revolution. But it's doubtful they are a majority. When the Poles or chuck the whole revolution. But it's doubtful they are a majority. When the Poles or Czechs looked West they saw the glitter of Germany. To their East they saw the disaster that is the Soviet Union. But what do Cubans see? Either the impossible dream of Miami, or more likely the desolation that is Haiti, or the food riots in more developed Venezuela and Argentina. They see the Mexican tourists who traveled on my plane and were reminded by the tour guides that here, in Havana, they *could* drink the water and walk the streets freely at night without fear of assault.

Thinking about Cuba's future puts to the test not only the Cubans' capacity for self-examination and criticism, but also raises the question of what political choices we, as Americans, are willing to permit the Third World. If we automatically discount the possibility of a revolution reforming itself and surviving, then the only alternatives we offer an underdeveloped nation like Cuba are to be an Albania or a Panama, if not an El Salvador.

I have come here to see how real Cuba's three-year-old program of "rectification"—the rather cumbersome name for Castro's half-a-*glasnost*—is, and if it can improve the revolution without reforming it out of existence.

I spent most of my time with journalists

and writers based on a simple formula: if there is to be any sort of reform in Cuba, it must be preceded or at least accompanied by some public debate. What solutions can there be unless there is a recognition of the problem. I had been in Cuba several times since 1980, but not at all in the last five years. Yet this is the first time ever I did not get blank looks when the subject was broached. Nowadays, this is all that any and everybody wants to talk about.

"Really for the last two years there has been a much more open climate. People speak up with no fear. Often absolutely nothing gets accomplished, but at least there is an environment for criticism," says Miguel Angel, the fiftyish, veteran journalist and party member, a friend of mine, who has volunteered a week of his time to help me negotiate the bureaucracy. He spoke to me while we drove, in my Havan-Auto Rent-a-Car, on our way to my first appointment. And this was to be only the first of many similar frank dialogues I would have with him during that week, almost always in the rented Jetta as we noodled among Soviet-built Fiats and cannibalized '54 Fords.

"The informational ice was broken in '87 when a magazine published an article entitled Sandra's Case that for the first time dealt honestly with prostitution in Havana. Criticism has broadened since then," Miguel Angel continues. "But it's still centered on specifics, not the system. Especially since the collapse of Eastern Europe, there is a fear of opening up cracks; cracks that could be pried wide open."

"The official line here is that in Eastern Europe there were abuses, mistakes, errors. Errors? Balls! Those weren't errors. Those were horrors! That wasn't a socialist camp; it was a socialist clique! But what else can our party say other than that it was errors? To say anything else would be to admit they lied to the people, and to themselves, for 30 years about Eastern Europe."

We pulled to the curb. "Here you can get a good reading on official thinking," he said. Because "here"—the site of one of my first meetings—was the headquarters of *Moncada* magazine, the official organ of the militarized Ministry of the Interior, home not only to the Fire Department, but also to the National Revolutionary Police and the secret State Security. If there is a hard-line in Cuba, this is its bastion.

Up the elevator to the fourth floor, through double oak doors and into an air-conditioned conference room that materialized as the the worst sort of nightmare; at least to reporters like me who spend most of their time in Latin America.

Seated around the table were 18 people in military uniform.

This, at least in a place like Chile or El Salvador, is usually your last earthly vision. But, hey, these guys (and women), uniformed military journalists really, could actually talk. And listen. And even debate. And they didn't have to shave their hands every morning. Chalk up one point for the Cuban Revolution.

Though I must admit I got very little chance to probe their official thoughts. They had decided to interview *me*, instead of vice versa. So excited were they to have a real American journalist in front of them (even if he was from the *Voice*), that our two hours were spent answering *their* questions about Hunter Thompson, Norman Mailer, Joan Didion, Frances FitzGerald, the rise and fall of American New Journalism, and the social significance, if any, of *Bonfire of the Vanities.* Then a volley of questions about what reporting techniques I use. And then some jokes about how the silly "Russian advisers who used to work here in the ministry tried to convince people that we shouldn't put out a magazine."

Our encounter ends with Moncada's director, Colonel Ricardo Martinez (who had helped put Fidel's original clandestine radio on the air during the revolution), putting his arm around me and asking would I please go over the last 12 or 15 issues of his magazine before I leave Cuba and write him up a critique of everything I find wrong. And, oh yes, please take a look at the current issue's article "This Is The Truth," because it's the first time anyone can remember that an article has appeared apologizing for the four-year incarceration of four incorrectly convicted people.

My next two afternoons are filled with similar meetings at the Cuban Journalists Union (UPEC), where in two separate, three-hour sessions, attended by some 40 reporters and writers, I'm invited to freely trash the Cuban press—which I do with some abandon—and then am roundly congratulated for giving the best talk in recent times. Well, really the second-best talk, because everyone is still buzzing about the 10-day marathon staged by Mexican anarchist novelist and journalist Paco Igacio Taibo II, who kicked off his UPEC conferences with the now immortalized one-liner about the Cuban Communist Party daily: "Brothers and sisters: *Granma* is the worst goddamned newpaper in the en-tire hemisphere!"

Many of the reporters I met credit UPEC's new president, Julio Garcia—a Fidel confidant—with helping infuse Cuban journalism with a dose of critical oxygen just when it was on the verge of asphyxiating itself. Garcia was among the most cautious officials I spoke with, and in that sense, his openness is even more striking. "Cuban journalism has nothing to learn from the Stalinist model. I would travel to Eastern Europe and after one week I felt like a Martian, totally deprived of all information about the world," Garcia told me. "We are unquestionably at a historic turn-

ing point. The worst aspect of all this copying of East Europe that went on here was the loss of our national culture, which by nature is very open. Cuba has suffered great isolation and backwardness. We need a renewal in every aspect of our society."

That sentiment was echoed in conversations with the editors of *Juventud Rebelde,* Cuba's national afternoon daily. Thirty-year-old foreign editor Ignacio Hernandez—formerly a top official of the Communist Youth—agrees. "The world is changing. Things can no longer be looked at in terms of right and wrong. Now people must be given a chance to make up their own minds. Much of what we have here is a copy of the socialist countries, including our political structures. And everything we have copied has turned out like shit! What we do on our own is always better. So it is time to make changes, but in a Cuban way."

What changes if any, then, are evident in journalism and literature? Castro recently signed an agreement with Ted Turner, and every Friday night Cuban TV carries a soon-to-be-expanded half-hour package of CNN. National radio's nightly two-hour news magazine, *El Exclusivo,* has been so aggressive in exposing high-level corruption and inefficiency (not shying away from ambushing cabinet ministers with the most embarrassing of allegations) that it is affectionately referred to by people in the street as "Los Terroristas." Coverage of Eastern European events in the daily press has been expanded and frequently relies on Western sources such as AP, UPI, and ANSA. The dailies are also beginning to carry reports of economic mismanagement, equivalent to the first tentative probes of the Soviet press in the earliest phase of *glasnost.* Cuban reporters are given a daily 40-page roundup of the world press, including the most critical articles on Cuba.

The leadership of the Cuban Writers Union has been reinvigorated and is peopled by writers who in the past were considered being just short of Enemies Of The State. The union's quarterly journal, among the most open in Latin America, is edited by prize-winning novelist Pablo Armando Fernandez, whose works did not see light during the entire decade of the 1970s (see, "All We Have Are Mosquitoes, Cubans, and the Revolution," for an in-depth interview with Armando Fernandez). He has filled the journal not only with such decidedly noncommunist figures as Argentina's Jorge Luis Borges, but also with Cuban authors such as Manuel Diaz Martinez, Jose Rodriguez Feo, Cesar Lopez, Luis Aguero, Jose Yanes, Delfin Prats, Miguel Barnet, and others, many of whom in the past were considered taboo because of suspect politics or unorthodox personal lives.

On the other hand, last year the hard-liners won one debate and, in an absurd move, outlawed the circulation of two *Sovi-*

et journals accused of being too liberal. All in all, the *apertura*—the information opening—is only partial, uneven, tenuous, and bereft of future guarantees. The brightest and most articulate official I met, the youthful editor-in-chief of *Juventud Rebelde,* Jose Vidal, was concerned that the deepening economic crisis could lead to a political clampdown. "Too often we have confused unity with uniformity. So we have to continue opening up the debate. The biggest mistake we could make would be to halt this process of change. But we have to do it without providing an opening for the enemy. We have to move slowly but surely. The problem is that the atmosphere of economic crisis, perhaps the worst Cuba has ever faced, just doesn't favor the opening up of debate."

How bad is that economic crisis? Bad enough so that the morning after Fidel's speech, the streets of Havana were already filled with bitter jokes. "What problem is Fidel going to have during the 'Special Economic Period'?" asks the most repeated barb. Answer: "During the 'Special Period,' Fidel will continue as *Commandante.* But Hunger will be General."

Walking through central, colonial Havana, the distortions in the economy came out and grabbed me. Cubans were nowhere near hungry. But their economy is so obviously fragile that it is easy to imagine it crumbling overnight under the stress of total Soviet cut off. People were undeniably healthy, well-groomed and well-dressed by Latin American standards. But the shops, stores, and services melded into a surreal tableau. In Cuba, everything is state-owned. So the streets are lined with hundreds of seemingly individual and distinct shops, but nearly each is selling only a few items, sometimes a single product, like plastic hair barrettes. And almost always, only items imported from the East are available.

Miguel Angel and another journalist and friend, Teresita, gave me the walking tour of Havana's "shopping district." The economic crisis in Cuba has been a permanent fact of life for 30 years but with the aid cut off from the East "we are really feeling it now," said Miguel Angel. We stood in line in front of the Pizzeria Napoles, a counter that opened on the sidewalk, with no signs, no seats, and which, for a peso, served up a single glob of cheese pizza delivered on newsprint. "In the provinces the bread ration has been cut from four ounces to three. There are no eggs this week in all of Havana, by the summer they'll be back on the ration card," Miguel Angel added. "Since the beginning of this year the Russians are making us pay for goods in hard currency and we are buying a lot less. I don't think it will be long now before almost everything is rationed, and in smaller amounts."

After our pizza, we stopped on a corner

where a snow-cone vendor had set up a colorful wooden cart. From a block of ice he scraped chips into a wax-paper cone and then poured sweet cherry syrup over it. "This is a Kafkaesque, absurd system," said Teresita, a longtime Communist militant. "Even this snow-cone operation is owned by the state. Imagine the bureaucracy involved. This vendor has to buy his ice from a central warehouse. That warehouse has its own administrators. He has an administrator and so on."

A department store we entered looked like the dregs of a California yard sale. The chintziest plastic barrette costs three pesos. One Russian-made aluminum watchband, occupying an otherwise deserted display case, costs 15 pesos—half a week's salary. A pair of Chinese-made polyester pants, 65 pesos. Chinese blue jeans, 100 pesos. Not only are these goods scarce and of poor quality, they are also prohibitively expensive.

"Essential items on the ration card are dirt cheap," Miguel Angel explained. "Items off the card are enormously expensive. As a journalist I have a good salary—300 pesos a month. In my house there are four adults. Three of us work. But with only 30 pesos we can buy *everything* that the card allows us. We get five pounds of rice per person per month at six cents a pound. It's really free. Same for oil, sugar, salt, beans, and three-quarters of a pound of meat per person. What you get on the card is just enough to get by on. Anything else you have to buy in the open market and there you can pay three pesos for the same pound of rice that costs six cents on the card. So every Cuban has got a lot of money, and very little to buy, except some extra food, and of course books—which are very, very cheap."

In fact, we ran into a knot of excited people on the street scooping up the newest shipment of books. Heller's *Trampa 22*, Vidal's *Burr*, and Graves's *Hercules y Yo*, all at the ridiculously low price of one peso.

Another ritual pit stop with Miguel Angel and Teresita, six or seven times each day, called for a dark, rich *cafecito*. This time we have come into a cavernous bar that has one item on the menu: "Coffee—10 cents." One middle-aged black woman with a scarf on her head slowly—v-e-r-y s-l-o-w-l-y—tends to each customer. "Unanimously people think that small services like these should be privatized," Juan Carlos said as he impatiently tapped the counter. "I'm not talking about giving up the revolution, about privatizing natural resources or major industries. I'm talking about making life a bit more rational. But government policy on this is still unyielding." The coffee was finally poured. "Take this coffee stand," Miguel Angel said. "It only sells coffee. But you know we Cubans like to drink ice water after our coffee. You know that in *all* of Havana you can't get a single glass of cold water. Watch."

"Comrade, can you spare me a glass of ice water?" he asked the waitress.

"Freezer's broken," she responded, shrugging her shoulders.

Miguel Angel shook his head at me. "Of course the freezer works. The real problem is that the person who works behind the counter has no reason to give you a glass of water, unless she just wants to create more work for herself."

Teresita added: "And what's worse, she makes a fortune. Her salary is 120 pesos a month but I guarantee she takes home more than a journalist. There's no one to look after her. How can a single employer, the state, keep everyone accountable? She must pocket at least another 15 or 20 pesos a day."

On the way back to our car, I was spotted by two teenagers who correctly took me for a foreigner. The black market hustle began; the tiresome dance that every tourist, every foreign vistor finds on almost any corner in Havana: Do I want to sell them dollars—which Cubans are not allowed to possess—at 10 times the official rate? Do I want to buy export-quality cigars—supposedly sold only for dollars to foreigners—at half the price? Can I go into the hard currency stores—from which Cubans are banned—and buy them something with the $20 bill they want to slip me?

Miguel Angel was angered by the hustle, but not surprised: "The lack of consumer goods creates among many people an obsession with consumerism, sometimes bordering on the hallucinatory. I can remember as a boy seeing a magazine ad that said, 'This Buick Can Be Yours' and knowing very well it couldn't. But today when you talk to young people, when you talk to them about the revolution, about how they have gotten their education because of the revolution, of how they have a career opportunity because of the revolution, they say, 'Thank you very much. We support the revolution. We don't want to go backward. But we *also* want all those other things we hear about and see. And we want them *now.*' "

We got back to Teresita's Polish-made Fiat only to find that, in our absence, someone had boosted her almost-impossible-to-replace spare tire.

After a cool-down smoke looking over the *malecon*—the miles-long Havana sea wall—Miguel Angel was still brooding over the teenagers and the burglary. "There's a lot of tension building up. A new generation pushing to get in and finding all places are taken by the original generation of the revolution," he said. "This generation that is in power can keep this revolution together this year, the next, and even beyond. But they are getting old. At most they have a decade left in power. Then what? I can explain to you how we got to this point. I have no idea how we will get out."

Sebastian, a middle-aged novelist, a self-described "unconditional devotee" of the revolution, had concluded there was no way out. During a long afternoon of conversation and coffee he argued that the future of Cuba depended exclusively on the person of Fidel Castro—and that Castro showed no sign of changing.

"Fidel Castro is an Absolute Christian, a Total Idealist, a man without a reverse gear. He is absolutely pure, absolutely committed to socialism as he understands it, though he has never really understood Marxism at all. He is a man given over 100 per cent to his nation. But he has administered this nation like it was his father's farm. If he likes you, you're in, and if he doesn't, you are out. He has built a hand-picked pyramid structure with Fidel Castro at the top and with revolution tucked away inside Fidel Castro's pocket. He has created a structure in which there is no one to replace him. There are no government and party institutions that work here. Fidel, with the best of motivation, has stuck his fingers into everything. And if you look around you, you will see that everything he has touched has turned to shit. Is he a military genius? Yes. Is he a diplomatic and foreign affairs genius? Yes. But does he know how to run an entire country? Look around you."

This was a painful talk for Sebastian, who said he had never spoken like this before to a foreign reporter. "The day my balls filled to overflowing was a couple of years ago when Fidel came on TV to explain—to fully explain—how one of his favored appointees, Luis Orlando Dominguez, had been caught building a private mansion, how he had been caught with cars, hundreds of thousands of dollars, mistresses, the whole sordid scenario." He pauses and rubs his hand over his face. "I really expected Fidel to finally make the self-criticism he owed to the country. I mean Dominguez was a creature of Fidel's inner group, a favorite of Fidel. If Fidel likes you, you feel you have a blaring green light. Answer me, how is it possible that Dominguez could rob, traffic, speculate without State Security finding out? I can only conclude that he was a figure made untouchable by his relationship to Fidel and no one dared speak out. Fidel got on the air and denounced Dominguez as a traitor. OK. But why didn't Fidel admit that it was he who gave this man such free reign?

"Fidel is still the revolution. He holds all the strings. No one can think about organizing against him. A military movement? A mass movement against Fidel? You've got to be joking! Anyway, the Cubans *love* him. They really do. They love him. Fidel

Interview With Writer Pablo Armando Fernandez

All We Have Are Mosquitoes, Cubans, and the Revolution

When writer Pablo Armando Fernandez celebrated his 60th birthday last month, Fidel Castro showed up at the party, took Armando in his arms, and gave him a big kiss.

But Armando has not always been in such favor. Shortly after winning the coveted Casa De Las Americas prize for his 1969 novel, *Los Niños De Despiden*, Armando became a nonperson for almost a decade, never to be published. Without ever apologizing for his views, without any revision, without any recanting, he now enjoys national prestige. We spoke over a long lobster dinner at the Hemingway Marina, an exclusive tourist complex that accepts only foreign currency.

"There are two classes of citizens in Cuba," Armando said as we ordered. "Tourists with dollars who can go to the best restaurants, and the rest of us Cubans."

Marc Cooper: Is this revolution done for?

Pablo Armando: Oh my God! That's like asking me, Is Cuba done for? Cuba *is* the revolution. We possess no other wealth other than our revolution. We have no gold, no energy, no forests, no big rivers. All we have are mosquitos, Cubans, and the Revolution. And of those three, the worthiest is the Revolution. It will not only be preserved, it will be improved.

Cooper: And yet, in Eastern Europe, other societies that called themselves revolutionary evaporated overnight.

Armando: There was never a revolution in Eastern Europe. When the world was divided after the Second World War between the powerful American Empire and the decaying Russian Empire, then those old Tsarist dependencies became 'socialist.' But there was no revolution. And they didn't want one. They were bureaucratic, very repressive, backward states.

Cooper: Aren't you uncomfortable with so much power being in the hands of Fidel?

Armando: I can't think of any society other than ours where *so* many people exercise power. Foreigners say Fidel holds all the power. But the truth, in Cuba, is that if I become the administrator of even a small shop, I alone decide when and if I will sell the potatoes, when and if the rice will be put on the shelf; or if I run a restaurant I will give the tables to my friends and ignore the line of people in front. This is what

happens every day. A bureaucratic structure that leads to errors and problems.

Cooper: Yet what we say in the United States is that the fall of the Eastern European regimes is our historical vindication; that to be afraid of communism was to have been right.

Armando: What's happened in Eastern Europe may make some of you think you were right. These people lacked freedom, they were unhappy. Fine, soon they will be happier; they will be unemployed, they will have prostitution, bag ladies, street beggars, they will have all the horrors that capitalist countries with unhealthy economies, like Poland and Hungary, experience. So, we'll see. If they succeed and in one or two or five years and there is no unemployment, and there is health care and there is good education and there are all the beauties and bounties of life blooming there, well . . . then they were right.

But if you are going to replace police terror with the terror of the daily death of hunger then you have done nothing. Both are evil. What is sad is that these people never found a way out. What is really painful is to think of how these Eastern Europeans will become Cheap Labor, the servants, the maids, the butlers of Western Europe. They will be the waiters. They will do *all* the dirty work for the more developed countries.

In any case, we are going to be better off without Eastern Europe. At least now our errors will be our own, we will have no one else to blame.

Cooper: You will still have the U.S. to blame.

Armando: I think it's very healthy for Cuba to be opposed by the United States. It brings us closer together! [Laughs] The United States and the blockade can be blamed for a lot of our troubles, but not all of them. When our bananas sit and rot on a dock, it has nothing to do with imperialism! But now with Eastern Europe gone, if our bureaucracy remains in place we can no longer say, well, that's the way our socialist brothers and sisters live. In that sense, we are better off alone.

Cooper: But one doesn't get the feeling in the streets of Cuba that people are concerned about being ever more isolated.

Armando: We are islanders, and islanders never think of isolation. It is very beautiful,

or perhaps very sad, but Cubans are very narcissist. The only border we have is the sea. And when we come to the shore and look at the water, all we see is our own reflection, an eternal reproduction. And we leave very self-satisfied. I think it will be healthy for us to be alone for the very first time, alone and narcissistic. We will be better off. I am not afraid.

Cooper: Just last night, Fidel warned Cuba that the worst of economic times might be just around the corner. You can't deny that with the aid cutoff from the East, things are likely to get very tight around here. That's why in Miami and in Washington they are counting down your days.

Armando: Cuba is no Poland! And Cuba is no Panama! Neither of those two things are going to happen here! But even if the bombs start falling on us as we speak tonight, this will not be Panama. Our country has been preparing for this for 30 years. The bombs that fell on Panama were a warning, a reminder to the rest of Central America and the Caribbean. But we are not going to sit in the bar and sip drinks under the rockets as some did in Panama. The U.S. can give it a try. But they better not try here! If we are attacked, millions of Cubans will die. But so will millions of Americans. No one knows what would happen if an island disappeared. Because surely, we would disappear before surrender. Probably, the two oceans would sweep over us and meet and the currents would carry up the Mississippi River and overflow the plains.

Cooper: In the meantime, Washington says Cuba is drowning, asphyxiated by a failed ideology.

Armando: Oh yes! They are so happy now. They are celebrating. For them the world has ended. History has ended. Ideology has ended. How very silly to think that! Communism has not disappeared. The utopia of socialism and communism is not going to disappear as long as there are exploiters and exploited. You have to be very foolish to think people are very contented with having one piece of bread to eat while others throw meat to their dogs. I didn't have to read Marx to know the difference. Because I had those divisions in my own family. With my own mouth I could taste the difference between a spoon of silver and one of tin.

Cooper: Beyond ideological considerations, in purely practical terms, it would seem that this is an ideal moment for the U.S. to normalize relations with Cuba and fill the void left by the East. Yet, all we have seen so far is stepped-up hostility....

Armando: People who rule empires are totally convinced they are superior. But mostly, the Americans are scared. They are scared because the United States is not a country, it is a capitalist enterprise. It's not a nation. Nothing sustains that country other than capitalism. If they lose what they sell and buy they will have nothing else. Even in your writing. There is no body of critical literature as poignant, as passionate, as violent, as courageous, as brave as that of North America. There is so much acute

criticism of your society. But it is astounding, because it is a way of exorcising evil, yet the evil is always there. When a black writer writes about the suffering in the ghetto, everyone says "OK. Isn't that wonderful that he's written that. Now we all know about that awful suffering." And the writer becomes famous and a film is made and he or she becomes wealthy. And nothing happens! It's really amazing. What country in the world talks more about drugs and yet has so many drug addicts? They talk about the superiority of the white race, but everyday your country is ever less white. The new immigrants are younger, they come from stronger races, and the whites become very weak, very decadent. Very old.

Cooper: And very frightened.

Armando: Yes. And it has all become so vulgar, so common. I mean that whole script about Noriega was so poorly written! In the '40s they would have made a much better film of that! But they are so scared. They've been scared since the 19th century. They are scared of Moby Dick. You Americans will be eternally hunting Moby Dick. The metpahor of the eternal hunt, of the hunter and the hunted, has become the destiny of the United States. In the 18th century Moby Dick was white. This century it became red. Maybe it will now become blue or green. Why don't they just forget Moby Dick? Moby Dick will do them no harm. If they do not free themselves of this curse, then eventually the Hunter will have to become the Hunted.

—M.C.

---

is like that crazy grandfather we all have. The old guy who never stops telling stories, the old man who steals your wallet, the guy that embarrasses you in front of friends, the guy who is a giant pain in the nuts, but whom you love dearly. That's Fidel. And all this talk about rectification? It's just chatter, that's all."

After a week among journalists and writers, almost uniformly optimistic about the possibility of some sort of significant opening, Sebastian's dark vision, honestly, left me worried and confused.

"I was born here and live here and *I* am totally confused," admitted Enrique, a writer and translator whom my friends had described as the "most critical" voice among them. His parents were members of the pre Castro Communists. Enrique has never joined Fidel's party.

"If you think you see forward movement and backward movement, then you are seeing our reality. Inside the highest levels of the government there are those who want to democratize, who want to decentralize power. And there are also those who are no less than ferocious dogmatists who feel there is no need to debate anything. But I want to debate a lot of things. Like why in Cuba there continue to exist two certain social groups: a privileged bureaucracy on the one hand, and criminals and traffickers on the other. And you know both groups have much in common. It wouldn't be so easy to sell stolen goods here if it were not so easy to steal them from state warehouses.

"Socialism is morally much simpler than capitalism. That's why the sinful apple is so much more deadly when plucked from a socialist tree."

Is the confusion, I asked, over whether or not to just scrap socialism as the Eastern Europeans have?

"No," Enrique answered. "Unlike Eastern Europe we are not debating a return to capitalism. I can't think of any way of living other than in socialism. But I can think of a hundred ways of dying every day that aren't. One thing is clear to most all Cubans: socialism and national independence in Cuba are inseparable. The confusion is over how to make socialism work. Some think you do so by opening up and giving more power to the people. Others think you do that by yelling slogans at the people. But this much is for sure: When the Yankees machine-gun a Cuban boat, or when Bush puts a balloon in the sky to impose TV Martí on us, I, for one don't feel the need any longer to debate with the dogmatists. My conflict with them evaporates. What I want to do, instead, is go out and grab some fucking U.S. marine by the balls! In this sense, the greatest support for our dogmatists comes from the United States."

Carlos Fuentes recenty wrote that for Cubans the Cold War is not over. When I was last here five years ago, I spent my final night in Havana listening to Ronald Reagan make a menacing special transmission to Cuba over the Voice of America. Tonight, my last night in Cuba, I walk under the yellowish sulfur lights of the *malecon*. The surf pounds the seawall and lovers perched atop it snuggle closer together in the face of an encroaching cold front. I shiver, too.

Over the VOA's preposterously named Radio Martí, a Cuban on the gringo payroll excitedly announces that in just a few more days experimental transmissions of TV Martí will begin. With an initial outlay of $40 million, the Bush Administration has permanently anchored a weather balloon

10,000 feet above the Florida coastline and will soon start bombarding Cuban homes with images of *Kate & Allie* and, presumably, Elliot & Ollie.

The old black fisherman leaning over the *malecon* next to me is facing due north, separated from Florida, tonight, by only 90 miles of dark ocean. But his mind is on his drop line. Around his palm and index finger he has wrapped a swath of electrical tape to keep from being cut by the nylon line that is being violently tugged by the current. His pants are stained and threadbare. The flannel shirt over his T-shirt is tattered and buttonless. He is, he tells me, a retired janitor. His pension is only 100 pesos a month.

"Is that enough to live on?" I ask.

"Barely, not really. But my children help me. One's a doctor. My girl is an engineer."

"Have you ever thought about going over there?" I say, pointing toward Florida.

"No. I'm a revolutionary."

"What has this revolution given you?"

"It's not a question of the revolution giving me anything. That's not the point." He takes his drop line and wedges it between two rocks so he can devote his attention to me. "The problem is people. Humans. Humans are capable of acts of great barbarity. Of becoming a Hitler, of killing millions of people. But we humans are also capable of very beautiful things. Of helping someone injured in the street. Or of taking one loaf of bread and cutting up it so all can eat, even if it's very little.

"In every country in the world there are bad people, little Hitlers, you know. And there are good people. The only difference is that some societies teach you and reward you for being one way. And other places, teach you to be the other. How you turn out is up to you."

Chadli's Perestroika

Rachid Tlemçani

Rachid Tlemçani teaches political science at the University of Algiers. His book, State and Revolution in Algeria, *was published by Westview Press in 1987.*

Until October 1988, the most severe challenge to Algerian President Chadli Benjedid's perestroika came not in industrial plants or in party forums. Instead, it came in the form of street protests by masses of disaffected, unemployed and marginalized young people refusing to be manipulated by the state. The most important was the November 1986 protests of students in Constantine which led to riots throughout the eastern region.[1]

In early October 1988, the capital of Algiers and other major cities, including Annaba in the east and Oran in the west, erupted into violence which spread to many provincial cities and towns. The authorities declared a state of emergency and imposed martial law in Algiers and its peripheral cities. The riots, according to official figures, left 159 dead, many more injured and 7,000 arrested, as well as material damage of more than $20 million.

Many in Algeria believe that, confronted with an impending systemic crisis, a faction of the political leadership stirred up these "October events" as an instrument to unleash a "democratic opening" and political reforms that would reinforce the "economic liberalization" that Benjedid has been pushing since he assumed power in 1979. Certainly the October events have given violent impetus to the political reforms which the Benjedid regime had timorously initiated.

Transferring Legitimacy

The social conflict that erupted in the streets calls into question the legitimacy of the political establishment rooted in the national liberation struggle, namely, the "historic chiefs" who launched the war of national liberation in 1954. The National Liberation Front (FLN) in 1954 had itself emerged out of the contending political parties which comprised the Algerian liberation movement. Then at independence, after some internecine violence, Ahmad Ben Bella, with the military support of the ALN (National Liberation Army) general staff headed by Houari Boumedienne, was able to take over state power. Ben Bella's dictatorial tendencies soon provoked factionalism on the one hand and alienated the working masses from political participation on the other. In 1963, political authorities consented to subordinate the spontaneous workers' self-management movement to the control of the state technocrats.

Boumedienne's coup in 1965 hardly caused a ripple in Algerian society, already inured to the authoritarianism of the political system. By 1968 Boumedienne had eliminated armed opposition to his regime—Tahar Zbiri's coup in 1967—and forced most of the political opposition abroad. Boumedienne's regime was able to stabilize the political situation sufficiently to proceed with state-building and industrialization.

A special FLN Congress in 1980, more than a year after Boumedienne's death, evaluated the economic and social developments of his era, highlighting the shortcomings of the drive for heavy industrialization. The introduction to the report clearly intimates a shift towards a new political economy. By this time, the state bourgeoisie had clearly split into two wings: one group favored strengthening the state sector and opposed any "political liberalization" of Algerian socialism; the second, headed by Chadli Benjedid, favored "economic liberalization."

At the FLN's Fifth Congress in 1983, Chadli endeavored to eliminate the last vestiges of the Boumedienne period, ousting several key figures from the FLN Central Committee and other main organs. After his reelection in 1984 as president, though, the coalition of groups made up of the defenders of Boumedienne's "revolutionary achievements" continued to confront Chadli. Strangely enough, Muhammad Cherif Messadia, whom Chadli made head of the FLN in 1983, led this coalition and became a serious contender to Chadli's growing power. It was only after the events of October 1988 that Chadli could oust Messadia. But earlier the president did make changes in the upper echelons of state institutions, especially the military.[2] In retrospect, this seemed to signal that the People's National Army was being prepared to intervene in the ongoing conflict within the state apparatus.

Politically, Chadli pursued a cautious policy as president. He eliminated exit visa requirements for travel abroad. He released political prisoners like Ben Bella, who moved to France and organized the Algerian Democratic Movement (MDA). In 1984, Chadli allowed the return of certain political figures and amnestied others—Benyoucef Ben Khedda, for instance, former head of the pre-independence provisional government, who in 1989 organized the Umma (Nation) Party with the aim of implementing the *shari'a* (Islamic law). Chadli's perestroika aimed to reinforce his power base by fragmenting the opposition.

In April 1987, under Amnesty International pressure, the government approved the Algerian Human Rights League.* In July 1987, parliament passed a bill allowing associations to

---

* In 1989 a second organization, the Algerian Human Rights Defense League, was formed, and in January 1990, the government approved a local chapter of Amnesty International.

 From *Middle East Report*, March/April 1990, pp. 14–18. Middle East Report, MERIP, 1500 Massachusetts Ave., Suite 119, Washington, DC 20005.

operate outside the FLN's control. These associations evolved in various domains—sports, social and cultural. Since October 1988, the number of associations has rapidly mushroomed throughout the country—to approximately 12,000 by January 1990. But "bureaucratic politics"—the heavy hand of the FLN—remain as important as ever, making them ineffective and unable to contribute to a social dynamic which will bring about social democracy in Algeria.

The real political shift came with the February 23, 1989, referendum to amend the 1976 Constitution. The new text, supposedly designed to produce what the intelligentsia calls a "state of law," in fact reinforces the president's power.[3] The president can indefinitely renew his terms of office; he appoints the prime minister and can dismiss him without a vote of no-confidence from the parliament. In September 1989, Chadli terminated Prime Minister Kasdi Merbah on the grounds that Merbah did not push political liberalization hard enough. Those close to the pinnacle of power, however, say Merbah had risen as a serious contender to Chadli's control.

The 1989 constitution severely restricts the parliament's autonomy. It is automatically dissolved by two consecutive votes of no-confidence. Needless to say, the parliament has no authority over military affairs, which remains under the president. To complete the edifice of the so-called Second Republic, Chadli's third term has produced a series of bills on elections, mass media and political parties, to name a few, all these issued from the "president's circle." In a word, the president of the "state of law" is empowered with all the attributes of an enlightened shaikh.

The new constitution makes no reference to socialism or the ruling FLN. It recognizes the right to establish "associations of political character," although taking into account the new precarious balance of power stemming from the October events, this clause aims essentially at reinvigorating the "ministry of mobilization"—the FLN—by "modernizing" the ruling party. Existing political opposition such as the Socialist Vanguard Party (PAGS, the former Communist Party), the Islamist and the social-democratic trends would remain incorporated inside the FLN, allowing the FLN with its 500,000 militants to remain the hegemonic party. By January 1990, there were 20 legal political parties, three of which call for implementing *shari'a* as the fundamental law in Algeria. Two other parties have applied for legal approval.[4]

All the parties pontificate about Chadli's slogans—"production and efficiency, free enterprise and social justice"—but none project concrete proposals to tackle seriously the potential collapse of the national economy. No wonder: all the leaders of these new parties have been members of the previous or current regimes. Thirty-five years after the FLN's birth, they still refer to the "political heritage of liberation war."[5] The PPA, the Popular Party of Algeria, is the only party the political establishment has refused to sanction. The growing Islamist movement, meanwhile, is seriously challenging the "soft state."[6]

New Economic Policy?

Boumedienne gave priority to industrial development over agricultural development, spending oil revenues to import the most sophisticated technology at the expense of consumer goods, housing and employment. Some 48 percent of this industrial investment was spent in hydrocarbons and only 15 percent of total investment went to agriculture. Rapid economic growth took precedence over both social equality and political participation.

Algeria reached a critical juncture even before the fall of oil revenues in the mid-1980s. Algerian state capitalism no longer had the capacity to insure at the same time its developmental and its welfare functions. Yet any thorough reforms would severely threaten the very foundation of Algeria's political rule, based on mismanagement and corruption, patronage and privilege, and coercion—in a word, the politics of authoritarianism.

Chadli's strategy was a package of administrative and economic reforms designed to restructure and decentralize the "industrializing industries." Breaking up the giant state corporations, some planners argued, would disperse political and economic decision-making. But did the deficits of the state firms owe to the technocrats' autonomy from political control?[7] Sonatrach, the state-run oil and gas company employing 100,000 persons, now comprises 13 specialized units. Sixty-six giant firms were broken into 474 specialized firms known as Public Economic Enterprises (EPEs). Provincially-controlled firms were also broken down from 500 into 1,865 units in 1985. The number of provinces (*wilaya*) increased from 31 to 48, and communes from 704 to 1,541.[8] Bureaucratic personnel, "conventional" rather than "developmental," grew noticeably.

Related measures allow the EPEs to form their own capital base so as to plow back their profits, while depriving the EPEs of subsidized state bank financing. This means the EPEs have to pay commercial rates while divesting their welfare functions—e.g., job security, transportation and housing. The government, meanwhile, has implemented a system of shareholding to encourage privatization of the public sector.

Since 1982, the state has also worked to establish more joint-venture firms with foreign capital, especially in tourist industries, housing and raw materials prospecting. Until the October events, foreign capital had been reluctant to invest in Algeria. Since October 1988, Algeria has revised legislation to make joint-ventures more attractive, but foreign capital remains skeptical.

Private Sector, State Bourgeoisie

The private industrial sector is important in Algeria. The 1963 and 1966 investment codes regulated its legal existence during the Boumedienne era, when the regime considered it "parasitic." The 1982 investment law, though, accords it a "positive role," complementing the activities of the public sector and providing consumer goods oriented to short-term profits. The state sector traditionally produced inputs for the private sector at low cost, often with no national or international competition.

In 1982, the private industrial sector employed more than a quarter of the industrial workforce, and accounted for more than 40 percent of the national value-added outside agriculture in 1989. As a result of the recent measures favoring private investment, the Chambre Nationale de Commerce (CNC) counted 2,364 private new projects in the current year. The real figures are much higher, because many entrepreneurs avoid the complications of recording their projects with the CNC. According to the state sector, though, Algerian entrepreneurs have not played by the "rules of the game." They have not invested in the areas designated to create jobs in the interior. They also took advantage of the backward fiscal system and paid few taxes.

The paucity of reliable data on this sector leads one to speculate as to the relations between the Algerian entrepreneurs and the bureaucratic bourgeoisie. People believe that many private firms are owned by members of the ruling class; on the record they belong to their relatives and friends. A survey in 1982-83 found that out of 1331 entrepreneurs, 40 percent had been state managers or military officers.[9] By 1981 the state bourgeoisie had acquired a great many of the 200,000 residential and business properties which had been abandoned by French settlers in 1962 at ridiculous prices. This measure, as well as the 1987 law on land reform, permitted certain people to become extremely wealthy overnight.

Algeria's decade of perestroika has fostered a culture of corruption. Today private wealth is amassed conspicuously and flagrantly. Private fortunes smuggled abroad are enough, according to some estimates, for Algeria to pay back its $25 billion foreign debt. As in Egypt, Chadli's *infitah* (economic opening) has produced a "new class" within the bourgeoisie while living and working conditions of the overwhelming majority of people have declined precipitously.

The most recent official figures show five percent of the population earning 45 percent of the national income, while 50 percent of Algerians earn less then 22 percent.[10] Wage disparity now exceeds 20 to 1. The declining quality of life can also be seen in unemployment and underemployment, inadequate food supplies and derelict social services. Between 1985 and 1987, male unemployment increased dramatically. A job is no longer a sure thing for a college graduate. The tourists now attracted to Algeria see large numbers of these young men standing around on every street corner. If one adds women to these figures—they are not, by and large, tabulated in the official data—one can plainly infer that the "Egyptianization" has virtually marginalized two-thirds of the Algerian labor force. No wonder the disaffected youth turn to the mosques and the soccer stadiums and to street protests to vent their frustrations.

Above all, Algeria faces an explosive housing shortage. In 1990, the country has a deficit of 2 million dwelling units. Since the October events, the housing crisis has stirred up further disturbances and riots throughout the country. I would estimate that more than half of the towns and cities in the country have seen at least one serious incident of social unrest. Labor strikes have also increased dramatically. In the 1980s, there were no more than 70 strikes per month in the public sector. Since the "October events," this sector has been disrupted by a wave of labor protest unprecedented in Algerian history. Last year, the ministry of labor recorded a loss of 2 million labor days—an average of 250 strikes per month.[11]

Chadli's perestroika has been less the outcome of Algerian class dynamics than the country's mode of integration into the world economy. This adjustment could have only succeeded if the state had, for instance, put into practice in the 1980s a radical reform of the system of taxation. Instead, emphasis has been laid on reducing industrialization and cutting consumer subsidies while deregulating prices in the national market.[12]

Politics and Islam

In Algeria, Islam is a source of cultural identity. During colonial rule, it served as a factor of national cohesion and a creative force against foreign rule. The recent rise of an Islamist movement signifies that official Islam and state reformism have together failed to incorporate popular Islam or to modernize society. The minister of religious affairs has virtually total authority over religious matters. He administers all religious schools and hires imams—the bureaucrats in cloaks who preached the state's Friday sermons in the 1970s. The ministry also sponsored seminars and monitored a wide range of religiously-related activities. Attendance at official mosques in Algiers by the mid-1970s resembled church attendance in Moscow.

Boumedienne subsequently made bold moves that have favored a resurgence of Islamist politics. One was a sudden and rowdy campaign to "Arabize" street and shop signs, in spite of the fact that more than 60 percent of the population could not read Arabic. Boumedienne used Islamism to counterbalance communist penetration into the state apparatus. Now the Islamist trend capitalizes on the grievances of university graduates who find themselves destined for "dead-end jobs," as nearly all positions in the private as well as the public sector require French and to some extent English as working languages.[13]

Since the October events, the Islamists have been exceedingly active. They obstreperously demand "purification" measures—for example, the elimination of coeducational schooling, the Arabization of the medical schools and colleges of technology, and the substitution of English for French as Algeria's second language.

It seems the Islamist movement has intensified its strategy of penetrating state institutions, especially the educational system. During the October 1988 events, the Islamist militants did not violently intervene against the regime, in spite of provocation by unknown people who fired random shots at mosques. The Islamic Salvation Front (FIS), the main Islamist organization, was formally sanctioned a few months later even though it contravened the proscription against religious political parties in the July 1989 political parties bill.

The most visible manifestation of the challenge to secularism is the growth of street mosques and prayer rooms in factories, schools and government offices. Using electronic amplification in these places, imams loudly preach against "infidels" and women who do not follow "Islamic norms." Cassettes of sermons and speeches by eastern theologians allow Algerian fundamentalists to follow trends from the other side of the Arab world. This heavy drive forced debate over coeducation for the first time in Algeria's political history at the November 1989 FLN meeting.

It seems clear that transforming authoritarianism into a

democratic political system is not on Chadli's agenda. The November 1989 reintegration of Boumedienne's close associates into the FLN Central Committee means that Algeria's "legitimation crisis" will surely erupt again in the near future. Unemployment continues to grow and urban conditions worsen, creating conditions for a "law and order" crisis and intervention by the military.

Footnotes

1 The first challenge goes back to 1980, when public discontent erupted in Tizi-Duzou in three days of riots against all symbols of state authority.

2 J. Entelis, "Algeria Under Chadli: Liberalization without Democratization or, Perestroika, Yes; Glasnost, No!," *Middle East Insight* 6,3 (Fall 1988), p. 59.

3 El-Hadi Chalabi, "Métamorphose d'une Constitution-loi" *Sou'al*, #9-10 (July 1989), p. 22.

4 *El Moudjahid*, January 21, 1990.

5 R. Radjala, *L'opposition Algérienne* (Paris: L'Harmattan, 1988), p. 13.

6 N. Ayubi, "Bureaucracy and Development in Egypt Today," *JAAS* 24,1-2 (Jan-April 1989), p. 66.

7 R. Tlemçani and W. Hansen, "Development and the State in Post-Colonial Algeria," *JAAS*, vol. 24 (1989).

8 M. Bennoune, *The Making of Contemporary Algeria, 1830-1987* (Cambridge University Press, 1988), pp. 265-66.

9 D. Liabes, "Entreprises, Entrepreneurs et Bourgeoisie Industrielle en Algérie—Elements d'une Sociologie de l'entreprendre," (Paris: Ph.D., Université de Paris VII, 1988), p. 606.

10 K. Aomar, "Les années de l'anesthésie," in *Algérie-Actualités* #1257 (November 16-22, 1989).

11 *El Moudjahid*, January 29, 1990.

12 G. Luciani, "Economic Foundations of Democracy and Authoritarianism: The Arab World in Comparative Perspective," *Arab Studies Quarterly*, vol. 10, no. 4.

13 R. Tlemçani, *State and Revolution in Algeria* (London: Zed Books, 1986 and Boulder: Westview Press, 1987), p. 197.

Map by Dave Herring

AFTER THE FALL OF A DICTATOR

Paraguay's Generalissimo left behind a banana republic. Now an elected President promises law and democracy. The people are both pleasantly surprised and quietly skeptical.

Mac Margolis

Mac Margolis, who travels widely from his base in Brazil, is a longtime observer of Latin America, writing for Newsweek, The Christian Science Monitor, *and other publications.*

Late last February, in the anxious days after the fall of Paraguayan dictator Alfredo Stroessner, a policeman came to Benjamin Arditi's house. The young political scientist took a deep breath and slowly opened the door. In the bad old days, when Paraguay was run by the Southern Hemisphere's most unshakable dictatorship, a house call by a police officer could be cause for dread. This was, after all, the republic of Generalissimo Stroessner, who ruled this small South American country with an iron hand, and often an iron heel. Political opposition was gagged by official censorship or driven underground. Dissidents were routinely jailed and packed off into exile, if they were lucky, or, if not, they might be found bobbing face-down in the Rio Paraguay.

But Arditi noticed something was different. The officer had come not in a dun-colored van and escorted by machine-gun toting guards but alone and on a bicycle. The caller, it seemed, was an envoy of the chief of Asunción police, who kindly requested an audience to hear Señor Arditi's views on the then pending elections.

On a later afternoon in Asunción, Arditi recalled the fright of that day, and his surprise at the unlikely whirl of events that have swept up Paraguay since. "It hurts to say," Arditi said, "but when you thought of Paraguay in the past, you had to think of a banana republic." He spoke in the restaurant of a popular downtown hotel, where government officials and dissidents mingled easily and exchanged Latin-style *abrazos* (embraces). "But now it looks as if things are beginning to change."

In fact, a lot is different in Paraguay since Feb. 2, when Gen. Andrés Rodríguez, First Army Division Commander, rolled his tanks into the street to topple the Stroessner regime. Even as the smoke was clearing and the shell-pocked military ramparts being repaired along Mariscal López Avenue, Rodríguez had issued a flurry of reforms. Thousands of Paraguayan exiles were allowed to return. The Paraguayan media were unmuzzled, including the nettlesome tabloid ABC Color; which began publishing in April after five years of silence. Four clandestine political parties were recognized, and a handful of new ones blossomed, including the ultra-right-wing National Socialist Party and the leftist Workers' Party.

Most important, not only did Rodríguez carry through with elections for president and Congress, but the May 1 balloting was hailed by Paraguayans and international observers alike as the first genuine vote the country has had in memory.

This bold Paraguayan political opening was closely orchestrated, of course. Rodríguez, who claimed he took up the sword to restore order and democracy, did not hesitate to call upon the autocratic legacy of the *ancien régime*. He sprang the election a mere three months after the coup. The short span was perfectly legal—according to the Constitution that Stroessner wrote—but left the opposition, hounded and silenced for three decades, at a nearly impossible disadvantage.

Rodríguez also got a boost from the electoral law, another holdover from the Stroessner era, prohibiting alliances among parties—and therefore fracturing the opposition. (The law, patterned after that of Italian dictator Mussolini in the 1930s, also rewards the party that gets a mere plurality of votes with two-thirds of the 108 seats in Congress.)

Not that Rodríguez needed the advantage. He won comfortably, taking 74% of the presidential ballots while his nearest rival, Domingo Laíno, the tireless and tousle-haired candidate for the Authentic Racial Liberal Party (PLRA), took 20%. Laíno, who has lost count of the number of times he was jailed under Stroessner, did win a Senate seat.

Election day was peppered with the usual fraud accusations ("phantoms" voted while legitimate voters were inexplicably stricken from the registry) but not enough to significantly alter the result, according to dozens of foreign poll watchers. Indeed, the irregularities were surprisingly modest compared to the ballot-stuffing heyday of the recent past. (So modern was Paraguay, ran the derisive joke of the Generalissimo's time, that the election results were known hours before the polls closed.)

Stated oversimply, the May vote was basically one of gratitude. In February General Rodríguez rid the country of an aged and tottering dictator who had overstayed his welcome and whose regime was rotting from within. Three months later, Paraguayans returned the favor. Rodríguez now has what every generalissimo pines for: legitimacy. There is much speculation as to what, and how much, he is going to do with this mandate.

He has many promises to keep. Rodríguez has repeatedly pledged to support "democracy" and to abide by the rule of law in a nation accustomed to neither. He has announced plans to call a constituent assembly to reform the Constitution, a document disfigured by three decades of personal fiat. Now safely elected, he is also expected to rewrite the electoral law, to allow alliances, and to implement a system of true proportional representation.

Like Benjamin Arditi, many Paraguayans seem pleasantly surprised by the changes they have seen and skeptical about those promised. Changes of this order have not been routine in Paraguay, which has caromed between fits of anarchy and the tyranny of career *caudillos*. The republic's first ruler, José Gaspar Rodríguez de Francia, governed for almost three decades, completely shutting down Paraguay to trade and even to visitors. He was known, fittingly, as "El Supremo." Later came the two-decade reign of the enlightened autocrat Cárlos Antonio López, who built South America's first rail and telegraph system. He was succeeded in 1862 by his son, Francisco Solano López, basically a warlord who plunged the nation into a disastrous five-year war against Brazil, Argentina, and Uruguay, which wiped out half of Paraguay's population. But it was under the 34-year tenure of Stroessner that this California-sized nation of 4 million had become the bad joke of nationhood, the "democracy" where one man could win seven consecutive elections and which turned smuggling into an honorable vocation.

The stereotypical mantle of Latin tyrant didn't always fit this corpulent descendant of a Bavarian brewer, however. Though he was implacable with his foes, for the most part Stroessner's authority did not depend on thumb screws or cattle prods but instead on a more prosaic kind of terror. He survived by turning this state into a private fief, based on the pillars of the armed forces, the ruling Colorado Party, and the bureaucracy. The party divided the country into "secciónales," or wards, administered like a vast patronage machine. It was the Colorado machine that paved roads, lit streets, and disbursed jobs. The fate of each citizen in each region depended on the distribution, or the denial, of such largess.

As long as Paraguay grew and developed, which it did for nearly 30 of Stroessner's 34 years, the common Paraguayan was content. The appeal was understandable. In a continent roiled by violent disputes and dirty wars between guerrillas and the military, Paraguay was a placid island of prosperity. For years, Stroessner could confidently say that peace and tranquility meant more to his people than democracy and liberty.

Thus cemented into power, Stroessner erected many monuments to himself. His name was attached to the second city (Puerto Pres. Stroessner, now Ciudad del Este), Asunción's international airport (Aeropuerto Presidente Stroessner), countless streets and highways. There was even a Stroessner polka. So ubiquitous was his influence that he became a noun (people still talk about Stroessnerism) and an adjective (to be Stroessnerist was to be imperious, despotic). The height of this carefully sculpted idolatry came in May 1988 during Pope John Paul II's visit, when Stroessner's minions plastered Asunción's edifices with posters bearing his image in tandem with the pontiff's, like running mates in some celestial election.

But as the events of last February showed, even the most deified of *caudillos* have clay boots. Stroessner fell much as he had come to power, in a palace coup led by some of his seniormost servants, and applauded by the people he had made his subjects.

Many fear that the hero of the day, General Rodríguez, could easily become another *caudillo*. On the surface, he makes a disappointing despot. The general who spent half his 65 years in khaki can now be frequently seen in a sport shirt wading through crowds, dispensing bear hugs to adoring peasants and patting the heads of youngsters. He has given his palace handlers constant headaches with his habit of halting abruptly for impromptu press conferences. Since the February coup, he has worn an almost indelible smile that gives him a mien somewhere between affable and jolly.

His doubters note that these gestures are basically political theater. Human rights advocates, especially, contend that the coup d'etat, though welcome, does not wash him clean of the three decades he spent loyally at Stroessner's side. Though the new Paraguayan authorities have taken to calling the bygone era "the long, dark night," it is basically a marketing ploy to repackage an old product. Foreign Minister Luiz Maria Argaña, a longtime senior aide of Stroessner's, has gone on record saying that his former boss had "32 or 33 years of a really great government."

The "long, dark night," then, was more like a brownout, dating exactly from August 1987 when the so-called militants, an upstart faction, seized control of the Colorado Party from the traditionalist faction in a raucous convention. Led by a nefarious cabal dubbed the "four golden names" (basically Stroessner's kitchen cabinet), the militants took advantage of the aging dictator to set up their own private kingdom within the kingdom.

Dissidents in the Colorado Party have produced documents charging the foursome with commanding a nethereconomy of smuggled goods, extortion, irregular levies, and ample use of public funds for private lucre. Some 25 government officials currently stand accused of corruption and, in an unexpected move last September, the courts ordered three Army generals who collaborated with the Stroessner regime to return $11.2 million they allegedly embezzled from public coffers.

Perhaps the militants' greatest sin, however, was their pedigree. They were self-made men, from rude beginnings, who had bullied their way into the system run for nearly a century by the blue-blooded Colorado traditionalists.

When the militants were deposed and many of the blue bloods returned to power under Rodríguez, one Western diplomat in Asunción commented: "This was not a coup, really, but a *Putsch*" (something like a revolt of the *avec culottes*). Yet indications are that Rodríguez may be carving his own way. Though aided by the traditionalists, he has composed a ministry not only of politicians but of businessmen, such as Commerce and Industry Minister Antonio Zuccolillo, and technocrats, such as Finance Minister Enzo Debernardi. It is this cabinet that implemented an economic reform at least as startling as the political changes.

The government has put up for sale white elephants like the money-draining state cement plant and the steel company, Acepar, now more than $200 million in debt. Virtually overnight, the government eliminated the system of preferential exchange rates, which artificially inflated the worth of the national currency, the *guaraní*, and granted state companies a festival of cheap dollar imports, courtesy of the public coffers. "They have implemented an IMF program without the IMF," said one ecstatic Western embassy official in reference to the austerity often imposed by the IMF (International Monetary Fund) when aiding distressed economies.

The economic overhauling may be prudent economics, but it could be dicey politics. The blow against money-guzzling state enterprises also threatens the system of encrusted privileges that kept Stroessner's underlings fat and happy.

But if Rodríguez is worried, he doesn't let on. He seems still to be basking in his newfound role as man of the people. It may be too soon to pass judgment on his tender opening to democracy. But in a country where one patriarch survived autumn after autumn, citizens have been pleasantly surprised by this year's unexpected Paraguayan spring.

MENDING BROKEN BURMA

An assassinated leader's daughter comes back to serve her country as it reels from popular uprising, military massacre, economic crisis, and the globe's longest civil war.

Clayton Jones

Clayton Jones, Manila-based correspondent of The Christian Science Monitor, *travels often throughout Southeast Asia.*

ANY FUTURE DEMONSTRATORS FOR democracy in Burma face a new weapon: elephants. The hulking beasts are the most conspicuous inhabitants of a new zoo that was hastily erected in historic Mandalay earlier this year at the behest of the Burmese Army. The zoo rises on a flat field at the foot of Mandalay Hill—occupying the same spot where, last August, hundreds of thousands of protesters, led by Buddhist monks with shaven heads and ocher robes, had set up their command after taking over the city during a brief national uprising.

It was after the Army retook Mandalay on Sept. 18—as martial law was imposed nationwide—that someone got the bright idea that a zoo with elephants could block this strategic spot from further outbreaks of the people's power. But before martial law, for five gleeful weeks, while soldiers cowered in their barracks, the people of Mandalay ran Burma's second largest city—the nation's business and religious center, its former capital under the last king, a city known for dreams and romance.

NOTE: As this article was written, Burma's military ruler decreed a name change for his nation (Myanmar) and its capital, Rangoon (Yangon). To avoid complexity, and let the new name stand the test of time and politics, we have retained the familiar terms.

"We felt free, like we had real democracy," recalls a young Buddhist monk, Nayaka, whose monastery now secretly gives lectures on "people's power."

People-run Mandalay received little attention outside Burma, which had cut itself off from the world since 1962. Yet, to make a Western comparison to the takeover, it was as if the clergy and citizens of New York had defied police and politicians to run the city from Central Park—without guns.

Mandalay's untelevised mutiny may be a foretaste of events to come in Burma. It was a potent sign of nascent democratic will, cloaked with the sanctifying robes of Buddha's spiritual sons, triumphant for a spell over an acquiescent military.

"When the monks joined in with the people, we knew we had something," says a Western diplomat in Rangoon. "They're like a checkered flag [recognizing a winner] at a car race."

But, when martial law came last September, hundreds of monks and lay people were arrested. Dozens of others fled to border areas or went underground. Now the people of Mandalay cower before the soldiers, instead of vice versa.

"Our Burmese people are like a bottle of soda," says the nation's most famous comedian, Zargana, a protest leader jailed for seven months after telling anti-Army jokes." Shu-u-u-PA! They pop off. But then they stay calm and quiet."

The similarity to what happened eight months

later in Beijing is striking. In Burma's case, the world caught only a bare glimpse of the Burmese Army's trigger-happy massacre in 1988. What started with brutal suppression of a Rangoon tea-shop brawl in March eventually escalated to millions of Burmese chanting "democracy" on the streets of almost every city. Since the Burmese language lacks a word for democracy, protesters use the English word. (By democracy most Burmese simply mean freedom, Zargana notes.)

As in Beijing this year, soldiers killed hundreds of demonstrators, most of them students, temporarily quelling protests but leaving the people seething. Two big massacres took place in towns near Mandalay.

Now despised and feared, the Army has become a virtual occupation force in its own country, compounding what was already an Orwellian nightmare of spies, doublespeak propaganda, curfews, and petty state control of daily life.

The idea that people have rights in their relation to the state is new to Burma. Besieged by public enthusiasm for this concept, the regime goes to bizarre lengths to win loyalties (doubling wages for civil servants in April) or to prevent more protests (building the Mandalay zoo). The Army recently sponsored a rock concert to allow youth to let off a little steam, but then it packed the stadium with soldiers to keep order and to prevent dancing, which was outlawed in 1975.

Burma is a country full of contradictions. Its people are highly literate but remain among the world's poorest. Underpopulated and naturally rich though Burma is—sitting at the foot of four rivers flowing from the Himalayas—it is a land whose poor suffer malnutrition. About the size of Texas, Burma somehow remains one country despite suffering the world's longest civil war—between a Burman majority and frontier ethnic groups.

On the surface, Burma appears to be struggling toward democracy, like many other one-party or military-dominated states in Asia. After the horrid violence of last year, the Army felt compelled to promise an election, scheduled sometime before May 1990.

But few Burmese think the Army will accept being ruled by a multi-party civilian government. Government spokesman Ohn Kyaw responds to such an idea by saying: "We Buddhists say that when you bend your elbow, anything can happen—snap—in the split of a second." The Army threatens to postpone the election if social order fails to meet its expectations.

"What is good or bad for the country lies in the hand of the Army," says the government spokesman.

Advocates of democracy admit their cause is hindered by Burma's isolation, extreme poverty, and an acute divisiveness and distrust among Burmese. "The government can just divide, divide, divide the people so that we cannot get solidarity," says comedian Zargana.

Student groups and the newly formed political parties are almost hopelessly fragmented; they reflect the backbiting traits portrayed in George Orwell's "Burmese Days." Some fear that the Army is arranging a repeat of the chaotic 1950s politics which brought it to power in 1962. Or that the Army might revive Burman fear of other nationalities to justify military domination.

"We've had 27 years of building socialism," quips Zargana. "Now we will have 27 years of fighting for democracy."

Longtime leader Ne Win, who was Army chief when he stomped out democracy in the 1962 coup, still keeps a private grip on power. To appease rioters last year, he put forth three new public leaders in succession, the latest being Army Chief of Staff Gen. Saw Maung, who took power Sept. 18 in a reassertion of Army dominance.

As an original hero of the struggle for independence from Britain, Ne Win was a close subordinate to the founding father of modern Burma, Aung San, who was assassinated in 1947. Ne Win has built up Aung San's image until it is larger than life and has made selective use of the dead hero's history to justify Army rule.

Aung San Suu Kyi, the daughter of Aung San, seeks to reclaim her father's legacy from Ne Win. She had been living in Britain with her husband, an Oxford don, and their two children. She returned to Burma last year.

Young and charismatic, Aung San Suu Kyi now heads the biggest of the government-regulated political parties, the National League for Democracy (NLD). She fearlessly travels the length of Burma, despite very constricting campaigning rules and petty harassment—including detention—by the Army. Her popularity grows steadily as she exploits the glory of her father's name and articulates peasant disgust with the Army.

"My father didn't build up the Burmese Army in order to oppress the people," says Aung San Suu Kyi, who professes to be building only a political movement for democracy, not a springboard for her to win an election. Her chief ally in the NLD, Tin Oo, a former Army chief of staff under Ne Win, believes peasants hold deep animosity toward the military because it has forced them to sell rice at low prices.

Ne Win's power rests almost solely on his appeal to top officers in the Army. Despite the slaughter last year, his personal sway over his men has not been broken. Most of all, he can always find soldiers who will shoot—even at others who defect.

"If the people look at you with hurt or hate in their eyes," Ne Win once told troops in a statement he might now regret, "then you must examine yourselves and change your ways."

Starting in 1986, Ne Win did begin to make big changes. After realizing the economic failure of his unique style of socialism, he made a humbling request of the United Nations to list Burma as a "least developed" nation. He then began to free up markets.

2. PEOPLE, POWER, AND LEADERSHIP

But, in a move typical of his economic mismanagement, Ne Win demonetized high-value currency notes, offering no compensation. The instant poverty for many Burmese was tinder for social revolt. He has also botched management of rice, the prime staple, the price of which has soared nearly tenfold in two years. The Burmese like to tell an old tale of a king who bungled a hunt by letting the big deer escape. Rather than face the truth of his mistake, he looked for a scapegoat, as Ne Win often has.

Ne Win's most immediate worry is a potential split in Army ranks. Many officers know that their reputation with the people is low. Several hundred soldiers broke ranks during the height of the shooting last year. The intelligence chief, Brig. Gen. Khin Nyunt, who wields power perhaps second to Ne Win, gains no friends by setting spies on combat officers or being close to Ne Win's powerful daughter, Sanda Win.

"The more they claim that the Army will never be split, the more it means there are signs of factionalism," says Tin Oo. "Young soldiers are less enamored with Ne Win and are just indoctrinated to be loyal."

Three of nine field commanders are thought to favor civilian rule. But they face a dilemma: how to arrange a guarantee from any future leader, such as Aung San Suu Kyi, that no reprisals will be made against them. That bargain has yet to be struck.

"It's possible that some [commanders] have a greater sense of fairness than others," says Aung San Suu Kyi. "There are some Army officers who don't like what is going on and who think it is a far more honorable cause to get out of politics. They may be afraid or they may be weak. Or they may be waiting to see how the wind blows."

Ne Win would probably not believe in a guarantee for his safety in return for stepping down. "He expects reprisals from the people," says Tin Oo. "He can see what happened to Somoza in Nicaragua and Marcos in the Philippines." Ne Win himself once posed the dilemma for any Army that takes power, asking how you let go of a tiger's tail once you've grabbed it.

Keeping troops ignorant of political reality is vital to Ne Win. Soldiers who listen to a BBC shortwave broadcast about events in Burma face court-martial. To persuade soldiers to shoot monks on the front lines last year, the soldiers were told that the monks were fakes, troublemakers donning religious garb for protection.

Last December, the military kicked out all monks from its camps to prevent the seeds of rebellion from being planted. "Officially, we can't talk to the Army," says a Rangoon monk. "But about 10% of [the soldiers] tell us that they are unhappy."

The order of Buddhist monks known as the *sangha* is the only nationally organized institution in Burma other than the Army. First in 1965, and again more successfully in 1980, Ne Win tried to set up controls over the *sangha*.

"As long as we support them, they support us," says a civilian official in the Ministry for Home and Religious Affairs.

The moral leadership of the *sangha* has always been a threat to Burmese rulers. Monasteries are launching pads for protests, sanctuaries for political outlaws. Some ancient Burmese kings fell when top monks withdrew a spiritual mandate of *sangha* support. Their role is crucial today in a nation that, except for the Army and a very thin middle class, is largely peasant.

Many monks, especially young firebrands, still chafe at the government's move to register all monks, put spies in monasteries, and defrock rebellious monks.

Monks have tremendous prestige with the people for their sacrifice in renouncing worldly life. Their role is part priest, part counselor, part social worker. Buddhism's influence in Burma runs deep, weakened only slightly by modern education and technology.

As self-designated mendicants, monks depend on the people for support. Each morning they walk barefoot door to door, collecting food for their daily meal from faithful who believe that they gain "merit" for later lives by offering alms to the spiritual descendants of Buddha (Siddhartha Gautama), born about 563 B.C., who founded Buddhism.

Burma has over 120,000 monks, and another 180,000 novices (those under 20). Almost every boy goes into a monastery to be educated for at least a short period of time. Some stay for life, and many alternate between monastic living and a secular life. Women, too, have their own monasteries.

In theory, the monks are apolitical. "To wear the yellow robes is to be finished with laymen's affairs," contends government spokesman Ohn Kyaw. "If they want to be active, they can take off the yellow robe and be politicians."

But monks live with an unresolved dilemma. They seek spiritual good for society by drawing away from it. When society obviously needs help, such as in the fight against the British that led to independence 41 years ago, the monks are quick to the barricades. They are Burma's "yellow army" in reserve.

"Monks did oppose the British," admits the Ministry of Home and Religious Affairs official mentioned above. "So being political became a tradition. But to stop that, we centralized in 1980."

Before then, Burmese Buddhism had at least nine sects, often feuding. Today, the sects find an uneasy unity under the central leadership of the State Sangha Maha Nayaka Committee, run by 47 elderly monks who are elected every five years, the next time being in 1990.

Signs of anti-government dissent are showing in the *sangha* leadership, says U Nu, the Buddhist scholar and former prime minister ousted by Ne Win in 1958, re-elected prime minister in 1960, and driven out for good in Ne Win's March 1962 coup. The present *sangha* chairman, Abhidajja Maha

Rata Guru, has lately not appeared at official functions. Some top monks complain of being forced "to wear the mouth of Ne Win."

Aung San Suu Kyi makes a point of meeting top monks during her campaign, and performing Buddhist rituals at temples. "I would say that 99.99% of the *sangha* are on the side of what they consider is the rightful side of democracy," she says.

Still, most top monks have kept quiet. Some fear losing privileges, such as overseas travel. Others fear being defrocked. Some believe in a fundamental Buddhist line of total patience and the futility of revolt.

These days, monks show touches of modernity. In 1982, Mandalay monks rioted when they couldn't get tickets to a boxing match. Young ones are less likely to obey an order to stay away from a rally. Some monks end a day of reading scripture by watching racy pirated videotapes.

During the 1988 Mandalay people's takeover, some monks had an air of arrogance. They barked orders to people while they rode around on motorcycles. They ran the television station, directed traffic, pressured merchants to lower prices. An elderly monk hired a bicycle taxi to patrol back streets for any sign of approaching military. One captured thief was tied to a pole outside the train station and told to yell "I am a thief" for hours. If he stopped, a monk whipped his legs.

The monks organized daily marches, with members of each profession walking by row in their respective uniforms. But the marches did not start until after the monks had finished their breakfast at 10 a.m. each day.

The monks had almost the entire city of half a million in their palms. On Sept. 10 a rumor spread that the Mandalay Army commander, Tun Kyi, might defect. The next day the government in Rangoon announced it would punish anyone trying to split the Army.

"The monks will influence events because they still enjoy the support of the people," says U Nu.

"As a matter of fact, it is not just Buddhism. Burmese temperament is very sensitive."

The existence of a new underground organization of young monks, with about 5,000 members, sends shivers down the Army's spine. The group can rally people for a revolt, or sway votes if a fair election is actually held. When these young monks called for a strike in January, soldiers invaded monasteries to quash it. Special distributions of cooking oil and rice were later made to many monks, part of the campaign to buy loyalty. But the *sangha's* independence and power rest to a degree on a Buddhist spirit of anti-materialism.

Until 1980, Ne Win may have made a strategic mistake by breaking from a tradition of Burmese kings who lavishly supported the *sangha*. Instead, Ne Win banked on winning support from the people by promising economic growth. His socialism has failed, however, and he is quickly backpedaling to free-market policies and to controlling the *sangha*. But it may be too late.

Since 1980, Ne Win has sponsored the building of a large eight-sided Buddhist pagoda in the shadow of the country's most sacred pagoda, the Shwedagon in Rangoon. His pagoda's tall spire sparkles with rare jewels. For a price, the people can view the gems through a telescope.

Since the introduction of Theravada Buddhism well over a millennium ago, Burmese kings have left behind thousands of giant temples to show they had good karma and to earn merit in the next life. "May I for this meritorious act obtain a good rebirth," states a common inscription on such temples.

These costly projects gave rise to a Burmese proverb about the burden of taxes to build them: "The pagoda is finished, but the country is in ruin."

The pagoda of Ne Win, whose name means "bright sun," is just about finished, and the proverb is finding a new popularity. Some Burmese speculate that Ne Win's sun, now 27 years in the sky, may be about to set.

Stability, Crisis, and Revolution

- The Middle East (Articles 12-14)
- Latin America (Articles 15-17)
- Africa (Articles 18-19)
- Other Third World Areas (Articles 20-21)

In assessing the root causes of most Third World conflicts (e.g., those in Nicaragua, El Salvador, South Africa, Lebanon, the Philippines), one is left with myriad unanswered and perhaps unanswerable questions regarding rights, responsibilities, claims, and blame. These questions include, among others: Did the government achieve power legitimately? If not, who speaks for the people? Does the head of state possess sufficient authority to rule? If not, how does this affect the decision-making process? Do the people enjoy true freedom? If not, is real freedom possible? Are democratic rights respected? If not, is the government justified in limiting individual freedom in order to promote unity, stability, and peace? Is the government capable of solving basic social problems? If not, who is? Is war inevitable? If not, why do nations continue to expand their military arsenals? Is economic progress possible? If not, what factors preclude success?

In any society, there are two systems of government—the myth system and the operational system. One part of the myth system consists of the stories that people like to

tell one another. Some of these stories are romantic tales that have been handed down from generation to generation to glorify a nation's history. Another part of the myth system is dictated by political theory, idealism, and even by a healthy fear of such persistent human vices as greed, corruption, and nepotism. When the myth system deliberately refuses to take account of these human failings, it represents the political equivalent of whistling past a graveyard.

The operational system describes how things actually work. The myth system and the operational system cannot be the same for two important reasons. First, people wish to take bribes, help their relatives, further their economic interests, gratify their vanity, and work as little as possible. Second, the myth system always reaches for the ideal, which means that there will probably be design defects in the myth system's plan which will make it impossible to construct a truly functional government according to the myth. Yet, the myth system affects the operational system in a constructive way. It provides a standard by which the operational system can be judged; deviations from the myth's ideals arouse guilt and shame among those in the operational system.

The divergence between the myth and operational systems is important to bear in mind when studying Third World governments. Indeed, there is an inherent tension between what political theory tells the people ought to happen in their society and what actually occurs in the day-to-day operations of their government. For example, the Salvadoran people love democracy—having long been denied it—but are willing to support a regime, at least temporarily, that endorses democratic rights while limiting individual freedoms.

According to the myth system, the developing nations, like other countries in the industrialized world, routinely denounce the evils of international violence. Indeed, the myth system requires governments to eschew armed conflict in favor of peaceful negotiations. Yet, the operational system demonstrates the unreality of such claims in many Third World countries. Despite the fact that sanity and survival would seem to dictate peaceful solutions to international problems, many developing nations continue to wage brutal wars with dire political consequences.

The myth system tells us that war is bad—that it should be avoided at all costs. But is it always bad? It depends on a country's objectives. In the case of some Third World nations, it may actually rescue a country from economic depression, reduce unemployment, or enable a despot to silence the opposition. At times, war is initiated to promote national sovereignty, territoriality, and strength. It may also foster such national goals as unity, cohesion, and stability. In most cases, the proponents of war are far more organized, influential, and vocal than those who advocate peace. War fever can easily be mobilized by economic, ideological, dynastic, political, and other sources of international conflict.

The supreme challenge of any real government is not to design an ideal system based on unrealistic theoretical assumptions, but rather to meld political institutions and human nature—with all their vices and imperfections—so that they work together more or less acceptably. Analyze the international crises explored in this unit in the context of the myth-operational system—that is, probe beneath the official pronouncements, with an eye to understanding what makes the engine run. In this regard, remember that politics is the study of power: how to get it, how to keep it, and how to use it. Unfortunately, this definition often describes the relations of nations as they battle for the real-world advantages of power, influence, and authority.

Looking Ahead: Challenge Questions

What are the chief obstacles preventing the establishment of a Palestinian state?

How has the Palestine Liberation Organization benefited from the actions of the Intifada?

Would nonviolence accelerate the Palestinians' goal for an independent homeland?

Why did the international press corps and outside observers fail to predict the outcome of the Nicaraguan election?

Why does the United States hold most of the cards in Panama?

To what extent is Colombia's ruling elite responsible for the problems that grip that country?

In the wake of the release of jailed activist Nelson Mandela, what should the African National Congress do to avoid losing ground, not only to the government, but to other political rivals?

Why have the United States and the Soviet Union abandoned their efforts to end the war, famine, and repression that plague Ethiopia?

Is China responsible for the rise of the Khmer Rouge?

What, if anything, can be done to prevent a new round of genocide in Cambodia?

What factors have contributed to India's quiet emergence as a leading industrial, military, and agricultural force?

What are the major economic and social challenges that threaten to undermine India's progress?

■ BEYOND THE *INTIFADA*

The Struggle to Build a Nation

DAOUD KUTTAB

Daoud Kuttab is a Palestinian journalist and West Bank correspondent for As-Senara, *a Nazareth Arabic weekly, and for* Middle East International *and* Mideast Mirror.

East Jerusalem

After twenty-one years of Israeli occupation of the West Bank and Gaza Strip, the Palestinian people are getting closer than ever to fulfilling their aspiration of living in a free and independent state. By combining popular unarmed protests with intensive communal organization and an increasingly pragmatic political offensive, the Palestinians now stand to achieve more this year than they have in many—though substantial obstacles remain.

Contrary to perceptions in the West, the efforts of the *intifada* have not been restricted to demonstrations and throwing stones. Since the coalescence at the beginning of January of the Unified National Leadership of the Uprising, an underground command comprising representatives from each of the main Palestine Liberation Organization factions—Yasir Arafat's Fatah, the largest; George Habash's Popular Front for the Liberation of Palestine; Nayef Hawatmeh's Democratic Front for the Liberation of Palestine; the Palestine Communist Party; and Islamic Jihad—a great deal of effort has been expended on developing the internal front. Palestinians have begun to boycott Israeli-made products to which there are Palestinian alternatives, like cigarettes, soft drinks, food products, clothing and drugs. Israeli-appointed mayors, policemen and civil administration officials have been asked to resign. Workers in Jewish settlements have been urged to stop working and Palestinian labor in Israel has been disrupted by weekly strikes.

This largely negative protest campaign has been complemented by efforts to develop local resources through a vast expansion of home and community gardening, to encourage work in Palestinian factories and, most important, to create an alternative governmental structure through the effort of self-reliant popular committees. So far, the boycott campaign has been quite successful: Most of the policemen and appointed mayors have resigned and many communities, like Beit Sahour, Bethany and Bani Neim, have resisted for

months Israeli pressure to pay taxes. But it is the growing strength of independent Palestinian communal organizations that most threatens Israel's grip on the territories. Thus, in recent weeks the Israelis have targeted the popular committees, detaining members without trial and deporting many of them. Israeli Defense Minister Yitzhak Rabin has issued a military order declaring membership in or contribution to the popular committees a crime punishable by up to ten years in prison.

The *intifada* is now poised to move into a new phase. At the end of July, while Palestinians here were discussing ways of broadening their civil disobedience campaign, King Hussein of Jordan decided to break his country's legal and administrative ties to the West Bank. This Jordanian move pushed to the fore options for unilateral Palestinian actions that were until then only talked about in theory. One that has gained popularity in the occupied territories is for Palestinians to declare independence based on the United Nations partition plan of 1947, which calls for the creation of an Arab state and a Jewish state in mandatory Palestine (a move that would explicitly recognize the legitimacy of the Jewish state of Israel); to establish a provisional government (made up of Palestinians in the occupied territories and outside); and to seek Arab and international recognition of this newly declared state.

Israel has already rejected this idea; however, as Sari Nusseibeh, a professor at Bir Zeit University, argues, the concept would gain a momentum of its own that would make it difficult to discourage. Writing in August in the Paris-based Arab weekly *Al Yom al Saba*, Nusseibeh says that the plan would give Palestinians in the occupied territories a big morale boost, and change the focus from the P.L.O. recognizing Israel to the world community recognizing the Palestinian state. Nusseibeh argues that this would increase pressure on Israel to go to an international conference and would greatly improve Palestinians' bargaining position in any negotiations.

A second option that has been suggested is for the P.L.O. to set up a government-in-exile. In fact, this idea has been supported for years by some Arab regimes because it would mean the conversion of the P.L.O. from a revolutionary organization into a predominantly political one. Many Palestinians oppose this suggestion, arguing that it was the P.L.O.'s military activities that put the Palestinian issue on the international agenda in the first place and forced its adversaries to take it seriously. However, the *intifada*'s mass unarmed protests make armed struggle unnecessary and possibly counterproductive, and could complement the activities of a government-in-exile. Nevertheless, one drawback is that such a body would exclude Palestinians in the occupied territories, the very ones laying so much of the foundation for the new state.

The third option currently being discussed is to seek international or U.N. custodianship of the occupied territories until a settlement is reached. This was one of the first demands of the uprising and one that the P.L.O. has gone on record as supporting. But while there is consensus, few Palestinians believe that this option could be implemented because it would need Israel's consent. Hence many here worry that much effort could be wasted on an idea that is a "nonstarter" during this crucial period.

Any of these options, or even a mixture, could very well be adopted at the next session of the Palestine National Council (P.N.C.), expected to take place this month. But whatever happens, it will not answer all the questions on the minds of Palestinians here. For example, the relationship between the P.L.O. and the new body (be it a provisional government or government in exile) will have to be hammered out. One suggestion is that the government will be the body with power. The P.L.O. could then become a "Palestinian Agency" handling relations with Palestinians around the world in the same way that the Jewish Agency was reorganized after the Israeli government was declared in 1948. Or, the P.L.O. could continue to possess superior power, with relations between it and the Palestinian government similar to those in the Eastern bloc between the Communist Party and the state. Either way, the role of Arafat is uncertain. Some feel that he should head the government in order to give it legitimacy and power. Others, who feel that Western recognition is the main reason for setting up the provisional or exile government, think its president should be a Palestinian outside the P.L.O. in order to improve the likelihood that key Western countries will recognize this new formation.

The Unified National Leadership has been the driving force pushing the P.L.O. toward a pragmatic position. At the end of August, leaflet No. 24 called on the P.N.C. to come up with a "clear and comprehensive political program that will increase international support for the Palestinian cause." Many here see this language as a signal to the P.L.O. to adopt measures that will include some type of recognition of Israel— mutual or unilateral, conditional or unconditional. Palestinians here want the coming P.N.C. meeting to reap the political fruits of the uprising. In the event that the meeting is inconclusive, the uprising leadership may decide to cut its

losses, freeze the *intifada* in order to allow Palestinians to catch their breath and wait for a better opportunity (and wiser leadership) to rise again some years down the line.

But even if the emerging political initiative comes to nought, those who are betting that the Palestinians will beg King Hussein to rescind his decision will be disappointed. Palestinian civil servants who used to be paid by Jordan want to participate with the rest of the community in the struggle. Though many have not suffered at all during the *intifada*, they say that if a little financial sacrifice will bring the founding of a state closer, then they will make it. In any case, existing institutions have for the past twenty-one years been undergoing a process of "Palestinianization." Even before the *intifada*, their ties with Jordan were becoming largely *pro forma*, an umbilical cord that needed to be cut before the baby could begin to live on its own. No matter what decisions the P.L.O. ultimately makes regarding political strategy, Palestinians "on the inside" are already moving to fill the vacuum left by Hussein—by setting up their own procedures for accrediting professionals, by supervising their own education system, by taking over the cooperative system of agricultural marketing, by creating Palestinian credit institutions and by providing emergency health-care and police services.

Lack of political movement may fuel an emerging fundamentalist side to the uprising. For many years, the Moslem Brotherhood was tolerated by the Israelis as a conservative force that concentrated solely on social and religious issues. But one of the early achievements of the *intifada* was the incorporation of Islamic Jihad, a new Islamic fundamentalist group. This group began to attract attention last year after several highly visible anti-Israeli actions, including an attack on Israeli soldiers in Jerusalem, an escape from a Gaza prison and confrontations with Israeli security personnel. In response, the Islamic Resistance Movement, or Hamas, was founded last February as a more activist wing of the Moslem Brotherhood. Unlike Islamic Jihad, which identifies with the mainstream of the P.L.O., Hamas's covenant, published in August, calls for "the liberation of all of Palestine by *jihad* [holy war]." Since the beginning of the uprising, the Israelis have cracked down on Islamic Jihad, arresting and deporting most of its leaders, while they have turned a blind eye to Hamas's divisive activities. So far the Unified National Leadership has also refrained from confronting Hamas so as not to weaken the national struggle.

The *intifada* and the emerging pragmatic approach toward Israel reflect a long evolution in Palestinian thinking and experience. Palestinians admit that in the first years of occupation they were baffled by Israel, by the money that started to pour in from working inside the Green Line and by some of the liberties that then–Defense Minister Moshe Dayan was allowing in his "open bridges policy." Then Israel's economic boom ended in the early 1970s and Jewish settlement under both the Labor and Likud governments began to eat up more than 52 percent of Palestinian land in the West Bank. When an "iron fist" policy replaced Dayan's "liberalism," the Palestinian resistance began spreading and taking root.

It took some time before this resistance matured into its present effective and popular force. The P.L.O.'s commitment to the slogan "armed struggle" was not very effective in the occupied territories. Palestinians living in the West Bank and Gaza Strip had no weapons or military training. The countries that had controlled the occupied territories before 1967, Jordan and Egypt, had refused to arm the population or to allow the development of any political or organizational infrastructure. And after the Israeli occupation of 1967, those two countries, along with Syria, refused to allow Palestinian commandos to use their territory to launch attacks against Israel or to smuggle in weapons. The longer Israel occupied the territories, the more difficult it became to carry out the armed struggle the P.L.O. had considered the "only way to liberate Palestine."

Hence, this approach began to change officially after the twelfth session of the P.N.C., in 1974, when the P.L.O. decided that armed struggle was "one of the ways to liberate Palestine," along with "political, popular and diplomatic struggle." It was also during this important session that the P.L.O. dropped its goal of achieving a "democratic secular state" in all of Palestine and accepted the idea of "an independent Palestinian state in any territory that Israel withdraws from." But it wasn't until the 1976 victories of pro-P.L.O. candidates in West Bank municipal elections and the strong rejection by West Bank and Gaza activists of the autonomy scheme envisioned by the Camp David Accords that the P.L.O. started to change its emphasis in the occupied territories to one of political and grass-roots struggle. By the late 1970s many of these popularly elected mayors had formed a National Guidance Committee and had started to act on behalf of the P.L.O. in the occupied territories. After a short period of Israeli permissiveness, when Ezer Weizman was Defense Minister of a Likud government, under pressure from Jewish settlers the Israeli government cracked down on the committee, deporting and dismissing most of the leaders who constituted its core. Three mayors also were the targets of assassination attempts by the Jewish terrorist underground.

In reaction, the major P.L.O. factions started putting their efforts, time and money into establishing grass-roots organizations in the occupied territories, following the example of the Palestine Communist Party, whose members and leadership are primarily in the occupied territories. The Social Youth movement (Shabibeh), by far the most important of these grass-roots organizations, was formed in 1982 and at first concerned itself with social, cultural and sports issues. The Boy Scout–like nature of the movement made it attractive to Palestinian youths, and within a few years it had hundreds of chapters throughout the occupied territories. Majed, a 23-year-old member of the Shabibeh in the Balatta camp and a former member of the Bir Zeit student council, explains, "Youths belonging to the movement would clean up cemeteries, pave roads, build retaining walls and conduct lectures. In many refugee camps where the Israelis had closed the UNRWA [United Nations Relief Works Administration] centers, the movement formed football teams that competed with other Palestinian clubs. They also visited families of those in prison and who were injured or killed by the Israelis."

Similar efforts were exerted in building up Palestinian trade unions, popular women's committees and high school and university student unions [see Joost R. Hiltermann, "Force for Change in the West Bank," *The Nation*, October 3, 1987]. These grass-roots efforts were given a big push after the expulsion of the P.L.O. from Lebanon. The loss of the Lebanese front and pressure on P.L.O. leaders in Jordan provided the perfect opportunity for a serious development of the "western front," as the P.L.O. called the occupied territories. With the help of Arab countries, a joint P.L.O.-Jordan committee was established to support the *sumud* ("steadfastness") of Palestinians under occupation. The late Khalil al-Wazir (Abu Jihad) headed the Palestinian side of the joint committee and used his post during the early 1980s to establish and support a wide network within the occupied territories that later became very useful in consolidating and directing the uprising.

After the initial outbreak of demonstrations last December, it didn't take Palestinians long before they figured out that in order for the *intifada* to last, Palestinians had to pull together. The curfews imposed by the Israeli authorities on the refugee camps were the trigger for the first collective action among Palestinians. Committees were set up to provide the necessary food and medical supplies for the besieged Gaza refugee camps. These new support committees represented the multipartisan scope of Palestinian activists. Later the committees grew and expanded their goals. Local neighborhood committees became responsible for alternative education, health needs, guard duties and agriculture. They have now become the backbone of the uprising, comprising as many as a hundred small committees in each of the major cities and up to ten in every refugee camp and village. The process of leadership developed from the base up.

From these groups emerged the Unified National Leadership of the Uprising, responsible for making major decisions on a national basis and for writing and distributing leaflets that direct protest activities. Decisions of the Unified Leadership are made unanimously and after consultation with the local committees. The success of the uprising is to a large degree the result of democratic decision-making, unification of the community, the creativity of the leadership and its pragmatism in dealing with important issues. When the Israeli authorities closed all the schools in the West Bank, the Unified Leadership encouraged the committees to start community teaching programs while pressing the Israelis to reopen the schools. When the Israelis opened the schools, the leadership encouraged the students and teachers to go back and make up their lost courses. Similarly, when shops here in East Jerusalem were closed in a merchants' strike for more than forty days, the command called on them to open for three hours a day so that Palestinians would not have to go to the Israeli side of Jerusalem to purchase their food.

The leadership of the uprising has taken special care, in resisting the Israeli occupation of the West Bank and Gaza Strip, not to oppose the existence of the state of Israel. In urging protest activities, the leadership's leaflets call for attacks against "the forces of occupation" and on workers to boycott their jobs in Jewish settlements in the occupied territories. The leadership has not called for any acts against the Israelis or Israel itself. In March and again last summer, two leaflets were printed in Hebrew and distributed to soldiers assuring them that "we are not against you or your state, we want our independence." The Hebrew leaflet called on soldiers to stop "beating us and instead to go to the beach and relax rather than be part of an occupation army."

Whether the P.L.O. will capitalize on the successes of the *intifada* or squander the current opportunity cannot be foretold. The uprising command may be a powerful new force in Palestinian politics, but it is not the only one. The nine-month-old awakening of the West Bank and Gaza, however, has opened a new chapter in the history of the Palestinian community: A state is being born.

GUNLESS IN GAZA

As Israelis debate the uses of military force,
Palestinians debate the uses of nonviolence.

Helena Cobban

British-born Helena Cobban is a Mideast special-
ist who has contributed to The Christian Science
Monitor, *National Public Radio, and other news*
organizations. A guest scholar at the Brookings
Institution last year, she is currently a visiting
peace fellow at George Mason University in Fair-
fax, Virginia.

RIVING SOUTH FROM JERUSALEM, YOU TURN
left just before Bethlehem's Manger
Square. The road descends rapidly, past
square-built stone houses gay with the
greenness of grapevines. There are some
signs for "Shepherds' Field," then before you
know it you are in Beit Sahour.

The orderly, middle-class look of this small
town gives little away to casual visitors. But the
people here, most of them well-educated Palestinian Christians, are at the forefront of a new
movement, a veritable revolution within the
Palestinians' now-aging nationalist "revolution."
This new movement has already shown a dramatic potential to unlock the long-frozen Mideast
peace process: It is the move by the Palestinians
of the occupied territories toward using the tactics of nonviolent civil disobedience, though they
clearly do not go all the way in this direction.

I visited Beit Sahour last summer as part of a
lengthy investigation into Israeli and Palestinian
conclusions about the usefulness of nonviolent
tactics in their long struggle.

Beit Sahour was in the middle of a lengthy
tax-resistance campaign. The week before, the
Israelis had responded by seizing goods belonging to some of the town's most prominent citizens.
They took the entire stock held by two pharma-
cists as well as a carpenter's woodworking
machines and the stock of a grocer estimated in
the hundreds of thousands of dollars. (In October
the tax collectors again appeared in Beit Sahour.

Operating as before under cover of a military cur-
few, they hauled away furniture and other household goods from the homes of alleged defaulters.)

One person I talked to in Beit Sahour was
A.B., a thoughtful family head in his mid-40s. He
asked that his name not be used, since many
townsfolk had already been taken to prison
camps under Israel's provisions for detention
without charge or trial. A.B. estimated that 95%
of the residents of the community were participating in the tax strike.

"Why do we refuse to pay taxes?" he asked.
"Because our taxes only go to the Israeli army to
buy more bullets. But when our municipality
needed new roads, we had to go begging elsewhere for the money to finance them."

The tax resisters of Beit Sahour see themselves as part and parcel of the broader nationalist movement that, under the leadership of the
Palestine Liberation Organization, seeks to
replace Israel's military occupation with an independent Palestinian state. But for many longtime
PLO activists, especially those forbidden access to
their homeland, the emergence of a nonviolent
trend inside the movement presents a challenging
new conundrum. For nearly a quarter of a century,
after all, these activists (terrorists to the Israelis,
liberation fighters to Palestinians) had tried to liberate their historical homeland from Israel
through "armed struggle." Tens of thousands of
Palestinians (as opposed to hundreds of Israelis)

From *World Monitor*, March 1990, pp. 57–58, 60, 62, 64. Copyright © Helena Cobban. Reprinted by permission.

*f the intifada turned into armed struggle, then that would turn all the Israeli factions that now support us, against us,' a Palestinian organizer in East Jerusalem warned.*

died in those campaigns. But not an inch of the homeland was liberated.

INTERNATIONAL DIPLOMACY WAS ABUZZ

Cut to December 1987. The unarmed uprising launched that month by Palestinians resident in the homeland brought, by comparison, fairly impressive results. Within half a year, international diplomacy was abuzz with plans for rolling back Israel's occupation from the West Bank and Gaza in exchange for Palestinian agreement to recognize and live in peace with Israel. By late 1989, with the uprising (*intifada*) still continuing, the Palestinians looked much nearer to acquiring the national rights they sought than they had just two years before. And all this, for casualties that—while they exceed 500 killed by the Israelis, and many thousands wounded—still remain much lower than those of the years of armed struggle.

The continued harshness of the Israeli occupation and the almost daily deaths it has imposed on the Palestinians have brought many of the "resident" Palestinians close to the boiling point. Nevertheless, as of this writing, the discipline with which they continued to wage their *intifada* continued to be effective. No Palestinians had cracked under the pressure and taken up arms in anger against the Israelis. And the timetables of basically nonviolent activities announced in the nationalists' clandestine leaflets—days and part-days for strikes, peaceful marches to religious sites, cultural and economic activities—were still greeted with near-total observance.

Despite the constraints the *intifada*'s leaders placed on the use of force, the *intifada* has never been totally nonviolent. Any young Israeli soldier who has been surrounded by Palestinian youngsters throwing stones can attest to that. (So can I. I came under a brief stoning in a Palestinian refugee camp, early in the *intifada*. And I'm not ashamed to admit that it was a frightening experience.)

Against this background, Palestinian activists both inside and outside their homeland were debating whether increasing the nonviolent component of their struggle might hasten achievement of their national goals. Or was it the case, as I also heard argued, that in the end "the Israelis would listen to nothing but the language of force," so the Palestinians should start preparing to step up the violence?

NEUTRALIZING ISRAEL'S ARMS

Faisal Husseini is the doyen of the activists in the "resident" wing of the movement. Son of a famous Palestinian military leader of the 1940s, Husseini nowadays uses his persuasive charm (and fluent Hebrew) to discuss the need for Palestinian rights with as broad a spectrum of Israelis as possible.

"We reached the conclusion, over a long period of time," he told me in an interview last summer, "that if you confront a superior force, you have two major options to deal with it. Either you should build your own forces until you can achieve superiority, or you should reduce or neutralize the other force. The *intifada* has done this. It has neutralized Israel's atom bombs, its Phantoms, tanks, heavy guns, and everything. It has forced them to fight us using a single bullet, a nightstick, tear gas, or clubs."

The Israelis have also tried to counter the *intifada* by detaining suspected leaders. Husseini himself has served a number of terms under Israel's provisions for detention without trial. Most recently he was detained in January this year.

The day before our summer meeting, Israeli authorities had extended a closure order—for an additional 12 months—on the think tank Husseini heads. So we had to hold our conversation in Husseini's bustling family home, at the foot of the Mount of Olives. The dusty streets and walls outside were bright with painted Palestinian slogans.

Like many of the other activists I interviewed, he had come to see that the traditional repertory of nonviolent actions also has a positive value of its own. Peaceful mass gatherings, strikes, tax resistance, and self-sufficiency campaigns—all can play a real role in the process of nation-building. Beit Sahour's A.B. put this process at the center of what the *intifada* meant to him. "The real *intifada* has nothing to do with violence," he stressed.

A.B. was quite confident that, despite all the material and human losses the Israelis could inflict, it was improbable that the *intifada* could be crushed by force. Everyone I interviewed agreed.

Gaza lawyer Raji Surani said, "The Israelis made a mistake, from the beginning of the *intifada* on, by inflicting so much pain, humiliation, and especially the mass arrests." Surani often spends long days trying to locate missing Palestinians within the overcrowded Israeli prison camps. He knows how vital that work is, since he, like Husseini, is one of the camp system's many thousands of "graduates." Nevertheless, his overall judgment was: "The people here have a strategic optimism. Their psychology became an offensive psychology—even though they are tired, exhausted, bleeding."

Still there was no blanket agreement on which way the *intifada* should continue in the future.

One powerful argument I heard for moving further toward nonviolent tactics was that, in any conflict, the means one chooses should be related to the end one seeks. "The currently stated goal of the PLO is to establish an independent Palestinian state alongside Israel," said one East Jerusalem organizer. "If we want to reassure the Israelis that they can be safe alongside such a state, then we should cut our violence against them to the minimum. But if the *intifada* turned into armed struggle, then that would turn all the Israeli factions that now support us, against us."

The Palestinian proponent of nonviolence who is probably best known in the West is Mubarak Awad, a genial Palestinian-American who was thrown out of his native Jerusalem by the Israelis just a few months into the *intifada*. Awad is a veteran student of nonviolent tactics. He compared the Palestinians' adherence to the *intifada*'s program with the extent of Mahatma Gandhi's support among the Indians, or Martin Luther King Jr.'s support from African-Americans.

CAMPAIGN COULD ESCALATE

"The conditions are very ripe for escalating the civil disobedience dimensions of the *intifada*," he told me from Washington, D.C. "Twenty-three months of *intifada* have given us the lesson that small-scale instances of civil disobedience have been successful, so a larger-scale campaign could be even more so."

In the occupied territories, however, even most of those Palestinians who favored cutting the violence completely, like Beit Sahour's A.B., expressed pessimism that this cutoff could be achieved in the near future. "It is improbable, because the Israelis are pressing down on us so hard that people are extremely angry," he said.

"Violence begets violence," said Gaza's Surani, while a philosophical friend of his offered the view that "if violence means trying to impose your will on another, then the occupation is the root of the violence here."

Other arguments against relying on nonviolence centered on the logistic difficulties involved. The Palestinians were intensely aware that 22 years of occupation had left most of their communities dependent on the Israeli economy. In Gaza, for example, some 50,000 Palestinians were still commuting to jobs in Israel every day—except for those six or seven days a month that the *intifada*'s secret leadership declares a general strike. The hard-earned shekels that the workers brought home were the major source of income for Gaza's 630,000 Palestinians. Could the community withstand cutting even this tie in a move toward total nonviolent disengagement?

A TWO-WEEK PROTEST STRIKE

This argument raged throughout last summer. At the end of August, the *intifada*'s secret leadership tried a limited experiment, calling a two-week strike to protest a new Israeli administrative control measure. That strike was nearly completely observed, but the subsequent judgment reportedly remained mixed as to whether an even longer strike would be worth the pain the Gazans would have to suffer in order to stage it.

The pain that the *intifada*—or more often, the Israelis' retribution for it—has brought to the resident Palestinians was evident. A middle-class Gazan gave me detailed accounts of how, under cover of the nightly curfews, Israeli soldiers would move through the dwellings on an entire city block, smashing the residents' household goods or, on occasion, taking valuables.

"No Palestinian can feel secure," this man, a respected employee of an international organization, quietly concluded. "The soldiers can enter your home at any time, take your belongings, or take any family member into custody. Sometimes it takes days or weeks to find the people they take away." (Israel's regulations for detention of Palestinians without charge or trial were changed over the summer, doubling the previous period of six months for which it is allowed.)

While the residents of the occupied territories continued to debate the future of the *intifada*, Palestinian leaders outside their homeland brought their own historical experience to this issue. These leaders, who include all the publicly named leaders of the PLO, all grew to maturity in the bitterness of those Palestinian communities of refugees who were dispersed from their former homes in the fighting of 1948 and never allowed back.

In the Palestinian view of history, 1948 represented a historic "disaster," an event during which their old way of life was crushed forever by the victorious Israelis. Traumatized by the impotence and rage they felt, they invested the concept of military power with enormous mystique. For the nationalist movement that emerged in the 1950s—the movement that became today's PLO—the idea of "armed struggle" assumed almost mythic proportions.

Most military specialists who study the area agree that overthrowing the Israeli state through armed struggle was never a realistic option for the Palestinians. For some years, the PLO activists hoped they could, through their own guerrilla actions, spark a bigger war with Israel in which the large Arab armies would help them regain their homeland. That did not work either, as the 1967 and 1973 Arab-Israeli wars showed. And in 1982 the Israelis inflicted a crushing battlefield defeat on the PLO's remaining military infrastructure in Lebanon.

In addition to the interviews I conducted in the occupied areas, I was also able to discuss the issue of violence versus nonviolence with a number of PLO activists and leaders in their headquarters in far-off Tunis. They agreed with their compatriots "on the inside" that the 1982 defeat had been cru-

If the present PLO leadership is unable to demonstrate the longer-term value of restraint, a number of organized groups will be in a good position to take over.

cial in forcing them to reassess the relative value of armed versus unarmed tactics. Several of them noted that the PLO's longtime military leader, Khalil Wazir—who was assassinated by an Israeli hitsquad in April 1988 in Tunis—had played a key role in this rethinking.

'OFFENSIVE NONVIOLENCE'

Faisal Husseini in Jerusalem concurred. "From 1985 on, Wazir was clearly talking about the need for civil disobedience and what we came to call 'offensive nonviolence,'" Husseini said. "I saw him as a man who first and foremost cared about his people, rather than being fascinated with military affairs for their own sake. And after all, in a movement like ours, who was better to legitimize the turn toward nonviolence than the veritable father of our armed struggle?"

PLO discussions about stepping up the nonviolent part of their campaign may have started soon after 1982, but it still took the outbreak of the *intifada* to demonstrate the value of nonviolent tactics. In an interview in his heavily guarded office in a Tunis suburb, PLO Executive Committee member Yasser Abed Rabboo recalled, "Before the *intifada*, anyone who questioned the value of armed struggle was considered a traitor." But now, he said, the PLO had learned valuable new lessons about the value of nonviolence—and these lessons had come from the underground activists in the occupied territories.

Abed Rabboo is a smart political thinker who, since December 1988, has headed the PLO's delegation to the US-PLO dialogue. "The development of nonviolent tactics there was not so much a single decision as a constant development throughout two decades of Israeli occupation," he explained. He also confirmed what many Palestinians had previously claimed—that early in the *intifada* the on-site Palestinians had taken an explicit decision not to use firearms. "That decision came from the people on the inside," he said. "It was a good decision, because it gave them self-reliance and saved them from the illusion of deliverance from the outside."

How long that decision will stand, no one can tell. Already a small number of Palestinian residents of the territories have cracked under the pressure of Israeli measures and run amok inside Israel with knives, with bare hands, or even, in one tragic incident last summer, by plunging a civilian bus over a precipice, killing 16 Israelis. Arms have also been used to kill Palestinians identified as collaborators.

Meanwhile, a fairly vocal group within the occupied areas argues that the Palestinians' restraint cannot last forever. Though all the nationalist groups dissociated themselves from the bus incident, few Palestinian voices openly condemned it. I even heard some Palestinians applaud it. "Maybe that's the path we all ought to take," said an older man, a hotel worker. "Our people die like flies in the refugee camps, but it seems the Israelis take no notice of that. Is our blood cheaper than theirs?"

Waiting in the wings to capitalize on such feelings of anger are a number of organized groups that, if the present PLO leadership is unable to demonstrate the longer-term value of restraint, will be in a good position to take over the leadership of the movement. One of these is the shadowy Islamic Jihad. When I interviewed one of their organizers in Gaza, he warned that "the form of confrontation may develop into the use of arms at the popular level."

For the moment, groups like Islamic Jihad are content to give the PLO leaders their tacit backing. But they have put the PLO on notice that they expect to see the PLO's move toward political moderation, and the nonviolent tactics it has espoused, bring results before the Palestinians' pain becomes too much to bear.

A TICKING ALARM CLOCK

The debate in the Palestinian community between advocates and opponents of nonviolence is now like a ticking alarm clock. If the alarm bell of an eruption of violence should go off, then the whole region might be plunged into war, causing tragedies to all of its peoples. But for the moment, the debate goes along more quietly as Palestinians give each other support in the daily round. Just such small moments of encouragement sustained the residents of Beit Sahour during last fall's confrontation with the Israelis. For 42 days the Israeli military maintained a state of siege in the town, while Defense Minister Yitzhak Rabin vowed he would break the will of its tax resisters. The tax collectors hauled away household goods that the Palestinians valued at $8 million, but still the townsfolk refused to pay Israel's taxes.

The people of Beit Sahour emerged from that difficult encounter with their community and nationalist spirit unbroken. Over the months ahead, they and their compatriots will decide whether nonviolent tactics are the wave of the future—and whether these tactics can bring Palestinians the solid nationalist gains they seek.

Iraq's Power Grab

Audacious and ruthless, Saddam Hussein seizes tiny Kuwait—and no one is sure where his ambition will end

LISA BEYER

With hindsight it looks so obvious, so wickedly brilliant. There sat Kuwait, fat and ripe, bulging with enormous reserves of oil and cash, boasting an excellent port on the Persian Gulf—and utterly incapable of defending itself against Iraq's proficient war machine. Saddam Hussein, hungry for money but greedier still for regional dominance, knew before the first of his soldiers crossed the border that it would be a walkover—and it was. In 12 hours, Kuwait was his.

With his brief romp through the desert, the imperious Iraqi President doubled the oil under his control to some 20% of the world's known reserves; only Saudi Arabia, with 25%, has more. He strengthened his claim to the position he has long coveted: overlord of the Arab world. And he made the entire world quake, weak-kneed, at his raw power. Not since the brilliant military leader Nebuchadnezzar ruled the Babylonian Empire more than two millenniums ago had Baghdad exercised such sway.

Just how far will Saddam Hussein's lust for power carry him? By provoking the first major military conflict of the post–cold war era, he provided the maiden test of the proposition that the U.S. and the Soviet Union can create more peace working together than apart. As recently as a year ago, such an incursion in the Middle East would probably have caused a fearsome rift between the superpowers. But in the summer of 1990, the Iraqi blitz prompted

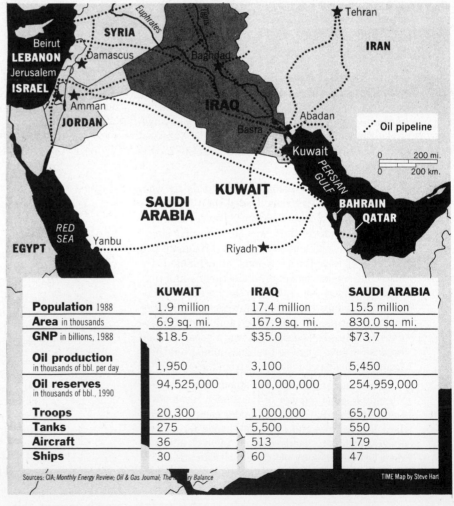

	KUWAIT	IRAQ	SAUDI ARABIA
Population 1988	1.9 million	17.4 million	15.5 million
Area in thousands	6.9 sq. mi.	167.9 sq. mi.	830.0 sq. mi.
GNP in billions, 1988	$18.5	$35.0	$73.7
Oil production in thousands of bbl. per day	1,950	3,100	5,450
Oil reserves in thousands of bbl., 1990	94,525,000	100,000,000	254,959,000
Troops	20,300	1,000,000	65,700
Tanks	275	5,500	550
Aircraft	36	513	179
Ships	30	60	47

Sources: CIA; *Monthly Energy Review; Oil & Gas Journal; The Military Balance*

TIME Map by Steve Hart

Washington and Moscow to act in stunning unanimity, each abhorring the raid and demanding, in an unprecedented joint statement, that the invaders retreat. That position was also endorsed by the United Nations Security Council. While all parties were clearly loath to take on the mightiest army in the Arab world—a force of 1 million fighting men—the rare convergence of views raised the possibility that Iraq's expansionism can somehow be contained.

Or can it? To Saddam, the end of the cold war, the breakup of the Soviet empire and America's re-evaluation of its military spending offered a safe opening for his claims of hegemony. He has the army, the arsenal and the audacity to pursue his grand ambition to rule the region—or rock the world. In effect, Saddam has leveled a brazen challenge: Stop me if you can. Last weekend one of his spokesmen snarled that if anyone moved against Iraqi forces, Baghdad would "chop off his arm from the shoulder."

Saddam's power grab is a bold reminder of the role brute force will always play in the history of nations. Without the threat of escalation to superpower conflict, countries with sophisticated weapons and thuggish rulers will try to take advantage of the shifting international climate to assert their will. The threat to U.S. interests is not some distant danger. It is very real, and not only because of the region's oil reserves. Does America really want to let the Saddams of the world shape the new global power structure?

Saddam's aggression immediately cast the financial markets into turmoil. Some economists believe that even a slight surge in prices could push America's economy, already weakened by sluggish demand, the federal deficit and the S&L crisis, over the brink into recession. Perhaps more important, Saddam's move on the Middle East is an unexpected test of whether nations will pay the necessary price to assure peace and stability in the new global climate. Said a senior State Department official: "You just cannot allow this kind of behavior to go unchecked."

But Saddam is not easily intimidated. He is convinced that no nation has the nerve to take him on. His conquest might have been deterred, but undoing it now will be nigh impossible. Baghdad radio warned that Iraq would "make Kuwait a graveyard for those who launch any aggression." The feckless international response to his muscle flexing during the past decade has nourished his belief that he has little to fear if he misbehaves. A loner, he has rarely if ever been told no— probably because the few who tried to do so tended to wind up dead. So no one can be very sure what, if any, message will derail his ruthless drive to be the paramount power in the Persian Gulf. Fortunately, Saddam has few friends around the globe, and his trucu-

lence is knitting unlikely partners into a broad-based opposition.

The emerging harmony of international opinion, however, was scant consolation for Kuwait, since no one appeared actually willing to come to the defense of the tiny state and its 1.9 million people. While Iraq in the face of the world's condemnation promised to bring its troops home beginning five days after the invasion, a subsequent announcement made nonsense of that pledge. Baghdad said it was raising a new army for Kuwait in which—surprise— 100,000 Iraqis had volunteered to serve. What's more, Baghdad named a new government, composed of nine Kuwaiti army officers, that would clearly be a puppet regime. For all practical purposes, Iraq has annexed its southern neighbor.

Iraq's land grab drew inevitable comparisons with the 1930s, when Hitler began to gobble up Europe in pieces small enough not to provoke a military response by the other powers of the day. It did not take long before fears grew that Iraq, having devoured Kuwait, would turn next to other appetizing and vulnerable gulf nations—most notably Saudi Arabia, the richest of them all. The extent to which the NATO countries, the Soviet Union and the threatened Arab states move to thwart Saddam will determine whether they have learned the lesson of history or are doomed to repeat it.

Even in the fine points of his strategy, Saddam evoked echoes of the past. He excited his people with impassioned speeches full of grievances toward their neighbor. He exploited a border dispute, scheduled negotiating sessions that were intended all along to be fruitless, and cooked up a request for intervention by supposedly downtrodden locals. The invasion sequence itself was classic '30s: bluff, feint and grab.

Baghdad's bitterest complaint against Kuwait was that the gulf state had been grossly overproducing oil in violation of OPEC quotas. Combined with similar cheating by the United Arab Emirates, Kuwait's excess pumping had depressed the average price of an OPEC barrel nearly $7. Iraq, which relies on oil for 95% of its export revenues, claims that every $1 drop in the price of a barrel of oil costs it $1 billion a year. As Saddam saw it, the Kuwaitis might as well have been stealing from his treasury.

That business, however, was supposedly settled late last month at OPEC's midyear meeting in Geneva. Just before that session began, Saddam resorted to outright intimidation: he marched his 30,000-strong élite Republican Guard, the troops who did the toughest fighting in the gulf war, to the Kuwaiti border. Through Egyptian President Hosni Mubarak, who called the spat "a cloud that will pass with the wind"—a comment he would soon bitterly regret—Saddam promised he would not

attack his neighbor, at least for the moment. Still, Kuwait and the U.A.E. got the hint, meekly agreed to abide by their production caps and consented to the first hike in OPEC's target price in four years.

But rather than pull its forces back, Iraq sent in 70,000 reinforcements. Saddam had other scores to settle with Kuwait. There was the quarrel over the rich Rumaila oil field, a finger-shaped deposit whose tip reaches just into frontier territory claimed by both Iraq and Kuwait. Baghdad insists that when its attention was turned to fighting Iran in 1980, Kuwait surreptitiously moved the border 2.5 miles north to tap into Rumaila. Now Saddam wants $2.4 billion in compensation for oil he claims Kuwait withdrew.

Then there was Baghdad's insistence that Kuwait forgive $10 billion to $20 billion in loans it extended to help fund Iraq's eight-year war against Iran. Saddam, who started the conflict, maintains that he fought off Iranian fundamentalism on behalf of all Arabs and is therefore entitled to relief from the entire $30 billion to $40 billion debt he racked up with the rest of the Arab world.

Finally, Iraq saw in Kuwait a way to compensate for the disadvantages—enormous for an oil exporter—of being virtually landlocked. Iraq has just 18 miles of shoreline, and most of that is blocked by Kuwait's Bubiyan Island. Baghdad has long pressed Kuwait to cede or lease Bubiyan Island, but the Kuwaitis refused, figuring they would never get it back. Then there is Iraq's long-standing claim that all of Kuwait rightfully belongs to it. Once part of the province of Basra under the Ottoman Empire, Kuwait has never been acknowledged as a separate entity by Baghdad. Iraq tried to reclaim the land by force in 1961, when Britain granted Kuwait independence, and again in 1973 and 1976.

All the points of discord between Iraq and Kuwait were on the agenda of talks between the two countries last Wednesday. From the outset the Kuwaitis made it clear that they were willing to pay Baghdad a sizable sum for peace. But the Iraqis, who demanded Kuwait's total capitulation on every count, were determined to see the negotiations break down. After a fruitless two hours, they did. At exactly 2 the next morning, the 100,000 Iraqi soldiers massed on the border—a force nearly five times as great as the entire Kuwaiti military— spilled south. Two additional commando units swarmed in by air and sea.

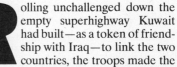 olling unchallenged down the empty superhighway Kuwait had built—as a token of friendship with Iraq—to link the two countries, the troops made the 37 miles to the capital, Kuwait City, in just four hours. "It was chaos in the streets," said Stephanie McGehee, a photographer

who witnessed the attack. Panicked residents tried to flee south toward Saudi Arabia, but the Iraqis forced people out of their autos and angrily ripped out car phones—no rarity in a country with so many wealthy citizens—presumably because they could be used to communicate troop positions.

While an estimated 300 Iraqi tanks prowled the city, an additional 50 surrounded the Emir's palace and the nearby U.S. embassy. But the Emir, Sheik Jaber al-Ahmed al-Sabah, and his family were able to flee to Saudi Arabia by helicopter. Though the invaders had quickly seized Kuwait's radio and television station, a hidden transmitter continued to broadcast exhortations to resist the raiding foreigners and pleas for help from other Arab states. "O Arabs, Kuwait's blood and honor are being violated. Rush to its rescue!" cried a voice thought to be the crown prince's. "The children, the women, the old men of Kuwait are calling on you."

Though help never came, Kuwaiti troops put up small pockets of resistance. At the palace, the country's symbolic heart, the Kuwaitis held their own through a two-hour artillery barrage. During the battle, the Emir's younger brother Fahd was killed. The Iraqi force assigned to secure the oil rigs off Kuwait's shores saw the most action. Kuwaiti troops and missile boats managed to sink and burn an unknown number of Iraqi landing craft and escort ships. By early afternoon, however, nearly all Kuwait's guns had been silenced. In all, it is estimated that 200 Kuwaitis were killed in the assault. No figure for Iraqi casualties was available.

Concocting the flimsiest of excuses for an invasion, the Iraqis announced that they had entered the country at the invitation of the Free Interim Government, which had supposedly seized control of the country from the Emir. This previously unknown organization was said to be made up of "young revolutionaries." But no one bought the tale. "Instead of staging a coup d'état before the invasion, they got it the wrong way around," said Thomas Pickering, Washington's U.N. ambassador.

To one and all, it was obvious that the Iraqi assault was, as President Bush termed it, "naked aggression." Resource-rich but sparse in people, Kuwait was a timely acquisition—an act of piracy, pure and simple—for Iraq, whose war with Iran left the country with $70 billion in debts and tremendous reconstruction costs. While Saddam does not face an immediate cash shortage, he is intent on proceeding with some $40 billion worth of self-memorializing development projects that he has been unable to finance. Among them: the Baghdad metro, 2,000 miles of railway and two gigantic hydroelectric dams. Now Saddam can not only pocket the profits of Kuwait's oil wells but also manipulate their production levels to ensure a high price for his own oil.

Kuwaitis carrying portraits of their deposed Emir demonstrate at the Iraqi embassy in London

Iraq promised to withdraw its troops in stages, but the pledge was widely disbelieved.

Equally tantalizing were Kuwait's enormous investments overseas, estimated at $100 billion, which provide the gulf state with more than $6 billion a year, a sum roughly equivalent to its oil revenues. What's more, Iraq's new piece of real estate, which includes Port Ahmadia and 120 miles of coastline, gives it direct access to the Persian Gulf.

Of course, Saddam had more on his mind than money. Having won—by his lights—the war against Iran, he is intent on making himself the new Gamal Abdel Nasser, master and hero of the entire Arab world. As Robert E. Hunter, former director of Middle East affairs for the National Security Council, points out, "If you're going to run a protection racket, every once in a while you have to blow up a dry cleaner."

No country that shares a border with Iraq can rest easy. It is obvious that Saddam has the military might to seize more territory in the gulf, and he could move—who knows?—into Jordan or Syria as well, a prospect that raises anxieties in Israel. The first modern Arab invasion of another Arab state has broken the myth of family that held those competing states in check. But even if Saddam reins in his soldiers, the threat that he might loose them will scare his Arab neighbors into submission. They will find it easier and the better part of valor to knuckle under.

Nor can they necessarily count on foreign help. Kuwait pleaded for military intervention. "My friend, we are desperate for any kind of assistance we can get," said Sheik Saud Nasir Al-Sabah, Kuwait's ambassador to the U.S., addressing a reporter. But the immediate international response smelled of appeasement. Although the U.S.

moved to position three of its aircraft carriers in the region, President Bush at first said his government was not "discussing intervention." The Arab League met for a full day in Cairo and was unable to come up with even an expression of concern.

Soon enough, however, the danger of allowing Saddam to get away with murder began to sink in. The U.S. State Department reported that some of the Iraqi invaders had moved to within five miles of the border with Saudi Arabia. Though the Saudis have stockpiled tens of billions of dollars' worth of Western military hardware over the years, they have only a 65,000-man armed force that is no match for the Iraqis. Holding that neighbor under its guns, Iraq would control more than 44% of the world's proven oil reserves. Suddenly backbones straightened up. Bush said he was not ruling out a counterstrike and warned later that Iraq would be attacking U.S. "vital interests" if it took on Saudi Arabia. His aides asserted that Washington had unspecified "contingency plans" in the event of an Iraqi move beyond Kuwait. Bucking itself up, the Arab League, though rejecting foreign interference, condemned the invasion and demanded an immediate withdrawal.

In a compelling display of the new relationship between the superpowers, U.S. Secretary of State James Baker quickly flew to Moscow to consult with his Soviet counterpart, Eduard Shevardnadze. After what Shevardnadze called "a rather unusual meeting," the two issued a rare communiqué, the first team effort by the superpowers to muster global support to halt a regional war. Decrying the "brutal and illegal" Iraqi attack, the two countries called on all nations to join in an arms embargo of the aggressor state. Signing the statement, Shevardnadze allowed, was "rather difficult" for the Soviet Union, since Iraq had long been a close client. But, he said, the joint declaration was "more consistent with the new political thinking."

For the moment, the consensus seemed to be that it was more prudent to try to squeeze Saddam dry than to outgun him. "There are two approaches to the problem: confrontation or asphyxiation," said a Western diplomat in Cairo. "Asphyxiation is the best, but it requires the complete cooperation of all the countries if it is going to work." The U.S. immediately froze Iraqi assets and imposed a boycott on Iraqi oil. Last weekend the European Community adopted those measures, banning arms sales to Baghdad and adding on a boycott of Kuwaiti oil. The U.S. and the European countries have also frozen Kuwaiti assets to keep the Iraqis from getting their hands on them. Japan asked its financial institutions to follow suit.

Whatever countermeasures are taken, they had better be decisive. "The invasion is the first fundamental challenge to the new superpower order," says John Hannah of the Washington Institute for Near East Policy. The implications of failure are underscored by the fact that Iraq, with its less than punctilious attachment to the rules of civilized conduct, is thought to be three to 10 years away from possessing a nuclear bomb. Already Iraq is one of the world's largest producers of chemical weapons, and Saddam has shown he is willing to use them not only to subdue his external enemies but also to cow his own compatriots.

As with any bully, the key to taming Saddam is to make sure he gets away with nothing. Given "the mind-set of a person as ruthless as he is," says a high-level U.S. State Department official, "unless you meet this kind of aggressive behavior very firmly, he's encouraged to try again, and you'll pay a substantial price later." What the U.S., the other Arabs and the rest of the international community must come to terms with is that the time to draw a line in the sand is now.

—Reported by William Dowell/Cairo, J.F.O. McAllister/Washington and Christopher Ogden/Moscow

Master of His Universe

Iraq's dictator seems capable of doing anything to get his way

OTTO FRIEDRICH

Nebuchadnezzar . . . was driven from men, and did eat grass as oxen . . .
—The Book of Daniel 4: 33

What kind of man would cold-bloodedly gobble up a neighboring country? What kind of man would try to assassinate a Prime Minister? What kind of a man gasses undefended villages or executes his closet colleagues? What kind of a man, in short, is Iraq's President-for-Life Saddam Hussein?

The heir, it would seem, of the fierce and bloodthirsty Mesopotamian kings who once ruled the civilized world. Many of those ancient potentates met terrible ends—when they made the mistake of relaxing their grip for an instant. Saddam is determined not to repeat their fate.

When Israeli intelligence agents gave an anonymous sample of Saddam's handwriting to a leading graphologist recently, the analyst said the writer suffered from severe megalomania with symptoms of paranoia. Graphology is even less of a science than long-distance psychiatry, but there is other evidence besides the loops and whorls of script. Saddam had himself photographed not long ago in a replica of the war chariot of Nebuchadnezzar, the Babylonian king whom Saddam apparently reveres as his hero. Despite a bout of insanity, which is recounted in *The Book of Daniel*, Nebuchadnezzar made his name in history by destroying Jerusalem in 587 B.C. and driving its inhabitants into 70 years of captivity. It is fair warning.

Like those forebears, Saddam is by no means crazy. Rather, he is a man willing to do almost anything to get what he wants—and he wants to dominate the Middle East much as Nebuchadnezzar once did. "He is an extremely shrewd, cold-blooded, clever thug," says a senior British diplomat who has dealt with him. "Human life means nothing to him." He plays the complex game of Middle East politics by the bareknuckle rules of the region. Says another diplomat: "He does what he thinks is expedient. He is not driven by ideology or whim. He coldly calculates every move. He is simply a brutal and very clever pragmatist." Adds TIME correspondent Dan Goodgame: "On meeting him, a visitor is first struck by his eyes, crackling with alertness and at the same time cold and remorseless as snake eyes on the sides of dice. They are the eyes of a killer."

The origins of Saddam's killer instinct go back to his roots in Tikrit, 100 miles north of Baghdad. Born in 1937 the son of peasants, he was orphaned at the age of nine months and raised by an uncle, and army officer named Khairallah Talfah, who hated Britain's domination of Iraq's puppet monarchy. At his knee, the boy learned the ways of intrigue and sneak attack, until Talfah joined in a abortive anti-British coup in 1941 and was imprisoned. Saddam did not attend school until the age of nine and later, when he applied for admission to the élite Baghdad Military Academy, he was rejected for poor grades. It was a devastating blow, instilling, say Israeli analysts, an obsession with the use of military force. Though Saddam now likes to parade around in self-designed military uniforms, it was only after he came to power that he could make himself a full general.

The nearest he ever got to combat was assassination. As a student, he had joined the Baath Party, an underground anti-Western, pan-Arab socialist movement. The party put him on a team assigned to murder Iraq's military ruler, Abdul Karim Kassem. Saddam and his confederates sprayed Kassem's station wagon with machine-gun fire as it sped through downtown Baghdad, but they missed their target. Although bodyguards killed several of the assailants, Saddam escaped with a bullet in his left leg. In the glorified words of his own hagiography—the truth is less dramatic—he carved out the bullet himself with a razor dipped in iodine, then disguised himself as a Bedouin tribesman, swam across the Tigris River, stole a donkey and fled across the desert to Syria. He was captured and jailed, but supposedly word of his adventures reached Egypt's President Gamal Abdel Nasser, who was then a charismatic exponent of pan-Arabism. Nasser got Saddam transferred to Cairo, and became another hero.

At 25, Saddam began studying law, but his heart was in other things. According to one anecdote, Saddam was exasperated when his Cairo classmates sat around in cafés and debated the fine points of local politics. "Why argue?" Saddam shouted. "Why don't you just take out a gun and shoot him?"

Saddam returned to Baghdad in 1963 and started organizing a militia for the Baath party, which finally succeeded in grabbing power permanently in 1968. Under the nominal leadership of General Ahmed Hassan al-Bakr, the man who held the real control was his relative Saddam Hussein. Keeping things in the family, Saddam married another relative, Sajida Talfah, the daughter of the officer who had raised him.

Al-Bakr retired in 1979, and that left Saddam completely in charge. He celebrated by ordering the execution of 21 Cabinet members, including one of his closest comrades, on dubious charges of treason. "He who is closest to me is farthest from me when he does wrong," said Saddam.

According to a British diplomat, on other occasions Saddam took a band of Cabinet ministers and aides down to Baghdad's central prison to serve as the firing squad for a number of political prisoners. "It was to ensure loyalty through common guilt," says the British official. It also reminds his colleagues what their own destiny might be. Amnesty International has estimated the number of executions in Iraq at hundreds a year, and the secret police are everywhere. Torture is commonplace. It is a crime to own a typewriter without police permission. It is death to speak against the "Father-Leader." Says a Western official: "Everyone knows that no one is safe."

Yet in 1980 Saddam nearly brought his regime to ruin when he attacked Iran. He had once given refuge to the Ayatullah Khomeini, then, under pressure from the Shah, expelled him. Not only did Saddam want disputed territory, but he was also provoked when Khomeini began calling for the overthrow of Saddam's "blasphemous" regime. He is a Sunni Muslim, though most Iraqis belong to the rival Shi-'ite branch, as did Khomeini. Saddam responded by invading, confident that his powerful, Soviet-equipped army could easily smash the Ayatullah's ragtag militia, but the Iranians fought back. When the going got especially rough, Saddam turned to poison gas, a horror weapon outlawed after World War I.

Not so much popular as feared at home, he is equally ruthless in preserving his power. He is omnipresent, his face, sometimes several feet high, adorning every city block. His picture hangs in every office, every shop, even most private homes, lest the dreaded secret police pay a call. Those who don't conform pay. A senior general once warned him, according to an Iraqi informant, that an attack he had ordered would lead to very high casualties. Saddam invited the general into the next room to dis-

cuss the matter. After the door closed behind them, a shot rang out. Saddam returned alone, stuffing his pistol into his holster.

While fighting the Iranians, Saddam was also waging war against the rebellious Kurds, who make up about 19% of Iraq's population. There too he relied on poison gas, not against invading soldiers but against civilians, women and children. It took eight years for the gulf war to end in a stalemate, with a loss of an estimated 75,000 to 150,000 Iraqi lives and the country's economy in ruins. To rebuild from the wreckage, Saddam needed more oil revenues, and when Kuwait interfered with his plans, he reached—as ever—for his pistol.

What distinguishes Saddam from the rulers of other lands is that he is not content merely to "be" President. He has a vision—some would say a delusion—of grandeur for himself and for Iraq, but the only ways he knows to pursue the dream are to kill and bully and take.

—Reported by Dan Goodgame/ Washington and William Mader/London

Nicaragua's Election: Who Really Won?

Managua

IN TODAY'S MEDIATED world, truth lies not so much in the eye of the beholder as in the eye of the reporter. We tend to believe that what "happened" is actually what radio, TV and newspapers tell us has happened. Unfortunately, the difference between this mediated reality and *real* reality was very apparent in the recent election in Nicaragua.

This is not to say the media lied; they got the facts straight. And most certainly they did not ignore what was going on. During the week prior to the February 25 elections, more than 2,300 accredited press agents poured into this tiny country of only 1.75 million voters—a figure that works out to about one reporter for every 750 people who went to the polls.

In the weeks prior to the election little was written in the mainstream U.S. press about Nicaragua. Except for the serious papers such as the *New York Times*, the *Washington Post* and the *Los Angeles Times* and a few special-interest dailies such as the *Miami Herald*, most newspapers contained no coverage at all. Television was almost as complete a void, unless one sought out the few pieces on CNN or Monitor News. Consequently, the average informed American, and even the above-average opinion leader, was doing well to know that there was to be an election between the revolutionary Sandinistas and an opposition coalition, that the election was to be monitored by the United Nations, and that the outcome could have a marked effect on the future of the contras.

Then, during the week just before the election, news coverage expanded enormously. For newspapers in which Nicaragua previously had not existed, suddenly it was front-page news. The national papers carried three and four stories each day. The major TV networks pooled a satellite uplink from the Olaf Palme press center in Managua.

The press got most of the story right about the election monitoring in which the United Nations, the Organization of American States, the Carter Center and more than 100 other invited observer groups, including an international ecumenical observation team from the World Council of Churches, the Lutheran World Federation, the United States Catholic Conference, and the Latin American Council of Churches, were engaged. They told how the UN and OAS had sent teams two months earlier to oversee the setup of the governing electoral authority, the procedures for forming political parties, the rules regarding public rallies and voter registration, and the use of the media.

But much more was said about the quantity and quality of the election observers than about the fact that the Sandinistas had *voluntarily* welcomed an unprecedented intrusion into their internal election process. Never before had an autonomous, sovereign nation agreed to accept the monitoring of its own election process in as much detail as the Sandinista government did in Nicaragua, but this was scarcely mentioned in press accounts.

The reason why so many officials and private citizens from Europe, Latin America and the United States became involved in the observation was also largely unspoken: without international certification that the election was fair, the United States would be able to cry "foul" and refuse to change its policy of helping to demolish the Nicaraguan economy. But Elliot Richardson, head of the UN observers, reported on the day before the election that "though not free of fault, the election process has worked remarkably well. . . . The people of Nicaragua will be able to go to the polls and exercise free choice tomorrow, and we believe the counting process will work fairly and well."

And the people lined up all day to cast their votes. By an almost 15 percent margin, they voted for Violeta Chamorro and the National Opposition Union (UNO) rather than for President Daniel Ortega and the Sandinistas.

The results shocked many in Nicaragua, including both political parties themselves. Several of the most reliable polls had predicted just the reverse, a Sandinista win over UNO by a margin of about 15 percentage points. After all, UNO was a loose coalition of 14 groups ranging from center-left to the far right, hampered by a fuzzy platform and presidential and vice-presidential candidates who constantly fought one another. The UNO candidate, a 60-year-old widow of an assassinated newspaper editor who had crusaded 15 years ago against the Somoza regime, had been born into a wealthy farming family, and only reluctantly accepted the nomination. She admitted during the campaign that she was unfamiliar with many of her party's own position papers. Also, the UNO coalition faced serious financial problems. Although it had to accept the stigma of depending on U.S. funding, most of the funds arrived much too late in the campaign. And UNO had made a serious tactical mistake: when the United States invaded Panama, an event which enraged the average Nicaraguan, UNO refused to condemn it. Polls showed that half the nation believed that UNO was "too closely tied to the contras," and 45 percent of the voters agreed with the statement that "Violeta Chamorro is a puppet of the United States." On a less ideological note, I made a careful tally of attendance at each party's closing rally in Managua. UNO's was attended by about 60,000, while the Sandinistas' brought together a tremendous crowd of more than half a million.

SO WHAT HAPPENED to bring about an election result that confounded so many polltakers, reporters and observers—people who were sure that if fair elections were held, the Sandinistas would win hands down?

The U.S. press generally interpreted the results in political terms, as a victory of democracy over communism. On the day after the election the *New York Times* wrote that the opposition "crushed" Ortega, thus "bringing an end to 10 turbulent years of Sandinista rule." It explained that the vote "prepares the ground for the first democratic transfer of power that this country has known, a turnover that parallels to some degree the changes in Eastern Europe, where Communism has little by little given way to democratic change."

While such reporting is not false, it also is not true, if we mean reality rather than facts. For by and large the popular press in its coverage of Nicaragua left out the *context* of reality: the environment, the history and ultimately the meaning.

The symbolic environment supplied by both print and electronic media was primarily people—pictures of Ortega, Chamorro, Richardson, Jimmy Carter, or João Baena Soares of the OAS, in various combinations—or perhaps an aerial photo of a rally, a group of contras on patrol or a police officer swinging his club. But the true symbolic environment in Nicaragua today, the environment that controls the people's reality, is the picture of near-total national devastation—whole sections of farming lands unusable because of a decade of war; 30 blocks of downtown Managua in rubble and weeds, destroyed by the 1974 earthquake and never rebuilt because millions of dollars in relief funds were quietly siphoned off by the Somoza family; once middle-class families now unbelievably poor, because the U.S. embargo and blockade has driven prices up 34,000 percent in 1988, another 1,500 percent in 1989. What was in people's minds was gripping poverty, not ideological discussions, international observers or rallies.

The historical context provided by the press, when any was provided at all, began at the point the Sandinistas took over the country in 1979 and then documented the frustrations of U.S. policy in attempting to overthrow the Sandinistas. For Nicaraguans, the 1979 overthrow of Somoza was the culmination, not the beginning, of their century-old struggle against U.S. control. As Ortega said in almost every speech, "We are not communists; we are not capitalists; we are Sandinistas." But when the United States refused to assist, the Sandinistas accepted aid from Cuba and the Soviet Union—an unforgivable act in the eyes of Washington, but understandable in Nicaragua's historical context.

WHAT, THEN, is the meaning of the election? To most of the media it meant that the people chose to oust a socialist state for a democracy. There is truth in this. The Sandinistas, like most groups in power, clearly took advantage of their position. While they redistributed land to more than 100,000 farmers, the Sandinistas also established the Ministry of the Interior, a large security apparatus with its own internal army. They imposed universal conscription, which took young men off the farms. They created a huge bureaucracy, which became a power base for the party faithful but hindered what small opportunities remained for growth and development. In the last days of the campaign, for example, it was not lost on the people that the cost of the tremendous rally in Managua—the thousands of flags, hundreds of banners and government trucks, the balloons and fireworks—was paid by the desperately poor. The people chose to oust a system that was not working.

But this vote was not, as most portrayed it, a decision to reject one ideology in favor of another. Most Nicaraguans simply were exhausted. They were tired and hungry. Above all, they wanted the war to end. They voted *against* more revolution, more fighting, more hunger, more deprivation. Like most Americans, they voted their stomachs and their pocketbooks. They voted to say "Uncle," because they simply couldn't take it any longer.

Thus, ironically, U.S. policy toward Nicaragua has succeeded, but not in the same sense that the popular press portrays the victory. For a decade U.S. policy has been to devastate Nicaragua in every way possible in order to oust the Sandinistas, who dared to insist that their nation was sovereign and independent. That policy has now succeeded, but at the price of destroying the well-being of an entire people.

If this is what really happened, then many questions remain. Will Ortega be able to head off military action by the radical left in his party? Will UNO be able to hold together enough of its splinter groups to govern? Will the contras lay down their guns and return to their farms? Will the people be able to survive the transition?

But the most important questions involve the United States. Will it withdraw support for the contras? Will it lift its economic embargo and allow Nicaragua to sell to its largest natural market? Will it agree to the judgment of the World Court and make reparations to Nicaragua for the injuries the U.S. has caused for more than a decade? Will it provide aid to a people devastated by its own policies?

A few in the popular media are asking these questions, but not many. To most the fact is merely that the U.S. "beat" the Sandinistas, and while that is true, it also is not what really happened.

William F. Fore

PANAMA: WHOSE AGENDA?
ONE CRISIS MAY LEAD TO ANOTHER

PHILLIP BERRYMAN

Phillip Berryman, a writer and translator, lived in Panama and Guatemala for twelve years. A revised version of his Inside Central America *(Pantheon) will be published this fall.*

hen General Manuel Noriega walked out of the nunciature, Panama's fifteen days in the spotlight ended. A CNN reporter waiting in line for his boarding pass candidly told me they were now shifting their attention to the Soviet Union. Developments in Panama, however, are sure to resurface as policy problems for the United States. At the moment, concerns focus around U.S. responsibility for economic reactivation. Over the longer run the future of the U.S. military bases in Panama is likely to prove problematic. One indication is the fact that a U.S. congressman just back from a trip to Panama could breezily summarized his understanding of the 1977 Carter-Torrijos Treaties this way: "the Panamanians get the canal and we get the bases"—seemingly unaware that the treaties oblige the United States to give up the bases by the end of 1999.

The base issue should be kept in mind in connection with what I see as the most positive outcome of the invasion, the possibility that the new Panamanian government might opt not to have an army.

Demilitarization has considerable rational appeal. Panama does not have to defend its borders; on one side stands armyless Costa Rica, and on the other, the eastern half of the country leading to Colombia is a dense jungle with no road of any sort. Panamanians see themselves as a trading country, and would like to assert their neutrality. If they had only a police force and not an army lusting after late model weapons, the savings could be applied to education, health care, and other programs, as is done in Costa Rica.

In addition to such rational considerations, one can sense a visceral reaction to the country's recent experience. Repudiation of the Noriega regime is universal; in addition, some people, particularly those involved in the Civic Crusade, which led the anti-Noriega campaign and is the core of the new government, see the twenty-one years of military rule, including the populism of General Omar Torrijos (1968-1981), as negative.

As Vice-President and Minister of the Interior Ricardo Arias Calderon explained the plan to me, the bulk of the new Public Force would carry out police functions. In addition there is to be a small, professionally trained body for carrying out investigation, and some specialized combat units for dealing with serious armed threats, whether from potential guerrilla groups or possibly international drug rings. Many of the functions that Noriega's military had carried out, such as running the prison system, immigration, and transportation, would pass into civilian hands, and the new security bodies will no longer be financially independent but will be accountable to civilian authorities.

Two immediate difficulties come to mind. The crucial question is not whether a security force be designated an army or a police force, but how it behaves. Labor leaders with whom I talked strongly suspected that the new government would be repressive. They are convinced that with Panama awash in weapons, the wealthy might easily pay to have their dirty work done by death squads, as in Guatemala or El Salvador. One economist believes that the government will inevitably have to use repression to quell dissent against the economic policies it will be forced to enact. More than one person sensed a witch hunt in the making. "Communism may be dead," observed a priest, "but anti-communism isn't."

Nationalists fear that demilitarization would make it all the easier for the United States to argue its need to retain the bases since Panama would obviously be unable to defend the canal. Ironically, whereas in neighboring Central America the business sector relies on military repression, in Panama the same sector is the most enthusiastic over the possibility of demilitarization, while it is nationalists and the miniscule Left that is most suspicious of the proposal.

It is worth noting that the Santa Fe Committee, whose 1980 report served as a blueprint for the Reagan administration's Latin America policy, in a similar document issued in 1988 looked beyond the Noriega crisis to assert the need for discussions on "a realistic defense of the canal after the year 2000," which would include "the United States's retention of limited facilities in Panama...for proper force projection throughout the Western Hemisphere."

Actually the canal seems largely indefensible. Destruction of the dams that maintain the water level of Gatun Lake at its center would in effect pull the plug on the canal and put it out of commission for a long time. Or, as a former U.S. military attaché speculated on "Nightline," terrorists could attack ships passing through the canal to the point where insurance companies would no longer issue policies. Small specialized units could patrol the areas around the canal for such eventualities, but no conceivable Panamanian force could defend the canal from a strategic air attack. In fact, the best guarantee for the safety of the canal would be a stable, prosperous, peaceful—even demilitarized—Panama.

The Santa Fe Committee's "proper force projection" no doubt means the ability to intervene militarily in Latin America, carry out military exercises and surveillance, or simply to intimidate putative enemies. As the Pentagon and its allies scramble for a new raison d'être in the post-cold-war world, Panama may assume even greater importance.

Vice-President Arias Calderon believes the possibility of Panama's internal demilitarization can be unlinked from that of the bases and he implied that the changes sweeping the world should eventually make it easier for the United States to relinquish the bases as the treaty demands.

Thus Panama's hopeful steps toward demilitarization are taking place in an atmosphere of ambiguity. In that connection it may be germane to recall that Costa Rica's decision to abolish its army was not immaculately conceived. It was the outgrowth of the 1948 civil war in which two thousand people died. The war was fought against a coalition that had instituted social reforms—which the leader of the opposing and ultimately winning side, Jose Figueres, largely adopted. In abolishing the army, Figueres calculated that he was eliminating a potential threat to himself, should he become president.

Some Panamanians are more concerned about a crime wave with which the still small Public Force seems unable to cope. Unprecedented numbers of people are joining gun clubs to learn how to shoot.

The most pressing immediate concern is economic reactivation. Unemployment is estimated at around 35 percent. In cash terms the greatest cost incurred in the invasion was not the physical destruction, calculated to be $100 million, but the looting, in which merchants lost an estimated $700 million in merchandise and $200 million in plant and equipment. These losses, plus the effects of the U.S. economic sanctions, whose burden fell on the business community and the general public more than on Noriega himself, explain why Panamanians were saying the U.S. should provide $1.5 to $2 billion in new aid.

The Bush administration has accepted responsibility for the physical reconstruction, but regards the loss from the looting as an insurance matter. Predictably, the insurance companies, most of them foreign, argue that they are not liable for acts of war, while the merchants' representatives view the looting as robbery, for which they are covered. President Guillermo Endara welcomed the Bush administration's proposal of $1 billion in aid, half of which is to be used for debt servicing—the Noriega government stopped payment a couple of years ago—and the other half for development projects and economic reactivation.

Panama's economic future seems to entail more than reactivating the existing economy. As an economist explained it to me, the deeper economic crisis antedates Noriega's fallout with the United States. Although it has an agro-export sector (bananas, coffee, beef, sugar), Panama's economic mainspring has been its "transit function": during colonial times, the gold shipped through Panamanian ports to Spain; during the California gold rush, a transisthmian railroad; and during this century, the canal. Starting in the 1960s Panama became a major finance center to the point where it now has 110 banks (only 17 of them Panamanian). Since its currency is the dollar, Panama has been an attractive place for Latin American oligarchs and businesses to keep deposits—and inevitably for money laundering. In the early 1980s deposits reached $32 billion (as compared with the country's GNP of $5 billion at that point). Panama was also a haven for "paper" companies. Through internal transactions with their Panamanian affiliates, transnational companies can evade taxes. The Free Trade Zone in Colon functions essentially as a

warehouse operation for merchandise, largely Japanese, destined for sale in Latin America and the Caribbean. In the go-go atmosphere of economic growth, the Torrijos government could continue to borrow. The numerous high rises visible in TV reporting on the invasion reflected the period of expanding banks, financial services, and borrowing.

The Latin American economic decline and debt crisis brought that kind of growth to a screeching halt in 1982. Deposits plateaued and then declined (to $8 billion today) and the market for the goods of the Free Zone fell off. Increasing the debt was no longer an option, and in fact even under Noriega the International Monetary Fund and the World Bank began to pressure Panama toward structural adjustment (reduced public expenditures, and in a more general sense reorienting the economy away from services and toward production). Labor leaders and economists fear that the new government will take steps in this direction. Possibilities suggested to me include Hong Kong-style industries (perhaps with capital from Chinese fleeing Hong Kong) and efforts to stimulate nontraditional agricultural exports. Although the new government will be trying to stimulate employment, it will be laying off large numbers of government workers. Thus observers expect that the economic measures may produce social discontent, which the government might find it necessary to quell with repression.

The Bush administration is already urging Panama to modify its bank secrecy laws to enable U.S. authorities to investigate suspected money laundering. However, a representative of the Banking Association of Panama assumed it was in Panama's interests to maintain its present legislation. He also told me that the amount of money laundered in Panama is not as large as is often imagined.

Panama's political future is unclear. No one doubts that the ticket headed by Guillermo Endara won the election last May overwhelmingly—I heard no calls for new elections. Moreover, those occupying cabinet and other top administrative positions are acknowledged to be upright and competent. To some observers, however, they look like a rerun of pre-1968 civilian politics. Unless the new government can take measures that serve the needs of the poor majority, both urban and rural, many Panamanians might sour on the new order.

One test of whether the new government is truly democratic will be its tolerance for a broad spectrum of opposition. That might include some version of "Torrijismo," labor movements, and pressure groups from popular sectors.

These various issues—demilitarization, the bases, economic recovery, the political future—all point toward the U.S., which holds most of the cards. Bush administration representatives insist publicly that the new Panamanian government must rapidly take charge. However, accompanying the crucial U.S. dollars is a large contingent of military and civilian planners and experts, who, one fears, may constitute a shadow government, laying down the parameters and leaving only the execution (and unpopular decisions) to the Panamanian government. Installed by U.S. troops and dependent on massive aid, the new government will have little leverage when it comes to defending Panamanian interests in any clash with the Bush administration.

The U.S. invasion to resolve one crisis may engender others.

The People's War

Jenny Pearce

O N AUGUST 18, 1989, LUIS CARLOS GALAN, front-runner for the Liberal Party presidential nomination and likely winner in elections due in May, was shot dead while addressing a crowd in Soacha, on the outskirts of Bogotá. The assassination took place in front of television cameras and in spite of the presence of Galán's 22 bodyguards. All evidence indicates that the killing was ordered by some of the country's most powerful traffickers in cocaine, the Medellín cartel.

The cartel had already killed a justice minister (Rodrigo Lara Bonilla); the editor of the leading daily, *El Espectador* (Guillermo Cano); an attorney general (Carlos Mauro Hoyos); and the leader of the Left opposition movement, Unión Patriótica (Jaime Pardo Leal). Dozens of judges, magistrates, policemen, soldiers and other members of the establishment had also been murdered to persuade the government to abandon its efforts to prosecute the drug lords. Colombian journalist Antonio Caballero calls this the "commercial war," waged by the cartel to protect its business interests.[1]

There is another war, with a great many more victims —in this case mostly from the lower echelons of Colombian society: the "political war" or the "dirty war." In it the cartel does not stand alone, but is allied with businessmen, landowners and members of the armed forces. Since 1986, this war has taken the lives of 8,000 peasants, workers, opposition politicians and left-wing activists.[2]

Among the victims was Daniel Espitia, the national treasurer of the peasant movement (ANUC), who was shot dead by paid assassins on August 9 of last year. He was an organizer in the city of Montería in Córdoba, where 20,000 refugees from political killings and army bombings of peasant villages live in miserable shanty towns. His brother had been killed in 1988 along with 15 others including several children; his father was assassinated early last year, and his wife had left him because she could no longer stand the fear in which they lived.

The world's press often describes Colombia as the most democratic country in Latin America, due to its regular elections and stable two-party system. Political violence is thus presented as senseless acts carried out by evil men—paramilitary groups, drug traffickers and guerrillas—with the armed forces and police only incidentally involved. In reality, Colombia lives under an anachronistic political order which defends an extreme concentration of wealth and power.[3] Political violence is better understood as the result of the elite's desire to preserve its privileges.

During the 1970s, Colombia's poor and excluded formed massive and combative movements, which soon overflowed the rigid boundaries of the political system. Entire towns went on strike to protest the lack of basic services. Peasants invaded lands and labor organized in factories and on plantations. A new generation of guerrilla armies emerged and found increasing support. By the mid-1980s these movements were challenging the hegemony of the traditional parties.

The "political war" was launched to crush these efforts to organize for change. In the 1950s Colombia's ruling class led its people into one of the bloodiest civil wars of the twentieth century, La Violencia, in which as many as 350,000 died.[4] Three decades later that class is unleashing a wave of right-wing terror against people who demand their rights.

Violence is not the route preferred by all of the ruling elite. Modernizing politicians, President Virgilio Barco among them, have sought a way out of the crisis by opening the system up to some democratic participation, strengthening the state, and making it capable of relieving some of the greatest suffering of the poor. The national political class, however, is weak and divided, and the fear of losing power and privilege has kept reforms at an eternal impasse in Congress. Lacking a consensus for either reform or repression, the state has abandoned the fight to local elites—including cattle ranchers, businessmen and regional political bosses, in alliance with army officers and drug traffickers—who have opted for "private justice" as their best bet to maintain the status quo.

The private and violent settling of accounts for political purposes is not new in Colombia. Landowners and political bosses made use of both the paid assassin, the *pájaro*, and private paramilitary armies during La Violencia. But the amount of money cocaine generated turned the *pájaro* into the *sicario*, a well-equipped and well-trained professional. In 1973, with 19.8 murders for every 100,000 inhabitants, Colombia was one of the most violent countries in the world—compared, for instance, to Thailand (15.6), Mexico (13), United States (9.7) or France (0.8). By 1978, the figure was 27 per 100,000. But with the cocaine boom of the 1980s, the homicide rate zoomed to 70 per 100,000 in 1988.[5]

From *NACLA Report on the Americas*, Vol. XXIII, No. 6, April 1990, pp. 13–21, 38–39. NACLA, North American Congress on Latin America, Inc., 475 Riverside Drive, Suite 454, New York, NY 10115.

3. STABILITY, CRISIS, AND REVOLUTION: Latin America

Today's political violence overwhelmingly affects the poor. Peasants make up the majority of the victims who could be identified, with 840 in 1988. In some places militant labor suffers most. During 1988 and the first two months of 1989, over 230 union leaders and activists were victims of politically motivated killings.[6] Eleven trade unionists at the Nare Cement works in the Magdalena Medio region were killed, including the union's president, vice-president and treasurer; others fled the region. In 1989 African palm workers in the departments of César, Santander and Norte de Santander protested the murders of ten of their members. Ninety-nine members of the teachers union have been killed over the past three years, and death threats forced nearly a thousand to leave their jobs and homes. In January 1989 the oil workers union broke off contract talks with the state company fearing for the lives of its negotiators.

Paramilitary forces also target priests and members of religious communities who work with the poor. On January 17, 1988, Father Jaime Restrepo López, parish priest of San José del Nus in the department of Antioquia, was shot dead as he prepared to say mass. On June 1, 1989, Father Sergio Restrepo, Jesuit priest of Tierralta in the department of Córdoba, who had been working with the Sinú Indian community, was shot dead near his church.

In the departments of Meta and Antioquia, attacks have been particularly systematic against left-wing politicians of the Unión Patriótica (UP) movement. In these and other regions the UP has lost over a thousand people since 1985; two other left-wing groups, A Luchar and the Frente Popular have lost 100 and 50 activists respectively. "These are neither errors, acts of vengeance, nor irra-

tional acts on the part of some madmen who joined forces to slaughter Colombians hither and yon," said a former attorney general, Dr. Horacio Serpa Uribe. "These events bear all the characteristics of political crimes, committed to punish those belonging to certain parties or adhering to certain ideologies, or to intimidate entire communities, to maintain a certain economic status quo or to prevent the rise of certain forms of popular expression."[7]

COLOMBIAN NOBEL LAUREATE GABRIEL García Márquez scoffs at his country's democracy. "We are acting, thinking, conceiving...not a real country, but one of paper," he said last year. "The Constitution, the laws...everything in Colombia is magnificent, everything on paper. It has no connection with reality."[8] The paper Colombia is constitutional and legalistic, boasting all the trappings of a modern polity. But there is also a "real" Colombia where the rule of law barely holds, deprivation and poverty are the norm, and democracy is just a word on a historic document.

For many years loyalty to the two traditional political parties, Conservative and Liberal, was the link between the two worlds, sealed through generations of bloody vendettas in which people fought and died on behalf of one or the other faction of the ruling oligarchy. This culminated in the late 1940s and 1950s in La Violencia. The political order forged then remains the basis of the Colombian system to this day. Social and economic reality, however, has changed profoundly. Between 1964 and 1985 the rural population grew less than 10%, while the urban population more than doubled to 19 million, out

Cali squatters show the remains of their homes after police eviction: Lack of housing and services has spawned massive and combative "civic movements"

Joe Fish/Impact Visuals

of a total of 29 million. Despite steady economic growth, the rise in urban population was not accompanied by matching increases in employment opportunities, or the provision of fundamental services or housing.

The Colombia of macro-economic statistics is a success story. It avoided the sudden swings from radical populist to radical monetarist policies which have characterized many Latin American economies. And unlike most of its neighbors, Colombia paid its debts and sustained steady growth even through the regional depression of the 1980s. But the very nature of economic modernization and growth sowed the seeds of political rebellion.

In the countryside, rapacious cattle ranchers forced thousands of peasants off their lands. These peasants poured into urban slums or colonized the forests and lowland plains. In both cases they were virtually abandoned without credit or infrastructure. In the towns and cities, where there were only 500,000 manufacturing jobs in 1985, illegal activities flourished and the informal sector grew to provide over half of all employment.[9]

Unlike the economy, the political order based on oligarchic power and family patrimonies failed to modernize. It remained closed, unable to offer channels for demands to be heard or reforms that might meet the aspirations of the country's poor majority.[10] It depended, as it always had, on capturing the vote of a population essentially excluded from any genuine participation or influence in political life.

The 1958 National Front pact, by which the two parties agreed to govern in coalition and alternate in the presidency for the next 16 years, ended La Violencia by offering guarantees of patronage and power to both parties. The selection of the president and other high officials came to be achieved through delicate secret negotiations among a few party leaders, within each party, and, finally, between parties. The same political families, fathers and sons, who had dominated the country's political history remained in power.

While party rivalry diminished, political battles continued—not over policy but over access to government resources. The business associations (*gremios*) maintained direct contact with the top levels of government to ensure that the economy served the interests of those who owned it. The people remained at the margins of political life, to be manipulated as "electoral capital" by party bosses and their henchmen. Although the pact lasted formally only until 1974, power-sharing arrangements have continued.[11]

This situation was hardly conducive to the emergence of a participatory political culture, let alone a sense of loyalty to the polity as such. The two parties quickly suppressed any attempt by a politician to make a direct appeal to the people. They controlled all the major means of communication, and the economics of electoral campaigns made it difficult for opposition parties to compete. The growth of third forces, such as the Revolutionary Liberal Movement (MRL) in the early 1960s and the National Popular Alliance (ANAPO) in the middle of that decade, was dealt with by co-option or fraud.[12]

The decline of party struggle also meant the gradual decline of party loyalties, the heart of Colombia's social fabric. In the countryside, the *caciques*—often natural leaders with personal influence over servile peasant communities—traditionally could be counted on to bring

In the shadow of the other coca: squatters in Bogotá

out the vote. Colombia's shift to a predominantly urban society brought with it a new form of clientelism (the trading of favors in return for political loyalty) which fed on the deprivation, unemployment and powerlessness of the urban poor. Those with power acted as brokers between the population and the source of benefits and services, exchanging these for the only leverage available to the poor, their vote. The personal loyalties of the past became pragmatic loyalties. The parties lost their mystique but retained their influence through material favors. The professional politician replaced the old-style political boss with his "natural" claim to leadership.[13]

While *caciquismo* and clientelism sustained local party control in many areas, particularly in the countryside, fewer and fewer people actually voted. The 1986 presidential election, held during a period of intense political debate and following improvements in the registration process, attracted just over 50% of the potential vote. Of the six presidential elections since 1966, only three attracted more than half the registered electorate, and only two brought out more than half the eligible electorate.[14]

With high levels of abstention, the bosses had to mobilize fewer votes to secure a victory, removing the incentive to develop strong party institutions or accommodate opposition interests. Though it faced a growing social catastrophe in the burgeoning cities, local government actually did less and less. So little got done at the local level that people had no choice but to seek solutions outside the system.

EFFORTS TO BUILD AN EFFECTIVE INDEPENDent grassroots movement in the 1970s faced many difficulties. The traditional party machines intervened to manipulate and divide. Elitism and sectarianism characterized the Left, replicating much of the paternalism of traditional patronage politics. However, the movement grew across the country and across the political spectrum. Indians demanded territorial and cultural rights in the South, banana workers waged a bloody battle for basic union recognition in the North, peasants fought for land and squatters for basic services in the East, and Blacks organized for the first time in Colombia's most backward department of Chocó in the West. In the smaller towns multi-class civic protests over lack of services became widespread, while in the larger cities labor sought to break free from the shackles of traditional party control.

The peasant movement, led by the National Peasant Association (ANUC), was at the forefront of people's struggles in the first half of the 1970s. After abandoning state sponsorship, it grew into the most militant popular organization in the country's history, only to face gradual defeat, division and demoralization after 1974. The community-based urban civic movements then took the lead with numerous strikes, culminating in the successful national civic strike of 1977. Meanwhile, urban labor also became more militant, with public-sector workers leading the strike activity of the late 1970s.

Between 1979 and 1981, President Julio César Turbay Ayala sponsored repressive legislation to restrict popular mobilization. This prompted the movements to seek national coordination and to create expressly political vehicles for challenging the hermetic political and social order. The indigenous movement set up the National Organization of Indigenous People of Colombia (ONIC). The trade unions and civic movement moved toward unity, and those factions of ANUC which refused to capitulate to the government began rebuilding.

At the same time, repression drove others closer to the various guerrilla organizations, which showed some capacity to defend the movements under fire. Colombia has a long history of armed struggle, but only since the 1960s have independent guerrilla movements begun to pose an alternative structure of power. At least one guerrilla movement, the Revolutionary Armed Forces of Colombia (FARC), emerged directly out of peasants' experiences in certain regions during La Violencia. A handful of today's commanders were legendary guerrilla-bandits during La Violencia.

But the new movements were primarily children of their times. In the wake of the Cuban Revolution, a student leader, Antonio Larrota, organized the Workers, Students and Peasants Movement (MOEC). He was killed in 1961 while trying to establish a guerrilla center (*foco*) in the north of the Cauca Valley. A few years later Tulio Bayer, of MOEC, and Rosendo Colmenares, a veteran of the Liberal guerrilla experience of the 1950s, were killed leading a similar attempt in Vichada in the eastern plains. By 1964, MOEC had collapsed into factions.

Fabio Vásquez and a small group of mostly student activists, strongly influenced by Cuba and MOEC, set up the Army of National Liberation (ELN) in 1964, after receiving basic military training in Havana. Their first *foco* was near San Vicente de Chucurí in the south of Santander, a region with a tradition of struggle, having housed the *Comunero* revolt in 1781, as well as the peasant leagues of the 1920s and Rafael Rangel's Liberal guerrillas in the 1950s. Latin America's first guerrilla

THE MEDIA: A FAMILY AFFAIR

POLITICS IN COLOMBIA IS VERY MUCH A FAMily business. Journalist and writer Apolinar Díaz Callejo described it as "hereditary power without monarchy." This is nowhere more evident than in ownership of the media.

The major dailies, *El Tiempo* and *El Espectador*, belong to different factions of the Liberal party. *El Tiempo*, the more conservative of the two, is owned by a great Liberal political family, the Santos. The present editor, Hernando Santos, boasted of the election of Virgilio Barco: "We didn't make the new president, but *El Tiempo* certainly was an important factor in getting him nominated. At first we were virtually the only ones fighting for him."

La República (Conservative) is owned by the family of former President Mariano Ospina Pérez. *El Siglo* (Conservative) is controlled by the infamous political family of Alvaro Gómez Hurtado. *Nueva Frontera* (Liberal) is edited by former President Carlos Lleras Restrepo, *Guión* (Conservative) by former President Misael Pastrana Borrero, *La Prensa* (Conservative) by Pastrana Borrero's son, and the weekly *Semana* by the son of Liberal ex-President Alfonso López Michelsen.

Incredibly, all the major television news programs are run by the children of former presidents:
—"Noticiero de la 7" by Felipe López Caballero, son of López Michelsen, grandson of ex-President López Pumarejo;
—"Noticiero 24" by Mauricio Gómez, son of Alvaro Gómez Hurtado, and grandson of Conservative Party godfather Laureano Gómez;
—"Noticiero Crypton" by Diana Turbay Quintero, daughter of ex-President Turbay Ayala;
—"Noticiero TV Hoy" by Andrés Pastrana, son of ex-President Misael Pastrana Borrero; and
—"Telenoticiero de Mediodía" by María de Rosario de Ortiz Santos, from the Santos family of *El Tiempo* and ex-President Eduardo Santos. **JPS**

priest, Camilo Torres, joined them the following year, only to be killed four months later.

The Popular Liberation Army (EPL), formally founded in 1967, is the armed wing of the Chinese-line Marxist-Leninist Communist Party (PCC-ML). The PCC-ML broke away from the Moscow-line Communist Party (PCC) in 1965 as a result of the Sino-Soviet split, and began working among the peasants of Alto Sinú in Córdoba and the Bajo Cauca, a region in which the Liberal guerrilla Julio Guerra had influence.

By the mid-1970s these movements were in deep crisis and faced virtual defeat. They had failed to win broad support and were hard put to battle the large and well-equipped Colombian army. Only the FARC, with its very particular origins and character, survived the 1970s with most of its original objectives intact. But in the meantime, a second generation of guerrilla movements had begun to form: Most importantly, some former members of the FARC joined with a sector of ANAPO in 1973, to found the April 19th Movement, M-19.

M-19, a radical, nationalist and palpably Colombian phenomenon, attracted a broader base of sympathy and support than any previous group, particularly from urban middle-class youth. In 1973, 60% of Colombians were living in urban areas and M-19 was the first guerrilla group to acknowledge this demographic shift. Their urban work gave new impetus to the armed struggle, a

THE MILITARY MIND

General Rafael Peña Ríos retired from active military service at the end of 1987 at the age of 49. He had been fighting guerrillas since he was sixteen. He graduated first of 800 officers in the Chief of Staff's course at Fort Leavenworth, and was commander of the XII Brigade in Caquetá. In March 1988 he gave his first interview to Plinio Apuleyo Mendoza of El Tiempo, *from which this is drawn.*

Are we at war, General?

We are at war. Just as they created two Vietnams, two Koreas, there could be a Colombia divided into two.

What is happening? Why isn't there an effective military response to armed insurrection?

In order to develop, the *guerrilla* needs three supports: one political, another social and the third economic. At this moment it has all of them. The political support it was lacking, it obtained through the peace agreements. Movements arose which weren't aiming to integrate the guerrillas into legal activity, but were simply their political projection, not explicit but camouflaged. Each guerrilla organization has its political movement, broad in some cases, narrow in others.

Don't you think that the political groups are one thing and the guerrillas another? The confusion of these two is dangerous. The linking of the UP and the FARC has produced many assassinations.

The violence of the so-called paramilitary groups comes from the transparent relationship between political groups and guerrilla groups. It wouldn't have arisen if from the beginning in the agreements the former were made responsible for what the latter did.

Some years back, General, the army had more initiative, it confronted the guerrillas, it defeated them, it recovered stolen arms. Nothing of that is seen today.

The army lost its capacity for combat, because it was taken away. It was taken away at the very moment when military justice was deprived of its function of judging public order crimes...at the moment army commanders began to face charges, when their hands were tied. The army lost the protection of the state....The basic problem is that the army is not being used as a military force. It is being used as a preventive force, as a civic force. Not even as a police force, because the police have more powers. A simple interrogation carried out by a military authority has no legal validity. It is not, as it should be, a force of repression.

Repression is a taboo word...

The function of the army with respect to subversion is repression. But today you can't shoot before you're shot at. The Statute for Defense of Democracy was left with no backbone when the Supreme Court annulled the right of the armed forces to carry out searches....We are not asking for a licence to kill. But just to arrest, search, keep a detainee for eight or ten days and carry out an interrogation...

Don't you believe in a political solution to the problem of subversion?

I don't. The aim of these groups is subversive, that is the seizure of power by arms to change a system and a society. It is not insurgency, it is subversion....Insurgency corresponds to political, economic and social problems. When those problems disappear, so does insurgency. If new political spaces and reforms are open, insurgency loses its reason for being. Subversion, no. It accepts dialogue for purely tactical reasons, to strengthen itself, but it never abandons its objectives....Here, there are politicians who say that we must enter into dialogue with the guerrillas. They are people who already accept defeat and who want to win their [the guerrillas'] favor or that of political groups in certain regions for electoral interests or for protection.

How to defend the country better, General?

We must recognize that there are insufficient troops to protect the thousand municipalities. Besides, civil support to the police is not allowed as it is not legal. That would create armed self-defense or paramilitary groups, it is thought. We are at war, that is forgotten...

And how do you defeat the guerrillas militarily? Is it possible within the institutional framework of a democratic system, without recourse to a dictatorship, which the democrats, the immense majority of the country, all reject?

It is possible. But the nation has to make the firm decision to confront subversion as an adversary, an enemy. It must be defeated. And in this struggle, all institutions must take part; the Supreme Court must take into account the reason of state, the fact of a country in danger, and not abstract legal considerations. If there is will on the part of the government, will from the parties, will from the court and the judiciary, will from parliament, the armed forces will have the will to fight and win....They don't have it now for lack of support. Many officers say, Why should we get ourselves killed for those who judge us without taking into account that we contribute our dead?

General, the country is aware of that. But it won't accept the dirty war. It doesn't want torture, disappearances. The complicity of the army in these activities has been condemned. For a democrat, that is to be rejected.

That dirty war exists, but the army is not linked to it. It is caused by private initiatives, due to the absence and weakness of the state and also to the pain caused by the subversive groups. An energetic state would make the dirty war unnecessary.

What do you call an energetic state?

A state which gives us the instruments to act. It must create legislation which supports our operations. It must create legislation which protects the army's witnesses. Which makes it possible to take special measures, to restrict freedom at a given moment. I am not speaking of arbitrariness nor of despotism, but rather of the institutional framework adequate for a war situation.

If this doesn't happen what will?

A very serious power vacuum. Nothing will remain as an alternative, neither one of the parties, nor the church, nor, as people have come to think, the armed forces. Only subversion. It is the only organized force with a vision.　§

struggle which the repressive tactics of the government of the late 1970s fueled rather than checked.

Other new guerrilla movements appeared in the 1970s and 1980s: Workers Self-Defense (ADO), the indigenous group Quintín Lame in Cauca, MIR-Patria Libre and the Workers' Revolutionary Party (PRT). From the ashes of the old EPL and ELN, movements emerged which threw off their Chinese or Cuban ideological straitjackets and sought to root themselves more firmly in Colombian reality. During these years, economic developments in the countryside, particularly in regions of colonization or expanding commercial agriculture, encouraged peasants to turn to an option—guerrilla warfare—that offered defense against landowners, and a political project in which they figured as actors and subjects.

THE RESURGENCE OF GUERRILLA MOVEments coincided with a deepening crisis in the traditional political parties. Despite a growing awareness during the 1970s that "something was wrong," the political class was slow to recognize the need for reform. Fierce debates over how to bring about political reform have been a common feature of Colombian politics since 1973, but few reforms have ever made the statute book. Politicians find it easier to use the party machines than to challenge them. And repression, the elite was to discover, can buy as much time, if not more, as reform.

The 1978 election, with its poor turnout, represented a low point for the political system. The new president, Turbay Ayala, had engaged in all sorts of political machinations and the election took place amid accusations of fraud and drug-financed campaigns. People were taking their opposition into the streets for want of any other political channel. Social unrest had grown under Turbay's predecessor and the national civic strike of 1977 led to calls from the army for strong state action. Turbay responded with a draconian security statute.

Since 1947, Colombia has lived almost permanently under state of siege. A series of decrees gradually increased the armed forces' control over affairs of public order, and diminished the ability of civilian authorities to protect the public against abuse. Turbay expanded both the army's power to arrest and the kinds of crimes tried by military court. Peasant and labor organizers and suspected guerrillas were arrested; many were tortured.

Antagonism to Turbay's sleazy practices and repressive policies eventually split the Liberals. In 1980 Sen. Luis Carlos Galán led an anti-corruption faction out of the party to found Nuevo Liberalismo. Even with the barriers to third party candidates, he managed to win 10.9% of the vote in the 1982 elections against the official Liberal candidate, former President Alfonso López Michelsen.

The anti-Turbay backlash certainly contributed to the victory in that election of Conservative candidate Belisario Betancur. He succeeded by appealing beyond the party machinery to the people, particularly the urban middle class. He spoke of reform, and was viewed as making a serious effort to deal with the violence—not just political violence, but also criminal violence, which had reached epidemic proportions in the cities by the early 1980s.

Betancur launched an audacious initiative for negotiating peace with the guerrillas, and dedicated himself to the Contadora Group working for peace in Central America. He paid less attention to political reforms at home and had no substantial economic and social program with which to back up his peace initiatives. He faced strong opposition from within his own party; and, while a few selected Liberals participated in his government, the rest opposed him from their congressional majority and blocked any significant reform.[15] The paramilitary Right, meanwhile, drowned his peace initiative in blood by stepping up the dirty war against guerrilla sympathizers.

BY 1986, COLOMBIA'S POPULAR MOVEMENTS had reached a new stage, qualitatively and quantitatively. A more educated population was less willing to be

manipulated. No longer would they put up with conditions tolerated at the beginning of the 1960s. People were organizing around their real needs and sought no mediation from the parties.

These movements brought people into political life in an unprecedented way, forcing both the orthodox and revolutionary Left to question the elitism of the past and show greater respect for popular organizations and their autonomy. In 1986 the country's first independent labor confederation, the United Confederation of Workers (CUT), was formed, with the majority of the country's trade unions affiliated.

Perhaps more significant were the newer "civic" movements, which brought people together on the basis of interests shared by a local community, sector or region—such as the lack of water, sewers or other municipal services—rather than the traditional class-based trade unionism. These movements view the fundamental contradiction in society less as that between capital and wage labor (which has won some privileges) than between capital and the excluded (unemployed, underemployed, street vendors, etc.) who are denied the means to a livelihood. Not concerned with the seizure of state power, these movements attempt to build alternatives from below, independent not only of the traditional parties, but also of the orthodoxies of the Marxist Left and the various strategies of armed struggle. But with hardly any time to consolidate, these young and fragile movements soon found themselves working in semi-clandestinity and subjected to systematic violent repression.

While the worst of the 1970s sectarianism had diminished, the Left remained locked in debate over whether the popular movements should seek reforms through existing institutions, or a radical transformation of Colombian society as a whole. The Left made two attempts to work within the electoral system during the Betancur administration. Most important was the Unión Patriótica (UP), a coalition of the Communist Party and several small left parties, founded in 1985 by the FARC guerrillas as a result of peace accords signed with Betancur. The effort was principally intended to be a vehicle for the guerrillas to enter the political arena. Making use of the PCC political machinery, the UP successfully established itself as the country's third political force and main opposition party.

The second attempt was the Frente Popular (FP), which the PCC-ML set up in an effort to widen its political influence. Like the UP, the FP was meant to provide a way for broad sectors, rather than just the parties' own members, to participate. In the 1986 presidential election the UP won 4.5% of the vote, the largest in the history of the Left, and 14 UP candidates were elected to Congress. The "dirty war" was immediately stepped up, and UP and FP politicians began to be murdered en masse by right-wing death squads. The FARC hastily returned to armed struggle.

Those who opposed electoral politics and the peace plan gathered together in another movement, A Luchar, in 1984. These included a number of independent workers' collectives, some factory-based groups, the Movement for Bread and Liberty (MPL), the Trotskyist Socialist Workers Party (PST)—part of which later withdrew—and the Revolutionary Socialist Party (PSR). A Luchar's combative politics (the name means "to struggle") won it influence in the peasant and, to a lesser extent, the workers movement. Many of A Luchar's members had strong sympathies for the ELN guerrillas, but no formal organic ties exist. The organization grew rapidly, mainly because many people on the Left distrusted Betancur's peace plan and feared that raising false expectations would damage the movement as a whole.

The three political organizations, UP, FP, and A Luchar, had very different ideas about how to work with grassroots movements. In joining forces to support the third national civic strike of 1985, for example, FP and UP sought to call for greater democracy and the fulfillment of the peace agreements; A Luchar wanted to protest the government's demagogic behavior on the peace issue. They nonetheless cooperated over minimal common demands: respect for human rights, dismantling the paramilitary groups, the defense of national sovereignty.[16] Each had lost hundreds of lives and endured considerable repression in exchange for a tiny opening in the political system. The traditional elite seemed unlikely to allow more than a minimal participation of opposition forces.

THOUGH THE 1985 STORMING OF THE PALace of Justice and the subsequent massacre severely weakened the M-19, guerrilla activity as a whole escalated in the mid-1980s.[17] The ELN in particular, which had not entered into Betancur's "national dialogue," grew considerably. No reliable information exists on exactly how many guerrillas there are, though some suggest a figure of around 12,000. By 1987 they were operating in 339 of the country's 1,009 municipalities, a considerable geographical area, covering all the departments except Guajira, Chocó, Nariño and the *comisarias* of Amazonas and Vaupés. No longer confined to isolated marginal regions, they had grown strong in areas of strategic economic importance, such as the Magdalena Medio and Urabá. They were weakest, however, in the urban areas, particularly the large cities.[18]

Each movement had a regional base. The FARC, with nearly 50 fronts, covered the largest area, and was strongest in places of peasant colonization—the eastern plains, the Magdalena Medio, the Alto Magdalena and in some parts of the South and East. The ELN was strongest in the Northeast, particularly Arauca, along the frontier with Venezuela and in the east of Antioquia. The EPL was strongest in Urabá, Córdoba and Antioquia, and had a small operational base in Norte de Santander and Putumayo. M-19's operational base was in the Southeast, in Valle, Cauca and Tolima.

Despite serious strategic differences, six guerrilla organizations took the first remarkable step towards coordinating their activities in 1985, which culminated in October 1987 with the formation of the Simón Bolívar Guerrilla Coordinating Body (CGSB), made up of ELN, M-19, Quintín Lame, FARC and the Revolutionary Workers Party (PRT). Among these groups, FARC and ELN stood at opposite ends of the tactical and strategic spectrum. FARC viewed its military prowess as the bargaining power necessary to force an opening in the political system, and as a defense against the armed forces, landowners and drug traffickers. Though increasingly at odds with its civilian allies, the UP and PCC, it endorsed their efforts to broaden support and further test the electoral waters.

ELN, on the other hand, clearly sought to seize power.[19] The group won support and made large sums of money by kidnapping oil executives and forcing their companies to

---

SMALL-TOWN LIFE IN THE MAGDALENA MEDIO

THE PEOPLE HAD NEVER SEEN THEM LIKE THAT. With their heads shaved and their faces painted black, the soldiers began to come out of the Luciano D'Luyer barracks in San Vicente de Chucurí at 6 p.m. on February 5, 1989. During the past week, when the army was patrolling the streets and people were forced to hide in their homes, slogans were painted on walls and notes were put under doors. They announced the imminent "cleansing" of San Vicente of the guerrillas and their collaborators, and were signed by the paramilitary command, "Colonel Rogelio Correa Campos."

That Sunday evening, the mayor and town councilors went to the battalion commander to ask for an explanation. "The army has more than ten uniforms; that is one and they are entitled to go out into the streets like that," the commander told them. As night fell, the sounds of machine-gun fire, bombs and grenades filled the town. One grenade exploded in a house, killing a four-year-old boy instantly and wounding his grandmother and mother. An elderly nun saw a bullet hit her bedroom. The next day, the civil authorities again asked the commander for explanations. "In the evening, a group of guerrillas tried to take the town, the soldiers went out and followed them and there was a confrontation," he answered.

On March 16, community organizations, the town council and the mayor sponsored a Forum for Life and Democracy in order to discuss with regional and national authorities measures to bring peace to the region. Only a few regional politicians showed up; national and departmental authorities refused. After the forum, military operations in the neighboring villages intensified. According to the president of the municipal council, Adolfo Muñoz, peasants talked of nearly 40 dead and many wounded who could not be brought to the towns because the army stopped them. More than 500 families fled.

Curiously, say council representatives, people are being forced out from the most productive lands, which are then being repopulated with people close to the paramilitary. The area is rich in farmland and pasture, oil, gas and coal. San Vicente is the third most important municipality in the department of Santander, with 85,000 inhabitants, of which 45,000 live in the urban area. It was the zone which mobilized most people during the regional civic strike in 1987 and the peasant marches of May 1988. During the October 27, 1988 national civic strike residents paralyzed the town for eight hours.

Military attacks have sparked town officials to unite irrespective of party in a Common Front for Life and Democracy, as agreed at the March 16 forum. After that event, Rafael Gómez, commander of the D'Luyer battalion, wrote the mayor asking for tapes of the speeches and a list of participants. He hadn't attended himself, "because I knew that there would only be attacks on the army." §

Source: *Colombia Hoy*, March and April 1989.

---

invest in health, education, water and sewerage in the areas in which it operates. But its primary activity today is blowing up oil pipelines, a tactic which engendered intense debate on the Left. The campaign was launched at the end of 1986 under the slogan "Awake Colombia...

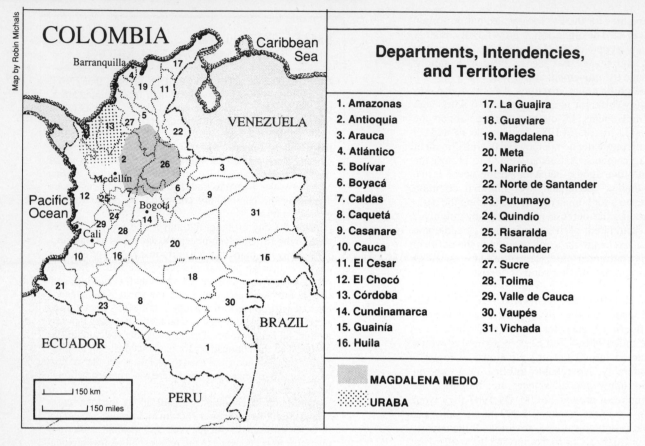

Map by Robin Michals

COLOMBIA

Departments, Intendencies, and Territories

1. Amazonas	17. La Guajira
2. Antioquia	18. Guaviare
3. Arauca	19. Magdalena
4. Atlántico	20. Meta
5. Bolívar	21. Nariño
6. Boyacá	22. Norte de Santander
7. Caldas	23. Putumayo
8. Caquetá	24. Quindío
9. Casanare	25. Risaralda
10. Cauca	26. Santander
11. El Cesar	27. Sucre
12. El Chocó	28. Tolima
13. Córdoba	29. Valle de Cauca
14. Cundinamarca	30. Vaupés
15. Guainía	31. Vichada
16. Huila	

MAGDALENA MEDIO

URABA

they are stealing the oil." It has cost the government millions in lost revenues and, between early 1988 and mid-1989 alone, nearly $400 million in damage to pipelines. By 1989, the ELN had generated a considerable level of debate about national energy policy.[20]

As popular support for Colombia's guerrilla movements began to build, the "dirty war" moved to close it off. (The war affected primarily sympathizers and innocents, not combatants.) Incorporating the large numbers of civilians under threat into the guerrilla movements was impossible. And guerrilla weakness in urban areas meant that revolution—and an end to the war—was not on the horizon. The guerrillas had to decide how to use their armed strength. Should they, as the ELN wished, deepen the revolutionary process through a prolonged popular war? Or, as the EPL insisted, find political openings by uniting all forces against "fascism"? Or, as the FARC and M-19 argued from their different perspectives, win reforms and the right to participate in the electoral process?

References

The People's War

1. *El Espectador* (Bogotá), Oct. 1, 1989. According to Hernando Gómez Buendía, director of the Institute of Liberal Studies, between 1979 and 1989, seven magistrates, 41 judges and over 200 investigators and auxiliaries were killed by the drug mafia. *Economía Colombiana* (Bogotá), Oct/Nov 1989.

2. Monitoring of the press by the human rights office of the Jesuit research body CINEP, as well as the Church's Justicia y Paz, came up with a figure of 8,150, which includes "social clean-up" (*limpieza social*) murders of homosexuals, criminals, and prostitutes, as well as killings that are known to be political. It does not include murders whose motive is unknown, of which there were 2,729 during 1989, up to Nov. 15.

3. It is often noted that Colombia has a relatively large middle class, but official income distribution figures show that the middle 30% receives only 28% of total income. Given the average per capita income of $1,372, the "middle class" is more likely made up of those who have access to some form of wage employment, rather than well-paid professionals.

4. La Violencia began as a final attempt by the ruling Conservative Party to crush the Liberal Party by outright massacre. The Liberals responded with guerrilla warfare and massacres of their own. It is usually dated from the 1948 assassination of populist Liberal leader Jorge Eliécer Gaitán. The signing of the National Front pact by the two parties in 1957 brought it formally to a close, although related banditry and violence continued until 1965.

5. 1973 figures come from a Departamento Administrativo Nacional de Estadística (DANE) study quoted in Alvaro Avila Bernal, *Corrupción y expoliación en América Latina* (Bogotá: Grijalbo, 1987), p. 150. 1978 and 1988 statistics are calculated from DANE figures reported in Latin American Newsletters *Andean Report*, July 27, 1989. One study found that in Cali the number of murders with firearms grew from 51% of all murders in 1980 to 85% in 1986, and in Medellín from 40% in 1979 to 76% in 1985. Gonzalo Sánchez et al, *Colombia: Violencia y Democracia* (Bogotá: Universidad Nacional de Colombia, Colciencias, 1988).

6. *Colombia Hoy* (Bogotá), No. 65, Feb. 1989, p. 9 and 11; *Cien Días* (Bogotá), March 1989, p.10; Amnesty International, *Colombia Human Rights Developments—"Death Squads" on the Defensive?*, (London, Sept. 1989).

7. *El Tiempo* (Bogotá), Aug. 6, 1988.

8. *Semana*, March 20, 1989.

9. Alvaro Reyes Posada, "Tendencias del empleo y la distribución del ingreso," in José Antonio Ocampo and Manuel Ramírez (eds.), *El problema laboral colombiano: informes de la Misión Chenery*, (Bogotá: Contraloría General de la República, 1987). Other peasants, drawn by rumors of riches, headed for the gold-producing areas of northeast Antioquia and the emerald mines of

eastern Boyacá, each of which became notorious centers of violent conflict.

10. One example of the failure of reform attempts is agrarian reform. From 1961 to 1985 the agrarian reform institute INCORA bought up 472,470 hectares and expropriated 66,035 more. This land was distributed to 30,000 families. An additional 350,000 hectares were "ceded" to INCORA, but that was mostly barren land. INCORA also distributed just under five million hectares of public lands, mostly in colonization areas where lack of infrastructure and credit, and constant harassment by cattle ranchers have forced peasants into bankruptcy or coca farming. Julio César Quintero Latorre, ¿Qué pasó con la Tierra Prometida? (Bogotá: CINEP, 1988), pp. 39-44.

11. Neither of the traditional parties would accept a government-opposition formula, which would relegate its influence to Congress. Colombia was governed by de facto coalition rule in one way or another until 1986 when, for the first time since bipartisan government was developed, Virgilio Barco's Liberal administration ruled without the participation of the Conservatives. The perception that a party could only survive if it had access to government coffers is deeply rooted in the political culture. A sample of private-sector, government and party leaders in 1977 and 1978 showed that two-thirds were unequivocal on this issue. One Liberal politician claimed that opposition movements or party factions could survive only four to five years without access to state resources and bureaucratic posts. (Jonathan Hartlyn, *The Politics of Coalition Rule in Colombia* (Cambridge: Cambridge University Press, 1988).

12. MRL was set up by Alfonso López Michelson as a Liberal Party faction in opposition to the National Front pact. After a strong showing in the 1960 legislative elections and the symbolic 1962 presidential vote—in which the Conservatives were guaranteed victory by pact—the government offered it access to high office in return for rejoining the Liberal mainstream. ANAPO led Gen. Rojas Pinilla's (president 1953-57) efforts to make a political comeback in the 1966 elections, and presented the National Front with its first major challenge. Rojas won 38.7% of the vote on April 19 of that year (to Pastrana's 40.3%) but is widely believed to have been deprived of victory by fraud. ANAPO activists went on to co-found the M-19 guerrilla movement, named after the date of the alleged fraud.

13. For people at the local level, government came to be personified in the professional political fixer. University professor Eduardo Díaz Uribe described the role: "From the installation of electricity, the construction of a bridge, a school or of a health post, to the most everyday things such as medical attention, a job, agricultural credit etc. [all] are considered the product of his action or of his benevolence, they are his works. 'Look at this health center. The Guerras put it there'....'The light in this district was given by Martínez Simahán'....'The sewerage system was put in by Dajer.'" Eduardo Díaz Uribe, *El clientelismo en Colombia* (Bogotá: El Ancora, 1986), p. 46.

14. Elections to the legislature attracted even lower turnouts, an average of 40.3% from 1958 to 1978, with only 33.4% voting in 1978. Abstentions in the big cities were notorious; in the 1976 legislative elections in Bogotá, 80% did not vote. A study of municipal elections (undertaken in 1986) concluded that since 1981, 88% of municipalities have given a majority to the same political party. [Patricia Pinzón, *La oposición política en Colombia: aproximación*

al itinerario de las fórmulas (Bogotá: FESCOL, 1986), p. 9.] Pinzón also found that in 1984, 35% of the municipalities were still giving 80% majorities to one party. In only one-third of the municipalities was there anything resembling genuine competition. Abstentions were high even before the National Front, and the Front's first presidential election attracted nearly 58% of the registered electorate. The 1970 election, with ANAPO in the ascendent, brought a much larger turnout (52.5%) than the 40.1% in 1966. The first competitive presidential election in 1974 brought a 58.1% turnout. But in 1978 only 40.9% voted.

15. Though it had taken years to get through Congress, a constitutional amendment allowing the direct election of mayors was finally approved in December 1985. Other reforms dealt with some overt abuses of the bipartisan system, for instance one member from a third party was to be allowed to join three members of the traditional parties on a new National Electoral Council. But other reforms, including attempts to limit and account for campaign funds and to give minority parties more access to legislative posts, failed to get through Congress, and the two parties failed to agree on how to end Article 120 which perpetuated their coalition rule.

16. In September 1988 the three announced their intention to join forces in a political front (Frente Político de Convergencia), but it had great difficulty getting off the ground. The UP saw it as broadly based and encompassing both the Left and other progressive forces; similarly, the FP saw it as generally anti-imperialist and anti-fascist; but A Luchar saw it solely as a front of the Left.

17. About 40 M-19 guerrillas stormed the Palace of Justice on November 6, 1985, and took over 100 people hostage, including the entire Supreme Court. Within an hour the building was surrounded by troops and tanks. The 28-hour army siege that followed left the building gutted and 95 dead, including all the guerrillas and 12 Supreme Court justices. No negotiations were attempted.

18. Alejandro Reyes Posada and Ana María Bejarano, "Conflictos agrarios y luchas armadas en la Colombia contemporánea: una visión geográfica," *Análisis Político* (Bogotá), No. 5, Sept./Dec. 1988. By 1986, the urban cells of M-19, the only group to mount significant urban operations, had been all but wiped out. In March of this year, M-19 signed a peace accord with President Barco. Their rural forces handed over their weapons in return for guarantees that they could safely participate in electoral politics. They ran candidates in the March elections.

19. The ELN's growth between 1986 and the end of 1988 (which it estimated at 500%) was rapid. [Marta Harnecker, *Reportajes sobre Colombia: entrevista a dirigentes de la UCELN* (Quito: Quimera, 1988) p. 87.] In June 1987 it merged with the MIR-Patria Libre (a split from the PCC-ML) and was subsequently known as the Unión Camilista-ELN (UCELN). In 1987 it held its first national assembly which elected the national leadership.

20. Among the guerrillas' demands have been the resignation of the minister responsible for oil and of the president of ECOPETROL, the nationalization of the Caño Limón oil field, an end to contracts with foreign companies and a nationwide forum to discuss oil policy. In November 1989 the government did agree to an energy forum in which the ELN could make its case. The minister of mines did resign, and the ELN stopped blowing up the pipeline. For the first time, the national press began to debate the energy issue, the role of the multinationals and the nature of the contracts signed with them.

South Africa on the Move

"Whether South Africa's transition will lead, with a minimum of violence, to a multiparty nonracial democracy is unclear. At least that future appears possible. But the legacy of apartheid, the scars of violence and the polarization of society have left their mark."

PAULINE H. BAKER

Senior Associate, Carnegie Endowment for International Peace
Pauline H. Baker is the author of *The United States and South Africa: The Reagan Years* (New York: Ford Foundation–Foreign Policy Association, 1989).

JUST as 1989 was a watershed year for East Europe, 1990 is a historic turning point for South Africa. The year marked a new international environment, a new regional situation and, most dramatically, a new initiative by South Africa's President Frederik W. de Klerk to break the country's racial impasse. From revolutionary upheaval and economic decline in the 1980's, South Africa seems poised—albeit delicately—on a threshold of change that will result in a totally different political dynamic in the 1990's.

"The old South Africa is burdened by inheritances from many sources of the past which are really blocks around our neck," said de Klerk. "We're getting rid of those blocks. . . . That is why things are so dynamic in South Africa."[1] De Klerk's remarks were made in a televised interview with ABC correspondent Ted Koppel, after the February 11 release of Nelson Mandela, the country's most respected black nationalist, who spent 27 years in prison.

The interview itself was an extraordinary event. Having been all but excluded because of tight censorship imposed during the four-year state of emergency, the international media flooded the country with a press corps of 2,000 to cover the Mandela story. All the major American television networks broadcast Mandela's historic walk to freedom, live from South Africa. Virtually overnight, the world's major pariah state was catapulted into the international spotlight, this time inspiring hope rather than despair.

By releasing Mandela from prison, de Klerk began to release whites from their self-inflicted international isolation. He first took some small steps to test the political waters. Within the first 100 days of taking office, he released eight political prisoners of Mandela's generation, seven of whom were leaders of the African National Congress (ANC) and one who belonged to the breakaway Pan-Africanist Congress (PAC), an organization that is more sus-picious of the role of whites and of negotiations. He also permitted mass demonstrations to celebrate the freedom of these leaders; he desegregated beaches; and he designated four undeveloped areas as mixed residential zones.

However, the most important action taken by the South African President to pave the way for Mandela's release was the dismantling of the state security management system. In effect, this was a secret parallel government built up by then-President P.W. Botha as part of the counterrevolutionary strategy the government adopted to confront black unrest. Hundreds of committees blanketed the country, from the State Security Council at the top to provincial and municipal councils at the bottom.

Dominated by the security and intelligence forces, this apparatus of control had multiple functions, including citizen surveillance, welfare distribution and the counter-organization of the black population to create an alternative leadership willing to cooperate with the state. With this machinery, the government grew more repressive than it had been in any other period in the country's history. Within the last five years, 5,000 people died because of political unrest and more than 30,000 were jailed without charge.

In addition, de Klerk shifted decision-making control back into civilian hands by cutting in half the two-year compulsory military service for whites, reducing the military budget, ending cross-border raids against neighboring states, and suspending military assistance to rebel groups in Mozambique and Angola. These measures reduced the power of the "securocrats," the political class of military, police and intelligence chiefs who, together with an inner circle of ministers and functionaries, were in charge of crushing the revolutionary uprising of 1984–1987.

These actions went a long way toward demilitarizing society, but the threat of right-wing violence and conservative opposition remains. Many white security officers, especially in the police, are supporters of the Conservative party (CP), the official parliamentary opposition that captured 30 percent of the white electorate, or approximately 680,000 votes, in the September, 1989, election. The CP accuses de Klerk of treason and vows to rally 1 million whites in a campaign to stop him.

In addition, neo-Nazi groups, like the Afrikaner Weerstandsbeweging (AWB), the Afrikaner Resistance Movement, represent dangerous pockets of opposition. The AWB has a paramilitary wing, a youth brigade modeled on the German SS (Nazi elite police) and a fiery leader, Eugene Terre Blanche, a former police officer and an admirer of Adolf Hitler. Formed in 1973, the AWB has been shaken by recent scandals and infighting, spawning a splintering of the far right into a cluster of organizations that insist on a hard-line apartheid ideology. Another, possibly more serious, concern is the existence of extremists within the security forces. The army and the police have been implicated in charges of "death squads" that engage in political assassinations, prompting de Klerk to establish a special judicial commission to investigate the allegations.

Notwithstanding the intransigence of the right, de Klerk probably won more white support than he lost when he crossed the proverbial Rubicon. Clearly, he picked up supporters of the Democratic party, a newly formed alliance of liberal whites that captured over 20 percent of the electorate in the last election by campaigning on a one-person, one-vote platform. In fact, although most whites are anxious about the future, they were relieved at de Klerk's actions. Students and the business community welcomed the breakthrough, openly demonstrating their support and placing advertisements in newspapers to greet Mandela. (Only a few years ago, the chief executive of Barclays National Bank was publicly castigated by President Botha and subjected to a judicial inquiry for financing a newspaper advertisement that called for the very steps de Klerk is taking.)

On the day he was freed, thousands of ordinary whites lined the streets to cheer Mandela as he made his way to Cape Town, displaying an outpouring of emotion and support that amazed the black hero. Actually, many whites—perhaps even the majority — have been ahead of the government in wanting genuine reforms. De Klerk's actions thus represent a shrewd political calculation. He has shed the far right and has consolidated his political power among the rest of the white population, reducing the decade-long erosion of support in the ruling National party's electoral base.

The most dramatic political move de Klerk made before Mandela's historic walk to freedom, however, was taken on February 2, exactly one year to the day after the resignation of President Botha as head of the National party. In a speech at the opening of Parliament in Cape Town, de Klerk announced the legalization of the ANC and the PAC, both of which had been banned for 30 years, and the South African Communist party (SACP), which had been banned for 40 years. Restrictions were also ended on 33 other anti-apartheid organizations operating within South Africa. In addition, de Klerk announced the release of many political prisoners, a selective relaxation of media censorship, the intended repeal of the Separate Amenities Act (which segregates public facilities) and the suspension of executions until new regulations make the death penalty more difficult to impose. Eight days later, the state President revealed at a news conference that Mandela would be released from prison unconditionally.

Although it was anticipated for months, Mandela's release rejuvenated the country's black population more than the legalization of the ANC and other proscribed organizations a week earlier. Mandela had achieved a stature of Olympian proportions. His calm self-confidence, regal bearing and principled defiance symbolized the irrepressible resistance of black people. His remarks during his first days of freedom were directed not to the world community, but to his people, his party and his country. Mandela restated his loyalty to the ANC, reiterated his belief in the philosophy of non-racialism, and reassured whites that he was sensitive to their concerns. He called de Klerk a "man of integrity." But he affirmed his intention to use all means possible, including the "armed struggle," to pursue full political rights for blacks.

THE REACTION

Despite the euphoria of the moment, the hard reality was that apartheid remained in force, negotiations seemed a long way off and contentious issues were left unresolved. De Klerk reserved powers that ensured he would remain in control, triggering objections from the ANC. The ANC insisted on freedom for all political prisoners, including hundreds whom de Klerk refused to release because they had been convicted of violent crimes. The ANC also called for an end to the state of emergency, which permitted troops to remain in the black townships and gave the police extraordinary powers to contain dissent. And the ANC wanted to obtain guarantees of immunity from arrest for returning exiles, including members of the ANC's military wing. Despite these stumbling blocks, the ANC national executive committee decided at a meeting on February 16 at its exile headquarters in Lusaka, Zambia, to resume activities openly inside South Africa and to prepare for direct contacts with the government.

The international community applauded de Klerk for his bold decisions and praised the ANC for its willingness to respond to the challenge.

United States President George Bush invited de Klerk and Mandela separately to the White House. British Prime Minister Margaret Thatcher, an ardent opponent of sanctions, defied her European Community partners and unilaterally lifted the British voluntary ban on new investments. And foreign investors rushed to purchase South African stocks with renewed optimism about the future.[2]

In the week following the legalization of anti-apartheid organizations, $400 million in new funds poured into the country. In the first two months of the year, in fact, foreign reserves increased by $1 billion, a tantalizing foretaste of the payoffs that could come from a comprehensive political settlement. The market dipped after Mandela endorsed the nationalization of key sectors of the economy, but the rapid response of the private sector to fast-breaking developments and the generally positive reaction of foreign leaders buoyed hopes in spite of this volatility. "It is likely that every hiccup in talks between the ANC and Pretoria could move the market quickly in one direction or another," noted *The New York Times*.[3] But a director of one of South Africa's brokerage houses calmly observed that "everyone here thinks [Mandela] is doing no more than staking out his position from where he will negotiate."[4]

As difficult as it was for Pretoria and the ANC to have come this far, the hard part had only just begun. The government's initiative and the ANC's response were decisions made by caucuses within each political grouping. Apart from Mandela's contacts with the government during his internment, no negotiations had taken place, no elections had been held and no legislation had been enacted to institutionalize the process. The curtain is therefore going up on a new type of engagement that will pit two old antagonists in a wholly untested political arena. The ruling Nationalist party will be moving out of power while the ANC and other extraparliamentary groups, power brokers and anti-apartheid allies will be moving in.

The negotiations, if and when they take place, will be burdened by a deep legacy of distrust, divided constituencies, and a complex political tapestry that includes dedicated ideologues and militant rivals standing in the wings who claim to be the true torchbearers of African and Afrikaner nationalisms. For that reason, the process must be as inclusive and democratic as possible from the outset. As Thabo Mbeki, ANC secretary for international affairs, warned, "it must be stated plainly that no South African can now be certain that negotiations, once they start, will succeed."[5]

THE INTERNATIONAL ENVIRONMENT

The changes that took place in South Africa oc-

curred against a backdrop of a radically changing world order. Mandela walked out of prison at the moment when the Communist party of the Soviet Union was deciding to permit a multiparty system and ownership of private property, steps that repudiated not only former Soviet leader Joseph Stalin, but Karl Marx and V.I. Lenin as well. Mandela went into jail at the height of the cold war; he came out as it was drawing to a close.

The ANC had been witness to decades of sweeping global changes, none of which had previously had much impact on the struggle inside South Africa. Formed in 1912, before other nationalist movements emerged in sub-Saharan Africa, the ANC saw the rise and fall of communism, the consolidation and collapse of colonialism, the success of the American civil rights movement, and the march to majority rule and independence of the rest of the African continent, including—in 1990—neighboring Namibia, Africa's last colony.

At the same time, South Africa is no longer the white citadel it used to be. Its military forces, though still strong, discovered in the 1980's that there were limits to its ability to achieve its objectives in the region and to suppress internal black dissent. The South African economy is dependent on international trade and foreign capital as never before. Sophisticated communications have undermined the work of censors, exposing whites and blacks to ideas that can no longer be kept out. And internal demographic and political trends are breaking down white enclaves of privilege. The walls of apartheid have been crumbling under the cumulative weight of these trends just as the walls of communism have been crumbling under similar pressures in East Europe.

Among the most interesting examples of the effect of world developments on South Africa are developments in the Eastern bloc. The rapid pace of change there has set new international standards for democratization, heightening pressures on Pretoria for black enfranchisement. The spectacle of popular masses overthrowing tyrannies once thought impregnable has encouraged Pretoria's leaders to get ahead of the trend.

But developments in East Europe and the Soviet Union have also eased the transition because of the diminished threat of communism. Moscow's policy change in southern Africa, which began to be evident some years ago, dismayed Pretoria at first, but was eventually taken seriously. The Soviet Union downplayed the "armed struggle," put aside the goal of socialism, cautioned its allies not to meddle with the productive sectors of the economy and advised blacks to take account of white fears. These shifts suggested to Pretoria that the military capabilities of the ANC were being weakened as the Soviet Union fostered a political settlement. It "created a scenario," said de Klerk, "where the Communist threat . . . lost its sting."[6]

Joe Slovo, the leader of the South African Communist party, revealed how the ripples of Soviet "new thinking" had reached the distant shores of Africa, affecting anti-apartheid forces as well. Slovo questioned the wisdom of nationalization, pointing out that state domination of the economy is a feature of apartheid. And he rejected the one-party state as incompatible with democracy. "We have to face up to our failure in East Europe," he said. "We have to recognize that those were popular revolts against unpopular regimes. It's no good complaining that this was some kind of capitalist conspiracy. We did it all on our own."[7]

There have been more subtle, but no less significant, shifts in the West, particularly in the United States. Washington not only distanced itself from Pretoria as a result of a bitter national debate over President Ronald Reagan's policy toward South Africa, but Congress took tangible steps to encourage the end of apartheid. In 1986, sanctions became the law of the land in the country recognized as the leader of the free world.

Wanting to avoid confrontation with Congress over this issue, the administration of President George Bush has been sensitive to public sentiment. The administration appears to be more willing than the Reagan administration to cultivate sustained and high-level contacts with anti-apartheid leaders, both through its embassies in the region and in Washington, D.C. One of President Bush's first moves was to invite Albertina Sisulu (the wife of Mandela's colleague Walter Sisulu), a widely respected anti-apartheid voice who was banned at the time, to the White House.

The administration is also more balanced in its assessment of the impact of sanctions, despite the President's personal lack of enthusiasm for these measures. Assistant Secretary of State for African Affairs Herman J. Cohen noted that sanctions have had an effect on white South African thinking. He and other members of the administration have consulted on Capital Hill with leading sanctions supporters, including members of the Black Caucus. By nurturing a bipartisan consensus, the administration has thus far been able to maintain some influence on the situation, including credibility with blacks and a working relationship with whites in South Africa.

The most concrete result of its efforts was an agreement between the Executive Branch and Congress in 1989 to delay pressing for more sanctions for a period of six to nine months to "give de Klerk a chance." If that consensus is sustained, the United States could facilitate negotiations. A tilt in the other direction that would lift sanctions prematurely, however, could divide American opinion, squander American leverage and paralyze Washington in a pointless debate.

The conciliatory approach adopted by the Bush administration is based on a recognition that South Africa has become a domestic political issue. No other major Western ally has a grass-roots constituency of comparable weight, one that sees South Africa not in strategic or economic terms, but overwhelmingly as a human rights problem.

As a consequence, George Bush's approach to South Africa has been linked closely to contemporary partisan politics. A decision by the Republican National Committee to try to win more African-American votes in the 1990 election is a key element in this calculation, especially in light of recent gains made by this constituency in local and state politics, notably, the election of Douglas Wilder as governor of Virginia and David N. Dinkins as mayor of New York.

Many southern white congressmen are also in office thanks to African-American votes. The visit of civil rights leader Jesse Jackson to South Africa, which coincided with Mandela's release, was the most recent reminder of this political reality. Among other advantages, the trip provided an opportunity for one of the most celebrated African-American leaders to help shape the American response.

The debate over South Africa has also reached a new audience in the wider American public. Increasingly, analysts have acknowledged that sanctions have helped put the South African economy in a straitjacket of debt, capital outflow and loss of credit that affected white attitudes.

Stephen Lewis, author of *The Economics of Apartheid,* estimated the loss of capital to the South African economy at roughly $2 billion a year. "Economic pressures have played a major role in forcing the South African government to change its policies on a wide range of issues from labor reform to the release of political prisoners," he wrote.[8] William Claiborne, a correspondent for the *Washington Post,* admitted that

> I . . . remained [skeptical] . . . for a good part of my [three-and-a-half-year] tour in South Africa. It seemed to me that punitive economic sanctions might be effective as a threat, but once they were imposed the stiff-necked, self-reliant nature of the Afrikaners who rule this country would come to the surface . . . and [they would] perhaps become even more intractable . . . I was wrong. For all of their faults . . . sanctions were beginning to work, finally.[9]

A new regional calculus also emerged in 1989. The Angolan-Namibian agreement signed in December, 1988, set in motion a process that had multiple repercussions. First, it gave South Africa an internationally recognized role as a peacemaker in the region, despite earlier policies that had contributed to conflict in the area. Second, it helped reduce cold war tensions in Africa. The Soviet Union supported the agreement, which called for the removal of Cuban troops from Angola over a 27-month period. Third, it launched Namibia, a territory that South Africa had controlled since World War I, on the road to democracy, providing a model of peaceful racial reconciliation on South Africa's doorstep.

Lastly, the agreement enabled South Africa to conclude a military retreat from the region without losing face. Although the civil war in Angola raged on with a new intensity and the insurgency in Mozambique was no closer to resolution, South Africa had officially withdrawn from these wars and pledged not to interfere, whatever happened to the Union for the Total Independence of Angola (UNITA) and the Mozambican National Resistance (Renamo), anti-government guerrilla groups that were Pretoria's clients.

Furthermore, while the agreement was being negotiated and implemented, the Angolan and Mozambican governments embarked on economic and political reforms, with the latter—formerly one of Africa's most committed socialist states—rejecting Marxism-Leninism. Even the ANC guerrilla threat was reduced. As part of the accord, military camps that had been located in Angola before the Angolan-Namibian agreement were moved to Tanzania and Uganda. There were now "no immediate prospects of inflicting an all-around military defeat on the enemy," noted the South African Communist party in a document assessing the new strategic situation in the region.[10] However, in August, 1989, the ANC launched a fresh diplomatic offensive with its adoption of the Harare Declaration, which set forth a plan for negotiations. The document was endorsed by the Front-Line States, the Non-Aligned Movement, the Organization of African States and, with some modification, the United Nations General Assembly.

Internal pressures within South Africa also mounted. Having been battered severely by the state of emergency, anti-apartheid forces began a defiance campaign of nonviolent resistance. Detainees arrested under emergency regulations went on a hunger strike, forcing the government to negotiate their release with leaders of the Mass Democratic Movement, as the anti-apartheid forces restyled themselves after their organizations were banned. Some prisoners escaped from custody and took refuge in foreign embassies. Those who were placed under restriction ignored government orders, defying Pretoria to rearrest them in peaceful protests. Sit-ins were organized, political rallies convened, and negotiations with local authorities started to resolve some of the burning issues in the black townships, like housing and education. Blacks were moving—literally—into cities, universities, hospitals, recreational areas and public facilities that had been historically reserved for whites.

Politically, the white community had also reached a moment of truth as the full implications of the results of the 1989 election set in. From that September poll, the Conservative party showed that, while it did not do as well as expected, it was there to stay. The rift in Afrikanerdom could not be healed. The Democratic party, doing better than expected, showed that a new challenge had emerged on the left. Marginal victories by the National party in several close constituencies raised the possibility of a hung Parliament in the next election, due in 1994.

The handwriting was on the wall: either the National party had to make a political breakthrough or it would be caught in a political vise. A party man all his life, de Klerk saw the tides of world opinion, white fragmentation and the resurgence of black resistance playing against the white establishment.

At this juncture, South Africa's future depends on how the two primary actors—the ANC and the National party government—play their cards. The situation has never looked more promising, but it is also highly dangerous. Expectations are running ahead of negotiations; rhetoric is glossing over real political differences; and time is not on anyone's side. The National party must reach a settlement before the next election, when it could be voted out of office. The ANC must move quickly or it may lose ground, not only to the government, but to other political rivals.

South Africa may well enter a period of political realignment that will cut across racial barriers even before a transition to a new government takes place. That would be a hopeful sign, leading to the creation of a new body politic. But before that occurs, Pretoria must shift from unilateral reforms to multilateral negotiations, and the ANC must make the transition from liberation struggle to participatory politics.

If an elected body, a constitutional convention or a constituent assembly, is convened, a national debate could take place that would permit all groups and alliances to test their political strength and their political ideas. Whatever mechanism is used it must be democratic or it could invite outside interference, provoke renewed conflict and lose international credibility.

Whether South Africa's transition will lead, with a minimum of violence, to a multiparty, nonracial democracy is unclear. At least that future appears possible. But the legacy of apartheid, the scars of violence and the polarization of society have left their mark. Without a commitment by all major parties to a common future, South Africa could still plunge into the abyss of race war or the violent throes of partition. The range of alternative outcomes is as broad in South Africa as it is in East Europe, and democracy hangs in the balance.

---

[1]"ABC Nightline," interview with F.W. de Klerk, President of South Africa, February 13, 1990.

[2]*Washington Post,* February 9, 1990; and *The New York Times,* February 6, 1990.

[3]*The New York Times,* February 18, 1990.

[4]Ibid.

[5]*The New York Times,* February 4, 1990.

[6]"ABC Nightline," op. cit.

[7]*Washington Post,* January 21, 1990.

[8]Stephen R. Lewis Jr., *The Economics of Apartheid* (New York and London: Council on Foreign Relations Press, 1989), p. 167. See also *Washington Post,* February 18, 1990.

[9]*Washington Post,* January 14, 1990.

[10]"The Path to Power," as quoted in *The Weekly Mail* (Johannesburg), January 18, 1990, p. 11.

The apocalypse in Ethiopia

Grain burns in a starving nation as another dictator's days dwindle

Gaunt nomads paw through smoldering piles of grain in the bombed-out Red Sea port of Massawa, scuttling to salvage a few sacks of food that are all that remain of 50,000 tons of aid once destined for Ethiopia's war-scarred Eritrea province. These ghosts of the ruins load what they find onto camels for a grim trek into the drought-stricken countryside, where as many as 1.9 million people are starving. Most days, the scavengers must dive for cover amid the charred hulks of Soviet-built T-55 tanks and United Nations relief trucks when Ethiopian jets scream back to drop more bombs and napalm on the port, which was captured by the Eritrean People's Liberation Front (EPLF) last month.

War, famine and superpower competition have tortured northern Ethiopia since the early 1960s. Now, however, a major rebel offensive is closing in on the Marxist regime that President Mengistu Haile Miriam has held together with brutal repression, ideological bombast and $11 billion in Soviet aid. After years of jockeying for influence in Ethiopia, Moscow and Washington now have decided the region is not much of a strategic prize after all. These changes may finally write an end to Africa's longest-running civil war: Eritrea's three-decade struggle for autonomy or independence. But they may come too late to save either those facing starvation in Eritrea or the millions facing famine in Tigré province and elsewhere in the Red Sea hinterland.

Mengistu's position has become increasingly vulnerable since the EPLF overran Massawa in mid-February after one of the fiercest battles in Africa since World War II. Just a few days before the rebel attack, Soviet arms were still flowing through the port to the 120,000-strong Ethiopian Second Revolutionary Army. With that lifeline cut, Mengistu's biggest and best front-line force is cut off and running short of food, fuel and wa-

ter in Asmara, the Eritrean provincial capital, and a nearby garrison town. EPLF forces are already within 30 miles of Asmara; they need to advance only about 12 more miles to bring the city's airport under artillery fire that would smash the Second Army's tenuous air-supply route from Addis Ababa, the national capital.

Mengistu has been in trouble before but survived because of the loyalty of his military, the guile of his East German-staffed intelligence service and the open checkbook of his Kremlin supporters. All three of those props are now missing or seriously weakened. Despite bloody purges of Army officers—including executions carried out personally by Mengistu—the military no longer shares its leader's enthusiasm for continuing the war at any cost. An attempted coup against Mengistu last May failed largely because the plot was discovered in advance by East German security advisers. But those advisers were called home even before East Germany voted out the Communists. Diplomats in Addis Ababa say another major military defeat, such as the fall of Asmara, could trigger a new coup attempt that would have much greater chances of success.

GARY VISGAITIS—*USN&WR*

Public support for Mengistu was revived briefly last fall, when his forces stopped an offensive by another breakaway rebel group, the Tigréan People's Liberation Front (TPLF), within 200 miles of Addis Ababa. But steadily worsening food shortages, relentless poverty and widespread fears about a new round of press-gang conscription of teenagers have soured the mood in the capital. Few people put much stock in Mengistu's March 5 attempt to get in step with *perestroika* by publicly embracing capitalism—tabbed a "deathbed conversion" by one Western diplomat—or his proposal to replace the country's rigid Stalinist system with a mixed economy. "Mengistu has lived his whole life as a thug, a murderer and a Marxist," says a senior U.S. official. "Suddenly he turns capitalist. That's bull."

Where have all the Russians gone? Capitalist or Communist, the Ethiopian dictator now seems to hold little attraction for the Kremlin, which once backed him lavishly. When Eritrean rebels attacked Massawa in 1977 and 1978, Soviet warships shelled the port and saved Mengistu's forces from certain defeat. For years, Moscow automatically replaced tanks, artillery and rifles captured by the EPLF. As recently as last May, Western officials say, there were 5,000 Soviet advisers working with the Ethiopian Army.

All this began to change sometime in 1988 as Mikhail Gorbachev's reformers questioned the value of fighting proxy wars in the Third World and Mengistu's forces looked increasingly incapable of defeating the rebels, no matter how much help they received from Moscow. By early this year, the Soviets had moved from publicly warning Mengistu that his war was unwinnable—widely interpreted as backstage support for negotiated settlements with the rebels—to actually cutting back support for his regime. This time, no Soviet ships arrived to save Massawa. And Moscow reportedly rejected an appeal to use its giant Antonov cargo planes, which are still sitting on the tarmac at Addis Ababa, to supply the besieged Second Army in Asmara.

Then last week the Soviet ambassador in Sudan, which also serves as a staging base for famine-relief operations, announced that all Soviet advisers had been pulled out of Ethiopia's battle zones. The envoy, Valeri Soukhine, told the Reuter news agency that hundreds of advisers had withdrawn to Addis Ababa, where some will continue working while others return home. Soukhine said that even though Moscow might renew an arms-supply agreement that expires this year, "we don't have any counselors or experts or technicians helping to fight or advising" in Ethiopia.

Mengistu is receiving new assistance from Israel, which re-established diplomatic relations with Ethiopia last December as a step toward getting exit visas for some 10,000 Falasha Jews who live

there. Although Israeli officials flatly deny that any lethal aid is included in the aid package, Western diplomats in Addis Ababa report that Israeli advisers and military supplies, including cluster bombs, already are arriving. The EPLF makes similar claims of Israeli involvement. "We know that the Israelis have been supplying bombs for the Ethiopian Air Force and that there has been a resumption of cooperation in areas like intelligence and information," EPLF Secretary General Isais Aferwoki told *U.S. News* last week.

The full impact of the Massawa fighting on famine relief is uncertain but could be devastating. The port would be serviceable within a few days if Mengistu halted the daily bombing by accepting a U.S.-backed EPLF proposal to make it an "open city" for shipping grain to starving civilians on both sides. The chances of that happening appear just as slim as the prospect of concluding other agreements that would let relief convoys across battle

lines before summer rains make roads impassable.

Meanwhile, Ethiopians who know little about politics but much about hunger are beginning to trek long distances across the parched countryside. When Hamid Nur, a 54-year-old peasant, heard a rumor that food salvaged from Massawa would be handed out, he walked 24 hours to get enough grain to keep his family alive for a month.

If hundreds of thousands of people starve, as in 1984-85, it would be a grimly fitting counterpart to a recent discovery on a former Ethiopian Army compound near Massawa: Fifty large ammunition crates stuffed full of human bones. The victims were probably soldiers killed in Mengistu's purges, not in combat. Their burial site—set up almost as a kind of shrine—likely will not be the last such find as Mengistu's bloodstained regime collapses on itself.

by Eric Ransdell in Massawa

CAMBODIA AND
THE INTERNATIONAL COMMUNITY

Stephen J. Solarz

Stephen J. Solarz (D-N.Y.) has served in Congress since 1975, and has been Chairman of the House Subcommittee on Asian and Pacific Affairs since 1981. He has visited Cambodia three times, most recently in March 1989.

The Cambodian endgame has entered a new and critical stage. The regime installed in Phnom Penh by Vietnam eleven years ago—the People's Republic of Kampuchea—continues to hold sway over the major cities and most of the countryside. But with the withdrawal of Vietnamese combat forces in September 1989, its capacity to counter the Khmer Rouge remains in serious doubt, and it is entirely possible that Pol Pot could battle his way back to power in Phnom Penh.[1]

Continued fighting in Cambodia serves the interests of the Khmer Rouge. Sustained by a mixture of intimidation and indoctrination, as well as Chinese support and Thai sanctuary, the Khmer Rouge is once again a fanatical and formidable force. It has given up neither its goal of regaining power by whatever means necessary nor its xenophobic brand of communism. The best way to prevent the Khmer Rouge from returning to power is to shift the conflict from the battlefield to the ballot box.

Clearly, the best outcome for Cambodia would be a comprehensive political settlement that demilitarized the internal struggle, neutralized Cambodia as an arena for superpower and regional rivalry, and gave the Khmer people an opportunity for free and fair elections. In the last three years there has been a variety of efforts to produce such a settlement. All have failed, however, largely because the formulas put forward have been more unacceptable to the parties concerned than a continuation of the conflict itself.

In the absence of a settlement the most that Cambodia can hope for is to become a kind of Southeast Asian Lebanon, condemned to continuous civil strife and economic deprivation. In a worst-case scenario Cambodia could even witness a resumption of the Killing Fields should Pol Pot and the Khmer Rouge return to power.

In response to the diplomatic deadlock and deteriorating military situation, the Australian foreign minister, Gareth Evans, has launched a new initiative designed to end the fighting and give the Cambodian people an opportunity to determine their own destiny. The core of the Australian proposal—that the United Nations assume responsibility for the administration of Cambodia during the interim period between the establishment of a ceasefire and the emergence of a new government following an internationally supervised election—has attracted an unprecedented consensus among the great powers. In view of the difficulties the Cambodians have had in reaching agreement among themselves on almost all issues, the fate of Canberra's initiative will probably be a litmus test for the possibility of any agreement at all. Indeed, it does not seem an exaggeration to suggest that the Australian proposal constitutes the last best hope for a peaceful resolution of the Cambodian conflict. No less certain is the danger the Khmer Rouge poses for Cambodians if negotiations fail.

The chances for a comprehensive political settlement in Cambodia are not high. Yet no one knows whether a mutually acceptable agreement is impossible or merely difficult. In view of the consequences of a continuation of the conflict, it would be a serious political and moral mistake to let the fear of failure preclude the possibility of an overall settlement. Indeed, if the international community neglects the nation's bloody past, defenseless Cambodians may be condemned to repeat it.

II

For the United States, Cambodia is primarily a moral and humanitarian issue. For the countries of Southeast Asia, it is strategically important because of its geographical position as a potential buffer state for both Vietnam and Thailand. Hanoi has traditionally sought to dominate Phnom Penh or at least deny hegemony to Bangkok. Thailand would prefer to keep Cambodia in its sphere of influence or at least out of Vietnam's. Thailand's partners in the Association of Southeast Asian Nations (ASEAN)—Brunei, Indonesia, Malaysia, the Philippines and Singapore—have all sought to keep Vietnam out of Cambodia, both to support Thailand's strategic objective and to reaffirm the principles of nonintervention and self-determination.[2] Cambodia has also been the object of great-power conflicts. Beijing's primary objective has been to have a client in power in Phnom Penh and, failing that, to support resistance to Vietnamese hegemony in Indochina, while Moscow has supported Hanoi as a counterweight to Beijing.

There is, however, a precedent for isolating Cambodia from regional and superpower conflict. Once Cambodia became independent from the French in 1953, its ruler, Prince Norodom Sihanouk, sought to preserve autonomy through a policy of neutrality. For more than a decade he succeeded in steering a course among Thailand, South Vietnam and the United States on the one hand, and North Vietnam and China on the other. With the coming of the Vietnam War, however, super-

Reprinted by permission of Foreign Affairs, Vol. 69, No. 2, Spring 1990, pp. 99–115. Copyright © 1990 by the Council on Foreign Relations, Inc.

power involvement in Southeast Asia intensified and the vise constraining Cambodian independence tightened. The prince had to concede the eastern portion of the country as a logistics base to North Vietnam and turn a blind eye to the massive American bombing campaign that followed.

Compounding the difficulty of Sihanouk's effort to preserve his country's stability and independence was the evolution of the Cambodian Communist Party. The movement was originally led by individuals who traced their ancestry to the anti-French struggle of the Viet Minh. Challenging them was a group of nationalistic intellectuals who regarded Hanoi's guidance of their party as a type of colonialism. The latter group, led by Pol Pot (né Saloth Sar), gained preeminence in 1960. Five years later, when Vietnam and China urged the Cambodian Communist Party to cease its challenge to Sihanouk's regime—as the expedient price of Sihanouk's tolerance of the Vietnamese presence in the eastern part of the country—Pol Pot refused. At the same time, these "Khmers Rouges" supplemented their disdain for the norms of proletarian internationalism with an ultra-radical approach to the revolution within, a metastasis of China's Cultural Revolution. Thus were sown the seeds of auto-genocide.

Beset on all sides, the prince was deposed in 1970 by Lon Nol, whose forces in turn proved unable to stave off the victory of the Khmer Rouge in April 1975. Once in power Pol Pot proceeded to depopulate the cities, slaughter the educated, and impose an unrelenting program of forced-draft economic development. When communism did not materialize overnight, the revolution began to devour itself, with some elements of the party escaping to Vietnam. Thousands of cadres were tortured and murdered in Tuol Sleng, a special concentration camp in Phnom Penh for party members. Close to 30 percent of the population died as a result of Khmer Rouge misrule.

In Southeast Asia, nationalism triumphed over ideology after 1975. The Khmer Rouge xenophobia for the Vietnamese and China's rivalry with Vietnam shattered the facade of Asian communist unity. The split deepened between China (which backed the Khmer Rouge) and the Soviet Union (which increasingly favored Vietnam). In late 1978, Vietnam invaded Cambodia to end the latter's challenges to its territorial integrity.[3] Hanoi quickly took over most of the country and installed the remnants of the pro-Vietnamese wing of the Cambodian communist movement as the People's Republic of Kampuchea.

Vietnam's victory produced a strategic nightmare for both China and Thailand. Beijing faced powerful "barbarians" to both the north and the south, which it renamed "global and regional hegemonists." Bangkok saw its traditional buffer occupied by its historic adversary. Thailand and China then conspired to redress the balance of power by an act of complete moral cynicism—the resurrection of the nearly devastated Khmer Rouge. Pol Pot's forces became the lever for removing Vietnam from Cambodia, or at least a rein to render it incapable of aggression elsewhere.

The United States and the rest of ASEAN went along, sometimes reluctantly, with this strategy. In order to put the best light on it and to provide a counterweight to the Khmer Rouge, two small political groupings—the Khmer People's National Liberation Front and the National Front for an Independent, Neutral, Peaceful and Cooperative Cambodia, led respectively by former Prime Minister Son Sann and Prince Sihanouk—were joined with the Khmer Rouge in 1982 to form a Coalition Government of Democratic Kampuchea. The CGDK was imposed on Sihanouk and Son Sann to prevent the United Nations from substituting the PRK for the Khmer Rouge as the occupant of Cambodia's seat in the United Nations or from declaring the seat vacant. From a Leninist perspective this coalition was a classic united front, in which

communists used "royalists" and "bourgeois nationalists" to promote their interests.[4]

In time Cambodia became Vietnam's Vietnam, an obstacle to Vietnam's economic development and a drain on Soviet-supplied resources. As Moscow's interest in regional conflicts waned under Mikhail Gorbachev's leadership, Hanoi resorted to its own version of "Vietnamization." It made commitments—which few believed at the time—to withdraw its forces by 1990, and worked to build up the PRK regime—now led by Hun Sen, a former Khmer Rouge regimental commander—as an economic, political and military bulwark strong enough to withstand a challenge by the Khmer Rouge. At the same time, Vietnam sought a political settlement in which its adversaries would accept the legitimacy of the PRK. Not until the summer of 1988, however, did the international community take seriously the possibility that Vietnamese forces would indeed withdraw from Cambodia and leave the world to face the problem that remained: an armed and revitalized Khmer Rouge.

III

The tortuous process of finding a negotiated settlement to the Cambodian problem has been long and complex, usually conducted under a glare of publicity, marked first by signs of progress but then followed by bitter reversals. A number of different approaches have been tried, but all the formulas required the verified end of foreign engagement in the military struggle in Cambodia: the total withdrawal of Vietnamese troops, the end of Thai sanctuaries for the Khmer Rouge and the noncommunist resistance (NCR), and the end of external support for the Khmer factions. All envisage some type of election as a necessary act of self-determination by the Cambodian people.

The core disagreement concerns the political arrangement that will exist in Cambodia from the time a settlement is concluded until the emergence of a new, electorally legitimate government. On this question, there have been two basic approaches. The first advocates the creation of a quadripartite interim government in which all four factions, including the Khmer Rouge, share power. The second plan argues for the preservation of the current PRK regime, supplemented by mechanisms that provide some role for all four factions. Neither of these approaches has been acceptable to all the parties concerned.

The quadripartite formula was the proposal of Prince Sihanouk in his capacity as president of the CGDK. It is supported by his coalition partners (Son Sann and the Khmer Rouge), by China and the ASEAN countries, and was generally endorsed by the United States. As originally tabled at the Paris conference in August 1989, it envisaged the simultaneous dissolution of the CGDK and the PRK as legal entities, and the sharing of ministerial power on a four-party basis. The Sihanouk proposal included, under U.N. aegis, an international peacekeeping force and international supervision of elections. The four military forces would be either disbanded or reduced to 10,000 fighters each, pending the creation of new Cambodian armed forces.

The basic PRK proposal, which was also presented at the Paris conference by Prime Minister Hun Sen, called for a ceasefire in place and a continuation of the political status quo—the PRK regime—until general elections. A supreme steering council would be established, composed of representatives of the PRK, the CGDK and a number of unaffiliated Khmers. The supreme steering council, under international supervision, would create an electoral system and conduct elections. An international control mechanism would verify the end of external assistance, but there would be no provision for peacekeeping forces. Nor would this control commission be under U.N. aegis since, in Phnom Penh's view, the United

Nations had shown itself to be biased by passing resolutions hostile to the PRK and by continuing to seat the CGDK. In the hard-line version of the PRK proposal, the Khmer Rouge military and political organizations would be abolished and their leaders punished. In other versions, Khmer Rouge fighters who laid down their arms would be reincorporated into the political life of the country.

Each of these proposals has been consistently rejected. The CGDK has opposed the standard PRK proposal because it would legitimize a regime imposed on the Cambodian people by force of Vietnamese arms. Moreover, the CGDK argues, the PRK's control of the administrative apparatus would virtually guarantee a victory by Hun Sen in any election, thereby depriving the Cambodian people of the opportunity to freely and fairly determine their own destiny and denying the other factions any chance of gaining power.

On the other hand, the PRK has rejected the CGDK proposal, claiming that its effect would be to legitimize the Khmer Rouge and delegitimize the PRK, whose ideological raison d'être has been unyielding opposition to "the Pol Pot clique." Moreover, the PRK believes that a quadripartite approach would give the Khmer Rouge a better opportunity to come to power than it would have in the absence of a political settlement. Hun Sen has expressed the fear that his party, as only one element of a coalition government, would be outvoted by the other three factions. The Khmer Rouge would therefore be able to subvert the government from within while attacking it from without.

Advocates of a quadripartite approach answer Hun Sen's objections by asserting that the Khmer Rouge does not wish to regain exclusive power in Phnom Penh. As evidence they point to the five pledges of Khmer Rouge representatives at the Paris conference:
—support for Sihanouk's leadership;
—support for disarmament of all the factions;
—support for a strong international peacekeeping force under U.N. auspices;
—conditional support for internationally supervised elections and the promise to abide by the outcome;
—willingness not to insist on equal power-sharing in the quadripartite interim authority.

Some argue that the Khmer Rouge pledges should be put to the test. Pinning one's faith in the quadripartite proposal on such promises is a dangerous and perhaps deadly gamble on the goodwill of a movement for which truth—let alone decency—has been a totally alien concept. Moreover, the U.S. government and most independent observers believe that the objective of the Khmer Rouge is to regain its monopoly of power by whatever means necessary. The continued harsh treatment of civilians in refugee camps by the Khmer Rouge belies any claims of a more humane approach. The claim by the Khmer Rouge that Pol Pot has "retired" when, in fact, he continues to dominate and direct the Khmer Rouge is persuasive evidence of its continued passion for prevarication. Finally, its characterization of the auto-genocide as a "mistake" indicates that all it has learned from the past is the need to employ euphemisms to divert international attention from its barbarous record.

IV

Inhibiting the search for a negotiated settlement has been a reluctance on the part of the parties concerned to summon the political will to make the necessary concessions. Hun Sen and his colleagues clearly believe that their survival depends upon isolating the Khmer Rouge as a military and political force. As former Khmer Rouge officials who know first-hand the duplicity and treachery to which Pol Pot will resort to achieve his goals, the PRK leaders wish to minimize the size of the arena in which the Khmer Rouge will be able to operate. They also know the political benefits that will flow to them if they can keep world attention focused on the horrors of Pol Pot's rule and the need to prevent its resurrection in the future.

Hun Sen has therefore insisted on the preservation of the PRK regime. He has been willing to include Sihanouk in a purely symbolic role—reigning but not ruling—because that would legitimate the PRK regime without forcing it to relinquish any power. But he is prepared to go his own way if the prince continues to reject cooperation.

Hun Sen's confidence was buoyed for a while by apparent cracks in the policy consensus in Thailand. Since late 1988, Prime Minister Chatchai Choonhavan has taken a much softer line on Cambodia than his predecessor and the Thai foreign ministry and army. Chatchai appeared willing to recognize the "reality" of the PRK regime once Vietnam withdrew, and favored turning the Indochina battlefield into a marketplace dominated by Bangkok. He toyed with the ideas of denying sanctuary on Thai soil to the three wings of the resistance and of choking off the supply of Chinese military assistance to them—actions that the PRK and Vietnam believe would cause the Khmer Rouge and the NCR to wither on the vine and guarantee Phnom Penh's ability to contain them. Chatchai's initiative took its most visible form in January 1989 when Hun Sen visited Bangkok at the prime minister's invitation. He has subsequently backed away from his proposals because he was unwilling to accept a break with China, which took a dim view of his move toward Hun Sen. Yet as long as the PRK believes that the Chatchai card might be played, and the Khmer Rouge rendered impotent as a result, its incentive for compromise tends to remain low.

Sihanouk's political constraint stems from his dependence on China. Always aware of Chinese influence, the prince in the last decade has had also to rely on Beijing for diplomatic and financial support and for material assistance to the NCR. In exchange for Chinese aid, Sihanouk has given China a veto, in effect, over his negotiating proposals. Although he knows the dangers posed by the Khmer Rouge—many members of the royal family met their end in the Killing Fields—Sihanouk has vigorously advocated a quadripartite interim government. In public defense of that proposal he asserts that it would be easier to "keep an eye on" and control the Khmer Rouge if it were included in an interim regime than if it remained in the jungle. In his franker moments, he admits that his hands are tied with a Chinese knot.

For this reason Sihanouk has been reluctant to consider what would be a morally more acceptable alignment: a tripartite coalition arrangement in which he and Son Sann would join with the PRK against the Khmer Rouge. By joining Hun Sen, Sihanouk would burn his bridges to China without any advance guarantee of a new patron in order to provide the role of front man for the pro-Vietnam wing of the Cambodian communist movement, just as he has in the past given respectability to the Khmer Rouge. In any event, it appears that although Hun Sen has offered Sihanouk the position of chief of state in his regime and posts for some of his followers, he has not proposed a genuine power-sharing arrangement.[5]

In November, in the wake of the failure of the Cambodian factions to resolve their differences at the Paris conference, Australian Foreign Minister Evans proposed establishing a U.N.-supervised interim administration as a way of removing the key obstacle to a political settlement and bringing the conflict to an end. His proposal emphasizes the following elements of a comprehensive settlement:
—a U.N. peacekeeping force that would be responsible for implementing a ceasefire in cantonments, disarming the forces, destroying military stockpiles and monitoring the ceasefire;
—internationally supervised elections to select a constituent assembly;
—an internationally supervised end to external sanctuaries

and external assistance for military purposes to all parties;
—a massive international program of relief, rehabilitation and reconstruction in Cambodia;
—permitting civilians in all camps associated with the resistance factions to have freedom of movement to return to their place of origin or to accompany their faction back into Cambodia.

In order to break the logjam on interim political arrangements, the Evans initiative would have the United Nations play a significant role in governing Cambodia between the time an agreement is reached and the emergence of a new Cambodian government. An enhanced U.N. role that would supervise an interim Cambodian administration creatively circumvents Hun Sen's objection to the inclusion of the Khmer Rouge in a coalition government and the CGDK's objection to recognizing the PRK regime as the basis for a settlement.

The U.N. secretary general, with the agreement of all parties concerned, would appoint a special representative to serve as head of an interim authority. He and the international civil servants he brings with him would supervise the existing bureaucracy, although the depth of U.N. involvement is still a matter for negotiations. The four factions would continue to exist at least as political parties (but not as coalition partners in an interim government). Whether the PRK and the CGDK would cease to exist as legal entities is as yet unresolved.[6]

The initial positive responses from most of the parties, including Vietnam and the PRK, were somewhat encouraging. The main point of contention is how the concept will be fleshed out. China still prefers the quadripartite interim proposal, but if that approach is not acceptable it is prepared to support "in principle" a supervisory role for the United Nations. Only the Khmer Rouge has displayed some public resistance.

More disquieting have been the results of initial soundings concerning the U.N. role in administering Cambodia during the interim period. Understandably, Hun Sen has asked for a minimum of U.N. interference in the running of the country. The Chinese, on the other hand, have argued for a root-and-branch removal of PRK officials. In effect, the disagreement over power-sharing that derailed the 1989 Paris conference has been transposed into the U.N. frame of reference. Yet because the concept of U.N. supervision of the interim administration is designed to circumvent the stalemate over power-sharing, negotiations will run aground unless the four factions and their partners can reach a compromise on this central issue.

The U.N.-based settlement should have a better chance of being accepted than previously rejected proposals because it would give something to everyone and requires capitulation by no one. For the NCR, such an agreement would put an end to the fighting in Cambodia, provide for the presence of an international peacekeeping force and avoid a legitimation of the PRK. It would also give them the opportunity through free and fair elections to shape Cambodia's political future, and thus reduce the political advantage that Hun Sen might otherwise gain from control of the administrative apparatus.

A U.N. agreement on Cambodia would also enable China and the ASEAN countries to verify the Vietnamese withdrawal and deny Hanoi the victory of international acceptance for the PRK regime. China would then be able to tell the Khmer Rouge that it is on a par with the other parties. Furthermore, by facilitating a settlement, Beijing could reduce some of the international notoriety it earned in the Tienanmen massacre.

Although the Khmer Rouge would gain the dissolution of the PRK regime, it is less inclined to go along with a U.N. formula than the other factions because its prospects for seizing power would clearly diminish. Yet Beijing is the key: if China supports the formula, the Khmer Rouge would probably be compelled to go along, given its dependence on China. The prospects for a settlement therefore depend, among other things, on China's willingness and ability to deliver the Khmer Rouge.[7]

For the PRK, it would secure an end to the fighting, a cessation of Chinese support for Pol Pot, the exclusion of the Khmer Rouge from the interim administration, an opportunity to do well in the elections, increased foreign assistance, enhanced international legitimacy, and perhaps a share of the Cambodian seat at the United Nations.

For Vietnam, a U.N. agreement would provide the opportunity for Hanoi's leaders to end their international isolation and provide their protégé, Hun Sen, with the possibility of a significant political role in the new government. An accord would also reduce the chances that Vietnamese troops would have to return to Cambodia to prevent a Khmer Rouge victory.

An agreement would allow the Soviet Union to end its involvement in another regional conflict—certainly more cleanly than was the case in Afghanistan—and gain the benefit of a further reduction in East-West tension. Moreover, a U.N. solution would be consistent with the growing emphasis in Soviet foreign policy on using the United Nations as the mechanism for resolving regional disputes. The United States would also achieve its policy objectives—an act of self-determination for the Cambodian people and some certainty that the Khmer Rouge will not return to power.

Whether the United Nations should shoulder the burden that Foreign Minister Evans has suggested, and whether the governments and taxpayers of wealthy countries are willing to pay the price, reflects the more basic problem of political will. Without a willingness on behalf of all parties to the Cambodian conflict to take risks for the sake of the Khmer people, no settlement will ever be possible. It is the task of diplomacy to determine whether a compromise can be reached, and given the consequences should negotiations fail, it is important to make the effort.

Will the Cambodian factions accept a U.N.-supervised interim administration? If China supports the Evans formula, or does not actively oppose it, Sihanouk will probably jump at the chance to appear more independent.[8] More problematic are the motives of the two communist factions. If neither is truly willing, despite its public statements, to run the risk of a contest for power through internationally supervised elections, then there will never be a political settlement. If Hun Sen in fact is able to contain his adversaries close to the Thai-Cambodian border, then he will probably expect the international community to confer legitimacy on him. If the Khmer Rouge believes that, even without Chinese support, it can seize power through armed struggle at an acceptable cost, it will probably not be willing to subject itself to the popular will.

Between these two scenarios, however, may exist a zone of opportunity in which the risks of a continuing struggle outweigh those of a political settlement that seeks to demilitarize the conflict, particularly if external backers choose to cut their losses. In that zone of opportunity lies the proposal for a U.N.-supervised interim administration. Hun Sen and Pol Pot should be put to the test.

v

During the ten years that Vietnam occupied Cambodia, the United States, haunted by its Indochina nightmare, tended to follow the lead of China and the ASEAN countries. Washington took a back seat in defining the shape of a political settlement, and was reluctant to provide assistance for the noncommunist resistance. When the United States decided to provide aid, it was only of a non-lethal character and was given on the condition that it not enhance, directly or indirectly, the fighting capacity of the Khmer Rouge. There have been U.S. proposals to provide lethal aid for the forces of Sihanouk and

Son Sann, but the requisite political consensus has been lacking and no such aid has been provided.[9]

Although Washington had no role in developing Sihanouk's quadripartite formula, the United States became associated with it. At the same time, the Bush administration was unable to dispel the serious concerns that such an agreement would provide Pol Pot with his best chance of returning to power, and that Sihanouk appeared to be acting less and less as a symbol of Cambodian nationalism and more and more like a front man for China and the Khmer Rouge. Whether these concerns were well founded or not, their existence made it difficult to build a broad and sustainable consensus for U.S. policy.

The current U.S. objectives in Cambodia are to secure a verified withdrawal of Vietnamese forces, bring an end to the fighting, prevent the Khmer Rouge from returning to power, and encourage Cambodian self-determination. In pursuit of those goals and in the wake of the positive response to Foreign Minister Evans' initiative regarding interim political arrangements, the United States has undertaken to build consensus among the permanent members of the Security Council on all the elements of a U.N.-based comprehensive settlement. The first stage of this process occurred in mid-January 1990 in Paris, when officials at the level of assistant secretary exchanged views on a peacekeeping force, elections, costs and so on. The result was a "summary of conclusions" that expressed agreement on "an enhanced U.N. role in the resolution of the Cambodian problem," and consensus on most of the elements of a settlement.

On the critical point of a U.N.-supervised interim administration not even a vague public agreement was achieved, but that is not surprising given the preliminary stage of the discussions. Presumably, U.S. officials will attempt to forge consensus around some variant of the Evans initiative, in part because they know that it is probably the only idea left for cutting the Gordian knot of power-sharing.

In addition to playing the important role of building a great-power agreement, Washington should also undertake several bilateral initiatives. It should urge Moscow to cease military aid to the Hun Sen regime, and encourage Bangkok to inhibit Khmer Rouge activities and secure greater freedom for the civilians under Khmer Rouge control. To make the proposal as attractive as possible to Vietnam, the United States should be prepared to offer full normalization of relations, including the establishment of a diplomatic mission in Hanoi, and the elimination of the embargo on trade and investment. Given Vietnam's economic crisis and Hanoi's desire to break out of its isolation, a U.S. offer to open a new chapter in the relations between the two countries should be a powerful incentive for Vietnam to cooperate in the search for a Cambodian settlement.[10]

Because China has been the sole supporter of the Khmer Rouge, and because the Khmer Rouge will probably not agree to a reasonable settlement without Chinese pressure, Washington should:

—inform Beijing of the importance it attaches to China's role in this issue;
—explicitly reject the quadripartite formula, which the United States previously had quietly endorsed and which China continues to support, in order to make clear to Beijing that there can be no fallback from the U.N. formula;
—call on Beijing to immediately end its support for the Khmer Rouge;
—promise an improvement in U.S.-China relations if Beijing gets the Khmer Rouge to agree to a settlement.

Securing genuine Chinese endorsement of a U.N.-based settlement for Cambodia would be one way for the administration to prove that the dispatch to China of National Security Adviser Brent Scowcroft and Undersecretary of State Lawrence Eagleburger in July and December 1989 was justified.

The Chinese have indicated that they do not want the Khmer Rouge to return to exclusive power, and that if Pol Pot rejected a reasonable settlement, China would end its assistance to the Khmer Rouge. If Khmer Rouge intransigence results in a breakdown of negotiations, therefore, it will still result in a cutting of the Chinese lifeline, the probable emergence of a coalition of Cambodian factions opposed to Pol Pot, and the end of Thai sanctuary for the Khmer Rouge, thus greatly reducing the threat it poses. At best, the U.N. approach will produce a negotiated settlement that puts the Khmer Rouge in a political box. At a minimum, it could serve to place the Khmer Rouge in isolation—which is precisely where it belongs.

Others have argued that because a settlement is highly unlikely, the United States should recognize the PRK regime as the strongest bulwark against the Khmer Rouge and even provide it with assistance. If a political settlement on any terms is impossible, the international community may confront a choice between supporting the PRK or watching the Khmer Rouge return to power. Indeed, if the Evans-U.N. formula fails, Western governments such as Britain and France may well be forced to yield to the pressure of anti-Khmer Rouge public opinion and begin opening embassies in Phnom Penh. They will surely be unwilling to continue voting at the United Nations to give the Cambodian seat to the Khmer Rouge and its noncommunist partners in the CGDK.

Choosing between the PRK and the Khmer Rouge would present the United States with a Hobson's choice. Support for the Khmer Rouge would be, of course, utterly unthinkable. Yet backing Hun Sen is hardly an enticing proposition. In the first place, the PRK may prove to be quite weak, even with U.S. support, when confronted by the full force of the Khmer Rouge. If the United States were to provide support to the PRK regime—whether political or military as well—it would probably not make much difference in stopping the Khmer Rouge.[11]

In any case, building political support for U.S. recognition of the PRK, even on anti-Khmer Rouge grounds, would not be easy. Hun Sen's party remains a Leninist party both organizationally and ideologically. The PRK's leaders are tainted, moreover, by a sordid past. Most of the members of the PRK politburo are former Khmer Rouge who were part of the killing machine established by Pol Pot. They defected to Vietnam not for reasons of principle but because they were about to be devoured themselves. Having ridden into Phnom Penh on Vietnamese tanks, they then engaged in human rights abuses that, according to Amnesty International, included the execution, incarceration and torture of thousands.

It is doubtful, therefore, that either the Bush administration or Congress would be willing to materially support the Hun Sen regime—even though, should the Australian initiative fail, U.S. support for the PRK would clearly be the lesser of two evils.

The only way to avoid the difficult choice between the Khmer Rouge and PRK and the best way to achieve U.S. objectives—the most important of which is to prevent the Khmer Rouge from returning to power—is to secure a sound political settlement in Cambodia. If Washington were to recognize the regime in Phnom Penh before the search for a political settlement was exhausted, Hun Sen would inevitably conclude that time was on his side and he would undoubtedly be less willing to make the kind of concessions necessary for an agreement. Furthermore, siding now with the PRK, thereby greatly reducing the prospects for a comprehensive settlement, would rule out the other major objectives of American policy—true independence for Cambodia and self-determination of the Cambodian people.

Prior to the Vietnamese invasion of Cambodia in December 1978, no country lifted a finger to stop the slaughter by the Khmer Rouge of innocent people. While a powerful moral argument might be made for an international police action to prevent a Khmer Rouge return to power again, the prospects for such an initiative in 1990 are as slim as they were in 1975. Regrettably, there are limits to what people of goodwill can do to stop inhumanity and injustice.

Yet the impossibility of stopping some abuses in the past is no justification for doing nothing when new disasters loom in the future. If the international community truly believes that humane treatment of the defenseless is a norm that should be applied wherever possible, it must act now and to the utter limits of its capacity to block a new round of genocide in Cambodia. Even if chronic civil war is the ultimate outcome in that country, it is not an acceptable one as long as a satisfactory political settlement remains possible. Cambodians have suffered too long because of the moral cynicism of others. We degrade our own values if we unnecessarily permit them to suffer any longer.

---

[1] In late February, news reports indicated that Vietnam sent elite combat units back into Cambodia at the end of October 1989. This both restores the Vietnamese presence to the agenda of issues to be addressed in a political settlement and indicates the fragility of the PRK hold on the country.

[2] This pattern began in the fifteenth century, with the Vietnamese and Thai courts trying to control Cambodia or at least bar the other's influence. The most common scenario before the arrival of French colonialism was for factions in the Khmer court to seek the aid of Hanoi or Bangkok, each of which was all too willing to use the conflict to wrest control of zones of Cambodian territory and otherwise protect their interests.

[3] In a conversation in 1981, Foreign Minister Nguyen Co Thach told me that Vietnam's motivation for intervening was not to protect the human rights of the Cambodian people,

which Hanoi regarded as Cambodia's internal affair, but to bring an end to a series of destructive cross-border raids by the Khmer Rouge. He said nothing about Vietnam's historical ambition to establish an Indochinese federation under its control, which presumably was one of Hanoi's motives as well.

[4] This was not the first time that Prince Sihanouk entered into an alliance with the Khmer Rouge. After his fall in 1970, he lent support to Pol Pot's cause. Khmer Rouge cadres carried his picture as a kind of revolutionary icon. Far more than the American bombing, the willingness of Prince Sihanouk to let the Khmer Rouge recruit and mobilize in his name was a key factor in its ultimate triumph. It was a mistake of disastrous proportions for which the prince has never forgiven himself.

[5] Sihanouk's objections aside, a tripartite arrangement has other problems. It would neither stop the fighting nor guarantee an end to Chinese assistance. Furthermore, any type of international presence under United Nations auspices would be impossible, since the United Nations only enters situations where all parties agree, and China would certainly veto a U.N. role under such an agreement.

[6] Cambodia's seat at the United Nations, now under the exclusive control of the CGDK, would either be declared vacant or filled in a way acceptable to each of the factions, thereby giving Hun Sen, who has criticized the United Nations for being biased in the past, some assurance that it would be more objective in the future.

[7] Some have objected to the Australian initiative because it would give the Khmer Rouge the right to participate in elections. Yet if there is to be a settlement that ends the fighting and permits an act of self-determination by the Cambodian people, the Khmer Rouge leaders will have to be included as participants, albeit in a way that reduces the risks that they could undermine the settlement. If they cannot even participate in the elections—which they are sure to lose—they and their Chinese patrons will never agree to a settlement in the first place and the fighting will continue.

[8] Prince Sihanouk's latest resignation, in January 1990, appears designed to distance himself from the Khmer Rouge now that a political settlement seems to be in the cards. Realistically speaking, however, he will probably preserve the possibility of a return to the Chinese-Khmer Rouge fold in case the U.N. formula does not result in a settlement, particularly if Beijing is the only certain source of weapons for his troops.

[9] Although it is conceivable that minimal amounts of assistance intended for the NCR have ended up in Khmer Rouge hands, such "leakage" is insignificant, since the total amount of aid reaching the NCR is a fraction of what the Khmer Rouge receives from China.

[10] It would be a mistake to establish diplomatic relations and lift the embargo before the outcome of this round of negotiations is clear. If we were to do so, it would significantly diminish Hanoi's incentive to exercise leverage on Hun Sen in order to facilitate a settlement. Once a settlement is achieved, we should move swiftly to normalize relations between the United States and Vietnam.

[11] The failure of the Lon Nol regime to defeat the Khmer Rouge after receiving over $1 billion in U.S. military aid from 1970 to 1975 suggests that American backing alone hardly constitutes an adequate basis for preventing the return of the Khmer Rouge. Then, as now, Pol Pot's opponents did not lack for military equipment. Now, as then, the deficiency lies in the areas of leadership, morale, training and so on.

PASSAGE TO POWER

*The world's most populous democracy is quietly emerging
as a leading industrial, military, and agricultural force.
Why do homelessness and starvation persist?*

Brahma Chellaney

*Brahma Chellaney is a widely experienced Indian
journalist and columnist who writes for Indian
Express and Nucleonics Week. He has been doing
research in the US at the Kennedy School at Harvard University and the Brookings Institution in
Washington.*

ATYEN G. PITRODA IS NO POLITICIAN. But today he wields more power and influence than most of India's federal ministers. In less than five years the 46-year-old industrialist, formerly based in Chicago, has established himself as the symbol of India's technological revolution.

Popularly known as "Sam" Pitroda, he is a scientist, a technocrat, and a policymaker. But, most important, he is India's telecommunications czar—a man in a hurry to drastically revamp India's notorious telephone system and locally design and manufacture sophisticated telecommunications equipment. Since Pitroda was closely identified with former Prime Minister Rajiv Gandhi (who also made him czar over immunization, drinking water, literacy, oilseeds, and dairy products), the new government of V.P. Singh appears to be trying to curb his power.

In a country where the loud-mouthed, pot-bellied politician has legendarily ruled the roost, Pitroda has been seen as a harbinger of change. A man who brooks no bureaucratic delays in his plans to transform India into a technological giant. "I thrive on work—that's my kick," says Pitroda.

Like Japan, India may have reached the point where the squabbling and corruption of its political factions can tarnish but not slow the growth of its economic and technological power. India has come a long way since it gained independence from British colonial rule a little more than 40 years ago. In the West, images of India remain stereotyped. A land of poverty, snake charmers, elephants, election violence, and slums. But in reality the world's most populous democracy is quietly becoming a leading industrial and military power. Pitroda is just one symbol of the change sweeping this country of 800 million people.

• India now has the world's third largest pool of scientific manpower, just after the superpowers. It is producing scientists, engineers, and doctors at a rate that by far outstrips its economy's capacity to absorb them, resulting in a heavy brain drain.

• India has the world's fourth largest military machine, after the US, Soviet Union, and China.

• India has achieved not only agricultural self-sufficiency but also, at the moment, a glut.

The land of the holy Ganges is industrializing rapidly. As an Indian living in the United States, I sometimes forget this myself. But the change strikes you instantly when you revisit your country. And the longer you have been away, the more acute the change appears. In 1988, when I returned home to New Delhi, I could not believe how the city's road traffic and pollution had grown. It seemed as if driving in Manhattan was easier and safer than driving in the Indian capital. I am told the city's traffic has become five times bigger in less than one decade. The Indian-made cars,

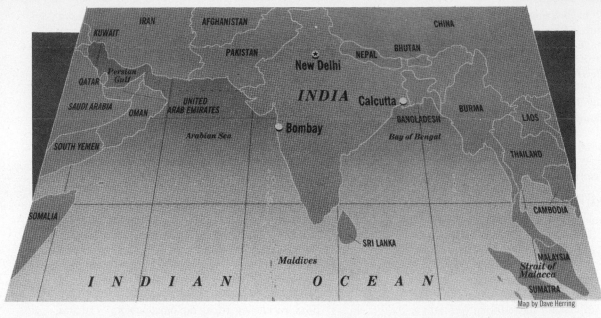

Map by Dave Herring

motorcycles, and scooters that clog the traffic are only one example of the industrialization. A drive into the countryside shows that the entire society is being transformed. Television antennas perch atop many village homes, small diesel generators at wayside shops beat the perennial power outages, and modern agricultural machinery operates on farms.

India's agriculture, long dependent on the vagaries of nature, has come of age. Despite a severe nationwide drought in 1987, the country's real gross national product (significantly dependent on agriculture) grew by almost 11% the following year—the highest rate in more than 12 years. In contrast, the droughts of the 1960s and '70s left the economy crippled for three to four years at one go. Today, government granaries overflow.

NEW BALLISTIC MISSILE
Economic liberalization, introduced in 1984 by the Gandhi government, has spurred industrial production, foreign investment, and the growth of high-technology industries. New factories producing computers, electronics, and telecommunications equipment have mushroomed across the nation in the past five years.

A large military buildup, fueled in part by a desire to be recognized as a world power, has accompanied the economic progress. The government has a multibillion-dollar military research program, aimed at achieving an independent weapons-production capability. The latest success in indigenous research came in May when military scientists test-launched India's first intermediate-range ballistic missile, the "Agni" or Fire.

"Agni is a technological strength," says Dr. Abdul Kalam, director of the government-run Defense Research and Development Organization, which spearheads the military research drive. "Strength respects strength. Weaklings are not honored. So we should be strong." Dr. Kalam, a

Muslim in a predominantly Hindu country, is the country's chief missile scientist.

Despite its impressive scientific strides and its emergence as a technological leader of the third world, India remains a country of sharp contrasts. Tradition coexists with modernity. Mud-and-thatch hovels stand beside elegant high-rise buildings and luxury hotels. Farmers produce bumper harvests, but many Indians still starve.

The benefits of industrialization have obviously not percolated to the entire society. An estimated 288 million Indians, or 36% of the population, live below the government's own poverty income line. This has spurred criticism of the government's capital intensive, Western-style industrialization drive. Critics contend that the government should pursue labor-intensive development programs to tackle rampant poverty and unemployment in the countryside and stem the influx of villagers into city slums. These critics draw inspiration from the writings of the late Indian independence leader and father of the nation, Mahatma Gandhi, who advocated making village economy self-reliant.

INDUSTRY AMID POVERTY
There apparently is some merit in the criticism that large plants built with heavy capital investments do not necessarily contribute to the development of a region. The northeastern state of Bihar is the site of India's biggest steel and mining industries, but it also is the country's poorest region.

A current people's movement in central India typifies the problems facing Indian industrialization. The unrest was sparked by the government's clearing of thousands of acres of virgin forests to build a massive electricity plant and a dam in a backward district. The action has uprooted a large number of tribespeople, who traditionally depend on the forests for survival, and angered environmentalists, who fear it may make the area flood-prone. Joined by "Gandhian" critics of Western-style industrialization, the local people have staged sit-ins and disrupted development work in the region.

Power shortage is the biggest bottleneck in the Indian industralization drive, and probably no region needs electricity as desperately as the area troubled by the protests. Although power generation increased by 9.5% nationwide in 1988, and the government planned to raise it by another 14% in 1989, chronic electricity shortages continue to curtail industrial production and parboil people seeking comfort from the Indian heat under ceiling fans that don't work.

LOOSENING SOCIALISM

Despite the criticism of the country's development planning, it is the emphasis on building modern capital-intensive industries and investing large resources in high technology that is transforming India into an important industrial and military power. Successive governments since independence have emphasized national self-reliance, which has been the motto of Indian planning. This inevitably has made the mastering of complex technologies a key element of development.

Economic expansion has been accelerated in recent years by the loosening of India's socialist-style economic system and the shift toward market orientation under Rajiv Gandhi. The government lifted regulations on many industries and simplified industrial licensing for small and medium companies. Only the large industrial conglomerates remain within the straitjacket of India's monopoly and licensing laws. With the world trend against socialized industry, India's liberalization is not likely to be reversed.

A liberal Indian patent law—an irritant in US-Indian economic relations—has helped make the country's pharmaceutical industry one of the largest in the world. India is a major exporter of bulk drugs to the Soviet Union, Europe, and North America, with exports soaring 700% in four years.

GROWING AMERICAN INVESTMENT

Attracting foreign investment is an important government goal. The long-delayed approval of a Pepsico joint venture last year, despite a domestic furor, appeared to be a calculated political move to signal India's growing willingness to accept foreign investment. Procedures are being streamlined for foreign investors in high-tech.

"We will also have to take a second look at 100% export-oriented units and the free trade zones," said Gandhi's Commerce Minister Dinesh Singh. "These schemes exist in a number of countries, but their procedures are simpler. Companies are allowed to bring in machinery free of tax. We tend to get tied to the hang-ups of the past. Here, they have to acquire licenses more or less on the lines of companies in the domestic market. There are restrictions on their entering the domestic tariff area. We could stick to them, and foreign companies

would still come. But if we want to expand, more facilities will have to be provided."

The new business climate in India is providing American, European, and Japanese firms major opportunities to invest in high-technology sectors, particularly electronics, telecommunications, computers, oil and gas exploration, and power plants. A string of US companies has started investing in India, including Texas Instruments, Du Pont, Hewlett-Packard, Amoco, General Electric, Texaco, and Chevron.

One major reason for the growing American investment in India is Washington's willingness to grant high-technology export licenses. That in itself is a reflection of the closer political ties that are developing between the United States and India. After more than two decades of troubled relations, the world's two largest democracies appear ready not to allow their geopolitical differences to get in the way of improved political and economic relations. As one American diplomat puts it: "The idea is, 'Let's do business without harping on our differences or treading on each other's toes.' " In 1988 the US administration granted $703 million worth of license approvals for advanced technology sales to India—compared with a mere $22.7 million worth of export licenses five years earlier.

The Indian boom, aided by foreign investments and collaborations and import liberalization, is expected to continue. It already has spawned the third largest community of shareholders—12 million—after those in the United States and Japan.

Rising prosperity in the country is helping the consumer electronics industry, which is growing at a galloping pace of almost 90% a year. Consumer electronics now accounts for about four-fifths of all electronics production in India.

SLICE OF THE SOFTWARE MARKET

Another sign of change in Indian society is the computers that dot many offices. The computer hardware industry is growing rapidly. The government had believed that India's large pool of skilled English-speaking engineers and scientists would help it win a slice of the world software market. Indeed, software exports have risen sixfold in two years. But they are far below the government's export targets.

The biggest technological revolution taking place today in India, however, is in telecommunications. The country's antiquated, overburdened telephone system has been considered one of the world's worst. There is no nationwide direct-dial network, and getting even a local call through can at times be a torture: One often gets a wrong number or a cross-connection, or the phone might just go "dead" after a number is dialed.

The Indian phone system not only is a source of harassment to the public but also is being blamed for straining the country's relations with Nepal. Gandhi says that, before he imposed a trade cutoff with Nepal, he called the royal palace in Kathmandu to discuss ways to defuse the crisis, but was told King Birendra was away on a hunting expedition. Nepal, however, insists no such call was received by the palace. Knowing how the phone system works, many an Indian seems to believe that Gandhi may have reached a "wrong number" and spoken with someone pretending to be at the royal palace.

RETURN OF THE MODERNIZER

Pitroda, who gave up a flourishing business empire in the United States to return to his native country, is trying to modernize the Indian phone system with digital technology. He is a strong advocate of producing telecommunications equipment within India. Says Pitroda: "You can import special equipment but not things like phone instruments and switching equipment. These are things we can make ourselves. My problem [on imports] comes from the fact that we have a lot of talent. We have 800 million people. We can rule the world if we want to."

He went to the United States at the age of 21 with just $400 in his pocket, he says. After graduate study in Illinois, he joined General Telephone and Electronics to work on digital electronic switching systems. In a few years, he became a vice-president of Rockwell International, and later established two of his own telecommunications companies.

Pitroda went back to India in 1984 and convinced Gandhi that he could locally develop digital telephone exchanges with a research grant of $24 million. In three years, as his friendship with Gandhi deepened, he was appointed Gandhi's adviser on technology missions.

Today Pitroda wears several hats, and this is winning him some enemies. He is India's telecommunications secretary, the chairman of the powerful Telecommunications Commission (which was his own brainchild), the head of the Center for Development of Telematics, and the chief of the five technology missions mentioned earlier. In addition, he advised Gandhi on a host of matters.

Critics say Pitroda has more than he can chew. But his many supporters call Pitroda a symbol of the newly emerging India, a country impatient to catch up with the industrial revolution it missed because of colonial rule, a country buoyant about its future.

REGIONAL SUPERPOWER

While the pace of industrialization is bound to accelerate over the next decade, it is the country's technological advances in the nuclear, military, and space fields that are increasingly attracting the attention of the world. In less than one decade India has emerged as a regional superpower through an awesome defense buildup and an increasingly assertive role in South Asia as exemplified by its military intervention in Sri Lanka and the Maldives and the trade blockade of Nepal.

"Is Super India emerging as the Big Bully?" asked a screaming cover-page headline in a recent issue of the widely circulated newsmagazine The Illustrated Weekly of India. The article argued that India's image among its neighbors had become one of a "bully on the block" because of its desire to be the "lord of the region." Although many Indians take pride in their country's new image as an emerging world military power, the article reflected the unease of some scholars and lawmakers over the government's willingness to take on the role of a regional policeman.

Defense policymakers currently are concentrating on two goals: developing advanced weapons systems locally and building the Indian Navy into the undisputed leader of the region stretching from Africa to Southeast Asia. The naval buildup, which has included the acquisition of a Soviet-leased nuclear-powered submarine, has been propelled by arguments that India historically has been vulnerable to invaders who came by sea such as the British. Two countries that border the Indian Ocean, Australia and Indonesia, view the buildup with considerable unease.

Prof. M.G.K. Menon, now minister for science and technology, cited two reasons for India's advances in military research and development:

• The establishment of an integrated research structure under the umbrella of the Defense Ministry.

• Long-term defense planning.

"We have moved from improvements and adaptations [in weapons systems] to clear-cut and fairly large projects based on long-term defense planning," Professor Menon said in an interview.

THREE HIGH-TECH LEADERS

Menon, Kalam, and Pitroda, three of the leaders of India's technological revolution, have one thing in common: They received their training in the United States. The half million Indians residing in the United States and the hundreds more who go there every year for graduate study provide an important link between the two nations.

In addition to Agni, India has test-fired a shorter-range ballistic missile, the "Prithvi," which like Agni can carry a nuclear payload. It also has developed a sophisticated anti-tank missile, two types of surface-to-air and air-to-ground missiles, a high-explosive incendiary system, and rocket boosters for launching pilotless aircraft. The Indians also are trying to build their own nuclear submarines, light combat aircraft, and an aircraft carrier battle group. The weapons projects have spurred progress in allied fields such as metallurgy and space research. The government reported last year that its scientists have succeeded in producing maraging steel, a rare alloy used in uranium enrichment and the manufacture of nuclear bombs.

India can readily build a small nuclear arsenal, and there are indications that scientists at Bombay's Bhabha Atomic Research Center have been working on weapon designs for more than 15 years. But most accounts suggest that India actually has not assembled any nuclear weapons despite detonating an atomic device in 1974.

MORE PLUTONIUM THAN CHINA

The country's nuclear military potential flows from its large civilian power program. With its emphasis on developing plutonium recycling and fast-breeder reactors, India is likely to have a massive stockpile of weapons-usable plutonium in 25 years. At its current rate of production, the country will have accumulated more weapons-grade plutonium by 1998 than its archrival China now has in its nuclear arsenal.

India has launched an ambitious nuclear power expansion program. With seven reactors in operation, it is currently constructing another seven reactors, importing two from the Soviet Union, and planning to build 10 others over the next nine years at a time when the rest of the world, with the exclusion of Japan, is scaling back nuclear construction work. In addition, it is building a new nuclear research complex and a second fuel-fabrication facility. The nuclear power sector, however, has been burdened by cost overruns, production slippages, and design and equipment problems, and it seems unlikely that the country will achieve its target of generating 10% of its total electricity requirements from atomic energy by the year 2000.

Unlike nuclear science, the civilian applications of space technology are having a significant impact on Indian society and industry. Satellites now provide extensive telecommunications, broadcast, meteorological, navigation, and earth-resources survey services in India. About 182 space-linked stations have brought television to more than 80% of the country's villages. Sociologists say that television programs on improved farming techniques, family planning, disease control, and animal husbandry have promoted social and economic change in rural communities.

India surprised the world in 1980 by placing a satellite in orbit. But in recent years the space program, which employs more than 10,000 scientists at two dozen research facilities, has experienced some setbacks. Twice, the Augmented Satellite Launch Vehicle, designed to place a 330-pound satellite with a sophisticated guidance system in low-earth orbit, has crashed into the sea after takeoff.

TV THE HOMOGENIZER

The proliferation of televisions and videocassette recorders in Indian society is one yardstick of the rising economic prosperity. More than five million TVs were sold to the Indian public in 1988 alone. Television has emerged as a very powerful entertainment and communications medium in a multicultural country in which dozens of languages are spoken. Sociologists debate whether television in the long run could homogenize Indian society without dismantling cultural and ethnic identities.

India's society already is undergoing a major social transformation in response to economic change. Two of the most significant developments have been the emergence of a large and burgeoning urban middle class and, in the countryside, the growth of a politically powerful "kulak" class like the wealthy farmers who resisted collectivization in the Soviet Union.

The introduction of modern technology to farms and heavy government subsidies on seeds, fertilizers, machinery, and farm produce have helped foster economic prosperity in large parts of rural India. A big class of wealthy farmers has emerged from caste groups that traditionally have had a low ranking in the social hierarchy.

FARMERS WITH CLOUT

Atrocities against the untouchables or landless peasants traditionally have been associated with the Brahmins, the Rajputs, and other upper castes. Although upper-caste discrimination and persecution of the untouchables persists in varying degrees, a majority of reported attacks on the outcasts involve this new class of socially backward but economically prosperous farmers. Such farmers also have political clout because they make up about one-fifth of a typical rural constituency and tend to vote en bloc for a candidate in elections.

The rapid growth of a large urban middle class is reflected in the mushrooming of fancy beauty parlors in Calcutta, the addition of 10,000 vehicles every month to New Delhi streets, and the half-million-dollar apartments in Bombay. New Delhi's Punjabi-speaking "yuppie" is locally described as a "puppie": He drives a gaudily decked-out car, visits a video library daily, and eats dinner in an expensive restaurant. There are so many "puppies" getting married at five-star hotels that wedding receptions yield more profit than room occupancy at some of the luxury hotels.

Some Indian analysts see a link between the "money culture" symbolized by the middle classes and the rapid erosion of traditional values and morality in urban India. Corruption is rampant and it often goes hand-in-hand with India's proverbial red tape. Government clerks, for example, are routinely bribed to "push" files for quicker action on them. There is widespread concern that corruption might turn into a way of life in Indian society.

Modern technology, meanwhile, is doing wonders to Indian traditions. National newspapers now offer computer matchmaking services to those who advertise in their matrimonial columns, making the task easier for parents trying to arrange the marriage of their children in the Indian tradition. Astrologers, who play an important role in Hindu ritual, are using computers to prepare and analyze horoscopes. As a result, a new elite astrological class of "computer babas" has emerged.

TWO MOST PRESSING ISSUES

Although India's technological momentum seems irreversible, the nation faces several major economic and social challenges. The two most pressing issues are food distribution and homelessness.

Despite the country's record foodgrain production of more than 160 million tons in 1988-89, there have been reports of starvation in the southeastern state of Orissa.

Unemployment in the countryside is driving hundreds of thousands of poor into the cities every year and creating larger and larger slums. About 40 million Indians, or 25% of the urban population, "live in slums and under conditions of multiple deprivation," the National Commission on Urbanization said in a recent report. The report warned that at the present rate of urban migration, every second city resident in the country would be a slum-dweller by the year 2001.

The government has pledged to remove homelessness by the turn of the century, but with no coherent national housing policy, that is widely seen as a hollow promise. The slum-dwellers in Bombay, whose plight was portrayed in the movie "Salaam Bombay," face a constant struggle to keep their shanties from being bulldozed by the city government.

Raj Mangal lives in a jute-and-bamboo hovel with his wife and three children in Bombay's fashionable seaside Cuffe Parade neighborhood. According to Mangal, he has had to rebuild his tiny home 24 times in one year because of demolitions by the city's "anti-slum squad." Mangal is one of the 4.5 million faceless slum-dwellers who do not exist in the city's records.

WORLD'S MOST POPULOUS NATION?

India's population currently grows at a rate of 2% per year, and the country is poised to overtake China as the world's most populous nation. Contraceptives, sterilization, and abortion are available free of charge, but the backlash triggered by the coercive family-planning policy of the mid-1970s still deters policymakers and politicians from advocating tough birth control measures.

Another problem facing the government is the runaway spending triggered by economic liberalization. The country's foreign debt has climbed 65% in four years and foreign exchange reserves have dipped so low as to cover barely 2 1/2 months of imports. Indian economists are concerned that the country may be heading into a Latin American-type debt trap. With an external debt of $47 billion, India now is the fourth largest debtor nation after Argentina, Mexico, and Brazil. Policymakers, however, believe that the debt situation is manageable.

Nationalism, burgeoning forces of technology, and a national consensus on a self-reliant policy are expected to accelerate India's economic march. As the world appears to head into a multipolar power structure, the newly emerging India—viewed by many international scholars as a major power in the making—is carving out a special place for itself in global politics.

The Limits
of American Power

Many Americans believe—and correctly so—that United States foreign policy is, at times, both difficult to explain and difficult to predict. In their view, American policy lacks coherence and consistency, which undermines unity at home and support abroad. Legislative-executive conflict, political discord, the absence of clearly defined goals, and numerous legal vagaries all contribute to the foreign policy maze that continues to baffle both pundits and lay citizens.

To understand foreign policy-making, it is necessary to possess sufficient information. In some cases, however, the problem is not a lack of information but too much information. Still, possessing information alone is not sufficient; to understand the contradictions and nuances of the policy-making process, one must ask the right sorts of questions. In this regard, it may prove useful to posit several alternative models that have been developed by political scientists to assess foreign policy decisions.

The most widely accepted approach is the strategic or rational model. According to this approach, state leaders can be viewed as "solitary actors," seeking to advance their objectives in the international arena. This action-reaction model attempts to explain each response as a rational calculation to counterbalance a move by the other side. Like all models, it has strengths and limitations. Its principal advantage is its simplicity, in that it permits one to analyze foreign policy decisions with a minimum of complexity. On the other hand, it understates the impact of sundry domestic and international actors. In addition, it assumes a level of rationality that is rarely present in the formulation and implementation of foreign policy decisions.

The second approach is the decision-making model, which is considerably more complex. This approach focuses on numerous internal and external factors that shape foreign policy choices. It places special emphasis on the weight assigned to the determining factors by official decisionmakers. Its salient advantage is that it underscores the significance of the human factor—that is, the motivations of official policymakers, the flow of information among them, and the impact of various alternatives on their decisions.

The bureaucratic politics model not only examines the major players in the foreign policy process, but highlights the role played by top bureaucrats who are involved in the process. It is based on the assumption that, in many cases, important decisions are influenced by high-level bureaucrats, who frequently possess greater expertise than the elected politicians who actively solicit their advice and assistance. Additionally, these bureaucrats are intimately involved in the implementation of foreign policy directives and, like all bureaucrats, can choose to implement a policy, do so reluctantly, or refuse to act at all. The primary limitation of this model is the tendency to overestimate the role of bureaucrats in the policy process.

The adaptive approach attempts to analyze foreign policy decisions by examining the ways in which nations respond to the opportunities and constraints imposed by their international environments. This model maintains that official state actions are often defined by the environment in which the states function. Clearly, the adaptive capacities of states differ, based both on their desire to act and their ability to do so. In reality, a state's ability to act is, to a large extent, the product of its political allegiances, geographical position, and military strength.

Finally, the incremental decision-making model views foreign policy decisions as an ongoing series of small forward steps, each based on the actions that preceded it. It challenges the rational-actor model, arguing that the lack of certainty and information, combined with the large number of foreign policy actors, preclude comprehensive rational calculation. Rather than weighing every possible option, top decisionmakers tend to concentrate on those alternatives that reflect past policy.

As you read the following articles, consider the above models. These approaches will help you to define a policy, evaluate its strengths and weaknesses, identify key actors, and suggest viable alternatives. Remember, however, that foreign policy defies simple explanation—it is rarely the product of any *one* model. Moreover, foreign policy is the result of numerous domestic and international considerations, any one or a combination of which may bear heavily on the action taken. And keep in mind that American foreign policy can rarely be explained in terms of good guys and bad guys; nations tend to act on the basis of self-interest, even if that means signing a pact with the devil.

Looking Ahead: Challenge Questions

Why should the United States be concerned about the Third World?

When, if ever, should the United States intervene to affect political conditions in the developing world?

Should the United States adopt a conciliatory noninterventionist posture toward the Third World as a means of reducing the risk of American military involvement in that part of the world?

Should the United States ever support or recognize a Third World dictatorship?

Does the United States have a moral obligation to provide humanitarian assistance to refugees?

What major developments have forced the United States to reassess its security needs in Southeast Asia?

Would decreasing U.S. activity in South Asia undermine actual and potential American interests?

Why have the new Central American presidents been slow to embrace the cause of economic integration?

Policies Toward the Third World

Seyom Brown
Brandeis University

To those people in the huts and villages of half the globe struggling to break the bonds of mass misery, we pledge our best efforts to help them help themselves, for whatever period is required—not because the Communists may be doing it, not because we seek their votes, but because it is right.

—John F. Kennedy (Inaugural Address, January 20, 1961)

United States policies toward the so-called Third World—the nonindustrialized countries outside of Europe, most of which are former colonies of one or another of the European powers—are ostensibly for the purpose of furthering the development of economically underdeveloped or politically fragile countries. Presumably, special United States help or intervention is required by many of these countries for them to tend adequately to their people's material needs and to maintain internal peace and independence from foreign domination.

But *why* should the condition of such Third World countries be of major concern to the United States? The answers encountered in the policy community range from narrow self-interest concerns to universal imperatives to alleviate the suffering of others wherever in the world they might reside. Each answer has its own rationale and generates its own objections.

NATIONAL SELF-INTEREST RATIONALE

United States government programs to help other countries develop economically rarely obtain congressional majorities to fund them unless a convincing case can be made that the United States itself will benefit from such a diversion of the taxpayers' money from domestic programs. This condition often is satisfied by Buy American provisos stipulated by Congress on financial credits extended to countries that need money to purchase equipment, technology, or experts for their economic development projects. Such strings, of course, are not possible to attach to U.S. contributions to international development agencies, such as the World Bank or regional development banks, nor are they appropriate to attach to U.S. loans to governments to help them balance their budgets and pay off existing foreign debts.

In cases where immediate or quick payback through purchase of U.S. goods and services is inappropriate, other—indirect—benefits to the United States usually have to be demonstrated to gain congressional approval of a foreign assistance program. These indirect benefits to the United States can be economic, political, or both.

Straight grants, concessional loans, and associated economic assistance to particular developing countries or to multinational regional development banks often will be championed as important stimulants to the economic growth of the recipients; and purportedly, the resulting economic growth will provide new markets for U.S. products and new opportunities for U.S. investments, including the location of subsidiaries of multinational corporations. These types of benefits to the United States private economic sector were a large part of the rationale in President Reagan's 1982 Caribbean Basin Development Initiative.[1] Though philosophically opposed to heavy reliance on market distorting mechanisms such as government-to-government loans at concessionary interest rates, free enterprisers such as Ronald Reagan and his economic advisers are willing to resort to them temporarily because they provide seed money for generating an initial development cycle. Then, the loans can, presumably, be eliminated as the potential for growth in the aided countries begins to attract private investment.[2]

Often the economic self-interest rationale for foreign assistance is less direct, focusing on the effects of the economic aid on the political conditions within the recipient countries—conditions that are thought to be inhibiting what would otherwise be a profitable market for U.S. products and a stable source of inputs for U.S. industrial processes. The political disorder that disrupts normal commerce is attributed to the resentment of the poor alienated masses who have lost all hope of improving their lives within the system and thus can be mobilized into radical revolutionary movements willing to use violence to topple the existing order. Progress in economic development is a necessary precondition, so the argument goes, for the minimum public order, which in turn, is the precondition for a degree of economic development that will allow for mutually profitable commerce with the United States.

The political self-interest rationale for the United States helping economically disadvantaged countries has two facets: (1) To the extent such help does indeed relieve economic conditions that otherwise would lead to widespread despair, alienation, and susceptibility to radical revolutionary mobilization, the opportunities for the Soviet Union and its friends to make easy gains among the world's poor will be reduced; and (2) To the degree that U.S. economic aid is perceived by recipients as essential to their development efforts, the United States will gain gratitude that can be cashed in, so to speak, for at least informal commitments by the recipients not to become client states of the Soviet Union or for political support (perhaps in votes in international agencies) on issues of importance to the United States. From some recipient governments, particularly those that want financial or other help in building up their military establishments, the quid pro quo for United States aid can be base rights and servicing facilities for U.S. aircraft and naval vessels, permission for the U.S. to operate intelligence gathering stations, or a formal mutual security alliance.

WORLD-INTEREST RATIONALE

A broader national-interest rationale, sometimes called enlightened self-interest, holds that the United States will fare best in a world community where countries not only respect one another but assume some responsibility for one another's well-being, especially in cases of dire need.

A minimum starting point toward such a world community, it is argued, would be for the United States to accede to the request of developing countries that each affluent country devote some specified fraction of its annual gross national product (GNP) to improving the lot of poor countries—without political or economic strings attached. (The standard figure asked by the coalition of developing countries is seven-tenths of one percent of an industrial country's GNP).

In a more elaborate and generous gesture, the United States could embrace the philosophy and something like the general program of action put forward by the Brandt Commission in 1980:* The Brandt Commission argued that a major effort by the more affluent countries to cooperate with the poorer nations in reducing the gap between the rich and the suffering poor was required in the interests of world survival:

> Continued rapid population growth in the next century could make the world unmanageable; but that growth can only be forestalled if action is taken to combat poverty in this century. Much

*Willy Brandt, the former chancellor of the Federal Republic of Germany, at the suggestion of World Bank President Robert McNamara, appointed a commission of distinguished persons in 1978 to study the international issues arising from the economic and social disparities of the world and to recommend remedies. In addition to Brandt, the members were Edward Heath (Conservative prime minister of the United Kingdom, 1970-1974), Olaf Palme (prime minister of Sweden, 1969-1976), Peter G. Peterson (United States secretary of commerce, 1972-1973), Eduardo Frei Monyalva (president of Chile, 1964-1970), Adam Malik (vice president of Indonesia, 1977-1978, and minister of foreign affairs, 1966-1979), Layachi Yaker (minister of commerce of Algeria, 1969-1977), Antoine Kipsa Dakoure (minister of commerce of Upper Volta, 1970-1976), Rodrigo Botero Montoya (minister of finance of Colombia, 1974-1976), Lakshmit Kant Jha (Indian ambassador to the United States, 1970-1973), Haruki Mori (Japanese ambassador to the United Kingdom, 1972-1975), Joe Morris (Canadian labor leader and chairman of the International Labor Organization Governing Body, 1977-1978), Abdlatif Y. Al-Hamad (prominent Kuwaiti economist), Khatijah Ahmad (prominent Malaysian banker and economist), and Katherine Graham (publisher of the *Washington Post*).

the same is true for the biological environment, which is threatened with destruction in many countries as a direct result of poverty—though in others as a result of ill-considered technological decisions and patterns of industrial growth. These problems—nuclear weapons proliferation is another—can only be solved by North and South acting in cooperation, and their mutual interests in doing so are only too obvious. The conquest of poverty and the promotion of sustainable growth are matters not just of the survival of the poor, but of everyone.[3]

Specifically, the United States would endorse and contribute to raising at least $8 billion annually for a special fund to overcome food deficits in poor countries through a broad program of increased food production and agricultural development. The United States would resist pressures from special industry and labor groups for protection against Third World products. The United States would support the use of the reserve assets of the International Monetary Fund (IMF), principally the Special Drawing Rights, to help developing countries with their financial problems. The United States, in addition to meeting the 0.7 percent target for official development assistance, would support certain forms of automatic international taxation to raise funds from those with great wealth to be transferred to the world's poor. (The Brandt Commission, in some of its most controversial proposals, suggested taxes on international trade, especially on arms exports, and taxes on users of the international "commons" areas—the ocean beyond national jurisdiction, the atmosphere, and outer space.) And the United States would be more responsive than it has been to price-stabilization agreements with the producers of basic commodities subject to devastating fluctuations in the international market.

The United States would also attempt to promote a more cooperative relationship with developing countries by allowing them more decision-making weight in international institutions affecting their welfare, such as the IMF and the World Bank and by moving more in the direction of one-nation-one-vote arrangements in new institutions, such as those being set up to regulate the exploitation of minerals on the deep seabed.[4]

The Brandt Commission's recommendation for global negotiations, including periodic summit meetings among world leaders, to move toward the more "equitable world order" envisioned in its report, would be responded to positively, not begrudgingly in the manner of the Reagan administration, if this basically generous and accommodating approach to Third World demands for a restructured global political economy were to become United States policy.

Some Americans agree with Willy Brandt that "What is now on the agenda (and should be supported) is a rearrangement of international relations, the building of a new order and a new kind of comprehensive approach to the problems of development."[5] But clearly, not all Americans agree.

The Case Against a Policy of Apolitical Generosity

Three kinds of objections to generous foreign assistance programs are raised in public and internal government debates over the ways and extent to which the United States should attempt to help the world's poor. The first, which can be called *economic nationalism,* emphasizes the need to tend to problems at home before devoting resources to the welfare of others. The second, the *conservative realpolitik* stance, is fearful of disruptions to the global political and economic status quo that are resulting from the unrealistic expectations and demands stimulated by the notion that there should be a global social-welfare approach to the world's poor. The third kind of objection, arguing from the premises of *classical economics,* holds that the best path for increasing everyone's well-being lies in a free international market, the emergence of which is retarded by the market-distorting effects of artificial affluent-to-poor resource transfers.

Economic nationalism. Nationalistic objections to substantial programs of special assistance to economically disadvantaged countries are of two sorts: (1) those stressing that charity begins at home; and (2) those concerned over the presumed loss of U.S. profits and jobs that could result from giving the disadvantaged countries special subsidies and privileges to compete in the market.

In a domestic United States political and economic environment dominated by demands to cut down government expenditures and reduce taxes on personal and corporate incomes, the popular saying that charity begins at home has greater consequences for foreign assistance programs than it normally does.

Even in the relatively good economic conditions of the 1950s and early 1960s, policymakers advocating increased resource transfers to the disadvantaged countries had great difficulty in convincing their fellow Americans that it was just as important to spend the United States taxpayers' money on helping the poor in India and Peru as on helping the poor in Harlem and Appalachia. Therefore, during this period, the cold war rationale of competing with the Soviets for influence in the Third World was invoked to justify foreign resource transfers. Economic development assistance was subordinated to or made an adjunct of "security assistance," and claimants in the United States government for such resources for foreign assistance programs competed with one another to demonstrate the country or region within their bureaucratic responsibility would "go communist" or align with the Sino-Soviet bloc if the United States failed to come to its aid.

In the early 1980s, the burden of proof carried by the advocates of foreign development assistance became heavier than ever. Public funds for this purpose were harder to come by than at any time since the end of World War II. This meant that political merit criteria would push aside most other considerations in the allocation of scarce resources, and the definitions of political merit would be narrowly drawn to virtually exclude that which did not add to U.S. power in its global rivalry with the Soviet Union.

Conservative realpolitik. International disorder, chaos, disruptions in the normal functioning of the global economy, and opportunities for the Soviet Union and other opponents of the United States to fish in troubled waters are the likely results, from the conservative perspective, of giving in to demands to share wealth and power with the Third World. The inequality of nations, it is argued, is not a superficial condition imposed on the world by a few selfish and venal leaders, but rather it is the product of a long and profound process of historical evolution of the nation-state system itself. The nation-state system is structured around the norm of autonomous national political economies, each sovereign over its own resources, and an orderly system of trade and bargaining between the nation-states, sustained by the great powers. To grant the argument being pushed by Third World leaders and their supporters in the more developed countries that the affluent and powerful nations have a duty to share their wealth and power in the name of global social justice is to undermine the legitimacy of the evolved international order before the groundwork for any viable alternative world order has been laid. Such action will stimulate unrealistic demands, which will have to go unmet and which in turn, therefore, will intensify the frustrations and anger of the

have-nots and prevent the reasoned discourse and moderate policies necessary for international peace and security.

The conservatives are particularly adamant in opposing attempts by developing countries to democratize the structure of international institutions, such as the International Monetary Fund, the General Agreements on Tariffs and Trade, the International Maritime Consultative Organization, and the International Telecommunications Union, set up to ensure an orderly functioning of the international economy and commerce. Decision-making weight in these bodies characteristically rests with those countries with the most real resource power in the economic sector to be regulated. Moves in the direction of a one-country-one-vote decision process in such institutions will, according to conservatives, make for irresponsible decisions and will simply drive away the holders of real resources whose participation in any case is voluntary. Similar objections are raised to proposals to give developing countries more power in the allocation and approval of loans by the World Bank, which gets most of its resources from affluent governments and private corporations. If the World Bank's Board of Governors no longer represents the contributors when it sets the terms on loans, then the sources of the Bank's assets will dry up because the contributors will either revert to bilateral negotiations with recipients or form new multilateral lending consortia under the control of the donor countries.

This basic conservative stance was reflected in the Reagan administration's efforts to alter the Law of the Sea treaty provisions subjecting deep seabed mining and mineral exploitation to regulation by a thirty-six-nation council in which the United States, Japan, West Germany, Britain, and France could be outvoted by a combination of Third World and Warsaw Pact countries. The Reagan administration, in voting against the treaty in the spring of 1982, indicated it could not accept a seabed council weighted against those countries with the heaviest investments in seabed mining.[6]

Classical economics. A third kind of objection to generous international income redistribution policies normally finds expression in the Treasury Department and among a large portion—perhaps a majority—of academic economists at American universities. The classical economists want to remove most man-made barriers to the free exchange of goods in the international market. From their point of view, anything that prevents individuals from buying as cheaply as possible and selling to the highest bidder anywhere in the world is unjust. International free trade—or as close an approximation to it as possible—supposedly will result in the greatest good for the greatest number of people. It will induce procurers to locate where the factors of production (natural resources, labor, capital, managerial capabilities) can be obtained most efficiently and therefore result in goods that can be sold more cheaply. Everyone benefits. According to the classical theory, this basic free market process will tend toward a global distribution of production, and thus income earning capabilities, on the basis of the comparative advantage of various societies in providing factors of production more efficiently for certain kinds of products. This dynamic, in turn, will produce a specialization of production by particular societies and presumably therefore provide each of them with secure sources of income.

Ronald Reagan has been a devotee of the classical economic notions and has stated that they are the official premises of his administration's economic policies toward developing countries: "The societies which have achieved the most spectacular broad-based economic progress in the shortest period of time . . . be-

118

lieve in the magic of the marketplace," he told the Board of Governors of the International Monetary Fund and the World Bank. "My own government is committed to policies of free trade, unrestricted investment and open capital markets."[7]

Any program to correct the flow of trade and investments (and their rewards in the form of income) that naturally occurs in the free market is, by these lights, considered to be a harmful distortion of those processes that eventually will stimulate the most economic development. Large-scale official development assistance, concessional loans and debt forgiveness, and any form of international taxation are prime examples of such distortive mechanisms and must be opposed.

Responding to Specific Economic Demands[8]

The various philosophical stances toward social justice claims of developing countries can be seen in debates in the United States policy community over how to respond to many of the specific demands put forward by the Third World coalition at successive meetings of the United Nations Conference on Trade and Development (UNCTAD) and at Special Sessions of the United Nations General Assembly (especially the sixth and seventh Special Sessions of 1974 and 1975).

On commodity agreements. The case for assuring that developing country producers of basic commodities (mostly agricultural products and other raw materials) receive minimum or floor prices, or for indexing the prices of such commodities to the international market prices of industrial goods, rests on claims of fairness as well as United States self-interest. It is grossly inequitable, so the argument goes, that poor countries with economies highly dependent upon export earnings from one or a few basic commodities should be thrown into sudden and severe depressions because of a slackening of international demand for these commodities or a decline in real earnings in relation to goods they must import. The more diversified economies of the affluent countries are better able to absorb demand and price changes in particular sectors. (Indeed, most of them subsidize their own vulnerable sectors, like grain farmers, with price supports and government purchasing arrangements.) Simple fairness, therefore, requires international guarantees to poor countries against disastrous export-income losses that are no fault of their own. Some participants in the U.S. policy debates over providing special protection to the disadvantaged commodity producers also grant the argument of many Third World people that the industrial countries bear a special responsibility for redressing the existing disparities because it was they—the former colonial imperialists—who allegedly forced a specialization of one or a small number of primary products on their colonies in previous centuries. The U.S. self-interest argument for commodity price-stabilization schemes merely emphasizes the connection between having reliable markets for U.S. exports in the Third World and providing the developing countries with assured means of earning what they need to pay for U.S. goods. Surely, it is argued, guarantees of an equitable relationship between industrial prices and prices for primary commodity imports couldn't *hurt* the United States economy.

Objections to commodity agreements center on both their desirability and their practicality. According to the orthodox free traders, everyone loses over the long run by making purchasers of any goods pay more than they would if prices were allowed to reflect supply and demand. Especially where price declines reflect the entry into the market of new producers, the development of more efficient means of production, or the use of better substitutes, efforts to prop up commodity prices are unfair to the consumers—many of whom may also be poor. Artificially pegging the price of raw rubber to the price of automobiles and other manufactured goods, for example, will only increase the costs to everyone, rich and poor alike, of getting from place to place; and, the marginal increases are likely to hurt the poor more than the rich. Moreover, it is argued, such artificial pricing arrangements will either feed on themselves, by attracting even more producers into a particular commodity line and thus requiring even heavier controls on prices (most likely in the form of production quotas), or else they will collapse when the number of new producers extends supply beyond the point where restraining competitive selling underneath fixed prices is feasible.

Another type of objection challenges the relevance of commodity agreements to the global rich-poor gap. Those who produce commodities for exports, it is pointed out, are not necessarily poor. Most of the large industrial countries are also raw material producers and exporters. Furthermore, within the poor countries themselves, the exporting sectors are the most affluent and resistant to income redistribution policies and other social reforms in their own societies. More often than not, their profits are reinvested in banks and corporations outside of their own countries; and sometimes, as in the so-called banana republics of Central America, they operate in cahoots with foreign-owned multinational corporations to keep control of the economies and political systems of their countries.

On tariff preferences. Discrimination in favor of the products of developing countries by allowing them duty-free or low tariff entry into the United States market is one of the ways that these countries and advocates of their cause within the U.S. see to help them earn foreign exchange and diversify their economies. Some preferences were granted by the European Community and Japan in 1971 and then by the United States in 1975. The European countries have extended trading privileges in the Common Market to their former colonies, while denying them to other countries. Similarly, the United States, in President Reagan's Caribbean Basin Development Plan, favors a subset of developing countries willing to cooperate with the United States in political as well as economic matters affecting the hemisphere.

Objections to the extension of tariff preferences come not only from particular industry and labor groups that fear their products will be undersold, but also from supporters of the Most Favored Nation (MFN) principle of the General Agreements on Tariffs and Trade. In the eyes of many, MFN is the heart of the GATT system of nondiscriminatory trade in that it states that all nations shall have access to a country's market equal to the most favored nation. Without such a rule, the world economy would evolve into rivalrous trading blocs antithetical to the goal of universal free trade. But advocates of tariff preferences for developing countries cite the long tolerance of the United States for European Economic Community (EEC) trading arrangements that discriminate against nonmembers—especially during the years of post-World War II reconstruction of the European economy—as a precedent for compromising with GATT principles when an important world-order objective is served thereby.

On official development assistance. Support for the proposition that affluent industrial countries should appropriate 0.7 percent of their gross national product to development assistance for disadvantaged countries (as recommended in various UN resolutions and the Brandt report) is very thin in the United States policy community and probably even thinner on the part of the general public. The small minority that argues for such an obligatory donation takes its stand largely on the premise that the world has become an interdependent community and on the ethi-

119

cal postulate that in a community the affluent are duty bound to help the poor. Some geopolitically oriented public officials, while not wanting to be tied to any specific percentage of GNP, regard official development assistance as a useful tool of foreign policy because it provides the government with leverage that is lacking in resources transferred through the private sector or through multilateral institutions.

Those who advocate a generous response to the needs of disadvantaged countries worry that bilateral foreign assistance will be used primarily to pressure recipient countries to conform to United States foreign policy objectives. In order to gain congressional majorities, the sponsors of foreign aid legislation must often accept a variety of rides to their bills, ranging from Buy American provisions, to human rights stipulations, to guarantees against expropriation of U.S. corporations. Economic development functions of the resource transfers more often than not are subordinated to the particular hobby horses of congressmen whose votes are required. Rather modest levels of transfers are burdened beyond their carrying capacity with the result that few if any of the hoped-for effects—least of all economic development—are realized; and, neither the United States as donor nor the recipient countries are satisfied. Instead it is just as likely that both sides become increasingly disenchanted, if not bitter, with each other.

Because government-to-government development aid is tempting for the donor country to use as a lever on the recipients, many developing countries would prefer to receive help from international institutions; and the constituency in the United States policy community championing selfless assistance to developing countries tends to support such a funnelling of aid through multilateral rather than bilateral arrangements. Yet not all developing countries want to compete equally against each other for the limited funds of international and regional banks. Some countries, particularly those that are favored military and ideological allies of the United States (like Guatemala or Thailand), are anxious to preserve their position as the preferred beneficiaries of any U.S. generosity. And the congressional and administrative backers of particular allies are equally desirous of keeping direct control of the resource transfers so that they can be used as rewards to those foreign regimes presumed to be most supportive of U.S. policies.

Thus, even controversies over basic types of official development assistance—multilateral versus bilateral—are, at base, debates over the extent to which the United States should be pursuing a long-term, politically neutral strategy of helping developing countries, as opposed to a more politicized strategy of attempting to affect immediate international alignment and ideological character of Third World countries. Equally important decisions on if and how much a particular country should be helped are infused with these controversies over the basic purposes of foreign assistance as well as arguments over whether the countries are politically and economically worthy of aid.

On debt and balance-of-payments relief. There is controversy over how to respond to the fact that, even with the availability of low interest loans and other concessionary resource transfers, many a developing country is unable to increase its national income enough to pay its debts to foreign lenders at previously negotiated rates. (Put another way, if the debts were to be repaid at the agreed rates, the debtor nation would substantially wipe out its annual margin of economic growth or, in extreme cases, even suffer a decline in national income.) Developing countries have been pressing for payments moratoria on such accumulated external debts.

The main argument for such additional concessions to developing countries is that without them the purposes of the original loans—to allow the recipients to generate development investments that would be unavailable out of current earnings—would be negated, and they would be unable to sustain their economic growth; worse yet, they might fall into total bankruptcy. The main arguments against debt moratoria are (1) that they would constitute, in fact, an additional loan by those who had already extended help at concessional rates of interest, and that these lenders (including many nongovernmental contributors to the resources of financial institutions) would be driven away from future lending to developing countries if this becomes the pattern; (2) that debt moratoria tend to reinforce weak economic performance; and (3) that better risk borrowers, therefore, will have less funds available to them.

Although there is no agreement among United States policymakers on debt moratoria as a general policy, there is a consensus that the issue should be approached on a country-by-country basis to determine both the legitimate need and the consequences of a moratorium in each particular case. This, of course, provides just one more entry point for injecting political considerations into development financing, especially when the question is about debts owed the United States government directly.

Closely related to the debt problem are the severe balance of international payments deficits frequently incurred by developing countries, which are caused largely by their export earnings dropping far below their expenditures on imports. There is general support among United States policymakers for helping developing countries overcome temporary balance-of-payments deficits so that they can continue to purchase needed imports during a period of declining exports; the normal source for obtaining such additional financial reserves is the International Monetary Fund or regional multigovernmental financial facilities. Controversy, however, surrounds proposals to allocate Special Drawing Rights (SDRs) against the IMF funds to developing countries with balance-of-payments difficulties—that is, to have the needy countries obtain a larger share of IMF credits than they would have under normal IMF criteria. Some policymakers favor this SDR-development link, while others are against mixing development issues with the main purpose of SDRs—namely, to provide sufficient liquidity to tide high levels of international trade over the reserve depletions suffered periodically by major trading countries.

Opponents of the SDR link argue that a diversion of SDRs to development purposes may reduce their availability for this primary role of avoiding severe international recessions that might accompany constrictions in trade when there are liquidity bottlenecks in the system. Advocates of the SDR link to development aid contend that the amounts of SDRs transferred to developing countries need not be of such magnitude to detract from the larger liquidity providing functions of the IMF and that the principle problems with the SDR link are technical and administrative and can be overcome if the moral commitment is there.

THE POLITICAL INTERVENTION TRILEMMA*

When it comes to the issue of whether, under what circumstances, and how the United States should intervene to affect

*The material in this section is adapted from my essay, "The Trilemma of U.S. Foreign Policy," *AEI Foreign and Defense Review,* Vol. II., No. 5 (1980), pp.2-4.

the *political* conditions in Third World countries, the debates become most intense for they reach to the very essence of what the United States stands for in the world. Three alternative philosophies contend for basic acceptance as U.S. policy:

1. *Help friendly regimes secure themselves against U.S. adversaries.* This policy—reflected in the 1984 report by President Reagan's Commission on Central America, headed by Henry Kissinger—rests on the geopolitical premise that the most important determinants of United States support are a country's international alignments in the big power games of vital interest to the U.S.: the U.S.-Soviet rivalry and the efforts of the industrialized countries to maintain access to the world's energy resources and other critical raw materials. A regime's domestic characteristics are of little account when it is on our side in these international power games. Dictators and democrats, conservatives and reformers, fascists and communists—all are, in principle, equally acceptable as allies of the United States as long as their international interests converge with ours.[9]

In practice, this policy normally inclines the United States more toward rightist than leftist regimes. Leftist governments are suspected of having a basic animus against the United States as the leading capitalist power and of being supported by movements hostile to the United States. Rightist governments are presumed to be motivated more purely by practical considerations of power and thus will be more grateful for whatever tangible assistance the United States can provide them against their internal and external opponents. They are believed to be dependent for their political survival on domestic, commercial, and military classes, and deathly afraid of what would befall them if the leftists, especially those friendly to the Soviet Union, gained control. In the Reagan administration's lexicon, rightist regimes of an undemocratic character warranting U.S. support are called "authoritarian" while leftist regimes of an undemocratic character are called "totalitarian" and normally would not warrant U.S. support (China being a glaring exception).[10]

United States assistance to regimes warranting U.S. support on the above grounds takes several forms: generous financial credits, technology transfers, military and police training programs, and a permissive weapons sales policy—all of which constitute in fact, if not by explicit design, a rather significant intervention into the domestic affairs of the client country to help keep the existing regime in power. Occasionally this policy—appropriately called "conservative *realpolitik*"—can take the form of U.S. attempts to destabilize potentially shaky leftist governments. (These attempts might be overt through highly restrictive lending and commercial policies or covert through assistance to opposition groups.)[11]

The main problem with the conservative *realpolitik* policy is that a United States-supported regime, such as the autocracy of the Shah of Iran, may lose credibility with its own people and succumb to a sudden coup or a long germinating swell of popular discontent. In such cases, the United States may find its reputation sullied by its close association with the deposed government. Moreover, the elements engineering the coup or directing the revolution might have aligned themselves with our major international rivals to counterbalance U.S. support for the established government.

Defenders of the conservative *realpolitik* policy grant these risks but argue that the world political arena, particularly the volatile Third World, is by its very nature an uncertain field of competition. Either we accept the risks and participate vigorously on behalf of our friends, or we leave the field open to our major rivals who will intervene to tip local balances in favor of themselves and their friends—cumulatively, the global balance of power as well.

2. *Identify the United States with "progressive" regimes and political movements.*[12] The basic premise of this policy is that the dominant forces in world politics are those working to equalize the distribution of wealth, broaden political participation, and expand human rights. This is assumed to be the outgrowth of the universal spread of literacy and the accompanying exposure of the world's peoples to Lockean and Marxist ideas; namely, that all persons are to be regarded as equal in their basic rights to life, opportunity for economic betterment, and political activity; that governments are legitimate only to the extent that they rest on the consent of the governed; and (in some socialist variants) that disparities in wealth and socioeconomic class are to be eliminated.

From this point of view, United States success in the global rivalry with the Soviet Union, and U.S. international influence in general, will depend on the resourcefulness of this country in championing *two* movements—those for liberty and those for equality. The United States, because of the philosophical roots of its independence movement and constitutional system, the evolution of its humane domestic social welfare policies, and the main thrust of its best foreign policy traditions of anticolonialism and antiautocracy, can credibly identify its basic liberal ethos with the reformist forces of the contemporary world.

Proponents of the policy like to emphasize that they are not motivated primarily by altruism or even idealism. The policy is designed, they contend, to drive a wedge between the communists and the democratic progressives by providing the latter with sufficient financial, organizational, and military resources to allow them to operate separately from communist-organized leftist coalitions. If the United States were to provide hope and concrete assistance to the noncommunist left, then this country—not the Soviet Union and Cuba—would be the reformers. In addition to reducing the U.S.SR's prospects of gaining new clients and satellites, such a policy, if it were well executed, presumably would gain the United States long term access to petroleum resources, other raw materials, and important geopolitical bases in the Third World.

There are problems, however, with this "progressive" interventionary policy also: To be successful it requires almost omniscient knowledge about who's who and what's what in the political life of complex and unfamiliar societies. Despite our best efforts, the regimes or movements supported might fail. Equally important, political leaders whom we may believe to be "progressive" might, once they assume power, turn out to be autocratic and brutal. The ideologies they express concerning human rights, economic egalitarianism, and democratic constitutionalism may be nothing more than instruments to garner popular support on the march to power, only to be discarded for instruments of oppression designed to eliminate their opponents once they are in control. Moreover, a posture of nationalist nonalignment vis-à-vis the U.S.-Soviet rivalry might also prove to be little more than a temporary expedient to gain international support, whereas the deeper commitments of Marxist elements in a "progressive" regime might incline it toward the Soviet Union.

The United States certainly has the option of withdrawing its support from those who have betrayed our faith in them. But unless such withdrawal of support is accompanied by an active policy of destabilizing the regime in power—with all the risks that entails—it will be viewed as a futile gesture, only increas-

4. LIMITS OF AMERICAN POWER

ing the opportunities for our major rivals to make the regime more completely dependent on them. Furthermore, if such second-thought reversals tend to become characteristic of U.S. policy, the global influence of the United States will be weakened by an embarrassing reputation for inconstancy and incompetence.

3. *Maintain a posture of scrupulous neutrality toward indigenous rivals for power in other countries.*[13] This policy does not prevent the United States from assisting those currently in power in worthwhile projects nor from vigorously objecting to policies that might injure U.S. interests or seriously offend basic American values. Nor does it deny the United States the option of counterintervention when our international rivals have intervened in regional or local conflicts. But it does attempt to preserve a clear-cut distinction between projects and policies on the one hand and other personalities and parties on the other. Official and unofficial contacts with various elements of the opposition would be regarded as a normal feature of U.S. relations with other countries. In the event that internal turmoil erupts in countries with which this country has diplomatic relations, the United States would insist on keeping communications open with persons and groups that do not necessarily have the government's official sanction.

Under such a noninterventionist policy, the United States government would not support political activity or cause anti-regime groups to agitate. It would be official U.S. policy, however, to encourage foreign governments to allow transnational organizations, such as labor unions, churches, human rights groups, that support their fellow members across nation-state lines. Furthermore, the United States could make it clear that it would be strongly biased against funding or promoting projects of regimes that systematically suppressed dissent or political opposition.

The United States need not dispense with a capacity to change a local political situation that is detrimental to important U.S. interests or to affect the outcome of an ongoing local conflict whose results, in the absence of such intervention, would substantially injure important U.S. interests. Nevertheless, the basic policy would be one of nonintervention in the affairs of other countries. The advocates of intervention would have to demonstrate that a situation requires U.S. intervention and that the costs and risks of such action are less than the costs and risks of no action at all.

The problem with such a noninterventionist stance is that it could well tempt major adversaries of the United States (the Soviet Union in particular) to intervene first in situations that are below the threshold of a U.S. interventionist reponse, to establish a *fait accompli*, and to thrust on to the United States the awesome responsibility of choosing between initiating or avoiding a large-scale confrontation.

Advocates of this policy, therefore, usually are also advocates

of international conflict control mechanisms, international peace-keeping forces, UN-supervised (or other international or regional agency) cease-fires and elections, international arbitration, and the like to prevent deteriorating local and regional situations from giving our adversaries the pretext for unilateral intervention. Even if the international presence does not succeed in settling a conflict or stabilizing a deteriorating situation, it can provide a buffer against competitive outside interventions of the type that could spark a larger conflagration.

NOTES

1. Ronald Reagan, Address to the Organization of American States, February 24, 1982, U.S. Department of State, Current Policy, No. 370.

2. Ronald Reagan, Address to the Board of Governors of the International Monetary Fund and the World Bank, September 29, 1981, *Weekly Compilation of Presidential Documents*, Vol. 17, No. 4, pp. 1052-1055.

3. *North-South: A Program for Survival* (Cambridge, Massachusetts: MIT Press, 1980), p. 75.

4. *Ibid.*, the whole report.

5. *Ibid.*, p. 18.

6. Department of State, "Law of the Sea: January-February 1982," *Current Policy*, No. 371.

7. Ronald Reagan, Address of September 29, 1981, *Weekly Compilation of Presidential Documents*, Vol. 17, No. 4, pp. 1052-1055.

8. On the responses in the U.S. policy community to specific demands of the Third World countries, see Richard N. Cooper, "A New International Order for Economic Gain," *Foreign Policy*, No. 26 (Spring 1977), pp. 65-120; and Roger D. Hansen, "North-South Policy—What's the Problem?" *Foreign Affairs*, Vol. 58, No. 5 (Summer 1980), pp. 1084-1103.

9. The archpractioner of the conservative *realpolitik* approach toward the Third World was Henry Kissinger during the period 1969-1975. See his retrospective defense of the U.S. support for the Shah of Iran in his *The White House Years* (Boston: Little, Brown, 1979), pp. 1258-1264. See also my book, *The Crises of Power* (New York: Columbia University Press, 1979), pp. 107-140.

10. Jeane Kirkpatrick's "Dictatorships and Double Standards," *Commentary*, Vol. 68, No. 5 (November 1979), pp. 34-35, developed the distinction between "authoritarian" and "totalitarian" regimes and so pleased President-elect Reagan that he appointed her ambassador to the United Nations.

11. Justifications for U.S. interventions to destabilize leftist governments are found in the following policy statements by the Reagan administration: Ronald Reagan, Address to the Organization of American States, February 24, 1982, Department of State, *Current Policy*, No. 370; Ronald Reagan, Address before the British Parliament, June 8, 1982, *Current Policy*, No. 399; Richard Halloran, "Reagan Aide Tells of New Strategy on Soviet Threat," *New York Times*, May 22, 1982.

12. The principal Third World development initiatives of the Kennedy administration were an expression of the "progressive" interventionist stance, although the public presentation of these policies tended to stress the purely economic objectives. The political interventionary premises are detailed in Arthur M. Schlesinger, Jr., *A Thousand Days: John F. Kennedy in the White House* (Boston: Houghton-Mifflin, 1965), pp. 195-196.

13. The aloof noninterventionist rationale is most clearly articulated by J. William Fulbright, *The Arrogance of Power* (New York: Vintage Books, 1967). It also finds articulation in George F. Kennan, *The Cloud of Danger: Current Realities of American Foreign Policy* (Boston: Little, Brown, 1977). A pragmatic version of this approach, fused somewhat with interventionist reformism, was advocated in the Carter administration by Cyrus Vance. See his *Hard Choices: Critical Years in America's Foreign Policy* (New York: Simon and Schuster, 1983).

The U.S. and
Third-World Dictatorships:
A Case for Benign Detachment

The U.S.'s current foreign policy "tragically identifies the U.S. and—even worse—its capitalist democratic system with the most reactionary elements around the globe."

Ted Galen Carpenter

Mr. Carpenter is a foreign policy analyst at the Cato Institute, Washington, D.C.

IT is a central dilemma of contemporary American foreign policy that the world's leading capitalist democracy must confront an environment in which a majority of nations are neither capitalist nor democratic. U.S. leaders have rarely exhibited ingenuity or grace in handling this delicate and often frustrating situation.

The current turmoil in Central America is illustrative of a larger problem. American officials assert that this vital region is under assault from doctrinaire communist revolutionaries trained, funded, and controlled by the Soviet Union. Danger to the well-being of the U.S. is immediate and serious, Administration spokesmen argue, and it is imperative that the Marxist-Leninist tide be prevented from engulfing Central America. Accomplishing this objective requires a confrontational posture toward the communist beachhead (Nicaragua) combined with massive support for all "friendly" regimes, ranging from democratic Costa Rica to autocratic Guatemala. Washington's Central American policy displays in microcosm most of the faulty assumptions underlying America's approach to the entire Third World.

The current strategy of the U.S. betrays a virtual siege mentality. It was not always thus. Throughout the 19th century, U.S. policymakers exuded confidence that the rest of the world would emulate America's political and economic system, seeing the U.S. as a "beacon on the hill" guiding humanity to a better future. As late as the 1940's, most Americans and their political representatives still believed that democracy would triumph as a universal system. The prospective breakup of the European colonial empires throughout Asia and Africa was generally viewed as an opportunity, not a calamity. Scores of new nations would emerge from that process, and Americans were confident that most would choose the path of democracy and free enterprise, thus isolating the Soviet Union and its coterie of Marxist-Leninist dictatorships in Eastern Europe.

The actual results were acutely disappointing. No wave of new democracies occurred in this "Third World"; instead, decolonization produced a plethora of dictatorships, some of which appeared distressingly friendly to Moscow. This development was especially disturbing to Washington since it took place at a time when America's Cold War confrontation with the U.S.S.R. was at its most virulent. The nature and magnitude of that struggle caused American leaders to view the Third World primarily as another arena in the conflict. Consequently, the proliferation of left-wing revolutionary movements and governments seemed to undermine America's own security and well-being.

Washington's response to this adversity has been a particularly simplistic and unfortunate one. American leaders increasingly regarded any anti-communist regime, however repressive and undemocratic it might be at home, as an "ally," a "force for stability," and even a "friend." At the same time, they viewed leftist governments—even those under democratic procedures—as little more than Soviet surrogates, or at least targets of opportunity for communist machinations.

A portent of this mind-set among the U.S. policymakers surfaced during the earliest stages of the Cold War. Pres. Harry Truman's enunciation of the so-called Truman Doctrine in 1947 proclaimed the willingness of the U.S. to assist friendly governments resisting not only external aggression, but also "armed minorities" in their own midst. It was an ominous passage, for the U.S. was arrogating the right to intervene in the internal affairs of other nations to help preserve regimes deemed friendly to American interests. Although Washington had engaged in such conduct throughout Central America and the Caribbean for several decades, those incidents were a geographical aberration in what was otherwise a noninterventionist foreign policy. The Truman Doctrine raised the specter that America's meddlesome paternalism in one region might now be applied on a global basis.

Although Truman stressed that the *status quo* was not "sacred," his doctrine soon made the U.S. a patron of repressive, reactionary regimes around the world. It was a measure of how far that trend had developed by 1961 that Pres. John F. Kennedy could proclaim in his inaugural address America's determination to "support any friend, oppose any foe" in the battle against world communism. Today, leading foreign policy spokesmen such as Henry Kissinger, Alexander Haig, and Jeane Kirkpatrick express a fondness for "friendly" authoritarian regimes that would have seemed incomprehensible to most Americans only a few decades ago.

A false realism as well as moral insensitivity characterize American policy toward Third World dictatorships. There is a disturbing tendency to view such regimes in caricature, regarding right-wing governments as valuable friends whose repressive excesses must be ignored or excused, while perceiving leftist insurgent movements and governments as mortal threats to America's national interest, justifying a posture of unrelenting hostility. For example, the Reagan Administration pursues a confrontational policy toward the Marxist government of Nicaragua, terminating all aid programs, imposing a trade embargo, and supporting rebel guerrillas. At the same time, Washington lavishes economic and military aid upon equally repressive "allies" in South Korea, Taiwan, Zaire, and elsewhere.

The consequences of this simplistic and morally inconsistent strategy are highly unfortunate. America finds itself involved far too often in futile or mutually destructive confrontations with left-wing regimes. Even worse is the evolution of a cozy relationship between Washington and a host of right-wing authoritarian governments. A pervasive perception of the U.S. as the sponsor and protector of such dictatorships has undermined America's credibility as a spokesman for democracy, caused Third World peoples to equate both capitalism and democracy with U.S. hegemony, and established a milieu for rabidly anti-American revolutions. It is an approach that creates a massive reservoir of ill will and, in the long run, weakens rather than strengthens America's national security.

4. LIMITS OF AMERICAN POWER

A flawed policy

Washington's policy toward Third World dictatorships is seriously flawed in several respects. One fundamental defect is the tendency to view largely internal struggles exclusively through the prism of America's ongoing cold war with the Soviet Union. Secretary of State John Foster Dulles was an early practitioner of this parochial viewpoint during the 1950's, when he insisted that the emerging nations of Asia and Africa "choose sides" in that conflict. Nonalignment or neutralism Dulles viewed as moral cowardice or tacit support for the U.S.S.R. Such an attitude only antagonized nonaligned leaders who were concerned primarily with charting a postcolonial political and economic course for their new nations and cared little about an acrimonious competition between two alien superpowers. The chilly relationship between India, the Third World's leading democracy, and the U.S. throughout this period was due in large part to Washington's hostility toward Prime Minister Jawaharlal Nehru's policy of nonalignment.

American policymakers have learned few lessons from Dulles' errors in the subsequent quarter-century. During the 1960's, Washington still saw internal political conflicts in nations as diverse as Vietnam and the Dominican Republic exclusively as skirmishes in the larger Cold War. A decade after the victory of one faction in the complex tribal, linguistic, and economic struggle in Angola, former Secretary of State Henry Kissinger describes that war as part of "an unprecedented Soviet geopolitical offensive" on a global scale. Kissinger's former boss, Gerald Ford, likewise interprets the episode purely as a struggle between "pro-Communist" and "pro-West" forces. Former UN Ambassador Jeane Kirkpatrick views such countries as Mozambique and Nicaragua not as nations in their own right, but as components of the Soviet empire. Similarly, Pres. Reagan's bipartisan commission on Central America describes the multifaceted conflicts of that troubled region as part of a Soviet-Cuban "geo-strategic challenge" to the U.S.

This failure to understand the complexities and ambiguities of Third World power rivalries has impelled the U.S. to adopt misguided and counterproductive strategies. One manifestation is an uncritical willingness to embrace repressive regimes if they possess sufficient anti-communist credentials.

At times, this tendency has proven more than a trifle embarrassing. During a toast to the Shah of Iran on New Year's Eve, 1977, Pres. Jimmy Carter lavished praise on that autocratic monarch: "Iran, because of the great leadership of the Shah, is an island of stability in one of the more troubled areas of the world. This is a great tribute to you, Your Majesty, and to your leadership, and to the respect and admiration and love which your people give to you." Apparently concluding that America's vocal enthusiasm for the Shah and his policies during the previous quarter-century did not link the U.S. sufficiently to his fate, the President emphasized: "We have no other nation on earth who [sic] is closer to us in planning for our mutual military security."

Barely a year later, the Shah's regime lay in ruins, soon to be replaced by a virulently anti-American government. Carter's assumption that the Shah was loved by the Iranian people was a classic case of wishful thinking. CIA operatives in the field warned their superiors that the American perception was a delusion, but those reports were ignored because they did not reflect established policy. Blind to reality, the Carter Administration identified itself and American security interests with a regime that was already careening toward oblivion.

One might think that American leaders would have gained some humility from the wreckage of Iranian policy and at least learned to curb vocal expressions of support for right-wing autocrats. Unfortunately, that has not been the case. Less than four years after Carter's gaffe, Vice Pres. George Bush fawned over Philippine dictator Ferdinand Marcos: "We stand with you sir. . . . We love your adherence to democratic principle [sic] and to the democratic processes. And we will not leave you in isolation."

It is a considerable understatement to suggest that the burgeoning Philippine opposition (which contained many legitimate democrats, such as Salvador Laurel and Butz Aquino) did not appreciate effusive praise for the man who suspended the national constitution, declared martial law, governed by decree, and imprisoned political opponents to perpetuate his own power. From the standpoint of long-term American interests (not to mention common decency and historical accuracy), Bush should have considered how a successor Philippine government might perceive his enthusiasm for Marcos. During his second presidential campaign debate with Walter Mondale, Reagan not only defended this nation's intimate relationship with the Marcos regime, but also implied that the only alternative to Marcos was a communist takeover—which proved to be a gross distortion of reality.

Ill-considered hyperbole with respect to right-wing autocratic governments places the U.S. in an awkward, even hypocritical posture. Equally unfortunate is the extensive and at times highly visible material assistance that Washington gives such regimes. For more than three decades, the U.S. helped train and equip the military force that the Somoza family used to dominate Nicaragua and systematically loot that nation. Similarly, the American government provided lavish military hardware to the Shah of Iran as well as "security" and "counterinsurgency" training to SAVAK, the Shah's infamous secret police. Throughout the same period, Washington gave similar assistance to a succession of Brazilian military governments, a parade of Guatemalan dictatorships, the junta that ruled from 1967 to 1974, and several other repressive governments. Most recently, the U.S. gave the Marcos regime economic and military aid totaling more than $227,000,000, plus millions more in payments for the military installations at Clark Field and Subic Bay. Despite ample signs of that government's increasingly shaky tenure, the Reagan Administration asked Congress to increase aid by nearly 20%. Congress exhibited little enthusiasm for that approach, approving instead a significantly smaller sum and attaching various "human rights" restrictions.

Warm public endorsements of autocratic regimes combined with substantial (at times lavish) material support produce an explosive mixture that repeatedly damages American prestige and credibility. Many of those governments retain only the most precarious hold on power, lacking significant popular support and depending heavily upon the use of terror to intimidate opponents. When repressive tactics no longer prove sufficient, the dictatorships can collapse with dramatic suddenness—as in Iran. American patronage thus causes the U.S. to become closely identified with hated governments and their policies. The domestic populations see those regimes as little more than American clients—extensions of U.S. power. Consequently, they do not view the ouster of a repressive autocrat as merely an internal political change, but as the eradication of American domination.

Moreover, there is a virtual reflex action to repudiate everything American—including capitalist economics and Western-style democracy. The U.S. unwittingly contributes to that process. By portraying corrupt, autocratic rulers as symbols of the "free world," we risk having long-suffering populations take us at our word. They do not see capitalism and democracy as those systems operate in the West, enabling people to achieve prosperity and individual freedom. Instead, Third World people identify free enterprise and democratic values with the corruption and repression they have endured. Historian Walter LaFeber, in *Inevitable Revolutions*, describes how that reasoning has worked in Central America: "U.S. citizens see [capitalist democracy] as having given them the highest standard of living and the most open society in the world. Many Central Americans have increasingly associated capitalism with a brutal oligarchy-military complex that has been supported by U.S. policies—and armies."

Hostility to the left

The flip side of Washington's promiscuous enthusiasm for right-wing autocrats is an equally pervasive hostility toward leftist Third World regimes and insurgent movements. There have been occasional exceptions to this rule throughout the Cold War era. For example, the U.S. developed a cordial relationship with communist Yugoslavia after Premier Josef Tito broke with the Soviet Union in 1948. A similar process occurred during the early 1970's, when the Nixon Administration engineered a rapprochement with China, ending more than two decades of frigid hostility. These achievements are instructive and should have demonstrated to American policymakers that it is possible for the U.S. to coexist with Marxist regimes. However, that lesson has not been learned, and such incidents of enlightenment stand as graphic exceptions to an otherwise dreary record.

More typical of America's posture is the ongoing feud with the Cuban government of Fidel Castro. The campaign to oust or, failing that, to make him a hemispheric pariah, was shortsighted, futile, and counterproductive from the outset. It served only to give him a largely undeserved status as a principled, courageous revolutionary and to drive his government into Moscow's willing embrace. Soviet defector Arkady Shevchenko recalls a 1960 conversation with Nikita Khrushchev in which the latter viewed America's hostility toward Cuba with undisguised glee. Describing U.S. efforts to "drive Castro to the wall" instead of establishing normal relations as "stupid," Khrushchev accurately predicted that "Castro will have to gravitate to us like an iron filing to a magnet."

Apparently having learned little from the Cuban experience, the Reagan Administration seems determined to make the same errors with the Sandinista government of Nicaragua. Washington's attempts to isolate the Managua regime diplomatically, the imposition of economic sanctions, the "covert" funding of the contra guerrillas, and the use of apocalyptic rhetoric to describe the internal struggle for power in that country all seem like an eerie case of *deja vu*. Reagan's depiction of the contras as "the moral equal" of America's own Founding Fathers constitutes ample evidence that U.S. policymakers have not learned to view Third World power struggles with even modest sophistication. One need not romanticize the Sandinista regime, excuse its suppression of political dissent, or rationalize its acts of brutality (*e.g.*, the treatment of the Miskito Indians), as the American political left is prone to do, to advocate a more restrained and detached policy. Administration leaders fear that Nicaragua will become a Soviet satellite in Central America; Washington's current belligerent course virtually guarantees that outcome. As in the case of Cuba nearly three decades ago, the U.S. is creating a self-fulfilling prophecy.

The American government's hostility toward left-wing regimes in the Third World has even extended to *democratic* governments with a leftist slant. An early victim of this antipathy was Iranian Prime Minister Mohammed Mossadegh. Evidence now clearly shows extensive CIA involvement (including planning and funding) in the 1953 royalist coup that enabled the Shah to establish himself as an absolute monarch. Mossadegh's "crime" was not that he was communist, but that he advocated policies inimical to powerful Anglo-American economic interests. A year later, the left-leaning reformist government of Jacobo Arbenz in Guatemala suffered the same fate. This time, American complicity in the overthrow of a democratically elected government was even more blatant. The U.S. Ambassador to Guatemala reportedly boasted that he had brought the counterrevolution to a successful conclusion barely "forty-five minutes behind schedule." Even Reagan's bipartisan commission on Central America concedes U.S. assistance in the coup, and Washington's role has been amply documented elsewhere.

Buoyed by such successes, the U.S. helped oust Patrice Lumumba, the first elected Prime Minister of the Congo (now Zaire), in 1960. Like Mossadegh and Arbenz, Lumumba had committed the unpardonable sin of soliciting communist support. There is also some evidence of American complicity in the 1973 military coup that toppled the government of Chilean Pres. Salvador Allende. We do know that the Nixon Administration sought to thwart Allende's election in 1970, discussed a coup with disgruntled elements of the military immediately following that election, and ordered steps to isolate and destabilize the new government economically. No less a figure than Henry Kissinger, then serving as National Security Advisor, concedes that the U.S. authorized covert payments of more than $8,800,000 to opponents of the Allende government during the three years preceding the coup. Given the relatively modest size of the Chilean economy and population, an infusion of such an amount of money certainly created a considerable political impact, but Kissinger and Nixon both blame Allende's downfall entirely on internal factors. The Marxist president's pursuit of disastrous economic programs together with his systematic attempts to undercut the conservative middle class and harass political opponents undoubtedly galvanized the opposition, weakening his already precarious political position. Nevertheless, it would be naive to accept at face value the Nixon Administration's protestations of innocence regarding the coup, especially in light of Kissinger's ominous assertion that Allende was "not merely an economic nuisance or a political critic but a geopolitical challenge."

It is reprehensible for a government that preaches the virtues of noninterference in the internal affairs of other nations to have amassed such a record of interference. The level of shame mounts when American meddling undermines a sister democracy and helps install a repressive autocracy. Yet, in Iran, Guatemala, Zaire, and Chile, that was precisely what happened. Post-Mossadegh Iran endured the Shah's corrupt authoritarianism for 25 years before desperately embracing the fanaticism of the Ayatollah Khomeini. Guatemala after Arbenz has witnessed a dreary succession of military dictatorships, each one rivaling its predecessor in brutality. The ouster of Patrice Lumumba facilitated the rise to power of Mobuto Sese Seko in Zaire. His regime is regarded as one of the most corrupt and repressive on any continent.

Perhaps Chile is the saddest case of all. Although deified by Western liberals, Allende had his unsavory qualities. His enthusiasm for Marxist economic bromides pushed his nation to the brink of disaster. He also exhibited a nasty authoritarian streak of his own, including an intolerance of political critics. Nevertheless, his actions remained (although sometimes just barely) within constitutional bounds. Moreover, he was the last in an unbroken series of democratically elected rulers stretching back more than four decades—an impressive record in Latin America. The Pinochet dictatorship that replaced Allende is conspicuous for its brutal and systematic violation of individual liberties. Yet, Kissinger can assert that the "change in government in Chile was on balance favorable—even from the point of view of human rights." Such a view reflects either willful blindness or an astounding cynicism.

Strategic, economic, and ideological justifications

Those individuals who justify America's existing policy toward the Third World cite strategic, economic, and ideological considerations. On the strategic level, they argue that the U.S. must prevent geographically important regions from falling under the sway of regimes subservient to the Soviet Union. Otherwise, a shift in the balance of global military power could jeopardize American security interests, perhaps even imperil the nation's continued existence. Economically, the U.S. must maintain access to vital supplies of raw materials and keep markets open for American products and investments. It is not possible, this argument holds, for an economy based upon free enterprise to endure if the world is dominated by state-run Marxist systems. Finally, beyond questions of strategic and economic self-interest, the U.S. must thwart communist expansionism in the Third World to ensure that America and its democratic allies do not become islands in a global sea of hostile, totalitarian dictatorships.

All these arguments possess a certain facile appeal, but they hold up only if one accepts some very dubious conceptions of America's strategic, economic, and ideological interests. Moreover, proponents have often employed these arguments as transparent rationalizations for questionable foreign policy initiatives.

The notion that the United States must assist and defend right-wing regimes while opposing leftist insurgencies or governments for its own strategic self-interest depends on several important subsidiary assumptions. Those who justify America's Third World policy on this basis generally define "strategic interests" in a most expansive manner. In its crudest form, this approach regards Third World states as little more than bases or forward staging areas for American military power. Such a rationale is convincing only if one assumes that the United States truly possesses "vital" strategic interests in regions as diverse as Southeast Asia, the Persian Gulf, Central Africa, and South America, and that successor regimes in regional "keystone" nations would be hostile to those interests.

One can and should question whether the U.S. actually has strategic interests, vital or otherwise, in areas thousands of miles removed from its own shores. How a plethora of small, often militarily insignificant nations, governed by unpopular and unstable regimes, could augment U.S. strength in a showdown with the Soviet Union is a mystery. One could make a more plausible argument that attempts to prop up tottering allies weaken America's security. These efforts drain U.S. financial resources and stretch defense forces dangerously thin. Worst of all is the risk that a crumbling Third World ally could become an arena for ill-advised American military adventures. As we saw in Vietnam, the entrance to such quagmires is easier to find than the exit.

The inordinate fear of successor governments is equally dubious, for it assumes that such regimes would inevitably be leftwing and subservient to Moscow. Neither assumption is necessarily warranted. The ouster of a right-wing autocracy does not lead ineluctably to a radical leftist government. Vigorous democracies succeeded rightist dictatorships in Portugal and Greece. Moreover, even in cases where a staunchly leftist government does emerge, subservience to Moscow can not be assumed. Such pessimism may have had some validity in the bipolar ideological environment of the late 1940's and early 1950's, but, given the diffusion of power away from both Moscow and Washington in the past 30 years, it is now dangerously obsolete. When China and the U.S.S.R. are mortal adversaries, Yugoslavia charts a consistently independent course, and such a country as Rumania—in Moscow's own geopolitical "backyard"—dares exhibit maverick tendencies on selected foreign policy issues, the assumption that a Marxist Third World state will be merely a Soviet stooge is clearly unwarranted.

Economic factors

The economic thesis for current U.S. foreign policy is no more persuasive than the strategic rationale. Assumptions that rightist governments serve as pliant instruments of American economic objectives or that left-wing regimes become commercial adversaries can not be sustained as a general rule. It is true that countries ruled by right-wing autocrats tend to be friendlier arenas for U.S. investment, but the price in bureaucratic restrictions and "commissions" (i.e., bribes) to key officials is often very high. Moreover, governments of whatever ideological stripe usually operate according to principles of economic self-interest, which may or may not correspond to American desires.

Washington received a rude awakening on that score in the 1970's, when its closest Middle East allies—Iran and Saudi Arabia—helped engineer OPEC's massive oil price hikes. Neither U.S. client was willing to forgo financial gain out of any sense of gratitude for political and military support. Much the same situation occurred in 1980, when the Carter Administration invoked a grain embargo against the Soviet Union for the latter's invasion of Afghanistan. The U.S. encouraged, even pressured, its allies to cooperate in that boycott. Nevertheless, the Argentine military junta, a regime that the U.S. had routinely counted upon to stem the tide of leftist insurgency in Latin America, promptly seized the opportunity to boost its grain sales to the U.S.S.R.

Just as right-wing regimes exhibit a stubborn independence on economic matters, revolutionary leftist governments are not inherent commercial enemies. When the U.S. has allowed trade with leftist countries to occur, that trade has usually flourished. The lucrative oil and mineral commerce with the Marxist government of Angola is a case in point. Similarly, once the emotional feud with mainland China ceased in the 1970's, commercial and investment opportunities for the United States also began to emerge. Although a Marxist state dominating the global market in some vital commodity might conceivably attempt to blackmail the U.S., that danger is both remote and theoretical.

Economic realities exert a powerful influence that often transcends purely political considerations. Most Third World governments, whether right-wing or left-wing, benefit from extensive commercial ties with the industrialized West, particularly the U.S. America is often the principal market for their exports and is a vital source of developmental capital. Revolutionary rhetoric, even when sincerely believed, can not change that fundamental equation. It is no coincidence that Third World governments have rarely instituted economic boycotts; most embargoes originate as a deliberate U.S. policy to punish perceived political misdeeds.

Rather than adopting economic sanctions as a device for political intimidation, the U.S. should relish the prospect of promoting commercial connections to the greatest extent possible. Nothing would more readily provide evidence to left-wing leaders that a system based on private property and incentives is vastly superior to the lumbering inefficiencies of Marxist central planning. On those rare occasions when the U.S. has pursued a conciliatory, rather than a truculent and confrontational, approach, the results have been gratifying. The Marxist regime in Mozambique, for instance, first looked to the Soviet bloc for economic as well as ideological guidance, only to confront arrogant Russian imperialism and a recipe for economic disaster. The disillusioned leadership now has begun to turn away from the U.S.S.R. and open its country to Western trade and investment, a process that is likely to accelerate in the coming years.

The most misguided justification for America's attachment to right-wing Third World states lies in the realm of politics and ideology. Proponents assume an underlying ideological affinity between authoritarian systems and Western democracies. They insist that, while rightist regimes may be repressive, such governments are natural U.S. allies in the struggle against world communism. Conversely, revolutionary leftist movements are "totalitarian" in origin and constitute accretions to the power of that global menace.

No one has advanced this thesis more passionately and at greater length than former U.S. Ambassador to the United Nations Jeane Kirkpatrick. While conceding that "traditional" autocracies sometimes engage in practices that offend American "sensibilities," Kirkpatrick clearly finds those regimes more palatable than their leftist adversaries. She asserts that "traditional authoritarian governments are less repressive than revolutionary autocracies," are "more susceptible to liberalization," and are "more compatible with U.S. interests." That being the case, American aid to keep such friendly regimes in power is not only justified, but becomes something akin to a moral imperative.

Even if one concedes that the repression practiced by leftist dictatorships is more pervasive and severe than that of right-wing dictatorships, a more fundamental issue still exists—American complicity. The U.S. has neither the power nor the requisite moral mandate to eradicate injustice and oppression in the world. At the same time, as the most powerful and visible symbol of democracy, America does have an obligation not to become a participant in acts of repression and brutality. Our sponsorship of right-wing autocracies violates that crucial responsibility. Assisting dictatorial regimes makes the U.S. government (and by extension the public that elects it) an accomplice in the suppression of other people's liberty. In a profound way, such complicity constitutes a stain on our democratic heritage.

Kirkpatrick's contention that traditional autocracies are more susceptible to liberalization likewise misses a fundamental point. She asserts that autocratic regimes sometimes "evolve" into more democratic forms, whereas no analogous case exists with respect to revolutionary socialist governments. Yet, her own examples—Spain, Greece, and Brazil—do not involve evolutionary transformations, but, rather, the *restoration* of democratic systems that right-wing elements had destroyed. History demonstrates that, while communist revolutionaries oust competing repressive systems, rightist insurgents habitually overthrow democratically elected governments. There is only one instance of a successful communist uprising against an established democracy—the takeover of Czechoslovakia in March, 1948. Conversely, right-wing coups and revolutions have erased numerous democratic regimes. Spain (1936), Guatemala (1954), Brazil (1964), Greece (1967), the Philippines (1972), Chile (1973), and Argentina (1976) represent only the most prominent examples. It may be more difficult to eradicate leftist (especially totalitarian) systems than it is to replace rightist regimes, but rightwing autocratic movements pose the more lethal threat to functioning democracies. No fact more effectively demolishes the naive notion of an underlying affinity between democracies and rightist dictatorships. The two systems are not allies; they are inherent adversaries.

An alternative

A new foreign policy must eschew inconsistent moral posturing as well as amoral geopolitics. The most constructive alternative would stress "benign detachment" toward all Third World dictatorships, whatever their ideological orientation.

The concept of benign detachment is grounded in the indisputable reality that, for the foreseeable future, the U.S. will confront a Third World environment in which a majority of nations are undemocratic. It would unquestionably prove easier to function in a community of capitalist democracies, but we do not have that luxury. Democracy and capitalism may emerge as powerful doctrines throughout the Third World, but such a transformation would be long-term, reflecting indigenous historical experiences. We certainly can not hasten that process by abandoning our own ideals and embracing reactionary autocrats. In the interim, the U.S. must learn to coexist with a variety of dictatorships. Benign detachment represents the most productive and least intrusive method of achieving that objective.

This approach would reject the simplistic categorization of right-wing regimes as friends and Marxist governments as enemies. It would require redefining America's national interests in a more circumspect manner. No longer should Washington conclude that the survival of a reactionary dictatorship, no matter how repressive, corrupt, and unstable it might be, somehow enhances the security of the U.S. A policy of benign detachment would likewise repudiate the notion that there is an underlying kinship between rightist autocracies and Western democracies. Rightwing dictatorships are just as alien to our values as their left-wing counterparts.

America's primary objective should be a more restrained and even-handed policy toward repressive Third World regimes. Cordial diplomatic and economic relations should be encouraged with *all* governments that are willing to reciprocate, be they democratic, authoritarian, royalist, or Marxist. This would require normalizing diplomatic and commercial relations with such countries as Cuba, Nicaragua, and Vietnam while curtailing aid to so-called allies.

Conservatives invariably protest that this position is a manifestation of a liberal double standard. It is not. In fact, conservatives ignore the actual effects such policies have had in the past. Take the case of mainland China. Throughout the 1950's and 1960's, Washington's attempts to isolate the People's Republic of China only caused that nation to turn inward and fester, producing a particularly oppressive and regimented system. Since the U.S. abandoned its misguided strategy in the early 1970's, China has become a far more open and progressive nation. Deng Xiaoping and his followers now eagerly welcome Western trade and investment, particularly in the field of high technology. Equally important are the changes sweeping the domestic economy. Chinese officials are dismantling crucial elements of Marxist central planning, decentralizing production, creating incentives, and even legalizing certain forms of private property. All those developments should be gratifying to Americans who believe in the virtues of a market economy. Moreover, the first, albeit hesitant, signs of political liberalization in China are beginning to emerge. Prominent Chinese spokesmen even assert publicly that Karl Marx was not infallible and that many of his ideas are irrelevant in the modern era—sentiments that would have merited the death sentence only a few years ago.

While the U.S. initiative in establishing cordial political and economic relations with China can not account entirely for this movement toward liberalization, there is no question that it helps facilitate progressive trends. Conservatives who advocate isolating Cuba, Vietnam, Nicaragua, and other Marxist nations would do well to ponder that point. Liberals who endorse economic sanctions against South Africa should consider whether their suggested strategy is not counterproductive as well.

A policy of benign detachment is not isolationist—at least insofar as that term is used to describe a xenophobic, "storm shelter" approach to world affairs. Quite the contrary, it adopts a tolerant and optimistic outlook, seeing Third World states not merely as pawns in America's cold war with the Soviet Union, but as unique and diverse entities. Extensive economic relations are not merely acceptable, they are essential to enhancing the ultimate appeal of capitalism and democracy. There is even room for American mediation efforts to help resolve internecine or regional conflicts, provided that all parties to a dispute desire such assistance and our role harbors no danger of political or military entanglements. The U.S. need not practice a surly isolation. America can be an active participant in Third World affairs, but the nature of such interaction must be limited, consistent, and nonintrusive.

A policy of benign detachment would bring numerous benefits to the U.S. No longer would America be perceived as the patron of repressive, decaying dictatorships, or as the principal obstacle to indigenous change in the Third World. Our current foreign policy tragically identifies the U.S. and—even worse—its capitalist democratic system with the most reactionary elements around the globe. This foolish posture enables the Soviet Union to pose as the champion of both democracy and Third World nationalism. It is time that America recaptured that moral high ground. If the U.S. allowed the people of Third World nations to work out their own destinies instead of trying to enlist them as unwilling combatants in the Cold War, Russia's hypocritical, grasping imperialism would soon stand exposed. Moscow, not Washington, might well become the principal target of nationalistic wrath throughout Asia, Africa, and Latin America. Moreover, the inherent inequities and inefficiencies of Marxist economics would soon become evident to all but the most rabid ideologues.

Equally important, a conciliatory noninterventionist posture toward the Third World would reduce the risk of U.S. military involvement in complex quarrels generally not relevant to American security. Savings in terms of both dollars and lives could be enormous. Our current policy threatens to format a plethora of "brush fire" conflicts with all the attendant expense, bitterness, and divisiveness that characterized the Vietnam War.

Finally, and not the least important, reducing our Third World commitments would put an end to the hypocrisy that has pervaded U.S. relations with countries in the Third World. It is debilitating for a society that honors democracy and fundamental human rights to embrace regimes that scorn both values. A nation that believes in human liberty has no need for, and should not want, "friends" who routinely practice the worst forms of repression. A policy of detachment would restore a badly needed sense of honor and consistency to American foreign policy.

'The Third World Is Not a Hopeless Place'

But to help, the former president argues, we must be more than patrons—
we must become partners.

Jimmy Carter

Former president Jimmy Carter is founder of the Atlanta-based Carter Center, a nonprofit institution dedicated to alleviating conflict and suffering around the world. He is also a distinguished professor at Emory University.

I HAPPEN TO BE A FARMER. My mother was a registered nurse, so I have a connection with health care. The environment has always concerned me. At The Carter Center in Atlanta, we try to combine agriculture, health care, and environmental quality work in a number of places around the world. We have projects in China, Bangladesh, Pakistan, Tanzania, Uganda, Kenya, Ghana, Nigeria, Zambia, and other countries. With various political and economic interests competing throughout the world for influence, it's hard to find ways in which agriculture, health care, and environmental preservation can be pursued together.

It's easy to blame people who are cutting down trees. In countries such as Sudan, where 260,000 people died last year from war, or Ethiopia, or Somalia, or Mozambique—it's easy to say that if they can't prevent the civil war, somehow or another, they deserve to suffer. It's easy to blame them; it's easy to blame our own government, or outside sources, for the problems. We always know the answers for other people. But, ultimately, we not only want a good life for ourselves, we want a good life for others as well.

What is the mechanism, or the means, by which we can cross the chasm between ourselves and others around the world who can actually implement what we want to accomplish? I believe the means consist of establishing trust by producing results at the grassroots level, and by this immediate benefit convincing the political leadership of the world (including the leadership in this country) that long-term planning of food produc-

tion, health care, and environmental preservation must be done together, as was envisioned in the process begun when I commissioned the Global 2000 report during my presidency. This one-year study assessed the probable changes in the world's population and environment through the end of the century and was to serve as the foundation of future planning.

IN THE LAST TWENTY YEARS, the per-capita production of food grain across Africa has actually gone down. The average African is now consuming seventy calories fewer per day than twenty years ago.

I'm the only president who ever visited Africa. Sometimes the leaders there have to be convinced, contrary to their natural inclination, that what we from The Carter Center are trying to do in health, population, environmental work, and food production is best for their country. I sit at the table with the king or the president or the prime minister, and because I was president they generally bring in all their cabinet officers. I bring with me people such as Dr. Norman Borlaug, who was a Nobel Laureate for his work in the green revolution, and The Carter Center's executive director, Dr. William Foege, who orchestrated the campaign to eradicate smallpox from the Earth, and we tell these leaders what we hope to accomplish in their country. Our purpose at the meeting is to get the country's key people convinced that what we're proposing can benefit them. If they're not convinced, then we are going to be dealing with third-level bureaucrats, not with key cabinet ministers. And nothing will be accomplished.

In January 1986 I made my first trip to Ghana, primarily to talk about food production. That year we got forty farmers to participate in our Global 2000 program. Twenty planted corn, and twenty

planted sorghum; each planted about one acre of demonstration plots using traditional farming practices, and one acre using an improved kind of seed and a moderate amount of fertilizer. We didn't bring any mechanization; the farmers still plant with a pointed stick and cultivate with a hoe. But the demonstration plots were so successful—on average tripling the previous yield—that we jumped in 1987 from forty farmers to twelve hundred. In 1988, Global 2000 had sixteen thousand, and in 1989 eighty-five thousand Ghanaian farmers were participating in our program.

We also teach farmers environmentally sound growing techniques. They plant now in contour rows, to stave off erosion. Instead of slash-and-burn techniques—where they would burn off an area of forest, plant it for one year, and then move on to another area—farmers now plant using enough fertilizer so that they can repeatedly grow crops on the same plot of land. That means the forest can be saved. And we have only three foreign employees in Ghana: two Mexicans and one Korean. All the rest of the workers are Ghanaians, so at the end of five years (1991) we plan to withdraw from Ghana, leaving that nation self-sufficient in food production.

Ethiopia is another example of a country in which we have to prove the immediate benefit of our work before we can get started on the road to long-term solutions. The war in Ethiopia between the government and the Eritrean People's Liberation Front—over whether Eritrea should be a part of Ethiopia or have the right to self-determination—is twenty-nine years old. Both sides are Marxist. A million people have died in this war, not only as a result of bombs, bullets, and shells, but also from starvation, malnutrition, and diarrhea among children as a direct result of lack of food.

Ethiopia is the poorest country in the

By Jimmy Carter. From *New Age Journal*, March/April 1990, pp. 52–54, 132–134. Adapted from a speech given at the Globescope Pacific Conference in October 1989.

world, with a per-capita income of one hundred thirty dollars. Farmers there produce only four bags of grain per acre. It's impossible to get people in such poverty to worry about environmental issues. It's impossible to gain their confidence or forge partnerships with just words. They're starving. So what we at The Carter Center try to do first is get Dr. Borlaug's staff to show farmers how to triple or even quadruple production of grain per acre. When we show a direct and identifiable benefit to the people, the leaders see a political benefit, and that short-term gain gives them enough confidence in us to listen to environmental discussions. I might add that in spite of its being the poorest nation on Earth, Ethiopia spends 60 percent of its total national wealth on weapons. [*Editors' Note:* The Carter Center's International Negotiation Network was successful in arranging preliminary talks between Ethiopia's warring parties, at which they agreed for the first time in nearly three decades to embark on full-scale peace negotiations in 1990.]

IT'S EASY TO CRITICIZE the Third World for its burgeoning population, but deeply related to the problem of too many people is wasteful consumption. I have four children and six grandchildren. It's sobering to me to know that each one of them, and Rosalynn and I, consumes fifteen times as much of the world's limited

At the end of five years we plan to withdraw from Ghana, leaving that nation self-sufficient in food production.

resources as does the average citizen in India. When we worry about population growth in India, when we tell them they ought to be ashamed, we ought to remember that fifteen children in India are not going to deplete the world's supply of vital resources any more in the future than one child born in America. Perhaps, in addition to efforts directed at population control in India, we should exert some self-discipline to conserve resources. When I left office we had, after a lot of heartache and struggle, reduced our dependence on imported oil to about 30 percent of total use. Now it's back up to 50 percent, and going up

every day. The developed world has got to realize that a large part of the responsibility to conserve resources is still ours.

We also need to change our dependence on weapons production and weapons sales overseas as a basic foundation for jobs in this country. It costs about one million dollars in defense expenditures to create one job—a vast inefficiency. But we have been so seduced, so influenced, so outspent—so outbribed, you might say—in the

Courtesy Global 2000

It's impossible to get people in poverty to worry about environmental issues. So first we try to show farmers how to triple or even quadruple production of grain per acre. When we show a direct benefit to the people, that gives leaders enough confidence in us to listen to environmental discussions.

Above: A Zambian farmer learns corn-planting techniques.

When we worry about population growth in India, we ought to remember that fifteen children there are not going to deplete the world's resources any more than one child born in America.

Congress of the United States by the defense industry that it's almost impossible to prevail when you want to cut back on unnecessary expenditures.

Another inefficiency: The US Agency for International Development program (USAID), which was supposed to be designed for sustainable development in the Third World, is almost totally incompetent. The Carnegie Foundation and The Carter Center, looking to the application of science and technology to improve the quality of life in the Third World, recently did a definitive analysis of USAID. Of the $11 billion spent annually, $10 million goes to Israel every day, about two thirds of that amount goes to Egypt, and a huge part of the remainder goes to finance purchases of weapons from American manufacturers. This leaves about $2.1 billion a year to actually improve the lives of people overseas. Of that $2.1 billion, 80 percent goes to administrative costs: It costs us eighty cents of every dollar to finance the expenditure of twenty cents of aid in the Third World.

Japan also budgets about $11 billion for overseas aid. What they do is go to the leaders of the poor nations and say, "We have $26 million to spend on health care in your country. What is the best way to spend it?" And with minimal administrative costs, with practically no staff in the country, they work harmoniously with that country's minister of health, spending the money for safe water or to provide immunization programs. This is not purely altruistic on the part of the Japanese, because they are planting small seeds of help that in the future will pay richly in friendship, partnership, and availability of increasingly scarce natural resources. They will also reap a benefit in commerce, creating markets for Japanese consumer prod-

I wish the major universities in the West would adopt a Third World country, giving students an opportunity to learn things about the developing world they might otherwise never know.

ucts. You can't do that when you spend eighty cents of every dollar on administrative costs.

IN WORKING WITH the developing world, you see the relationships between health care and other problems, such as illiteracy. Here's an example, and an opportunity for people who work in telecommunications research and development:

A lot of the most arable land in the Third World has not even been planted because of two afflictions: Guinea worm and river blindness. Guinea worm, which most Americans have never heard of, affects ten million people a year. It's a parasite people get from drinking impure water. The water contains the worm's egg, and inside the human body that egg grows into a worm a meter long in twelve months. The worm then emerges through the skin, leaving a horrible sore.

River blindness is caused by the sting of a fly found along fast-flowing streams. Sometimes you go to villages where 35 percent of the adults are blind; you see adults walking around holding one end of a stick with a little five-year-old child holding the other end, acting as a seeing-eye baby. And you know that if something isn't done, that child will be blind someday, too.

We have treatments for both these conditions, donated by US corporations such as Merck and Company, and we can go in with them. In fact, the Global 2000 program and other health care

organizations have targeted 1995 as the year by which Guinea worm will be eradicated. But remember, we're trying to teach people to take care of themselves. So there's another problem: How do you educate people who are basically illiterate about the cause of Guinea worm or river blindness? We ran our first test case in Pakistan, in a place where only 12 percent of the men, and almost no women, were literate. There are currently two ways to communicate with these people. One is through radio, and the other is by giving them printed cartoons that tell the story in pictures. These are not very efficient methods, and so there's a need for telecommunications people to get involved, to invent a way to communicate health information to people who are illiterate. Long-term planners can see that these problems—health care and illiteracy—are related.

The world political situation, far from being hopeless, offers opportunities to help everywhere. I wish the major universities throughout the West would, in effect, adopt a Third World country. The University of Georgia has a great agricultural school and a great forestry school, and could go to a country such as Haiti and ask, "What can we do to help you to provide jobs, replant your forests, improve tourism, educate your people, build better homes, establish democracy?" Haiti would accept a university, whereas it would never accept any intrusion from the US government (most countries won't, by the way). Working with major corporations in our country and others, the university could bring in students and give them an opportunity to help, and in the process those students would learn things about the developing world they might otherwise never know.

Rosalynn and I are volunteers with Habitat for Humanity, which builds housing for homeless people. In June we're going to Tijuana to build a hundred homes on a barren hillside in a desperately poor area. It's arid, so there aren't many trees. We've used wood, two-by-four studs, before. Now we're working on a problem: How are we going to build

It's easy to criticize the Third World for its burgeoning population, but related to the problem of too many people is wasteful consumption—the developed world has got to realize that a large part of the responsibility to conserve resources is still ours.

adobe block homes with inexperienced volunteers who lack masonry skills? We'll find a way, but the point is we'll do it with absolutely no government money, and in the process we'll develop innovative ways for inexperienced people, in arid parts of the world at least, to build homes at very low cost.

I would like to see the Global 2000 process revived. It was killed when I left Washington, because of a political aversion to long-term planning with an emphasis on the environment. It ought to be resurrected and concentrated in the National Academy of Sciences, not in the federal government. It ought to be supported by the major corporations. It wouldn't take much money. This we can do collectively, as men and women committed to sustainable development, to a better quality of life, for all those on Earth.

I don't have any sense of impending doom or despair. I think that things can be changed. If you look at the face of just one Ghanaian farmer who for the first time is producing sixteen bags of sorghum or corn where previously there were just three or four bags, and see how eager he is to join our program of environmental work as well, you know the Third World is not a hopeless place. The people there are waiting to be partners with people here in seeing that everybody on Earth can have a better way of life.

Refugee Concerns and U.S. Interests

Jonathan Moore

Ambassador Jonathan Moore is U.S. coordinator for refugees.

The United States has a historical, nonpartisan, priority commitment to humanitarian assistance to refugees. Americans care about refugees because we are a compassionate people, because we ourselves are a nation of global ties, and because our national interests abroad involve us inextricably in refugees' fates.

When waves of humanity surge across borders, it matters little whether the persons arriving are legally eligible to be considered refugees, displaced persons, or persons of concern under the UN High Commissioner for Refugees' extended mandate. At the beginning, they are fearful, hungry, sick, fleeing people. The world's response is to care for them, provide them the necessities of life, and sort out identities, priorities, and criteria later.

It is generally accepted that the present refugee population worldwide numbers over 12 million, with millions more who are displaced or "at risk" in "refugee-like circumstances." Africa is the area most extensively affected. Mozambican refugees have fled to all surrounding countries; one-tenth of the population is outside of Mozambique. Malawi hosts some 500,000 Mozambican refugees; the Republic of South Africa has approximately 200,000 within its borders. Refugees of the fighting in Angola have also spread to neighboring areas. In Ethiopia, warfare, repressive government policies such as forced resettlement, and tribal persecution have forced well over one million people into exile. Sudan is host to some 650,000 refugees from Ethiopia, plus several hundred thousand more from Uganda and Chad. Throughout Africa, drought, famine, and feeble economies have exacerbated refugee movements provoked by insurgencies.

In Southeast Asia, the aftermath of the Vietnam War has caused the flight of 1.3 million refugees from Vietnam, Laos, and Cambodia. The flow of boat people leaving Vietnam continues at a rate exceeding 20,000 people annually; smaller numbers of refugees continue to leave Laos. Thailand is the most heavily impacted country in the region: It is the first asylum of some 130,000 refugees and hosts a population of some 260,000 Cambodian "displaced persons," located in camps near the Thai-Cambodian border, who have fled the Vietnamese occupation.

The oldest refugee situation in the world is that of the Palestinians in the Middle East, a refugee community now in its third generation. More than two million Palestinians in Israel's Occupied Territories, Lebanon, Jordan, and Syria are registered to receive international assistance.

Refugees from Eastern Europe and the Soviet Union, including Jewish émigrés, also continue to seek asylum. Well-established procedures to process them exist in Western Europe and the major resettlement countries: Australia, Canada, Israel, and the United States. In the last 10 years, 185,000 of these people have sought a new life in America.

In Central America, the total number of acknowledged refugees in first asylum within the region is more than 300,000.

The best news in the world refugee panorama is for the more than five million Afghan refugees in Pakistan and Iran. With the signing of the Geneva peace accords on Afghanistan in April and the withdrawal of Soviet troops from their homeland, these Afghans can get poised for the trek home, after as many as eight years in refugee camps. As the largest international refugee repatriation since World War II, the Afghan return will require a tremendous effort and coordination of international organizations and major donor countries, including the United States, under the aegis of the UN special coordinator.

Wherever they are, refugees live in dislocated, deprived, ambiguous circumstances and face bleak futures. Once described as "human rights violations made

The United States ranks 8th among the top 20 in contributions to international refugee assistance funds.

visible," most refugees are victims of violence—whether wrought by the countries they have fled, the wars they bring with them, hostile local populations, or their own factionalism. The countries to which they flee are often among the world's poorest. The average per capita GNP for the primary nations of first asylum is about $800 per year.

An ambitious international system of multilateral and bilateral programs involving a wide range of collaborating agencies administers basic assistance to refugees. These services include: life-sustaining food, water, shelter, medical supplies, and health aid; education; protection and security; development and impact assistance; and resettlement. Partners in the effort include multilateral agencies led by the UNHCR and the UN Relief and Works Agency for Palestinian Refugees in the Near East (UNRWA); specialized international organizations such as the International Committee of the Red Cross

(ICRC) and the Intergovernmental Committee for Migration; a multitude of private, nonprofit, voluntary agencies with enormous commitment and skill; and nations that receive refugees, donate money, resettle refugees, and in some instances facilitate their return.

Needs not met

Unfortunately, immediate assistance needs for refugees are not being met adequately, either in terms of the international aspirations expressed in the 1951 Geneva Convention on refugees and its Protocol or of our own national values. A major challenge for the international community is to care for refugees and keep them from becoming physically or emotionally exhausted, until return to their homes or other permanent solutions are possible.

In raw dollar terms, international assistance levels appear to keep pace with the enlarging refugee population. Total contributions to the main international refugee assistance organizations —UNHCR, UNRWA, and ICRC —have increased in the past three years to almost $700 million annually. But the sad reality is that the reach of these humanitarian programs is substantially less than what is required, and budget requests are heavily influenced by the limited contributions obtainable.

This year, emergency appeals from international refugee organizations are up, but it remains unclear how well the international community will respond. Those of the ICRC alone are 46 percent above last year's appeals for the ICRC's important relief and protection work in Africa, Southeast Asia, Central America, Afghanistan, and the Middle East. This year's U.S. response is running $8 million lower than last year's, and the president's $50 million fund for meeting unpredictable emergencies has been depleted to $12.6 million without having been replenished over a two-year period.

In absolute terms, the United States remains well in the fore-

front of overall contributors to international refugee organizations. This year, the U.S. government will spend $176.2 million to support refugee assistance programs. The next largest donor, the European Community (EC), contributes about half that. Yet, in the short run, our national commitment to deficit reduction places real constraints on us. Our assistance contributions this year are 9 percent under 1987 levels, and the U.S. contribution to the ICRC is down from 22 percent to 11 percent. Similarly, our traditional 30 percent contribution to the UNHCR has dropped to 23 percent. The cut from $67 million to $61.3 million in the U.S. contribution to UNRWA's program for Palestinian refugees is particularly wrenching during this sensitive period of tragic events in the Occupied Territories.

Compared with other major donors, the United States ranks 8th among the top 20 in contributions to international refugee assistance funds when measured on the basis of the per capita donor population. This is up from 12th in 1980 but down from 5th in 1985. Per capita contributions from Nordic countries, consistently at the top of the list, have jumped from $2.50 to over $4.00 in the past three years; and EC coun-

More than 20,000 Vietnamese flee their communist homeland annually.

tries among the top 20 have more than doubled their average per capita contributions to $1.50. On the other hand, U.S. per capita contributions have stagnated below $1.00.

Immediate, emergency, and temporary assistance is critical, and we can never fail to provide it. But what happens next? What possibilities exist between meeting the emergency and attacking the root causes of refugee problems? Classically, the international community relies on three "durable solutions" as long-run alternatives to immediate assistance in place:

● Repatriation—voluntary return to the country from which the refugees fled;

● Local integration—establishing new homes in the country of first asylum; and

● Third country resettlement —transporting and transplanting refugees to a distant country where there is an opportunity to begin a new life.

Ideally, resettlement to a third country should be the last option considered, for adjustment to a totally new environment requires a tremendous effort on the part of the refugees and those taking them in. The process is expensive as well as difficult, and many refugees cannot meet the requirements necessary for permanent admission to third countries. There is also the risk that the possibility of resettlement will have a "magnet effect" that attracts further refugee flows.

Resettlement remains a viable but costly option for a limited few. About one-third of the U.S. refugee assistance budget of $448 million for fiscal year 1988 is allocated for the resettlement of roughly 68,000 refugees in this country, and the rest goes for international assistance in place, benefiting roughly 12 million refugees. Resettlement can be the solution for only about 1 percent of the world's refugees.

First asylum countries are among the poorest in the world, in addition to struggling under the burden of newly arrived populations in need of assistance. Although the response of first asylum countries has been remark-

able, in the long run they are unlikely to provide significant opportunities for the second durable solution—permanent local integration. In Africa, countries are less willing to accept, or their fragile economies are less able to bear, the weight of new populations. In Southeast Asia, where first asylum countries—supported by the UNHCR and the resettlement countries—have granted asylum to refugees for more than a decade, with no end in sight, pressures are accumulating to stem the flow. Prospects for refugees settling in the region are not bright.

Voluntary repatriation, the most desirable durable solution, is also the most difficult to achieve in many cases. For a person to be willing to return home, the conditions that forced him to become a refugee in the first place must be resolved. Too frequently, the causes of refugee flight are intractable and unlikely to disappear soon.

We believe that more situations where repatriation is possible must be encouraged and will develop. In Africa, more than a dozen repatriations are occurring or have taken place recently: to Ethiopia from Sudan, Somalia, and Djibouti; to Chad from the Central African Republic, Sudan, and Cameroon; and to Uganda from Rwanda, Sudan, and Zaire. Yet, Africa is an exception in experiencing repatriation.

Preventing flows

While valuable options, the three durable solutions for refugees are today limited and insufficient in and of themselves. If we are really serious about aiding people in such a state of fear and discouragement that they are willing to abandon everything, we must not only "manage" refugees once they arrive in first asylum and press for all three durable solutions, but also find ways to achieve conditions that do not breed refugee flows.

Let me review some ongoing priorities and recent accomplishments to which the United States has contributed:

● The continuing generous resettlement of refugees in the United States, led by the government but in close collaboration with the private sector. Churches, community groups, and individuals all continue to sponsor refugees and help them in resettlement.

● The preservation of first asylum, particularly in Southeast Asia, where receiving countries once again face the possibility of more and more boat arrivals. We will continue to work with the international community for their support of resettlement.

● The resumption of the Orderly Departure Program from Vietnam, allowing refugees, including Amerasian children, to exit from Vietnam directly to the United States instead of trying to escape in unsafe boats.

● The resumption of exits from Cuba of political prisoners and their families, after a hiatus of several years.

● The increase of our ability to receive the growing numbers of Jews and Armenians emigrating from the Soviet Union.

● The establishment of effective relief programs for the massive numbers of refugees fleeing Mozambique.

● The securing of leadership within international organizations to assure effective management and use of scarce financial resources.

What we have accomplished is crucial, but is still inadequate to meet the growing needs. Yet we are committed to face the challenges ahead, spurred by the most powerful aspect of our refugee policy: our values and ideals, which are integral to broader U.S. foreign policy. The idealism inherent in refugee policy not only is essential to its own success but also can contribute to the character and conduct of overall foreign policy. We must include our most precious values to exert international leadership, which otherwise might be too susceptible to chauvinism or realpolitik. A dynamic commitment to humanitarian assistance to refugees helps assure that the human spirit and national foreign policy advance in union.

United States
Security Policy and ASEAN

Continuity and change in Southeast Asia are the focus of this issue. The introductory article explores how social and economic dynamism in the region is forcing the United States to reevaluate its security needs there. The author poses the central security question: "If superpower détente translates into a reduction of forward deployed forces in Southeast Asia during the 1990's, are the ASEAN states considering an alternative security posture?"

SHELDON W. SIMON

Sheldon W. Simon is a faculty associate of the Center for Asian Studies at Arizona State University (Tempe). A specialist on Asian security, his most recent book is *The Future of Asian-Pacific Security Collaboration* (Lexington, Mass.: Lexington Books, 1988). Research for this article was partially supported by travel grants from The Earhart Foundation (Ann Arbor) and the United States Information Agency.

WHAT happens if peace breaks out?" is a question applicable not only in Europe but in the Asian Pacific area as well. While superpower détente has become increasingly prominent in the late 1980's, its implications for United States diplomacy in Asia are complex. United States foreign policy in the Pacific followed two tracks during the years of Ronald Reagan's presidency. The dominant cold war track emphasized the importance of maintaining a strong navy and a strong air force along the Asian-Pacific rim to balance their growing Soviet counterparts and to reassure allies like Japan, South Korea, the Philippines and Thailand.

An increasingly important secondary track, however, seemed to conflict with the first. As United States budget and balance of payments deficits ballooned, Washington began pressing friends and allies to open their markets to American products and to raise the value of their currencies. These economic pressures have strained United States political-strategic relations with Asian nations, calling into question Washington's long-term ability to sustain a cold war posture through the 1990's.

As the decade closed, these strains were exacerbated by the détente process itself, which challenged the need for maintaining United States military dominance if the Soviet threat were declining. The confluence of economic strains and military relaxation portends troubled times for the Asian policy of President George Bush.

In effect, the Asian policy of the United States is in a period of transition. Alliances and the maintenance of an air and naval presence still contribute to stability; at the same time, however, they have become an economic burden to the United States and an affront to nationalist sensitivities in countries like South Korea and the Philippines. Nationalist pressures in an era of superpower détente, combined with the monetary costs of maintaining forward deployed forces, will inexorably lead to the reduction of United States forces in Southeast Asia over the next decade. If the size of Soviet deployments in Vietnam wanes, members of the Association of South East Asian Nations (ASEAN)[1] will view American ships and aircraft as increasingly irrelevant to their real security concerns: ethnic unrest, religious tensions and class-based turmoil over the distribution of the fruits of economic development.[2]

The movement toward democracy in Southeast Asia, leading to governments susceptible to popular pressure and shifting coalitions, will make United States policy more complicated on a daily basis. At the same time, there is consensus within ASEAN that only the United States is an acceptable provider of regional security. It is the only major power whose political motives are regarded as benign and whose open markets remain essential for regional prosperity. A United States commitment to Southeast Asian stability and development continues to form the basis of United States policy, even though the contribution Washington makes to regional economic goals is now shared with other donors, notably the countries of northeast Asia—Japan, South Korea and Taiwan. All three became major investors in ASEAN during the late 1980's.

As the United States reduces its military competition with the Soviet Union, it is simultaneously increasing economic pressure on allies like Thailand and the Philippines to open their own markets

to United States products in order to correct trade imbalances. United States officials have warned their Pacific allies that chronic trade imbalances must lead to defense budget cuts.[3] For example, the United States ambassador to Singapore has insisted that countries under the United States protective umbrella "should absorb more of the costs of that protection." Concern that Washington may press Japan to assume maritime security responsibilities in Southeast Asia may well be energizing recent efforts by Singapore, Malaysia and Indonesia to acquire new missile-armed aircraft and warships to protect adjacent South China Sea waters increasingly on their own.[4]

The ASEAN states are also aware of the decline of Soviet deployments in the South China Sea–Indian Ocean theater in recent years; they know that the Soviet Union is retiring ships more rapidly from the Pacific Fleet than it is commissioning new units. To ASEAN audiences, Soviet officials stress the fact that their naval presence is designed primarily to protect their own important sea lanes to the Soviet Far East, essential for Siberian development. No threat is intended, therefore, by the Soviet navy's operations in Southeast Asia.[5]

In a reduced external-threat environment, combined with American pressures for burden-sharing, United States relations with ASEAN may best be assessed by examining the policies dealing with three major current regional concerns. They include the future of the Philippine bases, which will affect the ability of the United States Navy and Air Force to maintain a permanent Southeast Asian presence; the future of Indochina, pending a Cambodian settlement and the prospect for a new ASEAN-Indochinese political-economic relationship; and the possibility of greater ASEAN defense collaboration as well as ASEAN's role in a larger Pacific Basin economic arrangement. The outcome of these issues could well determine Southeast Asian security in the 1990's.

THE PHILIPPINE BASES

The future of the Southeast Asian bases encompasses both United States facilities at Clark Air Base and Subic Bay Naval Station in the Philippines and Soviet facilities at Cam Ranh Bay and Danang in Vietnam.[6] Their disposition in the 1990's will affect the security policies of all Southeast Asian actors. The termination or even the diminution of forces at the bases would mean that the littoral states would become increasingly responsible for regional defense.

Philippine defense officials admit that their armed forces could not provide for external security were the Americans to leave abruptly.[7] Other

ASEAN members also fear that a precipitous United States withdrawal could bring Japanese, Chinese or even Indian naval forces into the region with unpredictable results. On the other hand, even staunch Filipino advocates of the bases agree that their years are numbered and that the facilities should be phased out by the turn of the century.[8] Achieving a gradual phaseout, however, is politically difficult.

Under the new Philippine constitution, the bases can be extended after 1991 only by treaty (not by executive agreement). Already, a decisive bloc of 11 Filipino senators have gone on record opposing renewal, a bloc large enough to prevent the ratification of any lease extension. Hoping to thwart the Senate preemption of the Philippine negotiating position (on which the prospect of considerable United States foreign aid depends), President Corazon Aquino has called for a national referendum on the bases. Assuming that Filipino voters support a lease renewal, public opinion could pressure the senators to drop their opposition.[9]

Because most Filipinos perceive the bases as relevant only to Asia-Pacific defense needs of the United States (and not to their own defense), their continuation is justified as a device to generate United States aid and investment. Manila insists, for example, that any new treaty address all funding provisions explicitly. However, no treaty can bind the United States Congress in advance on appropriations, because the House of Representatives must initiate all financing bills. Moreover, the United States has already raised its assistance package for the Philippines from $180 million in the 1983 bases review to an annual figure of $481 million from 1988 to 1991. This sum is independent of an additional $200 million that the United States has promised for each of the next five years under the Multilateral Assistance Initiative.[10] Given American fiscal constraints, it is unlikely that the United States Congress will be willing to raise the annual figure for the Philippines much beyond its current level.

Paradoxically, a five- or ten-year phaseout could actually accelerate a United States decision to leave the Philippines. Instead of investing further in bases it has agreed to leave, Washington would use its resources for future base sites and related alternatives, probably accelerating the withdrawal schedule from Clark and Subic Bay.[11]

An additional Philippine roadblock lies in the path of a successful lease extension. Article II of the Philippine constitution appears to prohibit nuclear weapons on Philippine territory "consistent with the national interest." Should this provision be interpreted to require that the United States reveal the presence of nuclear warheads on its ships and aircraft, Washington would almost certainly leave the bases.

As the negotiations for renewal begin in early 1990, Manila's talking points seem to focus on the issues of joint use by the Philippine armed forces and an increase in United States imports and investments. If the bases are to be renewed, then the United States must demonstrate sensitivity to the moderates among Philippine nationalists. Washington stresses that the bases are the country's second largest employer, providing jobs for almost 80,000 Filipinos, and that they contribute $1 billion to the economy annually, approximately five percent of gross national product (GNP).[12]

The United States will also be asked to give the Philippines a greater voice in military operations from the bases in Southeast Asia while simultaneously helping to build the Philippine navy and air force so that they, too, can deploy from the bases for external defense.

The politically risky connection between the bases and Philippine nationalism was dramatically illustrated in the December, 1989, sixth and bloodiest coup attempt by military elements against Aquino's government. In the first days, an air attack against Malacanang Palace (the President's quarters) led to Aquino's request for United States military assistance. The Bush administration obliged by sending F-4's from Clark Airfield to fly cover over the Philippine air base from which the mutineers had flown. No fire was exchanged; but the tactic achieved its desired effect by keeping Philippine planes on the ground during the fighting.

While the United States Air Force action was a bold demonstration of Washington's commitment to the Philippine government and to the democratic process in that country, political costs related directly to the bases negotiations. First, the intervention of United States forces in an internal Philippine political situation was probably in violation of Philippine-United States defense arrangements, which prohibit United States involvement in domestic affairs. Second, the United States effort to help President Aquino put down the coup made her vulnerable to nationalist allegations that her government is a lackey of the Americans.

Ironically, these developments could negatively affect the future of the bases. To refute the nationalists' argument, the Philippine government might attempt to attach so many conditions to United States use of the bases that their operational utility will disappear. It is worth noting that if military considerations alone had driven United States policy, Washington might well have decided to let the coup play out without United States interference. If the plotters had won and installed a

military-backed regime, renewal of the bases agreement would probably have been much easier. To its credit, the Bush administration acted in a broader political-strategic framework rather than a narrow military one.

THE SINGAPORE GAMBIT

In recent years, Philippine officials like Foreign Minister Raul Manglapus have urged other ASEAN states to share the burden of United States bases. In August, 1989, Singapore became the first ASEAN member to accept the challenge, setting off a heated debate in ASEAN councils over the association's preferred regional security future. This debate reveals the persistence of disagreement on the role of outside powers as ASEAN's protectors.

By offering to host a modest United States naval and air presence—just when Australian and New Zealand forces left Malaysia and Singapore—Singapore's Prime Minister Lee Kwan Yew reaffirmed his belief that the United States military has maintained the balance of power for all the Pacific and has provided the stable security environment within which the region's members could concentrate on export-led economic growth. According to Lee, these achievements should not be lightly dismissed in an emotional wave of nationalism.[13]

Although ASEAN solidarity was ultimately restored with respect to the Singapore offer when officials clarified the fact that the facilities would provide for only a token presence of United States air and naval forces, the controversy demonstrated that neither Singapore nor Thailand had yet come to accept regional neutralization as Southeast Asia's preferred security posture.

For Indonesia and Malaysia (for whom the creation of a Zone of Peace, Freedom and Neutrality (ZOPFAN) for Southeast Asia had been declared policy since the early 1970's), the existence of United States bases in both the Philippines and Singapore would appear to be a regression from the goal of excluding the armed forces of all external powers. A United States air base in Singapore would be particularly sensitive, because aircraft leaving or landing on that island automatically overfly Indonesian or Malaysian airspace. More subtly, Indonesian and Malaysian leaders interpreted Singapore's offer as a way to align with the United States less out of concern about the Soviet Union than to protect Singapore from any future threats from its immediate Malay neighbors.[14] Moreover, two ASEAN locations for the nuclear-weapon-equipped United States Navy would make a mockery of the association's 1987 call for the creation of a Southeast Asian nuclear-weapon-free zone.

Indonesia was particularly exercised that Singapore's offer would derail Jakarta's plans to become the dominant security actor in the region and the coordinator of ASEAN defense planning.[15] Jusuf Wanandi, director of Jakarta's Center for Strategic and International Studies, summed up Indonesia's dilemma by stating that his country wanted the United States to maintain a military presence in Southeast Asia but could not endorse long-term foreign bases in that region. Looking ahead, Wanandi foresaw the prospect of a joint United States-Japanese naval task force in Southeast Asia by the turn of the century as the American burden-sharing policy takes hold.[16]

By late 1989, the Singapore bases controversy had apparently been resolved. Singapore's offer had been redefined so that it merely formalized current practice, in which the United States Navy uses repair and bunkering facilities and the United States Air Force flies from Singapore in joint exercises.[17] Thus, ASEAN could state that there was no new bases arrangement in the region and no setback for ZOPFAN.

INDOCHINA'S FUTURE

The key to Indochina's future relationship with ASEAN will appear in the political resolution of the Cambodian imbroglio. Vietnam's decade-long occupation of Cambodia (1979–1989) constituted the last vestige of the cold war in Southeast Asia, in which a Soviet client confronted an array of Western-oriented opponents grouped around ASEAN. Unlike the first two Indochina wars, however, the United States declined to commit significant resources to this struggle, deferring instead to both ASEAN and China.

However, Washington's lack of initiative has left unresolved a central policy conflict between ASEAN and China: the latter has been in no hurry to end the Cambodian war, seeing it as an opportunity to punish Vietnam for defying China's strategic interests and to insure that Hanoi remains economically anemic. ASEAN, on the other hand, has no hidden agenda against Vietnam. Once Vietnamese forces are verifiably out of Cambodia and a coalition regime incorporating at least some of Prince Norodom Sihanouk's resistance forces is established in Phnom Penh, the ASEAN states are prepared to normalize relations with Vietnam, to encourage international assistance for its reconstruction, and even to consider some kind of formal relationship with Indochina.

The ASEAN orientation is epitomized by Thai Prime Minister Chatichai Choonhavan's plan to transform Indochina from a battlefield into a marketplace. Thai businessmen see Indochina both as a new source of raw materials and as a location for investment in labor-intensive manufacturing, once

Cambodia's future is resolved. Although some détente developed in the late 1980's between China and Vietnam, permitting unofficial cross-border trade between the two neighbors, China has not endorsed Chatichai's vision for a prosperous Indochina; this suggests that ASEAN and Chinese strategies will continue to diverge.

The failure of the Paris talks in the summer of 1989 to arrange a comprehensive settlement in Cambodia illustrated that neither Hanoi's client government led by Hun Sen nor the Khmer Rouge believed that it was necessary to compromise.[18] Each believed that it could ultimately prevail on the battlefield as long as the resistance had external sources of support through Thailand and as long as Hun Sen was sustained by the Soviet Union and Vietnam. United States intelligence sources claimed that the Soviet Union had doubled its military aid to Phnom Penh in 1989 over 1988 levels, including 100 T-54 tanks, armored vehicles, heavy artillery and 16 MiG-21 fighters.[19]

As fighting continues in Cambodia, United States policy and ASEAN preferences appear to be on separate paths, with Washington once again leaning more toward China's polarized vision of Southeast Asia than toward ASEAN's syncretic views. Thailand has indicated that it is prepared to tolerate a Cambodia under Vietnamese political influence so long as there are no Vietnamese forces there. Chatichai believes that over time Thailand's economic influence would more than compensate for Hanoi's relationship to the Phnom Penh government.[20] The United States insists, however, that only a comprehensive settlement based on Prince Sihanouk's demands for an interim four-part coalition government, including the Khmer Rouge (pending internationally supervised elections), will warrant United States diplomatic recognition of Vietnam.

United States policy toward Cambodia in 1989 was not a model of consistency, however, possibly reflecting differences within the Bush administration over such issues as the legitimacy of a Khmer Rouge role, whether Prince Sihanouk remains the best hope for a non-Communist Cambodia, and a residual desire to continue punishing Vietnam. High-level officials have variously stated that the United States will refuse to consider Khmer Rouge participation in a successor Cambodian government or that the Khmer Rouge should be included since Prince Sihanouk believes it is the only way to contain the Khmer Rouge before elections.[21]

The United States has not acknowledged that the only rule provided to Cambodia over the past decade is that of the Heng Samrin-Hun Sen regime. Insofar as administration and social services exist, they were created and implemented by the regime placed in power and subsidized by Hanoi and Moscow in 1979. The resistance has nothing to take its place. This reality would seem to undermine the American plan that the resistance should replace the Hun Sen government. Only a coalition that incorporates the latter is a meaningful alternative to the status quo. In fact, this preference was articulated by both United States Secretary of State James Baker and United States Vice President Dan Quayle in their addresses respectively to the ASEAN summit in July and, two weeks earlier, to the Heritage Foundation in Washington, D.C.

Yet by the fall of 1989, the Bush administration had resumed its earlier pro-China position in support of a Khmer Rouge role in an interim coalition government, refusing to deal with Hun Sen. Only active Vietnamese pressure on its ally to agree to a coalition government and subsequent elections supervised by the United Nations would lead to normalization of United States relations with both Hanoi and Phnom Penh.[22] By imposing these new conditions for normalization, the United States maintains an international embargo on trade, aid and investment, thus further punishing Hanoi— apparently the continuation of America's post-Vietnam war legacy. Any new movement toward a compromise coalition will apparently develop only after the Khmer contenders test each other further on the battlefield.

FUTURE REGIONAL SECURITY

If superpower détente translates into a reduction of forward deployed forces in Southeast Asia during the 1990's, are the ASEAN states considering an alternative security posture? Although a formal ASEAN defense arrangement is unlikely, the association's membership has developed norms and a structure for the management of disputes sufficiently successful that military budgets have been restrained. Moreover, through annual meetings with the world's major economic powers as dialogue partners, ASEAN has advanced its members' mutual interests in a global setting.

Militarily, two developments can be anticipated for the 1990's: a movement toward regional arms control and confidence-building measures (including the normalization of relations between ASEAN and Indochina); and efforts to effect higher forms of military cooperation within ASEAN. In 1989, Malaysian, Indonesian and Singaporean officials discussed prospects for ASEAN-wide maritime defense, including trilateral exercises. The establishment of a Thai-Chinese arms stockpile also points toward innovative security arrangements as a reduced United States presence seems probable, despite Malaysian and Indonesian objections to China as a long-term security threat.

However, the possibility of a United States exit from Southeast Asia apparently exacerbates the differences among ASEAN states' regional security views. Indonesia sees a great power withdrawal as the best opportunity to become the region's primary maritime power. Thailand, in contrast, believes that a relationship with China remains essential to balance Vietnam. Malaysia and Singapore seem to be leaning toward Indonesia if Indonesia agrees to develop a cooperative defense arrangement for the Malacca Straits. The Philippines is too weak militarily and economically to make a regional defense contribution.[23]

Other clouds on the ASEAN-United States horizon cover economic relations. The United States is either the first or the second largest trading partner with every ASEAN state except Brunei. All, except Brunei, are in trade surplus with the United States; and all have benefited in the past decade from America's open market and insatiable appetite for foreign products. As Washington tries to put its economic house in order, however, efforts to expand United States overseas markets are regarded in Southeast Asia as attacks on ASEAN's economic growth. Pressures on Singapore, Malaysia and Thailand to revalue their currencies and remove restrictions on the entry of foreign goods as well as the need for local legislation to protect American intellectual property rights (patents and copyrights, particularly for computer software and pharmaceuticals) have led to charges that the United States is undermining its friends' prosperity.[24]

THE PACIFIC POLITICAL ECONOMY

In an effort to transcend bilateral economic frictions and to develop a Pacific-wide forum to respond to the 1992 creation of a single European market, three major Pacific economic powers (the United States, Japan and Australia) convened the first ever East Asian-Pacific consultative conference in Canberra in early November, 1989. This unprecedented Pacific Rim conclave brought the United States, Canada, Japan, South Korea, Australia, New Zealand and the ASEAN states together, although it excluded Hong Kong, China and Taiwan for the time being because of the political sensitivity of their situations subsequent to China's crushing of the pro-democracy movement in Tiananmen Square in June, 1989.

The Pacific Rim gathering had its origin in a 1988 proposal by then Secretary of the Treasury James Baker, who believed that such a group would ensure a strong United States role in the Pacific, providing a counterweight to Japanese dominance. The group would also establish a formal link between the industrialized Group of Seven and Asia's newly industrializing countries (NIC's).[25]

ASEAN agreed to the initiative with reservations. The association did not want to see its own annual post-summit meetings with the industrial countries diluted in a larger organization. Malaysia, the Philippines and Indonesia were particularly wary, while Singapore and Thailand saw the enlarged economic consultative mechanism more positively, as an opportunity to discuss regionwide trade and investment expansion. Kuala Lumpur warned that the meeting "shouldn't degenerate into a forum where the richer countries say everyone must do this or that." Washington indicated it would like the Asia-Pacific group to take common stands on trade issues in such multilateral negotiations as the Uruguay round—the current round of UNCTAD (the United Nations Conference on Trade and Development).[26]

The Canberra meeting led to a number of agreements, including the creation of working groups to explore ways of increasing regional trade (already one-third of total world trade, or more than $200 billion in 1988), investment and technology transfer between rich and poor countries, and trade in services like telecommunications. New data systems will be devised to map these flows, which some officials foresee as eventually turning into a policy clearinghouse similar to the Paris-based Organization for Economic Cooperation and Development (OECD).[27]

In deference to ASEAN, the Asia-Pacific group agreed not to create a permanent secretariat and to convene every other meeting in an ASEAN state. (The next is scheduled for Singapore in mid-1990.) Among the issues of particular interest to ASEAN were the further opening of the Japanese market to add Japan to the United States as engines of growth for Southeast Asia and new investment and technology transfers to ASEAN to broaden its industrial base.[28]

While ASEAN apparently welcomes the new Asia-Pacific group's plans to promote more pan Pacific trade and investment, that welcome is tempered by Indonesia's concern that, just as the great powers may be leaving the region militarily, a new economic obstacle to Jakarta's regional prominence has appeared. To reassure Indonesia, other ASEAN states have tempered their enthusiasm for the Asia-Pacific conference, even though their own development may lie in the success of conference plans. The challenge to ASEAN solidarity in the 1990's may emanate as much from the global economic order as from regional military changes.

---

[1]The Association of South East Asian Nations (ASEAN) consists of Thailand, Malaysia, Singapore, Indonesia, the Philippines and Brunei.

[2]For a readable overview of the dilemmas facing the Bush administration's global policy, see Stanley Hoffmann, "What Should We Do in the World?" *The Atlantic*, October, 1989, pp. 84–96.

[3]Remarks by then Assistant Secretary of State-designate for East Asia and the Pacific Richard Armitage, cited by Michael Richardson, "The ASEAN Scene: Differences Mount as Tension Eases," *Pacific Defence Reporter*, June, 1989, p. 15.

[4]Ibid., pp. 15 and 18. Also see the address by Secretary of State James Baker to the Asia Society, June 26, 1989, in which he calls for a new Pacific partnership with Japan that will be "based on a global sharing of responsibilities," United States Department of State, *Current Policy*, No. 1185, p. 3.

[5]Statements by Commander in Chief of the Soviet Pacific Fleet Admiral Gennady A. Kvatov, as reported in Robert Horiguchi, "Eyewitness with the Pacific Fleet," *Pacific Defence Reporter*, August, 1989, pp. 8–9.

[6]Space limitations preclude a lengthy analysis of the domestic and international issues involved in the bases renewal question. Excellent reviews may be found in William Berry, *U.S. Bases in the Philippines: The Evolution of the Special Relationship* (Boulder: Westview Press, 1989), and Fred Greene, ed., *The Philippine Bases: Negotiating for the Future* (New York: Council on Foreign Relations, 1988).

[7]Statement by Defense Secretary Fidel Ramos as reported in *The Manila Chronicle*, August 22, 1989, in Foreign Broadcast Information Service, *East Asia Daily Report* (cited as FBIS), August 23, 1989, pp. 80–81.

[8]Thai, Singaporean and Malaysian leaders all prefer a continued United States presence in the Philippines. See, for example, both *Bangkok Post* and *Far Eastern Economic Review* (*FEER*) of August 24, 1989, p. 14. Defense Secretary Ramos has called for a one-time extension of the agreement to 1998, *Agence France-Presse* (Hong Kong), August 24, 1989, in FBIS, August 25, 1989, p. 38.

[9]*The Asian Wall Street Journal Weekly* (*AWSJ*), August 28, 1989, and Quezon City GMA7 Radio-Television Arts Network, October 16, 1989, in FBIS, October 17, 1989, pp. 42–43.

[10]A good discussion of these problems is found in Gregory P. Corning, "The Philippine Bases and U.S. Pacific Strategy" (a paper prepared for the annual meeting of the International Studies Association Section on Security Studies, Whittier, California, November 9–11, 1989), pp. 17 and 20.

[11]This argument was made by Larry Niksch of the Congressional Research Service in a paper to the Defense Intelligence College—U.S. Pacific Command Symposium, Honolulu, February 27–March 1, 1989, titled "U.S. Bases: Why They Are Important—How To Keep Them."

[12]*Philippine Daily Globe*, October 25, 1989, in FBIS, October 25, 1989, pp. 40–41.

[13]*The Straits Times* (Singapore), August 5, 1989, in FBIS, August 8, 1989, pp. 33–34.

[14]"Whistling Up a Storm," *FEER*, August 21, 1989, pp. 9–10; *Bernama* (Kuala Lumpur), August 28, 1989, in FBIS, August 29, 1989, pp. 45–46.

[15]See the editorial in *Jakarta Post*, August 8, 1989, in FBIS, August 11, 1989, p. 35.

[16]Author's interview, Los Angeles, September 9, 1989.

[17]*Bernama*, October 20, 1989, in FBIS, October 20, 1989, p. 36.

[18]A good review of the diplomatic and political positions of all Cambodian participants is found in Douglas Pike, "The Cambodian Peace Process: Summer of 1989," *Asian Survey*, September, 1989, pp. 842–852.

[19]This analysis was made by *FEER* correspondent Nayan Chanda in a presentation to the Asia Society, Los Angeles, September 8, 1989. Also see Paul Lewis, "Soviets Said to Double Cambodia Aid," *The New York Times*, October 6, 1989.

4. LIMITS OF AMERICAN POWER

[20]Mutthia Alagappa, "Malaysia's View of Cambodia," a presentation made to the Asia Society, Los Angeles, September 8, 1989.

[21]These contradictory views were expressed by Secretary Baker at the July ASEAN summit and later by Assistant Secretary of State for East Asia and the Pacific Richard Solomon in an address to the Asia Society, Los Angeles, September 8, 1989.

[22]Robert Pear, "U.S. Is Reassessing Indochina Policy," *The New York Times,* September 24, 1989. See also the report of United States presidential envoy General John Vessey's remarks in Bangkok in the *Bangkok Post,* November 1, 1989.

[23]These prospects are discussed by Donald E. Weatherbee, *ASEAN After Cambodia: Reordering Southeast Asia* (New York: The Asia Society, June, 1989), pp. 17–24.

[24]Karen Elliott House, "Mahathir Charges U.S. Is Trying To Hold Back Asian Growth," *The Asian Wall Street Journal Weekly (AWSJ)*, November 6, 1989.

[25]"Baker Proposes 'Pan-Pacific' Alliance," *AWSJ,* July 3, 1989.

[26]*Bangkok Post,* September 6, 1989; "Asia-Pacific Parley in Canberra Hoping to Lay the Groundwork for Cooperation," *AWSJ,* November 6, 1989.

[27]Jacqueline Rees, "First Step Taken," *FEER,* November 16, 1989, pp. 10–13.

[28]Charles Smith, "The Backroom Boys," *FEER,* November 16, 1989, p. 12.

The United States Role in the Middle East

This issue provides a broad overview of the changes in the Middle East during a period when new dimensions added to old tensions. As our introductory article indicates, the efforts of the new United States President underscore "his understanding of the continuing agenda for the United States in this area of the world — an area still in turmoil, awash in modern weaponry. . . . Thus 1989 proved to be a year in which a new administration began to shape its perspectives toward the region, but played a relatively modest role."

ROBERT E. HUNTER

Vice President, Regional Programs,
Center for Strategic and International Studies

Robert E. Hunter is vice president for regional programs and director of European Studies at the Center for Strategic and International Studies in Washington, D.C.

THE year 1989 began as a time of promise for United States foreign policy — in the Middle East and in many other parts of the globe. The cold war between the United States and the Soviet Union — the world's defining relationship for more than four decades — was beginning to change decisively. The Iran-Iraq War had finally come to an end. Soviet troops were to depart from Afghanistan by the middle of February. The United States had just decided to open a dialogue with the Palestine Liberation Organization (PLO) — perhaps not signaling a critical departure in Arab-Israeli peacemaking diplomacy, but at least indicating new avenues to explore. And the United States and the world awaited the inauguration of the forty-first United States President, George Herbert Walter Bush, who would lead his nation, its foreign policy and its engagement in the Middle East into a new decade.

Probably no factor defined the United States approach to the Middle East during 1989 more than a development that did not focus primarily on that region: the rapid shift in United States-Soviet relations or, more particularly, in Soviet attitudes toward the outside world. The principal locus of developments was elsewhere: in talks to control intercontinental-range nuclear weapons; in a gradual political thaw in Europe, which had been the primary area of the cold war; and in statements made by Soviet President Mikhail S. Gorbachev about playing a cooperative and conciliatory role in the international community. Clearly, two acts internal to the Soviet Union — the proclaiming of glasnost (openness) and perestroika (economic restructuring) — were having some impact on the way in which the Soviet Union would engage other states and define its security and political interests.

By the beginning of 1989, the United States had begun to pick up the signals relating to the Middle East as well as to other regions. During complex, indirect negotiations to encourage the PLO to meet United States conditions for a dialogue, Moscow clearly nudged the Palestinian leadership to take the plunge. In 1988, Soviet leaders had publicly chastised Syria for obduracy and were less than wholehearted in their support of Syrian requests either for political support or for advanced weaponry. The Soviet Union began to ease restrictions on the emigration of those people who wished to leave, including many Soviet Jews: clearly Moscow had calculated the costs in the Arab world of helping Israel to offset somewhat its loss of people (even though most emigrants from the Soviet Union preferred to go to the United States). And in the final stages of the Iran-Iraq War, Moscow worked for a cease-fire, both on its own and by supporting the efforts of others, including the United Nations (UN) Secretary General, Javier Pérez de Cuéllar.

Most important, as it became clear that there was a sea change in Soviet attitudes and policy, the United States began to recalculate its own policies, a process that was accelerated after President Bush stated his belief that the cold war was winding down and formally declared that the United States had a stake in Gorbachev's success and the success of perestroika. In fact, changing perceptions of the Soviet factor in the Middle East had an instrumental impact on calculations by the Bush administration about its own role in the region—at least in most areas. Only in southwest Asia and in the Persian Gulf was the Bush administration particularly concerned about Soviet objectives. Even with this exception, changes taking place in overall United States-Soviet relations led the Bush administration to make new assessments about the relative importance of the Middle East.

ONCE MORE INTO THE BREACH

For decades, judgments that new administrations have made about the Middle East have begun with the Arab-Israeli conflict. Until the Egyptian-Israeli peace treaty of 1979, that was true in large part because of the enduring risks of a major Arab-Israeli conflict and, with it, the risk of United States-Soviet confrontation, as happened at least to some degree in the wars of 1956, 1967 and 1973. At times, there was also the incipient threat of the so-called Arab oil weapon—the possibility that, in order to affect United States policy toward Israel and related issues, key Arab oil producers would use their economic leverage.

By the time of the inauguration of President Ronald Reagan in 1980, the new treaty had removed most of the risk of an Arab military attack on Israel—after all, Israel had succeeded against all comers and Egypt was out of the military balance. By the same token, the chances of a United States-Soviet confrontation had dropped precipitously. And despite continuing high oil prices, for a variety of reasons—including the preoccupation of Persian Gulf suppliers with events in revolutionary Iran—there was little prospect of an Arab oil embargo against the United States. Nevertheless, President Reagan had to make basic calculations about the Arab-Israeli conflict, if only because there was an ongoing peace process, based on the 1978 Camp David Accords, and all parties in the Middle East expected the United States to continue playing the role it had assumed more than a decade earlier.

By 1989, however, the region had successfully survived another eight years without major movement in peacemaking. It had weathered the assassination of Egyptian President Anwar Sadat, the Israeli invasion of Lebanon, the withdrawal of Jordan's King Hussein from the peace process in 1988 and the attenuation of the peace efforts undertaken by outgoing Secretary of State George P. Shultz—efforts that had never been given much chance nor much commitment on the part of the Reagan administration.

There was, however, the intifada, the Arab uprising in the West Bank and Gaza that had begun in December, 1987, and had led many American supporters of Israel for the first time to urge that the United States government take a leading role in peacemaking. After Israel restricted media access to the occupied territories in 1988, however, worldwide attention to the intifada had declined. It remained a criticial, perhaps decisive, question for the future of Israel, but it did not seem to the new administration to be the stuff of geostrategic challenge.

This seemed especially true because of the remarkable changes taking place in Soviet policy. Through 1987 and 1988, a key issue in the debate about peacemaking had been a potential role for the Soviet Union, which was petitioning widely for inclusion in the process. With the United States relatively unengaged, support had emerged everywhere in Europe and the Middle East, except in Israel, for an international conference that would include the five permanent members of the United Nations Security Council. That proposal was a code for bringing in the Soviet Union, and the idea was resisted, not only by Israeli Prime Minister Yitzhak Shamir and his Likud party, but also by many American and other outside observers who feared that such a step would enable the Soviet Union to meddle in the peace process without being required first to demonstrate willingness to take a responsible approach to complicated issues.

In 1989, however, what was happening elsewhere in United States-Soviet relations reduced the intensity of opposition to permitting Moscow to play a role: the Soviet Union no longer seemed poised to be a spoiler. Remarkably, pressure on the United States and Israel to include the Soviet Union in peacemaking also declined, perhaps in part because the Bush administration was apparently ready to become engaged in peacemaking, in contrast to the Reagan administration.

In fact, the peace process and the United States role in it were different in 1989. During the presidential campaign of 1988, various American groups had canvassed the possibilities for the new administration. The incoming Bush team believed that the politics of the individual parties in the region would have to evolve before the policies of the United States could be effective. This became known as the "ripening" process, a progressive changing of attitude both in Israel and among its potential interlocutors.

The decisive moment was the December 14, 1988, agreement by Secretary Shultz to open a dialogue with the PLO. In his judgment, PLO chairman Yasir Arafat had met three conditions set down by the United States, beginning with the United States commitment to Israel of September 1, 1975:

The United States will not recognize or negotiate with the Palestine Liberation Organization so long as [it] does not recognize Israel's right to exist and does not accept [UN] Security Council Resolutions 242 and 338.

The terms in which Arafat embraced the United States conditions were so carefully worded (along with the requirement that the PLO "renounce terrorism") that debate about his intentions would have been legitimate. Shultz, however, made a command decision: Arafat would be taken at his word and questioned no further. In so doing, the United States Secretary of State made a gift to President-elect George Bush. Whatever else might happen, the Bush administration would not have to decide whether to deal with the PLO.

In fact, this recognition gave point and purpose to the concept of "ripening." Israel's politics had to take account of the fact that its principal patron was accepting a legitimate role for the PLO. At the same time, Palestinian politics also had to change, as the PLO found itself talking directly to the United States, through representatives in Tunis. For the first time in its history, the PLO leadership had to accept responsibility for its actions as an indirect but acknowledged participant in the peace process. To this end, the Bush administration became reluctant to see violent acts committed against Israeli-styled "terrorism" or laid at the feet of the PLO.

In retrospect, the opening of the United States-PLO dialogue was a transforming moment in the history of Arab-Israeli relations. As 1989 progressed, it became clear that key points had become firmly established, whereas in the past there had been dispute or ambiguity. Henceforth, the primary issue between Israel and the Arabs was the Palestinian question; Israel's interlocutor was to be, in some guise, Palestinian, not another party like Egypt or Jordan — even if the latter were eventually involved in a final settlement. And, like it or not, the PLO would play a role, direct or indirect, even though the United States and Israeli governments still talked about potential differences between Palestinians living in the territories and those in the diaspora.

Although there were changes in the context within which avenues to peace were being debated, the Bush administration was not guided solely by perceptions of the relationship between the Arab-Israeli conflict and United States-Soviet relations. The threat of an Arab oil weapon seemed remote, although it might reemerge during the 1990's if the trend of rising United States dependence on imported oil continued unabated. But other developments increased United States sensitivity to the need for involvement, in addition to the traditional incentives provided by close American ties to and concern for the state of Israel. These developments included the likely proliferation within the region both of ballistic missiles and of unconventional weapons — especially chemical weapons. Further evidence also emerged that Israel had nuclear weapons and was cooperating with South Africa on the means of delivery. While the potential for interstate conflict remained low, certainly lower than the actuality of the intifada, the Bush administration decided that it could not adopt the passive role that had dominated most of the Reagan years.

THE ISRAELI INITIATIVE

But how to proceed? Following a classic American tactic of waiting to be asked for suggestions, Secretary of State James A. Baker called for "new ideas" on the part of the local parties and especially for concrete Israeli recommendations — a position underlined by Baker's hint that Israel might have to deal directly with the PLO. The United States challenge was accepted by Prime Minister Yitzhak Shamir, who was under pressure at home to be more accommodating in the face of the continuing Arab uprising. During a visit to Washington, D.C., in April, Shamir discussed his chosen route to peace and, on May 14, it was formally presented in full. This position was, in fact, derived from provisions of the Camp David Accords regarding autonomy for the territories — a process that had been effectively abandoned early in the Reagan administration. The Israeli plan provided for "free and democratic elections among the Palestinian Arab inhabitants of Judea, Samaria and the Gaza District," in order to choose "a representation" to "conduct negotiations for a transitional period of self-rule." Also as provided in the Accords, "at a later state, negotiations will be conducted for a permanent solution."

This was not a bold break with the past; indeed, it was clearly intended to exclude the PLO and to hold out the possibility of avoiding a trade of "land for peace." Predictably, the Arab states and the PLO dismissed the Israeli plan out of hand.

Having chosen to give up the initiative, the Bush administration faced a critical choice: whether to treat Shamir's proposal as an unattainable goal, perhaps a ploy to prevent serious negotiations, or to take it at face value and make it the basis for United States policy. The United States chose the latter course, even though it did not have much hope for success. At least in this way Israel would be actively involved in the process and the central point would be underlined: Israel had accepted the Palestinians as its negotiating partner.

The administration was obviously frustrated by the limited extent of the Israeli initiative, however. This was made evident in Secretary Baker's speech on May 22 to the annual Washington policy conference of the American-Israel Public Affairs Committee (AIPAC). He urged the Arabs to end the economic boycott of Israel and to stop trying to exclude it from the UN; and he urged the Palestinians to turn the intifada into a "dialogue of politics and diplomacy" with Israel. But he spoke even more bluntly to Israel which, he said, must give up "the unrealistic vision of a greater Israel" in order to gain peace. It must "forswear annexation" of its occupied territories, "stop settlement activity" and "reach out to the Palestinians as neighbors who deserve political rights."

This speech seemed to convey a United States intention to play an active role and to take an approach less sympathetic to Israeli concerns — at least to those of Prime Minister Shamir — than had been true of the Reagan administration. Curiously, there was little follow-up; the supporters of Shamir's position did not face active American opposition, nor were Shamir's opponents, including the Israeli Labor party, bolstered by United States activism.

Initiative thus passed to a third party, Egyptian President Hosni Mubarak, who (in July) presented a list of 10 points regarding elections that seemed patterned after Baker's AIPAC speech. He tried to pin down even more precisely, in terms favorable to Arab positions — like the participation of residents of East Jerusalem — the conditions for holding elections in the territories. While dismissed by Shamir — though largely accepted by Labor — this initiative formed the basis for a potential Israeli-Egyptian dialogue and kept the focus where Washington wanted it: on linking Israel and the Palestinians in the peace process and sustaining the basic validity of the Shamir proposal. Secretary Baker added five further points that attempted to promote the Egyptian role as a way station to engaging the Palestinians and to finding common ground. Again, the points stated, "the United States. . . . understands that elections and negotiations will be in accordance with the Israeli initiative." But Baker also tried to move beyond a process limited simply to the modalities of elections, to recognize that "the Palestinians will be free to raise issues that relate to their opinion on how to make elections and negotiations succeed." That, in effect, staked out a United States position: elections in the territories must be the start, not the end of the process.

Before the end of 1989, this sifting of fine points went further, including demands by the Israeli government — while declaring itself prepared to accept Baker's five points — that would exclude even an indirect role for the PLO in selecting representatives to talk about elections and that would limit discussion precisely to these modalities.

Thus the Bush administration continued to play a modest role as a potential broker between Israel and its neighbors, while working to make the basic principle of Israeli-Palestinian dialogue irreversible. Following years of stasis, the divided nature of the Israeli government, the departure of Jordan from the peace process and the opening of the United States-PLO dialogue, there was merit in focusing on the minutiae of modalities, although they were at least three levels away from discussions about critical issues of territory, people and peace. It is a gamble that may yet pay off with a basic realignment of the politics of the key parties; but that is far from assured.

With the Arab-Israeli conflict apparently so insignificant in comparison with the great leaps of European history and the basic reshaping of East-West relations, time seemed infinitely elastic in the Middle East in 1989. If history in this part of the world is any guide, however, that is unlikely to prove true; as so often in the past, time in the Middle East will probably work more strongly against political and human progress than for it. United States passivity — judged absolutely, though not in comparison with the flaccid period of the Reagan administration — has been most unwise.

TIE TO THE PERSIAN GULF

As in recent years, in 1989 the people of the United States were reminded of their inability to be isolated from events in the Middle East when, once again, an act of terrorism was vividly presented on television. On July 28, Israel kidnapped from Lebanon Sheik Abdul Karim Obeid, a Shiite Muslim leader who purportedly had been engaged in terrorism. This act, itself, was presumably a reflection of Prime Minister Shamir's political vulnerability after his meetings with Palestinian leaders, including avowed representatives of the PLO.

A shadowy group, the self-styled Organization of the Oppressed on Earth, promptly threatened to assassinate United States Marine Lieutenant Colonel William R. Higgins, an official of the United Nations Truce Supervision Organization who had been seized in February, 1988. On July 31, a videotape of Higgins's body hanging from a scaffold was distributed to the Western media — the shocking brutality of the videotape further evidence of the partnership of modern terrorism and television.

This was the first crisis of George Bush's presidency and one that he had learned to expect, after his eight years as Vice President during several hostage situations. He was faced with the same range of poor choices that had been available to his predecessors. These were essentially to use direct military force in Lebanon — thus potentially provoking more killings and breeding support for the terrorists because of the accidental death of civilians—or doing little or nothing to free the United States citizens who remained hostage in Lebanon. Indeed, a terrorist group, the Revolutionary Justice Organization, then threatened to hang another American hostage, Joseph Cicippio, at a date and time certain, and only provided a last-minute "reprieve" on August 3 after several days of manipulating the Western media and American sympathies.

Apparently recognizing his lack of desirable courses of action, Bush tried to steer between the different stances struck by earlier Presidents. He rushed back to Washington, D.C., from a trip around the country—thus seeming to highlight his own role in the crisis, as had former President Jimmy Carter. But he then began to go about a President's normal business, in order not to increase the price that the terrorists could exact in terms of national expectations. Like Ronald Reagan, Bush undertook a show of force, but he did not mislead the American people into believing that United States power could gain the unachievable. The President sent warnings; he developed and conducted a complex and far-flung diplomacy; and he sent United States ships both to the eastern Mediterranean Sea and to the vicinity of the Persian Gulf—near Iran, to which the terrorists in Lebanon said they owed their allegiance.

When the threat to kill Cicippio was lifted, American popular attention to the latest hostage crisis dissipated. In contrast to the period from 1979 to about the time of the Iran-contra scandal, the issue of American hostages no longer seemed to be a festering popular concern; it was rather a source of episodic outrage. In retrospect, President Bush proved to have conducted the crisis with virtually no lapses in judgment. Unable to affect events decisively—and certainly unwilling to give in to terrorists' demands—he was still able to combine both diplomacy and military maneuver in a blend that was satisfying to the American people. In competition with terrorists seeking to force his hand at home, he did not lose.

President Bush was obviously aware that the crisis surrounding the murder of Colonel Higgins was more complicated than many earlier terrorist outrages. Iran was implicated and reaction in the United States was intense concerning this latest involvement in terrorism by a country that had caused the United States so much grief. But which Iran? Since the death of Iran's Ayatollah Ruhollah Khomeini on June 3, 1989—and even well before then—a struggle for power in Teheran had begun. Divisions were not clear-cut, but generalizations were possible. The principle contenders could be

divided into "radicals" and "pragmatists." The former wished to fulfill what they believed to be Khomeini's revolutionary legacy; they favored a major role for the state in the economy and many of them were pro-Soviet, some intensely so. The "pragmatists," in contrast, seemed to recognize that Iran's survival depended on rebuilding a country shattered by eight years of devastation wrought by the war that Iraq began in 1980. This group—led by the man who became Iran's elected President, Ali Akbar Hashemi Rafsanjani—saw a more important role in the Iranian economy for the private sector and, whether by inclination or simply by necessity, opted for improved relations with the West. The West alone could provide the tools needed to rebuilt Iran, a point dramatized by Soviet confessions of economic failure.

Before coming to office in January, 1989, President Bush had apparently reached two conclusions based on his observation of the turmoil in Iran and in United States policy toward it during the Reagan years. He believed that the independence and integrity of Iran were important to the United States—this was the unrefuted strategic argument behind the "arms for hostages" dealings of 1985-1987; and he believed that Iranian leaders would be compelled to accept the importance of tolerable relations with the West after the cease-fire in the Iran-Iraq War.

Thus, in his inaugural address, President Bush held out an unexpected olive branch, intended in part for Iran and for anyone else with any influence over the hostage-takers in Lebanon:

> There are today Americans who are held against their will in foreign lands and Americans who are unaccounted for. Assistance can be shown here and will be long remembered. Goodwill begets goodwill. Good faith can be a spiral that endlessly moves on.

The road to "goodwill," however, proved to be long and rocky. Soon after President Bush issued this appeal, an accident of literature strengthened the hands of the so-called radicals in Iran, who still included Khomeini. A novel written by an Indian Muslim living in Great Britain, Salman Rushdie, gained widespread prominence. When it first appeared, *The Satanic Verses* had been condemned as blasphemous by many Muslims, Sunni and Shiite alike, especially in Saudi Arabia and Pakistan. Yet it was only in February, 1989, when a minor cleric in Iran called for a death sentence for Rushdie—and when Khomeini took up the standard—that the issue took on international proportions.

The Western rejection of threats against Rushdie had a significant political impact. For radicals in Iran, the pace of reconciliation with the West was slowed. Ironically, the summer crisis over the murder of Colonel Higgins allowed the subject of United States relations with Iran to reemerge. While many Americans believed that Iran should be held responsible, others believed that Rafsanjani was himself an intended political victim and that Iranian radicals and their allies in Lebanon were using this crisis to undermine him at home. Judging by President Bush's conduct of the crisis, this was apparently his view as well. He exerted enough pressure on Iran—a show of naval force—to permit Rafsanjani to compare it publicly with the accidental shooting down of an Iranian civilian airbus in July, 1988, by the U.S.S. *Vincennes,* an action that helped prompt Iran to accept the cease-fire with Iraq. But the President did not strike Iran. He used the occasion for indirect diplomacy and, at the end of the crisis, the United States government hinted that Iran had been helpful in its resolution.

For the Bush administration, therefore, a strategic course had been set—apparently deriving from the President's vision, not from the bureaucracy. As was implied in Bush's inaugural address, the United States would improve relations with Iran if Iran acted responsibly toward the outside world and, in particular, toward the United States.

For the Bush administration, however, there was a further reason to try to improve relations with Iran—a reason that seemed to be at variance with developments elsewhere in the world: the role of Soviet influence. In the region of southwest Asia and the Persian Gulf, unique among the world's most important areas, the Soviet Union continued to press its advantage—in Afghanistan through massive military aid to the Kabul regime, in Iran through diplomacy. This was made clear, for example, by a visit to Teheran by Soviet Foreign Minister Eduard Shevardnadze, even though he ostensibly focused on Soviet efforts to help resolve the hostage crisis.

In November, President Bush took one more step to show his own goodwill toward Iran and to enter the competition with the Soviet Union. He directed the release from escrow of $567 million in Iranian assets frozen in 1979. He related this act to the continued holding of hostages but also seemed to recognize the limits of Rafsanjani's influence:

I'd like to get this underbrush cleaned out now. I think they have made some positive statements, but I don't know whether it will work that way or not. I hope that they will do what they can to influence those who hold these hostages.

It was obvious that the United States could not act alone, that Rafsanjani was not master in his own house, that Iran could still move in ways hostile to the United States and to United States interests, that Soviet diplomats were in the game and that American public opinion was still skeptical of reconciliation with Iran.

For the United States, therefore, President Bush's efforts to create more flexibility in dealing with Iran underscored his understanding of the continuing agenda for the United States in this area of the world—an area still in turmoil, awash in modern weaponry, and, in the key country of Iran, still subject to competition for influence between the Soviet Union and the United States. Thus 1989 proved to be a year in which a new administration began to shape its perspectives toward the region, but played a relatively modest role. The year 1990 beckoned as a year in which United States intentions and its ability to affect events in the Middle East would be tested.

SAVING CENTRAL AMERICA

*With newly elected leaders, a
second try at a Common Market
and a little help from Mr.
Bush—a troubled region can
thrive again.*

Bruce Babbitt

*Bruce Babbitt, former governor of Arizona and a
candidate for the Democratic presidential nomination in 1988, has lived and traveled throughout
Latin America. In "Saving the Forest for the Trees
(WM, September 1989) he wrote about the Amazon
region, as he does in a forthcoming book. In
"Reviving Mexico" (WM, March 1989) he proposed
economic measures similar to some now being
carried out.*

Once upon a time there was a Central American
Common Market. It was created in 1961 by Guatemala, El Salvador, Honduras, Nicaragua, and
Costa Rica. Thereafter their economies grew and
grew at 6% per year. And then it all fell apart, and
the five countries declined into war and depression.

According to popular memory, this wondrous
economic machine was destroyed by a soccer game
between El Salvador and Honduras that turned into
a riot that led El Salvador to invade Honduras. The
"soccer war" was called off after a few days, but a
vengeful Honduras then stalked out of the Common
Market, triggering a downward spiral that eventually left five Central American countries in economic ruin.

Today, after a decade of bloody conflicts that
have cost 100,000 lives, created 2 million refugees,
transformed Latin military leaders into killers of
priests and nuns and United States political leaders
into lawbreakers, Central Americans are wistfully
looking back on those Common Market years as a
golden age of economic growth and wondering
whether that moment in history can ever be
recreated.

And now, quite unexpectedly, an opportunity is at
hand to pick up the shattered pieces and recreate a
new regional economy. The upset win of Violeta
Barrios de Chamorro in Nicaragua spells the end of
a failed Marxist economic experiment.

For the first time in history, the Central American countries including Panama have freely elected
leaders who advocate market economics. And prospects for regional peace seem to be improving by
the week.

Notwithstanding the political progress, the new
Central American presidents have been slow to take
up the cause of economic integration. Economic
survival and ending the warfare are the immediate
concerns. But after ten years of failure, Central
Americans also seem to be restrained by a lingering
sense of the futility of grand designs. Like the
protagonists in a García Márquez novel, they sometimes appear to be immobilized by historical failures that they are powerless to overcome.

However, recent events in Central America suggest just the opposite—that it is precisely the depth
and gravity of the economic crisis that provide the
opportunity for a fresh start.

4. LIMITS OF AMERICAN POWER

Just three years ago, it was a near hopeless political crisis that motivated five Central American presidents to take charge of their common political destiny. In August of 1987 they met in Guatemala and signed the accords known as Esquipulas II.

It was those accords, signed under pressure of taking the blame for failure, that took the initiative away from Ronald Reagan and set the five countries on the path of national reconciliation, free elections, and an end to civil war.

RISK-TAKERS

The principal authors of the Esquipulas accords are gone from the political stage: El Salvador's José Napoleón Duarte dead, Nicaragua's Daniel Ortega Saavedra defeated, Costa Rica's Oscar Arias Sánchez in constitutionally mandated retirement.

But their example, taking personal risks to reach a regional settlement not entirely acceptable to any of their constituents, suggests what could be done on the economic front by their successors.

A new Common Market is not likely to develop without strong leadership from the United States. And there is not much time, for the US attention span, always short for this region of the world, is already on the wane. With Daniel Ortega and Manuel Noriega—Panama's former strongman —out of the way, President Bush has turned toward Europe and the Soviet Union, leaving Vice-President Dan Quayle to patrol Central America. To be sure, the president quickly asked Congress for another $300 million in grants and subsidies for Nicaragua and $500 million for Panama, but those requests have about as much motivational appeal to impoverished countries as a rich uncle handing out quarters to his nephews.

The starting point on the path toward a new regional economy is to draw the correct lessons from the spectacular rise and gradual collapse of the first Common Market.

In reality, that Common Market was not destroyed by a soccer game or Latin temperament. It failed because it became too successful too quickly.

Trade within the region multiplied five times in the 1960s, and the result was large persistent trade imbalances between more developed countries, El Salvador and Guatemala, and the less developed countries, Honduras and Nicaragua.

REDUCED TO BARTER

Because neither the member countries nor the United States, their largest external trading partner,

had anticipated or prepared to deal with the unequal distribution of benefits, the predictable result was escalating trade warfare; protectionist measures followed by retaliation.

Nicaragua banned the import of rice from Guatemala, and Costa Rica cut off rice from El Salvador. El Salvador refused to buy Guatemalan cigarettes. Honduras withdrew from the Common Market altogether, and Nicaragua and Costa Rica responded with import licenses and quotas. As retaliation progressed, currencies lost convertibility, and the countries, beset by inflation and war, were reduced to barter trade in the manner of Eastern Europe or Africa.

The perception of winners and losers, created by unequal distribution of benefits in the initial phases of free trade, also took place in the evolution of the European Common Market. Shortly after World War II France found itself faced with account deficits. The French government suspended imports from Belgium and Switzerland. Other countries threatened to follow suit.

EUROPE'S LESSON

At that time, however, the United States recognized the problem and came to the rescue. It did so by diverting bilateral Marshall Plan aid programs into a multilateral institution called the European Payments Union (EPU). The payments union was simply a mechanism to smooth out the unequal distribution of benefits. The EPU provided currency support to clear the regional trading accounts of member countries. Within a few years the European countries developed their own adjustment mechanisms, and began the movement toward Common Market and on to Europe 1992.

The economic and social disparities among the Central American countries are vastly greater than those of postwar Europe, and free trade cannot develop without consistent national fiscal and monetary policies. But the economic lessons learned from the European experience are applicable. If the United States had been on hand in the 1970s with similar support in Central America, the course of history might have been quite different.

WASHINGTON'S SILENCE

The United States now has another chance to help initiate a new process of economic integration and to make it stick. One might ask why, in light of these previous experiences with Common Markets in Central America and Europe, no such proposal

The starting point on the path toward a new regional economy is to draw the correct lessons from the spectacular rise and gradual collapse of Central America's first Common Market.

has been forthcoming from Washington.

The likely answer, apart from neglect of large economic issues in general and Latin America in particular, is that US foreign aid bureaucracies do not like multilateral aid programs.

No US ambassador in Nicaragua or Guatemala is likely to be arguing for a regional economic plan that might diminish his own bilateral assistance budget. Congressmen prefer specific programs for specific constituencies. And it is hard to describe or photograph a payments union plan.

As a practical matter, this means that US leadership for regional integration must come, if at all, from the president and the secretary of state.

Reorienting the US aid program to foster economic integration does not necessarily mean more money—provided the US is willing to bundle some existing Agency for International Development (AID) programs into a multilateral context. Current aid to the Central American countries is about a billion dollars a year; perhaps 10% or 20% of that amount would be sufficient to fund a payments union as part of a market-oriented free-trade plan.

Without a functioning Common Market, it is hard to imagine how the Central American countries can ever consolidate their political progress by creating economic growth. The individual economies are simply too small to make their way alone in the global economy. Costa Rica and Panama each have fewer than 3 million people, Nicaraugua about 3.7 million, Honduras 5 million, El Salvador 6.3 million, and Guatemala 8.9 million. But together the countries constitute a respectable market of approximately 30 million.

With the example of Europe, the help of the United States, and some vision from its own political leaders, Central America could succeed on the second try.

Human Rights and Democratic Rule

In recent decades, the world community has become increasingly aware of and concerned about the extent and severity of human rights violations in the Third World. These abuses—which take sundry forms—are instituted in order to isolate or eliminate actual or potential political opponents who may pose a threat to the ruler or regime.

Since 1975, Third World governments have either ordered or condoned the political killings of hundreds of thousands of people by the army and police, other regular security forces, special units, and "death squads" sanctioned by official authorities. Typically, these killings occur outside the legal or judicial process; the victims are denied all constitutional protections. Political dissidents are frequently abducted, illegally detained, and/or tortured before they are murdered.

In some cases, the killings are orchestrated at the highest levels of the government. In others, the government either refuses to investigate the murders or refuses to adopt concrete measures to prevent further killings. When these murders are revealed, the governments usually deny that they occurred, blame their political opponents, or insist that they were the result of violent confrontations with government forces or of attempts by the victim to escape from official custody.

According to Amnesty International, political killings can be defined as "the unlawful and deliberate killings of persons by reason of their real or imputed political beliefs or activities, religion, other conscientiously held beliefs, ethnic origin, sex, color, or language, carried out by order of a government or with its complicity." These killings are committed in blatant violation of national and international law, and take place throughout the world, irrespective of political ideology. They range from individual assassinations to the indiscriminate slaughter of either members of opposition movements or ethnic groups.

In addition to political killings, many Third World governments also engage in the systematic violation of basic civil liberties, including freedom of speech, press, religion, assembly, and petition. In the case of political dissidents, governments regularly violate the constitutional safeguards of individuals who, in their view, pose a threat to their survival. Typical targets include politicians, government officials, judges, lawyers, military officers, unionists, journalists, teachers, students, and clerics. For example,
in Liberia, the government of President Samuel K. Doe illegally imprisoned hundreds of anti-Doe activists. Freedom fighters are routinely jailed in Liberia and elsewhere, not because they are convicted criminals, but because of what they represent—namely, a potent opposition voice with widespread popular support.

Government opponents who succeed in escaping imprisonment are frequently subjected to intimidation, harassment, and violence. Many are forced to adopt disguises, travel secretly, and find living quarters free of government surveillance. In many cases, opposition leaders are also forced to abandon their families, give up their careers, live in poverty, and survive as outlaws in their own land. In these instances, the government hopes to isolate the dissidents, discredit their reputations, and destroy their followings.

In many Third World nations, particularly those ruled by the gun, government officials employ even harsher measures, including kidnapping, torture, blackmail, death threats, and violence. Freedom fighters are denied the right to speak, write, organize, travel, and work. The courts exist in name only—they merely rubber-stamp the actions of high-level officials, who exert political pressure on judges to legitimize their conduct. Unless the judges acquiesce, they will be replaced, punished, or killed.

In many developing countries, the rights to life, liberty, and property exist only on paper—to be abridged at will by government officials. Freedom is permitted only to the extent that it serves the objectives of the government. Despots fear democratic rule because it encourages popular participation, which could ultimately bring down the government. This explains, in part, why many Third World governments are quick to silence opposition newspapers, suspend political parties, close churches, and impose martial law.

Looking Ahead: Challenge Questions

What can and should the United States do to protect human rights in the Third World?

Why is the West often willing to close its eyes to torture in the developing world?

What, if anything, can be done to protect the rights of prisoners in the Third World?

What explains the flight of the Vietnamese boat people?

Should the boat people be allowed to emigrate to the United States?

How real is the threat posed by the Cambodian Khmer Rouge?

What, if anything, can be done to neutralize the power of Pol Pot?

How have the Kurds been caught in the conflicting crosscurrents of nationalism and war in Asia Minor?

Is South African president F.W. de Klerk's plea for normalization and negotiation likely to succeed?

Why did President de Klerk release African National Congress leader Nelson Mandela and call for a new constitution in South Africa?

Is South Africa's apartheid system on the verge of collapse?

Why does Nelson Mandela continue to call for armed struggle against apartheid?

THE HUMAN RIGHTS IMPERATIVE

Cyrus R. Vance

CYRUS R. VANCE *was secretary of state from 1977 to 1980.*

The last 5 years have not been easy for those who believe that a commitment to human rights must be a central tenet of American foreign policy. The concept and definition of human rights have been twisted almost beyond recognition. Long-standing principles of international law and practice have been chipped away. Doublespeak has too often been the order of the day. Yet the time may be coming when Americans will be able to sweep aside the illusions and myths that have been used, often deliberately, to fog the human rights debate. The time may be coming when the opportunities presented by a strong human rights policy can again be seized.

These signs do not presage merely a belated recognition that former President Jimmy Carter was correct in committing U.S. foreign policy to human dignity and freedom. One can sense a rising desire among Americans to see a return to the fundamental beliefs on which their country's human rights policy must rest and from which it draws its strength. If so, and if their leaders will respond to this desire, Americans will be able again to pursue their ideals without sacrificing their traditional pragmatism.

President Ronald Reagan is fond of calling America a "city upon a hill." But the Puritan leader John Winthrop, who first uttered those words in the 17th century, intended them as a warning about the importance of adhering to the values that eventually shaped America's founding and development—particularly those later reflected in the U.S. Constitution in the Bill of Rights—not as a boast about military or economic power. As a country, America cannot be, as Reagan suggests, the "last, best hope of man on earth" unless it is prepared to restore to its rightful place in American national life respect for and protection of human rights at home and abroad.

Let me define what I mean by human rights. The most important human rights are those that protect the security of the person. Violations of such rights include genocide; slavery; torture; cruel, inhuman, and degrading treatment or punishment; arbitrary arrest or imprisonment; denial of fair trial; and invasion of the home. In the United States, many of these protections are enshrined in the Bill of Rights.

Second is that bundle of rights affecting the fulfillment of such vital needs as food, clothing, shelter, health care, and education—in the scheme of President Franklin Roosevelt's four freedoms, the freedom from want. Americans recognize that fulfilling these rights depends largely on the stage of a country's economic development. But the United States can and should help others attain these basic rights. Americans must never forget those whose empty stomachs and grinding poverty dominate their daily lives. Nor must they forget that governmental inaction, governmental indifference, and governmental corruption can threaten these rights just as seriously as the most dramatic acts of God.

Third, there is the right to enjoy civil and political liberties. These include not only freedom of speech, freedom of the press, freedom of religion, and freedom to assemble and to petition the government to redress grievances, which are guaranteed by the First Amendment to the Constitution, but also the right that most Americans take for granted—the freedom to move freely within and to and from one's own country.

Civil and political rights also must include the liberty to take part in government, the affirmation of Thomas Jefferson's declaration that the only just powers of a government are those derived from the consent of the governed. By exercising this freedom, citizens may insist that their government protect and promote their individual rights.

Finally, there is a basic human right to freedom from discrimination because of race, religion, color, or gender.

Almost all of these rights are recognized in the United Nations Universal Declaration of Human Rights, a document that the United States helped fashion and that draws heavily on the American Bill of Rights, the British Magna Carta, and the French Declaration of the Rights of Man and of the Citizen. Each of these documents has played a vital role in the historical evolution of respect for human rights. But after World War II, the world witnessed an unprecedented human rights revolution, including measures to institutionalize the international enforcement of human rights.

A genuine reversal of the administration's human rights policy could change profoundly the way America is seen in the world.

Until then, the idea that a regime could be held accountable to international standards and to the world for the treatment of its people was regarded largely as an idiosyncrasy of the democratic West, invoked only when it served a Western power's interests. A sovereign government, tradition held, could rule its people or its territory as it saw fit.

Even countries like the United States and Great Britain, which professed to follow higher standards, did not seem to believe that those standards applied to treatment of people without white skins. There was no international outcry when the United States used harsh methods to subdue opposition forces in the Philippines at the turn of the century or brutally drove native Americans onto reservations. The British could employ the most extreme tactics in repressing native populations around the globe, and few whites thought the worse of them for that. And countries without the respect for law were even less concerned about others' rights.

Such attitudes changed radically after World War II, principally because of the horror felt around the world when the Holocaust was exposed and when the full extent of Joseph Stalin's purges became clear. Individuals and countries suddenly realized that with-

out standards, there were also no limits. The war also revealed that the far-flung colonial systems were bankrupt. Great powers could no longer hold sway over peoples they had for so long considered, in the English writer Rudyard Kipling's words, "lesser breeds without the Law."

Against this historical background, substantial progress has been made over the last 40 years. Since 1945, the world has codified a wide range of human rights. That process is in itself an enormous achievement. The power of these codes is demonstrated when movements like Poland's outlawed independent trade union Solidarity cite international norms to justify popular demands for greater liberty. Even countries that show little respect for human rights feel a need to pay lip service to them. But codes alone are not enough. It also has been necessary to develop international institutions to implement them.

First, in 1945, the United Nations Charter was adopted, enshrining human rights both as a basic objective of the newly created body and as a universal obligation. Article 55 of the charter states that the United Nations shall promote "human rights and fundamental freedoms for all without distinction as to race, sex, language, or religion." Article 56 obliges member countries "to take joint and separate action in cooperation with the Organization" to achieve those purposes.

In 1946, the Commission on Human Rights was established in the United Nations; Eleanor Roosevelt, the former U.S. first lady, was elected its first chairman. In 1948 came the Universal Declaration of Human Rights, a basic though nonbinding declaration of principles of human rights and freedoms. The 1940s and 1950s also saw the drafting of the Convention on the Prevention and Punishment of the Crime of Genocide and the preparation of two separate human rights covenants—one on political and civil rights and the other covering economic, social, and cultural rights.

During much of the 1950s, Washington stood aloof from treaties furthering those rights and limited itself to supporting U.N. studies and advisory services. But during the 1960s, America resumed its leadership, and in 1965–1966, the two covenants were finally adopted by the United Nations and presented for ratification by member states.

Largely in response to American pressure, the world moved to implement these codes more effectively. To this end, Western Europe, the Americas, and later, Africa, established their own human rights institutions. On another front, the U.N. system for several years confined its public human rights activities to only three cases: Chile, Israel, and South Africa. But beginning in the Carter years, further U.S. prodding led the international community to broaden its concern to include the examination of human rights violations in many countries, including communist countries. Progress, though sometimes halting, has been made in a process that has no precedent.

Dangerous Illusions

Many opportunities and obstacles lie ahead. But first the illusions that cloud, and fallacies that subvert, American human rights policy must be dispelled. Only then can a coherent and determined course be charted.

The first and most dangerous illusion holds that pursuing values such as human rights in U.S. foreign policy is incompatible with pursuing U.S. national interests. This is nonsense. As Reagan stated in March 1986: "A foreign policy that ignored the fate of millions in the world who seek freedom would be a betrayal of our national heritage. Our own freedom, and that of our allies, could never be secure in a world where freedom was threatened everywhere else."

Moreover, no foreign policy can gain the American people's support unless it reflects their deeper values. Carter understood this when, as president, he championed human rights. In addition to enabling millions of people to live better lives, this commitment helped redeem U.S. foreign policy from the bitterness and divisions of the Vietnam War. It reassured the American people that the U.S. role abroad can have a purpose that they could all support.

Human rights policy also requires practical judgments. Americans must continually weigh how best to encourage progress while maintaining their ability to conduct necessary business with countries in which they have important security interests. But the United States must always bear in mind that the demand for individual freedom and human dignity cannot be quelled without sowing the seeds of discontent and violent convulsion. Thus supporting constructive change that enhances individual freedom is both morally right and in America's national interest.

Freedom is a universal right of all human beings. America's own national experience, as well as recent events in Argentina, Haiti, and the Philippines, attests to the power of the drive for freedom. In a profound sense, America's ideals and interests coincide, for the United States has a stake in the stability that comes when people can express their hopes and build their futures freely. In the long run,

no system is as solid as that built on the rock of freedom. But it is not enough simply to proclaim such general principles. The more difficult question remains: What means of support should be provided to those whose rights are denied or endangered? And to answer this question, two underlying groups of questions must be addressed.

First, what are the facts? What violations or deprivations are taking place? How extensive are they? Do they demonstrate a consistent pattern of gross violations of human rights? What is the degree of control and responsibility of the government involved? Will that government permit independent outside investigation?

Second, what can be done? Will U.S. actions help promote the overall cause of human rights? Can U.S. actions improve the specific conditions at hand, or could they make matters worse? Will other countries work with the United States? Does America's sense of values and decency demand that the country speak out or take action even where there is only a remote chance of making its influence felt?

If the United States is determined to act, many tools are available. They range from quiet diplomacy, to public pronouncements, to withholding economic or military assistance from the incumbent regime. In some cases, Washington may need to provide economic assistance to oppressed peoples and, in rare instances like Afghanistan, limited military aid. Where appropriate, the United States should take positive steps to encourage compliance with basic human rights norms. And America should strive to act in concert with other countries when possible.

A second illusion that must be exposed is one pushed by many critics of Carter's human rights focus. Wrapping themselves in a rhetorical cloak of democracy and freedom, these critics pursue a curious logic that leads them to support governments and groups that deny democracy and abuse freedom. They insist on drawing a distinction for foreign-policy purposes between "authoritarian" countries that are seen as friendly toward the United States and "totalitarian" states seen as hostile. Authoritarian governments, the argument continues, are less repressive than revolutionary autocracies, more susceptible to liberalization, and more compatible with U.S. interests. Generally speaking, it is said, anticommunist autocracies tolerate social inequities, brutality, and poverty while revolutionary autocracies create them.

Sadly, this specious distinction, rooted in America's former U.N. representative Jeane Kirkpatrick's November 1979 *Commentary* article "Dictatorships and Double Standards," became a central element of the new human rights policy set forth at the start of the Reagan administration. Kirkpatrick's thesis damaged America's image as a beacon of freedom and a wise and humane champion of human rights. If it were simply an academic exercise, this version of the authoritarian-totalitarian distinction might cause little mischief. But it has a deeper political purpose. The implication that such a distinction provides a basis for condoning terror and brutality if committed by authoritarian governments friendly to the United States is mind-boggling.

The suggestion that America should turn a blind eye to human rights violations by autocrats of any stripe is unacceptable. Such thinking is morally bankrupt and badly serves U.S. national interests. To the individual on the rack it makes no difference whether the torturer is right- or left-handed—it remains the rack. In short, a sound and balanced human rights policy requires condemnation of such conduct, no matter who the perpetrator is.

Recent events give some hope that this cruel and insensitive philosophy is being buried. In his March 14 message to Congress, Reagan stated that America opposes "tyranny in whatever form, whether of the left or the right." Debate over whether this statement reflects a policy reversal will continue until the new posture inspires a pattern of concrete actions. But it must not be perverted into a ploy to gain votes in Congress for increased military aid for the Nicaraguan *contra* rebels. A genuine reversal of the administration's human rights policy could change profoundly the way America is seen in the world and also unleash powerful forces that would encourage truly democratic alternatives. Such a policy surely would have strong bipartisan support.

A third human rights illusion, deriving from the second, is the fallacy inherent in the so-called Reagan Doctrine enunciated in the president's 1985 State of the Union address. Speaking about U.S. policy toward armed insurgencies against communist regimes, he declared: "We must not break faith with those who are risking their lives—on every continent, from Afghanistan to Nicaragua—to defy Soviet-supported aggression and secure rights which have been ours from birth. . . . Support for freedom fighters is self-defense."

No doubt there will be situations in which the United States should aid insurgencies—as in Afghanistan, where such aid promotes human rights and clearly serves American interests. There, the Soviet Union invaded a small neighboring country with overpowering military force, deposed the existing government, and imposed its own hand-picked government that, with the support of massive Soviet firepower, slaughtered tens of thousands of Afghans and turned millions more into refugees. It is critical to note that in supporting the Afghan rebels, Americans are not merely supporting an anticommunist rebellion. The United States is vindicating universal principles of international law and helping the Afghan people to determine their own future.

Yet the Reagan Doctrine, taking shelter under the banner of human rights, commits America to supporting anticommunist revolution wherever it arises. By implication, the doctrine offers no such assistance to opponents of other tyrannies. As the case of Nicaragua shows, the support the doctrine promises can include American arms. Consequently, despite repeated administration denials, the doctrine clearly holds out the possibility of ultimate intervention by U.S. forces.

This policy is both wrong and potentially dangerous to America's interests and its standing in the world. As with virtually all doctrines, it is automatic and inflexible by nature. That inflexibility blinds policymakers in a double sense. It blinds them to the realities and available alternatives in individual situations, and it blinds them to the principles of respect for national territorial sovereignty and nonintervention—cornerstones of international order.

The Reagan Doctrine's evident bias toward military options could easily prompt Washington to overlook better ways to achieve worthy goals. Even where economic incentives or restrictions may be sufficient, and even where U.S. policy may lack regional support and might work against broader U.S. interests, the Reagan Doctrine suggests that, at a minimum, America should fund military forces.

Beyond this strategic misconception, the Reagan Doctrine obscures the hard but essential questions of means and consequences. To avoid self-delusion, Americans must recognize that anticommunism cannot always be equated with democracy. Nor is anticommunism a shield against the consequences of unrealistic and imprudent action. At the very least, the United States must ask whom it intends to support. Do they believe in democratic values? Can they attract sufficient support in their country and region to govern if they take power? How would such a change affect the citizens of their country? Does America risk raising hopes or expectations that it cannot or will not fulfill? Can America deliver enough aid to decisively affect the outcome? Finally, will such a policy have the domestic support needed to sustain Washington's chosen course of action?

Ironically, many champions of the Reagan Doctrine call themselves realists. Yet any policy that tempts the country to ignore these basic questions cannot be called hardheaded or realistic. The doctrine's dogmatism and seductive ideological beckoning to leap before looking, are, in fact, strikingly unrealistic. So systematically ignoring the principles of sovereignty and nonintervention is not in America's national interest.

New Hope for Progress

A key strength of this country has always been its respect for law and moral values. To follow the Reagan Doctrine would undermine America's moral authority. What the United States and the Soviet Union have to offer the world must be distinguished by more than the simple declaration that, by definition, whatever Washington does is right and whatever Moscow does is wrong.

President John Kennedy once said that the United States is engaged in a "long, twilight struggle" in world affairs. But if that is so, America's principles and interests both are more likely to thrive if the country keeps faith with the ideals for which it struggles.

Principle must be the foundation of America's course for the future, but policy will be sustained only if it is also pragmatic. That must not mean that pragmatism should dominate. U.S. foreign policy must never become realpolitik unconnected with principle. Yet promoting ideals that have no chance of being put into practice risks becoming mere posturing. Nor should Americans focus simply on the great issues and ignore the fact that, at heart, human rights concern individual human beings. Indeed, it matters greatly what America can do in concrete cases, in individual countries, for any one person to live a better life.

The charge to U.S. human rights policy has rarely been put more clearly than by Felice Gaer, executive director of the International League for Human Rights. Testifying before a subcommittee of the House Committee on Foreign Affairs in February 1986, she said: "The United States needs to do more than make declarations and to provide free transport for fleeing dictators.... The U.S. Government has leverage to use—if it chooses to use it. It has the power to persuade governments."

The United States has many opportunities, and faces many problems, in trying to advance human rights abroad. In a few countries, there is reason to give thanks for recent progress. In others, recent shifts in stated U.S. policy provide hope for future progress.

Chile is a case in point. The regime of General Augusto Pinochet recently has increased pressure on Chilean defenders of human rights. Members of the Chilean Commission for Human Rights, the country's most important secular human rights organization, face almost daily threats, physical intimidation, and overt violence. Last November, the commission's office was invaded and ransacked. Its documents, compiled for a U.N. investigation, were confiscated by armed plainclothes police. The intruders beat the office caretaker with their fists and a revolver, causing a concussion. When the caretaker's daughters tried to help her, they were threatened with death. Before leaving, the invaders shouted, "Now you will know the hand of CNI [the Chilean national intelligence agency]."

On January 15, 1986, two commission officers were attacked and stoned in front of a police station by a mob of progovernment protesters while the civilian police stood idly by. The victims were the commission's president, Jaime Castillo, a founder and past president of the Christian Democratic party and former minister of justice in the democratic government of Eduardo Frei in the 1960s, and the commission's vice president, Maximo Pacheco, a former minister of education in the Frei government. The windows of the car in which they were riding were shattered by rocks, and Castillo was struck in the head with a rock and lacerated in the face and back by splintering glass. Fortunately, the two men were able to keep the car moving and escaped with their lives. Since then the pressure has continued. Pacheco has been harassed, his household servant kidnaped, and his daughter and her child subjected to threats of kidnaping and violence. The Chilean government has brushed aside all protests.

Despite such brutalities, there is still reason for hope. Chile does have a long tradition of popular rule before 1973—when Pinochet seized power in a bloody military coup—on which to build. A foundation for human rights does exist beneath the rubble created by the military dictatorship. Moreover, U.S. policy toward Chile has begun to change. From the outset, the Reagan administration opposed a U.N. resolution condemning Chile for human rights abuses. In March 1986, however, the administration changed its position and sponsored its own resolution condemning Chile. Much credit must go to America's courageous ambassador, Harry Barnes, Jr., to Secretary of

State George Shultz, and to those members of Congress who have long pressed the Chilean government to restore respect for human rights and to hold early, free, and fair elections.

In future dealings with Chile, the United States must make its views on human rights clear. Washington must stress that U.S.-Chilean relations will be affected by Santiago's conduct. America must state bluntly that unless Chile's human rights policies and conduct change, the United States will, among other actions, vote against all future international bank loans to Chile.

In Argentina, meanwhile, promise has become reality. Under the leadership of President Raúl Alfonsín, respect for freedom and for individual dignity has been restored to that country. As the publisher Jacobo Timerman—who was tortured under Argentina's old military regime—and others have pointed out, the Argentine people can be thankful to Americans who kept faith in the dark days of the late 1970s, when thousands of Argentines "disappeared" and many were murdered at the hands of the military.

Above all, Argentina's return to democracy is truly a triumph of popular courage and determination, a victory of the faith and will of the oppressed over their oppressors. Americans must continue to support the Alfonsín government both politically and economically as it confronts massive economic difficulties. Washington should be forthcoming and steady in providing help, bilaterally and through the international financial institutions.

Encouraging news recently has come from the Philippines and Haiti as well. In Haiti, the heir to one of the world's worst traditions of government finally was driven from power. This island country remains desperately poor and faces a difficult future. But at least its destiny is being determined largely by men and women who seek a better life for all Haitians. America can and must help, beginning with immediate emergency food aid, while it urgently assesses Haiti's longer-term needs. In the Philippines, the problems are even more complex, but the victory achieved is even more inspiring. All Americans have marveled at the magnificent commitment of the Filipino people to freedom, at the physical and moral courage of President Corazon Aquino, at the support of the Roman Catholic church under the leadership of Jaime Cardinal Sin, and at the unforgettable sight of peaceful, unarmed men and women facing down tanks and guns with their "prayers and presence." The United States should offer whatever support it can as that country seeks to rebuild both politically and economically.

One of the most striking developments of the 1980s has been the answer to Stalin's question concerning how many divisions the pope has. From Poland to the Philippines, the world has heard the answer: Quite a few. Much remains to be done in the Philippines, and the doing will not be easy. But what has been shown in Buenos Aires, in Port-au-Prince, and in Manila is that peaceful, democratic change is possible in today's world, that such change carries with it great promise, and that there is much that American human rights policies can do to promote it.

In many other countries the pace of change has been maddeningly slow, and in some, nonexistent. Both opportunities and pitfalls abound. This is particularly true in Central America, and nowhere more so than in Nicaragua. Furnishing military aid to the contras is a disastrous mistake. The United States should listen to the virtually unanimous advice of its Latin American neighbors who urge it not to give such aid and to give its full support instead to the Contadora process. Despite temporary setbacks, this regional peace effort provides a framework for ending Central America's agony while safeguarding the hemisphere's security interests. But whatever their viewpoint, Americans all should be able to agree that human rights are denied and abused in Nicaragua, and have been for decades—by the late dictator Anastasio Somoza Debayle and his supporters and by the Sandinistas. Americans must continue to demand an end to all such abuses.

To avoid self-delusion, Americans must recognize that anticommunism cannot always be equated with democracy.

In the Pacific, human rights are of special importance in South Korea. The United States has major national interests in South Korea and its future. Americans fought side by side with the South Korean people in defending the country. Seoul is an important ally, America's seventh largest trading partner, and a critical force for stability in Northeast Asia. And South Korea's future will be vitally affected by the way its government responds to popular demands for greater pluralism and respect for the rights and dignity of all of its citizens. America must exert its influence to that end. The next 3 years will be especially important as international attention to South Korea increases when Seoul hosts the Asian

Games in fall 1986 and the summer Olympic Games in 1988.

South Korea differs from the Philippines in its political traditions and cultural heritage. The Filipino people have democratic roots several decades long, while South Korea's slow movement toward more open government is a relatively recent development. These differences should caution Americans in drawing conclusions and predicting how each government will act to open up its society. Failure to be realistic can lead to false hopes and expectations.

This does not mean playing down human rights issues in U.S. relations with South Korea. Quite the contrary, as a friend and ally, the United States must speak more candidly and forcefully than it has about the need for South Korea's leaders to open up the political process more rapidly and to recognize and respect the right of all its citizens to be free from repression and secure from arbitrary arrest, imprisonment, and the invasion of their homes. A pragmatic as well as principled policy also would make clear that the United States will continue to help South Korea defend itself against the threat of attack from North Korea, while maintaining America's strong interest in South Korea's economic development and prosperity.

The Soviet Union clearly presents the most difficult problems in balancing human rights principles and pragmatism. Two critically important truths must always be kept in mind. First, human rights must always be on America's agenda with the Soviet Union. On that there can be no compromise. Second, human rights almost never can be on the agenda alone. The facts of the nuclear age require dealing with Moscow on matters that can determine the fate of the planet—avoiding nuclear war and preventing regional conflicts that could lead to nuclear war. No American government can honor its commitment to the human family if it fails to pursue human rights with Soviet leaders; it cannot honor its commitment, however, if it does not also pursue the cause of peace.

The United States must continue to prod the Soviet Union to honor its commitment to the human rights provisions of the Helsinki Final Act. America must also prod the Soviets to relax their grip on those people, from the dissident scientist Andrei Sakharov to thousands of unknown individuals, who are most oppressed by Soviet rule. America must do so because those individuals have few other advocates in world councils. America must do so because, in speaking out, it reminds the world of the difference between the vision of Jefferson and the perverse outlook of Stalin. And America must do so because it can have an effect. Sometimes America may act through quiet diplomacy; at other times, through forceful public statements. Still other situations may call for the use of incentives or rewards on the one hand and threats and punishments on the other.

Americans must also remember the special plight of Soviet Jewry. Specifically, Moscow must be pressed to increase the level of Jewish emigration at least to that achieved in the mid- and late 1970s. It was possible then; it should be possible now.

Since martial law crushed the Solidarity movement in December 1981, human rights conditions have been a major problem in Poland. American economic sanctions that initially were imposed have been dismantled step by step as the Polish government met certain conditions: Martial law was lifted and many political prisoners were released. The calibrated American response has been, on the whole, an intelligent application of U.S. human rights policy.

Yet despite what some take as normalization of the situation, the last year has seen severe incursions on academic freedom and purges, together with the harassment and even imprisonment of some of Solidarity's leading figures. Further U.S. assistance to help Poland overcome its economic catastrophe should be keyed to Warsaw's willingness to reverse the setbacks of the last year and to move toward genuine national reconciliation involving the Polish government, the Roman Catholic church, and Solidarity.

Finally, there is South Africa. The United States has maintained diplomatic relations with South Africa for many years. During World War II, although many of the strongest advocates of apartheid were pro-Nazi, the South African government itself fought with the Allies to free the peoples of Europe from fascist tyranny. South Africa is a source of important raw materials, occupying a strategic position along the sea routes running from the Indian Ocean and the Middle East into the Atlantic Ocean. Yet productive relations with South Africa are impossible because of sharp differences over apartheid, over the right of South Africa's blacks to live decent lives, and over their right to participate as full citizens in governing their country.

South Africa has institutionalized discrimination of the most vicious sort and resists fundamental change of this abhorrent system. What the United States seeks in the near term is clear: the dismantling of apartheid, root and branch, and the sharing of political power among whites, blacks, mixed-blood "Col-oreds," and Asians alike.

The United States should make unmistak-ably clear to President P. W. Botha and all South Africans that Americans are committed to the total abolition of apartheid and to genuine power sharing. The U.S. government must underscore that South Africa cannot adopt one policy for worldwide public con-sumption and a second, less stringent policy for private discussion in Pretoria. America must make unmistakably clear that time is running out and that major steps must be taken now. The South African government also must be told that, without prompt action, the United States will impose more stringent economic restrictions than those approved by Reagan in September 1985. And America should work with like-minded countries to pressure South Africa to make those decisions that are necessary now to stop further repres-sion and a bloody civil war later.

The world has a long agenda in the pursuit of human rights. There will be, I fear, no final victory over tyranny, no end to the challenge of helping people to live decent lives, free from oppression and indignity. But this gener-ation has set the highest standards for human rights in human history. It has achieved much; it has proved repeatedly that no idea is so compelling as the idea of human freedom. America was "conceived in Liberty, and dedi-cated to the proposition that all men are created equal." It is America's task, a century and a quarter after Abraham Lincoln spoke, to do its utmost to help redeem that promise for men and women everywhere.

The Fight to Stop
TORTURE

"In the midst of despair and degradation, tortured prisoners again and again have been lifted out of living death by the realization that fellow human beings—even those unknown and far away—are working to rescue them."

James David Barber

Dr. Barber is James B. Duke Professor of Political Science and Policy Studies, Duke University, Durham, N.C., and former chairman of the Board of Directors of Amnesty International USA.

AMERICA is a caring country. When drought hits the Southeast, farmers in the Midwest send hay—free of charge. Every year, Americans by the millions dig into their own pockets to help the helpless, at home and abroad. We could do more, but, through our churches and charities, we do try to demonstrate that we mean what we say when we speak of love and respect for our fellow human beings. No wonder then that it shocks Americans to learn that money we pay for taxes goes into the pockets of dictators who torture their own citizens.

Unbelievable as it sounds, there is no doubt of the truth that American money winds up supporting torturers. Extensive, detailed, carefully checked reports, spelling out names, dates, and places, are issued by Amnesty International, the worldwide human rights organization. These reports confirm the facts of torture and killing by a wide variety of governments, with different ideologies from left to right.

In too many cases, massive U.S. support goes to governments whose current human rights offenses are verified.

Take Turkey, for example. In 1986 alone, our taxes provided $738,841,000 to the Turkish government. Officials there keep claiming they are making "progress" in human rights. In fact, however, hundreds of Turkish citizens are in jail only for what they believe in or what ethnic group they belong to, and many are, at this moment, being subjected to crippling humiliation and pain. Men, women, and children in Turkish prisons are being shocked with electric rods, burnt with cigarettes, and sexually abused—not just now and then, but systematically, hour after hour.

In spite of Amnesty International's repeated appeals, the Turkish authorities still have to put a stop to torture in their jails. Day by day, Amnesty International is receiving new reports of Turkish torture.

The public relations blitz

Instead of wiping out torture in their police stations, Turkey has hired (at $1,000,000 a year) a high-powered public relations firm in Washington, D.C., Gray and Company, to bolster Turkey's public image and make sure Congress keeps the foreign aid money coming. That company represented "Baby Doc" Duvalier, Haiti's brutal dictator, before his overthrow. Experts in polling, advertising, and lobbying Congress and the Administration, Gray and Company says it is "proud to count among our professional staff" dozens of former top officials of the U.S. government who know how to influence national policy.

Turkey's tactics are not unique. Another big-time Washington lobby, headed by a former White House aide, was hired by South Korea (at $1,200,000) to "protect, manage, and expand trade and economic interests." Multi-page advertising sections, touting South Korea's economy, appear in news magazines. Meanwhile, South Korea demonstrates its contempt for free speech by locking up dissenters by the hundreds. One of their typical torture methods is to hang people upside down and force water through their nostrils.

Recently, the African revolutionary Jonas Savimbi came to Washington seeking support. His hired lobby firm, Black, Manafort, Stone, and Kelly, blitzed the Washington establishment, spending a reported $600,000, and won the Senate majority leader's support for massive military aid, despite Savimbi's record of locking up medics, foreigners, and other civilians who disagree with him. Savimbi's enemy, the Marxist government of Angola, has a similar record—and also has employed lobbyists in Washington.

Iraq's military forces, at war with Iran, recently arrested 300 children, to put pressure on their parents. Torture in Iraq has included roasting over fire prisoners tied to turning spits, among many other techniques. In Washington, Iraq's ambassador can get the help he needs to cover up these offenses from yet another professional lobby firm.

The list is long. China, South Africa, Mexico, Morocco, and both the government and the *contras* of Nicaragua have their lobbyists at work in Washington. Such clients spend an estimated $500,000,000 a year to persuade the American people and their elected representatives that they are worthy of American support, in spite of their violations of American values. They outspend human rights organizations like Amnesty International by at least 10 to one.

Why does it matter that these offending governments can recruit professional public relations experts in the U.S.? It matters because, as a recent report by the American Association for the Advancement of Science put it, "The most powerful weapon for preventing the use of torture is the mobilization of international opinion and pressure. It is the 'shame of exposure' that governments fear most." When it is revealed that Castro's Cuba, which advertises itself as a modern civilized nation, imprisoned and tormented prisoners of conscience for decades, the Cuban government gets upset. When Soviet Premier Gorbachev arrives in Paris for high-level talks with France's Pres. Mitterand and is met by demonstrators protesting the U.S.S.R.'s practices of starving, freezing, and drugging prisoners of conscience, he feels he must make an explanation. When world attention focuses on Indonesia because the Reagans are visiting there, and journalists discover that the Suharto government has systematically massacred thousands of people, Indonesia's reputation suffers in every capital around the world. The battle for world opinion is the key to the battle to stop human rights offenses. The public relations experts ought to join that battle on the side of those who demand that torture stop.

Instead, we confront sophisticated and subtle professionals whose strategies well may undercut the human rights movement. Their strongest tactic is diversion. For example, Turkey's lobbyist would rather have you think about their upcoming art exhibit or Turkey's tourist attractions than about their barbaric and degrading abuse of the helpless. When diversion doesn't work, the torturers may simply deny that they abuse prisoners (as Iraq does), despite the evidence, or point to statements in their constitution against torture (as Turkey does), as if their words could make up for their behavior.

When the facts can not be denied or evaded, the torturers reach for explanations they hope will seem convincing. The most common explanation is emergency. The nation is temporarily at war or momentarily threatened by subversion or invasion, so they must do whatever is necessary—torture included—to stop the enemy "just once." Almost always, "just once" turns out to be the precedent for torturing again, and again, and again—in short, for the establishment of torture as a regular feature of their security operations.

Justifying torture

When the news of regular, systematic human rights violations comes out, the torturers and their Washington lobbyists dream up theories to justify torture. For instance, they will argue that human rights conditions in their country are getting better—so be patient; or that, once they get their economy in order or their political system straightened out, they will surely stop butchering people. Such arguments will sound familiar to Americans who took part in the civil rights movement and so often were told to slow down and wait.

Other sophisticates will take off from the idea that different cultures naturally behave differently, and so we should not be indignant when some foreign nation has torture as one of its customs. Still others, obsessed with the question of who is most to blame, will be satisfied with delicate comparisons among human rights violators, as if, once we know whom to blame, we will have solved the problem.

Then there are the so-called "realists" who justify cruelty as necessary to protect a nation's security, not just from immediate threats, but from long-term enemies. Such "realists" forget what already has happened to rulers who systematically abused their own people—Hitler, Stalin, Duvalier, Marcos, the Shah of Iran, Somoza, Batista, the Argentine junta. In fact, torture undermines security.

These images and arguments in favor of torture can not stand up against a simple truth—as you read this, a person like you is being tortured! A person like you would include Laura Bonaparte's daughter. On Christmas Eve, Laura's phone rang. The voice said her daughter, Noni, had been taken away in an army jeep. Laura contacted the police. They said Noni had been killed in a skirmish with terrorists. Laura demanded her daughter's body. The police brought her a jar with a hand in it.

A person like you would be the father of a 12-year-old boy picked up by the police. The boy was brought home dead, his body marked all over with signs of torture.

A person like you would be a student forced to watch as his aged mother, 73 years old, was stripped naked and beaten, shocked, and burned, screaming in pain, in front of him.

Those are real cases, not made-up stories. All one has to do is to imagine that they describe your daughter, your son, your mother. Then, the fancy arguments justifying torture collapse.

The essential principle of human rights is the integrity of the individual. A person may be described with all sorts of labels, analyzed and categorized in every sort of way, but a person is the opposite of a thing. A person is to be seen as a complete being, a being who, by the right of his or her existence, is to be accorded dignity and respect.

This principle of individual integrity is illustrated starkly in a report from El Salvador in 1980. Six young labor leaders told of their friend who was taken by soldiers, tortured for days, and killed. His body was torn to pieces and the parts scattered in a ditch. His friends managed to collar the soldiers, "and we took them to the ditch and made them assemble our friend on the ground like a man, and ask forgiveness of the corpse." Then, they quietly let the soldiers go.

By contrast, the torturer's aim is to destroy the integrity of his victim, to transform a person into a thing, to shred his or her dignity. That is what none of us can decently tolerate.

There are no exceptions. The law is clear: "No one shall be subjected to torture or cruel, inhuman or degrading treatment or punishment," says the International Covenant on Civil and Political Rights. There is no way the rest of us can escape what Albert Camus called "the common lot of pain," unless we are willing to resign from the human race.

The common lot of pain links us to suffering, but it also links us to hope. In the midst of despair and degradation, tortured prisoners again and again have been lifted out of living death by the realization that fellow human beings—even those unknown and far away—are working to rescue them.

A grade-school teacher in Uruguay, who had to struggle with his asthma and torture at the same time, put it this way, in a letter to his Amnesty International adoption group in West Germany: "The task that you have been carrying out for years is a hand stretched out further than the iron bars of prison, which in our worst moments makes us feel that we are never alone, that there is always hope and a feeling of love that has no frontiers and no languages, and which is present to tell us of the constant struggle . . . of men and women of the world who want a more just humanity."

A 24-year old prisoner in Zimbabwe got a Christmas card from an Amnesty International member in Denmark. The prisoner wrote back: "When I received your Christmas card, I had food for the thought, I asked myself a question 'why does this person think of us in Zimbabwe, does he know me, what does it profit him to worry about me?' This at length came to my mind that 'we are linked together by common humanity and human needs and sympathies and we are all vessels of different colors and shapes of God-given lives.' "

The mother of a Soviet prisoner made her way from the Ukraine to the Soviet-Chinese border to visit her son. A scowling official told her that trouble was coming; letters from Amnesty International had been received, saying that, "On account of his religious beliefs A. Koplik did not take the military oath and is serving his sentence in the camp. We urge that he be released and returned to his family, that he be allowed to live in peace, and that his youth be taken into account." The official was disturbed: "Just how do they know his exact address, even his detachment number? How is it that your son has contacts abroad?" Two years later, he was released.

When we think of individuals, rather than abstractions, we recognize ourselves in the face of that other person. We sense that we might be in the same fix, were we not so lucky as to live in a free country. Unless we have put to death the conscience we were born with, we want to know what we can do about it.

An agenda for change

In the U.S. alone, Amnesty International has more than 500 groups and 160,000 members working to stop torture. Individual appeals for prisoners "adopted" by AI groups have contributed to the release of thousands of prisoners and thousands of others have been saved from torture. Worldwide, Amnesty International demands that every government:

● Order torture stopped under all circumstances.
● Bring every prisoner promptly before a judge and let his family, doctor, and lawyer visit him.
● Close down secret prisons and put out accurate information about which prisoners are where.
● Monitor prison procedures. Tell prisoners of their rights and how to register complaints. Inspect the prisons regularly.
● Investigate and report publicly on torture complaints and do not threaten witnesses.
● Throw out of court any statement made under torture.
● Make torturing a criminal offense in all cases.
● Arrest and prosecute alleged torturers wherever they are.
● Train police and military to refuse to torture, even if ordered to do so.
● Help torture victims get medical care, rehabilitation, and financial compensation.
● Press other governments to stop torture. Under no circumstances provide training or other aid for torturers.
● Sign and support international agreements to stop torture.

These specifics make a difference. In October, 1984, Congress passed and the President signed into law a definite American commitment against torture. The law sets out specific requirements for diplomats—to report regularly on human rights abuses overseas and to take specific steps to end them.

In Northern Ireland and in Brazil, changes have done away with systematic torture. From Guatemala, a leader of an Indian peasant farmer's association wrote that "The constant denunciations of Amnesty International have rescued from oblivion and anonymity the right to life of so many children, old people and others who have been persecuted, kidnapped, tortured and murdered by the successive military dictatorships which have been imposed on our people through blood and fire."

In the African nation of The Gambia, prisoners had long been locked in leg-irons. In 1982, Gambian Pres. Jawara wrote: "I must confess that I was shocked by this allegation. . . . In the light of Amnesty International's letter to me . . . I have come to the conclusion that it is time the use of leg-irons, inherited from the colonial era, was abolished entirely. I agree with Amnesty International that even security considerations cannot justify their use."

Clearly, human rights is now a worldwide concern, part of nearly every serious international negotiation. That is happening because concerned citizens on every continent have made up their minds not to let national boundaries get in the way of the implementation of our bedrock human values. It is happening because hundreds of thousands of people are not content to stand by and watch while victims are battered into madness and death. It is happening because the human rights movement has gone public, no longer confining itself to behind-the-scenes negotiations.

If the Turks, the South Koreans, the Angolans, the Iraqis, and other offending nations, as well as the lobbyists who represent them, want to improve their "image," they have one sure way to do so—cut out the practice of torture.

In the U.S., nearly all of us are descended from people who came here for freedom from the repression of human rights. Today, more and more citizens are raising the key questions with the representatives we send to Washington—our senators and Congressmen: "When is the government going to use its leverage to advance our national commitment to human decency? When are we going to show the world that we mean what we say—that 'all men are created equal' and that human beings everywhere have rights no government has the right to take away from them, namely 'life, liberty and the pursuit of happiness' "?

The Scandal of the Boat People

William McGurn

WILLIAM MCGURN, who formerly worked in Hong Kong for the *Asian Wall Street Journal*, is now Washington bureau chief of *National Review*.

FIFTY years ago a group of more than 900 Jewish refugees set sail from Nazi Germany to Cuba aboard the liner *St. Louis*, only to be turned away by officials there. The ship then made for the United States; it was intercepted off the coast of Miami, where the frightened passengers pleaded for admission. But the U.S. authorities refused, and the *St. Louis* was forced to return to Europe. More than half its passengers would be lost in the Holocaust.

Today the world shakes its collective head over the treatment of the *St. Louis*, but the underlying lesson has yet to be taken. For almost fifty years from the day the "Voyage of the Damned" was turned away, 65 nations were gathering under UN auspices in Geneva to contrive a legal means to send the boat people back to Vietnam, a country they had been fleeing ever since 1975 when it was unified by the Communist regime in Hanoi. The task in Geneva was a somewhat tricky one since there are international conventions, absent in 1939, that today prohibit the *refoulement*, or forced return, of refugees. But the countries of Southeast Asia had grown tired of the continued exodus out of Vietnam and wanted it stopped. They came to the conference determined to find a way around the new conventions, whatever it might take.

What it took, as things turned out, was nothing more difficult than a redefinition of the boat people—from "genuine refugees," who could not be returned against their will, to "economic migrants," who could. This distinction was invented by Great Britain, whose colonial government in Hong Kong had already used it unilaterally in screening new arrivals from Vietnam. With Britain again in the lead, Hong Kong's screening philosophy was adopted in Geneva and enshrined in a six-point comprehensive plan of action.

Reading this document, one might well conclude that the boat people represent the largest refugee problem in the world. In fact, they are today a relatively tiny percentage of the world's more than 14 million refugees; among those 14 million, Afghans, Ethiopians, and even Cambodians outnumber the Vietnamese. The reason the boat people have become so important has less to do with them than it does with the response of the countries upon whose shores they continue to land; in addition to Hong Kong, these countries include Thailand, Singapore, Malaysia, and Indonesia. Now that they have succeeded in getting the rest of the world to consider forced repatriation as a solution in the case of the Vietnamese, we can expect the same policy will sooner or later be applied to other groups of refugees as well.

THE story behind this cruel development begins with the fall of Saigon to North Vietnamese troops in April 1975. At that time about 130,000 South Vietnamese who had served the Thieu regime in either the army or the civil administration were evacuated; most of them resettled in the United States. Between then and mid-1978, another 30,000 or so sneaked out of the country, also resettling primarily in America.

But the real flight did not begin until mid-1978, when the new Communist government instituted harsh policies directed against the sizable Chinese minority who made up much of the merchant class in the South. Their predicament was exacerbated by Hanoi's growing ties with the Soviet Union and its concomitant estrangement from China. By mid-1978, the trickle of refugees leaving Vietnam had swelled into a torrent; even though ethnic Chinese accounted for only about 3 percent of the country's 50 million people, they were the majority of those fleeing, mostly by sea and mostly in leaky boats.

It was known almost from the start that many of these original boat people were bribing their way out. But what authorities in the region did not at first know was that the Vietnamese government itself (and not merely corrupt officials) was directly involved in the trafficking of refugees. By July 1979 when more than 200,000 boat people, mainly ethnic Chinese, had arrived on the shores of the nearby countries of Southeast Asia, it became clear that Hanoi not only was forcing them out but was running a profit on the side.

The reception was not friendly. Boat people were often killed or raped or robbed by Thai pirates. Singapore refused to allow them to land— Prime Minister Lee Kuan Yew spoke of the need to grow "calluses on your heart"—and Malaysia began towing them back out to sea. Thousands perished.

In response to this horrid situation, the United Nations High Commissioner for Refugees (UNHCR) called the first conference on the boat people. It was held in July 1979 in Geneva and was attended by 65 nations, including Vietnam. The deal negotiated there was relatively simple. The nations of Southeast Asia agreed to grant temporary refuge, or first asylum, to the boat people arriving at their borders. In return, Western governments such as the U.S., Great Britain, Australia, France, and Canada agreed to accept these refugees for permanent resettlement. In addition, a promise was extracted from the Vietnamese government to make "every effort to stop illegal departures" and to allow the foreign governments to set up an Orderly Departure Program (ODP) that would give Vietnamese a legal alternative to illegal boat departures.

For a time the Geneva solution interrupted the crisis, since refugees now at least had places to land. But since this arrangement did not address the root cause of the problem—i.e., the nature of the Communist government of Vietnam—the conditions that had precipitated the massive exodus were never dealt with. Consequently, beginning in 1986 the number of Vietnamese refugees began once again to increase dramatically, outstripping the pace of resettlement. This in turn created a growing population of "long-stayers" in the camps that had been set up in the region to accommodate the refugees under the terms of the Geneva agreement.

Looking at conditions in Vietnam, the rest of Asia correctly concluded that there was no end in sight to the potential outflow. The response this time was even uglier than before. Malaysia threatened to shut down all its refugee camps and send the Vietnamese packing. Singapore reasserted its policy of not allowing any refugee to set foot on its soil unless he could produce written acceptance for resettlement elsewhere. Indonesia fired on refugee craft, and Thailand started to push the boat people back to sea until an international outcry forced an official, though not always de-facto, reversal.

Yet the raw brutality of these stands pales beside the anti-refugee lead taken by British-ruled Hong Kong, the most prosperous enclave in the Orient. In fairness, it should be acknowledged that Hong Kong was initially one of the most open ports of asylum, but the colony had come to feel that its earlier generosity served only to attract ever more boatloads of people and thus to magnify the problem. Now Hong Kong began putting all its efforts into discouraging new boat people from coming and forcing back those who did arrive. It was in aid of this purpose that the British government invented the new category of "economic migrant." Although the term had no meaning in law, it provided a basis for cheating many refugees out of their international protections and stigmatizing them with the taint of opportunism.

It is a great irony that the local populace of Hong Kong should have been so unsympathetic to refugees at a moment when they themselves—fearful of what will happen when the colony is handed over by the British to Communist China in 1997—were arguing for immigrant rights abroad. But given that the colonial British government was already sending back three or four dozen people a day to Communist China, most of them relatives of Hong Kong locals, it might have been expected that similar treatment of strangers from Vietnam would arouse no great objection.

A further irony is that until now Communist Vietnam had habitually cited Article 13-II of the UN Declaration on Human Rights—which states that "[e]veryone has the right to leave any country, including his own, and to return to his country"—to justify the forced departure of the ethnic Chinese. But now the carrots dangled by London (financial aid, improved relations with others in the region, possibly a promise to pressure Washington to resume diplomatic ties with Vietnam) evidently had their effect. The face-saving solution was a new euphemism for forced repatriation: "orderly return." Under this formula, refugees were to be given a choice between prison in Hong Kong or voluntary return to Vietnam with a cash grant. But as many as 44,000 will be forcibly sent back, with Britain reportedly paying Vietnam $600 per person to cover the cost of resettlement.

At any rate, other Asian countries, seeing in the new British approach a chance to get rid of their own Vietnamese refugees, eagerly signed on. The result was the six-point comprehensive plan of action drafted in the spring of 1989 in Kuala Lumpur. This was adopted without revision in Geneva in July.

A fundamentally anti-refugee document, the plan represents the interests of the host nations who drew it up and not those seeking asylum, who had no say. Its six main provisons call for Vietnam to crack down on boat departures, for an expansion of the Orderly Departure Program, for a reaffirmed right to first asylum, for region-wide adoption of Hong Kong's screening policy, and for the return to Vietnam of those "determined not to be refugees."

In plain English the gist is that Vietnam should step up its repression to make it more difficult for boat people to leave, while the rest of the world redefines most of those who do manage to get out in a way that will allow other countries to send them back.

This last point is the critical one. Screening *without* forced repatriation for those who fail the test makes no sense; as Britain's then-Foreign

Minister, Sir Geoffrey Howe, told the assembled in Geneva, this is "the logic of screening." The conference did stop just short of explicitly endorsing forced repatriation, as the British wanted, but in section 6(c) it implicitly accepted Sir Geoffrey's hard logic: "If, after the passage of reasonable time, it becomes clear that voluntary repatriation is not making significant progress toward the desired objective, the alternatives recognized as being acceptable under international practices would be examined." The acquiescence of the UNHCR provided the moral imprimatur.

The response of the United States was jumbled. On the plus side, Deputy Secretary of State Lawrence Eagleburger told the Geneva conference that "the United States will remain unalterably opposed to the forced repatriation of Vietnamese asylum-seekers," a last-minute insertion included over the objections of many others in the State Department. It was a welcome, even heroic, move, as was the behind-the-scenes pressure on Great Britain not to return the boat people now in Hong Kong against their will. Recently President Bush reiterated his opposition to forced repatriation before an Asian-American audience at the White House.

But in the same speech at Geneva, Eagleburger unfortunately also endorsed the thrust of the plan. "The balance that has been struck is delicate," he said, "we should not seek to alter it." In this way, Washington put itself in an impossible predicament: opposing the obvious conclusions of a document whose logic—Sir Geoffrey's logic—it accepted. In practice this meant that the administration had abetted a process it was now powerless to stop.

WHERE the Bush administration ought to have objected is on screening itself, a policy that rests on a slippery slope of questionable assumptions. Even from a practical point of view, it is riddled with problems, beginning with the antipathy that exists between those arriving in Hong Kong (now mostly ethnic Vietnamese from the North) and the local translators (mostly ethnic Chinese). Even translators not hostile to the arrivals are unacquainted with the situation in Vietnam and of the people being interviewed. The Vietnamese themselves, moreover, do not distinguish between interviews and interrogation, and so their tendency is to clam up. For these reasons alone, various organizations of lawyers have objected to the Hong Kong program even without objecting to screening *per se*. The UNHCR, whose approval Britain is constantly citing in international forums, also is decidedly uneasy about the process.

There are problems as well with the way screening is administered. For example, no record is kept of the original responses in Vietnamese, in the event of an appeal. More importantly, people in the camps are not provided with adequate pre-screening counseling, or an explanation of refugee criteria and of their rights. They are not given enough information or guidance about their right to appeal, or how that appeal would be managed.

In the particular case of the boat people, there is a further complication posed by Vietnamese law. Those who escape are considered criminals, and under Vietnam's National Security Articles 85, 88, and 89 they are subject to harsh prosecution. A piece in the *South China Morning Post* in March quoted the immigration director for the Vietnamese Interior Ministry, Nguyen Can, as saying that anyone who in Vietnam helped organize illegal departures would face thirty years in jail, and that any escapee who upon failing the screening test did not opt for voluntary repatriation would be punished if forced back later. Whatever the status of people before they leave, these laws make them refugees once they have gone.

The most serious objections to screening, however, are philosophical. They start from the fact that screening began not as an effort to help "genuine" refugees but to pin the label of economic migrant on as many boat people as possible so that they could be subjected to forced repatriation. The British made this clear when they announced before screening even began that 90 percent of those arriving on Hong Kong's shores were not genuine refugees. Is it any surprise that the screening results conform to this preset figure? Is there any doubt that the results could be made to conform to *any* other figure?

The deepest question of all is whether the new distinction between genuine refugees and economic migrants has any validity when it comes to people who have escaped from totalitarian states. American law, following the lead of the 1951 UN Convention Relating to the Status of Refugees and its 1967 Protocol, defines as a refugee anyone "who is outside any country of such person's nationality . . . and who is unable or unwilling to return to . . . that country because of persecution or a well-founded fear of persecution on account of race, religion, nationality, membership in a particular social group, or political opinion."

Such language may be appropriate to old-style authoritarian regimes, where most people are left alone unless they belong to a specific group or have otherwise attracted the government's attention. But being singled out for "persecution" has no real meaning in totalitarian societies, where *blanket* persecution is the norm. The Convention's emphasis on the dispute of an individual (or his group) with the government unconsciously bases refugee criteria not on oppression but on discrimination, and leads to all manner of contradictions.

Just last year, for example, a judge in San Francisco granted asylum to a Chinese man who had been arrested at the airport while traveling on a phony Singaporean passport. The man asked for asylum because his wife had defied China's one-child policy; he said he would be persecuted if he returned. The Immigration and Naturalization Service (INS) opposed granting him refugee status. The judge did so anyway, but at least in part because the man was Catholic and hence opposed by religion to contraception and abortion. The implication appeared to be that non-Catholics subject to the same persecution would not be entitled to the same rights.

Or what about Ethiopia, where mass starvation has been brought about by Marxist-Leninist agricultural policies? Are those who flee that regime because they cannot feed their children any less genuine refugees than those who flee because of other objections? Indeed, trying to separate the economic from the political in a totalitarian society is like trying to separate the blue from the sky.

It is a symptom of our own overly politicized century that the only claims to refuge we accept are overt political statements or accidental membership in some ethnic or religious group, rather than the actual circumstances of repression. The more innocent the refugee, the less eligible he is for asylum, so long as everyone else is treated as wretchedly as he. This, in fact, is a chief argument used against the new wave of Vietnamese boat people from the North, where Communism has been established for decades. Presumably this means that they have had more time to grow accustomed to it.

Prior to becoming a party to the UN Protocol in 1980, the U.S. did take into account the special character of totalitarian oppression; it did so in a clause of its refugee law that referred to those fleeing "from any Communist or Communist-dominated country or area." Interpreted liberally, as it was, this meant that those coming from such countries were allowed in. The figures today suggest that U.S. policy would benefit from a return to that interpretation. For of the 14 million refugees in the world, the lion's share are those running from Communist regimes: 6 million from Afghanistan alone; at least 1 million from Ethiopia; more than 630,000 from Mozambique; almost 400,000 from Angola—not to mention the more than 450,000 from Laos, Cambodia, and Vietnam. These are not people with a "well-founded fear" of *individual* persecution. These are people fleeing a *system*.

This is neither to diminish nor to deny the claims of refugees from non-Communist countries who fit the present definition. Were there no Communism there would still be thousands of refugees with claims on our attention. But there is something perverse about a world that insists on solving the refugee problem while refusing to acknowledge the major driving force behind it.

Such an acknowledgment, of course, would be anathema to the United Nations, where a large chunk of the membership is made up of totalitarian states. It would also, by extension, be anathema to the UNHCR, a hideous international bureaucracy that has forfeited all respect among workers in the field because its greatest fear is offending a host government. (Recently the High Commissioner for Refugees, Jean-Pierre Hocke, was forced to resign; among the controversies during his tenure was his burning two years ago of an issue of *Refugees,* the official UNHCR publication, because it contained an article West Germany did not like.) It would also be anathema to an affected nation like Great Britain, which simply wants the boat people sent back, period.

Thus, instead of trying to pressure Vietnam into opening up its system so that people would no longer be so desperate to leave (something even East Germany recently began to do), the Geneva program tells Hanoi: get tough, and rewards will follow. To this message Hanoi has responded eagerly. Vietnamese officials report that in the first half of 1989, some 3,224 persons were arrested trying to leave, and 413 of these were sentenced to jail for up to twelve years. The Vietnamese navy has also been instructed to fire on boat people who refuse to stop. It is a safe bet that if Vietnam decided to collect its bribes and then sink all outgoing craft on the high seas, there would be no serious outcry from Malaysia, Indonesia, Singapore, Thailand, or Hong Kong.

The U.S. has shied away from criticism of screening *per se*, which is understandable since the INS uses much the same sort of rationale for denying entry to refugees from south of the border. This again points to an inherent problem in refugee policy: its complete dependence on the open doors of third countries. The different treatment accorded escaping East Germans and Vietnamese demonstrates that, in practice, UN guarantees of the right to leave are meaningless without a concomitant right to arrive. This further helps explain why even avowedly pro-refugee organizations such as Oxfam and UNHCR have signed onto the screening program: they believe that unless the numbers are reduced to appease host governments, the rights of all refugees will be jeopardized.

Others hope an expanded Orderly Departure Program will provide an alternative to risky escape on the high seas. But ODP is a specific program for a specific group of people, and most of those leaving by boat are not eligible for it. In July ODP was given a boost when Hanoi agreed to allow former reeducation-camp internees to apply for the ODP exit visas, after an earlier agreement to let out Amerasian children. This is welcome, but with a twenty-year backlog of perhaps 500,000 people, it is a fig-leaf solution.

For all the attention and debate they have attracted, the boat people—to say it again—represent neither the largest nor the most critical refugee problem in the world. Nor do the 107,721 boat people now languishing in various countries of Southeast Asia represent the kind of drain on resources that we see in Africa—in Malawi, for example, where 600,000 refugees from Mozambique appeared almost overnight. The sole reason there is a refugee "crisis" in Southeast Asia is that the assorted nations of the region no longer wish to take the boat people in.

The importance of the boat people, and the danger, thus lies in the precedent. In Geneva the world bowed to pressure from a few nations to rejiggle criteria in a way designed to scale back drastically the number of those who will be granted protection from oppression. There is no reason that Pakistan or the Sudan could not invoke the same principle to deport the large numbers of Afghans or Ethiopians there, moves that would likely also be very popular politically. Taken further, this principle might even be used by countries like Nicaragua to have their own escapees declared economic migrants as a means of getting international monies to bring them back home, as well as discrediting charges that people are leaving because of oppression.

None of this is to romanticize the refugees. In times of trial a given number of human beings will act with grace and dignity, just as another percentage will succumb to baser impulses; the Vietnamese are no exception. Every camp in Southeast Asia suffers from its share of prostitution, drug dealing, extortion, even murder, perhaps exacerbated by the miserable conditions in which the refugees are forced to live.

But these same refugees come off rather well when set against the actions of the states that want them out, whether it be Indonesian forces firing on their craft, Thai government officials ordering that boats be pushed back to sea (the new euphemism is "redirection"), or the British in Hong Kong taking advantage of ignorance to define the refugees out of sanctuary. Mrs. Thatcher's justification of this position before Parliament and on her recent visit to America reawakened eerie memories of a similar British argument over the forced repatriation of Russians after World War II. In Foreign Office minutes from June 1944, Sir Patrick Dean put it bluntly: "In due course all those with whom the Soviet authorities desire to deal must be handed over to them, and we are not concerned with the fact that they may be shot or otherwise more harshly dealt with than they might be under British law."

The boat people are not angels. They are human beings whose homeland has become so unlivable that they will leave behind everything they know and have to brave leaky boats, vicious pirates, uncertain seas, and possible arrest—all for the slight chance of starting life over again in another part of the world as complete strangers. If history teaches us anything, it is that average people do not make such a decision lightly; and indeed, although Vietnam has been invaded over its long history, never before was there such a flight out. The term "economic migrant," with its odor of money-grubbing opportunism, is a deliberate slander invented by free people to keep out others desperately seeking that same freedom. Its acceptance by the nations of the world at Geneva sadly illustrates that not much has changed since the *St. Louis* was turned around. Where refugees come from seems not to matter. What matters is where they are going.

The Second Coming Of Pol Pot

Fears of a return to the killing fields

ASIAWEEK

Has the Khmer Rouge cleaned up its act? As Vietnam pulls out of Cambodia, that question concerns the whole region. "Yes, we have," answer those infamous rulers of Cambodia from 1975 to 1979. They say they have pensioned off dreaded leader Pol Pot, eschewed their former ultra-leftist views, and now embrace liberal democracy. But the secretive group fiercely fends off all inquirers. And its national anthem, "Glorious April 17," named after the day on which it stormed Phnom Penh in 1975, remains unamended:

> Bright red blood that covers the towns and
>   plains of Kampuchea, our motherland,
> Sublime blood of workers and peasants,
> Sublime blood of revolutionary men and
>   women fighters,
> The blood changing into unrelenting hatred.

Recent incidents reported from Khmer Rouge camps on the Thai-Cambodian border provide evidence that some of the old ways have not changed. One evening 27-year-old Noeurn had just finished his meal of rice, dried fish, and vegetables. Suddenly, Khmer Rouge soldiers appeared. "They just asked him his name and shot him," recounts his widow, Rum.

On July 8, refugee officials found the partly buried body of a young man called Rath some distance from one of the

camps. Their investigations revealed that Rath had deserted his unit. He had apparently been executed with a single bullet in the back of the head.

Few are convinced that the Khmer Rouge has really changed. The leadership remains almost as inaccessible as it was before 1975. Reports indicate that it is forcing thousands of refugees from camps on the border back into Cambodia—a frightening echo of the brutal dislocations of Pol Pot days. Khmer Rouge authorities allow international aid officials only limited access to its camps to check that food and medical supplies go to civilians.

Vietnam has pledged to withdraw all of its troops from Cambodia by the end of 1990, even without a political settlement. Inevitably, there is mounting international concern that the Khmer Rouge is getting ready to stage a comeback. Accompanying that fear are nightmarish memories of the savage time when the black-clad Khmer Rouge guerrillas marched triumphantly into the capital, Phnom Penh. Overnight, every Cambodian became a peasant, a worker, or a soldier. Money was abolished. Private property ceased to exist. All shops and restaurants were closed. Henceforth, *angka*, "the organization," was to provide for everybody's needs.

Phnom Penh, swollen to a population of 3 million by refugees from the conflict in the countryside, was evacuated. Its residents were sent to work in the fields or on grandiose but ill-conceived construction projects. Hundreds of thousands died of exhaustion and starvation. Thousands of others were executed. Some 20,000 were tortured to

From the newsmagazine "Asiaweek" of Hong Kong

Reprinted from *World Press Review*, October 1988, pp. 25–28.

death in the capital's notorious Tuol Sleng detention center alone. Massive party purges took their toll of lives as the suspicious Khmer Rouge turned on itself.

Estimates of the total number of deaths from April, 1975, to 1979, when Vietnam drove the Khmer Rouge from Phnom Penh, hover at around 1.5 million, a fifth of the population. None of the Khmer Rouge leaders has paid for those crimes. Democratic Kampuchea, as it styles itself, retained its seat at the United Nations. It now shares that seat with its two resistance partners: the followers of Prince Norodom Sihanouk and the Khmer People's National Liberation Front (KPNLF).

The Khmer Rouge military high command is headed by former Defense Minister Son Sen, but Pol Pot is believed still to be in charge. Most of the members of his cabinet retain positions of authority. His barbaric lieutenants still roam free. Western calls to bring the leaders to trial have been muffled by ASEAN (the Association of Southeast Asian Nations, comprising Cambodia's non-communist neighbors) and by China, for they see the Khmer Rouge as their best weapon against the Vietnamese occupation. The estimated 30,000 members of Khmer Rouge make up the main fighting arm of the resistance.

"The Khmer Rouge have maintained their level of operations in a way the Sihanoukists and KPNLF have not," says a military analyst in Bangkok. He estimates that there are up to 22,000 Khmer Rouge guerrillas inside Cambodia at any one time, with the rest in border camps. About 20,000 women, he says, are mobilized for military operations and do much of the portering.

"The Vietnamese issue is almost resolved," said Prince Sihanouk recently. "Only the same problem of Pol Pot remains. This problem is returning to haunt us." The former king has never been comfortable with his alliance with the Khmer Rouge, who murdered several of his children and relatives. Today, he is the only leader acceptable to all Cambodian factions. His shocking resignation from the presidency of the resistance coalition in July appeared to set back the growing move to settle the conflict. Analysts in Bangkok think he may soon form a third front: an alternative to the Khmer Rouge and to the Vietnamese-installed Heng Samrin regime in Phnom Penh.

As the Vietnamese pull back, Khmer Rouge leaders seem preoccupied with moving the civilians under their control. At a camp on the northern sector of the Thai-Cambodia border, says an aid worker, "some 10 families are being trucked out daily, complete with their uprooted papaya trees." The worker thinks the plan is to relocate the bulk of the camp's 9,700 people, leaving only the crippled and the amputees. The camp commander, the young and powerful Look Van, is said to be a nephew of Pol Pot. Similar evacuations have been noted in two other northern camps with a combined population of 15,800.

Last May the UN cut off aid to one of the camps because its workers were repeatedly denied access. The UN has found it virtually impossible to monitor the use of its food aid. Rare headcounts conducted in the closed camps have uncovered cases of severe malnutrition. Look At, the aggressive Khmer Rouge camp commander at Huay Chan, bluntly told an aid team, "All we need from you is supplies. If you give us teaching materials on how to fight the Vietnamese, we accept. Otherwise, stay outside." Only one of the closed Khmer Rouge camps has an education program. As in the pre-1975 days, thousands of children are being molded into guerrilla fighters.

Hospital patients cannot seek treatment directly but must be selected. Khmer Rouge medics are said to be notorious for incorrect diagnoses. "Some 30 to 40 people are given appendectomies each month in Bo Rai," a Khmer Rouge camp, says a relief doctor. "That's equal to the figure for two months in the rest of the border camps." An apparent exception is Site 8, which houses some 40 percent of the estimated 82,000 people in Khmer Rouge camps.

Officials proudly point to the flourishing black market as a sign that the Khmer Rouge has embraced capitalism. General elections, they say, were held in February. Relief agencies and journalists have easy access. A Buddhist pagoda with a dozen monks is meant to show that religion is back in favor. But sources say an order in April warned that the safety of those who spoke against the Khmer Rouge would not be guaranteed.

On the military front, the Khmer Rouge has changed strategy in the past year. "They are trying to establish control over people rather than territory," says a Western diplomat. He and others note that the level of fighting has dropped despite recent shelling near the Thai border. "The Khmer Rouge have concluded that the Vietnamese are leaving and are trying to put themselves in the best position for a post-withdrawal situation—whether political or military," the diplomat says.

Khmer Rouge defectors say they were given orders last year to avoid clashes with Heng Samrin troops. Instead they were told to infiltrate village administrations and burn their buildings. The Phnom Penh government has acknowledged the village infiltration. Vietnam's pullback has aided the Khmer Rouge's village campaign. For the first time since the Vietnamese border offensive of 1984-85, the Thai-Cambodian frontier has become permeable.

Reports of arms caches being buried by the Khmer Rouge have gained circulation. But some sources maintain there has been no significant increase in logistics activities along the routes leading from the northwest to Phnom Penh. This suggests that the Khmer Rouge is not planning a major attack on the capital. The primary objective, say the sources, is to control the five provinces surrounding Tonle Sap. Another front runs along the Thai-Cambodian border, where the Khmer Rouge's apparent objective is to draw the Vietnamese troops to the frontier. But instead, the Vietnamese have been sending Phnom Penh troops to do the fighting. The final front, say these sources, is in and around Phnom Penh, where the Khmer Rouge aims to carry out sabotage.

International pressure is again building against the Khmer Rouge. Its strongest supporters, China and ASEAN, still want the group involved in a future government, but they now differentiate between the Khmer Rouge and its leaders. Recently, the Chinese have indicated that some would be put out to pasture. Phnom Penh has said it would accept the Khmer Rouge, minus Pol Pot and some of his "close associates," in a process of national reconciliation. But some say it is unlikely the Khmer Rouge could survive without Pol Pot. The political suicide being demanded of it may force a fight to the end.

Iraq's fleeing Kurds

Gary Thatcher
Staff writer of The Christian Science Monitor

Diyarbakir, Turkey

They are called Kurds. But they might be modern-day Gordians.

It was on the Anatolian highlands, in what is today Turkey, that the ancient Gordian civilization tied a knot that would not be undone until Alexander the Great cut it with his sword.

Now, the Kurds are creating a new Gordian knot for Turkey.

Thousands of Kurds are flooding into refugee camps here, claiming to have been driven from their homes in Iraq by the use of chemical weapons.

The horrors to which they claim to bear witness are impossible to confirm. The United States Senate was sufficiently convinced to vote economic sanctions against Iraq in retaliation. The US State Department harshly condemned the Iraqi regime of Saddam Hussein. And the human rights organization Amnesty International charged that Iraq is systematically trying to "eliminate" large numbers of Kurds.

The reason? The Iraqi Kurds supported Iran – and even fought for it – against their own government during the bitter eight-year-long Gulf war. With a cease-fire in that conflict now holding, it appears that President Hussein has unleashed his forces to exact revenge on the Kurds.

That marks the latest sad chapter in a history of dashed hopes, betrayal, and treachery against the Kurds. They are an ancient, non-Arab people, often caught in the conflicting crosscurrents of nationalism and war in Asia Minor. Many of the estimated 20 million Kurds spread across five countries nurture a vision of an independent "Kurdistan" encompassing their traditional homelands in Iraq, Iran, Turkey, the Soviet Union, and Syria.

But for the Kurds flooding into refugee camps here, that dream seems further away than ever. And for Turkey, the Kurds are a troubling presence that may well put its powers of patience, diplomacy, and tolerance to a most severe test.

Turkey has, for years, had its own problems with Kurdish separatism. It does not recognize the Kurds' language or culture, referring to the people as "mountain Turks."

Now, an influx of tens of thousands of embittered Kurds from Iraq could inflame separatist sentiments inside Turkey. Moreover, it could complicate relations with Iraq, and Iran, which supported them militarily.

The situation has focused extraordinary attention on Turkey. How it handles the influx of Kurds could have diplomatic repercussions among Turkey's NATO allies, as well as Europe and the Arab world.

With so many opportunities for complication and mistake, Turkey is moving swiftly to take control of the situation. Yet it is also avoiding entanglements with other countries or outside relief agencies, apparently to keep a free hand in dealing with the Kurds.

According to official figures, some 60,000 Kurds have fled here, and are now kept in 16 locations. Turkey is working at top speed to establish encampments and to provide medical and other services.

The effort is impressive. In two weeks, refugee settlements have sprung from the dusty flatlands of Turkey's southeast. Clinics, canteens, communal water taps, electric lights, toilets, and washing facilities are completed or under construction. Crushed-rock roadways cut a neat gridwork through rows and rows of white and green tents.

Some 10,000 Kurds have been settled in a camp outside Diyarbakir. Many of the men,

JOAN FORBES - STAFF

disarmed when they crossed the border, still wear the distinctive green uniforms of the *peshmargas* (guerrillas) that fought against Iraqi troops. And when they speak of the homes they left behind, they refer not to Iraq, but to the "freedom areas" – the building blocks of a nascent Kurdistan.

In this camp, there is a mixture of sullenness and anxiety, and of grieving at a loss common to refugee camps everywhere.

"These people had houses, and goats, and land where they came from," says 32-year-old guerrilla leader Akram Mayi.

Gesturing to a woman boiling water on a wood fire while a small child sits in the dust next to her, crying, he says, "Now, you see how we are forced to live."

It is, to be sure, an uncertain existence – the more so because of Turkey's ambivalent attitude. Indeed, Turkey has not even officially recognized them as refugees.

"We are not calling these groups refugees – yet," says Hayri Kozakcioglu, regional governor. "The reason is just because the word 'refugee' has very different legal meanings and understandings throughout the world. These groups haven't yet expressed their wishes about staying here. We understand they may go back to Iraq. So we call them Iraqis who are staying here awhile."

"And we are not calling [the places where they stay] camps. We are calling them temporary residential places."

Indeed, there are reports that some Kurds have been forced out of Turkey to seek sanctuary in Iran – a charge Ankara denies.

Indeed, Turkish officials have been at pains to be open about their handling of the Kurdish influx. The entire southeastern provincial areas, save for sensitive military installations and the security zones along the border, have been opened to foreign journalists. The government has laid telex, telephone, and telefax lines to Diyarbakir, and has made officials available for interviews.

It is because of this openness that complaints of the Kurds have surfaced. Some people have complained about the Spartan diet, centering on bread and rice, and the

security lights ablaze around the periphery.

"The food is very bad here. And there is no sleeping. No washing facilities. No bathing," Mr. Mayi says. "We need the help of the Red Cross. We want them to come here."

Turkey has allowed a few nongovernmental aid groups to conduct small-scale operations here. But it has not asked for large-scale foreign relief.

Indeed, it insists that it is coping well with the situation. A Monitor photographer, however, witnessed a demonstration against Saddam Hussein at a camp which escalated into a mass disturbance, with Turkish troops firing warning shots to restore order.

Despite the efforts – and accompanying costs – the Turkish government is playing down the need for outside help.

"Mostly, we are using the state's facilities to keep the spending figure low," says Mr. Kozakcioglu. "Well, maybe we've delayed some work in some villages. But we have enough supplies and food."

Farther south, near Kiziltepe, workers have, in just two weeks, built a camp that is expected to house 6,200 Kurds. A local official proudly displays the cinder-block kitchen and toilets that have been constructed, while two electricians nearby struggle with an octopus of electrical wires that will bring lights to every tent.

"It has been hard work," he says, "very hard work." Yet, he, too, plays down the cost – or the need for outside aid.

The reason is simple, a Western diplomat says. Outside aid, he says, comes with strings attached – legal restrictions and obligations on the treatment of refugees, and scrutiny. United Nations involvement, in particular, would vest the Kurds with a legal standing – and, perhaps eventually, a claim to permanent resettlement. It would also prevent deportation of Kurds back to Iraq.

Iraq has further complicated the situation by declaring an amnesty for refugees who want to return – undercutting Kurdish claims of persecution.

"Turkey is very sensitive to human rights issues," a diplomat says. "It has European aspirations, but it has to deal with Middle Eastern problems. And these two things are not easy to combine. I guess the Turks must be warring between the temptation to get rid of these people as quickly as possible, and the temptation to make a good impression on the world."

"For the sake of the region, for the sake of peace in this area, we must do something with them," says Governor Kozakcioglu.

"For now," says Mayi, the guerrilla, "our decision is to stay here." But he also makes clear that a longer-term goal - independence - remains. "We need our freedom. We need to be like all the peoples in the world. We need real autonomy. And we want peace."

Normalizing the Political Process in South Africa

THE TIME FOR NEGOTIATION HAS ARRIVED

F.W. de KLERK, *State President, Republic of South Africa*

Delivered to the Second Session of the Ninth Parliament of the Republic of South Africa, Cape Town, South Africa, February 2, 1990

MR. SPEAKER, Members of Parliament. The general election on September the 6th, 1989, placed our country irrevocably on the road of drastic change. Underlying this is the growing realisation by an increasing number of South Africans that only a negotiated understanding among the representative leaders of the entire population is able to ensure lasting peace.

The alternative is growing violence, tension and conflict. That is unacceptable and in nobody's interest. The well-being of all in this country is linked inextricably to the ability of the leaders to come to terms with one another on a new dispensation. No one can escape this simple truth.

On its part, the Government will accord the process of negotiation the highest priority. The aim is a totally new and just constitutional dispensation in which every inhabitant will enjoy equal rights, treatment and opportunity in every sphere of endeavour — constitutional, social and economic.

I hope that this new Parliament will play a constructive part in both the prelude to negotiations and the negotiating process itself. I wish to ask all of you who identify yourselves with the broad aim of a new South Africa, and that is the overwhelming majority:

—Let us put petty politics aside when we discuss the future during this Session.

—Help us build a broad consensus about the fundamentals of a new, realistic and democratic dispensation.

—Let us work together on a plan that will rid our country of suspicion and steer it away from domination and radicalism of any kind.

During the term of this new Parliament, we shall have to deal, complimentary to one another, with the normal processes of legislation and day-to-day government, as well as with the process of negotiation and renewal.

Within this framework I wish to deal first with several matters more closely concerned with the normal process of government before I turn specifically to negotiation and related issues.

1. Foreign Relations

The Government is aware of the important part the world at large has to play in the realisation of our country's national interests.

Without contact and co-operation with the rest of the world we cannot promote the well-being and security of our citizens. The dynamic developments in international politics have created new opportunities for South Africa as well. Important advances have been made, among other things, in our contacts abroad, especially where these were precluded previously by ideological considerations.

I hope this trend will be encouraged by the important change of climate that is taking place in South Africa.

For South Africa, indeed for the whole world, the past year has been one of change and major upheaval. In Eastern Europe and even the Soviet Union itself, political and economic upheaval surged forward in an unstoppable tide. At the same time, Beijing temporarily smothered with brutal violence the yearning of the people of the Chinese mainland for greater freedom.

The year of 1989 will go down in history as the year in which Stalinist Communism expired.

These developments will entail unpredictable consequences for Europe, but they will also be of decisive importance to Africa. The indications are that the countries of Eastern and Central Europe will receive greater attention, while it will decline in the case of Africa.

The collapse, particularly of the economic system in Eastern Europe, also serves as a warning to those who insist on persisting with it in Africa. Those who seek to force this failure of a system on South Africa, should engage in a total revision of their point of view. It should be clear to all that it is not the answer here either. The new situation in Eastern Europe also shows that foreign intervention is no recipe for domestic change. It never succeeds, regardless of its ideological motivation. The upheaval in Eastern Europe took place without the involvement of the Big Powers or of the United Nations.

The countries of Southern Africa are faced with a particular challenge: Southern Africa now has an historical opportunity to set aside its conflicts and ideological differences and draw up a joint programme of reconstruction.

It should be sufficiently attractive to ensure that the Southern African region obtains adequate investment and loan capital from the industrial countries of the world. Unless the countries of Southern Africa achieve stability and a common approach to economic development rapidly, they will be faced by further decline and ruin.

The Government is prepared to enter into discussions with other Southern African countries with the aim of formulating a realistic development plan. The Government believes that the obstacles in the way of a conference of Southern African states have now been removed sufficiently.

Hostile postures have to be replaced by cooperative ones; confrontation by contact; disengagement by engagement; slogans by deliberate debate.

The season of violence is over. The time for reconstruction and reconciliation has arrived.

Recently there have, indeed, been unusually positive results in South Africa's contacts and relations with other African

Reprinted from *Vital Speeches of the Day*, Vol. 56, No. 10, March 1, 1990, pp. 290–295, by permission.

states. During my visits to their countries I was received cordially, both in private and in public, by Presidents Mobutu, Chiassano, Houphouet-Boigny and Kaunda. These leaders expressed their sincere concern about the serious economic problems in our part of the world. They agreed that South Africa could and should play a positive part in regional cooperation and development.

Our positive contribution to the independence process in South West Africa has been recognised internationally. South Africa's good faith and reliability as a negotiator made a significant contribution to the success of the events. This, too, was not unnoticed. Similarly, our efforts to help bring an end to the domestic conflict situations in Mozambique and Angola have received positive acknowledgement.

At present the Government is involved in negotiations concerning our future relations with an independent Namibia and there are no reasons why good relations should not exist between the two countries. Namibia needs South Africa and we are prepared to play a constructive part.

Nearer home I paid fruitful visits to Venda, Transkei and Ciskei and intend visiting Bophuthatswana soon. In recent times there has been an interesting debate about the future relationship of the TBVC countries with South Africa and specifically about whether they should be re-incorporated into our country.

Without rejecting this idea out of hand, it should be borne in mind that it is but one of many possibilities. These countries are constitutionally independent. Any return to South Africa will have to be dealt with, not only by means of legislation in their parliaments, but also through legislation in this Parliament. Naturally this will have to be preceded by talks and agreements.

2. Human Rights

Some time ago the Government referred the question of the protection of fundamental human rights to the South African Law Commission. This resulted in the Law Commission's interim working document on individual and minority rights. It elicited substantial public interest.

I am satisfied that every individual and organisation in the country has had ample opportunity to make representations to the Law Commission, express criticism freely and make suggestions. At present, the Law Commission is considering the representations received. A final report is expected in the course of this year.

In view of the exceptional importance of the subject of human rights to our country and all its people, I wish to ask the Law Commission to accord this task high priority.

The whole question of protecting individual and minority rights, which includes collective rights and the rights of national groups, is still under consideration by the Law Commission. Therefore, it would be inappropriate of the Government to express a view on the details now. However, certain matters of principle have emerged fairly clearly and I wish to devote some remarks to them.

The Government accepts the principle of the recognition and protection of the fundamental individual rights which form the constitutional basis of most Western democracies. We acknowledge, too, that the most practical way of protecting those rights is vested in a declaration of rights justifiable by an independent judiciary. However, it is clear that a system for the protection of the rights of individuals, minorities and national entities has to form a well-rounded and balanced whole. South Africa has its own national composition and our constitutional

dispensation has to take this into account. The formal recognition of individual rights does not mean that the problems of a heterogeneous population will simply disappear. Any new constitution which disregards this reality will be inappropriate and even harmful.

Naturally, the protection of collective, minority and national rights may not bring about an imbalance in respect of individual rights. It is neither the Government's policy nor its intention that any group — in whichever way it may be defined — shall be favoured above or in relation to any of the others.

The Government is requesting the Law Commission to undertake further task and report on it. This task is directed at the balanced protection in a future constitution of the human rights of all our citizens, as well as of collective units, associations, minorities and nations. This investigation will also serve the purpose of supporting negotiations towards a new constitution.

The terms of reference also include:

— the identification of the main types and models of democratic constitutions which deserve consideration in the aforementioned context;

— an analysis of the ways in which the relevant rights are protected in every model; and

— possible methods by means of which such constitutions may be made to succeed and be safeguarded in a legitimate manner.

3. The Death Penalty

The death penalty has been the subject of intensive discussion in recent months. However, the Government has been giving its attention to this extremely sensitive issue for some time. On April the 27th, 1989, the honourable Minister of Justice indicated that there was merit in suggestions for reform in this area. Since 1988 in fact, my predecessor and I have been taking decisions on reprieves which have led, in proportion, to a drastic decline in executions.

We have now reached the position in which we are able to make concrete proposals for reform. After the Chief Justice was consulted, and he in turn had consulted the Bench, and after the Government had noted the opinions of academics and other interested parties, the Government decided on the following broad principles from a variety of available options:

— that reform in this area is indicated;

— that the death penalty should be limited as an option of sentence to extreme cases, and specifically through broadening judicial discretion in the imposition of sentence; and

— that an automatic right of appeal be granted to those under sentence of death.

Should these proposals be adopted, they should have a significant influence on the imposition of death sentences on the one hand, and on the other, should ensure that every case in which a person has been sentenced to death, will come to the attention of the Appellate Division.

These proposals require that everybody currently awaiting execution, be accorded the benefit of the proposed new approach. Therefore, all executions have been suspended and no executions will take place until Parliament has taken a final decision on the new proposals. In the event of the proposals being adopted, the case of every person involved will be dealt with in accordance with the new guidelines. In the meantime, no executions have taken place since November the 14th, 1989.

New and uncompleted cases will still be adjudicated in terms of the existing law. Only when the death sentence is imposed, will the new proposals be applied, as in the case of those currently awaiting execution.

The legislation concerned also entails other related principles which will be announced and elucidated in due course by the Minister of Justice. It will now be formulated in consultation with experts and be submitted to Parliament as soon as possible.

I wish to urge everybody to join us in dealing with this highly sensitive issue in a responsible manner.

4. Socio-economic Aspects

A changed dispensation implies far more than political and constitutional issues. It cannot be pursued successfully in isolation from problems in other spheres of life which demand practical solutions. Poverty, unemployment, housing shortages, inadequate education and training, illiteracy, health needs and numerous other problems still stand in the way of progress and prosperity and an improved quality of life.

The conservation of the physical and human environment is of cardinal importance to the quality of our existence. For this the Government is developing a strategy with the aid of an investigation by the President's Council.

All of these challenges are being dealt with urgently and comprehensively. The capability for this has to be created in an economically accountable manner. Consequently, existing strategies and aims are undergoing a comprehensive revision.

From this will emanate important policy announcements in the socio-economic sphere by the responsible Ministers during the course of the session. One matter about which it is possible to make a concrete announcement, is the Separate Amenities Act, 1953. Pursuant to my speech before the President's Council late last year, I announce that this Act will be repealed during this Session of Parliament.

The State cannot possibly deal alone with all of the social advancement our circumstances demand. The community at large, and especially the private sector, also have a major responsibility towards the welfare of our country and its people.

5. The Economy

A new South Africa is possible only if it is bolstered by a sound and growing economy, with particular emphasis on the creation of employment. With a view to this, the Government has taken thorough cognisance of the advice contained in numerous reports by a variety of advisory bodies. The central message is that South Africa, too, will have to make certain structural changes to its economy, just as its major trading partners had to do a decade or so ago.

The period of exceptionally high economic growth experienced by the Western world in the sixties, was brought to an end by the oil crisis in 1973. Drastic structural adaptations became inevitable for these countries, especially after the second oil crisis in 1979, when serious imbalances occurred in their economies. After considerable sacrifices, those countries which persevered with their structural adjustment programmes, recovered economically so that lengthy periods of high economic growth and low inflation were possible.

During that particular period, South Africa was protected temporarily by the rising gold price from the necessity of making similar adjustments immediately. In fact, the high gold price even brought prosperity with it for a while. The recovery of the world economy and the decline in the price of gold and other primary products, brought with them unhealthy trends. These included high inflation, a serious weakening in the productivity of capital, stagnation in the economy's ability to generate income and employment opportunities. All of this made a drastic structural adjustment of our economy inevitable.

The Government's basic point of departure is to reduce the role of the public sector in the economy and to give the private sector maximum opportunity for optimal performance. In this process, preference has to be given to allowing the market forces and a sound competitive structure to bring about the necessary adjustments.

Naturally, those who make and implement economic policy have a major responsibility at the same time to promote an environment optimally conducive to investment, job creation and economic growth by means of appropriate and properly co-ordinated fiscal and monetary policy. The Government remains committed to this balanced and practical approach.

By means of restricting capital expenditure in parastatal institutions, privatisation, deregulation and curtailing government expenditure, substantial progress has been made already towards reducing the role of the authorities in the economy. We shall persist with this in a well-considered way.

This does not mean that the State will forsake its indispensable development role, especially in our particular circumstances. On the contrary, it is the precise intention of the Government to concentrate an equitable portion of its capacity on these aims by means of the meticulous determination of priorities.

Following the progress that has been made in other areas of the economy in recent years, it is now opportune to give particular attention to the supply side of the economy.

Fundamental factors which will contribute to the success of this restructuring are:

—the gradual reduction of inflation to levels comparable to those of our principal trading partners;

—the encouragement of personal initiative and savings;

—the subjection of all economic decisions by the authorities to stringent financial measures and discipline;

—rapid progress with the reform of our system of taxation; and

—the encouragement of exports as the impetus for industrialisation and earning foreign exchange.

These and other adjustments, which will require sacrifices, have to be seen as prerequisites for a new period of sustained growth in productive employment in the nineties.

The Government has also noted with appreciation the manner in which the Reserve Bank has discharged its special responsibility in striving toward common goals.

The Government is very much aware of the necessity of proper co-ordination and consistent implementation of its economic policy. For this reason, the establishment of the necessary structures and expertise to ensure this co-ordination is being given preference. This applies both to the various functions within the Government and to the interaction between the authorities and the private sector.

This is obviously not the occasion for me to deal in greater detail with our total economic strategy or with the recent course of the economy.

I shall confine myself to a few specific remarks on one aspect of fiscal policy that has been a source of criticism of the Government for some time, namely State expenditure.

The Government's financial year ends only in two months' time and several other important economic indicators for the 1989 calendar year are still subject to refinements at this stage. Nonetheless, several important trends are becoming increasingly clear. I am grateful to be able to say that we have apparently succeeded to a substantial degree in achieving most of our economic aims in the past year.

In respect of Government expenditure, the budget for the current financial year will be the most accurate in many years. The financial figures will show:

—that Government expenditure is thoroughly under control;

—that our normal financing programme has not exerted any significant upward pressure on rates of interest; and

—that we will close the year with a surplus, even without taking the income from the privatisation of Iscor into account.

Without pre-empting this year's main budget, I wish to emphasise that it is also our intention to co-ordinate fiscal and monetary policy in the coming financial year in a way that will enable us to achieve the ensuing goals — namely:

—that the present downturn will take the form of a soft landing which will help to make adjustments as easy as possible;

—that our economy will consolidate before the next upward phase so that we will be able to grow from a sound base; and

—that we shall persist with the implementation of the required structural adaptations in respect, among other things, of the following; easing the tax burden, especially on individuals; sustained and adequate generation of surpluses on the current account of the balance of payments and the reconstruction of our gold and foreign exchange reserves.

It is a matter of considerable seriousness to the Government, especially in this particular period of our history, to promote a dynamic economy which will make it possible for increasing numbers of people to be employed and share in rising standards of living.

6. Negotiation

In conclusion, I wish to focus the spotlight on the process of negotiation and related issues. At this stage I am refraining deliberately from discussing the merits of numerous political questions which undoubtedly will be debated during the next few weeks. The focus, now, has to fall on negotiation.

Practically every leader agrees that negotiation is the key to reconciliation, peace and a new and just dispensation. However, numerous excuses for refusing to take part, are advanced. Some of the reasons being advanced are valid. Others are merely part of a political chess game. And while the game of chess proceeds, valuable time is being lost.

Against this background I committed the Government during my inauguration to giving active attention to the most important obstacles in the way of negotiation. Today I am able to announce far-reaching decisions in this connection.

I believe that these decisions will shape a new phase in which there will be a movement away from measures which have been seized upon as a justification for confrontation and violence. The emphasis has to move, and will move now, to a debate and discussion of political and economic points of view as part of the process of negotiation.

I wish to urge every political and community leader, in and outside Parliament, to approach the new opportunities which are being created, constructively. There is no time left for advancing all manner of new conditions that will delay the negotiating process.

The steps that have been decided, are the following:

—The prohibition of the African National Congress, the Pan Africanist Congress, the South African Communist Party and a number of subsidiary organisations is being rescinded.

—People serving prison sentences merely because they were members of one of these organisations or because they committed another offence which was merely an offence because a prohibition on one of the organisations was in force, will be identified and released. Prisoners who have been sentenced for other offences such as murder, terrorism or arson are not affected by this.

—The media emergency regulations as well as the education emergency regulations are being abolished in their entirety.

—The security emergency regulations will be amended to still make provision for effective control over visual material pertaining to scenes of unrest.

—The restrictions in terms of the emergency regulations on 33 organisations are being rescinded. The organisations include the following: National Education Crisis Committee, South African National Students Congress, United Democratic Front, Cosatu, Die Blanke Bevrydingsbeweging van Suid-Afrika.

—The conditions imposed in terms of the security emergency regulations on 374 people on their release, are being rescinded and the regulations which provide for such conditions are being abolished.

—The period of detention in terms of the security emergency regulations will be limited henceforth to six months. Detainees also acquire the right to legal representation and a medical practitioner of their own choosing.

These decisions by the Cabinet are in accordance with the Government's declared intention to normalise the political process in South Africa without jeopardising the maintenance of the good order. They were preceded by thorough and unanimous advice by a group of officials which included members of the security community.

Implementation will be immediate and, where necessary, notices will appear in the Government Gazette from tomorrow.

The most important facets of the advice the Government received in this connection, are the following:

—The events in the Soviet Union and Eastern Europe, to which I have referred already, weaken the capability of organisations which were previously supported strongly from those quarters.

—The activities of the organisations from which the prohibitions are now being lifted, no longer entail the same degree of threat to internal security which initially necessitated the imposition of the prohibitions.

—There have been important shifts of emphasis in the statements and points of view of the most important of the organisations concerned, which indicate a new approach and a preference for peaceful solutions.

—The South African Police is convinced that it is able, in the present circumstances, to combat violence and other crimes perpetrated also by members of these organisations and to bring offenders to justice without the aid of prohibitions on organisations.

About one matter there should be no doubt. The lifting of the prohibition on the said organisations does not signify in the least the approval or condonation of terrorism or crimes of violence committed under their banner or which may be perpetrated in the future. Equally, it should not be interpreted as a deviation from the Government's principles, among other things, against their economic policy and aspects of their constitutional policy. This will be dealt with in debate and negotiation.

At the same time I wish to emphasise that the maintenance of law and order dare not be jeopardised. The Government will not forsake its duty in this connection. Violence from whichever source, will be fought with all available might. Peaceful protest may not become the springboard for lawlessness, violence and intimidation. No democratic country can tolerate that.

Strong emphasis will be placed as well on even more effective law enforcement. Proper provision of manpower and means for the police and all who are involved with the enforcement of the law, will be ensured. In fact, the budget for the coming financial year will already begin to give effect to this.

I wish to thank the members of our security forces and related services for the dedicated service they have rendered the Republic of South Africa. Their dedication makes reform in a stable climate possible.

On the state of emergency I have been advised that an emergency situation, which justifies these special measures which have been retained, still exists. There is still conflict which is manifesting itself mainly in Natal, but as a consequence of the countrywide political power struggle. In addition, there are indications that radicals are still trying to disrupt the possibilities of negotiation by means of mass violence.

It is my intention to terminate the state of emergency completely as soon as circumstances justify it and I request the co-operation of everybody towards this end. Those responsible for unrest and conflict have to bear the blame for the continuing state of emergency. In the meantime, the state of emergency is inhibiting only those who use chaos and disorder as political instruments. Otherwise the rules of the game under the state of emergency are the same for everybody.

Against this background the Government is convinced that the decisions I have announced are justified from the security point of view. However, these decisions are justified from a political point of view as well.

Our country and all its people have been embroiled in conflict, tension and violent struggle for decades. It is time for us to break out of the cycle of violence and break through to peace and reconciliation. The silent majority is yearning for this. The youth deserve it.

With the steps the Government has taken it has proven its good faith and the table is laid for sensible leaders to begin talking about a new dispensation, to reach an understanding by way of dialogue and discussion.

The agenda is open and the overall aims to which we are aspiring should be acceptable to all reasonable South Africans.

Among other things, those aims include a new, democratic constitution; universal franchise; no domination; equality before an independent judiciary; the protection of minorities as well as of individual rights; freedom of religion; a sound economy based on proven economic principles and private enterprise; dynamic programmes directed at better education, health services, housing and social conditions for all.

In this connection Mr. Nelson Mandela could play an important part. The Government has noted that he has declared himself to be willing to make a constructive contribution to the peaceful political process in South Africa.

I wish to put it plainly that the Government has taken a firm decision to release Mr. Mandela unconditionally. I am serious about bringing this matter to finality without delay. The Government will make a decision soon on the date of his release. Unfortunately, a further short passage of time is unavoidable.

Normally there is a certain passage of time between the decision to release and the actual release because of logistical and administrative requirements. In the case of Mr. Mandela there are factors in the way of his immediate release, of which his personal circumstances and safety are not the least. He has not been an ordinary prisoner for quite some time. Because of that, his case requires particular circumspection.

Today's announcements, in particular, go to the heart of what Black leaders — also Mr. Mandela — have been advancing over the years as their reason for having resorted to violence. The allegation has been that the Government did not wish to talk to them and that they were deprived of their right to normal political activity by the prohibition of their organisations.

Without conceding that violence has ever been justified, I wish to say today to those who argued in this manner:

—The Government wishes to talk to all leaders who seek peace.

—The unconditional lifting of the prohibition on the said organisations places everybody in a position to pursue politics freely.

—The justification for violence which was always advanced, no longer exists.

These facts place everybody in South Africa before a fait accompli. On the basis of numerous previous statements there is no longer any reasonable excuse for the continuation of violence. The time for talking has arrived and whoever still makes excuses does not really wish to talk.

Therefore, I repeat my invitation with greater conviction than ever: Walk through the open door, take your place at the negotiating table together with the Government and other leaders who have important power bases inside and outside of Parliament.

Henceforth, everybody's political points of view will be tested against their realism, their workability and their fairness. The time of negotiation has arrived.

To those political leaders who have always resisted violence I say thank you for your principled stands. This includes all the leaders of parliamentary parties, leaders of important organisations and movements, such as Chief Minister Buthelezi, all of the other Chief Ministers and urban community leaders.

Through their participation and discussion they have made an important contribution to this moment in which the process of free political participation is able to be restored. Their places in the negotiating process are assured.

Conclusion

In my inaugural address I said the following:

"All reasonable people in this country — by far the majority — anxiously await a message of hope. It is our responsibility as leaders in all spheres to provide that message realistically, with courage and conviction. If we fail in that, the ensuing chaos, the demise of stability and progress, will for ever be held against us.

"History has thrust upon the leadership of this country the tremendous responsibility to turn our country away from its present direction of conflict and confrontation. Only we, the leaders of our peoples, can do it.

"The eyes of responsible governments across the world

are focused on us. The hopes of millions of South Africans are centered around us. The future of Southern Africa depends on us. We dare not falter or fail."

This is where we stand:

—Deeply under the impression of our responsibility.

—Humble in the face of the tremendous challenges ahead.

—Determined to move forward in faith and with conviction.

I ask of Parliament to assist me on the road ahead. There is much to be done.

I call on the international community to re-evaluate its position and to adopt a positive attitude towards the dynamic evolution which is taking place in South Africa.

I pray that the Almighty Lord will guide and sustain us on our course through unchartered waters and will bless your labours and deliberations.

Mr. Speaker, Members of Parliament, I now declare this Second Session of the Ninth Parliament of the Republic of South Africa to be duly opened.

Apartheid Has No Future

AFRICA IS OURS

NELSON MANDELA, *Member of the African National Congress*

Delivered to the Public, Cape Town, South Africa, February 11, 1990

AMANDLA! Amandla! i-Afrika, mayibuye! My friends, comrades and fellow South Africans, I greet you all in the name of peace, democracy and freedom for all. I stand here before you not as a prophet but as a humble servant of you, the people.

Your tireless and heroic sacrifices have made it possible for me to be here today. I therefore place the remaining years of my life in your hands.

On this day of my release, I extend my sincere and warmest gratitude to the millions of my compatriots and those in every corner of the globe who have campaigned tirelessly for my release.

I extend special greetings to the people of Cape Town, the city to which, which has been my home for three decades. Your mass marches and other forms of struggle have served as a constant source of strength to all political prisoners.

I salute the African National Congress. It has fulfilled our every expectation in its role as leader of the great march to freedom.

I salute our president, Comrade Oliver Tambo, for leading the A.N.C. even under the most difficult circumstances.

I salute the rank-and-file members of the A.N.C. You have sacrificed life and limb in the pursuit of the noble cause of our struggle.

I salute combatants of Umkonto We Sizwe, like Solomon Malhangu and Ashley Kriel, who have paid the ultimate price for the freedom of all South Africans.

I salute the South African Communist Party for its steady contribution to the struggle for democracy. You have survived 40 years of unrelenting persecution. The memory of great Communists like Moses Kotane, Yusuf Dacoo, Bram Fischer and Moses Madidha will be cherished for generations to come.

I salute General Secretary Joe Slovo, one of our finest patriots. We are heartened by the fact that the alliance between ourselves and the party remains as strong as it always was.

I salute the United Democratic Front, the National Education Crisis Committee, the South African Youth Congress, the Transvaal and Natal Indian Congresses. And Cosatu. And the many other formations of the mass democratic movement.

I also salute the Black Sash and the National Union of South African Students. We note with pride that you have acted as the conscience of white South Africans. Even during the darkest days in the history of our struggle, you held the flag of liberty high. The large-scale mass mobilization of the past few years is one of the key factors which led to the opening of the final chapter of our struggle.

I extend my greetings to the working class of our country. Your organized stance is the pride of our movement. You remain the most dependable force in the struggle to end exploitation and oppression.

I pay tribute — I pay tribute to the many religious communities who carried the campaign for justice forward when the organizations of our people were silenced.

I greet the traditional leaders of our country. Many among you continue to walk in the footsteps of great heroes like Hintsa and Sekhukhuni.

I pay tribute to the endless heroes of youth. You, the young lions. You the young lions have energized our entire struggle.

I pay tribute to the mothers and wives and sisters of our nation. You are the rock-hard foundation of our struggle. Apartheid has inflicted more pain on you than on anyone else. On this occasion, we thank the world — we thank the world community for their great contribution to the anti-apartheid struggle. Without your support our struggle would not have reached this advanced stage.

The sacrifice of the front-line states will be remembered by South Africans forever.

My salutations will be incomplete without expressing my deep appreciation for the strength given to me during my long and lonely years in prison by my beloved wife and family.

I am convinced that your pain and suffering was far greater than my own.

Reprinted from *Vital Speeches of the Day*, Vol. 56, No. 10, March 1, 1990, pp. 295–297, by permission.

Before I go any further, I wish to make the point that I intend making only a few preliminary comments at this stage. I will make a more complete statement only after I have had the opportunity to consult with my comrades.

Today the majority of South Africans, black and white, recognize that apartheid has no future. It has to be ended by our own decisive mass actions in order to build peace and security. The mass campaigns of defiance and other actions of our organizations and people can only culminate in the establishment of democracy.

The apartheid destruction on our subcontinent is incalculable. The fabric of family life of millions of my people has been shattered. Millions are homeless and unemployed.

Our economy — our economy lies in ruins and our people are embroiled in political strife. Our resort to the armed struggle in 1960 with the formation of the military wing of A.N.C., Umkonto We Sizwe, was a purely defensive action against the violence of apartheid.

The factors which necessitated the armed struggle still exist today. We have no option but to continue. We express the hope that a climate conducive to a negotiated settlement would be created soon so that there may no longer be the need for the armed struggle.

I am a loyal and disciplined member of the African National Congress. I am, therefore, in full agreement with all of its objectives, strategies and tactics.

The need to unite the people of our country is as important a task now as it always has been. No individual leader is able to take all these enormous tasks on his own. It is our task as leaders to place our views before our organization and to allow the democratic structures to decide on the way forward.

On the question of democratic practice, I feel duty bound to make the point that a leader of the movement is a person who has been democratically elected at a national conference. This is a principle which must be upheld without any exceptions.

Today, I wish to report to you that my talks with the Government have been aimed at normalizing the political situation in the country. We have not as yet begun discussing the basic demands of the struggle.

I wish to stress that I myself had at no time entered into negotiations about the future of our country, except to insist on a meeting between the A.N.C. and the Government.

Mr. de Klerk has gone further than any other Nationalist president in taking real steps to normalize the situation. However, there are further steps as outlined in the Harare Declaration that have to be met before negotiations on the basic demands of our people can begin.

I reiterate our call for inter alia the immediate ending of the state of emergency and the freeing of all, and not only some, political prisoners.

Only such a normalized situation which allows for free political activity can allow us to consult our people in order to obtain a mandate. The people need to be consulted on who will negotiate and on the content of such negotiations.

Negotiations cannot take place — negotiations cannot take up a place above the heads or behind the backs of our people. It is our belief that the future of our country can only be determined by a body which is democratically elected on a nonracial basis.

Negotiations on the dismantling of apartheid will have to address the overwhelming demand of our people for a democratic nonracial and unitary South Africa. There must be an end to white monopoly on political power.

And a fundamental restructuring of our political and economic systems to insure that the inequalities of apartheid are addressed and our society thoroughly democratized.

It must be added that Mr. de Klerk himself is a man of integrity who is acutely aware of the dangers of a public figure not honoring his undertakings. But as an organization, we base our policy and strategy on the harsh reality we are faced with, and this reality is that we are still suffering under the policies of the Nationalist Government.

Our struggle has reached a decisive moment. We call on our people to seize this moment so that the process toward democracy is rapid and uninterrupted. We have waited too long for our freedom. We can no longer wait. Now is the time to intensify the struggle on all fronts.

To relax our efforts now would be a mistake which generations to come will not be able to forgive. The sight of freedom looming on the horizon should encourage us to redouble our efforts. It is only through disciplined mass action that our victory can be assured.

We call on our white compatriots to join us in the shaping of a new South Africa. The freedom movement is the political home for you, too. We call on the international community to continue the campaign to isolate the apartheid regime.

To lift sanctions now would be to run the risk of aborting the process toward the complete eradication of apartheid. Our march to freedom is irreversible. We must not allow fear to stand in our way.

Universal suffrage on a common voters roll in a united democratic and nonracial South Africa is the only way to peace and racial harmony.

In conclusion, I wish to go to my own words during my trial in 1964. They are as true today as they were then. I wrote: I have fought against white domination, and I have fought against black domination. I have cherished the idea of a democratic and free society in which all persons live together in harmony and with equal opportunities.

It is an ideal which I hope to live for and to achieve. But if needs be, it is an ideal for which I am prepared to die.

My friends, I have no words of eloquence to offer today except to say that the remaining days of my life are in your hands.

I hope you will disperse with discipline. And not a single one of you should do anything which will make other people say that we can't control our own people.

Easing the Debt Crisis

Most political scientists and economists believe that the present international debt crisis represents a potential powder keg in the Third World, one that threatens to wreak havoc and instability in the developing nations. The situation is particularly acute in Latin America, where many nations face insurmountable problems in repaying their debts. For example, in the wake of a series of devastating earthquakes, Ecuador's president, Léon Febres Cordero, suspended—for the remainder of 1987—$1.3 billion in payments due on Ecuador's $8.2 billion foreign debt. In announcing the suspension, Cordero stated that Ecuador was incapable of both rebuilding that country's all-important oil pipeline and repaying the mounting interest on its escalating debt.

Ecuador is but one example of the increasing number of Latin American nations that have either unilaterally suspended their interest payments or requested the International Monetary Fund to reschedule those payments. In Latin America, the debt crisis has exacerbated an ever-widening economic crisis that dates back to the 1930s. Indeed, Latin America's population is now three to four times larger than it was in the 1930s, its social problems

have increased geometrically, and the purchasing power of its exports has plummeted to a record low.

The debt crisis has been fueled by a sharp decline in the terms of trade, high interest rates, the flight of capital, and unprecedented inflation. These and other developments have precipitated a dire economic crisis. To repay their debts, many Latin American countries will be forced to curtail badly needed programs and services, at enormous social costs.

It is questionable whether some of these nations can tolerate further sacrifices. For example, in the Dominican Republic—a more or less stable country—immediately following the implementation of the first of the IMF's measures, a spontaneous rebellion occurred. The army and police were summoned to quash the revolt, in which 50 people were killed and hundreds more were wounded. In Panama, measures aimed at balancing the budget brought hundreds of thousands of people into the streets. And in Bolivia—which has been virtually paralyzed by the debt crisis—inflation soared to over 2,300 percent in 1986.

Twenty-five years ago, Latin America was practically debt-free. Today, its debt amounts to over $400 billion. How was the money spent? Part of it was invested in weapons. In Argentina, for example, tens of billions of dollars was spent on military hardware. The same was true of Chile and other Latin American countries. Another part was either embezzled, stolen, or misappropriated. Still another part was returned to the United States and Europe as a result of the flight of capital. And last, another part was squandered on unnecessary or wasteful projects. Only a small part of the money was spent on essential programs and services.

As a result, many Latin American leaders argue that they cannot and should not be required to repay their debts, which they view as immoral. They ask: What benefits did the people derive from these expenditures? They contend that it would be much more moral to cancel the debt, which would benefit billions of people in Latin America, Africa, and Asia, 70 percent of the world's population. To do otherwise, they insist, would be to invite massive social upheaval.

Obviously, the lender nations disagree with this analysis. In March 1987, 44 countries assembled to discuss the deepening debt crisis in Latin America. At this conference, financial representatives from those nations debated a proposal which, its critics maintain, would give the United States veto power over how billions of dollars in new loans to Latin America will be allocated. Specifically, the debate focused on a U.S. proposal to exclude debtor countries from decisions on loans granted by the Inter-American Development Bank, which channels approximately $3 billion a year in loans to Latin America and the Caribbean.

The debt crisis has not only adversely affected the struggling masses in Latin America, but has seriously hurt American automobile workers in Detroit and farmers in Kansas. Some U.S. officials, like Senator Bill Bradley (D-NJ), believe that it is necessary to reduce both the principal and interest payments to banks and international lending organizations. For instance, in the two years after Mexico nearly defaulted in 1982, sales of U.S. construction equipment to Latin America experienced a sharp decline. During the 1980s, living standards dropped 8 percent in Mexico, 14 percent in Peru, 17 percent in Argentina, and 19 percent in Venezuela.

At the present time, the solution to the debt crisis rests with the industrialized world. Unless the lender nations propose bold new initiatives, they are likely to aggravate the situation and force the debtor nations to adopt extreme measures. They cannot afford to turn a deaf ear to the problem, as the crisis promises to grow increasingly worse. Before too much longer, Latin America and other Third World countries will impose their own solution, which could seriously jeopardize future relations. Clearly, both sides have made legitimate claims. The problem cannot be solved by rhetoric. It will require compromise, cooperation, and consensus. Both sides must rise to the challenge.

Looking Ahead: Challenge Questions

What are the principal causes of the international debt crisis?

How severe and widespread is the debt crisis?

Who are the major winners and losers in the debt crisis?

Who are the main villains on both the borrowing and lending sides of the debt crisis?

How has the debt crisis affected the Third World?

What are the major options for resolving the debt crisis?

Are there signs that economic prospects are starting to brighten in the developing world?

Is the Zambian economic adjustment approach likely to rescue that nation from its debtor status?

MORTGAGING A HOUSE OF CARDS

THE ETHICS OF INTERNATIONAL DEBT

KENNETH P. JAMESON

KENNETH P. JAMESON *is professor of economics at the University of Notre Dame. This article is adapted from a talk given at the Woodstock Forum, sponsored by the Woodstock Theological Center at Georgetown University.*

uring the humid summer of 1983, an unenviable Midwestern bank found itself at the center of the international debt crisis. That August, the Michigan National Bank sued Citibank. Michigan National had bought $5 million of a loan to Pemex, the Mexican state oil company. Pemex was unable to repay, even after the loan had been extended three times. Finally the bank, whose president was a fervent Mormon, decided that principle prohibited throwing bad money after good and refused to renew. Citibank attempted to renew the Pemex loan without permission. Michigan National Bank sued, thereby breaking the unity of banks in ''muddling through'' the crisis of unpayable loans.

Michigan National may have been correct legally. But the bank lost, and lost big. Observers said that the bank was going to feel a lot of heat. As one put it, ''I wouldn't be surprised if the auditors are there tomorrow.'' Later, ostensibly for other reasons, Michigan National's president was forced to step down, and he at one point faced penalties in the six-figure range for irregularities subsequently uncovered. Perhaps his problems are unrelated to the loan affair, but the story illustrates very clearly that there are big stakes in the debt game, that it is a political game, and that the whole structure resembles more a house of cards than a Gibraltar of financial security.

The basic facts on debt are clear: third-world debt now amounts to around $1 trillion, about half of which is in Latin America; the Latin American countries are now exporting capital to the U.S. to the tune of some $30 billion per year as a result of the debt; many major U.S. banks have third- world loans greater than their capital base, meaning that nonpayment would threaten the banks' survival. For example, one *Washington Post* article indicated that Chemical Bank's loans

to Mexico were 48.6 percent of its primary capital in 1986. Rather than dwell on these rather well-known matters, however, I would like to deal with three issues which relate to the moral issues and obligations that are posed by the current third-world debt crisis.

First is the question of who is to blame. In Catholic terms, what about sin, guilt, and punishment? I could make the case that the banks are to blame, that the third-world governments are to blame, that the elites of the third-world are to blame, that the OPEC countries are to blame, and probably that you and I are to blame as well. But that would not be a particularly useful approach. A better way might be to ask who is benefiting at this point from the operation of the debt game? If we could ascertain that, and if we could agree that there is something wrong with the game, then we could move to deal with it.

There are some clear winners in the present situation. The banks are the biggest winners, for although they would rather be out from under the loans, they are still collecting something on what were bad loans, what should have been clear losses. And even if they end up selling the loans at a discount of 30 percent for Chilean loans or of 75 percent for the Peruvian loans, they are getting back more than they should have expected had the firms they loaned to gone under and the loans simply been written off, or had the respective governments simply declared the loans unpayable.

Other winners are the private individuals and government officials of third-world countries who now have real estate or bank accounts outside of their own country as a result of their take from these loans. One study by Morgan Guaranty Trust estimated that the net debt of many of the Latin American countries would essentially be zero if extreme capital flight had not occurred.

There are clear losers as well. The poor and middle classes of the Latin American countries have seen twenty years of growth and development stripped away, as their governments have undertaken the recessionary steps the international structure requires of them. Their access to services such as education and health is being diminished, and there is evidence that malnutrition and infant mortality are increasing.

So presumably any steps to deal with the debt problem must make an assessment of who is to pay the cost, and it should be those who are benefiting from the continued existence of this house of cards.

y second point is to examine the various ways that the debt problem can be confronted. There are five general approaches.

● *Muddling through.* The argument is that the system has functioned since the 1982 Mexican debt crisis, and that policy should concentrate on continuing this experience with or without augmented financial flows. Perhaps the industrialized countries should stimulate their economies to aid third-world exports. Perhaps there should be new flows of capital from the banks and international institutions, as in the Baker Plan. Perhaps changes in commodity prices will begin to aid the debtors. Perhaps a decline in real interest rates will relieve the debt burden in some degree. But don't do anything to pull out one of the cards. This past August, Swiss Bank Corporation balked at putting up the money for the Mexican "rescue." As the headlines read: "Swiss Bank Jeopardized Mexican Rescue but Relented after Pressure by the IMF" (*Wall Street Journal,* August 13, 1986). If I were president of the bank, I'd be looking over my shoulder!

● *Redefinition of assets.* The loans could be sold to a new international bank at a discount, and that bank would then be the collecting agency, insulating present lender banks from the illiquidity problems of debtors. Or the loans could be swapped for assets such as plants and equipment. For example, in Bolivia, the most valuable asset is the national oil company. It could simply be sold to pay off the debt. The comic strip *Bloom County* actually anticipated this scenario some time ago, when Opus became dictator of Bolivia, and showed how ludicrous such an option is. Whether the loans were sold or swapped for assets, there would presumably be a write-down of the loans to reflect their current value. However, there would be no substantial change in the situation of the debtor countries; in the first case they would still have to pay the international bank, presumably on the full value of the debt; and in the second, they would lose control over the most profitable assets in their economy.

● *Share the cost.* Another approach would share the current adjustment costs among the banks, the debtors, and the beneficiaries of capital flight. Senator Bill Bradley's plan calls for a write-down of the loans by 3 percent per year over three years, so that the actual principal amount debtors have to pay is reduced, i.e., so that there is debt relief. Interest rates on the debt are also to be reduced, which would give liquidity relief. This would share adjustment between banks and countries. Some have suggested that the debtor countries, with the collaboration of the international banking system, simply call in the foreign assets of their nationals, as England and France did during World War I. Their citizens would be paid in bonds, but would certainly bear some of the costs of the adjustment. This would call upon the beneficiaries of capital flight to bear a portion of the burden.

● *Link to domestic performance.* Alan Garcia, the president of Peru, has declared that his country's payments will be dependent upon Peru's ability to pay, i.e., that payments will not exceed 10 percent of export earnings in a given year. The Cartagena Group of Latin American debtors will meet in April in search of a coordinated plan to limit the payment in some such way. Such an approach deals with the solvency and liquidity problems, and clearly indicates that the poor and middle classes of debtor countries will no longer pay the costs of adjusting. President Garcia's approach has not been particularly popular internationally, and Peru is an international pariah at this point. Nor does this solution solve the real long-term problem, for the unpaid interest is simply being added to the overall debt bill that remains. Nonetheless, the tying of payments to domestic economic performance is clearly going to become more common. The recent Mexican renegotiations for example, made some concessions to Mexico, taking into account the low price of oil and a low domestic growth rate.

● *Repudiation.* This has been the traditional way of dealing with the issue, going back in Latin America to the 1820s and 1830s. Until a few years ago, Peru's railroads were owned by the holders of bonds defaulted on in the 1860s. Fidel Castro has suggested this approach for Latin America, while at the same time paying his own debts. Even orthodox economic advisors have questioned whether new democratic governments should be required to pay debts contracted by military-civilian dictatorships. However, repudiation is a direct affront to the international banking system, and has not become an avowed policy, though Bolivia quietly quit paying in 1984 simply because it did not have the resources, and Nicaragua currently is not paying.

hich of these options might be most desirable and effective in dealing with this massive problem, particularly in light of the moral obligations that are involved? My criteria for choosing are two: first, that those who have benefited should bear the costs; and second, that the disruption of the structure should be minimized, if not avoided.

I dismiss muddling through, a process which at present allows the banks to benefit while the poor continue to pay. Redefining the assets would be preferable, only because it would increase the stability of the financial structure. But redefinition of assets has the same problems as muddling through. Repudiation, on the other hand, would be too disruptive, focusing the cost too completely on the banks, or on the American public, the lenders of last resort.

I would suggest that a combination of cost sharing and linkage to domestic performance would be the most effective and fairest approach. The present system is simply pyramiding added debt on top of the existing debt. As such, it is neither fair nor realistic: the debts themselves are unlikely ever to be paid, and their cost to the poor is unfair. Some write-down of the obligations of the debtors is therefore essential. A combination of lower interest rates and their linkage to the actual possibilities of a debtor country to pay in terms of its exports, would confront both the liquidity and solvency problems at a cost which would be more acceptable to the people of the indebted countries. Finally, there is no reason that a major beneficiary group, such as those who engaged in capital flight, should be protected from the required adjustments. Perhaps they stole it fair and square, to paraphrase former Senator Hayakawa, but there is no justification for allowing them to hide behind the faceless "international capital system." Clearly, this is a very good reason to interfere with capital markets and to bring them an order that will allow third-world countries to undertake development efforts with some assurance they won't be frustrated by capital drain to the safe haven of the U.S. Nor should the banks benefit from such deposits.

The debt problem is clearly a major challenge of the next several years. This is most acutely felt by the debtors whose economies are, for the most part, in disarray. But it should also be felt in the U.S. on moral grounds. The Catholic bishops pointed this out quite clearly in their recent pastoral on the economy when they called for systemic change of international economic institutions. But the need for change must be recognized by a much broader economic and political constituency. The economic interest of the United States lies with a prosperous and progressing third world, particularly in Latin America. This will occur only if meaningful steps for dealing with the debt problem are undertaken.

WILL THE PLANET PAY THE PRICE FOR THIRD WORLD DEBT?

The battle against the earth's destruction pits world leaders against an intractable foe: Poverty

The demonstrations in West Berlin last month stretched from the conference hall of the World Bank and the International Monetary Fund conclave to the golden arches of a McDonald's restaurant. Among the gripes: environmental destruction wreaked by projects financed by the World Bank, including the destruction of rain forests to make room for cattle grazing. By pushing hamburgers, chains like McDonald's Corp. must share part of the blame, the protesters said. They weren't the only ones concerned. In his address to the bankers, West German Chancellor Helmut Kohl warned darkly that unconstrained development "could prove disastrous for mankind."

In a year when a thinning ozone layer, a warming globe, and floating medical garbage have vied for front-page coverage, the politics of ecology has secured its place as a mainstream issue. But the battle against the earth's destruction pits world leaders against a foe much tougher than terrorists, drug-traffickers, or nuclear stockpiles: Third World poverty. As the planet warms partly from the effects of depleted rain forests from Indonesia to Brazil, the industrialized world is starting to feel the cost of Third World development as never before. The traditional paths to growth—building big dams, roadways, and the other megaprojects favored by international lending agencies—are thus coming under increasing scrutiny.

LOUDER VOICE. Just as the industrialized world is waking up to the consequences of such growth policies, poor countries are staggering under mountains of debt. Their desperation for cash—at any environmental cost—is only adding to the growing ecological crisis. Says José Lizárraga, Latin America director of the U.N. Environmental Program: "The debt crisis puts countries in a short-term frame of mind."

Even if the world's bankers were to forgive much of the debt, governments until recently had little incentive to devote scarce resources to saving forests and streams. Now, for the first time, they find themselves confronted with environmental movements at home. In Mexico, ecology activists supported opposition candidate Cuauhtémoc Cárdenas. In September environmentalists in São Paulo, Brazil, draped around the fence of the governor's palace a 2,500-meter-long petition calling for a new national preserve. Meanwhile, in Taiwan, strong support for the opposition Democratic Progressive Party forced the ruling Kuomintang to form an environmental protection agency and spend more money on cleanup projects. The broad shift toward pluralism that has swept from Brazil and Argentina to Korea and the Philippines in this decade is giving environmental groups a louder voice.

Still, neither the First nor Third World can deny that the developing countries' ability to support their mushrooming populations is increasingly dubious. In the next 60 years the world will grow from today's 5 billion people to between 11 billion and 14 billion, according to a U.N. report. Some 90% of this growth will occur in poor countries. Countries that are now hard-pressed to provide for their people will have to feed, clothe, house, and transport billions more within several decades. In preparing to face this task, they must make optimum use of their precious natural resources.

Yet throughout Africa and Latin America, debtor countries are cutting down forests, overusing fertilizers, and exhausting groundwater supplies in efforts to produce cash crops. In debt-ridden Brazil, for example, streams of impoverished settlers head west, hoping to cash in on abundant gold, tin, and land in the vast Amazon jungle. In the past decade settlers have slashed and burned enough forest to cover France. Each year, Brazilian scientists say, the cutting and burning of trees in the Amazon alone contributes as much as one-tenth of all the planet's principal greenhouse gas, carbon dioxide. As the world's largest rain forest shrinks, it absorbs less carbon dioxide and produces less oxygen. Worse yet, all of the world's rain forests are located in poor southern countries: Brazil, Zaire, Indonesia, and the Philippines.

In Central America, farmers douse their fields with megatons of pesticides long outlawed in the U.S. The result: Poisoned waters annually kill three of every 1,000 inhabitants, according to the U.S. Agency of International Development. Overuse of pesticides in Central America is also certain to affect the region's agricultural exports, three-quarters of which end up in the U.S.

'GREENING PROCESS.' With its enormous power over economic development—approving $17.5 billion for 217 projects this year—the World Bank is a highly visible target for environmental critics. Throughout its postwar history, the multination lending organization has enraged conservationists by funding ecologically unsound megaprojects. At the Berlin meeting, environmentalists from 20 nations presented a list of the World Bank's "dirty half-dozen"—six major projects that they say have damaged local environments. The projects range from a cattle-raising program in Botswana that has led to overgrazing to bank-backed overuse of pesticides in the Sudan.

Long before the meeting, however, attitudes had begun to change if slowly. Over the past five years the World Bank and its regional subsidiaries have begun what bank officials call "a greening process." A 60-person environmental department within the bank now oversees new projects. Still, environmentalists contend that ecology remains a mere tag-on item at the bank. "The types of projects coming out of the pipeline—the real test—have not changed significantly," says Brent Blackwelder, vice-president of the Environmental Policy Institute in Washington. Blackwelder claims that more than 90% of the bank's lending still goes to huge coal projects and big dams, such as the $10 billion Yangtze River Dan now under consideration for financing, which would force large-scale relocation.

QUANDARY. After getting an earful of suggestions at the Berlin meeting, World Bank Environmental Director Kenneth Piddington urged patience. "It's not a question of an institution like the bank turning green overnight," he said. "It's a long process." Other officials stress that the bank has limited clout in development financing. "A number of these [controversial] projects would have gone on with or without World Bank intervention," says Jeremy Warford, senior adviser in the bank's environmental department. "Environmentalists don't want to hear that."

Indeed, a World Bank report in September called on Brazil to curtail tax and agricultural incentives that are luring settlers and big farmers into the Amazon. Ironically, one of the problems mentioned in the report was the Brazilian Polonoroeste project, which features a large road through the jungle's southern rim. The World Bank has already invested $617 million in it. The Amazon controversy puts Brazil in a quandary. The country has a financial disaster on its hands: It pays more than $10 billion a year in interest on its $120 billion foreign debt, and inflation is nearing 1,000% annually. Rio de Janeiro just declared bankruptcy. Famine claims lives throughout the country's northeast.

Yet an accidental find of rich tin deposits deep in the Amazon has made Brazil a world leader in tin production. Now that it has found a source of precious revenue, the country is being told that for the good of the planet it must rein in Amazon development.

Worse, according to analysts at the World Wildlife Fund in Washington, Brazil needs to spend some $3 billion to $4 billion a year to protect the jungle and clean up the mess in its southern industrial region. Should Brazil be left to sort out the problems by itself? No way, says José Goldemberg, rector of the University of São Paulo. "If you leave industrializing countries alone, they will do nothing."

JAPAN'S ROLE. So desperate are they for cash that many leaders will look elsewhere for loans, despite warnings of dire ecological consequences. Many controversial projects are funded by the richest new power in international aid, Japan. The country is pouring into dams, roads, and railways from rain forests in Asia to the Brazilian Amazon. "The problem with Japan's aid," says Jonathan Holliman, a spokesman for Friends of the Earth Japan, "is that there is no environmental assessment."

In several cases, Japan has offered to pick up loans that other lending agencies have dropped for environmental reasons. In Thailand, critics say, Japan's Overseas Economic Cooperation Fund (OECF) was prepared to finance the Nam Choan Dam even after the World Bank backed away from the controversial project last spring. In the end, the Thai government shelved the project under pressure from environmentalists. Counters a Japanese Foreign Ministry official: "We try to improve the well-being of the recipient country, and instead we are accused of destroying the environment."

For decades, Chinese leaders have worried far more about industrial production than about the environment. One result is a green-brown smog the envelops Chinese cities. Citizens cover their mouths with scarves or masks on particularly thick days. Like London in the 1950s, Beijing suffers from extensive coal-burning: more than 20 million tons a year. More worrisome from a greenhouse perspective is China's plan to quadruple its coal consumption by the turn of the century.

With increased smog, environmental awareness is growing in China. In July the Beijing city government finally passed regulations to limit air pollution. And the *Guangming Daily* complained that China's pollution was "as heavy as that in the developed countries in the 1950s and 1960s."

DEBT SWAPS. Elsewhere, a few ingenious conservation schemes are sprouting. Last year several environmental groups, led by the World Wildlife Fund, began to finance conservation projects with debt-for-equity swaps. These swaps, now in vogue among investors in debtor countries, allow the environmental group to buy the countries' debt at a discount and cash it in for local currency. Rather than invest the money in a hotel or a factory, the environmentalists finance local conservation projects, thereby attacking both crushing problems of debt and environment at once. So far, several million dollars worth of such debt-for-nature deals have been done in Bolivia, Costa Rica, Ecuador, and the Philippines.

In Mexico City, dozens of bureaucrats work late hours in the Environmental Secretariat to complete the country's first set of environmental regulations before the new presidential administration takes office on Dec. 1. And for more than a year, public pressure forced the government to postpone loading the first reactor of the $3.5 billion Laguna Verde nuclear facility in the state of Vera Cruz. Meanwhile, environmentalists flexed their muscles before the recent presidential elections, reaping loads of promises from the candidates to attack the thick layer of smog that chokes the Valley of Mexico's approximately 20 million residents.

But in other regions of Mexico, as the population grows and the economy stagnates, once-great forests in the states of Michoacán and Chiapas are succumbing to a combination of small-time wood gatherers and lumber companies. This process, brought on by economic need and greed, already threatens to turn Haiti into a woodless wasteland and has turned formerly lush El Salvador into semi-desert. Those countries serve as grim reminders of the cycle of poverty that leads to environmental abuse. As the land fails, social tensions grow, sometimes exploding into war. Refugees flock to greener pastures, often chopping down trees along the way.

Cleaning up world development is too big a task for any one institution or country to handle alone. Even without the debt crisis, experts say, an environmental crisis would exist in the Third World, just as it does in the First. Treaties vowing cooperation to battle the greenhouse effect and ozone depletion are a promising start. But while leaders sign documents, peasants from Indonesia to Zaire continue to hack farm plots out of rain forests. The challenge at hand is not to preach to those people of the jungle's importance, but to offer them jobs that will leave it intact.

By Stephen Baker in Mexico City, with Jeffrey Ryser in São Paulo, William Glasgall in Berlin, Vicky Cahan in Washington, and bureau reports.

It Won't Go Away Alone

Christopher Korth

Christopher Korth is professor of economics at the University of South Carolina.

One of the most serious international economic and political problems today is the enormous amount of foreign debt owed by Third World countries. The burden of the debt problem, of course, varies significantly in different less developed countries (LDCs).

Some of these countries have indeed been able to avoid or overcome serious debt problems, thus creating a new category of new industrialized nations. Most of the success stories are in Asia—for example, Taiwan and South Korea. (Indeed, Taiwan has become a major capital exporter, and its government's international reserves are in excess of $70 billion.) However, most Third World countries are heavily burdened by their international debt.

Other LDCs, because of their extreme poverty and very poor credit prospects, share the dubious distinction of never having been able to borrow freely in the international private money and capital markets. Lenders, such as commercial banks and investors in the bond markets, have never found the prospects of returns attractive enough to make loans to these countries. As a result, these countries, "the poorest of the poor," have only been able to borrow from the governments of the wealthy countries and from international agencies, such as the International Development Association of the World Bank Group. Fortunately for those countries, loans from these official agencies are generally made on "concessionary" terms, with fixed, low-interest rates. Included in this group of the very poorest are such countries as Chad and Mali in Africa, Suriname and Guyana in Latin America, and Bangladesh and Burma in Asia.

Middle-income LDCs

Most of the current concern about the welfare of the Third World countries tends to focus on the middle-income LDCs. Among these are most of the largest LDCs, including those countries that had been widely considered the most promising in the Third World—Mexico, Brazil, Argentina, Venezuela, the Philippines, Indonesia, and Nigeria.

It is this last group, the middle-income Third World countries, whose international financial status has deteriorated most markedly. They have been the subject of greatest concern in recent years. This will focus primarily on this group.

The 1960s and early 1970s: The watershed to the international debt crisis was the oil-price hike in December 1973. Prior to that time, both the magnitude of the debt problem and the relations between the major lenders, regulators, and borrowing countries were very different than they are today.

By recent standards, the borrowing needs of most developing countries, and their total international debts, were relatively small. Most of the international loans to *all* developing countries came from foreign governments and international agencies (such as the International Monetary Fund, the World Bank, and the Inter-American Development Bank), and from trade credits from suppliers. The LDCs were generally unable to borrow from commercial banks or in the bond markets. Even the Brazils and the Mexicos generally could not borrow from commercial banks.

In addition to having more limited international

funding needs, the developing countries also benefited from economic conditions in the late 1960s and early 1970s. This made their international debts easier to service—both interest and principal. Interest rates were low. Exports from many developing countries were strong. Also, the prices of most of the major commodity exports from the LDCs were high (for example, between 1965 and 1975, the prices of major commodities rose more than 80 percent). As a result of these favorable conditions, serious financial problems at the time were infrequent: The debt burden was generally manageable.

The late 1970s and the 1980s: The 1970s saw ambitious economic expansion in many developing countries. That caused a sharp increase in their imports. There was also rapid inflation in most industrialized countries, causing the prices of manufactured products being imported by the LDCs to rise at the same time that the volume of imports was increasing. Although commodity prices (not only of oil, but of most primary products) remained strong through the end of the 1970s, the prolonged recession in the industrial world during the early 1980s substantially weakened most of those prices. A result of this combination of factors was a sharp deterioration in the balance of trade in most developing countries.

This was also a period in which most governments greatly increased their budget deficits. In many countries, subsidies on basic products (both domestically produced and imported) rose sharply —especially on food and fuel. Rising interest rates on foreign debts exacerbated the problem, which further aggravated the funding problems of these countries.

The role of commercial banks

As was noted above, before 1973, the role of commercial banks in lending to LDCs was small. For example, as recently as 1968, commercial banks had provided less than 6 percent of all the international funding needs for Latin America. Beginning in 1972, however, that relative importance grew rapidly. By 1973, the international banking share of all funding needs for Latin America had grown to 44 percent. The stage had been set for banks' critical role in helping alleviate the oil crisis that was to come in 1974.

After 1973, the OPEC governments, having received huge increases in revenues from their oil-price increases, deposited most of the funds in the international banks. Seeking profitable ways to invest such receipts, the banks proved only too willing to service the borrowing requirements of the developing countries. For example, in Latin America (the region most attractive to commercial banks), the banks' share of the region's international funding reached 70 percent in 1979, compared with 7 percent in 1968.

Major defaults among the developing countries were generally averted until the early 1980s. This was often less because of successful debt management by the borrowers than because the lenders loaned the borrowers the money to make payments on their loans.

Additional time was gained as a result of two developments for which neither the countries nor banks can take much credit: the drops in the price of oil and in interest rates. Although the steep decline in oil prices has hurt such oil-exporting countries as Indonesia, Mexico, and Nigeria (and the banks that had loaned to them), the lower interest rates have helped most LDCs.

Bad loans, borrowers, or creditors?

The current international debt situation (or the credit situation, as seen from the perspective of the lenders) is extremely grave. The villains in this scenario are numerous, and they exist on both the borrowing and lending sides. Heroes are few. The United States, still an economic superpower, is the largest debtor nation in the world. Although calls consistently come from Western Europe and Japan attempting to push Washington to get its economic house in order, in reality it is an awkward situation.

There can be little doubt that when the oil crisis arose in 1973–74, many borrowing countries (e.g., Brazil) did little to make economic adjustments to reduce the sharply increased import burden. As a result, their international debts rose rapidly. Other countries, once they were able to tap the international banks, borrowed for nonproductive, often frivolous reasons (e.g., an expensive Nigerian sports complex), and in some cases actually to finance fraudulent projects to benefit dishonest government officials.

For their part, commercial banks and other commercial lenders were Pollyannish in their optimism that countries could and would honor their international obligations. Banks competed aggressively to lend larger and larger sums. They scrambled to be the lead managers of large syndicated credits, and in the process dragged in smaller, less experienced banks. Unfortunately, the lenders did not exercise prudence in evaluating the creditworthiness of borrowers.

Were the loans bad? Many of them, yes. Were the borrowers bad? A few, yes, but many more were simply foolish. Were the bankers bad? Perhaps a few, but even more were foolish.

Lenders have been very slow to adjust to the credit burden that hangs over their heads. For too long, they deceived themselves, as well as bank regulators, into thinking that if they could only hang on, the crisis would pass. They were living in a dreamworld and, as we have seen, they were lucky.

However, although it took them a long time to react meaningfully, banks have in general made much more of an adjustment than have the borrowers. The results are generally beneficial for the individual banks and the credit system, as well. However, although some of the adjustments have also brought benefits for some of the borrowers, some of the other adjustments do not bode well for the less developed countries.

Although there has not been any systematic, comprehensive program undertaken by the international commercial banks to confront the threat of the debt overhang, most major banks have made no-

Mixed Reviews of the Baker Plan

The most celebrated comprehensive solution to the global debt crisis is the Baker Plan, which was presented by then-Secretary of the Treasury James Baker to the joint IMF-World Bank meeting in Seoul, Korea, in October 1985. It is a growth-oriented plan based on free market principles, as opposed to the traditional IMF austerity solutions for countries with severe balance-of-payments problems. Baker singled out 15 "middle income" countries as especially appropriate for the Baker Plan: Argentina, Bolivia, Brazil, Chile, Colombia, Ivory Coast, Ecuador, Mexico, Morocco, Nigeria, Peru, the Philippines, Uruguay, Venezuela, and Yugoslavia. Costa Rica and Jamaica have been mentioned sometimes in the context of the Baker Plan as part of the World Bank's "17 heavily indebted middle-income countries." (Incidentally, some analysts wonder why Bolivia made the list; it is so poor that it is the only one of the 17 countries that qualifies for International Development Assistance (IDA), the World Bank's special program for the poorest countries.)

Baker's initiative was prompted by the fact that in the fall of 1985, renewed momentum was needed to resolve the debt crisis. While progress had been made since the outbreak of the debt crisis in August 1982 in terms of debtor countries starting on the road to recovery and banks strengthening their balance sheets (capital to asset ratios, particularly the ratio of capital to Third World debt), falling commodity prices and related slow growth were seriously jeopardizing the debtor countries' standards of living and fragile democratic governments. Moreover, the economic weakness of these countries was exacerbating the U.S. trade deficit, as many of them had been traditional markets for U.S. exports.

Baker's initiative to promote structural reform and thereby break down entrenched inefficiencies was an ambitious one that required major financing, much of which would have to be external. In particular, Baker called on commercial banks to provide $20 billion in *new* loans over the following three years to the 15 countries that he identified as being most heavily in need. Additionally, he called on the multilateral development banks, notably the World Bank, to increase their disbursements by $3 billion a year. The new lending, however, was to be conditional on the recipient country undertaking significant free-market-oriented structural reforms.

Progress in implementing the Baker Plan is informally monitored by the Office of International Debt Policy of the U.S. Department of the Treasury. Its statistics show some degree of financial success. From October 1985 to the present, commercial banks have lent $17 billion in new money, while rescheduling $214 billion of old debt; concurrently, the IMF has disbursed $7.1 billion (Special Drawing Rights $5.2 billion), and the World Bank has committed $15.5 billion to the "Baker countries," most of which has been disbursed.

With respect to the degree of structural reform undertaken by the "Baker countries," the record is mixed. The three success stories are Colombia, Chile, and, to a lesser degree, Uruguay; they are approaching the point where they would qualify for new *voluntary* lending by the banks. Moreover, there have been some extensive reforms such as the Austral Plan in Argentina and the Tropical or Cruzado Plan in Brazil. Nonetheless, the reforms overall have been grossly inadequate in terms of the magnitude of the problems that these countries are facing.

—*Eugene Sarver*

ticeable individual adjustments. Their actions have served to reduce the seriousness of the international threat to the banks. However, the threat is still there, and many of the banks are removing themselves as much as possible from any new financial ties with the developing world.

Many international banks have enjoyed high profits during the past few years. As interest rates have declined, so has the cost of the banks' funding—and even more rapidly than have the rates charged to borrowers. Some banks have used this opportunity to reduce the amount of LDC credits on their balance sheets by taking a "hit" against profits or capital by writing down all or part of their exposure in certain countries or to certain borrowers.

Many banks have also increased their capital, which can be accomplished by keeping more retained earnings (when profits are high) or, even better,

increasing loan-loss reserves—with pretax money. The increase of capital can also be realized by issuing either stock or bonds. A larger capital base and loan-loss reserve reduce the banks' exposure to the threat of default on their LDC loans.

Selling and swapping loans: During the past several years, a secondary market in LDC loans has developed. Some of the discounts on LDC credits are very substantial. If a country has the resources, swaps could be a very wise investment—a chance to retire part of its debt at bargain prices. Bolivia was able to buy half of its international debt from its creditors at an average price of only twelve cents on the dollar.

However, many more LDC loans are being swapped or exchanged by the lenders than are being sold. Billions of dollars of such transactions have occurred every year for the past several years. In some cases, these "loan conversions" have involved debt for debt exchange. With these loan swaps (and also loan sales), the total amount of the borrower's debts generally remain unchanged—only the owner of those credits changes.

An increasingly popular form of loan conversion involves exchanging debt for equity. Swaps of loans for equity generally involve the debtor government as a party to the agreement and generally lead to a reduction of the borrower's total debts.

In addition to adjustments in assets and equity, there has also been a strong shift among the major international banks in policies, priorities, and even financial activities. These adjustments have helped buffer most of the banks against the threats from their LDC debt portfolios.

One change has been a strong shift away from a willingness by banks to lend to LDCs. They have already suffered large losses by excessive exposure to the LDCs. Still, huge potential losses remain. The threat leads to much worry and additional work for the bankers—and closer scrutiny by boards of directors and regulators.

At the same time, banks are being drawn to other markets in response to deregulation and competition from other types of financial institutions that threaten to erode banks' markets. In the United States, the advent of interstate banking, the rapid increase in competition from nonbanks (savings and loans associations, credit unions, nonbank credit cards, brokerage houses, and even retailers, such as Sears with its Discover card), the shift of traditional customers to direct funding in the money and capital markets (thus bypassing the commercial banks), and the progressive dismantling of the restrictions on investment banking are offering both opportunity and threat.

All of these developments pull bankers' attention away from the developing countries. So do the domestic problem areas of commercial banks: oil and natural gas, real estate, and agriculture. This shift of focus and the increased interest in nonlending activities (e.g., advisory services, such as mergers and acquisitions, and the underwriting of Eurobonds) that bring fees without adding assets (i.e., loans) to the books is not a passing fancy. It is a fundamental change in commercial banking, meaning that debtor countries are going to have increasing difficulty in finding commercial (private-sector) sources of financing.

Although the acuteness of the threat has declined, the international financial system remains allergic to further serious economic shocks—whether from rising oil prices, rising interest rates, default by a major borrower, or any of a variety of other potentially system-disrupting crises. Recovery remains tenuous, and the inaccessibility of the developing countries to the private financial markets remains a serious problem.

This is a potentially explosive situation. Both humanitarianism and the self-interest of the industrial countries dictate that serious efforts must be undertaken to ameliorate those conditions. However, without access to the private financial markets, there will not likely be sufficient funding for most of the countries.

What is needed is a comprehensive response to this dual threat. Short-term, ad hoc responses are wholly inadequate, yet they have been offered since the debt crisis began.

A comprehensive response to the debt problem must attack both dimensions of the situation—the threat of the overhang to debtors and creditors as well as the problem of access to future funding by the developing countries. The bottom line for the accomplishment of these two objectives is the protection and buttressing of the international financial system. Failing that, neither objective is attainable.

Solution of these problems requires the participation and cooperation of many groups: the debtors, the private creditors, the creditor governments, the international agencies, and perhaps even new participants (such as the insurance industry).

Hampering the task of resolving the crisis has been the reticence of any leader to initiate the process of comprehensive reform. Perhaps what is needed is another Bretton Woods conference bringing all the major parties together. The catalyst might be a major creditor government. It might be a major creditor bank. It could even be a critical debtor.

The most likely candidates for the role are the IMF and the World Bank. They will be critical in the success of any outcome, and both have the credibility and resources to get the process moving.*

---

* A more comprehensive discussion of the history and current status of Third World debt, and of the author's recommendations can be found in his article, "The Vulnerability of the International Financial System," in *Rekindling Development: Multinational Corporations and Third World Debt*, Lee A. Tavis, ed. (South Bend, Indiana: University of Notre Dame Press, 1988), 169–204.

A Way Out for the Debtors

Eugene Sarver

Eugene Sarver is author of The Eurocurrency Market Handbook *and is a professor at the Lubin Graduate School at Pace University in New York.*

The $1.2 trillion Third World debt crisis justifiably continues to attract global attention. It was the subject of an initiative by Treasury Secretary Baker in 1985 and very recently has been placed near the top of the agenda for the G-7 (group of seven leading industrial nations) meeting scheduled in early 1989. Even General Secretary Gorbachev focused attention on it in his December address to the United Nations in New York.

However, the General Secretary unfortunately reinforced the myth that the solution to the debt crisis is simply one of money—he spoke of debt forgiveness and very long-term reschedulings (a benevolent posture facilitated by the fact that Soviet debt exposures total less than 5 percent of Western exposures). To serious students of the debt crisis, the real solution requires throwing intelligence and integrity at it, not just more money.

The severity of the debt crisis can be measured in several ways, such as the amount of debt in arrears with respect to principal and even interest payments, or in the degree to which banks are willing to voluntarily lend money to debtor countries. However, an effective "quick" approach is simply to look at what discounts from face value that LDC (Less Developed Country) debt is trading at in the secondary market. While several brokerage houses and commercial banks such as Shearson and Citibank participate in the market, Salomon Brothers is a market leader and has provided its Indicative Prices for Less Developed Country Bank Loans.

On average, LDC debt trades at a 50 percent discount (see table), and as low as at a 98 percent discount, on the "bid" side for Nicaraguan debt. Moreover, many traditionally strong countries are currently trading debts at drastic discounts, such as: Argentina (82 percent), Brazil (61 percent), Mexico (57 percent), and Nigeria (76 percent).

The first myth to dispel is that the LDC countries simply borrowed too much. For example, South Korea borrowed approximately as much as Argentina, yet never had any problem repaying it. Indeed, developed countries borrow far vaster sums and rarely have a "debt crisis."

So what is the problem? The problem is that the LDCs have *not* invested the money in such a way as to produce an income stream of sufficient magnitude to make the requisite interest and principal payments. Why haven't they?

The wrong turn

First of all, a lot of money simply disappeared through capital flight, much of it to the United States. (Ironically, much of the capital flight was funneled out by the same banks that lent the money. While their institutional lending divisions were busy shoveling in the money, the equally industrious, bonus-oriented private international banking departments were busy taking the money out, explaining that "if we don't do it, some other bank will.") The Mexicans, who have exported as much as $70 billion (Bank for International Settlements [BIS] statistics show that Mexicans have over $30 billion alone in bank accounts in its reporting countries), seem to be reclaiming Texas, starting with Padre Island, while bankers have spoken pejoratively of Venezuela and Argentina as "revolving doors."

The enormous magnitude of the capital flight was due to several factors, including overvalued exchange rates that provided a highly temporary opportunity to buy "cheap dollars," negative real domestic interest rates (i.e., nominal interest rates *below* the inflation rate, causing the domestic investor to lose money), and a fear by the local plutocracy that their ill-gotten gains were in jeopardy.

Second, borrowed funds were used for unproductive consumer goods or military expenditures. Chile, for example, went on a spending spree in Asia, flooding its inadequate highway system with spiffy Japanese cars and its stores with low-priced dry goods from the "four tigers," (Hong Kong, Taiwan, South Korea, and Singapore). More reprehensibly, Argentina and Peru went on shopping expeditions for high-priced military hardware of no value whatever to their laboring classes. (Loaded up with war toys, Peru went on to fight an inconclusive war in the Ecuadorean jungle, and Argentina undertook its disastrous invasion of the Falkland Islands.)

Third, a lot of the money ended up simply financing huge government deficits, which approached as much as

16 percent of GNP in the case of Mexico. The magnitude of the fiscal deficits not only reflects excessive spending (including graft and short-term welfare measures to quell the masses), but shockingly low tax receipts. Massive tax evasion is commonplace in these countries, and the tax authorities have evinced little interest in rectifying it.

Fourth, in those few instances in which the borrowed money actually went to enhance productive capacity, the money frequently was invested in high-cost import substitution industries. Instead of being committed to industries in which the countries had a comparative advantage in the style of the export-oriented Asian economies, the money often was invested in high-cost input substitution industries.

Given the generally imprudent use of borrowed funds, it is surprising that the LDCs are not in worse shape. Some progress has been made, however, as lessons have been learned. Moreover, the LDCs have been influenced by the global shift from the public to the private sector, exemplified by the policies of such Western leaders as Reagan, Thatcher, Chirac, and now even Gorbachev via perestroika.

Needed: world response

As the global debt crisis is multidimensioned, so must be the solution. Although many of the problems are highly complex, others can be solved relatively easily if the political will is present.

Before listing a menu of necessary changes, it is vital to emphasize that the major problem is *not* a lack of resources, but rather a misallocation of them. Most of the economic advances of mankind are due less to movements along the production curve than to shifts in it. What this means is that most increases in production are not due to using factor inputs (labor, machinery, etc.), but rather to combining factor inputs in a more efficient way through advances in technology.

This general line of reasoning is emphasized by Edward J. Frydl, vice president and assistant director of research of the Federal Reserve Bank of New York and author (with Dorothy M. Sobol) of its study "A Perspective on the Debt Crisis." His research shows that the "Baker countries" generally have adequate savings ratios—it is just that the money is not optimally invested.

Some obvious recommendations are for the LDCs to substantially reduce corruption, which squander, so much money, to implement massive tax reform, and to improve tax collection efforts. These moves would significantly reduce the burdensome fiscal deficits that lie behind their excessive inflation and related lack of confidence.

Related necessities are not only to drastically reduce capital flight through tough, efficiently enforced

criminal penalties, but to promote repatriation of significant amounts of the LDC capital invested abroad. Given the fact that rates of return are significantly higher in the LDCs than in the industrialized countries, reinvestment should require merely a matter of developing workable administrative mechanisms and reasonable confidence levels.

Moving on to economic measures, a simple requirement would be to maintain a competitive as opposed to an overvalued exchange rate. While overvalued currencies are temporarily helpful in moderating inflation, the costs generally exceed the benefits as exports are reduced and imports and capital flight are encouraged. Given the high inflation rate of most LDCs, constant adjustments of their exchange rates are vital through "crawling peg" devaluations (systematic small ones), complemented by occasional "maxis" (large devaluations) if needed. Relatedly, export taxes should be avoided, as they have the same impact as overvalued exchange rates and result in suboptimal domestic resource allocations. Additionally, to implement an export-oriented policy, multiple exchange rates should be avoided. Such tiered systems, with a variety of financial and commercial rates, are condemned by the IMF and inevitably lead to economic inefficiencies.

Next, the LDCs should move drastically to reduce the size of the public sector, shifting their socialistic command economies to free-market economies. While perhaps 25 years ago, the scarcity of financial and human capital (skilled people) in the Third World justified government-owned business enterprises, that time is long past. Even countries as poor and socialistically doctrinaire as Tanzania are shifting toward private enterprise.

To accelerate the shift from public to private enterprise, foreign capital should be welcomed. Such investment, whether direct or via debt-equity swaps (whereby a foreign investor buys LDC debt at a discount and trades it with the LDC's central bank for local currency at or near face value to be used in a domestic equity investment), strengthens the country's financial position. Moreover, foreign investors bring not only capital but critically needed managerial skills and superior technologies.

A debt barometer: The magnitude of Third World debt can be understood by looking at the discounts below face value of less developed country debt in the secondary market.

Country	% of Face Value of Debt ($)				% of Face Value of Debt ($)	
	Bid	Offer		Country	Bid	Offer
Algeria	85.00	87.00		Nicaragua	2.00	4.00
Argentina	17.50	18.50		Nigeria	22.00	25.00
Bolivia	10.00	11.00		Panama	21.00	23.00
Brazil	36.75	39.75		Peru	5.00	6.00
Chile	53.25	54.25		Philippines	49.50	50.50
Colombia	55.00	57.00		Poland	34.50	36.50
Costa Rica	11.00	12.00		Romania	93.00	95.00
Dom. Rep.	21.50	23.50		Senegal	50.00	52.00
Ecuador	12.50	13.50		Sudan	2.00	5.00
Honduras	22.00	24.00		Uruguay	59.50	60.50
Ivory Coast	25.00	28.00		Venezuela	40.00	40.75
Jamaica	40.00	42.50		Yugoslavia	44.50	46.00
Mexico	42.50	43.25		Zaire	20.00	23.00
Morocco	48.50	50.00				

Source:Salomon Brothers, 11-23-88

RISKING THE LIFEBOAT

Having battled to keep Third World debtors afloat during seven years of crisis, the World Bank and the IMF are beginning to find they have an incipient debt problem of their own. Arrears on loans made by the two institutions are rising sharply, provoking mounting concern that the Bank and Fund may have to consider the unthinkable – reschedule the debts owed to them, or, probably more likely, concoct some alternative refinancing scheme to get them off the hook.

Publicly, IMF and Bank officials insist they have the situation under control. Together the agencies hold only about 15 per cent of total Third World debt, excluding short-term commercial claims, but there are signs that their position may become increasingly difficult.

Rescheduling or some other form of debt relief "will absolutely have to be faced by the multilaterals [the IMF and World Bank] in the next five years", says Mark Constantine, a veteran staff member on a key House of Representatives banking subcommittee. Princeton University economic analyst Peter Kennan says the IMF has maintained short-term and medium-term lending to some of the weakest economies in recent years, as "a response to the fact that these countries cannot repay what they owe. But the Fund is running out of time. It has found itself in the midst of the problem and cannot extricate itself. In fact, it's going in deeper." Unless economic conditions for the developing countries improve dramatically, "it's going to be harder for the Fund and the Bank to avoid the issue of rescheduling," Kennan says.

Talk of rescheduling amounts to heresy at both institutions. The Bank shudders at the idea because it fears, rightly, that such a move would jeopardise its rock-solid credit rating in the international capital markets, where the Bank raises most of the money it lends to the Third World. Since the Bank is considered such a good credit risk, it borrows relatively cheaply, and passes on some of the savings in its own loans. "We are an institution trying to recycle money from the capital markets," says Ishrat Husain, chief of the Bank's international finance and debt division. He believes it would be "suicidal" for the Bank

Arrears on World Bank and IMF loans to developing countries are mounting. Analysts are speculating that these agencies may have to think the unthinkable and consider rescheduling the debts owed to them.

to reschedule, since its own creditors would then raise the cost of their money – and the Third World would bear the brunt.

The IMF opposes rescheduling for different reasons. The agency does not borrow commercially, but operates like a revolving door, using repayments from one short-term loan to finance the next. Its fear is that rescheduling would tie up resources, undermining the institution's basic operating principle, although it has built up a huge cash reserve over the years.

Despite the arguments against rescheduling, the agencies may be forced to ease their claims on some borrowers in the next few years, if, as many experts fear, external financing and economic conditions in the Third World do not improve.

At present the IMF and the Bank are forced to cut off all lending to countries which fail to service their debts for more than six months. Each agency has taken this drastic step for nine countries. Six of them – Guyana, Liberia, Panama, Peru, Sierra Leone and Zambia – are in the dismal position of being shut out of both institutions. Once barred from the multilaterals' loans, a country's chances of getting back on its feet diminish greatly, because other creditors usually stop lending as well. Overdue payments of principal and interest to the Bank and Fund together total about US$5-billion. With interest rates at 7-8 per cent, interest arrears are compounding rapidly. The situation would worsen abruptly if a big debtor, such as Argentina, were to slide into more than six months of arrears.

The Bank has set aside about US$420-million in loan loss reserves and reckons last year's income would have been 25 per

cent higher were it not for unpaid debts. The IMF board, too, has had to cushion itself against loan loss, by levying new charges on all members. It became sufficiently alarmed last year to instal a special adviser on the issue, India's former director to the IMF board, Arjun Sengupta. Arrears, he says, are "a very serious problem" for the IMF, because, as a de facto rescheduling, they run counter to the agency's aim of recycling funds for short-term use.

Hopes for a breakthrough were raised earlier this year, when Guyana won a pledge of assistance from industrial nations in clearing its arrears, provided it

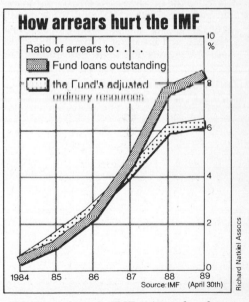

How arrears hurt the IMF

Ratio of arrears to . . . .
▨ Fund loans outstanding
▢ the Fund's adjusted ordinary resources

1984 85 86 87 88 89
Source: IMF (April 30th)

Richard Natkiel Assocs

sticks to a tough IMF-approved reform programme until the end of December. But the delicately constructed strategy looks likely to fail because of Guyana's dire economic circumstances. One IMF board member believes if that were to happen, the question of rescheduling or restructuring the arrears would be raised again.

Another concern is the increase in the Bank's and the IMF's share of developing country debt. By 1990, the Bank is expected to hold about US$50-billion in claims on 17 big debtors – double its shares of their combined debt just five years ago.

From *South*, The Third World Magazine, October 1989, pp. 21–23. Reprinted by permission of South Syndication Service.

6. EASING THE DEBT CRISIS

Although it has decreased its overall exposure since 1985, the IMF has been forced to make relatively large loans to poor African countries which were unable to repay the agency's expensive quick-fix loans in the early 1980s. By issuing these new loans at negligible interest and with longer maturities than regular IMF loans, the agency

STILL MOUNTING
Countries with accumulated arrears of principal and interest on IMF loans at 30 April

	Arrears (US$m)
Sudan	956.3
Zambia	790.0
Peru	716.3
Liberia	326.3
Panama	146.3
Vietnam	125.0
Guyana	115.0
Sierra Leone	75.0
Somalia	75.0
Total	**3325.2**

Source: IMF

hopes to avoid another repayments problem, but analysts like Kennan believe it may have thrown good money after bad. The agency has also softened its standards for approving regular loans, for example to Argentina and Zaire, sources contend.

The multilateral agencies' exposure, and thus their risk, will increase further if the Brady plan for reducing commercial debts proceeds as planned. The strategy involves enticing commercial banks to reduce the loan, or the interest on their current loans, by offering Bank, IMF and other public guarantees for the remaining debt. Since the IMF and the Bank plan to lend borrowers the money for their guarantees, the

agencies' exposure to troubled debtors will increase. "It is a risk," says one Bank official, "but it's a risk the board has decided to take."

The problem is not just the increase in the stock of debt, but the nature of the payments falling due. Since the agencies do not reschedule, an increase in their share of claims gives their big borrowers less breathing space if, as seems likely, they run into debt-servicing difficulties in the future. So far, debtor countries have won considerable relief through reschedulings by commercial banks and industrial country governments.

With no viable alternatives to the plan in sight, the IMF and Bank are hoping that a couple of key possibilities will work in their favour. If debt reduction works as planned, borrowers struggling with heavy commercial claims will be economically

FALLING BEHIND WITH THE PAYMENTS
(A) Countries more than six months overdue on debt repayments and interest to the World Bank as at June 30
(B) Sums overdue to World Bank for more than 30 days, but less than six months at June 30 (US$m)

	A Total overdue		B Total overdue
Guyana	40	Argentina	53
Honduras	64	Brazil	41
Liberia	62	Côte d'Ivoire	20
Nicaragua	149	Egypt	50
Panama	137	El Salvador	9
Peru	512	Jamaica	12
Sierra Leone	4	Nigeria	38
Syria	173	Yugoslavia	19
Zambia	169	Other	44
Total	**1,310**	**Total**	**286**
		GRAND TOTAL = 1,596	

Source: World Bank

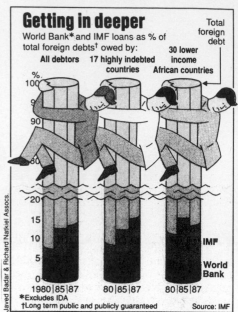

Getting in deeper
World Bank* and IMF loans as % of total foreign debts† owed by:
All debtors — 17 highly indebted countries — 30 lower income African countries
Total foreign debt
1980|85|87   80|85|87   80|85|87
*Excludes IDA
†Long term public and publicly guaranteed
IMF
World Bank
Javed Badar & Richard Natkiel Assocs.
Source: IMF

strengthened and better able to cope with the debts that remain. And if commercial banks resume new lending to their major debtors, the Bank and IMF will be able to hold their own exposure to a small proportion of countries' total debts. Then, since the agencies are considered first among all creditors when repayments are due, they will be fairly secure. If things do not work out as planned, however, the IMF and Bank will be in for a bumpy ride.

Samantha Sparks in Washington

Going it Alone

After abandoning an IMF-supported economic adjustment program in May, the Zambian government has launched its own reform effort. But donors warn that the new plan fails to come to grips with the fundamental issue—how to restructure the economy away from dependence on Zambia's finite copper resources.

ANDREW MELDRUM

Andrew Meldrum, an American journalist who has been based in Zimbabwe for six years, reports on southern Africa for The Guardian *of London, Agence France-Presse, and the Voice of America.*

Zambia

Something unusual in Africa, a four-lane divided highway, stretches through the 50 miles of rolling country-side between the copperbelt cities of Ndola and Kitwe.

The attractive, landscaped highway is testimony to the years when Zambia's copperbelt province was booming, providing the entire country with wealth.

In the 1960s, when the price of copper was high, Zambia was one of Africa's wealthiest countries, with one of the continent's highest per capita incomes. The copperbelt was the country's gleaming mining and industrial hub, a shiny and prosperous showcase of African development with new factories, roads, and modern cities.

In May this year, Zambia became Africa's economic equivalent of Brazil when it withdrew from an International Monetary Fund agreement, a dramatic demonstration of the country's fall from one of Africa's most prosperous nations to one of its most desperate debtors.

Today, the copperbelt cities are in what seems a chronic decline, compara-ble to Britain's depressed industrial north and America's "rustbelt" cities. Copper mining, the source of Zambia's wealth, is now blamed for its economic woes as the mineral has steadily lost value since 1974.

The highly urbanized copperbelt, which alone holds one-third of Zambia's 7 million people, now has a large and restive unemployed workforce as its industries operate at a fraction of their capacities due to the resulting chronic shortage of foreign currency.

The copperbelt cities—Ndola, Kitwe, Chingola, Mufulira, and Luanshya—were the flashpoints for the food riots in December last year that left 15 people dead and brought President Kenneth Kaunda's government to abandon an IMF economic restructuring program and limit payments on its $5.3 billion foreign debt to well under 10 percent of its annual export earnings.

"We used to call the copperbelt 'Africa's Switzerland' because we were building highways, factories, office buildings, schools, and hospitals," said a Zambian worker, remembering the boom years.

"I can remember when in school we would line up each day for a free glass of milk. Now the schools all have broken windows and many children cannot afford shoes," he said. "Of course, the free milk has been gone for a long time."

And the free schooling is gone, too. Unable to continue bearing the cost of education, the Zambian government, in its new post-IMF economic plan, began to charge parents for primary education through fees payable to local councils. Parents must meet secondary boarding school fees and industry is being asked to help pay for higher education costs.

Zambia's rich copper deposits, used by Africans for centuries for jewelry and wire, were exploited by British colonialists in the early 1920s. To obtain labor for the mines, the colonial authorities imposed a hut tax which forced peasant farmers to go to the mines to earn cash. Soon large populations sprang up around the mines and the colonial government kept urban food prices attractively low.

Today, Zambia has the highest percentage of urbanized population in Africa. Close to 45 percent of Zambia's people live in cities, compared with neighboring Zimbabwe's 15 percent or Malawi's 8 percent. One result is that Zambia's rural agricultural production has slumped and its fertile lands have not produced enough grain to feed the population for more than 10 years. The government has had to use valuable foreign currency to import the staple maize.

For years, economists have advised Zambia to diversify away from its total dependence on copper, which accounts for more than 90 percent of the country's $750 million in annual export earnings. Soon the country will be forced to become independent of copper earnings because mining experts say that by the year 2000, the copper deposits will be finished. Already the grade of copper has declined steeply, causing a fall in output by the state-controlled giant, Zambian Consolidated Copper Mines (ZCCM).

Yet the reliance on copper exports continues, largely because Zambia's industries are import-dependent.

"Zambia, along with Zimbabwe, has the most developed industrial infrastructure in sub-Saharan Africa," said a Scandinavian diplomat in Lusaka. "But Zambia's industrialization, much of it carried out in the 1960s, is unfortunately horizontal and too dependent upon foreign currency."

Many of Zambia's industries depend on imported raw materials and imported machinery, said the diplomat, and therefore the shortage of foreign currency has reduced the industries to functioning at about 30 percent of capacity.

That changed in 1986 when the IMF economic restructuring plan was in effect. Scarce foreign currency was auctioned off to the highest bidders each week. During the year and a half it was in operation, the auctioning system drastically devalued the Zambian kwacha from 2.20 kwacha to the dollar in October 1985 to 21 kwacha to the

"For years, economists have advised Zambia to diversify away from its total dependence on copper"

dollar in May 1987, when the currency auction was suspended.

Bankers and Western aid donors still praise the auction system as an efficient means of setting the kwacha at its proper value and of quickly distributing the foreign exchange.

"Any business or industry that needed to buy necessary spare parts or inputs could do so at the auction and they could get their factories going," said a Western diplomat. "During the auctioning, Zambian industry began to operate at better than 60 percent of capacity."

But since the May pull-out from the IMF program, the government has set the kwacha at eight to the dollar and has set up an unwieldy system to distribute foreign currency. Businessmen glumly report that industrial capacity is beginning a downward slide to the pre-auction 30 percent figure. The fixed rate of eight kwacha to the dollar makes Zambia's imports less expensive, but Lusaka's black market rate is at 20 kwacha to the dollar, indicating that the fixed rate values the kwacha too highly.

Perhaps the auctioning system alone would have been acceptable in Zambia, but it was coupled with IMF pressure on the Kaunda government to cut government spending on social services and to keep wages at a fixed rate while subsi-

dies on food were ended and food prices were allowed to increase dramatically.

Zambians had already seen their real per capita income fall by 45 percent over a 10-year period. When the price of the staple maize meal was increased 120 percent in December 1986, the people reacted violently. The increase raised a 50-kilo bag of the meal to the equivalent of $7.50, almost half the average monthly wage. The angry riots were not quelled until the price rise was rescinded.

After the food riots, the government tried to raise the price of fuel, but backed down after one day. With continued pressure from the IMF and with elections due in 1988, President Kaunda chose to break with the Fund on May 1, Workers Day, telling Zambians his government would restructure the economy in "a more humane way."

The Zambian withdrawal is a blow for the IMF. It had lent more to Zambia than to any other country in sub-Saharan Africa. An estimated $800 million is currently owed to the IMF, of which $100 million represents arrears in repayments. There were also crushing debt repayments, taking up well over 50 percent of Zambia's foreign exchange earnings. New IMF loans and donor assistance amounted to less than Zambia's loan repayments. Hence, the country, like much of the rest of Africa, was paying out more than it received.

Kenneth Kaunda dramatically unveiled Zambia's "go it alone" economic plan on national television in August, calling for Zambians to stimulate "growth from our own resources" and to support it with "discipline."

The Interim National Development Plan runs from July 1987 through December 1988 and charts spending of $412.5 million to generate 2.2 percent growth during the period.

The economic plan was greeted by a Western diplomat in Lusaka as "fairly laudable, surprisingly in line with the previous IMF plan, but too highly generalized a plan that is not easily translatable into practical policies."

According to government projections, the plan envisions a net 1988 budget deficit of $194 million, up from $187 million in 1987. Central to the new plan is the replacement of the auction system with a Foreign Exchange Management Committee to allocate the foreign exchange to key sectors of the economy. With the kwacha set at eight to the dollar, many businesses are clamoring for more foreign exchange and the new committee is charged with determining who will get the chronically short commodity.

"The great advantage of the auction was that it was a straightforward mechanism which effectively removed corruption from the system," said a Western diplomat. "In the new system, there are 13 signatures needed to apply for foreign exchange. Each of those signatures is a bureaucratic hurdle, with potential for corruption. Many feel that forex will gradually go back to those with the most influence."

The target areas for investment are mining and agriculture, with copper mining receiving $78.1 million, substantially up from the $10.7 million in the 1987 budget. The declining quality of Zambian copper means that new machinery and other major investments are needed to maintain its vital export earnings. Zam-

bia's copper mining giant, ZCCM, will receive 338 million kwacha of that total as part of its ongoing $300 million capital stock rehabilitation program.

However, according to economic analysts, the plan does not specify how it will solve ZCCM's chief problems—the high level of taxation on the mineral which makes it virtually impossible for the company to make a profit and its need for foreign currency.

Agriculture is seen as Zambia's only long-term hope to improve its economic performance, but again the plan does not clarify how existing problems in that sector are to be solved.

The small commercial farming sector will be encouraged to increase production of tobacco and sugar, especially for export sales. The export of horticultural fruits like strawberries is also suggested. The commercial sector already produces much of Zambia's wheat, dairy products, and vegetables, but the large-scale farmers are badly in need of foreign exchange for spare parts for tractors and other machinery and for new seeds and chemicals.

But the vast amount of Zambia's agriculture is in its peasant sector and this is where analysts fear that the new plan is not coming to grips with the country's pressing problems. Guaranteed prices of the staple, maize, to the rural smallholders have not been increased sufficiently to act as incentives for peasants to produce more, say agricultural experts. Instead, the government plan maintains the subsidies which keep the price of maize low for the urban population.

"Something needs to be done to improve the possibilities for the rural farmer," said an aid worker. "Even if the peasant earns more money, there is very little for him to buy with it in few, poorly stocked stores. There are not many good roads to receive seeds, fertilizers, and supplies, nor are there many schools or health facilities. These people do not have a voice."

Another problem, say aid officials and diplomats, is that the Ministry of Agriculture and the Ministry of Cooperatives are understood to be corrupt and inefficient. The government's National Agricultural Marketing Board is notoriously corrupt, and the United States is said to be pressing to allow the private sector to take over some of its functions.

"The government has long paid lip service to the need to improve the peasant agricultural sector. It is even talking of resettling some unemployed city-dwellers on peasant farms," said a long-time observer. "But there is no sign that it is doing anything to solve the problems."

In the face of this bleak economic outlook, there are a few positive signs. Canada, Denmark, and Sweden have converted some of their loans to Zambia to grants. Scandinavian support, in particular, remains strong. Despite Kaunda's urgings for self-sufficiency, there is no question that Zambia remains dependent upon foreign aid.

On a larger scale, the most heartening signs are those which indicate a new mood among the major Western financiers to come to the aid of sub-Saharan debtors like Zambia. "If Zambia's debt burden could be eased, that would be a great relief," said a British diplomat.

Other analysts point out that the economic course plotted in the new plan is not radically different from the previous IMF plan. They suggest that true to its name—Interim National Development Plan—the program could be a stop-gap measure to allow the domestic situation to cool a bit and enable Kaunda to win election to a sixth term of office in 1988, then return to the IMF for restructuring.

"We know we're not rich anymore. The workers certainly do not live like it anymore," said a copperbelt resident. "We have tightened our belts already—perhaps the government and its bureaucrats need to do the same thing now."

A World in Change

Sadly, the Third World—far more than the industrialized world—faces a host of urgent social problems. These include malnutrition, poverty, illiteracy, disease, pollution, overpopulation, and war. To a large extent, these ills stem from social, political, and economic inequality. Despite numerous efforts, the developing world has failed to close the ever-widening gap between the have and have-not nations.

Like its industrialized counterpart, the Third World is extremely pluralistic. Obviously, one cannot compare such "poor countries" as Nigeria and Mexico to the "poor, poor nations" of Haiti and Bangladesh. Indeed, some developing countries have proven far more successful than others in achieving stability, unity, and economic progress. As such, it is difficult, if not impossible, to make sweeping generalizations about the status of the Third World.

With this caveat in mind, it is still possible to identify the principal challenges facing the developing world, chief of which is the problem of war and civil strife. In several Third World nations, one can easily discern any number of organizations, states, and private individuals who are actively engaged in fomenting or supporting violent campaigns to accomplish their objectives. This is clearly the case in the Philippines, Nicaragua, Lebanon, South Africa, and elsewhere. The problem has grown increasingly acute due to the widespread manufacture and proliferation of armaments, which has become an important industry in some Third World countries.

The developing world also faces numerous economic problems, fueled in recent years by the banks and multinational corporations which have fostered increased financial dependency. These institutions wield significant power in many Third World countries, often to the detriment of the people they seek to serve. In some cases, these international organizations function independently of their parent governments, with little accountability or responsibility. This situation is due, in part, to the dismal economic conditions in many developing nations which possess inadequate resources, limited technology, and fragile political institutions.

Equally important is the problem of resources—that is, their control, conservation, and distribution. Third World nations, like many other countries, have squandered precious resources, ignored environmental warnings, failed to develop alternative energy sources, and refused to impose strict limits on population growth. Reckless disregard for the environment—in the form of air, land, and water pollution—could pose a major disaster. Moreover, future industrial development in the Third World threatens to intensify the problem.

The battle for human rights represents yet another threat to the future of the Third World. Countless developing countries practice widespread political repression. Today, many Third World peoples live in a permanent state of tyranny and oppression. The number of dictatorships has multiplied, and with them the use of kidnapping, torture, imprisonment, and assassination, which are commonplace in many developing nations.

The Third World is also plagued by problems of immigration, emigration, and statelessness. In some countries, the lack of economic opportunity and political freedom has encouraged many talented young people to migrate to other nations where life appears more rewarding. In addition, the intensification of racial, religious, and ethnic rivalries has produced a new wave of problems, causing some developing nations to impose tight new immigration restrictions or order mass expulsions.

In summary, one must ask: In what direction is the Third World headed? What new problems will it confront in the future? Is it reasonable to expect these nations—given their present economic conditions—to solve such critical problems as hunger, poverty, unemployment, and overpopulation? Clearly, solving the problems of the Third World will demand unprecedented resolve and ingenuity. The challenges of the future will require a major commitment of human and material resources. The developing world cannot continue to bury its head in the sand; it must meet the challenges of the twenty-first century head-on. Unless they act now, Third World nations may well lose many of the benefits of their hard-won independence and face a hostile world which has little if any interest in their future.

Looking Ahead: Challenge Questions

To what degree is the Western world responsible for the increase in international drug trafficking?

How has terrorism changed in recent years?

What should the main features of a successful counter-terrorist campaign be?

What dangers, if any, does the acquisition of ballistic missiles pose to the future of the Third World?

Why is the Third World fast becoming the global dump?

What, if anything, can be done to control the international shipment of waste?

Why do millions of people a year move to the large cities of Asia, Africa, and South America?

How have poor energy choices led to deforestation, desertification, indebtedness, and dependence in many developing nations?

Why is the problem of world hunger too big, too pervasive, and too permanent for any one country to solve alone?

Who is responsible for the misuse of pesticides in the developing world?

What lessons should the Third World learn from the Kerala experiment?

What major challenges are most likely to confront the Third World in the twenty-first century?

THE DRUG WAR

MARC W. CHERNICK

ALMOST MONTHLY, A FEELING OF COLLEC-
tive anguish seizes the political elite of Bogotá.
Estamos tocando fondo, people say. We have finally hit
bottom. In 1985 it was heard when the military massacred
guerrillas, Supreme Court justices and scores of trapped
hostages following the guerrilla takeover of the Palace of
Justice in the center of Bogotá. *Estamos tocando fondo*. It
was heard again in 1987 after the brutal assassination of
the president of the Unión Patriótica, the new left political
party, and again in 1988 after the killing of Colombia's independent attorney general.

Yet the despair rarely lasts. It is banished like an
unwelcome intruder, and then quickly forgotten when
several weeks pass without serious incident. Colombia's
elites have an extraordinary capacity for optimism and
self-delusion. They have an uncanny instinct for survival
amid an all-consuming violence in which many of them
are, directly and indirectly, victim and perpetrator. The
staccato interruptions caused by the major assassinations
only focus the mind temporarily.

It is more comfortable to understand the violence as an
aberration and to return to the familiar language of
"perfecting" Colombia's democracy. It is easier to ignore that, by 1988, more than 10 persons were being
murdered daily for ideological reasons, reaching a total of
3,011 *documented* political assassinations, and countless
others that were never reported.[1] And these are in addition
to the 379 members of the armed forces and 599 guerrillas
who died in combat during 1988 alone in a war that has
lasted for decades.[2] And, of course, then there are the
massive displacements of people and entire villages due
to stepped-up fighting in parts of the countryside. In these
and other regions, violence is a way of life. The people
have been *tocando fondo* for a very long time.

Yet the assassination of Senator Luis Carlos Galán, a
leading presidential candidate, on August 18, 1989, sent
shivers up and down the spine of Colombia's political
elite. Across five columns in large bold letters, the Bogotá
daily *La Prensa* summarized the mood that spread across
the country, but particularly across the wealthy residential
neighborhoods in the north of Bogotá, on the morning
after the assassination: *¡No puede ser no puede ser no
puede ser no puede ser no puede ser!* The headlines
screamed, it can't be, it can't be, it can't be, it can't be.
And for the leaders of Colombia's two ruling parties, the
Liberals and Conservatives, there was a sense that they
were exposed and vulnerable. The terror that had consumed the countryside was now being directed at them.

In the mid-1980s, the death squads began to target and
occasionally execute high political officials from the
traditional parties. On April 30, 1984, the cartels murdered the Justice Minister Rodrigo Lara Bonilla, in retaliation for his cooperation with U.S. Drug Enforcement
Administration agents and his high profile attack on the
drug trade. Six weeks earlier, Colombian police and DEA
officials had made the largest cocaine bust then on record
with the seizure of a huge refining plant on the Yarí River
belonging to the Medellín cartel.[3]

The assassination sparked the first of a series of declared "wars" by the government against the drug traffickers. The president at the time, Belisario Betancur,
invoked a state of siege, and went after traffickers, laboratories and property. He also reversed himself on the
controversial issue of extradition and announced that he
would implement the treaty signed with the United States
by the preceding government. The first extraditions in
early 1985 led to a spate of violence against Colombian
judges and a car bomb exploded outside the U.S. Embassy.

The first drug war soon subsided, however, and the
traffickers who had sought refuge in Panama returned
home within a year. While in Panama, the leading members of the Medellín cartel, Pablo Escobar, Jorge Ochoa
and Gonzalo Rodríguez Gacha, met with former President Alfonso López Michelsen and with Attorney General Carlos Jiménez Gómez on separate occasions. They
reportedly offered to invest their profits in the Colombian
economy, pay the national debt of over $12 billion and
dismantle cocaine production facilities—in exchange for
an amnesty and the right to return to the country.

Back then the drug wars were still a side show. National politics were focused on negotiations with the
guerrillas and the democratic opening of the political
system—upon which Betancur had staked his prestige.
Even the M-19 takeover of the Palace of Justice in the
center of Bogotá on November 6, 1985 was over the
breakdown of the initial peace accords signed with the
guerrillas. (Exhaustive journalistic and judicial inquiries
have shown that the mindless repetition by U.S. officials
that the takeover was financed and engineered by the drug
traffickers has no basis in fact.[4])

Yet the drug trade was already changing Colombian
society and was limiting Betancur's chances to achieve a
peaceful settlement of the guerrilla war. While Betancur
was offering guarantees for the incorporation of the
guerrilla movements into political life, the drug dealers, in

From *NACLA Report on the Americas*, Vol. XXIII, No. 6, April 1990, pp. 30–38, 40. NACLA, North American Congress on
Latin America, Inc., 475 Riverside Drive, Suite 454, New York, NY 10115.

alliance with members of the armed forces, began operating death squads against the new forms of political activism the president encouraged. While Betancur's peace commission initiated talks on agrarian reform, the cartels began to invest some of their profits in land, creating what political scientist Francisco Leal has called a counteragrarian reform. On the eve of the cease-fire agreements themselves, signed with four guerrilla movements, Betancur was forced to declare a state of siege in response to the killing of his justice minister, Rodrigo Lara Bonilla, by the cartels.

THE U.S. EMBASSY, LED BY AMBASSADOR Lewis Tambs, tried to turn the nation's focus toward drugs by proffering the thesis of the "narco-guerrilla." Guerrillas were certainly active in the regions where coca is grown, and they taxed coca much like they tax all the products of their zones, be they potatoes, yucca or petroleum. But coca production was the least profitable end of the drug business. The real money was going to those who processed coca into cocaine, and then marketed the drug. These were hardly guerrillas.

The most visible of the principal actors, the members of the Medellín cartel, were men from lower middle class urban backgrounds whose careers proved that trafficking in marijuana and cocaine was one of the few viable routes for economic and social advancement in Colombia's rigidly stratified society.[5] Many were petty criminals before getting involved in the drug trade, like Carlos Lehder who served time in a U.S. prison in the mid-1970s for car theft.

Most references to the drug "kingpins" or "barons" alude to this group of nouveau riche narco-entrepreneurs. But from the beginning there have also been drug lords who operate with a much lower profile. These businessmen form part of the traditional social and political structures of the country. One hears of the Medellín cartel and names like Rodriguez Gacha and Pablo Escobar. There is not much said about the Cali cartel, except that it is less confrontational and more closely linked to middle-class professionals. Again, we know names, such as Gilberto Rodríguez Oreguela, reported to be its maximum leader. Almost no reference is made to the Bogotá cartel, though it exists. Moreover, the regional groupings in Barranquilla, Santa Marta, Pereira and Bucaramanga all seem to be intertwined with the structures of local and regional power and operate with little fanfare. The "drug wars" rarely touch these people. In fact, many of them appear to be uncomfortable with the way Escobar and company behave.[6]

THE "DRUG WAR" WAS DECLARED ONCE again in late 1986 after the publisher of the Bogotá daily *El Espectador* was gunned down. He had led an anti-drug crusade and the paper publicly endorsed the extradition treaty. The new president, Virgilio Barco, ordered raids on the traffickers' properties and a general crackdown on their operations. Barco decreed a "statute for the defense of democracy," which echoed the worst state of siege abuses from earlier periods, particularly the national security statute of the Turbay administration (1978-1982). Like the previous two "wars," this drug war faded quickly. And, as before, the enhanced military and police powers were employed against the Left, the guerrillas and popular organizations.

In response to Barco's drug war, the Medellín traffickers hunted down former Minister of Justice Enrique Parejo, who had replaced Lara Bonilla, and gunned him down on the streets of Budapest, where he was serving as Colombia's ambassador. Parejo somehow survived. The peculiar choice of a victim half-way around the world led some to speculate that a loose pattern had emerged. Both Parejo and Lara Bonilla had aided Luis Carlos Galán in founding a dissident faction, known as Nuevo Liberalismo, to oppose corruption in the Liberal Party. They were the only cabinet members that represented this faction. Following the murder of Lara Bonilla, Galán declared: "In this moment, the drug traffic knows that its enemy is Nuevo Liberalismo and for that reason wants to destroy it."[7] In fact, it was Galán and Lara Bonilla who had spearheaded the fight to have drug lord Pablo Escobar booted out of Congress. (He had been elected as an alternate in 1982 on the Liberal Party ticket.)

Despite all this high-profile violence, the story of the 1980s was not the drug war—or wars, skirmishes really—but the dirty war. By the end of the decade the paramilitary groups, tolerated by some and actively endorsed by others as a counterweight to the guerrillas and the Left, had escaped even the control of the military. As the dirty war escalated, the victims were beginning to come from higher social and political strata, and it became increasingly difficult to discern motives. In 1988 and 1989, the federal attorney general and the governor as well as the police chief of Antioquia (where Medellín is situated) were killed.

It was the death of Galán, more than any other, that brought the violence home to the political class. Although the Medellín cartel did claim responsibility in press interviews in the days that followed, there was no obvious motive for his murder.[8] Despite his early rhetoric, he had backed down on the drug issue. Galán's murder was interpreted by the political class as a signal that the political assassinations had entered a new phase. The drug traffickers were not only fighting those elements of the state who directly threatened their commercial interests, or their welfare. They were now actively employing violence to influence the course of politics on the national level—against those who had wronged them in the past, and who might impede their position in the future. The most violent ones, grouped in the Medellín cartel, were in some sense declaring their intention to assert their authority nationally as they had come to do at the regional and local levels. Galán's murder was their debut on the national stage.

Moreover, it came immediately on the heels of the creation of a new political party, MORENA (Movimiento de Renovación Nacional), that was directly tied to the Medellín cartel and the far Right, and which DAS, the civilian secret police, had linked to the paramilitary death squads. MORENA's political program calls for the destruction of communism and the defense of private property, claiming the state has abandoned its duty.[9] It appeared that the Medellín cartel was beginning to get impatient with the traditional political class, and was trying to create its own vehicle. It is a classic story of economic wealth seeking political influence.

AT THE TIME OF GALAN'S DEATH, MOST OBservers saw only two real contenders for the presidency. There was Galán himself, who had just re-entered the party after spearheading Nuevo Liberalismo, which appealed mostly to the small but growing urban middle and professional classes. Yet the early luster of Galán's image as a progressive and renovating force had already worn thin.

Opposing him was Hernando Durán Dussán, the candidate of the business interests, producers groups and much of the Liberal political machine. Durán, who had denounced dialogue with the guerrilla movements, represents not only the Right of the Liberal Party, but the right wing of politics in Colombia. The most reactionary and violent members of Colombian society, the drug dealers-cum-landowners publicly declared their support for Durán Dussán when MORENA was founded. Said one of the founders in an interview: "All my life I have been a Liberal. I love the Liberal Party. If [MORENA] has revealed its preference for Doctor Durán Dussán, it is because the most serious and endemic problem the fatherland is suffering, is the [guerrilla] violence." Durán did

not disavow the support.[10] Some speculated at the time that the elimination of Galán would benefit Durán.

Galán was, to some extent, an outsider, but he always had the backing of important elements of the Liberal Party. And his stature rose in death. He was mourned as an insider. His body was displayed in the rotunda of the Capitol and lines of well-dressed people snaked around the Plaza Bolívar and along the Carrera Séptima, respectfully cordoned off by police barricades. The elite political class and the middle class were mourning a man who had now become, for them, a martyr. Populist political leader of the 1940s Jorge Eliécer Gaitán once observed that Colombia is divided into *el país político* and *el país nacional* (the country of the political class, and that of the rest of the nation). Each *país* has learned to mourn their own martyrs. Few Colombian leaders—not even Gaitán whose death on the streets of Bogotá in 1948 sparked an urban uprising and a decade of civil war—have been able to bridge the class chasm in Colombian politics.

THE PEACE PROCESS

IN 1982, THE NEWLY-ELECTED GOVERNMENT of Belisario Betancur set Colombian politics on an uncharted course. Although Colombian elites had always referred to their political system as a democracy, the new president called for a democratic opening—borrowing the language then current in the Southern Cone—to incorporate the nation's armed opposition into the political process. The first step was an unconditional amnesty, approved in November 1982.

Two years later, cease-fire agreements were signed with three of the principal insurgent groups: the April 19th Movement (M-19), the Revolutionary Armed Forces of Colombia (FARC) and the Popular Liberation Army (EPL). Peace gave the guerrillas a voice, but it exposed their leaders and supporters to paramilitary violence. M-19, the first to call for a peace process, suffered the worst. Even before the cease-fire accord was signed, one of their most prominent public figures, former Congressman Carlos Toledo Plata—who had accepted the amnesty and returned to his life as a physician after decades underground—was assassinated outside his home in Bucaramanga. Over the next few years, M-19 was to lose over a dozen senior leaders. Many of them were founders of the movement, such as Alvaro Fayad and Iván Marino Ospina, who fell victim to police bullets in luxury, residential neighborhoods in Bogotá and Cali.

M-19 was never a strong military force. It had gained political sympathy and strength through spectacular actions like the takeover of the Dominican Embassy in 1980, where 15 ambassadors, including the U.S. ambassador, were held hostage. That action focused world attention on the government's human rights abuses and torture of political prisoners. More importantly, it set the stage for the first negotiations between government and guerrillas in two decades of war. M-19's demands were minimal by most standards, but significant in the context of Colombia: an end to the state of siege, a cease-fire, and national dialogue.

In June 1985, M-19 claimed government betrayal and broke off talks only ten months after the first cease-fire was signed. It had been a stormy period of negotiations, ambushes, assassinations and, despite the formal cease-fire, open combat. In November of that year, M-19 guerrillas

stormed the Palace of Justice, taking hostage the entire Supreme Court. Their declarations at the time made clear their intent: to tell the nation and the world that the government had violated the peace accords and broken the cease-fire. M-19 expected the action, like the 1980 embassy takeover, would evoke sympathy. They miscalculated. The military responded with brutal force, retaking the building after twenty-eight hours of uninterrupted combat with mortars, rockets and tanks. In the end, eleven Supreme Court justices, thirty-four guerrillas and scores of others were dead or missing. Civilian authority was trampled; some called it a twenty-eight hour coup d'etat.

If the legitimacy of Colombia's regime had hit rock bottom, M-19, left with negligible strength and minimal support, had lost any pretense of presenting a viable alternative. When Betancur handed over power to Virgilio Barco in August of 1986, EPL had also pulled out of the cease-fire, leaving only FARC within it. Unlike M-19, FARC did not expose its leadership to the death squads. Instead, it created a new movement, the Unión Patriótica, using the already existing political machinery of the Communist Party of Colombia. Rarely has a political party been so brutally and barbarously repressed as the UP. In 1986, fourteen UP congressmen were elected; within a year, four had been assassinated. In all, over 1,000 UP members have been murdered. But FARC did benefit from the peace process. For the first time, its voice was heard directly in Colombian politics and not filtered through the roar of machine-gun fire.

Many in the political class felt that the original truce agreements Barco inherited, which allowed the guerrillas to form a political party without disarming, gave FARC an unfair advantage. Although the UP received only 4.5% of the vote in 1986, traditional party politicians complained that even that small percentage was won through intimidation and force, what they called "armed proselytizing." Barco concurred. From the outset he declared that all future discussions with the FARC would be limited to establishing an agenda for disarmament. Political reforms and other issues would no longer be considered.

Moreover, the government openly supported a new counterinsurgency campaign, and remained disturbingly

How different was the mood of the crowd at the funeral of Jaime Pardo Leal, the presidential candidate of the leftist Unión Patriótica in 1986 and the man who came to symbolize more than anyone else the possibility of transforming Colombia's decades-old guerrilla insurgency into a legal mass movement. Then the crowds were noticeably poorer, the color of their skin darker. On the evening of Pardo Leal's assassination, October 11, 1987, the frustration of the UP sympathizers erupted into riots and pitched battles with police in some urban barrios of Bogotá. The next day, a national strike was called to allow people to attend the fallen leader's funeral. Before the procession could begin, demonstrators and mourners clashed with police in riot gear. By late afternoon, a cloud of tear gas hung over the crowd outside the National Cathedral on the northeast corner of Bogotá's central plaza and burned the eyes of those attending the funeral mass inside.

Afterwards, the crowd marched down the Carrera Séptima defiantly, but slowly—as if to savor the grief—carrying the coffin of their slain leader away from the plaza, away from the Cathedral, the Palace of Justice, the Congress and the gilded city hall. As the parade advanced from block to block, a desperate mixture of angry demonstrators, petty criminals, juvenile delinquents and homeless children smashed windows, looted stores and threw molotov cocktails. Twenty blocks of storefronts and the lower floors of office buildings were burned by fire or gutted by looters before the procession turned down Calle 26 toward the National Cemetery.

Alongside and behind—always careful to maintain a distance of about two blocks from the marchers—were soldiers with machine guns and riot cops peering out from a wall of protective shields stamped "POLICIA." At the cemetery, masked guerrillas were poised atop the giant white stucco gates that frame the entrance, waving the flags of the nation's guerrilla movements and machine-gunning rounds of ammunition into the air. Here the

passive as paramilitary groups escalated the dirty war against FARC supporters. Not surprisingly, the cease-fire agreements were abandoned amid mutual recriminations. For the next two years, peace remained off the political agenda.

IN SPRING OF 1988, WHAT WAS LEFT OF THE M-19 kidnapped one of the leaders of the Conservative Party, Alvaro Gómez. He was not released until months later, when the Catholic Church agreed to host a new round of peace talks. The Barco administration was hesitant and refused to attend, but the pressure was on for a new peace strategy. On September 1, 1988 Barco announced that any group which demonstrated good faith in negotiations, following a period of unilateral cease-fire, could enter into discussions with presidential advisers over their future incorporation into political life. Such negotiations could not be indefinite, and the outcome had to be the surrender of the guerrillas' arms.

This did not appear to be much of a departure from earlier declarations. But to the surprise of many, M-19 took up the president's offer. It announced a unilateral cease-fire, and by January of 1989 was engaged in full-scale talks with the government. M-19's philosophy has always been more social democratic than Marxist-Leninist. It had been pushed out of the cities and was never able to reconstitute itself in the countryside. M-19's acceptance of Barco's proposals legitimized the government's contention that the other armed groups had no reason to continue fighting—a contention made with a straight face, even as the dirty war raged and Congress obstructed practically every reform proposed.

FARC leaders also declared a unilateral cease-fire and offered their own peace plan, but the military and government did not seem prepared to talk to them. The other large insurgent group, the National Liberation Army, ELN, announced that it would only discuss "humanizing the war." Both FARC and ELN had grown in the 1980s: ELN spectacularly in the areas of Arauca and Santander; FARC steadily in all areas of the country except the Magdalena Medio, where paramilitary violence was worst.

Throughout 1989, M-19 tried to link disarmament to permanent political reforms. By August, the government had agreed to create a one-time special nationwide electoral district exclusively for M-19, lowering the number of votes needed for electing a congressman.

Following the terms of Barco's proposal, M-19's leaders had gathered their men and arms in a camp in the north of Cauca, a mountainous zone just south of Cali. They only had about 500 fighters at the time, many of them young men recruited in the last year. In December they were to hand over their arms in Cali to an international delegation established under the auspices of the Socialist International. But all this depended on congressional approval; as could be expected, Congress failed to act. The president's advisers called this an unforeseen mishap; the arms transfer was postponed.

M-19 was left with very little to negotiate. It was not prepared to return to war, and the government was unable to offer any real concessions toward peace. In January, the leaders decided to go forward anyway. They would surrender their arms and transform their movement into a political party in exchange for a mere legal pardon. Barco decreed that pardon, and the two top *comandantes*, Carlos Pizarro León-Gómez and Antonio Navarro Wolf, left Cauca for Bogotá. Dressed more like bankers than guerrillas, they were received by the minister of government and the presidential advisers. After consulting with the leaders and ex-presidents of the Liberal and Conservative parties, Pizarro and Navarro launched their campaigns for mayor of Bogotá and Cali respectively. Neither stood a chance, but they hoped the campaigns would become the foundation of a new movement. It was not clear whether M-19's fate would be any different than that of the UP, which five years earlier was massacred for pursuing a similar objective.

M-19, once the self-proclaimed defender of Colombian nationalism and still in possession of Simón Bolívar's sword, which they stole from the national museum almost two decades ago, has come in from the cold. The day before the March 11 municipal and legislative elections, the group handed over its arms. Despite this dramatic act, the political system shows no sign of a real democratic opening. Meanwhile, the more powerful guerrilla movements are more active than ever. The government refuses to negotiate seriously. And Colombian politics continues as usual. **MWC§**

soldiers and police seem to have disappeared completely, abandoning the city burial grounds to the people, the revolutionaries and the few politicians that dared to enter. Among them was Luis Carlos Galán. The crowd booed and refused to let him speak. They yelled, ''This death belongs to the people.''

Less than two years later, a more subdued crowd gathered at the same cemetery for the funeral of Luis Carlos Galán. Galán was neither Gaitán nor Pardo Leal. The emotion stemmed more from the moving speech of Galán's teenage son who denounced the drug traffickers as traitors to the Colombian nation. ''These men are not Colombians,'' he repeated. The son, his mother and brothers at his side, his voice cracking as he held back the tears, called for the continuation of his father's work and, to the surprise of many, he anointed a young politician as his father's successor. That man was César Gaviria Trujillo, who was associated more with the outgoing government of Virgilio Barco than with Galán's Nuevo Liberalismo.

The new *galanista* candidate would soon become a major contender in the polls against Durán Dussán. Yet the pain and fright of the political class was not eased by the ascension of an inexperienced politician. Furthermore, beyond the mourning for Galán, there remained a palpable fear among all strata of Colombian society: the fear that the government had lost control, that a slide into chaos was imminent. And no side offered a clear sense of direction.

A S GALAN STRUGGLED IN HIS FINAL HOURS of life on the evening of August 18, 1989, President Barco appeared on television and declared, once again, an immediate war on drug trafficking. In rapid-fire manner, he issued decrees authorized under the state of siege provisions in Colombia's constitution. Barco announced that extradition would be reinstated, that bank accounts, farms, businesses and other assets of the drug traffickers would be confiscated, and he ordered the police and military to track down the traffickers themselves. Rewards of 100 million pesos (about $250,000) were offered on television and radio for information on the most notorious drug dealers of the Medellín cartel, Pablo Escobar Gaviria and Gonzalo Rodríguez Gacha. This time, it appeared that Barco was serious.

With the declaration of a real drug war, the political class found itself in a difficult position. Salomón Kalmanovitz, one of Colombia's foremost economists, estimates that the cocaine trade generates approximately $8 billion annually for the Colombian cartels. Of that, $1.5 billion is thought to be re-invested in Colombia, equivalent to 3% of the gross domestic product. That would be roughly equal to the gross earnings of Colombia's principal legal export, coffee, which in 1988 earned $1.6 billion.[11] The cartels have invested that money throughout the national economy, facilitated by the Central Bank's longstanding policy of accepting dollars without asking questions, in what has come to be known as the ''sinister window''—essentially a legal form of money laundering.

The influence of drug money was initially felt in the countryside, where the cartels scooped up farms in decline and under siege by the guerrillas. The new owners invested heavily to modernize and expand agricultural production. More importantly, they made enormous investments in security (the dirty war) which significantly reduced or annihilated labor demands, social pressures and guerrilla violence.

In addition to the widely publicized land acquisitions —estimated at one million hectares—the traffickers also invested heavily in the financial system, television and radio, drugstore chains and certain industries. Kalmanovitz calculates that the combined investments in land and productive activities account for 6% of the collective wealth of Colombia. The financial capacity of the cartels, of course, is much greater when one adds their deposits in international banks and their stockholdings in North America and Europe. These are calculated to exceed $30 billion, equivalent to two-thirds of the value of the nation's entire capital stock, housing and land.[12]

The cartels are in one sense just another powerful economic group in a nation with several privileged groups linked to different sources of productive wealth, such as coffee, petroleum, textiles, bananas, flowers, sugar and other primary and manufactured products. But they are more privileged than the others, since collectively they generate and have access to wealth which is many times greater.

Although there are core groups at the center of the drug trade, it is now virtually impossible to separate drug wealth from other wealth, and the investments of drug traffickers from those of other economic interest groups. When Barco declared his war on drugs, and a crackdown on the leaders of the drug trade, it was difficult to determine where the power of the traditional economic elites ended and that of the drug cartels began. Any serious crackdown would have major negative ramifications for the economy. Many were uneasy.

If economic integration had advanced relatively smoothly, and much of the new wealth had been incorporated into the relatively strong Colombian economy, the political integration of a new and powerful group of economic actors was another story. The Colombian elites have been unwilling to cede authority on the political terrain; much of the drug war is over this issue. MORENA, for example, was opposed by most traditional politicians. The Right is learning what the Left has known for decades: There is virtually no political space for alternative parties in Colombia outside of the two traditional parties.

What we are witnessing in Colombia is a conflict which is not unlike others in the past when new economic elites emerged with the advent of a new commodity-export boom. Much of the violence in the nineteenth century, and especially leading to the War of a Thousand Days at the turn of the century, related to the incorporation of a new coffee-exporting elite into the structures of the Liberal and Conservative Parties.[13]

If the past is any indication, the drug barons will eventually be integrated into the traditional parties, maybe siding more with one than the other. It is also probable that this integration will not be complete for another generation. It is the children of today's drug lords who will marry into the traditional families and become congressmen and cabinet ministers. They will be the heads of the financial and investment *gremios*. The current generation will be resisted, as happened, for example, when Pablo Escobar was removed from Congress. Thus far, the violence has not approached the magnitude produced by the emergence of the coffee-exporting elite. Yet it is inevitable and will continue, because the fight is over power, money and social position.

I N THE FIRST DAYS OF THE MOST RECENT drug war, Barco bared the teeth of the hated bilateral extradition treaty with the United States. He reinstated extradition by presidential decree, overriding a 1987 Supreme Court decision that found the treaty unconstitutional. In the conflict between the drug traffickers and the government, more blood has been spilled over this issue than any other. Barco also confiscated 989 buildings and ranches, 32,773 farm animals, 367 airplanes, 73 boats, 710 vehicles, 4.7 tons of cocaine, 1,279 guns and 25,000 rounds of ammunition in the first month.[14]

The traffickers, principally the Medellín cartel, responded with an escalating campaign of terror, burning the farms of regional politicians in Antioquia, and detonating bombs in banks, schools, newspaper offices, party headquarters, private homes in Bogotá, Cali, Medellín and Barranquilla. Their strategy was designed to pressure both the elites and the population to support a negotiated settlement.

In all their declarations, their preference for negotiations was paramount. Escobar released a communiqué the day after the assassination of Galán, in which he asserted that he was "tired of the legal charades that the government plays against [the Medellín cartel]. Now the contest will be with blood until the government accepts a dialogue." It continued, "We are in favor of peace. We have demanded it for all to hear, but we can't beg. How much blood would have been avoided after the conversations in Panama."[15]

Three issues became apparent as the war escalated: One, the conflict was over political power and not drug trafficking. The flow of drugs to the United States did not significantly diminish, and the military did not focus their efforts on destroying cocaine processing labs. Two, the government's efforts were directed at the handful of men in the Medellín cartel who were mounting the terrorist challenge. The other cartels, after the initial dragnets, were basically left alone. After a month, all efforts seemed directed at hunting and tracking down Pablo Escobar, Gonzalo Rodríguez Gacha, and Jorge Luis and Fabio Ochoa. The manhunt was often portrayed in the Colombian press in terms that evoked a Rambo thriller with elite forces surrounding remote jungle hideouts, and the good guys always just one step behind their man.[16]

The third issue was that, as violence escalated, the stakes grew higher, and compromise or negotiations less possible. The death of Galán struck hard at the political class. The random bombings of public spaces was a new and disconcerting form of violence for Colombia's urban populations. But soon the war moved to an entirely different plane: In September, an explosion leveled parts of the Bogotá daily, *El Espectador*; in November, a mid-air bombing killed all 101 passengers and six crew members aboard Avianca flight HK-1803 on a trip from Bogotá to Cali; and in December, the detonation of a huge truck bomb in front of the national police agency (DAS) headquarters, damaged buildings as far as twenty blocks away. Both sides were boxing each other into a corner.

The killing of "*El Mexicano*", Gonzalo Rodríguez Gacha, by Colombian police on December 15, seems to have provided the key for both sides to save face. Ro-

DOWN TO THE LAST DROP

C OCAINE IS NOT THE ONLY DRUG COLOMBIA exports. Its principal legal source of foreign exchange is coffee. More than 300,000 farmers cultivate the crop, with an additional 2 million people directly employed by the industry. Colombia's slice of the world coffee trade has been about 15% in recent years, second only to Brazil; Colombia is the largest exporter of the mild arabicas which are increasingly replacing robustas as the drink of choice.

Colombian coffee growers owe a debt of gratitude to the Cuban Revolution for 27 years of relative stability in world prices. The Kennedy administration, determined to stem the tide of Third World revolution with a program of capitalist social reform and development, initiated the International Coffee Agreement in 1962. Signed by 74 producer and consumer nations, the accord established a quota system based on annual estimates of demand. Latin America contributed 70% of global coffee production under the accord.

Since 1980 the price has ranged between $1.20 and $1.40 per pound. As the price moved up or down, quotas were eased or tightened. Last September 30 the 27-year-old accord expired and the price of Colombian coffee plummeted nearly 50%. The United States is demanding an overhaul of the quota system in favor of the arabicas and an end to the cutrate sale of surpluses to Eastern Europe. Although talks are scheduled for this spring, U.S. demands have already met strong opposition, particularly from Brazil, which concentrates production on standard robustas.

Until recently, the Colombian National Federation of Coffee Growers had been funding a project encouraging coca farmers to switch to coffee. Ironically, as the price of coffee continues its nose dive, out-of-work pickers are taking jobs harvesting and processing coca. The United States is the world's largest consumer of both cocaine and coffee.

Donna G. Ellaby§

dríguez Gacha was the head of military operations for the Medellín cartel. He seems to have been personally behind the campaign of terror from August to December. Borrowing a script from the guerrilla movements, the Medellín cartel orchestrated a few high level kidnappings, including the son of Barco's chief of staff. The kidnappings were carried out not because the traffickers were strapped for cash as some press accounts speculated. The drug barons were looking for, and found, political leverage.

The hostages were released after an exchange of letters in January of this year. The letters were written by "*Los Notables*" on one side, and "*Los Extraditables*" on the other. The first are a group of three former presidents, the archbishop of Bogotá and the president of the UP. With the exception of the latter, the list personifies the political class. The second are believed to represent the principal *capos* of the Medellín cartel. Their letter provided an opening for the government to back off: "We plainly share the criteria expressed by [Los Notables] concerning the survival of the state and of the democratically elected government in the face of persons and organizations that, as in our case, live at the margins of the law, combating its institutions and the very existence of the established legal order....Therefore, we accept the triumph of the state, of its institutions and of the legitimately constituted government."[17]

In the letter, they then offered a laundry list of concessions and gestures of good will that they are prepared to make: to mediate peace with the paramilitary, to suspend drug shipments, to hand over arms, explosives, laboratories, clandestine airstrips and hostages, as soon as they receive "legal and constitutional guarantees." Finally, they offered to suspend all violence against political, governmental and business leaders, as well as against journalists, police and military officers. The Medellín cartel seemed willing to take whatever steps necessary to be tried in their own country. "Better a tomb in Colombia than a jail cell in the United States," is the oft heard quote in Bogotá.

Barco soon rushed to declare victory in the war on drugs, repeating all the while that his government "will never negotiate with criminals." Indeed, drug terrorism directed against the state and the political class has practically disappeared since December. Both sides are working out the rules of a political modus vivendi.

Accommodation with this new group of elite actors will replenish and expand the political class. However, it does not bode well for the Left or for a democratic opening. Already, even as parts of Rodríguez Gacha's paramilitary apparatus are being successfully dismantled, there has not been a reduction of the dirty war against the Left. The presidential candidate of the UP claimed in an interview that 70 of the party's activists were murdered in the first two months of this year by paramilitary death squads.[18] He himself was killed on March 22. During the whole terrorist campaign of the drug barons, the entire question of the dirty war was removed from public debate. The primary legacy of the drug war may well be the development of new instruments of repression and intimidation: Random bombings now occur in public places frequented by the Left or in those communities that are most organized, as has happened in several of the poorer barrios of Bogotá.

THIS COMPLEX SITUATION HAS BEEN FURther complicated by the entry of the United States into the conflict. Mounting instability in the Andean region and extreme levels of violence both there and in the United States have propelled the coca and cocaine-producing nations into the forefront of U.S. foreign policy priorities, surpassing current commitments to Central America. Galán's body was not even buried when President Bush offered to send stockpiled U.S. military equipment and to extend an immediate $65 million emergency loan. This was the largest such loan ever rushed to a foreign nation and the first for anti-narcotics assistance.[19] Prior to 1988 the United States had only a relatively modest police training program in Colombia which operated under strict congressional controls.

In 1988, Congress authorized $15 million in special aid to the Colombian armed forces and $5 million for the protection of government officials from attacks by drug traffickers, in addition to sending a small number of military advisers. Last year, Congress directed the Export-Import Bank to make a $200 million loan to the Colombian defense ministry for the purchase of U.S. military equipment for that nation's war on drugs. On September 5, 1989, in his address to the nation, President Bush approved an additional $261 million to be divided among Colombia, Peru and Bolivia. Most recently, at the Cartagena summit attended by the presidents of Colombia, Peru, Bolivia and the United States, Bush offered

$430 million more in military and economic aid to the three countries.

Such a large and direct role by the United States in the Andean region is unprecedented. Many in Colombia, Peru and Bolivia believe that the aid is ill-conceived and potentially destabilizing. By strengthening the militaries of the three Andean nations—two of which, Colombia and Peru, are engaged in longstanding counterinsurgency efforts—the United States has launched itself into these guerrilla wars, thereby escalating and internationalizing the conflicts.

The armed forces of Colombia know how to recast the enemy to fit the needs of the United States. Just when most analysts had buried Lewis Tambs' notion of the narco-guerrilla, the Colombian defense ministry resurrected it. In his annual report to Congress this past July, Barco's defense minister stated: "The most important issue facing the forces of public order is the confrontation with the cartels of Cali and Medellín. But there exists a third cartel which is politically and socially more pernicious, harmful and dangerous for the institutional stability of the country. That cartel is the FARC [the pro-communist Revolutionary Armed Forces of Colombia]."[20]

Colombia's war on drugs has received widespread coverage in the U.S. press. The State Department and the media have expressed major sympathy for President Barco and his nation whose democratic institutions are threatened by ruthless drug barons. The story is one of good versus evil, of courageous leaders and journalists against vile criminals who stop at nothing. But what of Colombia's deep social conflicts? Of the rise of new social movements? Of the guerrilla war, the oldest in the Hemisphere? What of the dirty war that defined much of the 1980s, and of the links between drug traffickers and military officers? All of this is left unreported.

Barco's drug war is not the same one waged by the Bush administration. The United States is concerned with the flow of drugs from South America. The Colombian political class is interested in reducing the acts of narco-terrorism against the state. Even as Barco and his administration (perhaps prematurely) declare victory in the war on drugs, cocaine production and distribution continues to rise.[21] However, there is a point where the policies of the United States and the Colombian elite converge: fighting the guerrilla challenge.

While the elite may well sort out its conflicts with a nouveau riche that has already penetrated many areas of state and society, it has shown itself to be unable to address the serious social problems the nation faces—other than through violence. U.S. drug policy seems bound to lead this country to weigh in on the dirty side of Colombia's dirty war.

The Drug War

1. *Justicia y Paz* (Bogotá), Oct-Dec 1988, pp. 99-108.

2. Washington Office on Latin America, *Colombia Besieged: Political Violence and State Responsibility* (Washington, 1989), p.33. Also see, Americas Watch, The Killings in Colombia (New York, April 1989). And Comisión Andina de Juristas, *Colombia: El Derecho a la Justicia* (Lima, 1988).

3. Bruce M. Bagley, "Colombia and the War on Drugs," in *Foreign Affairs*, Vol. 67, No.1, Fall 1988.

4. See Manuel Vicente Peña Gomez, *Palacio de Justicia, Las 2*

Tomas (Bogotá: Fundacion Ciudad Abierta, 1986); Ramón Jimeno, *Noches de Lobos* (Bogotá: Siglo Veintiuno Editores, 1989).

5. See M. Arango and J. Child, *Narco-tráfico: Imperio de la Cocaína* (Medellín: Editorial Percepción, 1984).

6. Discussions of the two types of drug traffickers can be found in Bruce M. Bagley, ''The Colombian Connection: The Impact of Drug Traffic on Colombia'' in Deborah Pacini and Christine Franquemont, eds., *Coca and Cocaine: Effects on People and Policy in Latin America*, Cultural Survival Report No. 23 (Peterborouigh, New Hampshire: Transcript Printing Company, 1986), p.89-100.

7. Scott B. MacDonald, *Dancing on a Volcano* (New York: Praeger, 1988), p. 33.

8. See *Semana* (Bogotá), No. 398 (Dec. 1989), '''El Mexicano' habla sobre su guerra, su plata y su muerte.''

9. *La Prensa* (Bogotá), Aug. 18, 1989, ''Declaración de MORENA.''

10. Semana, Aug. 21, 1989, No. 380, '''Tenemos derecho a ejercer nuestro dominio político','' and ''MORENA Se Destapa.''

11. Colombia Information Service, *Colombia Today*, Vol. 24, No. 7 (1989/90).

12. Salomón Kalmanovitz, ''Los Efectos de la Lucha Contra El Tráfico.'' Universidad Nacional de Colombia (mimeo); Discussions with the author, January 1990.

13. See Charles Bergquist, *Coffee and Conflict in Colombia* (Durham, N.C.: Duke University Press, 1978).

14. Bruce M. Bagley, ''Dateline Drug Wars: Colombia: The Wrong Strategy,'' *Foreign Policy*, No. 77 (Winter 1989-90).

15. *La Prensa*, Aug. 19, 1989, p.17, ''Ahora la Cosa es Con Sangre, dijo Pablo Escobar.''

16. See *Semana* Nov. 28 and Dec. 4, 1989, No. 395, ''El Cerco: Toda la Historia de la Persecución a Pablo Escobar,'' p.24-30.

17. *Semana*, Jan. 23-30, 1990, ''Comunicado de ''los Extraditables,'' p. 25.

18. Ibid.

19. WOLA, *Colombia Besieged...*, p. 109.

20. *El Espectador*, p. 9A, July 21, 1989, ''Los Jucccs no Comprenden Problemática Militar.''

21. Barco understood this when he met Bush at the Cartagena drug summit: ''The best help that the United States and other industrialized nations can give us,'' he declared, ''is to commit their governments to reducing the demand for drugs.''*El Espectador*, p. 1B, Feb. 14, 1990, ''Entrevista con el Presidente Barco.''

UNMASKING TERRORISM

STATE-SPONSORED TERRORISM

Rushworth M. Kidder

The April 15 strike against Libya by US aircraft called dramatic attention to the growing involvement of states in sponsoring or supporting terrorism. While terrorists do not need help from a government to carry out their activities, the ready availability of money, weapons, safe havens, communications, and public support has made it easier for terrorists to attempt their objectives.

Rome

What he remembered later was the way their eyes glittered. And how, when they came into the slanting winter sunlight in the terminal at Rome's Leonardo da Vinci Airport from the automobile ramp outside, they walked unusually close together.

There were four of them, wearing long coats and scarfs pulled up nearly to their eyes. Amazing, he thought to himself later, that no one noticed them.

Later he learned they had also been high on drugs.

He was standing at a Trans World Airlines station next to the El Al Israel Airlines counter, waiting for a flight to Washington.

"I turned and saw them," recalls the American archaeology professor, a resident of Rome who prefers not to be named. "Then I turned back and was in conversation with one of the people I was in line with.

"The next thing we knew, we heard the sound of [grenades and] firing, and fortunately my companions and I hit the floor."

From where he lay, he could see the airport security forces returning fire — plainclothes men who suddenly produced long-barreled revolvers and, to identify themselves to one another, little paper hats. When it was over, he recalls, "there were a lot of shell casings on us and around us." One of the terrorists was 10 feet away.

The event described took place on the morning of Dec. 27, 1985 — the date of one of the most chilling incidents of international terrorism in recent years. Within minutes of each other, gunmen hurled grenades and opened fire at El Al counters in Rome and at Vienna's Schwechat Airport. Fourteen bystanders and four terrorists were killed at the two locations.

Who did it, and why?

In the days following, some of the possible motives began to grow clearer. A previously unknown group called the "Martyrs of Palestine" said the attacks were in retaliation for the Israeli bombing of the headquarters of the Palestine Liberation Organization (PLO) in Tunisia last

■ IRAN — A CASE STUDY

'The world's leading exporter of terrorism' is one of the ways the US State Department categorizes Iran. What methods does Iran use in sending violence abroad? What, exactly, does 'state sponsorship' mean for the Khomeini regime?

JOAN FORBES — STAFF

The incidents

Iranian terrorism catapulted into view in 1979, with the takeover of the United States Embassy in Tehran and the 444-day hostage-holding ordeal that followed.

In 1983, Islamic Jihad, a Shiite fundamentalist group operating under direct Iranian sponsorship, claimed responsibility for the devastating truck-bombings of the US Marine barracks at Beirut International Airport and of the French paratroop barracks two miles away, killing a total of 299 servicemen. Payment for those bombings reportedly passed to the terrorists via Iran's ambassador to Syria, Ali Akbar Mohtashami.

Later that year, Islamic Jihad exploded six bombs in Kuwait, including one at the US Embassy.

In July 1984, an Air France plane was hijacked and flown to Tehran; in December a Kuwaiti airliner was also hijacked to Tehran, where two American passengers were killed. The hijackers were reportedly driven from the airport in a limousine. By year's end, terrorism experts had counted more than 50 attacks involving Iranian support.

The major event of 1985 was the hijacking of TWA 847 to Beirut by members of the radical Shiite group Hizbullah (Party of God), who were later joined by members of a more moderate Shiite group, Amal.

The funding

According to a Washington representative of the People's Mujahideen Organization of Iran (a Paris-based opposition group that asserts it will overthrow the Khomeini regime within 18 months), Tehran is providing substantial financial support to terrorist groups in Lebanon. The spokesman claims that much of this support flows to three major Shiite groups: Hizbullah, Amal, and Tawheed. He cites reports in the Iranian government newspaper, Jomhouri, and Europe's leading Arabic-language newspaper, Al Arab, that Iran has given about $20 million to such groups.

The training

According to a report on state-sponsored terrorism prepared last summer for the US Senate Judiciary Committee, some 2,000 terrorists from more than 20 Islamic countries have received tactical training in Iran's holy city of Qom. Between 300 and 500 Shiites from Lebanon and Iraq have also received religious, political, and military training at Qom, which also appears to be the center for training suicide drivers.

This activity is ultimately overseen by the Ministry of Islamic Revolution in Tehran, headed by Ayatollah Hussein Ali Montazeri, who is Ayatollah Khomeini's handpicked successor.

The network

According to the Mujahideen organization, the Iranian regime operates an extensive network of potential terrorists in Europe. Said to be headquartered in West Germany, this network reportedly operates out of the Iranian Embassy in Bonn and makes use of the consulates in Berlin, Hamburg, and Munich, the Union of Islamic Associations, the House of Iran

State sponsorship takes many forms. It may come as direct financial aid.

■

Other assistance includes training in weaponry, explosives, methods of assassination, paramilitary tactics, and intelligence. These skills are taught at camps in Syria, Syrian-controlled eastern Lebanon, Libya, Iran, Nicaragua, and elsewhere.

in Cologne, the Hamburg mosque, the Iranian television office in Bonn, and the Iran Air office in Frankfurt. Embassy officials in Bonn reportedly engineered the 1984 hijacking of an Air France airliner to Tehran.

In 1984, Spanish police uncovered a plot by Iranian terrorists to blow up a Saudi airliner. The operation was being coordinated by the cultural affairs officer of the Iranian Embassy, and involved a substantial cache of weapons.

Last fall, an Italian newspaper reported that weapons were being stored in Iran's Vatican Embassy.

The tactics

In the past, the network has been used largely against anti-Khomeini Iranians living in exile. But terrorism experts are concerned that it could be activated for attacks against Europeans and Americans.

Last fall, French and Italian newspapers reported that an Iranian-controlled terrorist group with 400 forged passports was prepared to carry out attacks against US airlines.

The motivation

On the surface, Khomeini seems to be using terror to export his brand of fundamentalist Islamic revolution and to rid the Islamic world of Western influence.

His Iranian opponents charge that he has a far different motive: his own self-preservation. His government, they say, depends on external crisis to distract the populace from the failure of his domestic policies.

Mujahideen spokesman Shahin Gobadi estimates that since 1979 the Khomeini regime has executed 50,000 Iranians, imprisoned 140,000 others, and driven between 2 and 3 million into exile.

Czech Maj. Gen. Jan Sejna was one of the highest-ranking Communists ever to defect to the West.

He noted that the Czechoslovak intelligence service had extensive contacts with the IRA, had provided funds to the PLO, had developed a plan to terrorize Britain by poisoning the water supply, and had become involved in drug trafficking in Latin America in an effort to use drugs to destroy Western societies.

October. Western intelligence experts, however, pinned the blame on the notorious Abu Nidal group, a breakaway PLO faction, whose motives may have included a desire to embarrass PLO leader Yasser Arafat.

Whatever the intricacies of motivation, always a complex subject when analyzing the political affairs of the Middle East, one thing soon became clear: These Palestinian gunmen were not acting on their own. Behind their attacks lay a web of state sponsorship involving a number of countries.

Investigation of the airport attacks has revealed:

● The two attacks were probably masterminded in Libya, where Abu Nidal is thought to live now. Two days after the incidents, Libya described the operation as "heroic."

● The attackers made use of several Tunisian passports that had been confiscated from workers expelled from Libya earlier in the year. These passports were then probably turned over to the terrorists by Libyan authorities.

● The terrorists were trained in Iran and came to Europe through Syria, according to Italian police intelligence specialists.

● The gunmen used AKM assault rifles (a modern version of the Soviet Kalashnikov) manufactured less than a year before they were used and all traceable to the same serial number block from a Romanian factory, according to United States sources.

The nature of state support

How significant is state sponsorship — the organized support of independent terrorist organizations by governments?

That question was put to dozens of government officials, intelligence analysts, police and military officers,

and antiterrorism specialists from a number of countries in the last few months. Their answers provide some revealing insights.

State sponsorship is rapidly gaining recognition as a major item — maybe *the* major item — on today's antiterrorism agenda.

"International terrorism," Central Intelligence Agency (CIA) Director William J. Casey told a conference at Tufts University in 1985, "is inconceivable apart from the financial support, military training, and sanctuary provided to terrorists by certain states."

"Without states, [terrorist] groups couldn't maintain themselves," says Prof. Yehezkel Dror of the Hebrew University in Jerusalem. "They would be unpleasant but not very harmful without state support."

There is broad agreement that the list of worst offenders includes the Soviet Union and its East European satellites; the three major Middle East players (Iran, Syria, and Libya); and, to a lesser extent, Iraq, North Korea, South Yemen, Cuba, and Nicaragua.

There is, however, substantial divergence of opinion about the relative importance of states that support terrorism. Some European governments tend to play down the Soviet hand, while many US experts see it as significant. Many Europeans, and some Americans, feel that the US has overemphazed Libya's importance and boosted Col. Muammar Qaddaffi's image among Arab nations as a "Yank-buster."

Many agree, however, that Middle Eastern sponsorship of terrorism poses the most immediate threat: Of the 184 incidents of terrorism in Western Europe recorded by the US State Department for 1985, about 40 percent were related to Middle East groups or countries.

State sponsorship takes many forms. It may come as direct financial aid, allowing some terrorist leaders to live in posh North African seaside villas, travel to fancy hotels, and even maintain retirement funds.

Other assistance includes training for young recruits in weaponry, explosives, methods of assassination, paramilitary tactics, and intelligence gathering and analysis. These skills, along with ideology, are taught at dozens of camps in Syria, Syrian-controlled eastern Lebanon, Libya, Iran, Nicaragua, and elsewhere.

In addition, states can funnel funds and weapons through their embassies, establish safe houses among sympathizers in various countries, and provide weapons, transportation, intelligence, storage and planning facilities, and moral support. There is even a hierarchy among sponsoring states: "If you have an address in Moscow and you're a terrorist," says British antiterrorism expert Brian Crozier, "you've arrived, you've made it."

State sponsorship is difficult to prove, partly because to publicize evidence of links between states and terrorist groups might jeopardize the intelligence agents who gathered the evidence.

"Western governments know much more about international terrorist connections than they pretend to know," says a high-level official of the West German government in Bonn, "and yet they use this information less than they could be expected to."

Why support terror?

Why do states sponsor terrorism? Most do so because they reap clear benefits in political and foreign policy objectives.

First, terrorism can be cheap: A few thousand dollars spent on what some view as paramilitary activity can sometimes produce far more impact than millions spent in conventional warfare.

"To the degree [states] provide support," says Ambassador Edward Marks, a counterterrorism specialist on leave from the State Department, "they increase exponentially the capability of terrorist groups. Most of them are quite small. And here they are with airplane tickets, and money, and documents, and [rest and recreation] — all of that because they are getting support from a government."

Second, fueling conflicts by means of terrorist groups allows sponsoring states to maintain a façade of innocence. In their recently published book "Terrorism as State-Sponsored Covert Warfare," Ray. S. Cline and Yonah Alexander observe, "What sets apart the use of terrorism from more conventional forms of coercive force at a sovereign state's disposal, is the option of a plausible denial or lack of public accountability."

Beyond that, answers tend to vary from country to country.

Iran, which US State Department officials describe as "currently the world's leading supporter of terrorism," uses such tactics in its campaign to root out Western ideas from the Middle East and spread Ayatollah Ruhollah Khomeini's own brand of Islamic fundamentalism. Iran strongly supports the 800-member Hizbullah, or "Party of God," operating in Lebanon. As the region's major non-Arab state, Iran also uses terrorism to pursue centuries-old animosities with its Arab neighbors.

Syria, which plays host to such anti-Arafat Palestinian terrorist leaders as George Habbash, Ahmed Jabril, and Abu Musa, has a more secular view. Bordering on Israel (which it despises as an intruder into the region) and Lebanon (parts of which were partitioned off from Greater Syria in 1943 under Lebanon's French mandate),

Syria has territorial and political designs on these and other nations. As a Soviet client state, it also acts as a channel for Moscow's interests.

Libya, whose sponsorship of terrorism has attracted the most attention recently, may actually be a less significant player than either Iran or Syria. "If we look at the total volume of terrorist activity worldwide," says the Rand Corporation's Brian Jenkins, "those actions credited to Libyan sponsorship account for perhaps 3 or 4 percent of the total."

Colonel Qaddaffi has been a loud protagonist for terrorism, however, using it in particular as a tool against his Libyan enemies abroad, against Israel, America, and several European countries. At a meeting of 22 radical Arab groups hosted by Qaddaffi in Tripoli last February, the groups vowed to form a "revolutionary strike force and suicide squads" to strike at American targets.

At bottom lies Qaddaffi's desire to persuade other Arabs to join in some kind of pan-Arab union — with, presumably, Qaddaffi himself at the head.

Different though these three motivations are, there is "quite a lot in common between [these three nations]," according to University of Aberdeen scholar Paul Wilkinson. Noting that they are all "bitterly anti-American, anti-Zionist, anti-NATO," he says that "it wouldn't be surprising to find a sort of loose alliance among those states."

Such an alliance, in fact, may have been operating in the case of the Rome and Vienna massacres.

In the background, a bigger question remains: the role of the Soviets. For the most part, Soviet support for terrorist groups appears to flow through East Germany, Czechoslovakia, Bulgaria, Romania, and Cuba, all of which are active in promoting the destabilization of Western society.

For example, Czechoslovak Maj. Gen. Jan Sejna, one of the highest-ranking Communist officials ever to defect to the West, told interviewers from Tufts University last year that the Czech intelligence service, under the direct control of the Soviets, had "extensive" contacts with the Irish Republican Army, had provided substantial funds to the PLO, had developed a plan to terrorize Britain by poisoning the water supply, and had become involved in drug trafficking in Latin America in a conscious effort to use drugs to "destroy Western societies."

Miguel Bolaños Hunter, a former high-ranking Sandinista counterintelligence officer, told the same interviewers about the extent of Soviet, Cuban, East German, and Bulgarian involvement with Nicaragua. Speaking of the long-range plan to overthrow Mexico, he noted that "Ideologically, terror, as opposed to prolonged guerrilla warfare, is not a problem. The people in charge of subversion . . . don't care about blowing up a busload of people if that action will have the desired effect."

Britain's Lord Chalfont, a noted terrorism expert, comments that "There's absolutely no doubt that the Soviet Union, through the KGB and its various externalizations of the Kremlin, does clearly manipulate terrorism rather well."

But the trail is carefully disguised. Former CIA head Stansfield Turner, recalling his days in office, notes that "I never saw conclusive evidence of any state supporting indiscriminate terrorism — certainly no evidence that the Soviets train the PLO to go out and do whatever the PLO wanted to do.

"I don't say they don't do it; I'm saying it's circumstantial evidence and very largely inference as far as I've ever seen."

And as Rand Corporation scholar Paul B. Henze notes, Soviet sponsorship of terrorism is only one part of a larger picture.

"If the Soviets are supporting terrorism to the extent that I think they are," he says, "they don't call it that at all. They call it political operations to advance socialism.

"The context is subversion and destabilization; terrorism is only one aspect."

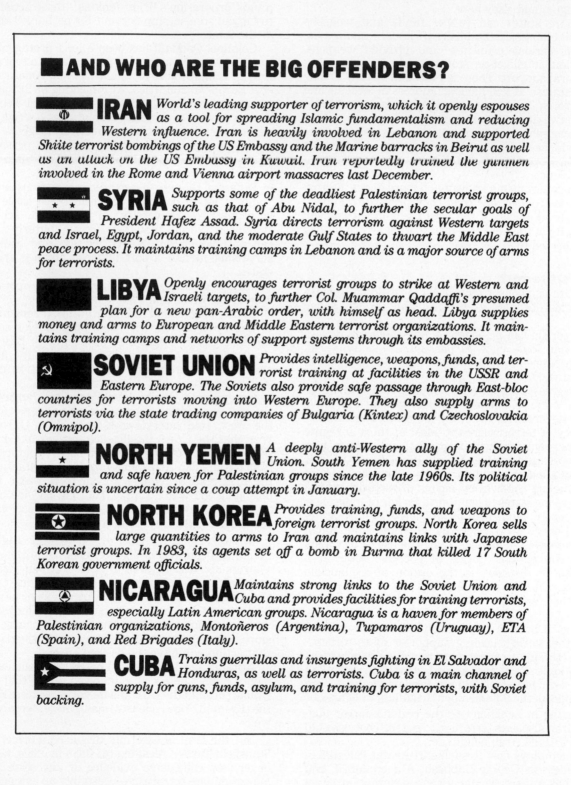

■AND WHO ARE THE BIG OFFENDERS?

IRAN *World's leading supporter of terrorism, which it openly espouses as a tool for spreading Islamic fundamentalism and reducing Western influence. Iran is heavily involved in Lebanon and supported Shiite terrorist bombings of the US Embassy and the Marine barracks in Beirut as well as an attack on the US Embassy in Kuwait. Iran reportedly trained the gunmen involved in the Rome and Vienna airport massacres last December.*

SYRIA *Supports some of the deadliest Palestinian terrorist groups, such as that of Abu Nidal, to further the secular goals of President Hafez Assad. Syria directs terrorism against Western targets and Israel, Egypt, Jordan, and the moderate Gulf States to thwart the Middle East peace process. It maintains training camps in Lebanon and is a major source of arms for terrorists.*

LIBYA *Openly encourages terrorist groups to strike at Western and Israeli targets, to further Col. Muammar Qaddafi's presumed plan for a new pan-Arabic order, with himself as head. Libya supplies money and arms to European and Middle Eastern terrorist organizations. It maintains training camps and networks of support systems through its embassies.*

SOVIET UNION *Provides intelligence, weapons, funds, and terrorist training at facilities in the USSR and Eastern Europe. The Soviets also provide safe passage through East-bloc countries for terrorists moving into Western Europe. They also supply arms to terrorists via the state trading companies of Bulgaria (Kintex) and Czechoslovakia (Omnipol).*

NORTH YEMEN *A deeply anti-Western ally of the Soviet Union. South Yemen has supplied training and safe haven for Palestinian groups since the late 1960s. Its political situation is uncertain since a coup attempt in January.*

NORTH KOREA *Provides training, funds, and weapons to foreign terrorist groups. North Korea sells large quantities to arms to Iran and maintains links with Japanese terrorist groups. In 1983, its agents set off a bomb in Burma that killed 17 South Korean government officials.*

NICARAGUA *Maintains strong links to the Soviet Union and Cuba and provides facilities for training terrorists, especially Latin American groups. Nicaragua is a haven for members of Palestinian organizations, Montoñeros (Argentina), Tupamaros (Uruguay), ETA (Spain), and Red Brigades (Italy).*

CUBA *Trains guerrillas and insurgents fighting in El Salvador and Honduras, as well as terrorists. Cuba is a main channel of supply for guns, funds, asylum, and training for terrorists, with Soviet backing.*

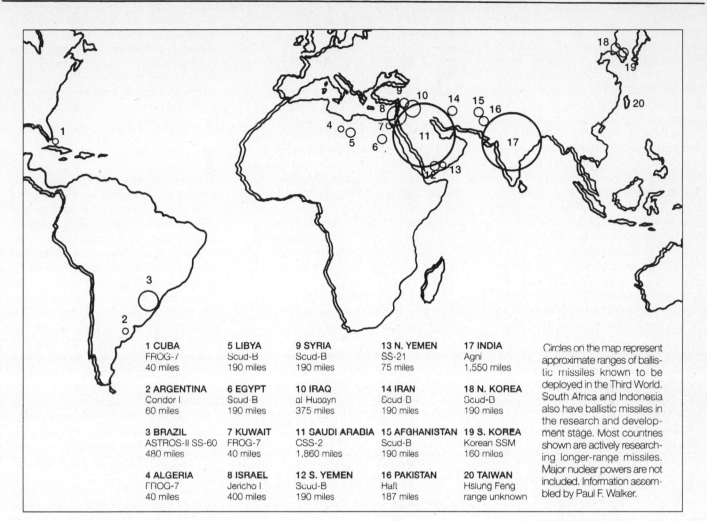

1 CUBA	5 LIBYA	9 SYRIA	13 N. YEMEN	17 INDIA
FROG-7	Scud-B	Scud-B	SS-21	Agni
40 miles	190 miles	190 miles	75 miles	1,550 miles
2 ARGENTINA	6 EGYPT	10 IRAQ	14 IRAN	18 N. KOREA
Condor I	Scud-B	al-Husayn	Scud-B	Scud-B
60 miles	190 miles	375 miles	190 miles	190 miles
3 BRAZIL	7 KUWAIT	11 SAUDI ARABIA	15 AFGHANISTAN	19 S. KOREA
ASTROS-II SS-60	FROG-7	CSS-2	Scud-B	Korean SSM
480 miles	40 miles	1,860 miles	190 miles	160 miles
4 ALGERIA	8 ISRAEL	12 S. YEMEN	16 PAKISTAN	20 TAIWAN
FROG-7	Jericho I	Scud-B	Haft	Hsiung Feng
40 miles	400 miles	190 miles	187 miles	range unknown

Circles on the map represent approximate ranges of ballistic missiles known to be deployed in the Third World. South Africa and Indonesia also have ballistic missiles in the research and development stage. Most countries shown are actively researching longer-range missiles. Major nuclear powers are not included. Information assembled by Paul F. Walker.

MISSILE MANIA
SOME RULES FOR THE GAME

JANNE E. NOLAN

Janne E. Nolan, a visiting fellow at the Brookings Institution in Washington, D.C., is the author of Guardians of the Arsenal: The Politics of Nuclear Strategy *(1989)*

Any system of control must respect the developing nations' struggle for independence.

Efforts to control the trade in military technology have traditionally focused on preventing Western technology from flowing east, and on preventing the spread of nuclear materials. But in the late 1980s, ballistic missiles became the currency of a new international security environment, as a number of developing countries heralded their entry into the missile age. Not coincidentally, most of the new missile producers are in regions of chronic tension where the interests of the great powers intersect.

For now, the significance of these programs may be more political than military. At a minimum, however, they demonstrate the developing nations' drive for military independence, sometimes regardless of political or economic consequences. And the fact that regional rivals have little common understanding of what constitutes stability, or of how to avoid provocation, suggests that the new missile age will be a turbulent one.

Industrialized nations have observed these developments with heightened concern. Yet the international consensus on controlling military exports, including missiles, is still very fragile. The only existing agreement is a consensual cartel of eight Western nations that manufacture ballistic missiles or their components—the United States, Britain, Canada, France, Italy, Japan, West Germany, and Spain. The Missile Technology Control Regime (MTCR), established in 1987, reflects the traditional view that the technical characteristics of ballistic missiles make them inherently destabilizing. But the regime has weak enforcement mechanisms, lacks an international agency to monitor compliance, and represents only a few of the current suppliers of missile technology.

It may already be too late to control the spread of ballistic missiles. Export controls are efforts by great powers to assert their prerogatives, and the foundations for those prerogatives are eroding quickly. Emerging regional powers are becoming less susceptible to coercion as they develop their own defense production capabilities. They see the denial of exports as discriminatory, and they accuse industrialized nations of hypocrisy when they denounce the legitimacy of ballistic missiles (or chemical or nuclear weapons). The new missile arsenals are obviously dwarfed by those of the five major nuclear powers. "It is fashionable among industrialized nations to deplore acquisition of high-technology weapons by developing nations," noted one Indian analyst recently, "but this moralistic stand is akin to drug pushers shedding tears about the weaknesses of drug addicts."[1]

Efforts to restrain missile programs are more likely to be effective if they are part of initiatives to end or contain regional conflicts. And these must be part of a broader effort to build a genuinely interdependent international system with codified, reliable means of resolving disputes peacefully. But how to encourage Third World countries to adopt nonaggressive and defensively oriented postures is not well understood.

Superpower-style arms control—limiting numbers and ranges of weapons, for example—seems an unpromising way to contain the threat of ballistic missiles in the Third World. The East-West military competition is relatively abstract, in contrast to the diffuse, highly volatile political and military conditions in those regions where missile proliferation is of most concern. And negotiated limitations depend on a measure of political accommodation among adversaries which does not exist in these regions.

To establish numerical ceilings, for example, the sides must agree on rough equivalencies among different weapon types, or agree to accept asymmetries, and they must agree that lower levels of weapons would improve stability. Negotiated limits derive from a common understanding of what is needed for overall military parity and stability, and these conditions must be within reach.

Defining regional balances in the Third World is extremely difficult. In the Middle East, for instance, Israel counts the inventories of the Arab and Persian Gulf states as a collective threat to its security. But the Arab states believe Israel's nuclear and missile capabilities vastly outweigh their own superiority in numbers. Both sides seek qualitative capabilities to offset the perceived threat. The problem is exacerbated by the Arab world's lack of political consensus, which would preclude any agreement requiring its forces to be counted collectively. Even defining the framework for negotiations can be complicated. Saudi Arabia, for example, sees both Iran and Israel as regional threats. In South Asia, India sees China as more important to its military calculus than Pakistan.

Negotiating numerical limits might seem more promising in Latin America, to mitigate the military and economic rivalry between Brazil and Argentina. Because these countries are producing missiles largely for export, however, economic or trade incentives may be more appropriate than arms control.

Range limits are also difficult to envisage. Israel, India, and Saudi Arabia already possess missiles that exceed the limits imposed by the U.S.-Soviet Intermediate-Range Nuclear Forces Treaty. And missile ranges can be increased by adjusting payloads or altering rocket engine efficiency. Restraints on such conversions would be difficult to enforce.

Instead of pursuing technical arms control measures, it would be more profitable to explore confidence- and security-building measures, including information and intelligence exchanges, on-site inspection of defense production and space launch facilities, and prior notification of missile tests. These mechanisms could help ease unwarranted suspicions about missile programs, limit their political and military consequences, and possibly reduce incentives to expand them. Although confidence-building measures only indicate political will and can be violated at any time, they can begin the process of broader accommodation. They can reduce tensions by taking the mystery out of rivals' military activities and providing channels for routine interaction.

Some regional measures have already been instituted or proposed: India and Pakistan have agreed not to attack each other's nuclear facilities and to begin negotiating a nuclear test ban. Argentina and Brazil inspect each other's nuclear facilities and have declared their nonhostile intent. And the United States has informally proposed encouraging Middle Eastern countries to abjure first use of ballistic missiles and to give prior notification of missile launches.

Other confidence- and security-building measures might be included in a missile restraint regime:

■ International safeguards could be applied at space launch facilities to insure that they are not being used to develop missiles.

■ An international space launch agency could grant nations access to space in return for giving up missile programs.

■ Missile forces might be kept unarmed and unfueled during peacetime, subject to monitoring.

■ Tests could be conducted only after notification, and away from rival territory.

■ Routine bilateral military exchanges could document the extent and pace of missile development plans and provide a forum for discussing security concerns.

Declarations of intent would not endure in a crisis, but they are important signs of political conciliation. On-site visits alone will not stop missile programs, but they can help reduce the reciprocal fears that fuel arms races.

Significant curbs on the demand for missiles will depend on reducing regional tensions, but incremental measures to enhance confidence will also help the broader objective. The great powers can encourage regional adversaries to pursue confidence-building measures. The United States and its allies could begin by helping countries develop routine consultative mechanisms, with which Third World governments are often genuinely unfamiliar. But the initiatives must come from the governments themselves and must reflect local realities.

It is even more important for the United States and Soviet Union to cooperate to stem conflict between nations they support. As the influence of both superpowers over their clients weakens, bilateral agreements will not be sufficient to contain future wars, but they are nevertheless vital. And, with the reconciliation of the superpowers, they now seem possible.

In June 1989 the chairman of the Joint Chiefs of Staff, Adm. William Crowe, and Soviet General Staff chief Sergei Akhromeyev signed an agreement to prevent and resolve crises arising from provocative activities by their respective armed forces. Although this was a technical accord, not a regional security agreement, it was inspired in part by the experience of the Iran-Iraq War, when, as one analyst put it, "American and Soviet forces sometimes operated in proximity to each other, leading both sides to recognize the need for a mechanism to coordinate their activities."[2] The nuclear risk reduction centers, established in Washington and Moscow in 1987, could be used for such communications.

But in the future, international agreements must elicit the support of both developing and developed states. An effort to broaden the Missile Technology Control Regime into an international treaty seems quixotic, at best. Developing countries would object to its discriminatory nature, and it does not cover other destabilizing weapons such as nonballistic missiles and aircraft. In fact the regime's success, such as it is, has derived from its modest goals and from the fact that it was negotiated out of the glare of the international spotlight.

Most proposals to restrain missiles show little sensitivity to developing states' ambitions to become equals in the international system. A first step might be to convene an international missile conference, under neutral auspices, to permit a full airing of all countries' views and to set a framework for cooperation. Modest agreements on some confidence- and security-building measures outlined here might be possible in the near future, and these might build momentum for more ambitious efforts.

The spread of ballistic missiles is a harbinger of future weapons proliferation. Industrial nations may find they are no longer able to use technological superiority to influence international events, and the quest for technological advantage will become ever more elusive. New generations of weapons may spread which could have even more adverse effects on international stability—precision-strike systems, biotechnologies, and antisatellite capabilities.

The developing countries must be taken seriously, and their interests must be recognized as enduring as well as diverse. Realism need not be the pretext for fatalism, however. The great powers must understand that although their leverage is limited, using it judiciously is as urgent as it is difficult. ■

1. C. Raja Mohan and K. Subrahmanyam, "High Technology Weapons in the Developing World," in Eric Arnett, ed., *New Technologies for Security and Arms Control: Threats and Promises* (Washington, D.C.: American Association for the Advancement of Science, 1989), p. 230.

2. Barrus M. Carnahan, "Decreasing the Danger in Military Activities: The Meaning of a New U.S.-Soviet Agreement," *Arms Control Today* (Aug. 1989), p. 13.

The North's Garbage Goes South

The Third World fears it will become the global dump

JEAN-PAUL DUFOUR AND CORINNE DENIS

This little prank cost us $2 million," says the visibly relieved owner of the Norwegian vessel *Banya*, "but I'm happy to see that ship sail." Off the West African coast of Guinea, in the warm dampness of a rainy July afternoon, his freighter moves slowly away, escorted by a naval patrol boat. In its hold is an unwanted cargo: more than 15,000 tons of toxic ash from garbage incinerators in Philadelphia.

It was unloaded last February on the island of Kassa, offshore from Conakry, the capital of Guinea, only to be hastily reloaded after Guinea arrested Norway's honorary consul-general, Sigmund Stroemme, and threatened to hold him until the waste was removed. Stroemme, who made the mistake of authorizing the import of the seafaring waste, was still not permitted to leave Guinea after the *Banya* set sail. And five Guineans were being held in jail.

A dozen similar incidents in which toxic waste has arrived from the West have recently occurred in Africa. Third World countries are offended at becoming "the garbage dumps of the rich." Europeans and Americans are discovering that protecting their environment can mean polluting other people's lands. Greenpeace and the European Environment Entente (EEE) have worked to expose such dumping.

In sending away the *Banya*, Guinea strictly applied a resolution adopted last May by the Organization of African Unity: "We declare that the dumping of industrial and nuclear wastes in Africa is a crime against Africans, and we condemn all companies that participate, in one way or another, in introducing these wastes into Africa. We ask them to clean up the areas already polluted."

The tough language was prompted by the dumping scandals of recent months. The most significant recent incident was at Koko, a port in southern Nigeria. Italians had to return and fetch some 10,000 barrels and 25 containers of particularly toxic industrial wastes that they had dumped. Much of it had simply been deposited on a Nigerian farmer's field, on the outskirts of a town of 6,000 people.

From the newsmagazine "L'Express" of Paris.

When this clandestine dump was discovered, the Nigerian government's reaction, like that in Guinea, was firm. The Nigerian ambassador in Rome was called home; two vessels in the port of Lagos were requisitioned; and about 15 people were arrested. According to Nigerian authorities, they "may face a firing squad."

The most sensational case may have been the odyssey of the *Zanoobia*. That freighter wandered for two months after recovering more than 2,000 tons of toxic waste from Syria, where it had been dumped after being rejected by Djibouti, Venezuela, and Sardinia. Finally, the ship had to return to its point of origin in Italy.

This year Guinea-Bissau canceled a contract to accept more than 3.5 million tons of dangerous waste after European ecologists revealed the agreement. By canceling the contract, this particularly poor country sacrificed annual income of $140 million, which is greater than its gross national product. Dignity has a great price.

Senegal has received and rejected offers to accept waste. But the Congo, Equatorial Guinea, Gabon, and Sierra Leone have all been accused of accepting dangerous wastes. Behind these incidents are secret deals involving phony companies based in Switzerland, Liechtenstein, Gibraltar, and the Isle of Man. Usually, embezzlement is involved.

The ash from Philadelphia was an exception. The Norwegian shipping companies involved—Torvald Klaveness and its affiliate Bulkhandling—are reputable, particularly in Conakry, where they ship out 5 million tons of bauxite a year. They protest any charge of impropriety, claiming that the ash can be recycled into top-quality cinder blocks and thereby assist the development of the country.

Originally, Guineans had no reason not to believe them. But when the Bulkhandling freighter unloaded the Philadelphia ash, the cargo was said only to be "raw building materials." The Norwegian shipper neglected to mention that it contained dioxins and heavy metals like lead and cadmium. The company did not mention that the shipment had already been refused by Panama, where it was supposed to serve as landfill.

Alerted by Greenpeace, the Guineans protested that

Reprinted from *World Press Review*, November 1989, pp. 30–32.

they had been defrauded. "Their reaction is excessive," replies Kaare Borch, vice-president of Torvald Klaveness. "They've been fooled by ecologists whose goals are not realistic in our industrialized world." Nobody was poisoned in Kassa, and contrary to the initial reports from Guinea the vegetation on this lush island did not completely shrivel up.

An official American study says the Philadelphia ash posed no danger to the inhabitants of Philadelphia. Still, they did not want it. And as for making cinder blocks, "It is technically feasible," says Bertrand Gontard, head of France's largest waste-processing plant. "In fact, we make them, but we would not take the risk of using them to build houses."

For two years, another shipment of ash from Philadelphia has been floating in the Atlantic on board the *Khiang Sea*, a freighter flying the Liberian flag. It has tried to unload the ash in the Bahamas, Bermuda, Honduras, the Dominican Republic, Guinea-Bissau, and Haiti, where the ashes were labeled "agricultural fertilizer." The *Khiang Sea* valiantly sails on. It was sighted off the coast of Senegal, and in August it was reportedly undergoing repairs in Yugoslavia.

"Philadelphia once sent its incinerator ashes by truck to a dump in Ohio," says a specialist. "That cost the city about $50 per ton. Bulkhandling probably put in a bid at $35 or $40 a ton. The cost of carrying the ashes to Guinea, however, is only about $20 per ton. And if they can be carried on the return leg of a journey to deliver Guinean bauxite to the U.S., you can imagine the savings." For more toxic wastes, the savings are bigger because the cost of their treatment and storage in the industrialized countries is even higher.

Until now, a bit of cleverness and unscrupulousness was enough to get Western wastes into the Third World. One old trick was to send them to a false address, preferably in some forlorn little port. The "lost" cargo would remain on the dock until somebody started worrying about the smell or people started falling ill. That usually took a few months, and by then it was impossible to trace the shipper.

For larger quantities, it is always possible to find some poor soul with a large, empty plot of land, hide the exact nature of the wastes, or hire a middleman willing to say or do anything for money. This was apparently the approach taken toward Nigeria and toward Lebanon, where 2,400 drums of toxic wastes were found in a vacant lot north of Beirut.

For "big deals," the best route is to deal directly with a cash-poor government. That is how it is done by one Italian-Swiss middleman, who tried to swing the "deal of the century" with Guinea-Bissau. First, you promise to respect "international standards" (which do not exist) and declare that the "big-hole technique" for disposing of wastes is "100 percent ecological." One may want to include the promise of building a waste-processing plant within an ill-defined, but reasonable, time.

For those who cannot embark on Third World adventures, there is a lot of potential in Europe. Turkey, for example, and Eastern European countries such as Rumania, Yugoslavia, East Germany, Hungary, and even the Soviet Union will accept wastes. The import of wastes represents a very attractive source of foreign earnings for them, as it does for the Third World. One advantage is that "these countries provide certificates of destruction," says an expert. In other words: "What they do with the stuff is none of my concern."

But today few countries are safe bets. In Rumania, seven people were recently sentenced to up to 18 years in prison, and several ministry officials were dismissed for "illegal storage of highly toxic chemical wastes." In Yugoslavia, officials are investigating the possible fraudulent entry of Dutch wastes that were reportedly sent there after being refused by Turkey.

In Western Europe there are significant differences in waste storage and processing costs. The main exporters are West Germany and the Netherlands, where strict laws—and the vigilance of ecological parties—lead to a scarcity of dumping sites and soaring waste-treatment costs. Britain, which offers unbeatable rates, is far and away the leading importer. It even practices "co-disposal," which involves mixing toxic wastes with household wastes.

The growing activity of middlemen—brokers of sorts who rack up small fortunes—is usually legal, but not always. The story of Simon Kemp, the Dutch "garbage king" arrested last June, is edifying. His company had been handling industrial and hospital wastes for 12 years. Officially, it was incinerated and disposed of at legal dumps. In fact, his trucks were said to have unloaded at hidden sites and in the rivers and forests of the Netherlands, France, and Belgium. This was only carrying on the tradition of the 1960s, when environmental protection was not yet a major concern. Wastes would often go to the nearest empty lot or into the nearest river. The Rhine was Europe's garbage pail.

Such irresponsibility has led developed countries to find and clean up polluted sites at great expense. With only about 100 "black spots" on its map, France is Europe's "cleanest" member. West Germany has located more than 1,000 dangerous waste sites, and Denmark has found 380. The U.S. has earmarked some $10 billion to clean up 20,000 such sites.

"In France, we have the technical means and professional skills necessary to manage our wastes," says Bertrand Gontard. With its processing unit and two incinerators, this plant can treat 160,000 tons of waste per year. "The ideal solution," says Gontard, "would be to treat wastes near the industrial zones, to avoid transporting dangerous materials over long distances." Unfortunately, even communities accustomed to foul smoke do not like that idea.

Concerned international agencies are mobilizing to control the international shipment of waste. The United Nations Environment Program is working to draft a convention that would regulate waste shipments. The UN experts are trying to strike a fair balance between advocates of "free trade," who oppose any regulation, and ecological activists in Greenpeace and the EEE, who favor a total prohibition on North-South transfers of waste.

Jean-Marie Junger, a representative on the European Commission, says, "It is not possible to halt waste trafficking overnight. A simple prohibition might be counterproductive if it encouraged fraud and led to the littering of Africa's beaches with waste cargo from ghost ships."

Only the Ruthless and Greedy Need Apply

A recent advertisement in the *International Herald Tribune* of Paris highlights the growing international nature of the toxic waste trade: "Thinking about making money? Hazardous toxic waste a billion-dollar-a-year business. Think about this! No experience necessary. No equipment needed. No educational requirements."

This ad also makes it clear that you do not need intelligence, knowledge, or skill to become a toxic-waste merchant.

What you may need, however, is ruthlessness and greed.

The dumping of untreated toxic waste can be extremely dangerous. Even so, there is evidence that some Third World nations, desperate for hard currency, have been tempted into colluding in massive dumping operations.

For the waste traders, the profits are vast. They buy and sell the waste like any other commodity. But because the original producer has no binding responsibility

for its final destination, it is traded as a liability rather than as an asset.

As it passes through different hands the price is forced down. Eventually the waste is bought by a broker who has negotiated a site in the Third World, either with willing government officials or enthusiastic local people.

"Let's all get rich quick!" is the attitude within the trade, says Michael Yokowitz of the Organization of Economic Cooperation and Development, which es-

FINANCIAL TIMES

timates that in 1987 waste disposal was a $20-billion-a-year business.

"These brokers are not so much cowboys as gentlemen cowboys who see the opportunity of making a fast buck," Yokowitz says.

"It's easy; anyone could do it. You register a private company and buy the waste, with no questions asked. Then you find a dump site, rent a ship, hire a crew, and retire early."

—*"Financial Times,"* London (independent).

Africans themselves are not opposed to regulation. "We are certainly going to have to learn to manage our wastes if we want to develop our industry properly," says Bakary Kanté, Senegal's director of the environment. "That means the transfer of technology, which will not happen if we take too rigid an attitude toward industrialized countries."

The UN experts propose that the contents of waste shipments be precisely defined and declared by the shipper. Moreover, the shipper should insure that the site where wastes are to be deposited has the necessary technical facilities. A secretariat would be set up to monitor all

of this and serve as technical adviser to governments.

"In the long run, these measures should discourage exports," says Alain Clerc, chairman of the working group on the convention. "If the provisions are applied, the costs of treatment and storage should be the same everywhere. Meanwhile, the developing countries, if they so desire, will have an opportunity to acquire the technology needed to process their own wastes."

Will we then be able to live at peace with our waste products? Before the 1970s, no one imagined that our garbage could become such a costly problem. We now know that, sooner or later, we will need global management of wastes that grow steadily in volume.

Third World Metropolises Are Becoming Monsters

Rural poverty drives millions to the slums

Jorge Wilheim can only study the uncontrollable growth of São Paulo, Brazil, from above. To keep tabs on this 60-mile-wide city, the city planner and state environmental minister takes regular helicopter flights over it. "Every time, I am amazed at how many new high-rises and developments there are," he says. The police department has added units to patrol the new streets, and their findings are added to existing city maps. But it is a constant race to keep up. "Often when we get calls, we have no idea where to go," says one police officer in the Copom precinct.

"São Paulo is developing so rapidly that it is impossible to lay hands on a map of the city: A new one would have to be issued every week," wrote the French ethnologist Claude Lévi-Strauss in his 1955 travel memoirs, *Tristes Tropiques* (Sad Tropics). Then the city had only 2.5 million inhabitants. Today's official estimates range between 17 million and 20 million.

A constant flood of newcomers, mostly unemployed field hands and farmers with their families, pours into the cement labyrinth of the Rodoviario Tietê terminal, one of the world's largest bus stations. Innocent, full of expectations, these new arrivals fill 2,000 buses a day, coming from all corners of the world's fourth-largest country. The journey usually eats up a family's meager savings. Their worldly possessions fit a few boxes, and their only assets walk beside them: their children. "Most of the migrants think São Paulo is some kind of El Dorado," says Cecília Rossi from the bus station's information window. "But many of them are robbed within hours of their arrival, and most will end up in the slums or on the street."

Currently, 300,000 people a year move to São Paulo. Similar numbers are moving to Rio de Janeiro, Caracas, and Mexico City. Around the world, several million people a year move to the urban centers of South America, Africa, and Asia. The people of the Third World are migrating toward their vision of the promised land, heedless of warnings from every international development agency

as well as the United Nations. Only half of the 9 million residents of Karachi, Pakistan, were born there. With 7 million inhabitants, Nigeria's capital, Lagos, is 20 times the size it was just 30 years ago. In China this spring, roughly 2.5 million people from the countryside moved into the prosperous city of Canton before authorities stopped the migration.

Third World cities are growing faster than predicted, and the UN now expects that by the year 2000, 17 of the world's 20 largest cities will be in the Third World. In 1980 it was only 11. With populations around 25 million, Mexico City and São Paulo will head the list. A few other metropolitan areas in the Third World are showing even higher growth rates, especially Indonesia's capital, Jakarta, and Kenya's Nairobi. Kenya's capital is a city of children, with nearly half of its 2 million inhabitants under the age of 16.

The Worldwatch Institute, an independent U.S. think tank, warns that this population explosion will stretch to the limit these cities' already overburdened infrastructures. The larger a city becomes, states a report from the Washington-based organization, the more complex and expensive are its social services. No one is placing any bets on when the first monster city will collapse. As New York City faced one fiscal crisis after another throughout the 1970s, many people suggested that the megalopolis of the Northern Hemisphere was ungovernable. Economic growth and infusions of money, however, brought economic prosperity back to New York. The cities of the Third World can expect no such economic miracle.

Among the problems affecting these cities today are: burgeoning dimensions that are already too big for politicians and police to control; steady increases in crime, which has become as much of a problem for most residents as the struggle for income; deep-rooted corruption in the public sector that has effectively prevented thorough reform efforts; steady population growth, which is minimizing and even reversing any progress made in sanitation, traffic, and public health; and, finally, the serious possibility of environmental disasters of unimagined se-

From the newsmagazine "Der Spiegel" of Hamburg.

Reprinted from *World Press Review*, October 1989, pp. 32–34.

verity. Stuttgart-based author Gerhard Schweizer, who traveled all over the world researching his book *Zeitbombe Stadt* (Cities as Time Bombs), argues that "revolutions today will be fostered primarily in the slums of our largest cities." As the slums "become more and more a heavy ring of poverty surrounding cities," Schweizer says, "they will become a key factor in politics, an unpredictable risk element in any policy objectives."

In many Third World cities—Nairobi and Manila, for example—half of the inhabitants live in slums. In Calcutta, the prototypical metro-disaster, the figure is 70 percent. And the percentages are increasing everywhere. In contrast to Europe's 19th-century industrial centers, where similar poverty reigned, these new mega-cities have no stable agricultural base to fall back on. Quite the contrary: As Worldwatch puts it, "Uncontrolled urban growth in the Third World is the result of failed economic and social policies—and is driven more by rural poverty than by urban wealth." Millions of farmers are not even bringing in a minimal harvest because of unequal land distribution and severe environmental degradation.

As the rural standard of living throughout the Third World has become gradually more disastrous, the cities of the Third World have been unable to produce enough jobs to support those fleeing the rural catastrophe. Too often, governments have favored prestigious, and expensive, high-technology industries over less glamorous, labor-intensive industries. To avoid "bread riots" in the cities, authorities have generally held prices on many staple goods unnaturally low, thereby enticing even more people to the cities. Now, incredible inflation rates—3,500 percent in Argentina, 1,000 percent in Brazil, 60 percent in Nigeria—and drastically higher rents are forcing even the upwardly mobile, such as office workers and skilled laborers, back into poverty. In Jakarta, many soldiers and bureaucrats live in shanties; they cannot afford the subsidized city housing offered to them.

Asia has employed useless measures to cover up the desperate need in the cities. The road to Bombay's airport is now bordered by brightly painted billboards that hide the hundreds of thousands of poor people occupying the neighboring slums. Manila's Tondo district is still fronted by the pretty cardboard walls that former First Lady Imelda Marcos had erected there to cover up the decay. Behind the walls, though, are the growing mountains of trash in which many people seek food and salable items.

Authorities in almost every country of the Third World thought that the only way to rid the cities of poverty was through forced slum clearance. But camps and housing projects on the edges of the city are useless to the poor. Most of the displaced people barely survive by begging and peddling in the city center, which often is five or six hours away by public transportation from the camps to which they have been moved. So they generally return to the city. Disappointed with the politicians, they reclaim land somewhere and erect more shantytowns from any materials they can find. The shantytowns go up without water connections, without electricity, and, most important, without any sewage systems. The politicians hardly care.

Soon enough, however, the politicians will bitterly regret this lack of concern. The health and environmental problems in the slums will start spilling into the more affluent parts of the cities. "These wild dumps are like automobiles without brakes," says an Indian residential planner. "Once the slums have become unlivable, the city will follow soon after."

São Paulo would need to devote its entire budget to sanitation and public works for 30 years to reach European standards for running water, sewage systems, and sewage treatment. Worldwatch worries that increasing water pollution may start to slow the cities' growth in a most brutal manner. Just like people in Africa's drought-stricken Sahel, residents of the cities may start dying for lack of potable water.

Ecologists' main enemy today, however, is air pollution. Many colonial powers unwittingly set up their chief trade centers in areas that, due to weather conditions, have become smog traps in the industrial era. Sixty percent of Calcutta's residents suffer from breathing disorders. In China's major cities, far more people die of lung cancer than do in the countryside—"chiefly because of the heavy air pollution," according to Canadian ecologist Vaclav Simil. In Jakarta, the airborne lead levels are 17 times higher than what the World Health Organization (WHO) believes to be dangerous. Carbon-monoxide poisoning is one of the most common causes of traffic deaths in São Paulo, where WHO standards would have dictated smog warnings on 226 days in 1987. This year city officials predict that the dirty yellow-gray clouds will hang over the city even more frequently.

Crime is changing the faces of cities. "I'm sick and tired of it," cries 24-year-old teacher Karin de Arruda Sampaio of the street crime in São Paulo. Youths have robbed her five times, taking both money and jewelry. Recently she threatened another would-be assailant with a knife. Her modest car now boasts an alarm system like those found on many other autos in São Paulo. The motor must be started within seven seconds after windows or doors are opened, or an alarm will go off. If she does not release a skillfully hidden valve, the fuel intake stops after a little more than a mile. She can lock all doors instantly with one button, and if anyone tries to reach into the car, she can raise all of the windows like guillotines in seconds. Even if she is dragged out of the car by auto thieves, she can still stop it with a remote-control device.

These security systems, however, have bred new approaches to crime. Now automobile thieves simply hijack owners along with their cars. And victims of crimes can no longer even count on popular sympathy. The public has long since been anesthetized to crime. São Paulo, with 4,444 murders, 170,000 armed robberies, and approximately 2 million thefts (80,000 cars), is easily the most crime-ridden city in the world.

Often the police only contribute to the violence. Inside one-and-a-half years, the police shot 975 "elements," as they call suspects, mostly because they offered "resistance to authority." Because the police view poverty alone as grounds for suspicion, they often patrol the slums as though they were in enemy territory. Naturally, they are greeted with general antipathy and hatred.

In contrast to Rio de Janeiro, where gangs and drug dealers have moved in with their own reign of terror, organized crime has not secured a foothold in São Paulo. Most thieves, as even the most conservative politicians agree, are driven by hunger. Unlike in the U.S., crime in São Paulo is not restricted to only a few sections of the city. Almost all supermarkets employ guards to inspect shoppers before letting them into the stores. Large shopping centers seem like armed bastions, and restaurants are as well protected as European banks.

In Nairobi, private security firms now form one of the largest sectors of the economy. In Jakarta and Lagos, homeowners take turns guarding their neighborhoods. Bangkok's Chulalongkorn University published a study that concluded, "The difficult conditions are leading, above all, to increased violence among children." In Karachi, Cairo, and Caracas, slum dwellers have already started riots and protests against the ruling authorities, and the military has often been called in during emergencies to keep the peace. The coming years will bring new problems, which should sharpen tensions further. In Mexico City, several million new jobs will have to be found by the year 2000 in order to keep even 60 percent of the population steadily employed.

"Nonetheless, the problems of the cities can be solved," says Jorge Wilheim. One of the few optimists to be found, Wilheim says, "We just need to address the critical areas." Technically, it is a matter of breaking these monster cities into smaller units, and giving greater authority to local districts, he continues. Poverty and homelessness, however, are "social problems, not municipal problems," says Wilheim.

"We have only been able to put out fires," says São Paulo Vice Mayor Luiz Eduardo Greenhalgh. He dreams of rooting out the corrupt bureaucrats, pushing through a solid municipal development plan, and narrowing the income gap between those in the highly protected wealthy sections of town and those in the slums. "Although the prognosis for São Paulo looks better than for many other Third World cities," he says, "we will never have a moment's peace."

WEEDING OUT WASTE
Energy Efficiency in the Third World

Ted Flanigan and Susan Hassol

Ted Flanigan is Director of the energy program of the Rocky Mountain Institute in Snowmass, Colorado. Susan Hassol is Associate Editor of IRT: Issues Review & Tracking, *a weekly energy newsbrief.*

FOR THE DEVELOPING world, meeting the growing energy needs of an ever-expanding population is critical to real development. Poor energy choices lead to deforestation and desertification on the one hand and indebtedness and dependence on the other. The average person in a developing country consumes less than one-sixth the energy consumed by a person from an industrialized country, and less than one-tenth as much as the average U.S. citizen. Much of this energy is used so inefficiently that the low levels of consumption correspond to even lower levels of energy sources. Often, this inefficiency is the result of suboptimal fuels being used for tasks, such as kerosene for lighting, because they are the only ones available.

The traditional response to such problems is expanding electrical supply to meet demand. But for much of the developing world, this is not feasible. It is far too costly and usually means adding to an already burgeoning debt. Utility borrowing in many developing countries already accounts for over one-third of total foreign debt. To meet its energy needs, the developing world will have to reevaluate its energy options.

Principles of Wise Energy Management

Two concepts regarding energy planning are of critical importance to the developing world's energy dilemma: "end use" and "least cost." An end-use approach to energy planning focuses on the energy services that are needed and then analyzes the most efficient means of delivering the desired service. This differs from traditional supply-oriented thinking which focuses on how much electricty, for example, we can produce and how to make it perform all end-uses, regardless of whether it is optimally matched to that use.

"Least-cost" refers to a method of energy planning that incorporates an end-use analysis to ascertain the least expensive means of meeting energy needs, considering all options, on both the demand and supply sides. Thus, where it is cheaper to save electricty than to produce it, or where it is cheaper to invest in indigenous renewables than buy imported oil, those options are chosen. The goal of this planning method is to provide the desired services at the lowest possible cost. Under least cost, total costs of an energy option, like environmental and social costs, that are difficult to quantify, can be factored in.

The Energy Efficiency Option

The preceding principles of energy planning suggest an underestimated "source" for increasing energy services—efficiency. Often referred to as "conservation," efficiency differs from conservation in an important way. Efficiency involves extracting the same or improved services from less energy through the use of advanced technologies, better matching of fuel to end-use and less wasteful practices. Conservation, on the other hand, implies a lower quality and quantity of services, such as being too cold in winter, or doing with lower levels of lighting than are needed. The efficiency discussed here is clearly of the first type, and is a cost-effective path to improving energy services in the developing world.

The Tata Study

A report of the Tata Energy Research Institute in India provides an example of efficiency's potential to improve energy services in the developing world. Currently, India's power system is unable to meet the peak demand for electricity. Load restrictions range from 10 to 50 percent and come into effect between 5 and 10 p.m. The Tata study was undertaken to explore strategies for dealing with this problem. The report looked at two options: adding new capacity, or managing demand by substitution and improved efficiency. "The addition of new capacity has always fallen short of targets over the different five-year plans, and shortfalls are also expected in the seventh five-year plan," notes the report. But in improving energy efficiency, there is much potential.

At peak demand, the report found, there was a sharp increase in the use of electric lighting in the residential and commercial sectors. The Tata research team then es-

Reprinted with permission of *Multinational Monitor*, January/February 1989, pp. 23–25. *Multinational Monitor*, P. O. Box 19405, Washington, DC 20036.

timated the contribution of lighting to the peak load and identified options to reduce this contribution. They found that in a representative sample area lighting accounted for 37 percent of the load at the peak of demand. That figure, they estimated, could be reduced significantly by improving efficiency. If all incandescents were replaced with higher efficiency flourescents, 10,000 MW of installed capacity could be saved, as well as large amounts of money in generation costs. And the annual return on expenditure for lamp substitution in electricity could save more than 50 percent.

Competitek Findings

The Tata Institute's findings are backed up by similar studies by the Rocky Mountain Institute's COMPETITEK (see box) team of energy researchers, whose work involves documenting advances in the rapidly changing field of energy-efficiency technology. In the United States it is technically possible, using commercially available and cost-effective technologies, to save 92 percent of all electricity used for lighting at a cost far below that of generating electricity in existing power plants, notes a COMPETITEK report. In fact, COMPETITEK's findings reveal that these savings can be acquired at what is referred to as a "negative net societal cost"—society actually saves more money than it invests in the efficient technologies, through reduced energy consumption and avoided replacement and maintenance costs. Since lighting accounts for about 25 percent of electricity used in the United States, and 25 to 40 percent of peak demand, such levels of savings could have enormous ramifications.

Preliminary research reveals that the technical potential for savings in other end-use areas is also substantial. In the area of appliances, which account for about half of U.S. residential consumption and a fifth of total electricity used, there is the potential to save 65 to 80 percent (13 to 17 percent of all electricity used). In space cooling, which consumes about 15 percent of all U.S. electricity, and 44 percent of summer peak loads, 80-90 percent could be saved (12 to 14 percent of all electricity used). Water heating (other than for industrial processes) accounts for 14 percent of residential use and 5 percent of total use, with savings of 65 to 85 percent possible, or 3 to 5 percent of total use. Preliminary research in the area of drivepower (including motors and their controls) shows similar potential for electricity savings with short paybacks.

Thailand, Kuwait, and Brazil

While this U.S. data is not directly transferable to developing countries, the implications are clear—there is a huge technical potential for saving energy without sacrificing quality of service, and with positive economic and environmental results. And increasingly, this is confirmed by studies in the developing world. For example, energy audits of 71 companies in Thailand suggest that total industrial electricity use (which accounts for 63 percent of the country's total consumption) could be cut by 7.7 percent through process improvements, 3.2 percent through equipment replacement, and 2.4 percent through simple housekeeping measures. All 13.3 percent of this savings potential is highly cost-effective and, if implemented along with similar oil conservation measures, could accelerate economic growth in Thailand.

COMPETITEK's findings in the area of space cooling are especially applicable to developing countries in warmer climates. In Kuwait, for example, air conditioning accounted for approximately 45 percent of total power consumption in 1983, and the fraction has been increasing. The 1986 preliminary COMPETITEK report on space cooling estimates a gross technical potential for savings in the order of 80-90 percent. Methods by which these savings can be accrued include reducing external heat gain using shading and spectrally selecting glazings; improving refrigerative systems; and using load management measures such as thermal energy storage systems.

A 1986 study of electric efficiency potential in Brazil in six end-use areas indicates possible savings of 20 percent for industrial motors, 50 percent for domestic refrigerators, 50 percent for domestic lighting, 20 percent for commercial motors, 60 percent for commercial lighting and 40 percent for street lighting. When these savings are aggregated, they equal almost 20 percent of Brazil's total electricity use. All of these savings could be provided through cost-effective technologies that are already available (some even manufactured) in Brazil. Furthermore, as COMPETITEK documents, the state-of-the-art in energy-efficient technologies is advancing so rapidly that many of the best current technologies were not even on the market two years ago when this study was conducted.

As significant as the enormous technical potential of efficiency is for all nations, the implications are especially profound for the developing world, where in many cases, as in the example of India, demand is not fully met. Even if a fraction of the technical potential in some of these end-

Sao Paulo, Brazil.

use areas was exploited, it might make the difference between meeting peak demand and not meeting it at all.

The Wider Benefits of the Efficiency Option

The benefits of pursuing efficiency in the developing world extend far beyond meeting electrical demand and saving money. Capital that would have been spent building additional power plants could be used to increase the scope of electrification, either by grid extension or investments in stand-alone renewable energy systems for remote villages. Because investing in efficiency is less costly than increasing supply, less debt would be added to the already heavy debt burden. Scarce resources could be channelled into essential health, education, welfare, and economic development activities. And the lower energy costs that result from increased efficiency could help to fuel economic growth.

Energy efficiency can also lead to increased employment. A recent study in the state of Karnataka in India showed that the industrial sector used 74 percent of the state's electricity, and that 18 electricity-intensive industries consumed two-thirds of that power, but provided only 7.8 percent of the jobs; the remaining 1,200 industries used just one-third of the power but provided 92.2 percent of the jobs. Thus, by choosing less energy-intensive industries, developing nations can direct the energy they use to creating more jobs.

Finally, opting for increased efficiency in lieu of supply expansion has beneficial environmental effects. Fewer hydroelectric developments will reduce the social and environmental havoc caused by large dams. Burning less fossil fuels will result in lower emissions of sulphur dioxide and nitrogen oxides. Using fuels more appropriately and efficiently will reduce the rate of deforestation and desertification. And the combined effects of reducing carbon dioxide-emitting fossil fuel use and reducing the rate of deforestation could help to alleviate the growing threat of global warming.

Implementation

Much of the funding and technical assistance for energy development projects comes from international lending and development institutions, such as the World Bank. These bodies have traditionally encouraged and funded supply expansion. Large-scale implementation of efficiency in developing countries will require these institutions to reevaluate their policies and begin to support energy efficiency improvements financially, technically and politically. In his 1986 study of end-use electrical efficiency for the World Bank, Howard Geller of the American Council for an Energy-Efficient Economy (ACEEE) details a strategy for implementing this change. A new report from ACEEE makes specific proposals for reforming international lending and development policies to reflect an emphasis on least-cost energy planning.

Lastly, the lack of a well defined energy infrastructure

Competitek

ROCKY MOUNTAIN INSTITUTE launched its COMPETITEK update service in January of 1988 to disseminate the breadth of information on new and advanced technologies and techniques for electric end-use efficiency. COMPETITEK's service is provided on an annual subscription basis to electric utilities, policy analysts, major end-users, etc. To date, COMPETITEK has over 50 subscribers in 12 countries, including major U.S. utilities such as Pacific Gas & Electric and South California Edison, major trade associations including the Electric Power Research Institute, and end-users including the Compaq Computer Corporation. Charter members also include such foreign organizations as the USSR Academy of Sciences; Energy, Mines and Resources Canada; the Italian Atomic and Alternative Energy Agency; the Tata Energy Institute of India; the Ministry of Energy, Mines and Resources in San Jose, Costa Rica; and several Swedish energy authorities. While marketing efforts have thus far focused on U.S. and European organizations, COMPETITEK's analysts believe that the potential for efficiency in the developing world is great and that their findings are clearly applicable there.

For an annual fee of $9,000, COMPETITEK provides subscribers with four components: (1) The State of the Art Series, including reports on Lighting, Drivepower, Appliances, Water Heating, Space Cooling, and Space Heating; (2) their Quarterly Updates; (3) The Implementation Series, topical papers on means of financing energy efficiency information and marketing programs, etc.; and (4) two-delegate participation in an annual COMPETITEK Forum held in Snowmass Village, Colorado.

For more information contact COMPETITEK, c/o Rocky Mountain Institute, 1739 Snowmass Creek Road, Snowmass, CO 81654-9199 (FAX: (303) 927-4178). —T.F. & S.H.

in much of the developing world makes the case for implementing energy efficiency stronger still. Since developing countries have less evolved infrastructures than those of the developed world, and therefore have not already installed the inefficient stock of electrical devices that are present in the United States and other developed countries, there is a tremendous potential to implement energy efficiency from the outset, driving economic growth and providing the important wider benefits mentioned above. Passing up the chance to influence these developing infrastructures positively would be a significant lost opportunity.

WORLD HUNGER AMIDST PLENTY

"If progress is to be made toward alleviating hunger and malnutrition, agricultural, trade, and food-distribution policies have to be approached from an international perspective and coordinated with monetary and fiscal policies."

John W. Helmuth

Dr. Helmuth, associate professor of economics and assistant administrator, Center for Agricultural and Rural Development, Iowa State University, Ames, served as executive coordinator of the 1988 World Food Conference.

EVERY three days, the same number of people die of starvation as were killed by the Hiroshima atomic bomb. Approximately 40,000 children die each day from starvation. Fifteen million people are dying each year from starvation, malnutrition, and hunger-related diseases. The numbers are staggering, incomprehensible.

Estimates of the total number of hungry in the world vary, depending on the criteria used to define the term. The World Bank estimates that, in 1980, there were 680,000,000 people, worldwide, who did not receive enough calories to prevent stunted growth and serious health risks. Most of the chronically malnourished are children. In 1980, 1,500,000,000 people did not receive enough calories to lead an active working life. Fifty percent (730,000,000) of these were living in developing countries, 40% (590,000,000) in low-income countries, and 10% (140,000,000) in middle-income countries.

The problem of hunger and malnutrition is not confined to developing nations. In the U.S., over 19,000,000 people were

Starving Nigerian boy is symbolic of the suffering of many children around the world due to insufficient food supplies, causing malnutrition and hunger-related diseases.

Reprinted from *USA Today Magazine*, March 1989, pp. 48–50. Copyright © 1989 by the Society for the Advancement of Education.

receiving food stamps as of May, 1987, and an average of 15-18,000,000 were receiving donated U.S. Department of Agriculture surplus commodities monthly.

Regardless of which numbers are used, or which measure is applied, the conclusion is inescapable—we live in a world stalked by the age-old specter of starvation. One-third of the Earth's population does not receive enough food to maintain an active working life, the economic loss is staggering, and the amount of human pain and suffering is incalculable. With all the relief efforts, government assistance, and private volunteer organizations combined, we are still in the dark ages in the battle against hunger.

The dreadful irony is that, during most of the 1980's, there was enough food to feed the hungry. Before the 1988 drought, food surpluses were five times larger than were needed for this purpose. Unfortunately, during 1975-86, non-emergency food aid to developing countries remained static at 7-9,000,000 tons per year. More than double that amount is needed. Now, the UN estimates world cereal stocks will fall by 80,000,000 tons as a result of the North American drought.

In 1900, the world population was almost 1,000,000,000. It took only until the 1920's for that population to double. By 1950, there were 2,500,000,000 people on Earth. That number doubled to 5,000,-000,000 in 1987. Six billion are predicted by 2000; 8,000,000,000 by 2025. It is estimated that more than 90% of the world's population growth occurring between now and the year 2025 will take place in the Third World—those very countries already plagued by hunger, malnutrition, and starvation.

One billion more people are being fed today than in the early 1970's, but the number of hungry people continues to increase. The 1988 drought is a vivid reminder that we must not relax if we are to make progress. Droughts and pest infestations are a constant menace to our food supply, but a more serious long-term threat may result from the continuing misuse of agricultural land. The World Food Council estimates that erosion, salinization, and desertification potentially could reduce the land area available for food production by 500,000,000 hectares in Asia, Africa, and Latin America.

Much of the world's ability to produce more than enough food is a result of the new high-yielding varieties of wheat and rice that were the vanguard of the Green Revolution of the 1970's. Now, however, most of the increases possible because of these new varieties have been realized. Future productivity gains may be much harder to accomplish and have to be achieved in much harsher environments on much less productive, marginal soils.

There are economic reasons behind the disparity between food availability in developed and developing countries. It is due in part to faster demand growth in developing countries (resulting from higher population growth rates) compared to supply growth; greater vulnerability of developing countries to drought, pests, and other natural disasters; a lack of the necessary food production and distribution infrastructure in developing countries; the economic policies of individual countries; the reduced purchasing power of developing countries due to adverse exchange rate shifts; worsening debt problems; and the slow economic growth of developing nations. Trade barriers by some countries compound the problems. These factors highlight the increasing difficulty developing nations face in trying to provide food for their populations.

Protectionist trade policies, in particular, have been shown to have detrimental impacts on their economic growth. Developed nations adopting more protectionist policies tend to experience lower economic growth rates in both the industrial and agricultural sectors. Developing nations adopting such policies tend to harm their long-run food production prospects. The free trade economies adjusted better to the economic shocks of the 1970's than did protectionist economies. Furthermore, the World Bank indicates that the adoption of new technology has been faster in less protectionist countries than in protectionist, developing countries.

The protectionist policies of certain countries not only have led to a decline in trade, but also to a national income loss. Developed nations engaging in high levels of agricultural intervention, such as the European Community and Japan, are experiencing significant domestic efficiency and real income losses, compared to the U.S. and Canada. The World Bank estimates that Europe and Japan incurred real income losses of about $24,000,000,000 and $27,000,000,000, respectively, in 1980-82 because of agricultural intervention in the grains, meat, dairy products, and sugar markets. The higher rates of protection for processed agricultural products in developed countries result in fewer exports by developing countries of value-added products that can generate needed foreign exchange. This protectionism on the part of developed countries blocks the process of industrial development in the less developed countries.

In addition to the adverse effects of protectionist policies, the governments of the U.S., Japan, and Europe annually are spending approximately $100,000,000,000 to provide income support to their farmers. In a period of growing surpluses, these agricultural subsidies are becoming more and more difficult to justify.

The macroeconomic policies of developed nations in the 1950's and 1960's resulted in a period of relative economic stability. Major changes in monetary policy during the 1970's, however, resulted in widely fluctuating interest and exchange rates. The economic shocks of the last two decades have resulted in significant deterioration in the terms of trade for most developing countries, persistently high interest rates, and reduced access to development loans. The financial capability of developing nations to deal with these problems has worsened significantly since 1980. In that year, 98 developing nations had a net financial inflow of $39,600,000,000, resulting from new development loans minus debt repayment. In 1984, the net inflow to developing nations had become a net outflow, which reached a negative $24,000,000,000 in 1986.

Developing nations are being forced to repay debts from previous years, are not obtaining new loans, and do not have the resources to cope with the food needs of their populations. During the 1970's, when developing countries had a net financial inflow, they were able to increase their average imports of food per person by almost seven percent per year. From 1980 to 1986, as their net financial inflow turned to a net financial outflow, average imports of food per person declined by three percent per year.

The internal policies of developing countries often add to the problem. Land-use policies, market intervention, and the heavy taxation of agriculture often stifle the agricultural development necessary for improved food availability.

The world food system

Research by the Food and Agriculture Program of the International Institute for Applied Systems Analysis (IIASA) has concluded that the problem of hunger amidst plenty stems from a malfunctioning of the world food system. While the economic, trade, and agricultural policies of individual countries may seem rational in the light of national goals toward food self-sufficiency and a viable domestic agricultural sector, taken together as a world food system, such policies are a failure. Nations pursuing their individual goals do not operate necessarily in the best interest of the world food system as a whole or of the world's hungry populations.

IIASA's economic models demonstrate that, while markets are an efficient way to allocate resources, they do not ensure a desirable distribution of income. The world food system is driven by markets that determine consumer food prices, and these markets adjust to changing circumstances in ways that leave the poor hungry because of a sheer lack of income. They can not earn needed income because they lack the productive resources of capital, tillable land, and marketable skills.

There is widespread recognition that the world faces a crisis in food production and distribution. The decade of the 1980's has been characterized by declining agricultural exports, increasing protectionism and trade tensions, agricultural prices dropping to the lowest real levels since the 1930's, and a pervasive economic crisis among farmers throughout the world. Government programs in developed countries have exacerbated the problems of low prices and surplus production, added billions of dollars to government expenditures, and continued to stifle the necessary development in food deficit countries.

There is no doubt that we face a crisis. What can be done? In 1974, the United Nations World Food Conference resolved that, by 1980, no child should go to bed hungry and no family should fear for tomorrow's food. The world has fallen far short of the lofty goal of that resolution.

Solutions to the problem are not easy to find. Direct food aid to the hungry is not a long-run solution, because it tends to reduce incentives for local food production. While direct food aid is vital as a short-run solution to crisis situations, more comprehensive solutions are needed that deal with the world food system as a whole and address the complicated interaction of the monetary, fiscal, agricultural, and trade policies of various nations.

The 1974 World Food Conference was a beginning. It expanded on efforts that had been under way for a number of years to document and quantify the nature and extent of the problem. The Rome Conference drew attention to world hunger and malnutrition and searched for ways to increase production to meet perceived shortages in the 1970's.

We face a different set of problems in the 1980's. The food shortages of the 1970's gave way to the surpluses of the 1980's and a period of nationalistic internalization—during which individual policies have been designed to help individual nations, but have harmed the poor nations.

Other conferences have struggled with the problem. A 1976 World Food Conference in Ames, Iowa, strived to broaden and intensify the involvement of scientists and educators and searched for ways to alleviate hunger and food shortages through interdisciplinary cooperation.

In April, 1988, the newly formed International Policy Council on Agriculture and Trade hosted a World Food Conference in Brussels, Belgium, that emphasized the need for agricultural policy change and highlighted the importance of trade policy reform, particularly between the U.S. and the European Community.

The most recent World Food Conference, hosted by Iowa State University, the Iowa Congressional delegation, and Iowa Gov. Terry Branstad was held in Des Moines in early June, 1988. With a theme of "Hunger in the Midst of Plenty: A World Policy Dilemma," the goal was to bring together world leaders from private industry, government, and academia to promote cooperation and the coordination of worldwide economic and agricultural policies through the exchange of ideas and information. More than 430 participants from 33 countries struggled with the general state of disarray in the production and distribution systems for food and other agricultural commodities.

Topics discussed included the glut in world markets of many major agricultural products; the widespread evidence of hunger and malnutrition; the enormous costs of agricultural production subsidies, which the national treasuries of many countries no longer can withstand; and trade patterns that continue to be distorted by government subsidies and protectionist policies.

The conference recognized that the symptoms of disarray stem from uncoordinated and *ad hoc* national economic policies, which are at the heart of the problems facing the world's food production and distribution systems. If progress is to be made toward alleviating hunger and malnutrition, agricultural, trade, and food-distribution policies have to be approached from an international perspective and coordinated with monetary and fiscal policies.

Hunger is a global problem, and global solutions must be found. In 1974, the problem was perceived as a technical one—how to produce enough food for the growing world population. Today, the problem is a political one—how to achieve cooperation among nations to equitably distribute the food that is available.

Recommendations

Eight broad recommendations for policy change were advanced by the 1988 World Food Conference:

● Developed countries should place increased emphasis on policies to stimulate economic growth in developing countries.

● Policy reform proposals explicitly should recognize impacts on poor and disenfranchised populations.

● Policy reform to make income transfers more explicit should be continued and accelerated.

● Policy harmonization should be emphasized in trade, exchange rate, monetary, and fiscal areas. A multilateral organization to develop a code for fiscal policy should be considered.

● Increased capacity for environmental assessment should be developed to help ensure sustainability. Assessments should be required of groups proposing policy change.

● A systematic means of restructuring Third World debt should be created.

● More realistic approaches to policy change should be developed, widely sharing the results of analysis, broadening participation, and directly addressing problems of adjustment, compensation, and changes in political and economic structure.

● Developed country donor organizations should broaden the set of nations in which they have programs and should target their efforts better.

There was consensus that income must be increased in developing countries and freer international trade policies need to be adopted. Freer trade can contribute to improvements in production efficiency and to a lower-cost world food supply. However, freer trade is not a simple solution. Policies encouraging it have differing impacts. Freer trade must be accompanied by compensation and adjustment policies that protect those who may be disenfranchised by changes in policy.

Perhaps the boldest recommendation to come from the 1988 World Food Conference was for a Marshall Plan for the 1990's and beyond. Envisioned as a jointly funded effort by major developed nations, this plan represents a significant long-run commitment to Third World development. It calls for pledges of institutional reform to stimulate economic growth in developing countries and bold and practical steps to resolve the Third World debt problem. Presently, less than one-half of one percent of the total world gross national product is devoted to economic development assistance, while approximately six percent goes for military expenditures.

The conclusion of the conference was that there needs to be a shift in priorities. Third World countries must have assistance in developing their entire infrastructures—education, health care, highways, harbors, and marketing and distribution systems—as well as their agricultural and industrial sectors.

Only through long-term, sustainable economic growth can the problem of starvation possibly be solved. When Third World nations are able to produce and sell the products efficiently for which they have a comparative advantage, they then will have command of the resources necessary to feed their populations. When economic development reaches this point, the investment of developed nations in economic assistance is returned many-fold.

The problem of world hunger is too big, too pervasive, and too permanent for any one country to solve alone. Its solution must be made the highest priority of all governments—of all humankind. That priority then must result in real, tangible, long-run action. All nations must work together against the common enemy. Only then will we stand a chance of knowing a world without hunger.

Concern Rising Over Harm From Pesticides in Third World

Marlise Simons

ROME

Arif Jamal, an agronomist and pesticide specialist, had traveled from Khartoum to tell the story haunting him since droves of animals were killed last August in the Dinder wildlife reserve in the Sudan.

Convinced that pesticide poisoning was to blame, he vainly pushed for an investigation by the Sudanese Government. Now, in frustration, he had come to a United Nations meeting here to show photographs of barrels found near the site of the slaughter. The barrels said: "Not registered for use in the United States of America."

"How can a country forbid a poison at home and yet manufacture it and sell it to other countries?" he asked. "Where is the morality of this? Are we supposed to be more resistant?"

Mr. Jamil's questions are at the heart of a long and intense battle between environmentalists and chemical companies over who is responsible for the misuse of pesticides in the third world. The use of some of these pesticides is barred or restricted in the countries that export them.

A new United Nations survey has underscored the extent to which misuse of pesticides has become the hidden price of the rush by third world countries to modernize their agriculture.

No Monitoring Systems

The survey, carried out by the United Nations Food and Agricultural Organization, found that "very toxic pesticides" are "widely available" in at least 85 developing countries. Further, it says, 80 of these countries have no adequate system to approve, register or monitor the material. They also lack information about hazards and do not have people trained to evaluate them.

Sales of agricultural chemicals to developing countries have grown rapidly. As a result, experts say, accidents and poisonings have sharply increased. World pesticide sales have nearly doubled since the mid-1970's to nearly $18 billion a year, and much of this growth has taken place in the third world.

Doctors and health experts working in Africa and Latin America tell tales of farm workers who use no protection because of the hot climate, of people storing water and food in empty poison containers and of mothers who unwittingly wash their children's hair with a lethal product, thinking it will kill lice.

The World Health Organization estimated that as many as one million people suffer acute poisoning from pesticides every year, among them many farmers in the third world. These cause an estimated 20,000 deaths a year, the organization said in 1986.

"Pesticides have done a lot of good for the world food supply and some of them are absolutely needed in health campaigns," said a diplomat from a European pesticide-exporting country, "but this picture is pretty disastrous."

Now, after a long fight to limit exports of products banned or restricted in the exporting countries, environmental groups appear to have made some gains. This month a United Nations committee agreed on the terms of the principle of prior informed consent, which requires countries to record on an international register the pesticides they are willing to buy and those they refuse.

Accidents and poisonings have grown rapidly, experts say.

Chemicals that have been refused may not be shipped to that country.

Initially, the procedure will be applied to nearly 60 pesticides, including such powerful ones as aldicarb, dieldrin, paraquat, chlordane and heptachlor.

The informed consent principle still needs to be formally endorsed in several United Nations bodies. But its significance was underlined by the presence of representatives of the chemical companies. In the past they have fought the concept, but they now say they will go along with it.

The United States annually exports about 500 million pounds of pesticides that are banned, restricted or not licensed for domestic use. American regulations require a maker to notify the Environmental Protection Agency about such shipments, and the agency must advise the receiving country. But agency officials said at Congressional hearings this month that documents on just 10 percent of the exports are filed with the E.P.A.

Most exporters claim exemption from the regulations under an E.P.A. policy that allows undocumented exports if the pesticides are similar to other approved pesticides.

'Public Kept in the Dark'

"The agency has created a loophole big enough to drive a Mack truck through," said Representative Michael Synar, Democrat of Oklahoma, who headed the hearings held by the House Energy and Commerce Committee's Subcommittee on Environment, Energy and Natural Resources. "The subcommittee investigation found that when it comes to the export of unregistered pesticides, foreign governments have been kept in the dark, the public has been kept in the dark and the agencies responsible for inspection of U.S. food imports have been kept in the dark."

An intense battle over hazardous pesticides is also taking place in the European Community, where proponents and opponents of tighter export controls have been arguing since 1986. Export restrictions on many dangerous chemicals may become mandatory for the 12 community members. West Germany, France and Switzerland, who with the United States are the world's leading pesticide exporters, have delayed a decision.

"Companies know they cannot keep swimming against the current," said a Dutch diplomat who asked not to be identified. "Pesticides have been receiving a lot of negative publicity."

Chemical companies argue that it is up to a buyer to decide if it wants a product. They note that DDT, banned in some countries, is made in India, which considers it vital in fighting malaria. Dieldrin, which is banned in many countries, was used by United Nations technicians to fight a locust plague in North Africa

The situation in Brazil illustrates some of the problems. Now one of the largest producers and consumers of agricultural chemicals in the third world, Brazil has a rural population that is close to 40 percent illiterate. In interviews earlier this year, agronomists said that even farmers who can read often find it difficult to understand the instructions for using the chemicals. More than 1,500 products are now widely available, and Government officials said

Brazil uses at least 10 products that are banned in the United States.

Workers Lack Protection

A pesticide inspector in Porto Alegre said existing rules are often ignored. The most toxic products, for example, require a permit, but salesmen overlook this. "Some places keep a stack of permits already signed by an agronomist," the inspector said.

Around Campinas, a farming region in southern Brazil, workers handling toxic products said they had no masks, rubber gloves, boots, head covers or other protection. Some said they would not use it anyway.

"It's unbearable," said Eduardo Garcia, an agronomist. "People suffocate in the heat." One of the greatest problems, he said, is that pesticides and protective clothing intended for colder climates have not been adapted for a tropical environment. Chemical companies have acknowledged the problem and say they are suitable protection.

One of the few studies available, a 1987 survey by the Department of Occupational Safety and Medicine of the Ministry of Labor, said that among more than 5,000 farm workers in eight states who handled pesticides, 28 of the men and women said they had already suffered poisonings.

"People only come here when they have accidents," said Dr. Ronan Vieira, who heads the department of toxicology at the University Hospital of Campinas. "But they don't make the connection

between their symptoms and slow poisoning." Moreover, he said, most doctors are not trained to establish the cause of symptoms like hair loss, eye and skin problems, and nausea.

Last year, after reports about pesticide abuse and accidents, Brazil's chemical companies began a television campaign to warn that misuse of pesticides could harm the environment. But Dr. Vieira and others complained that nothing was said about people.

'We Have No Laws'

Health experts at the United Nations said the misuse of pesticides is even more serious in Africa. "Some people use pesticides as a form of hunting," said Mr. Shamil, the agronomist. Talking of last year's slaughter at the Dinder reserve, he said farmers near the reserve decided to use pesticides because "there were too many birds" eating sorghum and millet. "So they put the poison in the puddles and lagoons," he said.

Mr. Shamil's photographs, which he said were taken at the reserve, showed barrels labeled as a concentrate of DDT and other chemicals, made in Delaware but not available in the United States. The poison, he said, had killed buffaloes, gazelles, lions and birds.

"What's worse," he said, "the animals were skinned, the meat dried and sold in the market." He is still trying to find out how the powerful pesticide entered Sudan. "We have no laws," he said. "There are no records."

THE KERALA EXPERIMENT

An Indian state chooses equity over growth

Richard Franke and
Barbara Chasin

RICHARD FRANKE is an anthropologist and BARBARA CHASIN a sociologist at Montclair State College in New Jersey. Susan Schacht, a member of the *Dollars & Sense* Collective, adapted this article from the authors' *Kerala: Radical Reform as Development in an Indian State* (Institute for Food and Development Policy, 1989). Franke and Chasin spent 1986 and 1987 as researchers at the Centre for Development Studies in Kerala.

"In the '60s and '70s, tremendous emphasis was put on how you get better GNP growth rates. But GNP growth rates can hide mass maldistribution of income. ... In the '90s, the target ought to be ... assuring safe water, assuring access to health services, assuring basic education."

— UNICEF director James Grant, delivering his agency's 1989 report.

At the southwest tip of India, the tiny state of Kerala is testing a rare approach to development. With a history of militant organizing — and several governments led by or including communists — Kerala has chosen equity before growth.

Like much of the Third World, this agrarian region of 27 million people wrestles with high unemployment and stagnant production, and it has no solutions on hand. If Kerala were a separate country, its per capita income would be the ninth lowest in the world.

Nevertheless, by redistributing what little they have, Keralites on the whole enjoy far better health, nutrition, and education than do other Indians or people in most developing nations (see tables). Material comforts are spread relatively evenly among men and women, farm workers and city dwellers, and high and low castes. A typical Indian dies at age 57, but a Keralite can expect to live to 68 — closer to the U.S. average of 75.

Kerala has made headway without the centralized power usually associated with radical change, so its successes — and failures — are especially relevant to reformers elsewhere who have no hope of immediate national power. While development theory usually focuses on entire countries, Kerala is one of 22 states in India. Ultimate control lies in New Delhi, which has never had a communist or leftist government. Often, policies from the center have blunted many of Kerala's reforms. The most important of these was the 1959 dismissal of Kerala's first elected communist government, delaying radical land reform. At least three times, New Delhi manipulated food supplies to undercut left-wing state administrations. During former Prime Minister Indira Gandhi's "emergency" of the mid-1970s, hundreds of leftists were arrested despite their longstanding commitment to democratic and parliamentary politics.

WHY KERALA?

Even within its limits, Kerala has provided its people with remarkable living standards for the Third World. Much of the explanation lies in the region's ecology, its history as a center of trade and British investment, and its long tradition of strong protest movements.

Kerala is a lush land of coconut groves, rice fields, and crowded hamlets. Along the Arabian Sea, Muslim fishing families eke out a poor living from their catch. Inland, women beat and pull apart rotted coconut husks, spin the fibers into a yarn called coir, and weave them into the mats that were a major export to Europe and the United States before synthetics took hold. Near the mountainous eastern border are pepper, rubber, coffee, and tea plantations. Cash crops cover 40% of the cultivated land. A few urban centers turn out food products, chemicals, plywood, fabrics, and other goods, but most wage work is in low-paid cottage industries or in the fields.

In Kerala, many decades of militant struggle by caste associations, peasants, and labor unions have brought radical reform.

From *Dollars & Sense*, May 1990, pp. 16–19. Reprinted by permission.

Quality of Life Indicators

	Kerala	India	Low-Income Countries	United States
Per capita GNP (in $)	182	290	200	17,480
Adult literacy rate (%)	78	43	na	96
Life expectancy (in years)	68	57	52	75
Infant mortality (per 1,000)	27	86	106	10
Birth rate (per 1,000)	22	32	43	16

Sources and notes: Kerala adult literacy rate, Government of Kerala, 1981 data; India and United States adult literacy rate, 1985 data; all other data, World Bank, 1988. Data for low-income countries is based on the average for 37 countries designated by the World Bank, excluding China and India. Kerala's per capita GNP was calculated at the rate of 13 rupees per U.S. dollar, the exchange rate in 1986-87.

In 1967, a communist-led coalition returned to power, and India's then-ruling Congress Party finally backed the growing movement for land reform. When Kerala abolished tenancy in 1969, a million and a half tenants won title to the rice fields they worked, their household gardens, or both. Landlords received compensation from the government and from tenants and turned to teaching, government jobs, or medium-scale farming.

Twice more, Kerala elected solidly leftist governments. Even when a coalition of left- and right-wing groups held sway through the 1970s, many progressive policies continued—due to persistent pressure from peasants and labor unions. The Left Democratic Front, a coalition of two communist and several smaller parties, has governed since 1987.

FRUITS OF STRUGGLE

Successive state administrations in Kerala have put equity and economic security ahead of growth. Thus, though their incomes are lower on average, Keralites eat as well or better than other Indians.

The government ensures minimum nutrition to just about everyone, largely through shops near almost every village that ration staples like rice and cooking oil at fixed prices. Some stores are cooperatives, but most are private businesses that receive a controlled profit. In addition, the government funds a daily school lunch program that first got off the ground in the 1960s with aid from CARE, a private U.S. relief agency. And at village nurseries, women's groups receive public money to cook daily meals for mothers and their infants.

Kerala has also outpaced India for decades in literacy, putting basic skills ahead of higher education. Almost three-fourths of Keralites can read and write; less than half are literate in the rest of India. Keralites lead the nation in newspaper readership.

Keralites have waged a sustained assault on the caste system as well—now officially illegal in India but in many ways intact. Some lower-caste members have risen to leadership in political parties and government ministries, and the cabinet elected in 1957 included four former untouchables.

During the course of a century, Kerala has moved to improve health through housing, sanitation, and immunization. In the 1970s, with state and national

The rich natural resources are fairly evenly distributed throughout the area, and so, in turn, are the people. Most of the state receives plenty of rainfall, so water hasn't been a major problem. Kerala has no great rural-urban distinction, so providing health care and education to this dense population costs less than elsewhere in India.

Kerala's past as a trading center may help explain the progressive outlook of many of its leaders. Though most Keralites are Hindu, international trade has brought settlers from around the globe since ancient times. The state has been exposed to the ideas and cultures of Greeks, Egyptians, Romans, Jews, Christians, and Muslims, most of whom came without conquest or bloodshed. Today, Christians and Muslims each make up 20% of the population. A small Jewish community lives in the port city of Cochin, a remnant of a larger group that figured in Kerala's ancient trade in spices and teak wood.

British imperialism led to the creation of a working class sooner in Kerala than elsewhere in India, and the process was far more intense. In the 19th century, British colonists set up rural industries and plantations, generating a large pool of landless laborers.

British rule also helped disrupt caste relations. Like the rest of India, Kerala has been steeped in the tradition of the caste system, which for centuries set everyone's social standing at birth—whom they could marry, what work they could do, which religious rituals they performed, how their bodies were dealt with at death. A tiny Brahmin elite owned most of the land. Below them, the ranks

descended to the untouchables, who were relegated to the most menial work.

In contrast to most of India, many decades of militant struggle by caste associations, peasants, and labor unions have brought radical reform. In 1893, a Kerala untouchable named Ayyankali traveled in a bullock cart along a public road. That simple act was a major public protest against caste restrictions: he should have walked, calling out his presence to all higher-caste people so they could avoid coming close to him. Ayyankali went on to help organize strikes by field laborers and campaigns to admit untouchable children to government schools.

As such movements grew, lower castes formed improvement associations that pressed for access to government jobs and education early in the 20th century. Moreover, time and again, tenant farmers rose up to fight a feudal system in which they rented from landlords at exorbitant prices. A bloody rebellion in 1920 spurred legislation but no real gains for the poorest tillers. A 1940s study in one part of the state found that peasants paid half to three-fourths of their gross returns to the classes above them.

In 1947, India won independence from Britain and after a decade established Kerala as one of 22 states. Voters elected a communist majority to the state legislature, with land reform high on the agenda. Pressure from landlords, however, led the national government to dismiss the state administration two years later, so in the late 1960s, 8% of landowners still owned 44% of all rented land. Tenants again rebelled, this time claiming their plots by planting red flags.

funds, Kerala built thousands of houses from wood, tile, and sun-dried brick for landless laborers, who had been living in dirt-floor huts that drew bacteria and mosquitoes. Kerala devotes more of its budget than any other Indian state to hospitals and clinics, and facilities are spread more evenly among urban and rural areas. One result: infant deaths in Kerala are a third as common as they are throughout India and only a fourth as frequent as in other poor countries.

While many Third World governments are cutting education and medical services to pay debts to banks in rich nations, Kerala has tried to expand school lunch and pension programs. Real per capita education spending rose 8% in 1987 but fell by almost 2% the next year, due to higher inflation. Health spending, even when corrected for inflation, rose about 12% in 1987 and 3% in 1988.

Despite Kerala's achievements in promoting social and economic justice, a stagnant economy limits progress. As in most of the Third World, children remain far below developed-nation standards in height and weight. Digestive problems from unclean drinking water are common. Most low-caste families are still farm laborers, and to help support the household, children must often skip school and work the fields. And the public programs are costly: in 1975, taxes soaked up 11% of average income, while the tax rates in most other Indian states were 6-10%.

Though Kerala ranks high among Indian states in land productivity, agricultural output isn't growing. Many small landowners have suffered from the falling price of rice relative to other products. They often lack the capital to plant more lucrative crops, such as coconuts or rubber.

Finally, massive unemployment, hovering at 25% in the mid-1980s, has proved intractable. Hundreds of thousands of Keralites have migrated to other parts of India, the Gulf states, or the West, where their education boosts their job prospects. A growing number of Keralite nurses work in the United States.

Some analysts, without offering conclusive evidence, argue that high wages cause Kerala's unemployment. Some cashew processors have moved across the state border in search of cheaper labor, but most of Kerala's unemployment predates wage increases won by unions in recent years.

In the face of these maladies, land

Provision of Basic Services, Late 1970s

	Rank of Kerala among All Indian States	% of Villages with Service in Kerala	% of Villages with Service in All India
Within 2 kilometers			
All-weather roads	1	98	46
Bus stops	1	98	40
Post offices	1	100	53
Primary schools	1	100	90
Secondary schools	1	99	44
Fair price (ration) shops	1	99	35
Health dispensaries	1	91	25
Health centers	1	47	12
Within 5 kilometers			
Higher education facilities	1	97	21
Hospitals	1	78	35
Fertilizer depots	1	93	44
Agricultural pump repairs shops	1	65	19
Veterinary dispensaries	1	82	45
Credit cooperative banks	1	96	61
Other banks	1	96	40
Seed stores	2	63	40
Storage and warehouses	4	34	21
Railway stations	8	23	18
In the village			
Drinking water	5	96	93
Electricity	3	97	33

Sources: Kerala: Radical Reform as Development in an Indian State, Institute for Food and Development Policy, 1989.

reform and welfare programs have provided some security, easing the hardship of joblessness and shielding the poor from global recessions. The state initiated unemployment insurance in 1981 and farm-worker pensions the following year. A pension of 720 rupees a year (about $48, or a fourth of the per capita income) seems a pittance, but it helps sustain 286,000 elderly agricultural workers who would otherwise depend entirely on impoverished offspring. Rural workers also have some assurance of food on the table from the garden plots they won in land reform.

A LESSON IN PROGRESS

Which is better, growth or redistribution? That choice drives much of the debate over Third World development.

Both would be nice, but if, as many believe, the two goals are incompatible, governments often must choose whether to boost production or to spread the wealth while accepting relative stagnation. Very few countries have managed both significant growth and redistribution. The economies of most of Latin America, the Middle East, Southeast Asia, and the Pacific Islands have grown considerably but with little or no redistribution. Most of Africa and South Asia have failed on both counts.

The prevailing U.S. view holds that if poor countries could get their economies to grow and modernize through private enterprise, they would eventually look like us. In the early stages of growth, inequality and poverty might increase, as they did in 19th century Europe, but eventually, distribution would become more just.

The radical response is that capitalism stands in the way of Third World progress. Rich countries extract income and resources from poor ones, repatriating profits and maintaining repressive military regimes. Revolution and a fundamental break with that pattern will pave the way for effective development.

Advocates of both positions can find strong support in the numbers. Higher per capita income does improve the overall health and education of a population. But for any given income, redistribution yields higher literacy rates, longer lives, and fewer infant deaths. And redistribution's benefits are greatest in the poorest countries.

In this debate, Kerala provides some but not all the answers. Redistribution by itself can't improve average income, and Kerala's reforms haven't raised agricultural production or eased unemployment—chronic Third World problems. The Left Democratic Front now in office has proposed to stimulate local investment in small-scale, rural industry, but it is too soon to tell whether the plans will generate many new jobs.

Still, Kerala has proven that radical reform can serve the poor even when per capita income is low. People's lives—the real bottom line of development—are better.

Grass-roots groups are our best hope for global prosperity and ecology

ALAN B. DURNING
WORLDWATCH INSTITUTE

Perhaps the most important political development of our time is one that receives little media coverage. While world leaders shake hands or trade accusations with one another, the people back at home set about changing the world in small ways: planting trees, stopping unwanted development projects, organizing cooperatives. Alan Durning, a researcher at the Worldwatch Institute in Washington, D.C., says that taken together, these grass-roots activists amount to today's leading political force fighting for economic justice and environmental safety. From Asian villages to Eastern European factories to U.S. neighborhoods, people are clamoring for the right to control their own futures.

Women on the banks of the Ganges may not be able to calculate an infant mortality rate, but they know all too well the helplessness and agony of holding a child as it dies of diarrhea. Residents along the lower reaches of the Mississippi may not be able to name the carcinogens and mutagens that nearby chemical factories pump into the air and water, but they know how many of their neighbors have suffered miscarriages or died of cancer. Forest dwellers in the Amazon basin cannot quantify the mass extinction of species now occurring around them, but they know what it is to watch their primeval homeland go up in smoke before advancing waves of cattle ranchers and developers.

These men and women in Bangladesh, Louisiana, and Brazil understand environmental degradation in its rawest forms. To them, creeping destruction of ecosystems has meant deteriorating health, lengthening workdays, and failing livelihoods. And it has pushed many of them to act. In villages, neighborhoods, and shantytowns around the world, people are coming together to challenge the forces of environmental and economic decline that endanger our communities and our planet.

In the face of such enormous threats, isolated grass-roots organizing efforts appear minuscule—10

women plant trees on a roadside, a local union strikes for a non-toxic workplace, an old man teaches neighborhood children to read—but, when added together, their impact has the potential to reshape the earth. Indeed, local activists form a front line in the worldwide struggle to end poverty and environmental destruction.

These grass-roots groups include workplace co-ops, suburban parents committees, peasant farmers unions, religious study groups, neighborhood action federations, tribal nations, and innumerable others. Although widely diverse in origins, these groups share a common capacity to utilize local knowledge and resources, to respond to problems rapidly and creatively, and to maintain the flexibility necessary to adapt to changing circumstances. In addition, although few groups use the term sustainable development, their agendas often embody this ideal. They want economic prosperity without sacrificing their

In villages, neighborhoods, and shantytowns around the world, people are coming together to challenge the forces that endanger our planet.

health or the prospects for their children.

All by itself this new wave of local activist organizations is nowhere near powerful enough to shift modern industrial society onto a more sustainable course of development. The work required—from slowing excessive population growth to reforesting the planet—will involve an unprecedented outpouring of human energy. Yet community groups, whose membership now numbers in the hundreds of millions worldwide, may be able to show the world how to tap the energy to perform these acts.

From *Utne Reader,* July/August 1989, pp. 40–49. Excerpted with permission from a paper prepared by the Worldwatch Institute "Action at the Grassroots: Fighting Poverty and Environmental Decline," *Worldwatch Paper 88.*

Grass-roots action is on the rise everywhere, from Eastern Europe's industrial heartland, where fledgling environmental movements are demanding that human health no longer be sacrificed for economic growth, to the Himalayan foothills, where multitudes of Indian villagers are organized to protect and reforest barren slopes. As environmental decay accelerates in industrial regions, local communities are organizing in growing numbers to protect themselves from chemical wastes, industrial pollution, and nuclear power installations. Meanwhile, in developing countries, deepening poverty combined with often catastrophic ecological degradation has led to the proliferation of grass-roots self-help movements.

In the Third World, especially, traditional tribal, village, and religious organizations—first disturbed by European colonialism—have been stretched and often dismantled by the great cultural upheavals of the 20th century: rapid population growth, urbanization, the advent of modern technology, and the spread of Western commercialism. Community groups have been formed in many places to meet the economic and social needs these traditional ties once fulfilled.

In the face of seemingly insurmountable problems, community groups around the planet have been able to accomplish phenomenal things.

■ In Lima's Villa El Salvador district, Peruvians have planted a half-million trees; built 26 schools, 150 daycare centers, and 300 community kitchens; and trained hundreds of door-to-door health workers. Despite the extreme poverty of the district's inhabitants and a population that has shot up to 300,000, illiteracy has fallen to 3 percent—one of the lowest rates in Latin America—and infant mortality is 40 percent below the national average. The ingredients of success have been a vast network of women's groups and the neighborhood association's democratic administrative structure, which extends down to representatives on each block.

■ In Dhandhuka, on the barren coastal plain of India's Gujarat state, a generation of excessive fuelwood gathering and overgrazing has led to desertification, which in turn has triggered social and economic disintegration. As cattle died of thirst, the children lost their milk, making them easy victims for the diseases that prey on the malnourished. Conflicts erupted over water that seeped into brackish wells, and in the worst years, four-fifths of the population had to migrate to survive. As in much of the world, fetching water in Dhandhuka is women's work. Thus it was the women who decided, upon talking with community organizers in 1981, to build a permanent reservoir to trap the seasonal rains. Migrant laborers described irrigation channels lined with plastic sheets they had seen elsewhere, and the villagers reasoned that a reservoir could be sealed the same way. After lengthy discussion and debate, the community agreed to the plan, and in 1986, all but a few stayed home during the dry season to get the job done. Moving thousands of tons of earth by hand, they finished the pool before the rains returned. The next dry season they were well-supplied, which inspired neighboring villages to plan their own reservoirs.

India's self-help movement traces its roots back to Gandhi.

Asia has by many accounts the most active grass-roots movement. India's self-help movement has a prized place in society, tracing its roots to Mahatma Gandhi's pioneering village development work 60 years ago. Gandhi aimed to build a just and humane society from the bottom up, starting with self-reliant villages based on renewable resources. Tens if not hundreds of thousands of local groups in India now wage the day-by-day struggle for development.

Across the region, community activism runs high. Three million Sri Lankans, for instance, participate in Sarvodaya Shramadana, a community development movement that combines Gandhian teachings with social action tenets of Theravada Buddhism. Sarvodaya mobilizes massive work teams to do everything from building roads to draining malarial ponds.

After Asia, Latin American communities are perhaps the most active. The event that sparked much of this work was the 1968 conference of Catholic Bishops in Medellin, Colombia, where the Roman Catholic Church fundamentally reoriented its social mission toward improving the lot of the poor. Since that time, millions of priests, nuns, and laypeople have fanned out into the back streets and hinterlands from Tierra del Fuego to the Rio Grande, dedicating themselves to creating a people's church embodied in neighborhood worship and action groups called Christian Base Communities. Brazil alone has 100,000 base communities, with at least three million members, and an equal number are spread across the rest of the continent.

Latin American political movements also laid the groundwork for current community self-help efforts. A decade ago, the rise and subsequent repression of Colombia's National Association of Small Farmers gave peasants experience with organizing that led to the abundance of community efforts today, including cooperative stores and environmental "green councils." In Nicaragua, the national uprising that overthrew the dictatorship of Anastasio Somoza in 1979 created a surge of grass-roots energy that flowed into thousands of new cooperatives, women's groups, and community-development projects.

Self-help organizations are relative newcomers to Africa, though traditional village institutions remain stronger here than in other regions. Nevertheless, in parts of Africa where political struggles have led to dramatic changes in political structures, local initiatives have sprung up in abundance. In Kenya, the *harambee* (let's pull together) movement began with

Sustainable success stories from the Third World

Environmental quality is not a luxury. Those who live beyond the borders of the world's industrial economy subsist on nature's surplus—soil fertility for food, stable hydrological cycles for water, and forests for fuel. Environmental degradation, consequently, has direct, tangible results: hunger, thirst, and fuel scarcity. No line can be drawn between economic development and environmental protection.

• The world's largest rain forest envelops the thousand tributaries of the Amazon River, forming a great fan that covers northern Brazil and spreads into Venezuela, Colombia, Ecuador, Peru, and Bolivia. The traditional inhabitants of this great basin include dozens of tribes of Indians and 300,000 rubber tappers, a guild of workers who earn their living by tapping the rubber trees spread through the region.

Since the 1960s, a series of powerful economic and political forces has brought waves of landless peasants and wealthy land-speculators into the jungles, where they have driven the rubber tappers out—sometimes at gunpoint. The newcomers proceed to clear-cut the woodlands and burn the fallen logs, causing unprecedented destruction and enormous releases of air pollution. In 1987 alone, an area almost the size of Maine went up in smoke.

In the late 1970s, a union of 30,000 rubber tappers from the remote Brazilian state of Acre decided to draw the line. At first, their tactics were simple and direct: Where the chain saws were working, men, women, and children would peacefully occupy the forest, putting their bodies in the path of destruction. This non-violent method was met with violent reprisals that continue today. Last December, two gunmen ambushed Francisco Mendes Filho, national leader of the rubber tappers union, killing him instantly.

The price of their struggle has been high, but the rubber tappers have made modest gains. Bolstered by an unprecedented alliance with indigenous tribes and the scattered beginnings of a nationwide rubber tappers' movement, the union has demanded an end to destruction of the land—and an end to violence against their members. They have helped reshape World Bank and Inter-American Development Bank lending policy by showing that, over the long run, natural-rubber production is more profitable and creates more employment per hectare than cattle ranching or farming. With help from interna-tional environmental groups, the union has called on the Brazilian government to set off large "extractive reserves" where tappers can carry on their way of life in perpetuity. And among the rubber trees of the Amazon forest, they have built community schools and health posts.

• Across the Pacific, Borneo's Dayak tribe has been less fortunate. The island's dense woodlands are a foundation of Malaysia's foreign-exchange/export strategy, providing the country with most of its billion-dollar annual hardwood trade. The Dayaks, however, want it lumbered only on a sustainable basis and have battled timber contractors by constructing roadblocks and appealing to European consumers to boycott Malaysian hardwoods. To date, government policies have stymied their efforts. The official attitude is summed up by state Minister of the Environment Datuk James Wong, himself a timber tycoon: "There is too much sympathy for the Dayaks. Their swidden lifestyle must be stamped out."

• The well-organized Kuna Indians of Panama, on the other hand, have been able to establish their homeland as a biological reserve, putting it off-limits to the settlers and cattle ranchers who, predictably, followed a new access road. In 1980 then-President Omar Torrijos demanded, "Why do you Kuna need so much land? You don't do anything with it . . . . If anyone else so much as cuts down a single tree, you shout and scream."

A local leader responded, "If I go to Panama City and stand in front of a pharmacy and, because I need medicine, pick up a rock and break the window, you would take me away and put me in jail. For me, the forest is my pharmacy. If I have sores on my legs, I go to the forest and get the medicine I need to cure them. The forest is also a great refrigerator. It keeps the food I need fresh. . . . So we Kuna need the forest, and we use it and we take much from it. But we can take what we need without having to destroy everything, as your people do."

• The world's most acclaimed community forest movement, Chipko, shows how grass-roots action to defend a resource can grow into far more. Born in the Garhwal hills of Uttar Pradesh, India, Chipko first drew fame for its sheer courage. In March 1973, as a timber company headed for the woods above one impoverished village, desperate local men, women, and children rushed ahead of them to *chipko* (literally, "hug" or "cling to") the trees, daring the loggers to let the axes fall on their backs.

Since its initial success, the movement has deepened its ecological understanding and, in the words of movement follower Vandana Shiva, "widened from embracing trees to embracing mountains and waters." In 1987, for example, activists formed a seven-month blockade at a limestone quarry that was recklessly destroying the ecosystem of an entire valley. Chipko has gone beyond resource protection to ecological management, restoration, and what members call "eco-development." The women who first guarded trees against loggers now plant trees, build soil-retention walls, and prepare village forestry plans.

• Grass-roots groups organize most readily to defend their resource base against the incursion of outsiders, but in the right circumstances they may organize to reverse deterioration driven by forces internal to the community.

As Kenya's forests shrink, thousands of women's groups, youth clubs, and harambee (let's pull together) societies have mounted local tree planting drives. The National Council of Women of Kenya inaugurated its Greenbelt Movement in 1977, calling on women's groups across the country to turn open spaces, school grounds, and roadsides into forests. More than a million trees in 1,000 greenbelts are now straining skyward, 20,000 mini-greenbelts have taken root, and 670 community tree nurseries are in place. Meanwhile, Kenya's largest women's development network, Maendeleo Ya Wanawake, with its 10,000 member groups, initiated a campaign in 1985 to construct improved, wood-saving cookstoves.

• An African federation popularly known as Naam is among the most successful of the world's grass-roots movements at mobilizing people to protect and restore natural resources in an area degraded from overuse. Building on pre-colonial self-help traditions, Naam taps vast stores of peasant knowledge, creativity, and energy to loosen the grip of poverty and ecological deterioration in the drought-prone Sahel region of West Africa. With origins in Burkina Faso, it now spills over under different names into Mauritania, Senegal, Mali, Niger, and Togo.

Each year during the dry season, thousands of Naam villages undertake projects chosen and de-

This farmer in the African nation of Mauritania tends her plot, which is part of a cooperative women's project.

signed with minimal assistance from outsiders. Along with five neighboring communities, for example, the settlement of Somiaga built a large dam and a series of check dams to trap drinking and irrigation water and to slow soil erosion. Villagers piled caged rocks by hand to form a dam four meters high and 180 meters long. Meanwhile, hundreds of Naam farmers have adopted a simple technique of soil and water conservation developed by Oxfam-UK, in which stones are piled in low rows along the contour to hold back the runoff from torrential rains. While halting soil loss, these *diguetes* increase crop yields dramatically.

—Alan B. Durning
The Progressive

Excerpted with permission from The Progressive *(April 1989). Subscriptions: $27.50/yr. (12 issues) from The Progressive, Box 54615, Boulder, CO 80321-4615. Back issues: $2.50. This originally appeared in the* Worldwatch Paper 88, "Action at the Grassroots."

People power transforms a St. Louis housing project

Bertha Gilkey lives today in Cochran Gardens, a St. Louis public housing project featuring flower-lined paths, trees and grass, play equipment for children, a beautiful and clean neighborhood, happy and trusting people. Gilkey grew up in the very same housing project when it was an ugly urban scar filled with broken windows, graffiti, rubbish, frequent shootings (both kinds), angry and fearful people. The change is one of the most dramatic stories dealing with government housing in our lifetime. And there might well have been no change at all except for Bertha Gilkey—and her hard, astute community organizing.

As a teenager she attended tenant meetings at a nearby church, and when she was 20 years old, Bertha was elected by the Cochran residents to chair their tenants' association. Since that time, the project has not been the same. Bertha had both short-range and long-range strategies, but she told me that she dared not tell anybody the long-range strategy. Nobody would have believed her.

Bertha and her group started with small things. What did people really want? What could actually be done? Everyone wanted a laundromat again. All of the project's previous ones had been vandalized. Bertha and her group began to organize other residents. "Let's get our laundromat locked," they said. "Locked?" Gilkey recalls, "When we took over, there were no locks. There was no doors! All the doors had been taken down." They got a new door from the city housing authority. Then the tenants had a fundraiser for a lock. Then for paint. The laundromat was a success. Next, the group organized to paint the hallways, floor by floor. "Everybody who lived on a floor was responsible for painting that floor," says Gilkey. "If you didn't paint that floor, it didn't happen. Kids who lived on a floor that hadn't been painted would come and look at the painted hallways and then go back and hassle their parents. The elderly who couldn't paint prepared lunch, so they could feel like they were a part of it, too."

While sprucing up the physical appearance of their building, Bertha and her organized tenants reintroduced a kind of conduct code for their unit. A committee established rules of behavior and elected monitors on each floor. No fights, no garbage out the windows, no loud disruptions, etc. Slowly people got the message. People got involved. Living conditions improved, bit by bit.

They renamed their unit the Dr. Martin Luther King Jr. Building. Symbols were important. "Everything we did, we had a party and a celebration," Gilkey says. "There would be a dedication for everything." Even the new laundromat had a ribbon-cutting.

Reaching the young people was another of Gilkey's key strategies. Changes were initiated in schools. "Kids wrote papers on 'What I Like about Living Here,' playing up the postive," Gilkey explains. "In the art class, they built a cardboard model of the housing project with street and playground. The principal put it in a glass dome with a sign that read 'Cochran.' Then kids could say, 'I live in that building.' Gradually, in an indirect way, we were rebuilding self-esteem, telling the kids it's all right to live in public housing."

Today Cochran Gardens high-rises are completely renovated. There is a community center, courtyards, tennis courts, playgrounds, and the Cochran Plaza town houses, built to reduce density in the complex. "But we had to fight the Housing Authority on that," Gilkey recalls. "When we got Cochran Plaza built, they said it was too beautiful for people from Cochran and started moving other people in. So we took them to court. The judge wrote a whole decision about how incompetent the Authority was. It was beautiful."

Cochran Gardens is one of four public housing projects in St. Louis managed by tenants. It is the centerpiece of an extensive network of non-profit housing developments and businesses owned and operated by the Tenant Management Council. Its other ventures include a catering service, health clinics, day-care centers, and a vocational training program. After showing me through Cochran Gardens, Bertha Gilkey asked rhetorically, "Isn't this beautiful? Isn't this the way poor people are supposed to live?"

How did all this happen? A lot of work, a lot of dedication, a lot of years. A lot of organizing. Gilkey sums it up: "Either you plan or they plan for you."

As I finished my visit to Cochran Gardens, Gilkey turned to me and said, smiling, "This goes against the grain, doesn't it? Poor people are to *be* managed. What we've done is cut through all the bullshit and said it doesn't take all that. People with degrees and credentials got us in this mess. All it takes is some basic skills."

I asked her about the principles that have created a success at Cochran: self-help, dignity, empowerment, responsibility. Are these transferable to any community? "Yes, yes," she smiled. "If we can do it in public housing, it can happen anywhere."

—Harry C. Boyte
Occasional Papers

Excerpted with permission from Occasional Papers *(Jan. 1989). Subscriptions: $7.50/yr. (3 issues) from Community Renewal Society, 332 S. Michigan Av., Chicago, IL 60604. Back issues: $2.50 from same address.*

independence in 1963 and, with encouragement from the national government, by the early '80s was contributing nearly one-third of all labor, materials, and finances invested in rural development. With Zimbabwe's transfer to black rule in 1980, a similar explosion in community organizing began, as thousands of women's community gardens and informal small-farmer associations formed.

A noteworthy characteristic of community movements throughout the Third World is the central role that women play. Women's traditional nurturing role may give them increased concern for the generations of their children and grandchildren, while their subordinate social status gives them more to gain from organizing.

Unfortunately, the map of Third World local action has several blank spaces. Independent community-level organizations concentrating on self-help are scarce or non-existent in the Middle East, China, north Africa, large patches of sub-Saharan Africa, and northeastern India. Likewise, remote regions in many countries lack grass-roots groups. Some of these

Women play a central role in many Third World community movements.

absences are a result of cultural, religious, or political factors, as in China, where state-sanctioned local groups monopolize grass-roots development. Northeastern India and sub-Saharan Africa, by contrast, are home to some of the poorest people on earth. The absence of local groups there may reflect a degree of misery that prevents energy from being expended on anything beyond survival.

Outside the Third World, grass-roots movements are also on the rise. In the Soviet Union and Eastern Europe, where officially sanctioned local organizations are numerous but largely controlled by state and party hierarchies, the political openness of this decade has brought a wave of independent citizens groups. (See "Independent activists challenge the status quo in Eastern Europe," *Utne Reader*, Jan./Feb. 1989.)

Environmental issues and grass-roots politics play a major role in the new nationalist movements rocking the USSR. In February 1988, thousands of Armenians, tired of bearing the brunt of pollution from the scores of local chemical facilities, demanded cancellation of a proposed plant near their capital city, Yerevan. Eight months later, 50,000 Latvians, Estonians, and Lithuanians linked arms in a human chain stretching 150 kilometers along the shore of the severely polluted Baltic Sea to protest Soviet planners' blatant disregard for the ecology of their homelands.

In those regions where nuclear power is still on a growth course—Japan, France, and Eastern Europe—anti-nuclear movements have grown dramatically since the 1986 explosion at Chernobyl. Intense popular opposition seems to follow nuclear power wherever it goes. In the Soviet Union, public protests have led to plans to close one operating nuclear reactor and to cancellation of at least five planned plants. In Japan, an unprecedented groundswell—the first nationwide movement on an environmental issue in the country's history—has enrolled tens of thousands of citizens with no past experience in political activism. Women in particular are joining in large numbers, apparently sensitized by fears of radioactive food imported from Europe after Chernobyl.

In Western industrial nations, community-based organizations set their sights on everything from local waste recycling to international trade and debt issues. The ascent of the German Green Party in the early '80s was partly a product of an evolution in this movement from local to national concerns. Inspired by their German counterpart, Green parties have sprung up in 16 European countries and already hold parliamentary seats in more than half of them.

Paralleling a steady rise in neighborhood organizing on local social and economic issues, the U.S. environmental movement experienced a marked grass-roots expansion in the early '80s. Local concern focuses particularly on toxic waste management, groundwater protection, and solid waste problems.

Midwives in the African nation of Rwanda gather leaves for traditional remedies that will be used in tandem with modern medicine.

Issue-oriented environmental activism is not peculiar to industrial lands. Just as grass-roots self-help movements have spread through the slums and countrysides of many developing nations, vocal advocates for environmental protection have emerged in most capital cities. Malaysia, India, Brazil, Argentina, Kenya, Mexico, Indonesia, Ecuador, Thailand, and other developing countries have all given birth to activist groups—largely since 1980. Sri Lanka alone has a congress of environmental groups with 100 members. Environmental movements and grass-roots development movements have also begun to work together.

Despite the heartening rise of grass-roots action, humanity is losing the struggle for sustainable development. For every peasant movement that reverses the topsoil erosion of valuable agricultural land, dozens more fail. For each neighborhood that rallies to replace a proposed garbage burner with a recycling program, many others remain mired in inaction. Spreading today's grass-roots mobilization to a larger share of the world's communities is a crucial step toward putting an end to the global scourges of poverty and environmental degradation.

All local groups eventually collide with forces they cannot control. Peasant associations cannot enact national or international agricultural policies or build roads to distant markets. Women's groups cannot develop and test modern contraceptive technologies or rewrite bank lending rules. Neighborhood committees cannot implement citywide recycling programs or give themselves a seat at the table in national energy planning. The greatest obstacle to community action is that communities cannot do it alone. Small may be beautiful, but it can also be insignificant.

The prospects for grass-roots progress against poverty are further limited in a world economy in which vested interests are deeply entrenched and power is concentrated in a few nations. Thus reforms at the international level are as important as those in the village

The largest challenge in reversing global ecological and economic deterioration is to forge an alliance between local groups and national governments. Only governments have the resources and authority to create the conditions for full-scale grass-roots mobilization. In the rare cases where national-local alliances have been forged, extraordinary gains have followed. South Korea and China have used village-level organizations to plant enormous expanses of trees, implement national population policies, and boost agricultural production. Zimbabwe has trained more than 500 community-selected family planners to improve

maternal and child health and control population growth. In the year after the 1979 Nicaraguan revolution, a massive literacy campaign sent 90,000 volunteers into the countryside; in one year, they raised literacy from 50 to 87 percent. Even under Ferdinand Marcos' repressive rule in the Philippines, the National Irrigation Administration amazingly transformed itself into a people-centered institution, cooperating with peasant associations.

Full-scale community-state alliances can come about only when a motivated and organized populace joins forces with responsive national leadership. But herein lies the greatest obstacle to mobilizing for pros-

A neighborhood group in the slums of Lima has built 26 schools and 150 day-care centers.

perity and ecology: Few leaders are committed to promoting popular organizations. Because government's first concern is almost always to retain political power, independent-minded grass-roots movements are generally seen as more of a threat than an ally. Unrepresentative elites rule many nations and all too often they crush popular movements rather than yield any of their privilege or power. Inevitably, self-help movements will clash with these forces, because like all development, self-help is inherently political: It is the struggle to control the future.

Essentially, grass-roots action on poverty and the environment comes down to the basic question of people's right to shape their own destiny. Around the world, community organizations are doing their best to put this participatory vision into practice, and they are simultaneously posing an even deeper question. In the world's impoverished south, it is phrased, "What is development?" In the industrial north, "What is progress?" Behind the words, however, is the same profoundly democratic refrain: What kind of society shall our nation be? What kind of lives shall our people lead? What kind of world shall we leave to our children?

Whether these scattered beginnings launched by grass-roots groups eventually rise in a global groundswell depends only on how many more individuals commit their creativity and energy to the challenge. The inescapable lesson for each of us is distilled in the words of Angeles Serrano, a grandmother and community activist from the slums of Manila. "Act, act, act. You can't just watch."

Index

Credits/ Acknowledgments

Cover design by Charles Vitalli

1. Understanding the Third World
Facing overview—United Nations photo by P. Teuscher. 24—Illustration by David Suter.

2. People, Power, and Leadership
Facing overview—United Nations photo by Y. Nagata. 41—Ministry of Information and Propaganda, Mexico.

3. Stability, Crisis, and Revolution
Facing overview—United Nations photo. 78—David Caulkin, AP.

4. Limits of American Power
Facing overview—United Nations photo by Jerry Frank.

5. Human Rights and Democratic Rule
Facing overview—United Nations photo.

6. Easing the Debt Crisis
Facing overview—United Nations photo by L. Barns. 196—*Africa Report.*

7. A World in Change
Facing overview—United Nations photo by John Isaac. 237—Photo by Maggie Murray Lee/UNICEF. 239—Photo by Bert Demmers/UNICEF.

ANNUAL EDITIONS ARTICLE REVIEW FORM

■ NAME: _____ DATE: _____

■ TITLE AND NUMBER OF ARTICLE: _____

■ BRIEFLY STATE THE MAIN IDEA OF THIS ARTICLE: _____

_____

_____

_____

_____

■ LIST THREE IMPORTANT FACTS THAT THE AUTHOR USES TO SUPPORT THE MAIN IDEA:

_____

_____

_____

_____

_____

_____

_____

■ WHAT INFORMATION OR IDEAS DISCUSSED IN THIS ARTICLE ARE ALSO DISCUSSED IN YOUR TEXTBOOK OR OTHER READING YOU HAVE DONE? LIST THE TEXTBOOK CHAPTERS AND PAGE NUMBERS:

_____

_____

_____

_____

_____

_____

_____

■ LIST ANY EXAMPLES OF BIAS OR FAULTY REASONING THAT YOU FOUND IN THE ARTICLE:

_____

_____

_____

_____

_____

■ LIST ANY NEW TERMS/CONCEPTS THAT WERE DISCUSSED IN THE ARTICLE AND WRITE A SHORT DEFINITION:

_____

_____

_____

_____

_____

*Your instructor may require you to use this Annual Editions Article Review Form in any number of ways: for articles that are assigned, for extra credit, as a tool to assist in developing assigned papers, or simply for your own reference. Even if it is not required, we encourage you to photocopy and use this page; you'll find that reflecting on the articles will greatly enhance the information from your text.

ANNUAL EDITIONS:
Third World 91/92
Article Rating Form

Here is an opportunity for you to have direct input into the next revision of this volume. We would like you to rate each of the 51 articles listed below, using the following scale:

1. **Excellent: should definitely be retained**
2. **Above average: should probably be retained**
3. **Below average: should probably be deleted**
4. **Poor: should definitely be deleted**

Your ratings will play a vital part in the next revision. So please mail this prepaid form to us just as soon as you complete it.
Thanks for your help!

Rating	Article	Rating	Article
	1. The Third World		28. Saving Central America
	2. Ethnocentrism and Third World Development		29. The Human Rights Imperative
	3. What the Third World Really Needs		30. The Fight to Stop Torture
	4. The North-South Affluence Gap		31. The Scandal of the Boat People
	5. Gorbachev's Global Doughnut: The Empire With a Hole in the Middle		32. The Second Coming of Pol Pot
	6. When Leaders Fall: Succession Systems in the Non-Industrialized World		33. Iraq's Fleeing Kurds
	7. Pakistan Under Benazir Bhutto		34. Normalizing the Political Process in South Africa: The Time for Negotiation Has Arrived
	8. Semper Fidel		35. Apartheid Has No Future: Africa Is Ours
	9. Chadli's Perestroika		36. Mortgaging a House of Cards: The Ethics of International Debt
	10. After the Fall of a Dictator		37. Will the Planet Pay the Price for Third World Debt?
	11. Mending Broken Burma		38. It Won't Go Away Alone
	12. The Struggle to Build a Nation		39. A Way Out for the Debtors
	13. Gunless in Gaza		40. Risking the Lifeboat
	14. Iraq's Power Grab		41. Going It Alone
	15. Nicaragua's Election: Who Really Won?		42. The Drug War
	16. Panama: Whose Agenda?		43. Unmasking Terrorism: The Fear of Fear Itself
	17. The People's War		44. Missile Mania: Some Rules for the Game
	18. South Africa on the Move		45. The North's Garbage Goes South
	19. The Apocalypse in Ethiopia		46. Third World Metropolises Are Becoming Monsters
	20. Cambodia and the International Community		47. Weeding Out Waste: Energy Efficiency in the Third World
	21. Passage to Power		48. World Hunger Amidst Plenty
	22. Policies Toward the Third World		49. Concern Rising Over Harm From Pesticides in Third World
	23. The U.S. and Third-World Dictatorships: A Case for Benign Detachment		50. The Kerala Experiment
	24. "The Third World Is Not a Hopeless Place"		51. Grass-Roots Groups Are Our Best Hope for Global Prosperity and Ecology
	25. Refugee Concerns and U.S. Interests		
	26. United States Security Policy and ASEAN		
	27. The United States Role in the Middle East		

(Continued on next page)

ABOUT YOU

Name_____ Date_____

Are you a teacher? ☐ Or student? ☐

Your School Name_____

Department _____

Address _____

City_____ State _____ Zip _____

School Telephone # _____

YOUR COMMENTS ARE IMPORTANT TO US!

Please fill in the following information:

For which course did you use this book? _____

Did you use a text with this Annual Edition? ☐ yes ☐ no

The title of the text? _____

What are your general reactions to the Annual Editions concept?

Have you read any particular articles recently that you think should be included in the next edition?

Are there any articles you feel should be replaced in the next edition? Why?

Are there other areas that you feel would utilize an Annual Edition?

May we contact you for editorial input?

May we quote you from above?

ANNUAL EDITIONS: Third World 91/92

BUSINESS REPLY MAIL

First Class   Permit No. 84   Guilford, CT

Postage will be paid by addressee

The Dushkin Publishing Group, Inc.
Sluice Dock
DPG **Guilford, Connecticut 06437**